Communications
in Computer and Infor

377

Sabu M. Thampi   Pradeep K. Atrey
Chun-I Fan   Gregorio Martinez Perez (Eds.)

Security in Computing and Communications

International Symposium, SSCC 2013
Mysore, India, August 22-24, 2013
Proceedings

 Springer

Volume Editors

Sabu M. Thampi
Indian Institute of Information Technology
and Management – Kerala (IIITM-K)
Trivandrum, Kerala, India
E-mail: smthampi@ieee.org

Pradeep K. Atrey
The University of Winnipeg, Canada
E-mail: p.atrey@uwinnipeg.ca

Chun-I Fan
National Sun Yat-sen University
Kaohsiung, Taiwan R.O.C.
E-mail: cifan@faculty.nsysu.edu.tw

Gregorio Martinez Perez
University of Murcia, Spain
E-mail: gregorio@um.es

ISSN 1865-0929   e-ISSN 1865-0937
ISBN 978-3-642-40575-4   e-ISBN 978-3-642-40576-1
DOI 10.1007/978-3-642-40576-1
Springer Heidelberg New York Dordrecht London

Library of Congress Control Number: 2013947418

CR Subject Classification (1998): K.6.5, C.2.0, K.4.4, D.4.6, H.2.7

Typesetting: Camera-ready by author, data conversion by Scientific Publishing Services, Chennai, India

Printed on acid-free paper

Springer is part of Springer Science+Business Media (www.springer.com)

Preface

Networking and distributed systems such as cloud-based data centers are increasingly being used for computation, communication, and storage of data. Since distributed systems generally include third-party servers, security in such systems is a very important issue. Despite many advances in the security field, current networking and distributed systems are considered highly vulnerable and can be easily compromised by attacks. Therefore, research on secure computing and communication has gained more and more attention and its major goal is to make systems measurable, available, sustainable, secure, and trustworthy.

The International Symposium on Security in Computing and Communications (SSCC) aims to provide the most relevant opportunity to bring together researchers and practitioners from both academia and industry to exchange their knowledge and discuss their research findings. This edition of SSCC was hosted by Sri Jayachamarajendra College of Engineering (SJCE), Mysore, India, during August 22–24, 2013. SSCC 2013 was co-located with the Second International Conference on Advances in Computing, Communications and Informatics (ICACCI 2013).

SSCC 2013 attracted 111 paper submissions. From these submissions, 24 papers were selected by the Technical Program Committee (TPC) for oral presentations and 15 papers for poster presentations. The TPC members and reviewers rigorously and independently examined all the papers. The authors of accepted papers made a considerable effort to take into account the comments in the version submitted to these proceedings.

Numerous people who contributed in the preparation of the final technical program of SSCC 2013 deserve appreciation. We thank all the authors who submitted their work, the symposium Chairs/Co-chairs, TPC members, and additional reviewers, who significantly contributed to the success of the SSCC 2013 paper review process under a tight schedule. The members of the Steering Committee ought to be thanked for their timely help and supervision. Our most sincere thanks go to all keynote speakers who shared with us their expertise and knowledge.

Many thanks go to the Organizing Committee members for taking care of the registration, logistics, and local arrangements for the symposium. We would also like to thank all those who contributed to the success of SSCC 2013 but whose names cannot be listed.

We wish to express our thanks to the editors of the *Communications in Computer and Information Science* series for agreeing to publish the proceedings in the series. We would also like to express our gratitude to the editorial team for producing such a wonderful quality proceedings book.

August 2013

Sabu M. Thampi
Pradeep K. Atrey
Chun-I Fan
Gregorio Martinez Perez

Organization

Steering Committee

John F. Buford	Avaya Labs Research, USA (Chair)
Xavier Fernando	Ryerson University, Canada
Peter Mueller	IBM Zurich Research Laboratory, Switzerland
Shambhu Upadhyaya	University at Buffalo, The State University of New York, USA
Raj Kumar Buyya	University of Melbourne, Australia
Chandrasekaran K.	NITK, India
Jaime Lloret Mauri	Polytechnic University of Valencia, Spain
Dapeng Oliver Wu	University of Florida, USA
David Meyer	Cisco Systems, USA
Ajith Abraham	MIR Labs, USA
Sattar B. Sadkhan A.L. Maliky (Chairman, IEEE Iraq Section)	University of Babylon, Iraq
Andreas Riener	University of Linz, Austria
Axel Sikora	University of Applied Sciences Offenburg, Germany
Bharat Jayaraman	University at Buffalo, The State University of New York, USA
Deepak Garg (Chair)	IEEE Computer Society Chapter, IEEE India Council & Thapar University, India
Dilip Krishnaswamy	Qualcomm Research Center, San Diego CA, USA
Narayan C. Debnath	Winona State University, Winona, USA
Selwyn Piramuthu	University of Florida, USA
Raghuram Krishnapuram	IBM Research, India
Theodore Stergiou	Intracom Telecom, Greece
V.N. Venkatakrishnan	University of Illinois at Chicago USA
Ananthram Swami	Army Research Laboratory, USA
Venugopal K.R.	Bangalore University, India
Adel M. Alimi	University of Sfax, Tunisia
Madhukar Pitke	Nicheken Technologies, India
Tamer ElBatt	Cairo University and Nile University, Egypt
Francesco Masulli	University of Genoa, Italy
Manish Parashar, Rutgers	The State University of New Jersey, USA
Sabu M. Thampi	IIITM-K, India
Anand R. Prasad	NEC, Japan

P. Nagabhushan   University of Mysore, India
Suash Deb (President)   Intl. Neural Network Society
                               (INNS), India Regional Chapter

Organizing Committee (SJCE)

Jagadguru Sri ShivarathriDeshikendraMahaswamiji (*Chief Patron*)
Sri B.N. Betkerur, Executive Secretary, JSS Mahavidyapeetha, Mysore (*Patron*)
M.H. Dhananjaya, Director-Technical Education Division, JSS
    Mahavidyapeetha, Mysore (*Patron*)
B.G. Sangameshwara, Principal, SJCE, Mysore (*Organizing Chair*)
V.N. ManjunathAradhya, Dept. of MCA, SJCE, Mysore (*Organizing Secretary*)

Advisory Committee

K. Chidananda Gowda
    (Former Vice Chancellor)   Kuvempu University, Shimoga
Y.N. Srikant (Dept. of CSA)   IISc, Bangalore
Mahadev Prasanna
    (Dept. of EE)   IIT-Guwahati, Guwahati
N.P. Gopalan (Dept. of
    Comp. Applications)   NIT-Trichy
G. Hemantha Kumar
    (DoS in Computer Science)   University of Mysore, Mysore
T.N. Nagabhushan (Principal)   JSSATE, Noida
Mritunjaya V. Latte (Principal)   JSSATE, Bangalore
C.R. Venugopal (Head – ECE)   SJCE, Mysore
C.N. Ravikumar (Head – CSE)   SJCE, Mysore
S.K. Padma (Head – ISE)   SJCE, Mysore
S.K. Niranjan (Dept. of MCA)   SJCE, Mysore
V. Vijaya Kumar (Dean)   GIET, Rajahmundry
Sudarshan Iyengar   IIT Ropar, Punjab

Technical Program Committee

General Chairs

Dapeng Oliver Wu   University of Florida, USA
Dilip Krishnaswamy   Qualcomm Research Center, San Diego,
                               USA
V.N. Venkatakrishnan   University of Illinois at Chicago, USA

Program Chairs

Chun-I Fan   National Sun Yat-sen University, Taiwan
Pradeep K. Atrey   The University of Winnipeg, Canada
Sabu M. Thampi   IIITM-K, India

TPC Members

Adlen Ksentini	University of Rennes 1 / IRISA Lab, France
Afrand Agah	West Chester University of Pennsylvania, USA
Agusti Solanas	Rovira i Virgili University, Spain
Ai-Chun Pang	National Taiwan University, Taiwan
Albert Levi	Sabanci University, Turkey
Andreas Wespi	IBM Zurich Research Laboratory, Switzerland
Aniruddha Bhattacharjya	Amrita School of Engineering, Banglore, India
Ankit Chaudhary	The University of Iowa, USA
Apostolos Fournaris	University of Patras, Greece
Ashok Kumar Das	IIIT Hyderabad, India
Bart De Decker	K. University Leuven, Belgium
Bartomeu Serra	Universitat de les Illes Balears, Spain
Bernd Becker	University of Freiburg, Germany
Bing Wu	Fayetteville State University, USA
Binod Kumar	Jayawant Technical Campus, Pune, India
Chin-Chen Chang	Feng Chia University, Taiwan
Christos Bouras	University of Patras and RACTI, Greece
Christos Dimitrakakis	EPFL, Switzerland
Christos Verikoukis	Telecommunications Technological Centre of Catalonia, Spain
Claudio Ardagna	Università degli Studi di Milano, Italy
Cristina Alcaraz Tello	University of Malaga, Spain
Delphine Christin	Technische Universität Darmstadt, Germany
Di Jin	Chrysler Group LLC, USA
Dibyendu Chakrabarti	Stevens Institute of Technology, USA
Dimitrios Stratogiannis	National Technical University of Athens, Greece
Eduardo Fernandez	Florida Atlantic University, USA
Edward Moreno	UFS - Federal University of Sergipe, Brazil
Erdal Cayirci	University of Stavanger, Norway
Feng Cheng	University of Potsdam, Germany
Flavio Lombardi	Università di Roma Tre, Italy
George Papadopoulos	Aristotle University of Thessaloniki, Greece
Ghazi Ben Ayed	University of Lausanne, Switzerland
Gheorghita Ghinea	Brunel University, UK
Giacomo Verticale	Politecnico di Milano, Italy
Giuseppe Raffa	Intel Corporation, USA
Gopal Patra	CSIR Centre for Mathematical Modelling and Computer Simulation, India
Gregorio Martinez Perez	University of Murcia, Spain
Grzegorz Kolaczek	Wroclaw University of Technology, Poland
Guang Tan	SIAT, Chinese Academy of Sciences, P.R. China
Harry Skianis	University of the Aegean, Greece

Huaqun Guo	Institute for Infocomm Research, A*STAR, Singapore
Hui Chen	Virginia State University, USA
Indrakshi Ray	Colorado State University, USA
Iwannis Stamatiou	University of Ioannina/CTI, Greece
Jalel Ben-Othman	University of Paris 13, France
Jerzy Konorski	Gdansk University of Technology, Poland
Jiankun Hu	University of New South Wales, Australia
Jiannong Cao	Hong Kong Polytechnic University, Hong Kong
Joni Da Silva Fraga	UFSC, Brazil
Kai Bu	The Hong Kong Polytechnic University, Hong Kong
Karima Boudaoud	University of Nice Sophia Antipolis, France
Kejie Lu	University of Puerto Rico at Mayaguez, Puerto Rico
Kevin Mills	National Institute of Standards and Technology, USA
Lau Lung	UFSC, Brazil
Luca Vollero	Università Campus Bio-Medico (Roma), Italy
Malamati Louta	University of Western Macedonia, Greece
Marek Klonowski	TU Wroclaw, Poland
Marius Marcu	Politehnica University of Timisoara, Romania
Mauricio Papa	The University of Tulsa, USA
Maurizio Aiello	National Research Council, Italy
Mesut Guenes	Freie Universität Berlin, Germany
Michele Pagano	University of Pisa, Italy
Nicolas Sklavos	Technological Educational Institute of Patras, Greece
Niki Pissinou	Florida International University, USA
Nikos Komninos	City University London, UK
Orazio Tomarchio	University of Catania, Italy
Panagiotis Sarigiannidis	University of Western Macedonia, Greece
Periklis Chatzimisios	Alexander TEI of Thessaloniki, Greece
Ping Yang	Binghamton University, USA
Rui Aguiar	University of Aveiro, Portugal
S. Kami Makki	Lamar University, USA
Sabrina Sicari	University of Insubria, Italy
Samad Kolahi	Unitec Institute of Technology, New Zealand
Sasan Adibi	Royal Melbourne Institute of Technology (RMIT), Australia
SeongHan Shin	AIST, Japan
Seyit Camtepe	Queensland University of Technology, Australia
Sghaier Guizani	Alfaisal University, Saudi Arabia
Sherali Zeadally	University of the District of Columbia, USA
Shu-Ching Chen	Florida International University, USA
Shuhui Yang	Purdue University Calumet, USA

Table of Contents

Regular Papers

Work-in-Progress

A Novel Approach for a Hardware-Based Secure Process Isolation in an Embedded System

Sunil Malipatlolla

OFFIS - Institute for Information Technology
26121 Oldenburg, Germany
sunil.malipatlolla@offis.de

Abstract. The need for a secure communication between two entities in a system is mandatory to protect the trustworthiness of the system. For example, consider an embedded system inside an automobile where two Electronic Control Units (ECUs) attached to a bus are communicating with each other. Such a system is rather secure against attacks from each other because the two ECUs and thus the tasks executing on them are physically separated from each other by design. However, this is not the case when two tasks, one of them being safety/security critical, execute on the same ECU in parallel because it opens an opportunity for a mutual impact by the tasks, for example, due to a shared resource such as the local memory. Thus, the goal of this contribution is to establish a secure isolation between such tasks to avoid an un-authorized communication and thus to build a trusted embedded system. Though, there exist approaches in the literature, for example, based on virtualization technology and others to address this issue, either they are only software-based or not suitable for embedded systems. In contrast, the proposed approach in here is not only hardware-based, which is more secure, but also lightweight in its design. In specific, the proposed approach, utilizes a security module with minimal Trusted Computing (TC) technology features tailored to the needs of a resource constrained embedded system. Additionally, a proof-of-concept implementation of the proposed approach is performed to illustrate the design feasibility.

Keywords: Secure Task/Process Communication, Trusted Computing, Embedded Systems.

1 Introduction and Related Work

Today there is a lot of progress in automotive electronics with many of the cars already containing multiple controllers networked together by a bus (e.g. CAN, Flexray) communication system. One such system is an abstract distributed system in which two Electronic Control Units (ECUs), which are physically separated from each other, communicate over an interconnecting bus. Further, such ECUs are rather secure against interference attacks from each other due to dedicated memories/processors and a defined channel access method, i.e., Time Division Multiple Access (TDMA), for the task execution. However, this type

Sabu M. Thampi et al. (Eds.): SSCC 2013, CCIS 377, pp. 1–9, 2013.

of security assumption is not valid when an ECU in such a system executes two tasks in parallel, one of them being safety/security critical and the other being non-critical. This is because, such a situation opens an opportunity for a mutual impact between the tasks, such as an unauthorized access of critical task data by a non-critical task, which creates new security concerns. For example, a security requirement by the system may be that the memory region where the critical task stores its data is not read or written by the non-critical task. Though, one approach to address this issue is to provide an isolated task execution and thus the memory isolation utilizing virtualization technology, it is only software-based. Further, there exists an approach, that utilizes the Trusted Computing (TC) technology combined with virtualization, thus providing the virtual Trusted Platform Module (vTPM) instances for the tasks [11]. However, such an approach is only partially hardware-based and it consumes plenty of platform resources, which is not desired in resource constrained embedded systems.

There exist two research projects, i.e., EVITA [11] and OVERSEE [2], in the automotive domain addressing the security in modern day cars. The goal of the first project is to design a Hardware Security Module (HSM) to provide an on-board secure communication in an automobile system. The HSM is equipped with variable TPM like security features and is protected against tampering and manipulations. The goal of the second project is to design a vehicular platform providing a protected run-time environment for execution of both manufacturer designed and/or third party applications adjacent to each other. The platform executes multiple applications in parallel in a secure manner by utilizing the well-known virtualization mechanism and a hardware security anchor i.e., the HSM, designed and implemented in the first project. In specific, each task from the group of tasks on a multifunctional ECU is run on a Virtual Machine (VM), which executes the software environment of the proprietary ECU and is strongly isolated from other VMs. However, combining the results from these two projects does not provide a complete hardware-based task isolation and thus it is less secure. Further, to achieve this isolation there is a need for an existence of strong binding between the VM and the HSM for preserving the platform integrity. In another work, the automotive industry consortium, AUTOSAR, specified the Crypto Service Manager (CSM), which provides a cryptographic functionality in an automobile, based on a software library or on a hardware module [3]. However, to the best of our knowledge, the issue of secure hardware-based task isolation on an ECU utilizing minimal security features is not yet addressed.

The rest of the paper is organized as follows. Section 2 gives a detailed description of the system under consideration and its operation. Section 3 illustrates the proposed approach for the secure task isolation on an ECU. Section 4 evaluates the approach with a proof-of-concept implementation on the hardware. Section 5 concludes the paper and gives some hints on future work.

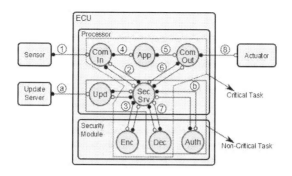

Fig. 1. System with an ECU Executing Two Tasks in Parallel

2   System Specification

An example system, which is the considered target system in this work, is detailed in the sequel. The system comprises of a sensor, an actuator, an ECU with a processor & a security module, and an update server as depicted in Figure 1. The system realizes a simple real-time control application, where sensor data are processed by the control application in order to operate the plant due to an actuator. The concrete control application is not of interest in the context of this paper. It might represent the engine control of a car, or a driver assistant system such as an Automatic Breaking System (ABS).

The scenario depicted in Figure 1 consists of the following flow: Sensor periodically delivers data from the plant over the bus (1), which is in an encrypted form to avoid its interception and later cloning by an attacker. The data is received by the input communication task ComIn, which is part of the Operating System (OS). Each time the input communication task receives a packet, it calls the security service (SecSrv), which is also part of the OS, for decryption of the packet (2). The security service provides the hardware abstraction for security operations, and schedules the service calls. The decryption call from the communication task is forwarded to the security module (3), which processes the packet data. The cryptographic operations of the security module modeled by Dec, Enc, and Auth are realized as hardware blocks. The decrypted data is sent back to the security service, which is in turn returned to the ComIn. Now the data is ready for transmission to the application (4), which is modeled by a single task App. The application task is activated by the incoming packet, and processes the sensor data. The controller implementation of the task calculates respective actuator data and sends it to the communication task ComOut (5) for transmission to the Actuator. However, before sending the data to the Actuator, the communication task again calls the security service (6), which in turn accesses the security module for data encryption (7). After Enc has encrypted the data, it is sent back to the communication task ComOut via SecSrv, which delivers the packet to the Actuator (8).

In essence, the described system provides a secure transfer of the data between the sensor and the actuator utilizing the encryption and decryption operations of the security module. All the tasks of the control application along with the corresponding cryptographic operations are grouped into a single block, depicted by a dotted boundary line and is referred to as *critical* task (c.f. Figure 1). A faulty operation of such a *critical* task causes the loss of fundamental system functionality and thus its secure operation must be ensured by the system.

Further, the target system supports a software update on it from outside i.e., manufacturer. To update the system with new software, the `UpdateServer` sends the data to the `Upd` task (a) via a communication medium (e.g., Internet) to the outside. This received data must be authenticity verified and decrypted before loading it into the system. For this, the `Upd` forwards the data to the `SecSrv`, which utilizes the `Auth` block of the security module (b). Only after a successful authentication, the data is decrypted and loaded into the system else it is rejected. The update application along with related cryptographic operations are also grouped into a single block, depicted by a thick boundary line and is referred to as *non-critical* task (c.f. Figure 1). Software update of the system is considered as an additional feature only here, thus the failure of such a *non-critical* task does not affect the fundamental functionality of the system.

To summarize, the considered target system has two tasks, i.e., a *critical* task and a *non-critical* task, executing in parallel on the same ECU with different functionalities. Thus it is mandatory for the user of such a system to avoid an interference between such tasks to provide a secure communication between them and consequently to safeguard the system.

3   Methodology

To achieve the goal of secure task communication, a feature referred to as remote attestation, defined by the Trusted Computing Group (TCG) [13], is utilized in here. The remote attestation is defined as the trustworthy reporting of the *platform status* of an entity to a remote entity when the latter makes such a request. Utilizing this feature, any malicious entity deceiving the remote entity may be detected. In this context, the entities are the executing tasks on the ECU of the target system whose inter-communication must be authorized. Furthermore, the tasks being on the same ECU within a single system, the feature may be referred to as local attestation. With reference to the tasks on the ECU, the *platform status* is the integrity measurement, which is the computed hash on executable binary of a given task. Then to attest itself, a task wishing to communicate with another task has to prove its integrity. For this, the security module of the target system is extended with necessary features as detailed in sequel. Additionally, the adversarial model in which the system has to operate is also illustrated.

3.1   Security Module

The security module inside the ECU of the system utilizes hardware blocks for cryptographic operations such as encryption, decryption, and authentication

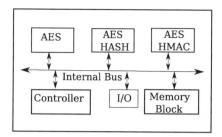

Fig. 2. Cryptographic Blocks of the Security Module

as depicted in Figure 2. These operations are all based on a single symmetric key block cipher algorithm, Advanced Encryption Standard (AES) [9]. Whereas, encryption and decryption operations utilize the *AES* block itself, authentication utilizes hash and Message Authentication Code (MAC) operations based on the same *AES* [8,10]. Such a block re-utilization feature not only makes the design of the security module easy but also consumes very few computational resources of the underlying platform.

As aforementioned, the security module has to support the integrity measurement and verification operations as a part of local attestation, which are handled by the *AES-Hash* and *AES-HMAC* blocks respectively. The *AES-Hash* provides a hash output of 128 Bit and the *AES-HMAC* utilizes a 128 Bit secret key for MAC comparison. To store the *AES* symmetric key and the MAC secret key, the module is extended with a memory (data buffer) block. In addition to holding these keys, this memory is assumed to be large enough (few tens of MB) to support computation and storage of hash values (integrity measurements) on all the binary executables of tasks on the ECU. The controller block is a finite state machine in design and manages all the cryptographic operations of the security module.

For example, consider the case that the *non-critical* task of the ECU wishes to communicate with the *critical* task of the ECU. In this case, the former task has to prove its integrity to the latter task, which in here is done through the security module. The pre-computed reference integrity measurements of both these tasks, at their first loading on the ECU, are stored inside the memory block of the security module. In specific, a set of registers, referred to as Platform Configuration Registers (PCRs) in TC terminology, store these values. At the next start-up of the system, an integrity measurement (i.e., hash) of the *non-critical* task is computed utilizing the *AES-Hash* block. This value is compared with the reference value inside the security module to decide on trustworthiness of the *non-critical* task. If the values match, it implies that there are no malicious modifications on the *non-critical* task and a communication with the *critical* task may be allowed else the communication is aborted. Thus, a secure communication between two tasks executing in parallel on the ECU is established utilizing the local attestation phenomenon. With this said, the security module is assumed to be the trust anchor and tampering with itself is considered as out of scope in this work.

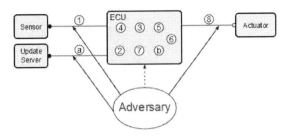

Fig. 3. Adversarial Model

3.2 Adversarial Model

To describe all possible attack points in the considered system, an adversarial model is formulated as depicted in Figure 3. The model highlights all the components (with a simplified ECU block) and the corresponding internal and external communication paths (i.e., numbered circles) of the original system (c.f. Figure 1). The adversary considered in the model is an active eavesdropper (c.f. Dolev-Yao Model [6]), i.e., someone who first taps the communication line to obtain messages and then tries everything in order to discover the plain text. In particular he is able to perform different types of attacks such as classical cryptanalysis and implementation attacks, as defined in taxonomy of cryptographic attacks by Popp in [12]. While classical cryptanalysis attacks include cloning by interception, replay, and man-in-the-middle attacks; the implementation attacks include side-channel analysis, reverse engineering, and others.

For our analysis, we assume that the attacker is only able to perform classical cryptanalytic attacks on the external communication links (indicated by thick arrows coming from adversary) i.e., from sensor to ECU, ECU to actuator, and update server to ECU. In specific, under cloning by interception attack, the adversary is capable of reading the packets being sent to the ECU and store them for use during a replay attack. Whereas in a man-in-the-middle attack, the adversary can either pose as an ECU to authenticate himself to the update server or vice versa. In the former case, he would know the content of the update data and in the latter he may update the ECU with a malicious data to destroy the system. However, to protect the systems against the classical cryptanalytic attacks, strong encryption and authentication techniques need to be utilized. With reference to this, the security module in here provides techniques such as confidentiality, integrity, and authenticity which overcome these attacks. We rule out the possibility of attacker being eavesdropping the ECU's internal communication (indicated by a dotted arrow coming from adversary) because such an attack implies that the attacker is having a physical access to the ECU and thus control the running OS and the tasks themselves.

Table 1. Resource Consumption of Security Module

Block	Regs.	LUTs	36Kbit BRAM
AES-128 bit	524	899	5
AES-Hash-Core	289	138	0
AES-HMAC-Core	294	184	0
Controller	662	453	0
Security Module	1769	1674	5

4 Implementation

The considered target system is a real-time system, which has to satisfy its real-time properties, such as meeting deadlines, in addition to guaranteeing the functional correctness. Thus, to guarantee these features of the system, the security module should perform its operations quickly and correctly. To illustrate this, a proof-of-concept implementation of the security module is performed on a *Xilinx* Virtex-5 Field Programmable Gate Array (FPGA) platform [1] and the corresponding resource consumption values are depicted in Table 1. Though, memory and I/O blocks are not mentioned in here, they are included as peripherals on the platform. The integrity measurements (i.e., hash values) are stored inside the Block Random Access Memory (BRAM) of the FPGA and the secret keys (symmetric and MAC) are stored in an external memory such as Flash. These memories are accessed accordingly through the respective memory controller interfaces as and when required by the security module. It can be seen that the security module consumes only 3% of the total available resources (with an additional few MB of working memory) on the considered FPGA, which justifies the term lightweight module used for it.

The core component of the security module is the *AES* core which determines the achievable speed of the local attestation phenomenon. The simulation results obtained utilizing *Xilinx* Isim simulator tool show that the time for 128 Bit data encryption, decryption, and authentication is $46\,ns$ for each operation. Given this, even if the size of the executable binary of the task is few tens of kb, the authentication operation is performed in less than $40\,\mu s$ when operating the security module at a frequency of 358 MHz. Furthermore, the security module in here communicates with the ECU via a Low-Pin-Count (LPC) bus [7]. LPC is a 4 Bit wide serial bus defined with a clock rate of 33 MHz. According to the specification [7], the transfer of 128 Bit data plus 16 Bit command requires about $1.46\,\mu s$, when the bus operates with typical timing parameters. In this context, the communication involving data transfer by ECU to the security module for authentication consumes around $2\,ms$ only. Thus, with a typical end-to-end deadline in a real-time system in the order of few tens of ms, such a configuration of the system is fast enough to establish a secure communication between the tasks while satisfying the timing requirements of the system.

To design and analyze the target system, the in-house tool referred to as *OrcaEdit*, which is integrated with a real-time analyzer is utilized. *OrcaEdit* is an

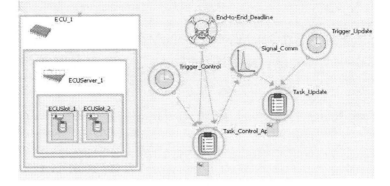

Fig. 4. Modeling and Analysis of Target System with OrcaEdit Tool

integrated development environment for modeling and analyzing real-time applications. A model created with *OrcaEdit* consists of the program structure and timing annotations in the form of so called *task networks*, and the underlying system architecture in form of ECUs and buses. Such a *task network* modeled for the target system is depicted in Figure 4. The *task network* comprises of several components such as a trigger, tasks, signals, ECU, and the interconnection between them. These components have connectors depicted on their outer edges which serve as the interacting points. Whereas the trigger represents a clock that is utilized for simulating the system, the tasks represent the functional software blocks with specific timing behavior, which in our case are the control and update applications. For a given task, the user may specify the entries such as the deadline, the memory usage, and the execution times (best-case and worst-case) on an ECU. A Signal is utilized to model communication between tasks and it represents a set of data that is sent from one task to another. An ECU represents a processor of a specific type that processes the modeled tasks and further enables their real-time analysis.

With the modeled system available in the background, a precise timing analysis based on real-time model-checking is performed [5]. To this end, the system is translated into a *UPPAAL* model with a set of timed-automata [4]. The result of such an analysis showed the satisfaction of the end-to-end deadline by the system with an established secure communication between the two tasks executing on the ECU.

5 Conclusion

In this contribution a hardware-based secure communication between two tasks executing in parallel on the ECU in an embedded system is established. For this, the proposed approach utilizes the fundamental feature, referred to as remote attestation, which is defined in the trusted computing technology. In specific, this feature is supported by the security module integrated in the system, which interfaces with the ECU over the standard LPC bus interface. In addition to performing the required cryptographic operations in quick time, this module consumes very few computational resources on the target platform thus making it suitable for the resource constrained embedded systems. A proof-of-concept implementation of the proposed approach utilizing the available tools is presented to show its feasibility. However, the proposed approach in here is applicable only for a distributed system architecture because when considering a multi-core system, additional interferences between various shared resources occur due to its higher complexity, which must also be taken into account.

Acknowledgement. This work was supported by the Federal Ministry for Education and Research (BMBF) Germany, under grant code 01IS110355M, in project "Automotive, Railway and Avionic Multicore System (ARAMiS)" The responsibility for the content of this publication lies with the author.

References

1. Xilinx, `http://www.xilinx.com/support/documentation/virtex-5.htm`
2. Groll, A., Holle, J., Ruland, C., Wolf, M., Wollinger, T., Zweers, F.: OVERSEE - A Secure and Open Communication and Runtime Platform for Innovative Automotive Applications. In: Proc. 7th Escar Conference - Embedded Security in Cars (2009)
3. Autosar, Org.: Specification of Crypto Service Manager (2011), `http://www.autosar.org/download/R4.0/` `AUTOSAR_SWS_CryptoServiceManager.pdf`
4. Behrmann, G., David, A., Larsen, K.G.: A Tutorial on Uppaal 2004-11-17. Tech. rep., Aalborg University, Denmark (November 2004)
5. Dierks, H., Metzner, A., Stierand, I.: Efficient Model-Checking for Real-Time Task Networks. In: International Conference on Embedded Software and Systems, ICESS (2009)
6. Dolev, D., Yao, A.C.: On the security of public key protocols. Tech. rep., Stanford, CA, USA (1981)
7. Intel: Low Pin Count (LPC) Interface Specification. Intel Corp. (August 2002)
8. National Institute of Standards and Technology (NIST): Secure Hash Standard, SHS (1995)
9. National Institute of Standards and Technology (NIST): Advanced Encryption Standard, AES (2001)
10. National Institute of Standards and Technology (NIST): The Keyed-Hash Message Authentication Code, HMAC (2002)
11. Perez, R., Sailer, R., van Doorn, L.: vtpm: virtualizing the trusted platform module. In: Proc. 15th Conf. on USENIX Security Symposium, pp. 305–320 (2006)
12. Popp, T.: An Introduction to Implementation Attacks and Countermeasures. In: Proceedings of IEEE/ACM International Conference on Formal Methods and Models for Co-Design (MEMOCODE 2009), pp. 108–115 (2009)
13. Trusted Computing Group, Inc.: Trusted Platform Module (TPM) specifications (2010), `http://www.trustedcomputinggroup.org/resources/tpm_main_specification`

Signature Embedding in the Functional Description of Reversible Circuit

Animesh Roy and Debasis Mitra

Department of Information Technology
National Institute of Technology, Durgapur, W.B., India

Abstract. In order to prevent unauthorized access and illegal redistribution during the exchange and distribution of Intellectual Properties (IPs), embedding ownership information has become inevitable. Recently, research on reversible circuits has drawn significant attention especially in the areas of digital signal processing, nano and quantum computing. The strategies employed for dealing with the security risks associated with the development and distribution of conventional digital circuits may not be directly applicable to reversible circuits. In this paper, we propose a simple technique to embed the owner's signature during the synthesis of a reversible circuit. The embedded signature can be used to prevent unauthorized access and/or illegal distribution of such circuits (or circuit descriptions). The proposed technique offers strong security as the signature is embedded as a functional part of the design, at the initial stage of the specification. Experimental results on benchmarks show that the owner's signature can be embedded without significant overhead.

Keywords: Intellectual property, reversible circuit, signature embedding.

1 Introduction

The market competition of worldwide digital integrated circuit (IC) industry helps itself to grow rapidly with more and more complex integrated digital chips. The integration of modern complex systems using reusable design components [5], has become one of the most important methodology for IC design. The extensive use of reusable modules, known as intellectual-property (IP) cores [4], is absolutely necessary for developing multi-million gate designs within a reasonable timeline. In IP-reuse based very large scale integration (VLSI) design methodology, various parts of a complex design, developed elsewhere, are usually reused among groups, companies, external IP providers. The sharing of IPs between authorities involves high security risk in today's competitive market. In order to prevent unauthorized access and illegal redistribution, embedding ownership information has become inevitable. Several works have been done so far to undertake security measures at different levels of conventional VLSI design [3,4,9,10,14,16]. Security risks involved in the various phases of development and distribution of VLSI circuits are dealt with strategies like licensing, watermarking, copyright and signature embedding to name a few.

Sabu M. Thampi et al. (Eds.): SSCC 2013, CCIS 377, pp. 10–17, 2013.

In recent years, reversible circuits have drawn significant interest in the areas like digital signal processing, quantum computing, and photonic and nano-computing technologies [2,7,8,11]. Security related issues discussed above are also pertinent in case of development and distribution of large and complex reversible circuits. However, to the best of our knowledge, no works have been reported in the literature till date dealing with the security concerns related to the design and distribution of reversible circuits.

In this paper, we propose a simple technique which can be adopted during the synthesis of reversible circuits to prevent unauthorized access and/or illegal distribution of such circuits (or circuit descriptions). The proposed technique guides the synthesis of a reversible circuit in such a way that only authorized users having proper license can get the proper functionality of the circuit. Moreover, to prevent illegal distribution of the circuit, the unique identification of the actual owner of the circuit (i.e., owner's signature) is embedded as a functional part of the design. The signature can be extracted on demand by the owner to prove her ownership. Experimental results on benchmark descriptions show that our proposed technique is able to embed the ownership information within the circuits with negligible increase in cost.

2 Proposed Methodology

For any deterministic device to be reversible, its input and output must be uniquely retrievable from each other [6]. In other words, the number of inputs and outputs of a reversible circuit must be same and there must be a one-to-one mapping between the input vectors and the output vectors. A detailed review of reversible logic and the synthesis of reversible circuits can be found in [6,8]. An irreversible function can be made reversible by appropriately adding extra input(s), output(s) or both and appropriately modifying the original specification. The modification is either performed prior to synthesis or in a unified approach during synthesis. The extra input(output) thus added to make a function reversible is called *constant input(garbage output)*.

Main aim of our proposed mechanism is to design a reversible circuit in such a way that only authorized users having proper license can get the proper functionality of the circuit. Moreover, to prevent illegal distribution of the circuit, the unique identification of the actual owner of the circuit is embedded (which can be extracted on demand by the owner only) in the form of a signature. Assuming a boolean irreversible function in the form of a truth table is given, we convert it to a primary reversible function with minimum number of garbage outputs and constant inputs by properly augmenting the truth table. When a reversible function has one or more constant inputs along with the normal inputs, the function generates desired outputs only for a particular combination of the constant inputs. The developer chooses a particular combination of constant inputs CI_k for which the reversible function is supposed to generate desired output. The bit values for the portions of the columns that correspond to this input combination under the normal outputs of the truth table are set accordingly (i.e., based on the desired outputs). This combination of constant inputs (i.e., CI_k) works as the license. With the synthesized circuit and the license in hand, an authorized user can set the constant inputs appropriately to achieve the desired functionality of the circuit. However, the license cannot prevent the security breach through unauthorized redistribution. An authorized user can illegally redistribute the license to others. In order to catch such violation of contract, we further propose a technique to embed the signature of the developer (owner) into the circuit. With her signature embedded within the circuit, the developer can extract it on-demand to prove her ownership. The entire procedure of embedding the owner's signature during synthesis of a reversible circuit is described below.

Step 1: Assuming the owner's signature to be an arbitrary-length string of alphabetical characters, a one-way hash function [13] is used to generate a unique fixed length bit-string. The length of the output string is chosen as 2^n, where n is total number of normal inputs of the reversible circuit. A combination of constant inputs CI_j other than the one for which the reversible function is supposed to generate desired-output is then chosen. A normal output NO_j of the circuit is also chosen. The 2^n bits long string generated by the hash function is then placed at the portion of the column representing NO_j that corresponds to CI_j. The combination of constant inputs CI_j, the output NO_j, the hash function, and the signature string (output of the hash function) all are kept as owner's secret information. The owner's signature is embedded under the normal output line to avoid intentional corruption of the signature by an intruder. In this case, the signature cannot be removed or modified without hampering the normal functionality of the circuit. If the signature is embedded under a garbage output, then that signature can be removed without hampering the normal functionality of the circuit. The procedure for selection of bit values for the remaining part of the truth table is described in the next step.

Step 2: It may be noted that bit values of the remaining part of the truth table do not have any impact on the desired functionality of the circuit. We may call them don't care bits. Hence, we select these values in such a way that the cost of implementation is minimized. Since quantum technology is the most predominant among the technologies that are supposed to use reversible gates and computation, *quantum cost* (QC) has emerged as one of the important metric in reversible circuit synthesis. QC of a circuit is defined as the number of elementary quantum operations required to realize the function. QC of each reversible gate of size 1 (e.g., NOT) and size 2 (e.g., CNOT) is taken as unity [1] and that of a circuit is calculated by counting the number of reversible gates of unit-cost required for its realization. QC of a reversible gate grows with the increase in the number of controls [1]. Accordingly, in order to minimize the quantum cost, the reversible circuit should be synthesized with minimum number of controls. The number of controls can be minimized by reducing the number of flipping of bits required to get the output vectors from the corresponding input vectors. So, we set the don't care bits in a way such that for all i, the output pattern (O_i) corresponding to a particular input pattern (I_i) can be obtained from I_i with minimum possible flipping of bits.

Step 3: The reversible function thus generated in the form of modified truth-table is applied to the Toffoli-synthesis technique [6]. We use Toffoli synthesis procedure as it tries to use narrow (with less controls) gates and hence the most popular option is used for reversible circuit synthesis.

As an illustrative example, let us consider the realization of the function shown in Table 1(a) which counts the number of 1's in a 4-bit input pattern. The input lines are denoted by a, b, c, and d respectively. The output lines are denoted by x, y, and z respectively. It is apparent that this function is irreversible. It may be noted that we must add at least three garbage outputs and two constant inputs to make it reversible. Let us denote the constant inputs by ci_1 and ci_2 respectively, and the garbage outputs by g_1, g_2, and g_3 respectively. The modified truth table is shown in Table 1(b). We assume that the output vector of the desired function can be observed through the normal outputs (i.e., x, y, and z) when the value of $ci_1 ci_2 = 01$. This particular combination of constant inputs works as the license for the authorized users.

Next, we generate the signature (string of bits) to be embedded in the circuit from the original signature of the owner (string of alphabetical characters). It may be noted that the total number of normal inputs (i.e., a, b, c, and d) is four. Hence, we need to choose the one-way hash function such that it generates a string of $2^4 = 16$ bits. Suppose, the output of the hash function is 0000111001010110. We further choose the combination of constant inputs (CI_j) as $ci_1 ci_2 = 10$ and normal output (NO_j) as x. We embed the signature by placing the string generated by the hash function in the portion of the column representing x that corresponds to $ci_1 ci_2 = 10$. Referring to Table 1(b), it is apparent that when $ci_1 ci_2 = 01$, values for the normal outputs x, y and z are determined by the desired functionality and can not be changed. However, we can choose the values for the garbage outputs g_1, g_2, and g_3 according to our convenience. When $ci_1 ci_2 = 10$, we have the owner's signature embedded under the normal output x. In this case, the bit values for the normal output x can not be changed, but the values for other outputs y, z, g_1, g_2, and g_3 can be taken according to our choice. When $ci_1 ci_2 = 00$ or $ci_1 ci_2 = 11$, all the six outputs (x, y, z, g_1, g_2, and g_3) can be considered as don't cares. As mentioned in Step 2, the don't care bits are chosen in a manner such that the quantum cost and the number of gates both are minimized. For example, let us consider the input pattern (I_i) 100000. The bit value corresponding to the output x is set to 0 for the signature and cannot be changed. Minimum flipping of bits occurs if we choose the bit values of the remaining five don't cares (y, z, g_1, g_2, and g_3) as 00000. This leads the entire output pattern (O_i) to be 000000, which has already been considered for another input pattern (010000). So, this output pattern cannot be taken. The entire output pattern becomes 010000 (not considered yet) if we choose the bit values of five don't cares as 10000. Hence, this output pattern is considered where just two bits need to be flipped to derive the output pattern from the corresponding input pattern. In this way, following the same procedure, bit values of other don't cares are set (Table 1(b)).

Table 1. Truth tables of (a) an irreversible function and (b) the corresponding reversible version

(a)

a	b	c	d	x	y	z
0	0	0	0	0	0	0
0	0	0	1	0	0	1
0	0	1	0	0	0	1
0	0	1	1	0	1	0
0	1	0	0	0	0	1
0	1	0	1	0	1	0
0	1	1	0	0	1	0
0	1	1	1	0	1	1
1	0	0	0	0	0	1
1	0	0	1	0	1	0
1	0	1	0	0	1	0
1	0	1	1	0	1	1
1	1	0	0	0	1	0
1	1	0	1	0	1	1
1	1	1	0	0	1	1
1	1	1	1	1	0	0

(b)

ci_1	ci_2	a	b	c	d	x	y	z	g_1	g_2	g_3
0	0	0	0	0	0	1	0	0	0	0	0
0	0	0	0	0	1	1	0	0	0	0	1
0	0	0	0	1	0	1	0	0	0	1	0
0	0	0	0	1	1	1	0	0	0	1	1
0	0	0	1	0	0	0	0	0	1	0	0
0	0	0	1	0	1	0	0	0	1	0	1
0	0	0	1	1	0	0	0	0	1	1	0
0	0	0	1	1	1	0	1	0	1	1	1
0	0	1	0	0	0	1	0	1	0	0	0
0	0	1	0	0	1	0	1	1	0	0	1
0	0	1	0	1	0	1	0	1	0	1	0
0	0	1	0	1	1	0	0	1	0	1	1
0	0	1	1	0	0	1	0	1	1	0	0
0	0	1	1	0	1	0	0	1	1	0	1
0	0	1	1	1	0	0	0	1	1	1	0
0	0	1	1	1	1	1	0	1	1	1	1
0	1	0	0	0	0	0	0	0	0	0	0
0	1	0	0	0	1	0	0	1	0	0	1
0	1	0	0	1	0	0	0	1	0	1	0
0	1	0	0	1	1	0	1	0	0	1	1
0	1	0	1	0	0	0	0	1	1	0	0
0	1	0	1	0	1	0	1	0	1	0	1
0	1	0	1	1	0	0	1	0	1	1	0
0	1	0	1	1	1	0	1	1	1	1	1
0	1	1	0	0	0	0	0	1	0	0	0
0	1	1	0	0	1	0	1	0	0	0	1
0	1	1	0	1	0	0	1	0	0	1	0
0	1	1	0	1	1	0	1	1	0	1	1
0	1	1	1	0	0	0	1	0	1	0	0
0	1	1	1	0	1	0	1	1	1	0	1
0	1	1	1	1	0	0	1	1	1	1	0
0	1	1	1	1	1	1	0	0	1	1	1
1	0	0	0	0	0	0	1	0	0	0	0
1	0	0	0	0	1	0	0	0	0	0	1
1	0	0	0	1	0	0	0	0	0	1	0
1	0	0	0	1	1	0	0	0	0	1	1
1	0	0	1	0	0	1	0	0	1	0	0
1	0	0	1	0	1	1	0	0	1	0	1
1	0	0	1	1	0	1	0	0	1	1	0
1	0	0	1	1	1	0	0	0	1	1	1
1	0	1	0	0	0	0	1	1	0	0	0
1	0	1	0	0	1	1	0	1	0	0	1
1	0	1	0	1	0	0	1	1	0	1	0
1	0	1	0	1	1	1	0	1	0	1	1
1	0	1	1	0	0	0	1	1	1	0	0
1	0	1	1	0	1	1	0	1	1	0	1
1	0	1	1	1	0	1	0	1	1	1	0
1	0	1	1	1	1	0	0	1	1	1	1
1	1	0	0	0	0	1	1	0	0	0	0
1	1	0	0	0	1	1	1	0	0	0	1
1	1	0	0	1	0	1	1	0	0	1	0
1	1	0	0	1	1	1	1	0	0	1	1
1	1	0	1	0	0	1	1	0	1	0	0
1	1	0	1	0	1	1	1	0	1	0	1
1	1	0	1	1	0	1	1	0	1	1	0
1	1	0	1	1	1	1	1	0	1	1	1
1	1	1	0	0	0	1	1	1	0	0	0
1	1	1	0	0	1	1	1	1	0	0	1
1	1	1	0	1	0	1	1	1	0	1	0
1	1	1	0	1	1	1	1	1	0	1	1
1	1	1	1	0	0	1	1	1	1	0	0
1	1	1	1	0	1	1	1	1	1	0	1
1	1	1	1	1	0	1	1	1	1	1	0
1	1	1	1	1	1	1	1	1	1	1	1

The final circuit (shown in Fig. 1) is then obtained by applying Toffoli synthesis technique. It may be noted that the desired functionality of the circuit can be achieved by setting the constant inputs $ci_1 ci_2 = 01$. Since, this information is available as license, it is apparent that only the user(s) having the valid license can use the circuit. Although, in this particular case, the desired combination of constant inputs can be obtained by trial and error method, it will hardly be so easy for large circuits where the number of constant inputs is high. In the case of an illegal redistribution of the license, the owner of the circuit can prove

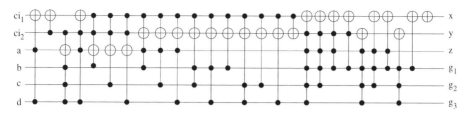

Fig. 1. Realization of the function of Table 1(b) using Toffoli gates

her ownership on-demand just by setting the constant inputs $ci_1ci_2 = 10$ and applying the sequence of all possible input patterns through the normal inputs and observing the responses at the normal output x. It is apparent that x will generate the signature string (0000111001010110) that was embedded.

3   Experimental Results

It may be noted that the proposed technique in this paper embeds the owner's signature at the behavioral level. The technique provides the maximum security, as the signature is embedded as a functional part of the design, at the initial stage of the specification. However, it seems that the signature embedding may incur some overhead in terms of gate count (GC) and/or the quantum cost (QC) of the final circuit thus obtained. To evaluate the effectiveness of the proposed technique, we have compared the synthesis results for various reversible benchmarks [15] with and without signature embedding.

Each benchmark description is fed to generalized Toffoli synthesis twice through *RevKit* [12], an open-source toolkit for reversible circuit design. In the case of synthesis without signature embedding, the description is fed directly, whereas in the case of signature embedding, the description is passed through the truth table augmentation block before it is fed to Toffoli synthesis. We have implemented the augmentation of the truth table for embedding owner's signature

Table 2. Evaluation of overhead incurred due to signature embedding

Circuit	Synthesis without signature embedding		Synthesis with signature embedding		Overhead (%)	
	GC	QC	GC	QC	GC	QC
1-bit adder	7	19	8	20	14.2	5.2
Mod-5	20	156	22	182	10	16.6
rd43	28	272	29	273	3.5	0.3
2-bit adder	36	396	36	460	0	16.1
Mod-7	27	243	28	272	3.7	11.9
rd53	47	909	54	1032	14.8	13.5
rd63	116	2601	107	2803	0	7.7
rd73	204	4713	205	5222	0.4	10.7

according to the proposed technique using a program written in C programming language. Table 2 shows the summary of experimental results for 8 benchmarks. It is apparent from the table that for most of the circuits, signature embedding incurs small overhead (less than 15% in terms of gate count and less than 17% in terms of quantum cost). It may be noted that for some circuits (e.g., rd63), signature embedding may result in better gate count.

4   Conclusions

A simple technique for embedding owner's signature in the functional description of reversible circuits has been proposed. The signature along with a license can prevent unauthorized use and/or illegal distribution of such circuit descriptions. The technique provides maximum security as the owner's signature is embedded as a functional part of the design. Experimental results on benchmarks show that owner's signature can be embedded without significant overhead.

Acknowledgements. The authors would like to thank Dr. Dipak Kumar Kole for his kind help.

References

1. Barenco, A., et al.: Elementary gates for quantum computation. The American Physical Society 52, 3457–3467 (1995)
2. Bennett, C.H.: Logical reversibility of computation. IBM J. Research and Development 17, 525–532 (1973)
3. Cui, A., Chnag, C.H., Tahar, S., Abdel-Hamid, A.T.: A robust FSM watermarking scheme for IP protection of sequential circuit design. IEEE Transactions on Computer-Aided Design of Integrated Circuits and Systems 30(5), 678–690 (2011)
4. Kahng, A.B., et al.: Watermarking techniques for intellectual property protection. In: ACM/IEEE Design Automation Conference, pp. 776–781 (1998)
5. Keating, M., Bricaud, P.: Reuse Methodology Manual for System-on-a-Chip Designs, 3rd edn. Kluwer, Norwell (2002)
6. Maslov, D.: Ph.D. Thesis on Reversible Logic Synthesis. The University of New Brunswick (2003)
7. Offermann, S., Wille, R., Drechsler, R.: Efficient realization of control logic in reversible circuits. In: Forum on Specification and Design Languages (FDL), Oldenburg, pp. 1–7 (2011)
8. Saeedi, M., Markov, I.L.: Synthesis and optimization of reversible circuits a survey. ACM Computing Surveys (CSUR) 45(52), 1–34 (2013)
9. Saha, D., Sur-Kolay, S.: Robust intellectual property protection of VLSI physical design. IET Computer & Digital Technique 4(5), 388–399 (2010)
10. Saha, D., Sur-Kolay, S.: Secure public verification of IP marks in FPGA design through a zero-knowledge protocol. IEEE Transaction on Very Large Scale Integration (VLSI) System PP(99), 1–9 (2011)
11. Shende, V.V., Prasad, A.K., Markov, I.L., Hayes, J.P.: Synthesis of reversible logic circuits. IEEE Transactions on Computer-Aided Design of Integrated Circuits and Systems 22(6), 710–722 (2003)

12. Soeken, M., Frehse, S., Wille, R., Drechsler, R.: RevKit: An open source toolkit for the design of reversible circuits. In: De Vos, A., Wille, R. (eds.) RC 2011. LNCS, vol. 7165, pp. 64–76. Springer, Heidelberg (2012), RevKit is available at `http://www.revkit.org`
13. Stallings, W.: Cryptography and Network Security, 5th edn. Prentice Hall (2011)
14. Sur-Kolay, S., Bhunia, S.: Intellectual property protection and security in system-on-chip design (tutorial). In: International Conference on VLSI Design (VLSID), pp. 18–19 (2012)
15. Wille, R., Große, D., Teuber, L., Dueck, G.W., Drechsler, R.: RevLib: An online resource for reversible functions and reversible circuits. In: Int'l Symp. on Multi-Valued Logic, pp. 220–225 (2008), RevLib is available at `http://www.revlib.org`
16. Xu, W., Zhu, Y.: A digital copyright protection scheme for soft-IP core based on FSMs. In: International Conference on Consumer Electronics, Communications and Networks (CECNet), pp. 3823–3826 (2011)

Detecting Laser Fault Injection
for Smart Cards Using Security Automata

Guillaume Bouffard, Bhagyalekshmy N. Thampi, and Jean-Louis Lanet

Smart Secure Devices (SSD) Team – University of Limoges
123 Avenue Albert Thomas, 87060 Limoges CEDEX, France
{guillaume.bouffard,bhagyalekshmy.narayanan-thampi}@xlim.fr,
jean-louis.lanet@unilim.fr

Abstract. Security and interoperability issues are increasing in smart card domain and it is important to analyze these issues carefully and implement appropriate countermeasures to mitigate them. Security issues involve attacks on smart cards which can lead to their abnormal behavior. Fault attacks are the most important among them and they can affect the program execution, smart card memory, etc. Detecting these abnormalities requires some redundancies, either by another code execution or by an equivalent representation. In this paper, we propose an automatic method to provide this redundancy using a security automaton as the main detection mechanism. This can enforce some trace properties on a smart card application, by using the combination of a static analysis and a dynamic monitoring. The security officer specifies the fragments of the code that must be protected against fault attacks and a program transformer produces an equivalent program that mesh a security automaton into the code according to the security requirements.

Keywords: Fault attacks, Trust, Smart Card, Security Automata, Countermeasure.

1 Introduction

Smart card is a small embedded chip/device which is commonly used in our day to day life for serving various purposes in banking, electronic passports, health insurance card, pay TV, SIM card, etc. It has efficient computing capabilities and security features for ensuring secure data transaction and storage. Many hardware and software attacks are performed to gain access to the assets stored inside a smart card. Since it contains sensitive information, it must be protected against attacks. The laser faults are the most difficult among them to be handled.

Fault Injection (FI) attacks can cause the perturbation of the chip registers (e.g., the program counter, the stack pointer, etc.), or the writable memory (variables and code modifications). If these perturbations are not detected in advance, an attacker can get illegal access to the data or services. Some redundancy is necessary to recognize the deviant behavior which can be provided by a security automaton and a reference monitor. This technique has emerged as a powerful

Sabu M. Thampi et al. (Eds.): SSCC 2013, CCIS 377, pp. 18–29, 2013.

and flexible method for enforcing security policies over untrusted code. The process verifies the dynamic security checks or a call to the security functions into the untrusted code by monitoring the evolution of a state machine.

In our work, we propose to implement the transition functions of such a state machine natively in the Java Card Virtual Machine (JCVM). For interoperability reasons, we implement a less efficient API to replace the transition functions and a static analyzer to verify the coherence of the security property.

This paper is organized as follows: section two describes the FI attacks on smart cards and their effects on program execution. The known detection mechanisms and their comparison are discussed in the third section. Section four presents our contributions and countermeasures. Final section gives the conclusions of our work.

2   Related Works

Aktug [1] defined a formal language for security policy specifications *ConSpec*, to prove statically that a monitor can be inlined into the program byte code, by adding first-order logic annotations. A weakest precondition computation was used here which works as same as the annotation propagation algorithm employed in [14] to produce a fully annotated, verifiable program for the Java Card. This allows the use of JML verification tools, to check the actual policy adherence. Such a static approach cannot be adopted here due to the dynamic nature of the attack.

As far as we know, the only application of the security automaton for smart card was presented in [13] where the concept of policy automaton which combines defeasible logic with the state machine. It represents complex policies as combinations of basic policies. A tool has been implemented for performing policy automaton analysis and checking policy conflicts and a code generator is used to implement the transition functions that creates a Java Card applet. It was concerned mainly to enforce invariants in the application.

3   Faults on Smart Cards

In general, a fault is an event that changes the behavior of a system such that the system no longer provides the expected service. It may not be only an internal event in the system but also, a change in the environment that causes a bit flip in the memory. However the fault (when activated), is the primary reason for the changes in the system that leads to an error which in turn causes a failure of the complete system. In order to avoid such a failure, faults have to be detected as early as possible and some actions must be carried out to correct or stop the service. Thus, it is necessary to analyze the errors generated by these faults more precisely. In the current smart card domain, fault attacks are the most difficult attacks to be tackled.

3.1   Fault Attacks

Smart card is a portable device which requires a smart card reader (provides external power and clock sources) to operate it. The reader can be replaced with specific equipment to perform the attacks. With short variations of the power supply it is possible to induce errors into the internal operations of the smart card. These perturbations are called spike attacks, which may induce errors in the program execution. Latter aims at confusing the program counter which can cause the improper working of conditional checks, decrease in loop counters and the execution of the arbitrary instructions. The reader like MP300 can also be used to provide glitch attack. A glitch [3,7,12] incorporates short deviations beyond the required tolerance from a standard signal bounds. They can be defined by a range of different parameters and can be used to inject memory faults as well as faulty execution behavior. Hence, the possible effects are same as in the spike attacks. If the chip is unpacked, such that the silicon layer is visible, it is possible to use a laser to induce perturbation in the memory cells [8]. These memory cells have been found to be sensitive to light. Due to photoelectric effect, modern lasers can be focused on relatively small regions of a chip, so that FI can be targeted well [4].

To prevent the occurrence of FI attacks, it is necessary to know its effects on the smart card. FI models have been already discussed in details in [6,20]. A widely accepted model corresponds to an attack that changes one byte at a precised and synchronized time [19]. An attack using the precise bit error model had been described in [18] which is not realistic on current smart cards due to the implementation of hardware security on memory (error correction and detection code or memory encryption) of modern components.

In real time, an attacker physically injects energy into a memory cell to switch its state. Thus up to the underlying technology, the memory will physically takes the value 0x00 or 0xFF. If memory is encrypted, the physical value becomes a random value[1].

3.2   Effects of Fault Attacks on the Program Execution

In this work, only a single fault will be considered. The proposed mechanism supports dual faults if the automaton is protected by some checksum method. An attacker can break the confidentiality and/or the integrity mechanisms incorporated in the card. The code integrity of the program ensures that the original installed code is the same as that executed by the card. The attacker can modify the value returned by a function to allow the execution of sensitive code without authorization. He can also generate a faulty condition to jump to a specific statement, avoid a given method invocation or ignore a condition loop.

The data of a program are also a sensitive asset to be protected. With a single fault, an attacker can permanently or temporarily modify sensitive information.

---

[1] More precisely, a value which depends on the data, the address, and an encryption key.

In particular, it can affect the variables used in any evaluation instruction like never start a loop, ignore initialization and so on. The smart card should ensure the confidentiality of the assets. The attacker may modify the data to be copied, from the application byte array or to the I/O smart card buffer by modifying the address of the buffer. Another way to obtain the asset is to change the number of bytes to be send in the buffer. This overflow provides information of data that follow the bytes sent from the application.

3.3   Fault Detection Mechanisms

The mechanisms for fault injection detection can be classified in to three countermeasure approaches: static, dynamic and mixed.

Static Countermeasure Approach. Static countermeasures ensure that each test is done correctly and/or the program Control Flow Graph (CFG) remains unchanged as described by the developer.

To verify if a test i.e., (a sensitive condition if) is done correctly, the usage of a redundancy *if-then-else* statement should improve the statement branching security. Indeed, if a fault is injected during an if condition, an attacker can execute a specific statement without a check. In real time, a second-order FI is difficult with a short delay between two injections. A second-order if statement is used to verify the requirements needed to access a critical operation to prevent the faulty execution of an *if-then-else* statement. An example of this kind of implementation is listed in the Listing 1.1 Second-order if statement.

Listing 1.1. Second-order if statement

```
// condition is a boolean
if (condition) {
  if (condition) {
    // Critical operation
  } else {/*Attack detected!*/
  }
} else {
  if (!condition) {
    // Access not allowed
  }else{/*Attack detected!*/}}
```

Listing 1.2. Step counter

```
short step_counter=0;
if (step_counter==0) {
  // Critical operation 1
  step_counter++;
} else {/*Attack detected!*/
  }
/* ... */
if (step_counter==1) {
  // Critical operation 2
  step_counter++;
}else{/*Attack detected!*/}
```

The problem with a second-order if condition is that the program CFG is not guaranteed. To ensure it, the developer can implement a step counter as described in the Listing 1.2. With this method, each node of the CFG, defined by the developer is verified during the runtime. If a node is executed with a step counter set with a wrong value, an incorrect behavior is detected.

Dynamic Countermeasure Approach. The smart card can implement countermeasures on dynamic elements (stack, heap, etc.) and thereby ensure integrity to prevent the modification of them. A checksum can be used to verify the manipulated value for each operation. Another low cost countermeasure approach, to protect stack element against FI attack was explained by Dubreuil *et al.* in [9]. Their countermeasure implements the principle of a dual stack where each value is pushed from the bottom and growing up into the element stack. In contrary, each reference is pushed from the top and growing down. This countermeasure protects smart card against type confusion attack.

As described before, a program's code is also an asset to be protected. In order to ensure the code confidentiality, the memory may be encrypted. For using a more affordable countermeasure, Barbu explained [4], a solution where the code is scrambled. Unfortunately, a brute force attack can bypass a scrambled memory. Razafindralambo *et al.* proposed in [16] a randomized scrambling which improves the code confidentiality.

Enabling all countermeasures during the whole program execution is not necessary and also it is more costlier for the card. Hence, to reduce the implementation cost of the countermeasure, Barbu *et al.* [5] described user-enabled countermeasure(s) where the developer can decide to enable a specific countermeasure for a code fragment.

Recently, Farissi *et al,* presented [10] an approach based on artificial intelligence and in particular neural networks. This mechanism is included in the JCVM. After a learning step, this mechanism can dynamically detect abnormal behavior of each smart card's program.

Mixed Countermeasure Approach. Unlike previous approaches, mixed methods use off-card operations where some computations are done for embedded runtime checks. This way offers a low cost because costly operations are realized outside the card.

To ensure the code integrity, Prevost *et al.* patented [15] a method where for each basic blocks of a program, a hash value is computed. The program is sent to the card with each basic block's hash. During the execution, the smart card verifies this value for each executed basic block and if a hashsum is wrong, an abnormal behavior is detected.

Sere [2], described three countermeasures, based on bit field, basic block and path check, to protect smart card against FI attacks. These countermeasures require off-card operations done during the compilation step to compute enough information to be provided to the smart card through a custom component. The smart card dynamically checks the correctness of the current CFG. Since there are off-card operations, this countermeasure has a low footprint in the smart card's runtime environment.

4   Security Automata and Execution Monitor

Detecting a deviant behavior is considered as a safety property, *i.e.* properties that state *nothing bad happens*. A safety property can be characterized by a set of disallowed finite execution based on regular expression. The authorized execution flow is a particular safety property which means that, the static control flow must match exactly the runtime execution flow without attacks. For preventing such attacks, we define several partial traces of events as the only authorized behaviors. A key point is that this property can be encoded by a finite state automaton, while the language recognized will be the set of all authorized partial traces of events.

4.1 Principle

In [17], Schneider defined a security automaton, based on Büchi automaton as a triple (Q, q_0, δ) where Q is a set of states, q_0 is the initial state and δ a transition function δ: (Q × I) → 2^Q. The set S is the input symbols, *i.e.* the set of security relevant actions. The security automaton processes a sequence of input symbols s_1, s_2, ... and the sequence of symbols is read as one input at a time. For each action, the state is evaluated by starting from the initial state s_0. As each s_i is read, the security automaton changes Q' in $\cup_{q\in Q'}\delta(s_i, q)$. If the security automaton can perform a transition according to the action, then the program is allowed to perform that action, otherwise the program is terminated. Such a mechanism can enforce a safety property as in the case for checking the correctness of the execution flow.

The property we want to implement is a redundancy of the control flow. In the first approach, the automaton that verifies the control flow could be inferred using an interprocedural CFG analysis. In a such a way, the initial state q_0 is represented by any method's entry point. S is made of all the byte codes that generate a modification of the control flow along with an abstract instruction *join* representing any other instructions pointed by a label. By definition, a basic block ends with a control flow instruction and starts either by a first instruction after control flow instructions or by an instruction preceding a label. When interpreting a byte code, the state machine checks if the transition generates an authorized partial trace. If not, it takes an appropriate countermeasure.

The transition functions are executed during byte code interpretation which follows the isolation principle of Schneider. Using a JCVM, it becomes obvious that the control of the security automaton will remain under the control of the runtime and the program cannot interfere with automaton's transitions. Thus, there is no possibility for an attacker to corrupt the automaton because of the Java sandbox model. Of course, the attacker can corrupt the automaton using the same means as he corrupted the execution flow. By hypothesis, we do not consider actually the double FI possibility for the attacker. If needed, it is possible to protect the automaton with an integrity check verified before each access to the automaton.

4.2 Implementation in a Java Card Virtual Machine

The control of the transition functions is quite obvious. Once the automaton array has been built during the linking process, each Java frame is improved with the value of the current state q_i. In the case of a multithreaded virtual machine, each thread manages the state of the current method security automaton in its own Java frame for each method.

Listing 1.3. Transition function for the IFLE byte code (next instruction)

```
1  int16  BC_ifle(void)  {
2      if  (SM[frame->currentState][INS]  != *vm_pc)
3          return  ACTION_BLOCK;
4      vm_sp--;
5      if  (vm_sp[0].i <= 0)  return  BC_goto();
6      if  (SM[frame->currentState][NEXT]  != state(vm_pc))
7          return  ACTION_BLOCK;
8      vm_pc += 2;
9      frame->currentState = SM[frame->currentState][NEXT];
10     return  ACTION_NONE;  }
```

The automaton is stored as an array with several columns like the next state, the destination state and the instruction that generates the end of the basic blocks. In the Listing 1.3, the test (in line 2) verifies that the currently executed byte code is the one stored in the method area. According to the fault model, a transient fault should have been generated during the instruction decoding phase. If it does not match, the JCVM stops the execution (line 3). If the evaluation condition is true, it jumps to the destination (line 5). Else, it checks if the next Java program pointer is a valid state for the current state of the automaton. If it is allowed, the automaton changes its state.

Listing 1.4. Transition function for the IFLE byte code (target jump)

```
1  int16  BC_goto(void)  {
2      vm_pc = vm_pc - 1 + GET_PC16;
3      if  (SM[frame->currentState][DEST]  != state(vm_pc))
4          return  ACTION_BLOCK;
5      frame->currentState = SM[frame->currentState][DEST];
6      return  ACTION_NONE;  }
```

In Listing 1.4, the last part of the IFLE byte code checks also if the destination Java program counter matches with the next state and update the current state.

Listing 1.5. Decoding an instruction

```
1      while (true)  { handler = bytecode_table[*vm_pc];
2                      vm_pc++; bc_action = handler();
```

In the decode phase of the instruction, the laser can hit the data bus while transferring the needed information from the memory. In this JCVM decode phase (Listing 1.5), the address of the byte code function is obtained in line 1. At that time, either the vm_pc or the handler can be corrupted. Thus, the byte code being executed is not the one stored in the memory. Therefore, we need to check the execution instruction is the same as that of the stored one.

The security automaton is build during the linking process of the Java Card applet. During the linking step, the method is processed byte code by byte code linearly, allowing to build the automaton array. Each state s_i corresponds to vm_pc start and vm_pc end; the function state(vm_pc) returns an index of the array corresponding to the state that includes the vm_pc.

Here, we presented the basic security automaton of the control flow redundancy which needs to be improved. In section 3.3, we have seen the possibility to skip an instruction or a call to a function. The granularity of the basic block is not enough to handle this issue and checking each instruction is not realistic. So, we need to find a trade off between the granularity and each instruction. We propose to insert calls to an abstract function setState(), in some sensitive code fragments. Being a control flow function, a call to a function will be directly included into the security automaton. Even if the latter is empty a call to a function costs a lot due to the built and the destruction of the frame. For that purpose, we developed a byte code analyzer that emulates this call. It takes the input as binary file (the CAP file) and extract all occurrences of the invokestatic instruction and replaces them by a simple goto instruction to the next line. It has the same semantics, *i.e.* an entry in the automaton array but it costs much less.

Listing 1.6. Inserting checks in a Java Card basic block

```
1 apdu.setIncomingAndReceive();
2 Util.arrayCopy(apduBuffer, (short) (ISO7816.OFFSET_CDATA), D,
3               (short) 0, (short) 4);
4 setState();
5 if (b == false) ISOException.throwIt(error_date);
6 tempo = Util.getShort(A, (short) 0);
7 setState();
8 k = 1;
9 (short) ((tempo >> k) / NbAmounts[0])
10 setState();
11 functionR(A, key, D);
12 setState();
```

The code presented in Listing 1.6 is extracted from the Internet protocol payment defined by Gemalto in [11]. We ensure that, the JCVM verifies if each step has been correctly passed in line 4, 7, 10 and 12. This corresponds to what is usually done in a Java Card secured development with step counters as shown in the Listing 1.2. However, it is integrated in a more general framework to automate the fault detection.

The Lightweight Version in the INOSSEM Project. The aim of the project INOSSEM is to guarantee a security interoperability between several smart card manufacturers. The security specification must be independent to the design of the JCVM. For that purpose, it has been decided to design the countermeasures as a Java API defining all the required services. The security automaton is one of the INOSSEM classes. The main drawback of this approach versus our native implementation is the cost of all the function calls. But on the other hand, the code fragment protected with the security automaton can be isolated from the rest of the application.

The call to the API methods that manages the transition functions of the security automaton should be explicitly written by the developer. The developer should only insert the call to the method `setState()` in his applet to have the guarantee that the JCVM will verify the control flow of this code fragment. A call to `endStateMachine()` checks the correct ending of the security automaton. Being under the control of the Java Card runtime, the isolation principle is still respected during the execution of the API.

The main difference is that the construction of the security automaton is delegated to the developer. He has to examine all the authorized traces and build the automaton. Exceptions that should occur during execution must also be a part of the authorized traces. The developers know which parts of their application is sensible and they focus on the protection of a particular code fragment. This leads to a new issue, the coherence of the security policy defined by the automaton.

Coherence of the Policy. If a developer specifies a security automaton that partially represents the CFG, the automaton could consider some illegal transitions while they are legal traces. In the example given in Fig. 1, we have the CFG at the left side and the specification of the security automaton at the right side.

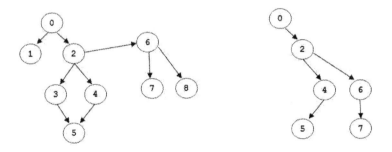

Fig. 1. Partial specification

The developer is only interested to protect some execution paths. He defines the following state sequences $\{q_0, q_2, q_4, q_5\}$ and $\{q_0, q_2, q_6, q_7\}$. If the sequence $\{q_0, q_2, q_3, q_5\}$ is executed, then in the state q_2, the automaton has to process a transition to the state q_3. It terminates the execution of the target while the execution path is valid. In fact, the security policy must be a subgraph of the control flow and thus, an edge must be added to the security automaton between the state q_2 and q_5. The verification of the coherence algorithm must check that the security automaton is a subgraph of the CFG. If the security automaton is a partial subgraph (i.e. every edges of the state of a CFG are not included), then the missing edges must be added to it. A specific action is to be done while

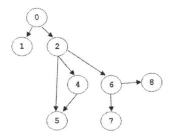

Fig. 2. Complete specification

reaching the end of the security automaton. Thus, all the terminal states must be added to the security automaton (q_1, q_8). The correct security automaton is given in Fig 2.

Each basic block can be split into several states as shown in Listing 1.6. For example, the state q_4 can be made of the sequence $\{q'_4, q''_4, q'''_4, \ldots\}$. In such a case, the security automaton is no more a subgraph of the CFG. While adding the edge for the closure, this sequence must be recognized as the state q_4. It is obvious to control the coherence for a simple automaton, like the one presented here. For real life examples, we need a static analyzer to check the coherence and build the automaton.

4.3 Static Analyzer and Code Meshing

Of course, this process is manageable automatically by a static analyzer before loading it into the card. The analyzer (SA) extracts the CFG (inter-class and interprocedural analysis) of the program from the source code, defining all the basic blocks. Then, it extracts the security automaton (call the API methods `setState()` and `endStateAutomaton()`) recognizing the state extension by subsequences when these calls are included within a basic block. It checks by comparing the security automaton and CFG if closure edges are missing and proposes through a graphical interface to the user to add the missing edges. The second step consists of initializing the state automaton object, defining all the states as final static fields and calling all the missing methods of the API: the `endStateMachine()` at the end of all the sink states.

Our prototype proposes also the possibility for the cards that do not implement the INOSSEM API to inline the security automaton into the application code with the two transition functions as shown in the Listing 1.7. Due to the fact that Java Card does not support multidimensional arrays, the security automaton must manage the index to simulate a matrix. The SA-Analyzer has filled the `securityAutomaton` array either with an index or the value `NO_STATE`. Then, if a `NO_STATE` is found for a transition, the method throws an exception.

The complexity of `setState()` is $\theta(1)$ while the complexity of `endStateMachine()` is $\theta(n)$, n being the maximum neighbors for all the nodes of the graph.

Listing 1.7. Inserting `setState` method

```
public void setState(short state) {
    if (securityAutomaton[(currentState*NB_COL)+state] !=
        NO_STATE)
        currentState = securityAutomaton
                        [currentState*NB_COL+state];
    else { ISOException.throwIt(ISO7816.SA_NO_SUCH_STATE); }
}
public void endStateMachine(short terminalState) {
    // checks if no successor
    for (short i = 0; i < NB_COL; i++) {
        if (securityAutomaton[currentState*NB_COL+i]
                    != NO_STATE)
            ISOException.throwIt(ISO7816.SA_NO_SUCH_STATE);
    } // then reinitialize the security automaton
    currentState = START_STATE_MACHINE; }
```

5   Conclusion

We have presented a general countermeasure in this paper, which can be applied to smart cards in order to detect FI attacks. The main idea was to provide redundancy of the control flow using a security automaton executed in the kernel mode. It allows to dynamically check the behavior of the program. We automatically generated the automaton during the linking process of the applet and for adding specific check points, we allow the developer to insert calls to a method `setState()`. For efficiency, we removed this call from the binary file and we replaced it by a simple `goto` which enforces the verification. In the second step, we applied this technique without modifying the JCVM by executing the transition functions in an API. We developed an analysis tool that checks the coherence of the security policy.

Of course, this technique is not limited to CFG properties but it can be used for more general security policy if they can be expressed as *safety properties*. In particular, it is interesting to check if some security commands have already been done before executing sensitive operation. Some are memorized in secured container (*i.e.* the PIN code field `isValidated`) but some of them use unprotected fields and could be subjected to FI attacks. The difficulty is to find the right trade off between a highly secured system with a poor performance or an efficient system with less security.

Acknowledgments. This work is partly funded by the French project IN-OSSEM (PIA-FSN2-Technologie de sécurité et résilience des réseaux).

References

1. Aktug, I.: Algorithmic Verification Techniques for Mobile Code. Ph.D. thesis, KTH, Theoretical Computer Science, TCS, qC 20100628 (2008)
2. Al Khary Sere, A.: Tissage de contremesures pour machines virtuelles embarquées. Ph.D. thesis, Université de Limoges (2010)

3. Anderson, R., Kuhn, M.: Low Cost Attacks on Tamper Resistant Devices. In: Christianson, B., Crispo, B., Lomas, M., Roe, M. (eds.) Security Protocols 1997. LNCS, vol. 1361, pp. 125–136. Springer, Heidelberg (1998)
4. Barbu, G.: On the security of Java Card platforms against hardware attacks. Ph.D. thesis, Grant-funded PhD with Oberthur Technologies and Télécom ParisTech (2012)
5. Barbu, G., Andouard, P., Giraud, C.: Dynamic Fault Injection Countermeasure A New Conception of Java Card Security. In: Mangard, S. (ed.) CARDIS 2012. LNCS, vol. 7771, pp. 16–30. Springer, Heidelberg (2013)
6. Blömer, J., Otto, M., Seifert, J.P.: A new CRT-RSA algorithm secure against bellcore attacks. In: Computer and Communications Security, pp. 311–320 (2003)
7. Boneh, D., DeMillo, R.A., Lipton, R.J.: On the importance of checking cryptographic protocols for faults. In: Fumy, W. (ed.) EUROCRYPT 1997. LNCS, vol. 1233, pp. 37–51. Springer, Heidelberg (1997)
8. Bouffard, G., Iguchi-Cartigny, J., Lanet, J.-L.: Combined Software and Hardware Attacks on the Java Card Control Flow. In: Prouff, E. (ed.) CARDIS 2011. LNCS, vol. 7079, pp. 283–296. Springer, Heidelberg (2011)
9. Dubreuil, J., Bouffard, G., Lanet, J.L., Iguchy-Cartigny, J.: Type classification against Fault Enabled Mutant in Java based Smart Card. In: ARES 2012, pp. 551–556. IEEE, Prague (2012)
10. Farissi, I.E., Azizi, M., Moussaoui, M., Lanet, J.L.: Neural network Vs Bayesian network to detect javacard mutants. In: Colloque International sur la Sécurité des Systèmes d'Information (CISSE), Kenitra Marocco (March 2013)
11. Girard, P., Villegas, K., Lanet, J.L., Plateaux, A.: A new payment protocol over the Internet. In: CRiSIS 2010, pp. 1–6 (2010)
12. Joye, M., Quisquater, J.J., Bao, F., Deng, R.H.: RSA-type signatures in the presence of transient faults. In: Darnell, M.J. (ed.) Cryptography and Coding 1997. LNCS, vol. 1355, pp. 155–160. Springer, Heidelberg (1997)
13. McDougall, M., Alur, R., Gunter, C.A.: A model-based approach to integrating security policies for embedded devices. In: 4th ACM International Conference on Embedded Software, EMSOFT 2004, pp. 211–219. ACM, New York (2004)
14. Pavlova, M., Barthe, G., Burdy, L., Huisman, M., Lanet, J.L.: Enforcing High-Level Security Properties for Applets. In: Quisquater, J.-J., Paradinas, P., Deswarte, Y., El Kalam, A.A. (eds.) Smart Card Research and Advanced Applications. IFIP, vol. 153, pp. 1–16. Springer, Heidelberg (2004)
15. Prevost, S., Sachdeva, K.: Application code integrity check during virtual machine runtime (August 2004)
16. Razafindralambo, T., Bouffard, G., Thampi, B.N., Lanet, J.-L.: A Dynamic Syntax Interpretation for Java Based Smart Card to Mitigate Logical Attacks. In: Thampi, S.M., Zomaya, A.Y., Strufe, T., Alcaraz Calero, J.M., Thomas, T. (eds.) SNDS 2012. CCIS, vol. 335, pp. 185–194. Springer, Heidelberg (2012)
17. Schneider, F.B.: Enforceable security policies. ACM Trans. Inf. Syst. Secur. 3(1), 30–50 (2000)
18. Skorobogatov, S.P., Anderson, R.: Optical Fault Induction Attacks. In: Kaliski Jr., B.S., Koç, Ç.K., Paar, C. (eds.) CHES 2002. LNCS, vol. 2523, pp. 31–48. Springer, Heidelberg (2003)
19. Vetillard, E., Ferrari, A.: Combined Attacks and Countermeasures. In: Gollmann, D., Lanet, J.-L., Iguchi-Cartigny, J. (eds.) CARDIS 2010. LNCS, vol. 6035, pp. 133–147. Springer, Heidelberg (2010)
20. Wagner, D.: Cryptanalysis of a provably secure CRT-RSA algorithm. In: 11th ACM Conference on Computer and Communications Security, pp. 92–97 (2004)

Virtual World Authentication Using the Smart Card Web Server

Lazaros Kyrillidis, Graham Hili, Sheila Cobourne, Keith Mayes,
and Konstantinos Markantonakis

Smart Card Centre, Information Security Group, Royal Holloway, Univ. of London,
Egham, Surrey, UK, TW20 0EX
{lazaros.kyrillidis.2011,graham.hili.2009,sheila.cobourne.2008,
keith.mayes,k.markantonakis}@rhul.ac.uk

Abstract. Virtual Worlds (VWs) are persistent, immersive digital environments, in which people utilise digital representation of themselves. Current management of VW identity is very limited, and security issues arise, such as identity theft. This paper proposes a two-factor user authentication scheme based on One Time Passwords (OTPs), exploiting a Smart Card Web Server (SCWS) hosted on the tamper-resistant Subscriber Identity Module (SIM) within the user's mobile phone. Additionally, geolocation attributes are used to compare phone and PC locations, introducing another obstacle for an attacker. A preliminary security analysis is done on the protocol, and future work is identified.

Keywords: Smart Card Web Server, Virtual Worlds, Authentication, Mobile phones, SIM cards, One Time Passwords.

1 Introduction

The term Virtual World (VW) has been defined as 'a synchronous, persistent network of people, represented as avatars, facilitated by networked computers' [1]. VWs are very popular: at the beginning of 2012, there were 1,921 million registered accounts in over 100 VWs [2]. Some VWs aim to mimic real life as closely as possible in a digital environment e.g. Second Life, by Linden Labs [3]. Others are designed as game environments, where the objective is to complete quests and enhance your avatar's skills and reputation, for example Blizzard's World of Warcraft [4]. Figure 1 shows a screenshot of a VW with an avatar. Authentication procedures for VW users are currently fairly limited, mostly relying on static, easily compromised username/password combinations. This can result in a number of security issues with real world consequences e.g. virtual goods/ identities can be stolen if an account is hacked, with the danger that the user's computer can then be compromised or real world identity theft could occur [5].

Using a mobile phone as a second factor in online authentication (i.e. something you have/something you know) should improve security. There are several existing mobile phone authentication options e.g. using SMS messages [6], or optical challenge-response procedures [7]. Mobile phone operating systems are

Sabu M. Thampi et al. (Eds.): SSCC 2013, CCIS 377, pp. 30–41, 2013.

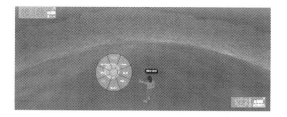

Fig. 1. Virtual World Avatar

increasingly becoming targets for malware, however [8]. Storing credentials in a tamper-resistant device, such as the Subscriber identity Module (SIM), is therefore a more attractive approach. This paper proposes a system that uses a SIM equipped with a Smart Card Web Server (SCWS) [9] in a One Time Password (OTP) authentication scheme. The SCWS/SIM is owned and operated by the Mobile Network Operator (MNO), and brings tightly managed web server functionality to the tamper-resistant SIM environment. Including geolocation [10] in the protocol introduces another obstacle for a potential attacker to overcome, by checking if the phone and PC are in the same geographical area. The aim is to significantly improve the security of the VW login, without unduly inconveniencing the user, and so enhance user and merchant confidence in VW security and services offered to users.

In this paper, the term SIM will be used generically to describe a type of smart card that consists of the Universal Integrated Circuit Card (UICC) and application software that allows telecommunication access; this is called the USIM (for 3G networks) or the SIM (for GSM networks) [11]. The paper is structured as follows: the technical architecture of VWs is outlined in Section 2 and information about the Smart Card Web Server is presented in Section 3. The proposed protocol is described in Section 4. A preliminary security analysis of the proposal is done in Section 5, before the paper reaches its conclusion in Section 6.

2   Virtual World Infrastructure

To connect to a VW the user needs client software, typically installed on a PC, represented as C1-C5 in Figure 2. The VW Client (VWC) can be regarded as a special kind of viewer or browser, in that the client gets data from a remote server, and renders it into a visual representation for the user to interact with. The VW environment is provided by the VW infrastructure i.e. a VW cloud consisting of a set of servers. There are load balancers, front end servers (denoted as S1,S2,S3 in Figure 2), and back end facilities usually composed of databases/VW rules which apply to interactions with objects/avatars inside the world. This infrastructure is subdivided into components and processes, used to conduct particular tasks and introduce modularity [12] [13]: e.g. a login component, a user component and a data component [14]. The proposal in this paper

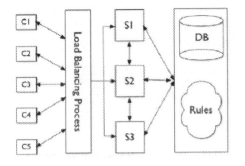

Fig. 2. Virtual World Infrastructure

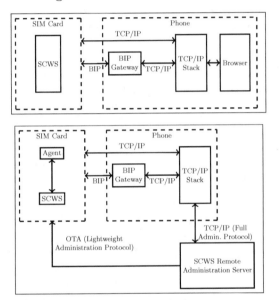

Fig. 3. SCWS Modes of Operation

is concerned with the Login Server processes which handle the initial request from the user to log into the world.

The next section now gives details about the operation of the Smart Card Web Server (SCWS) that will be used in the proposed authentication protocol.

3   The Smart Card Web Server (SCWS)

The Smart Card Web Server (SCWS) is a lightweight web server that is hosted on a SIM card and it is standardised by the Open Mobile Alliance [9]. The SCWS serves web pages locally to the handset's browser, either static or dynamically created HTML pages by java applets running inside the SIM. A SCWS can only be accessed locally by an HTTP(s) [15] client running on the handset, or from a remote entity, called the Remote Administration Server (RAS). Communication to/from the SCWS can take place in two ways:

Over the Bearer Independent Protocol (BIP): for SIMs without networking capabilities (older models and the Classic Edition of Java Card 3.0) [16]. A BIP gateway is utilised, that translates BIP commands (understood by the SIM) to proper TCP/IP communication expected by the browser (and vice versa).

Directly over HTTP : for Java Card 3.0 Connected Edition, that implements a TCP/IP stack.

SCWS content is remotely updated in a secure and managed manner. This remote administration for the SCWS can be done using the Lightweight Administration Protocol (LAP), or the Full Administration Protocol (FAP) (as shown in Figure 3). The LAP uses Over The Air (OTA) techniques for transferring small amounts of data e.g. a static HTML page. The FAP is used when the amount of data is relatively large e.g. a load of a java applet. In FAP, a remote entity (the MNO) connects with an on-card entity (the administration agent) and establishes a HTTPs connection in order to access and manage data on the SIM. Applets are transferred using procedures outlined in [17]. On-card events may trigger this communication, initiated by the local agent. External communication towards the SCWS is restricted to authorised entities i.e. the Remote Administration Server. The same applies for HTTP clients on the handset, where an Access Control Policy Enforcer may be in place controlling local access to the SCWS. The SCWS is particularly suited for use in an authentication protocol as the entire message flow is secured via standard HTTPs and the standard web browser on the phone is used. The SCWS is easily integrated with the VW web based environment, since it is web based itself and no specialised phone application is needed.

Now that VW technical architecture and the SIM/SCWS have been described, the proposed protocol will be detailed in the next section: however, necessary entities and assumptions, along with OTP processing and geolocation techniques will be outlined first.

4   The Proposed SCWS Authentication Protocol

4.1   Entities and Assumptions

Entities: The entities in the proposal are described in Table 1, and their relationship is shown in Figure 4. Notation used is in Table 2.

Assumptions: The following assumptions are made:

Business Relationships. The MNO has a business relationship with the VW developers, and has authorised their use of a Remote Administration Server to update the SCWS VW application and data.

Users Per SCWS. The mobile phone has a one-to-one mapping to the user, i.e. only one registered user can use a particular SCWS.

Table 1. Description of Entities needed

Notation	Description
VW	The Virtual World. Has details of all user credentials. It is responsible for checking user login details and creating one time passwords.
VWS	Virtual World Server. Provides back-end functionality for the VW, with all necessary information to keep the VW operating. It connects with back end processes such as the database and the login server.
LS	Login Server. Part of the Virtual World, this manages login details, authenticates users, creates the nonce (N) and OTP, then checks the OTP sent by the VWC.
SCWS	Smart Card Web Server. The user accesses the SCWS environment using a PIN. The SCWS uses a java applet to process and display the OTP.
AA	Administration Agent: an on-SIM entity that establishes a HTTPs connection with the RAS.
VWC	Virtual World Client. This is the interface presented to the user, installed on the user's PC. It provides just a graphical user interface, and is considered insecure.
RAS	Remote Administration Server. It updates the SCWS of a registered phone via the MNO's FAP, using HTTPs. It is a trusted entity, and can be operated by the MNO or a trusted third party. The RAS can also determine the phone's location (as it is a part of the MNO)
U	User. An individual who is registered with a VW

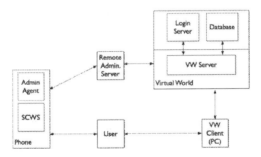

Fig. 4. Relationship between Entities

Registration. A secure user registration procedure is in place. The exact details are out of the scope of this paper, but a user must supply credentials such as mobile phone number/PIN so that the RAS can download the applet/credentials onto the correct phone and the PIN number can be used to create the OTP during the protocol. The VW authentication Java applet will then be installed on the user's SIM using the techniques described in Section 3, along with the user's PIN to access the SCWS. Additionally, during registration, a VW certificate will be installed on the user's VW Client to offer mutual authentication.

Channel Security. Channels between the RAS/ SCWS, and VWC/ VWS are considered secure, since all data in transit is protected by HTTPs.

4.2   One Time Passwords and Geolocation

One Time Passwords: Many VWs use a simple username/password as the user authentication mechanism at login, relying on static data for security; this may be captured and exploited via a range of IT security attacks. The general principle behind the proposed protocol is that an OTP generating process is done both at the VW back-end and by the SCWS, using a nonce N and the user's PIN. Thus the use of a static password is replaced by that of a dynamically created one on a separate personal device, using a tamper-resistant chip (the SIM), and connected via a different communications channel. Having an OTP password generator on the VW Server side means it benefits from the VW Server's existing security, which is reasonably expected to be of a considerably higher level than on the VW Client. The OTP should have a number of security properties: e.g. easy to compute, but very difficult to identify the PIN/ nonce used to create it; have a minimum length of 64bits (which can be condensed into a eight byte word); and be created using cryptographically-secure, standardised pseudo-random number generators such as RFC4226 [18]. A compromise of usability and security will be needed: e.g. a user may be prepared to type in a maximum of eight alphanumeric digits and so the OTP must be mapped to this field size; PIN size is crucial for the entropy of the OTP, however a small PIN size increases usability, but decreases security (and vice versa). Common practice for financial institutions and MNOs is to use sizes of 4 and 5 digits, with the maximum number of PIN entry attempts limited to 3 to protect against exhaustive (brute force) attacks .

Geolocation: The phone and VWC's locations are also used as a further obstacle for a potential attacker. The phone's location could be determined by either the cell towers of the mobile network or through the GPS adapter. Equivalently IP geolocation could be used to find the client's location. The authentication is successful if both locations are within a certain distance of each other. While IP geolocation is not extremely accurate, it is currently used by large organisations to counteract attacks originating some distance from the genuine user.

4.3   The Authentication Protocol

The steps in the protocol are now described (see Figure 5).

Step 1: The user initiates the VWC installed on their PC, and is requested to input their unique ID credentials (e.g. VW username/user ID)

Step 2: The VWC software initiates a secure connection (HTTPs) with the VWS. Both the VW Server and the VWC have a digital certificate, so that mutual authentication is achieved. The client software sends the ID credentials to the VWS over this secure channel.

Step 3: The VWS identifies this as a secure login request and passes it to the LS.

Table 2. Notation Table

Notation	Description
F	Function used for One Time Password generation
N	Nonce
ID	Any form of User Identity, like a username or other identifier
PIN	The PIN number that the user uses to login to the SCWS
OTP	One Time Password: The OTP that is generated as the result of function F in both the Login Server and the SCWS
Loc_{VWC}	The location of the VWC
Loc_{Phone}	The location of the Phone

Step 4: The LS checks the ID credentials: e.g. whether the user is already logged in, or has been banned due to some previous illicit action. If the credentials are acceptable, a time constrained authentication protocol is initialised. The LS creates a nonce (N), and an OTP in combination with the user's PIN i.e. $OTP = f(N,PIN)$. This OTP is stored securely in the LS. The VWS has substantial power, so OTP generation will not impact its performance. It must be noted that the OTP is only valid for a limited time period.

Step 5: The LS transmits N back to the VWS. Since both these servers are internal to the VW they are assumed to be secure and trusted.

Step 6: The VWS forwards N to the RAS. These entities also trust each other, and the connection between them is also established over a secure channel.

Step 7: The RAS determines the location of the phone (Loc_{Phone}) and returns it to the VWS.

Step 8: The VWS forwards the Loc_{Phone} to the LS.

Step 9: Once it receives N from the VWS, the RAS will establish an HTTPs connection with the user's SIM card and transfer N to the SCWS.

Step 10: Once N has been securely transferred to the SCWS, the user will connect to the SCWS via a link shown on the phone's browser. The user will be asked to input their PIN: if correct the OTP generation process is initialised.

Step 11: The PIN number is used as input to the same function used in the LS along with the nonce N that was received during step 9, to reproduce the OTP. This number is transformed into an eight byte alphanumeric string.

Step 12: The SCWS returns this string to the phone's browser via HTTPs.

Step 13: The user inputs the displayed OTP manually into the VWC. This is a time-constrained action; the LS must receive the OTP within a certain period.

Step 14: The entered OTP will be forwarded to the VWS (along with VWC's location Loc_{VWC}) over the previously established HTTPs connection.

Step 15: When the OTP/Loc_{VWC} pair reaches the VWS and is verified as authentic, it is forwarded to the LS.

Step 16: When the LS receives OTP/Loc_{VWC} pair, it will compare the OTP against the previously created OTP (Step 4) and check the location of the PC client Loc_{VWC} against the location of the phone Loc_{Phone} from (Step 8)

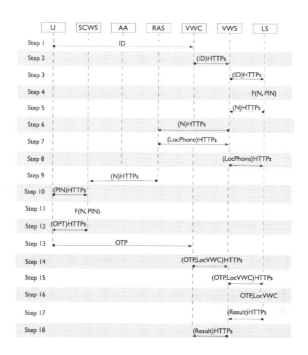

Fig. 5. Proposed Protocol Flow

Step 17: Successful checks authenticate the user on the LS: the VWS is notified.
Step 18: A message is sent to the VWC saying that the user is logged in. The VWC refreshes to the standard layout and user enters the VW.

A preliminary security analysis of the protocol will now be conducted.

5   Security Analysis of Protocol

The objective of this protocol is to give an assurance that if avatar X is in the Virtual World then we can reasonably assume that its legitimate real world controller (user X) has logged in by using two-factor authentication. The protocol also takes into consideration usability as one of the factors of security. There are several potential attack points which need to be considered with regard to the protocol's overall security, and these will be now analysed.

5.1   SCWS and Mobile Phone

Physical Security of the SIM: The SCWS is only accessible from the RAS or the phone browser and a malicious party needs to have physical access to the mobile phone to retrieve security information sent from the RAS. The information is processed by an applet on the tamper-resistant SIM/SCWS. To retrieve information about the applet /algorithms/ nonces used, etc, an attacker has to physically attack a SIM card or to know the correct SCWS PIN.

Web Based Attacks against the SCWS: The SCWS is a web server, and as such the OWASP top 10 attacks [19] may apply, but the potential to mount these from the phone browser is limited, and remote access to the SCWS is only permitted from the trusted RAS. The small attack surface of the restricted SCWS environment means that attackers have fewer opportunities to attack compared to a "traditional" web server. All web pages stored on the SCWS have little processing or scripting in them, which minimises attack potential.

Malware on the Phone: If phone malware steals the nonce from the SIM, it will still need the PIN number to generate the full OTP. If the malware is able to retrieve the OTP after this is created on the phone and/or is able to detect the phone's location, the attacker has to pass the OTP and the location information to a VWC before the legitimate user does so, which may represent a timing challenge. Malware on the phone alone, does not have the necessary potential to become a threat, since it also needs a PC client under the attacker's control to succeed with the attack.

Security of the RAS: The RAS is defined as a trusted entity in the assumptions, and therefore it is hard to attack. The RAS could be considered a single point of failure, but as it is owned/operated by an MNO or a trusted third party, it should have restricted and controlled physical access so any unauthorised usage will be difficult. In this proposal, it is used as a mere conduit between the VW Server and the SCWS, and does not store any secrets. The channel between the RAS and the SCWS is protected by HTTPs, and therefore has typical secure channel properties.

5.2   Virtual World Back-End Server

There is a generic attack which this protocol does not seek to address. If VW servers are compromised, this protocol will not protect the user or the VW developers. Malicious entities can get full control over the back end of the VW, and a user/avatar can then be impersonated. If the Login Server is compromised, the entire procedure fails and the malicious party can produce OTPs at will.

5.3   VW Client and Client PC

VWC and PC Security: The VW Client is the easiest target to attack. In current VW login procedures, if a malicious user steals a user ID/ password and downloads the appropriate VWC, a genuine user can be impersonated. However, in this proposed system, stealing the user ID is not enough to complete the login, as the user's SCWS/phone is also required. The advantage of this proposal compared to current practices is that if a static password is stolen, it can be used until the genuine user changes it, whereas with OTPs, an attacker gains access to one session only. Within this context, a reasonable compromise between security and usability is achieved. A highly motivated and knowledgeable attacker could still target a particular user/avatar, but the proposal sets more challenges for them to overcome.

Physical Compromise of the VWC: If there is a physical attack on the VWC equipment i.e. the computer is stolen, the malicious user will not be able to login into the VW system as the real authentication secret is sent to the phone. If the phone is stolen in addition to the computer then the attacker would also have to input the PIN on the phone to retrieve the OTP information from the SCWS, or physically attack the SCWS/SIM card.

Malware on the Client PC: If there is malware on the client computer e.g. a keylogger which records the OTP as it is input by the user [20], it will not gain any advantage, as the short validity period of the OTP means that authentication will probably complete before the malicious entity can mount an attack. If the malware is able to perform a DoS attack against the VWC, so that the user will not be able to submit the OTP, it still needs to spoof the IP address of the user. A certificate is also used to bind the VW Client to the VW Server, so malware would also have to steal or replicate this certificate for a successful attack. Although these attacks are possible, using the SCWS in conjunction with the PC will increase the complexity faced by malicious entities and may discourage less-motivated/unskilled attackers.

Mutual Authentication: In order to provide mutual authentication it is assumed that the VW Client is given a VW certificate during registration.

Data in Transit: Data in transit is protected by HTTPs at all stages: from phone browser to SCWS, RAS to SCWS and between the VWC and VWS. HTTPs is the de facto protocol used whenever security is needed on the web. There are recent attacks reported against HTTPs [21], but HTTPs provides reasonable protection against eavesdropping and man-in-the-middle attacks.

Replay Attacks: Replay attacks do not work as a particular OTP is used only once and is valid for a short time period.

Geolocation: IP spoofing [22] can also compromise the login process. IP geolocation can be spoofed by a motivated attacker [23], but including it in the protocol adds an additional obstacle for an attacker. Even though IP spoofing is not extremely difficult, the attacker also needs to know the location of the user/ phone at the exact time of the attack and simultaneously prevent the user from submitting the OTP through the genuine client. Geolocation checking is aimed against distant attackers, because if an attack is mounted within the genuine user's region it can be easily bypassed.

6   Conclusion

The relatively weak user authentication procedures employed by Virtual Worlds that rely on static username/password combinations lead to security issues such as identity theft. This paper has presented a method for using a phone, equipped with a Smart Card Web Server (SCWS) SIM, to enhance the login procedure of VWs by using One Time Passwords and location based checks. The use of standardised protocols (HTTPs, FAP), existing security hardware (SIM/SCWS) and secure communications, simplifies the design and operation of the proposal. A preliminary security analysis indicated that the proposal had promising capabilities to prevent unauthorised access to VWs. A more detailed analysis is required to fully understand its security properties and a practical implementation of the protocol would be useful to determine the speed of the various steps and how this would affect usability. Future work could also include an enhancement to the basic protocol to be used when a more advanced level of security is required (e.g. VW banking): this would involve a second OTP input to the SCWS, and sent to the VW via the RAS. The proposed protocol is believed to have security advantages over the current VW user ID/password login, so could form the basis of a new, more secure in-world experience for the millions of people who enjoy the freedoms and escapism that Virtual Worlds provide.

References

[1] Bell, M.: Virtual Worlds Research: Past, Present & Future July 2008: Toward a definition of "Virtual Worlds" (2008)

[2] KZero: Virtual worlds: Industry and user data universe (March 2012)

[3] Second Life Official Website, http://www.secondlife.com/

[4] World of Warcraft, http://eu.battle.net/wow/en/

[5] McGraw, G., Chow, M.: Guest editors' introduction: Securing online games: Safeguarding the future of software security: How world of warcraft almost ruined my credit rating. IEEE Security & Privacy, 11–12 (2009)

[6] Jorstad, I., Jonvik, T., et al.: Strong authentication with mobile phone as security token. In: Mobile Adhoc and Sensor Systems, MASS 2009, pp. 777–782. IEEE (2009)

[7] Vapen, A., Byers, D., Shahmehri, N.: 2-clickauth optical challenge-response authentication. In: Availability, Reliability, and Security, ARES 2010, pp. 79–86. IEEE (2010)

[8] Juniper Networks Inc.: Mobile Threats Report (2011)

[9] Open Mobile Alliance: Smartcard-Web-Server, Candidate Version 1.2, OMA-TS-Smartcard_Web_Server-V1_1_2-20120927-C, Open Mobile Alliance (OMA), Version 1.2 (September 27, 2012)

[10] Neustar: IP Geolocation: A Valuable Weapon to Fight Online Card-Not-Present Payment Fraud,
http://www.neustar.biz/enterprise/docs/whitepapers/ip-intelligence/geolocation-detecting-card-not-present-fraud.pdf

[11] Mayes, K.E., Markantonakis, K. (eds.): Smart Cards, Tokens, Security and Applications. Springer (2008)

[12] Calvin, J., Dickens, A., Gaines, B., Metzger, P., Miller, D., Owen, D.: The SIM-NET virtual world architecture. In: Virtual Reality Annual International Symposium, pp. 450–455. IEEE (1993)

[13] Frecon, E., Stenius, M.: DIVE: A scaleable network architecture for distributed virtual environments. In: Distributed Systems Engineering 5.3 (1998)

[14] Fernandes, S., Antonello, R., Moreira, J., Kamienski, C., Sadok, D.: Traffic analysis beyond this world: the case of Second Life. In: 17th International Workshop on Network and Operating Systems Support for Digital Audio and Video. University of Illinois, Urbana-Champaign (2007)

[15] RFC 2818: Hypertext Transfer Protocol over TLS protocol (May 2000), http://www.ietf.org/rfc/rfc2818.txt

[16] Oracle: Javacard v3.0 specifications, http://www.oracle.com/technetwork/java/javame/javacard/download/overview/index.html

[17] GlobalPlatform: Remote Application Management over HTTP Card Specification v2.2 Amendment B Version 1.1.1 (2012)

[18] RFC 4226: HOTP: An HMAC-Based One-Time Password Algorithm (December 2005), http://www.ietf.org/rfc/rfc4226.txt

[19] OWASP, The Open Web Application Security Project: OWASP Top Ten Project, https://www.owasp.org

[20] Shetty, S.: Symantec: Introduction to Spyware Keyloggers (November 2010), http://www.symantec.com/connect/articles/introduction-spyware-keyloggers

[21] Goodin, D.: Crack in Internet's foundation of trust allows HTTPS session hijacking (September 2012), http://arstechnica.com/security/2012/09/crime-hijacks-https-sessions/

[22] SANS Institute InfoSec Reading Room: Introduction to IP Spoofing (November 2000)

[23] Gill, P., Ganjali, Y., Wong, B., Lie, D.: Dude, where's that IP? Circumventing measurement-based IP geolocation. In: Proceedings of the 19th USENIX Conference on Security, Berkeley, CA, USA (2010)

A More Efficient and Secure Authentication Scheme over Insecure Networks Using Smart Cards

Chandra Sekhar Vorugunti[1,*] and Mrudula Sarvabhatla[2]

[1] Dhirubhai Ambani Institute of Information and Communication Technology,
Gandhi Nagar, India
Vorugunti_Chandra_Sekhar@daiict.ac.in
[2] Sri Venkateswara University, Tirupati, India
mrudula.s911@gmail.com

Abstract. In 2009, Xu et al. found that Lee et al.'s scheme is defenseless to offline password guessing attack. Xu et al. also indicated that Lee and Chiu's scheme is unguarded to forgery attack. Moreover, Lee and Chiu's scheme doesn't achieve mutual authentication and thus cannot resist malicious server attack. Xu et al. proposed an improved scheme. In 2010 Anil K Sarje et al. shown that Xu et al.'s scheme is vulnerable to forgery attack and proposed an improved scheme which preserves the merits of Xu et al. scheme and resists various attacks. In this paper we will show that Anil K Sarje et al. scheme cannot avoid any of the attacks they claimed that their scheme will resists. We then present our enhanced scheme to fix the vulnerabilities found in Anil K Sarje et al. scheme and various related dynamic identity based authentication schemes while preserving their merits.

Keywords: Smart card, Authentication, Authentication Protocols, Remote server Access.

1 Introduction

Remote user authentication is a mechanism in which a remote user is validated to access remote server resources or services over an insecure communication channel. Smart card based password authentication scheme is one of the most widely used technique for various kinds of authentication applications such as online banking, online shopping etc. Password authentication with smart cards is an efficient two-factor authentication mechanism to validate the legitimacy of a user.

In 2009, Xu et al. [2] found that Lee et al.'s [3] scheme is vulnerable to offline password guessing attack. Xu et al. also demonstrated that Lee and Chiu's [4] scheme is vulnerable to forgery attack. Furthermore, Lee and Chiu's scheme does not achieve mutual authentication and thus cannot resist malicious server attack. Therefore Sarje et al. proposed an improved scheme and claimed that improved scheme eliminates the security flaws in Xu et al.'s scheme. In this paper, we will show that the Sarje et al. [1] scheme is still vulnerable to all the attacks they claimed that their

---

* Corresponding author.

Sabu M. Thampi et al. (Eds.): SSCC 2013, CCIS 377, pp. 42–51, 2013.

scheme will resist i.e., user impersonation attack, server masquerade attack, stolen smart card attack, password guessing attack, Man in the Middle attack and fails to preserve user anonymity. We then propose an improvement scheme over Sarje et al.'s scheme to remedy their drawbacks.

The rest of the paper is organized as follows. In section 2 a brief review of Sarje et al.'s scheme is given. Section 3 describes the security weakness of Sarje et al. scheme. In section 4 our improved scheme is proposed and its security analyses are discussed in section 5. The cost and security comparison of various similar dynamic identity based authentication schemes are given in section 6 and section 7 provides the conclusion of the paper.

2   Review of Anil K Sarje et al.'s Scheme

In this section, we examine the improvement of Xu et al.'s authentication scheme using smart cards proposed by Sarje et al. [1] in 2010. The scheme is composed of three phases: the registration, login, and authentication phase.

2.1   Registration Phase

This phase is invoked whenever a user U_i registers with the remote system for the first time.

(R1) U_i selects his user identity ID_i, password P_i and submits the ID_i and P_i to the system S through a secure channel for registration.

(R2) S chooses a unique value y_i to each user U_i and computes the security parameters:

$$B_i \equiv H(ID_i)^{x+y}{}_i \bmod p \tag{1}$$

$$C_i \equiv H(ID_i)^{y}{}_i{}^{+P}{}_i \bmod p \tag{2}$$

The server S issues the smart card with security parameters $(B_i, C_i, H(\ ), p, q)$ to the user U_i where p, q are large prime numbers such that $q = 2p+1$. The server also stores identity ID_i of the user U_i in its database.

2.2   Login and Authentication Phase

Whenever the user intends to access the remote server S resources, the following procedure is performed.

(A1) U_i inserts his smart card into the card reader of a terminal and inputs his ID_i and P_i

(A2) The smart card computes:
$$C_i' \equiv C_i / H(ID_i)^{P}{}_i \bmod p \equiv H(ID_i)^{y}{}_i \bmod p$$
$$B_i' \equiv B_i / C_i' \equiv H(ID_i)^x \bmod p$$
$$D_i \equiv (B_i')^w \equiv H(ID_i)^{xw} \bmod p$$
$$E_i \equiv H(ID_i)^w \bmod p$$
$$M_i \equiv H(B_i' \mid C_i' \mid D_i \mid T)$$

where smart card chooses w belongs to $R \varepsilon Z_Q^*$ and T is the current time stamp of smartcard. Then smart card sends the login request message (ID_i, B_i, E_i, M_i, T) to the server S.

(A2) Compute: $h(x2 \mid y_i \mid b_i)^* = M_i \oplus T$, search for $h(x2 \mid y_i \mid b)^*$ in the database and extract $h(x2 \mid y_i \mid b_i)^*$, $ID_i \oplus h(x1)$, $h(x2) \oplus y_i$. As the server knows two secret keys x1, x2, h(x1), h(x2), it extracts ID_i, y_i from $ID_i \oplus h(x1)$, $h(x2) \oplus y_i$.

2.3   Verification Phase

After receiving U_i's login request message at time T^*, the server S performs the following steps:

(V1) The service provider server S verifies the received value of ID_i with stored value of ID_i in its database.

(V2) If $T^* - T \leq \Delta t$, S accepts U_i's login request else rejects the request where Δt is the valid time interval.

(V3) The server S computes:

$$B_i' \equiv H(ID_i)^x \bmod p$$
$$C_i' \equiv B_i / B_i' \equiv H(ID_i)^y{}_i \bmod p$$
$$D_i' \equiv E_i^x \equiv H(ID_i)^{xw} \bmod p$$
$$M_i' \equiv H(B_i' \mid C_i' \mid D_i' \mid T)$$

and compares M_i' with the received values of M_i. If both are equal then the user is authenticated else closes the connection.

Finally the server S and the user U_i agree on the common session key S.K = ($ID_i \mid C_i' \mid B_i' \mid T$) and all the subsequent messages are XORed with the session key S.K.

2.4   Password Change Phase

The user U_i can change his password without help of the server S. The user U_i inserts his smart card into the card reader and enters his ID_i and P_i. The smart card authenticates the user so that the user can instruct the smart card reader to change the password. Once the new password P_{new} entered by the user, the smart card replaces $C_i \equiv H(ID_i)^{y_i + P_i} \bmod p$ with $C_i^{new} = C_i / [H(ID_i)^{P_i}] *[H(ID_i)^{P_{inew}} \bmod p]$ and password gets changed.

3   Weakness of Anil K Sarje et al's Scheme

Sarje et al. [1] claimed that their scheme counters the weakness in Xu et al. [2] scheme i.e., forgery attack and resists various known attacks. In this section, we will show that Sarje et al.'s scheme cannot resists any of the attacks they claimed that their scheme will prevent and still vulnerable to revealing of secret key of server to legal user, user impersonation attack, server masquerade attack, man in the middle attack, fails to preserve mutual authentication and revealing of user password.

3.1   Revealing of User Secret Value Assigned by the Server to Legal User and Server Secret Value

A legal user U_i already knows his Identity ID_i and password P_i. After extracting B_i, C_i stored in his smart card by some means [2, 3, 10], U_i can perform guessing attack on (2) i.e. $C_i \equiv H(ID_i)^{y_i + P_i} \bmod p$, for y_i, as it is the only unknown value to the legal user in (2). Guess a secret value y_i^*, and check $C_i^* \equiv H(ID_i)^{y_i^* + P_i} \bmod p$. If they are equal then the secret value assigned by the server to user U_i is y_i^*. Otherwise E can repeat the process to get correct value y_i^*.

Once y_i is known to U_i, he can perform same guessing attack on (1) i.e., $B_i \equiv H(ID_i)^{x + y_i} \bmod p$. The only unknown value in (1) is x. Guess a secret value x^*, and check $B_i^* \equiv H(ID_i)^{x^* + y_i} \bmod p$. If they are equal then the secret key of server is x. Otherwise user can repeat the process to get correct value x^*.

3.2   Stolen Smart Card Attack Coupled with Insider Attack to Get Identity and Password of a Legal User

A legal adversary E, if gets the smart card of any valid user U_i of the system for a while or stolen the card, E can extract the secret data stored in U_i's smart card by some means [2, 3, 10] can get B_i, C_i.

Once U_i logs into the system, the legal adversary 'E' can capture login request with intermediate computational results $\{ID_i, B_i, E_i, M_i, T\}$ of user U_i, which a smart card sends to server. From this login request, E will come to know the identity ID_i of user U_i.

B.1) Through (3.1), E got the secret key of server S i.e., 'x' which is common to all the users.

B.2) E knows B_i of user U_i from the login request. Now E can perform guessing attack. Guess a secret value y_i^*, and check $B_i^* \equiv H(ID_i)^{x+y_i^*} \bmod p$. If they are equal then the secret value y_i assigned to user U_i is y_i^*. Otherwise user can repeat the process to get correct value y_i.

B.3) Now E knows x, y_i, ID_i of U_i. Calculate $B_i' = H(ID_i)^x \bmod p$

B.4) E knows C_i of user U_i, Now E can perform guessing attack. Guess a password p_i^* and check $C_i^* = H(ID_i)^{y_i + p_i^*} \bmod p$. If they are equal then the user password is p_i, otherwise user can repeat the process to get correct value p_i.

Hence in Anil K Sarje et al scheme, the biggest threat is the revealing of user password P_i, server secret key x.

3.3   User Impersonation Attack

An adversary 'E' who is a legal user can impersonate another legal user U_i of Server S as follows.

(1) Intercept the U_i login request message $\{ID_i, B_i, E_i, M_i, T\}$ and extract ID_i, B_i, E_i, M_i

where $B_i \equiv H(ID_i)^{x + y_i} \bmod p$

$E_i \equiv H(ID_i)^w \bmod p$

$M_i \equiv H(B_i' \mid C_i \mid D_i \mid T)$

(2) 'E' don't have to change ID_i, B_i, E_i as they are non-dependent on time, 'E' must frame $M_i^* \equiv H(B_i' \mid C_i' \mid D_i \mid T^*)$ at time T^* to impersonate as U_i. E must calculate B_i', C_i', D_i to frame M_i.

(3) $B_i' \equiv H(ID_i)^x$ mod p. from the login request, E knows the identity of user U_i and as discussed in (3.1) he gets 'x' and frames B_i' and $C_i' \equiv B_i/B_i'$. E will get B_i from the U_i login request message (1) and B_i' from (2) .

(4) $D_i = E_i^x$. As 'x' is a secret key of server and E gets x from (A) and E_i from the U_i login request message. From (1), (2), (3), (4) E can frame $M_i \equiv H(B_i' \mid C_i' \mid D_i \mid T^*)$

Whenever 'E' wants to impersonate 'U_i' he can send a fake login request message $\{ID_i, B_i, E_i, M_i, T^*\}$ at time T^* to S with proper T^*. It will pass the authentication process (V1), (V2), (V3) of S. Only value adversary needs to take care is T^*. E can find out the valid T^* by eaves dropping the communication between U and S.

3.4   Failure to Achieve Mutual Authentication

An adversary 'E' who is a legal user can perform Man in the middle attack as follows. Graphical View of Man in the middle attack in Anil K Sarje et al.'s scheme

User (U_i)   Adversary   Server (S)
                    (Adversary Intercepted 'x')

Login Phase
                    $\{ID_i, B_i, E_i, M_i, T\}$
    ──────────────────────────►

                    Compute:
                    $B_i' \equiv h(ID_i)^x$ mod p
                    $C_i' \equiv B_i/B_i'$
                    E will get B_i from U_i login request message
                    $D_i = E_i^x$.
                    frame $M_i^* \equiv h(B_i' \mid C_i' \mid D_i \mid T^*)$ where $T^*-T = \Delta t$

                            $\{ID_i, B_i, E_i, M_i, T^*\}$
                    ──────────────────────────►
                                        Compute:

                                $Bi' = H(ID_i)^x$ mod p
                                $C_i' = Bi / Bi' = H(ID_i)^{y_i}$ mod p
                                $D_i' = E_i^x = H(ID_i)^{xw}$ mod p
                                $M_i' = H(B_i \mid C_i' \mid D_i' \mid T^*)$.
                                Check M_i' computed $= M_i'$ received
frame $S.K_{U-A} \equiv (ID_i \mid C_i' \mid B_i' \mid T)$ frame $S.K_{A-S} \equiv (ID_i \mid C_i' \mid B_i' \mid T^*)$

4   Our Improved Scheme

In this section, we present an improved scheme over Anil K Sarje et al. [1] scheme to remedy their security flaws as mentioned above while preserving their merits. The proposed scheme is divided into four phases: the registration, login, authentication, and password change phases where the password change phase is similar to Sarje et al. scheme [1].

4.1   Registration Phase

This phase is invoked whenever a user U_i wants to register first time with the remote server S. The following steps are performed

(R1) The user U_i first chooses his identity ID_i and password PW_i, and a random number b_i.

(R2) U->S:$\{ID_i, PW_i, b_i\}$ through a secure communication channel

(R3) S computes:

$$B_i \equiv h(ID_i)^{(b_i | y_i) \cdot (x1 | x2) + (x2 | y_i)} \mod p \tag{2}$$

$$C_i \equiv h(ID_i)^{(b_i | PW_i) + (x2 | y_i)} \mod p \tag{2}$$

Where x1, x2 are the two secret keys of server S, 'y_i' is the secret value chosen by server S for each user U_i such that $(x1| y_i)$, $(x2| y_i)$ and $(b_i| y_i)$ are unique for each user. 'S' also selects a large prime number 'p'. The server stores ID_i, $(x2| y_i)$, $(b_i| y_i)$ for each user U_i.

(R4) S->U, a smart card containing B_i, C_i, h(.), p to the user U_i through a secure communication channel.

4.2   Login Phase

Whenever user wants to login into the remote server S, he inserts his smart card into the terminal and inputs his ID_i, PW_i and b_i. Then the smart card performs the following tasks.

(L1) Compute:

$$C_i' \equiv C_i / h(ID_i)^{(b_i | PW_i)} \mod p \equiv h(ID_i)^{(x2 | y_i)} \mod p$$
$$B_i' \equiv B_i / C_i' \equiv h(ID_i)^{(b_i | y_i) \cdot (x1 | x2)} \mod p$$
$$D_i \equiv (B_i')^w \equiv h(ID_i)^{w \cdot (b_i | y_i) \cdot (x1 | x2)} \mod p$$
$$E_i \equiv h(ID_i)^w \mod p$$
$$M_i \equiv h(B_i' | C_i' | D_i | T)$$

Smart card sends to you the login request:
Smart Card-> S: $\{ID_i, B_i, E_i, M_i, T\}$

4.3   Authentication Phase

On receiving the login request message at time T^* from U_i, S performs the following tasks:

(A1) Verify: $T^*-T \le \Delta t$ if yes, then proceeds for further computation

(A2) Verify: ID_i and indexes through the database for ID_i and retrieves ID_i, $(x2| y_i)$, $(b_i| y_i)$.

(A3) Compute: $C_i' \equiv h(ID_i)^{(x2 | y_i)} \mod p$ from extracted values of ID_i, $(x2| y_i)$.

(A4) Compute: $B_i' \equiv B_i / C_i'$ ('S' got B_i from login request and Ci' from (A3))

(A5) Compute: $D_i \equiv E_i^{(x1|x2)(b_i | y_i)}$ ('S' gets $(b_i| y_i)$ from its extracted values and S knows its secret keys x1, x2)

(A6) Compute $M_i \equiv h(B_i^{'} \mid C_i^{'} \mid D_i \mid T)$

(A7) If computed M_i in (A6) equals M_i received then the legality of the user is authenticated and 'S' proceeds further to establish the session else rejects the login request from user U_i and closes the connection.

(A8) S and U_i frames Session key $SK \equiv h(ID_i \mid C_i^{'} \mid B_i^{'} \mid T)$ afterwards all the messages are XORed with the session key so that only U_i and 'S' can retrieve the messages.

5   Security Analysis of Improved Scheme

In this section we discuss and demonstrate how our proposed scheme fixes the vulnerabilities found in Sarje et al. [1]'s scheme while preserving the merits of their scheme.

5.1   Prevention of Revealing of Secret Key of Server to Legal User

A legal user knows his Identity ID_i, random number b_i, and password PW_i. He can extract B_i, C_i from the smart card memory as discussed in [2,3,10,11]. A legal user from the extracted values of B_i, C_i can perform following operations.
Compute:

$$C_i^{'} \equiv C_i / h(ID_i)^{(b_i \mid PW_i)} \bmod p \equiv h(ID_i)^{(x2 \mid y_i)} \bmod p \tag{A.3}$$

$$B_i^{'} \equiv B_i / C_i^{'} \equiv h(ID_i)^{(b_i \mid y_i) \cdot (x1 \mid x2)} \bmod p \tag{A.2}$$

From the known values of ID_i, PW_i, b_i the legal user can perform guessing attack on (A.1) but U_i doesn't know either x2 or y_i, so guessing two unkowns simultaneously is computationally infeasible in real time. U_i can perform guessing attack on (A.1) for $(x2 \mid y_i)$ as a whole. Even U_i guesses the $(x2 \mid y_i)$ value correctly, it is only U_i specific and not useful to him to perform any attack on other user smart card. Similarly the case with (A.2). by getting B_i, C_i and computing $B_i^{'}$, $C_i^{'}$ user U_i doesn't get any info specific to server (x1, x2, y_i) and info specific to any other user of 'S'. Hence in our scheme the secret keys of the servers and y_i values are not revealed to any kind of user and the information guessed by one user U_i is of no use in guessing values of another user U_k.

5.2   Resistance to User Impersonation Attack

To impersonate a user U_i, a legal adversary E must fake a login message {ID_i, B_i, E_i, M_i, T} to the remote server S. To impersonate U_i, E must frame M_i correctly. To frame M_i, E must know $B_i^{'}$, $C_i^{'}$, D_i, T of U_i. E can get B_i, C_i from the stolen smart card of U_i. To frame $C_i^{'}$, E needs $h(ID_i)^{(b_i \mid PW_i)} \bmod p$, without knowing the password PW_i, b_i it is impossible to frame $C_i^{'}$, without Ci', $B_i^{'}$ cannot be framed. Hence in our scheme it is impossible for any kind of user to create a fake login message and impersonate a legal user U_i.

5.3   Resistance to Server Masquerade Attack

To masquerade as remote server S, an adversary E has to send U_i, a forged reply message XORed with SK as discussed in (A8). To frame SK, E must know C_i', B_i' of user U_i. We shown in 5.2, that it's impossible to guess or intercept C_i', B_i' by any kind of user. Hence in our scheme it is impossible for anyone to masquerade as server.

5.4   Resistance to Insider Attack

A legal adversary 'E', if stolen the smart card of the user U_i and captured B_i, C_i, later if U_i logs into the system and sends the login request through a public communication channel, E can capture the login request which a smart card sends to server, E have B_i, C_i and $\{ID_i, B_i, E_i, M_i, T\}$ of user U_i. It's not possible for an adversary E to find out any unknown values of user U_i. Hence our scheme provides resistant to offline password guessing attacks, stolen smart card attack, insider attack.

5.5   Prevention of Man in the Middle Attack

If we observe Sarje et al's [1] scheme, Man in the Middle attack graphical view, an adversary E, once performing the stolen smart card attack, can extract the information stored in the smart card and can perform guessing attack on 'x'. Once E gets the server secret key x, E can compute B_i', C_i', M_i, by computing B_i', C_i', M_i. E can frame a session key with server S and user U_i. It is not the case with our proposed scheme. No value of another valid user U_i can be intercepted or guessed by legal adversary E (also shown in 5.2 and 5.3). Hence it is not possible to frame a session key with server and user for an adversary. Hence our scheme is secure against Man in the Middle attack. As discussed above, E cannot frame a session key between User and Server, our scheme prevents Perfect Forward Secrecy (PFS) attack by E.

6   Cost and Security Analysis

In this section we analyze communication and computation cost required by our protocol and we compare the same with relevant protocols. We are also assuming the following things as similar to Sarje et al. scheme. The ID_i, PW_i, x1, x2, y_i, b_i, Time stamps all are128 bits. The output of Hash function is 128-bit. T_H, T_E, T_x, T_P denote the time complexity for hash function, exponential operation, XOR operation, public key operation. The time complexity associated with these operations can be roughly expressed as $T_P \gg T_E \gg T_H \approx T_R \gg T_x$. E1: The number of bits required to store the parameters C_i, B_i, $p = 3 * 128 = 384$ bits. E2: The communication cost of authentication i.e., the communication cost of $\{ID_i, B_i, E_i, M_i, T\} = 5 * 128 = 640$ bits. E3: Total time of all operations executed in the registration phase. In our scheme two exponential operations and one hash are performed to frame B_i and C_i. $E3 = 2T_E + 1T_H$. E4: The time spent by the user during the process of authentication $= 3T_E + 2T_H$. E5: The time spent by the server during the process of authentication $= 2T_E + 2T_H$.

Table 1. Efficiency comparison among various smart card scheme

	Proposed Scheme	Sarje et al [1]	Xu et al [2]	Yang et al [5]	Liao et al [6]	Lee-Chiu [4]	Lee et al [3]
E1 (bits)	512	512	512	896	512	640	128
E2 (bits)	5*128	5*128	8*128	10*128	6*128	4*128	5*128
E3	$2T_E+1T_H$	$2T_E+2T_H$	$1T_E+2T_H$	$2T_H+1T_R$	$1T_E+2T_H$	$1T_E+2T_H$	$1T_H+2T_X$
E4	$3T_E+2T_H$	$3T_E+3T_H$	$3T_E+5T_H$	$1T_E+1T_P$	$1T_E+3T_H$	$2T_E+2T_H+1T_X$	$3T_H+3T_X$
E5	$2T_E+2T_H$	$2T_E+3T_H$	$3T_E+4T_H$	$1T_E+1T_P$	$1T_E+3T_H$	$1T_E+2T_H+1T_X$	$4T_H+2T_X$
Total	$7T_E+5T_H$	$7T_E+8T_H$	$7T_E+11T_H$	$2T_E+2T+$ $2T_H+1T_R$	$3T_E+8T_H$	$4T_E+6T_H+2T_X$	$8T_H+7T_X$

The proposed scheme computation and communication cost is less than Sarje et al. [1], Xu et al. [2] schemes ,more than Liao et al. [6] scheme. But our scheme is highly secure compared to other schemes.

Table 2. Comparison of security features

Security feature	Bindu et al's scheme [7]	Anand et al. scheme [8]	Anil K Sarje et al. [1]	Our Proposed Scheme
Withstanding user impersonation attack	No	No	No	Yes
Withstanding server masquerading attack	No	No	No	Yes
Withstanding man in the middle attack	No	No	No	Yes
Achieving mutual authentication	No	No	No	Yes
Prevention of stolen smart card attack	No	No	No	Yes
Preventing DOS attack	No	No	No	Yes
Withstanding perfect forward secrecy attack	No	No	No	Yes

7   Conclusion

In this paper we have shown that Anil k Sarje et al. scheme cannot prevent any of the attacks they claimed that their scheme will prevent and vulnerable to numerous cryptographic attacks. As a part of our contribution, we have proposed an authentication scheme which is an improved version over various related authentication protocols, which requires minimum computation to achieve high level of security.

References

1. Sood, S.K., Sarje, A.K., Singh, K.: An improvement of Xu et al.'s authentication scheme using smart cards. In: COMPUTE 2010, Proceedings of the Third Annual ACM Bangalore Conference (2010)
2. Xu, J., Zhu, W.T., Feng, D.G.: An Improved Smart Card based Password Authentication Scheme with Provable Security. Computer Standards & Interfaces 31(4), 723–728 (2009)
3. Lee, S.W., Kim, H.S., Yoo, K.Y.: Improvement of Chien et al.'s Remote User Authentication Scheme using Smart Cards. Computer Standards & Interfaces 27(2), 181–183 (2005)
4. Lee, N.Y., Chiu, Y.C.: Improved Remote Authentication Scheme with Smart Card. Computer Standards & Interfaces 27(2), 177–180 (2005)
5. Yang, G., Wong, D.S., Wang, H., Deng, X.: Two-factor Mutual Authentication based on Smart Cards and Passwords. Journal of Computer and System Sciences 74(7), 1160–1172 (2008)
6. Liao, I.E., Lee, C.C., Hwang, M.S.: A Password Authentication Scheme over Insecure Networks. Journal of Computer and System Sciences 72(4), 727–740 (2006)
7. Bindu, C.S., Reddy, P.C.S., Satyanarayana, B.: Improved Remote User Authentication Scheme Preserving User Anonymity. International Journal of Computer Science and Network Security 8(3), 62–66 (2008)
8. Shoba Bindu, C., Misbahuddin, M., Ahmad, M.A., Ananda Rao, A., Muqist Khan, M.A.: A Novel Dynamic ID Based Remote User Authentication Scheme. International Journal of Computer Science and Network Security 8(3), 62–66 (2008)

A Combined Crypto-steganographic Approach for Information Hiding in Audio Signals Using Sub-band Coding, Compressive Sensing and Singular Value Decomposition

G. Jyothish Lal, V.K. Veena, and K.P. Soman

Centre for Excellence in Computational Engineering and Networking
Amrita Vishwa Vidyapeetham
Coimbatore-641112, India
jyothishlal@gmail.com

Abstract. In this paper, a new method of audio data security system is proposed, which uses the complementary services provided by steganography and cryptography. Here the audio data to be send secretly is encoded using the compressive measurements of the same and the resultant data is embedded in the perceptible band of the cover audio data using the SVD based watermarking algorithm. Thus the combination of these two methods enhances the protection against most serious attacks when audio signals are transmitted over an open channel. Decryption stage uses SVD based watermark extraction algorithm and L_1 optimization. Experimental results show that the combined system enhances the security of the audio data embedded.

Keywords: Sub-band coding, Compressive Sensing (CS), SVD, Combined Crypto-stegangraphy.

1 Introduction

The revolution in digital multimedia technologies changed the way in which digital data are transmitted through the transmission channel. Also, with the widespread use of Internet and freely available software's, the feasibility of redundant multimedia data for any kind of manipulation such as editing and distribution has increased. So there is a great concern over the security of these digital data. That is, any kind of unauthorized access should be denied to stop the piracy of data.

Cryptography and steganography are two widely used techniques for secure data communication over an open channel. Both these techniques manipulate digital content in order to encrypt or hide their existence respectively [1]. Cryptography encrypts the information by which data is difficult to read.In other words, it is the art of secure communication that protects the data by writing it in secret code. That is, data in the intelligible form is transformed into an unintelligible form. This transformation is called encryption. In this paper, the

Sabu M. Thampi et al. (Eds.): SSCC 2013, CCIS 377, pp. 52–62, 2013.

audio data is transformed into scrambled measurements which is also called cipher audio data. Decryption is the reverse process. The sender of the cipher audio data shares the decoding technique used for retrieving the original audio data. Cipher is a pair of algorithm that creates encryption and decryption. The operation of the cipher is controlled both by the algorithm and each instant by a secret key [2]. Steganography is a powerful security tool that provides a high level of security when it is combined with encryption [3]. It embeds the information on to a cover medium so that other person cannot know the presence of hidden information. This model mainly consists of message, carrier, embedding algorithm and stego key. Even though both methods provide security, it is a good practice to combine these two methods for better security. This paper uses SVD based watermarking as steganographic algorithm for hiding the secret audio data.

Information hiding or encoding is more challenging for audio data when compared to image or video data. This is because Human Auditory System (HAS) has a wide dynamic range when compared to Human Visual System (HVS) [4]. So encoding scheme for audio data takes advantages of the psycho acoustical masking property of HAS. This acoustic property implies that louder signal will mask the weaker signals. Thus human ear will not be able to perceive weaker sounds in the presence of louder sounds. This imperceptibility to weaker sounds is used in compression of audio data and embedding of secret information.

In the proposed combined Crypto-steganography method, prior to transmission, the cover audio data is compressed using Sub-band coding. The imperceptible frequency bands obtained after Sub-band coding are removed for efficient utilization of the constrained bandwidth. Then compressive measurements of the secret audio data are taken to embed in the perceptible frequency band of the cover audio data. These measurements are considered as encrypted representation of secret audio data. Additional encryption is provided by interleaving the measurements by a random permutation vector. In this paper, the next level of security to the compressed and scrambled measurements is provided with the aid of steganography. The encrypted audio data is embedded on to a carrier audio data by using SVD based watermarking. The resultant stego file is transmitted through the network. The proposed system proves to be more advantageous since the attention of an eavesdropper will be distracted by hiding the encrypted audio data in a cover medium. Also any attack towards Compressive Sensing technique is reduced. Furthermore, the channel capacity is efficiently utilized by the compressing both the cover audio data and secret audio data. Experimental results shows that combined security of Compressive Sensing and SVD watermarking is computationally more secure against attack on sensitive audio data.

This paper organized as follows. Section 2 provides a description about Subband coding. Section 3 provides a brief introduction about Compressive Sensing. Section 4 explains SVD based watermarking. Section 5 describes the combined Crypto-steganography encryption and decryption scheme. Section 6 gives the experimental results and finally section 7 concludes the paper.

2   Sub-band Coding for Audio Compression

The transmission of any signal through the constrained bandwidth demands the
signal bandwidth to be as small as possible. So there is a need for compression
of the signal. In the compression paradigm, Sub-band coding is one of the basic
methods of decomposition that breaks the signal or data into a number of different frequency bands [5,6,7]. These constituent parts will make up the source
signal. The data is divided into constituent frequency bands, typically 4 or 8,
by filter banks. Filter is a system that isolates a specific band of frequencies
based on some cut off value. It can be low pass, high pass, band pass etc. Here
in Sub-band coding, the compression of audio data uses the approach of passing the same through a bank of filters that will discard the information about
perceptually irrelevant bands.

Human ear has the deficiency of not hearing the weaker signal frequency in
the presence of a louder one. This is because louder sounds acts as a masker for
weaker sounds and human ear will not be able to perceive such sounds. This
deficiency is exploited in the data compression of audio signal through Sub-
band coding. The filters used in the process is known as Sub-band filters which
consists of cascaded low pass and high pass filter at each level. The pass band
of each filter determines the specific band of frequencies it can pass through.
The filtering operation is followed by down sampling to reduce the number of
samples. Fig. 1 show an audio data passed through eight band filter bank giving
four Sub-bands b0 to b3.

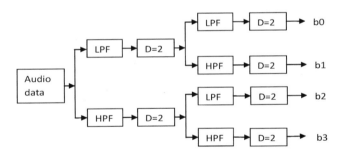

Fig. 1. Audio data passed through eight band filter bank. LPF and HPF denote low
pass filter and high pass filter, D=2 denotes decimation by 2

3   Compressive Sensing

Compressive Sensing (CS) is a recent technique in signal processing, which aims
at sparse signal acquisition and its recovery [8]. It is an entirely different method
from the traditional signal acquisition. Traditional methods follow Nyquist sampling theorem, which states that the sampling rate should be twice the maximum
signal frequency. This type of acquisition needs further compression of the acquired samples before transmission. This in turn increases the computation and

thereby consumption of the power of encoder device (often a battery operated device) also increases. So the target of Compressive Sensing is to reduce the consumption of resources. It could be the power or cost of the hardware.

CS tries to sense data from a fewer number of samples. That is, it directly acquires the compressed data. This is based on two principles namely sparsity and incoherence [9].

3.1 Sparsity and Incoherence

Compressive sampling relies on the sparse nature of the signal [10]. Many of the signals in nature are sparse in some domain, which means much of the transform domain coefficients are approximately zero and therefore does not contribute much to the signal intelligence. So these signals can be represented as in a concise manner when they are expressed in the proper basis Ψ. But, sensing in a sparse representation is not a good idea since the probability of finding out a non-zero coefficient is way too small. This demands sampling of the signal in another basis Φ. that can spread out the information contained in it. That is, both these bases are incoherent to each other. More precisely, the signal which has sparse representation in one domain will be spread out in the domain in which they are sensed.

Let x is an N-Point real valued signal which can be interpreted as $x = \Psi\theta$, where Ψ is a dictionary of size N×N that can give K sparse representation of x with K<<N and θ is the vector of scalar coefficients of x. This K sparse vector x is sampled with an orthogonalized random matrix Φ of size M×N to produce M<N compressive measurements y.

$$y = \Phi x = \Phi\Psi\theta \ . \tag{1}$$

The random measurements y will preserve the information present in x with high probability if M is taken in the order as follows.

$$M = O(K log(N/K)) \ . \tag{2}$$

3.2 Signal Reconstruction

The original signal can be reconstructed from the linear measurements if the sensing matrix Φ is known. But the system y =Φx is an under determined system since the number of rows of Φ is less than the number of samples N. Therefore, it will be having infinitely many solutions. However, the assumption of sparsity allows the recovery of unique solution via CS framework. Usually, least square techniques are used to find out that unique solution [11]. But an exact and computationally less complex recovery algorithm uses L_1 optimization which is also called basis pursuit algorithm, which can be formulated as:

$$\min \|\theta\|_1 \quad \text{subject to} \quad y = \Phi x = \Phi\Psi\theta \ . \tag{3}$$

4   SVD Based Watermarking Algorithm

SVD or Singular Value Decomposition has been employed for wide variety of image based application such as compression, hiding, watermarking etc [12,13]. SVD of any matrix A of size M×N can be represented as

$$A = U\Sigma V^T .$$ (4)

where U and V are orthogonal matrix and Σ is the diagonal matrix containing the singular values. The important feature of these singular values is that it undergoes slight variation only, when subjected to any kind of manipulation. This property is utilized in audio data hiding. The algorithm composed of an embedding stage to embed the watermark(W) in the cover data and an extraction stage to extract the watermark.

4.1   Embedding Algorithm

Initially, the audio signal is converted into 2-D matrix since SVD is a matrix decomposition technique. Then, SVD of this 2-D matrix is taken and the diagonal matrix formed (consisting of singular values) is added with matrix of scrambled measurements (W) with a scale factor α. Again, SVD of the new matrix Σ_n is taken and watermark matrix is formed by multiplying the matrix U, Σ_w and V^T. The algorithm is summarized as follows.

$$\left. \begin{array}{l} A = U\Sigma V^T \\ \Sigma_n = \Sigma + \alpha W \\ \Sigma_n = U_w \Sigma_w V_w^T \\ A_w = U \Sigma_w V^T \end{array} \right\} .$$ (5)

4.2   Extraction Algorithm

Algorithm requires U_w, Σ and V_w for extraction. It consists of the following steps.

$$\left. \begin{array}{l} A^*{}_w = U^* \Sigma^*{}_w V^{*T} \\ D^* = U_w \Sigma^*{}_w V_w^T \\ W^* = \frac{1}{\alpha}(D^* - \Sigma) \end{array} \right\} .$$ (6)

5   Combined Crypto-steganography

5.1   Sending Stage

In the sending stage, both the methods are combined by encrypting the message using cryptography and then hiding the encrypted message using steganography. Initially, the secret audio data is encrypted using Compressive Sensing. Encryption of the audio is done by performing a linear measurement step. It is achieved by using a measurement matrix. The measurement matrix is generated by using a secret key. The resulting encrypted and compressed measurements is further scrambled by interleaving process with the aid of a random permutation vector. Now, the scrambled measurements is converted into a matrix format, called cipher data. Then, the cover audio data used for embedding is decomposed into its constituent frequency bands using Sub-band coding. Only the perceptible band is taken and it is also transformed into a matrix format and the cipher audio data is embedded into it using SVD watermarking algorithm. The result is transformed back into 1-D audio signal, which is now called as the stego audio file. Fig. 2 shows the proposed combined encryption and embedding stage.

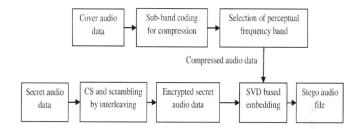

Fig. 2. Encryption and embedding stage

5.2   Receiving Stage

The receiving system performs the reverse operation of the sending system. Initially, the stego audio file is extracted using SVD based watermark extracting algorithm. The obtained scrambled audio data is is rearranged into original vector format by De-interleaving with the same permutation vector used at the sending stage. Finally, it is decrypted using L_1 optimization method. Fig. 3 shows the proposed combined extraction and decryption stage.

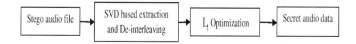

Fig. 3. Extraction and decryption stage

6   Experimental Results

For evaluation of the proposed method , a cover audio data sampled at 12000 Hz and secret audio data with sampling rate 8000 Hz were used. First decomposition stage of Sub-band coding divides the cover audio data into two half bands of 0-6000 Hz and 6000-12000 Hz respectively. This bandwidth division allows the reduction of number of samples via decimation process. Fig. 4 shows the cover

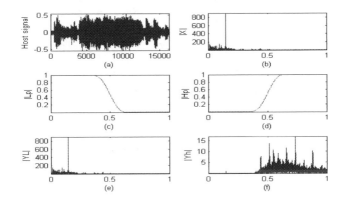

Fig. 4. (a) Cover audio signal or host signal; (b) its frequency response; (c) and (d) filter response of two filters; (e) and (f) lower and upper bands after filtering

audio signal with its frequency response, filter response of filters and the two speech bands in frequency domain.

The bands are again divided to form four bands b0 to b3 of 0-3000 Hz, 3000-6000 Hz, 6000-9000 Hz and 9000-12000 Hz respectively. Out of these bands, the louder frequency band b0 is taken for covert communication. Fig. 5 shows the frequency domain representation of four bands.

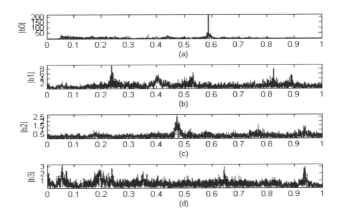

Fig. 5. Frequency domain representation of four bands

The secret audio data with 4096 samples is fed through a sparsification process before applying CS to it. More precisely, DCT coefficients for the secret audio data is calculated and small coefficients are eliminated based on a thresholding gateway. The lower and and upper bounds of the gateway used here are 0.05 and -0.06 respectively. Fig. 6 shows the sparsified DCT spectrum of secret audio data.

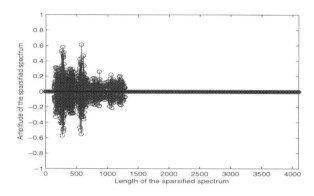

Fig. 6. Sparsified DCT spectrum of secret audio data

Then, this sparse vector is projected into a random measurement matrix. 2500 measurements were taken, which is further scrambled by interleaving process. Fig. 7 shows the compressed and encrypted secret audio data.

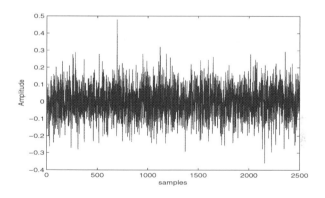

Fig. 7. Compressed and encrypted secret audio data

The cipher audio data in the matrix form is now embedded in the band b0 of cover audio data via SVD based embedding algorithm. Fig. 8 shows the stego audio file.

In the decryption stage, the scrambled audio data is extracted using the SVD based extraction algorithm. Then, with the help of the random permutation vector used at the sending stage, the measurements are sorted in the original order. After the extraction of the encrypted secret audio data, Compressive Sensing based reconstruction is performed to decrypt secret audio data. The reconstruction of the encrypted data is done with L_1 optimization. For subjective

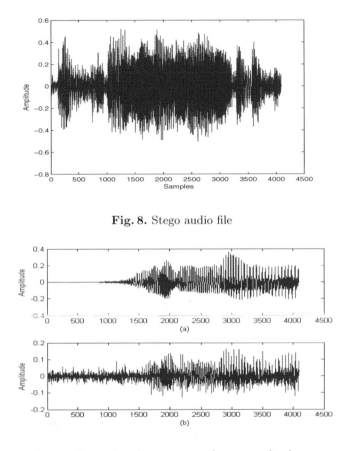

Fig. 8. Stego audio file

Fig. 9. Original and reconstructed secret audio data

analysis of the result obtained, IDCT of the reconstructed spectrum is taken. Figure 9 shows the original and reconstructed secret audio data.

The experiment is done on multiple audio files for different scale factors and the system is giving an absolute maximum error of 0.253 for the test data used here with an embedding strength of 0.5. Table 1 list out the maximum absolute error obtained for different scale factors.

Signal to Noise Ratio (SNR) values and Mean Opinion Score (MOS) grades are used for testing the inaudibility of the stego audio file, for different scale factors α. SNR value in dB is calculated based on the formula:

$$\text{SNR} = 20\log_{10}\left(\frac{\|F\|^2}{\|F - Fw\|^2}\right) . \tag{7}$$

where F and Fw denotes cover audio data and stego audio file in time domain. To calculate MOS grades, 5 people listened to cover audio file and stego audio file for 5 times (for different α values) and put their grades accordingly. Average

Table 1. Maximum absolute error obtained for 3 different scale factor α

Scale factor	Max. Absolute Error
0.2	0.295
0.3	0.287
0.5	0.253

Table 2. SNR and MOS obtained for 3 different scale factor α

Scale factor	SNR value in dB	MOS grade
0.2	36.3446	4.40
0.3	33.9042	4.20
0.5	29.2220	4.00

of these grades where taken as final MOS grade. The results demonstrate that the proposed system is highly efficient and a robust system. Table 2 list out the SNR values and MOS grades obtained for 3 different scale factors.

7 Conclusion

Neither cryptography nor steganography alone is a good way out for audio data security. So in this paper, we proposed the combination of cryptography and steganography by using Compressive Sensing and Singular Value Decomposition. The Sub-band coding technique allows better compression of the cover audio data, utilizing the deficiency of HAS. Besides providing compression, Compressive Sensing (followed by scrambling) gives better encryption for the secret audio data to be transmitted over the network. The use of SVD gives good result in audio data embedding. Unlike other transforms like DCT, DFT etc., SVD uses non fixed orthogonal bases. Thus, the combination of these two methods will enhance the security of the audio data embedded. The proposed approach proves to be a highly efficient method for covert communication of audio data in the near future and it fulfills requirements such as capacity, security and robustness to a great extend.

References

1. Raphael, A.J., Sundaram, V.: Cryptography and Steganography - A Survey. Int. J. Comp. Tech. Appl. 2(3), 626–630 (2011)
2. Swaminathan, S., Suganya, S.: Secured Information Transferring using Secured Cryptosystem. European Journal of Scientific Research 86(2), 180–184 (2012)
3. Nagham, H., Abid, Y., Badlishah Ahmad, R., Osamah Al-Qershi, M.: Image Steganography Techniques: An Overview. International Journal of Computer Science and Security (IJCSS) 6(3), 168–187 (2012)
4. Bender, W., Gruhl, D., Morimoto, N.: Techniques for data hiding. IBM Systems Journal 35(3), 313–336 (1996)
5. http://www.wikipedia.org/wiki/Sub-bandcoding (visited on March 2013)

6. Ramya, M., Sathyamoorthy, M.: Speech Coding by using Subband Coding. In: International Conference on Computing and Control Engineering (April 2012)
7. Chochiere, R.E., Webber, S.A., Flanagan, J.L.: Digital Coding of Speech in Subbands. Bell System Tech. J. 55(8), 1069–1085 (1976)
8. Donoho, D.L.: Compressed sensing. IEEE Trans. Inf. Theory 52(4), 1289–1306 (2006)
9. Candes, E., Wakin, M.: An introduction to compressive sampling- A sensing paradigm that goes against the common knowledge in data acquisition. IEEE Sig. Proc. Mag. 25(2), 21–30 (2008)
10. Orsdemir, A., Oktay Altun, H., Sharma, G., Mark Bocko, F.: On the security and robustness of encryption via compressed sensing. In: Proc. IEEE Military Communications Conference, MILCOM 2008, pp. 1–7 (November 2008)
11. Tropp, J.A., Gilbert, A.C.: Signal recovery from random measurements via orthogonal matching pursuit. IEEE Trans. Inf. Theory 52(12), 4655–4666 (2007)
12. Liu, R.Z., Tan, T.N.: An SVD-Based Watermarking Scheme for Protecting Rightful Ownership. IEEE Trans. on Multimedia 4(1), 121–128 (2002)
13. Andrews, H.C., Patterson, C.L.: Singular Value Decomposition (SVD) Image Coding. IEEE Trans. on Communications 24(4), 425–432 (2002)
14. Johnson, M., Ishwar, P., Prabhakaran, V.M., Schonberg, D., Ramchandran, K.: On compressing encrypted data. IEEE Trans. on Signal Processing 51, 2992–3006 (2004)
15. Venkata SaiManoj, I.: Cryptography and Steganography. International Journal of Computer Applications (0975 - 8887) 1(12), 63–68 (2010)

Random Key and Key Dependent S-box Generation for AES Cipher to Overcome Known Attacks

L.N. Pradeep and Aniruddha Bhattacharjya

Department of Computer Science and Engineering, Amrita School of Engineering
Amrita Vishwa VidyaPeetham, Bangalore, India
pradeep.vaishnav4@gmail.com, a_bhattacharjya@blr.amrita.edu

Abstract. Advanced Encryption Standard (AES) block cipher system is widely used in cryptographic applications. A nonlinear substitution operation is the main factor of the AES cipher system strength. The purpose of the proposed approach is to generate random session keys and use these keys to generate S-boxes. The random key generation will overcome the brute force attack and the key dependent S-box will make cipher resistant to linear and differential cryptanalysis.

Keywords: advanced encryption standard, key dependent s-boxes, random session key, generation algorithm.

1 Introduction

Cryptography has an important role in the security of data transmission and is the best method of data protection against passive and active fraud. The growing number communication users have led to increasing demand for security measures to protect data transmitted over open channels [1]. A cipher system is a set of reversible transformations from the set M of a plaintext into the set C of a cipher text. Each transformation depends on a secret key and the ciphering algorithm. In the block cipher system, the plaintext is divided into the blocks and the ciphering is carried out for the whole block [2]. Two general principles of block ciphers are diffusion and confusion. Diffusion is spreading of the influence of a one plaintext bit to many cipher text bits with intention to hide the statistical structure of the plaintext. Confusion is transformations that change dependence of the statistics of cipher text on the statistics of plaintext. In most cipher systems the diffusion and confusion is achieved by means of round repetition. Repeating a single round contributes to cipher's simplicity [3]. Modern block ciphers consist of four transformations: substitution, permutation, mixing, and key-adding [4].

Cryptographic objects are private key algorithms, public key algorithms and pseudorandom generators. Block ciphers transform usually the 128 or 256 bits string to a string of the same length under control of the secret key. Private key cryptography, such as DES [5], 3DES, and Advanced Encryption Standard (AES) [6], uses the same key for the sender and receiver to encrypt the plaintext and decrypt the cipher text. Private key cryptography is more suitable for the encryption of a large

Sabu M. Thampi et al. (Eds.): SSCC 2013, CCIS 377, pp. 63–69, 2013.
© Springer-Verlag Berlin Heidelberg 2013

amount of data. Public key cryptography, such as the Rivest-Shamir-Adleman (RSA) or Elliptic Curve algorithms, uses different keys for encryption and decryption. The AES algorithm defined by the National Institute of Standards and Technology of the United States has been accepted to replace DES as the new private key encryption algorithm. AES overpass DES in improved security because of larger key sizes. AES is suitable for 8 bit microprocessor platforms and 32 bit processors.

The use of random keys will overcome the brute force attack that can be launched on the AES cipher. A random key generation algorithm would take the initial 128bit key as input and will generate 128bit session keys.

Block cipher systems depend on the S-boxes, which are fixed and have no relation with the secret key. So the only changeable parameter is the secret key. Since the only nonlinear component of AES is S-boxes, they are an important source of cryptographic strength.

The use of key-dependent S-boxes in block cipher design has not been widely investigated in the literature. Research into S-box design has focused on determination of S-box properties which yield cryptographically strong ciphers, with the aim of selecting a small number of good S-boxes for use in a block cipher DES and CAST [7]. Some results have demonstrated that a randomly chosen S-box of sufficient size will have several of these desirable properties with high probability [8].

This paper outlines the work on design of a new random key generation and key-dependent S-boxes. Other systems using key-dependent S-boxes have been proposed in the past, the most well-known is Blowfish [9] and Khufu [10]. Each of these two systems uses the cryptosystem itself to generate the S-boxes. Our proposed algorithm has good cryptographic strength, with the added benefit that is resistant to linear and differential cryptanalysis, which requires that the S-boxes be known.

Along with this the random session keys generation will overcome any kind of brute force attack. The random session keys generated will produce different cipher texts for the same plain text for every session. This will lead to confusion and diffusion when brute force attackers try to hack it with different combination of keys.

A new method to generate key dependent S-boxes as a function of the secret key and a random session key generator will be presented. In the next section, we briefly introduce the AES algorithm. In the following two sections, we analyze AES S-boxes, differential and linear cryptanalysis. A central part of the paper describes the randomly key-dependent S-box and inverse S-box generation algorithm.

2   The AES Algorithm

The AES is a private key block cipher that processes data blocks of 128 bits with key length of 128, 192, or 256 bits. The AES algorithm's operations are performed on a 2-D array of 4 times 4 bytes called the State. The initial State is the plaintext and the final State is the ciphertext. The State consists of 4 rows of bytes. As the block length is 128 bits, each row of the State contains 4 bytes. The four bytes in each column form a 32 bit word. After an initial round key addition, a round function consisting of four transformations – SubBytes, ShiftRows, MixColumns and AddRoundKey is applied to each data block. The round function is applied 10, 12, or 14 times depending on the key length. AES-128 applies the round function 10 times, AES-192 – 12 times, and AES-256– 14 times. The transformations are reversible linear and non-linear operations to allow decryption using their inverses. Every transformation affects all bytes of the State. The transformation SubBytes is a nonlinear byte substitution that operates on each byte of the State using a table (S-box). The numbers of the table is computed by a finite field inversion followed by an affine transformation. The resulting table is called an S-box. The ShiftRows transformation is a circular shifting operation, which rotates the rows of the State with different numbers of bytes (offsets). The offset equals to the row index: the second row is shifted one byte to the left, the third row – two bytes to the left, the fourth row – three bytes to the left and first row – four bytes to the left. MixColumns transformation mixes the bytes in each column by multiplying the State with the polynomial modulo x^4+1. The State bytes are the coefficients of the polynomial. The AddRoundKey transformation is an XOR operation that adds the round key to the State in each round. The initial round key equals to secret key.

3   Random Session Key Generation

The random session keys are generated through a cryptographically generated random numbers. In this method we can take advantage of the encryption logic available to produce random numbers.

Counter with period N

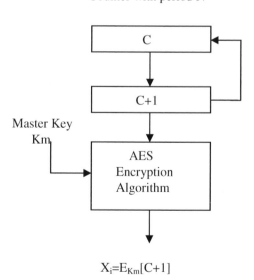

$$X_i = E_{Km}[C+1]$$

Fig. 1. Pseudorandom Number Generation from a Counter

The AES encryption algorithm is used as the heart of the pseudorandom number generation in Fig. 1. The procedure is to generate session keys from a master key Km, i.e., the 128 bit key to the main AES encryption algorithm. A counter with period N provides input to the encryption logic. In AES algorithm 128 bit keys are to be produced, so a counter with period 2^{128} is used. After each session key is produced the counter is incremented by one. Thus, the pseudorandom numbers produced by this scheme cycle through a full period: Each of the outputs X_0, X_1, X_2.... X_{N-1} is based on a different counter value and therefore $X_0 \neq X_1 \neq X_2.... \neq X_{N-1}$. Because the master key is protected, it is not computationally feasible to deduce any of the secret keys through knowledge of one or more earlier keys. In this way the same plain text can generate different cipher texts using session keys. Therefore brute force attackers will not be able to discover the key.

4   Substitution S-boxes

Substitution is a nonlinear transformation which performs confusion of bits. A nonlinear transformation is essential for every modern encryption algorithm and is proved to be a strong cryptographic primitive against linear and differential cryptanalysis. Nonlinear transformations are implemented as lookup tables (S-boxes). An S-box with p input bits and q output bits are denoted p → q. The DES uses eight 6→4 S-boxes. S-boxes are designed for software implementation on 8-bit processors. The block ciphers with 8→8 S-boxes are SAFER, SHARK, and AES. For processors with 32-bit or 64-bit words, S-boxes with more output bits provide high efficiency. The Snefru, Blowfish, CAST, and SQUARE use 8 → 32 S-boxes. The S-boxes can be selected at random as in Snefru, can be computed using a chaotic map, or have some mathematical structure over a finite Galois field. Examples of the last approach are SAFER, SHARK, and AES. S-boxes that depend on key values are slower but more secure than key independent ones.

In the AES, the S-box generate two transformations in the Galois fields GF(2) and $GF(2^8)$. S-box is a nonlinear transformation where each byte of the State is replaced by another byte using the substitution table. The first transformation: S-box finds the multiplication inverse of the byte in the field $GF(2^8)$. Since it is a algebraic expression, it is possible to mount algebraic attacks. Hence, it is followed by an affine transformation. The affine transformation is chosen in order to make the SubBytes a complex algebraic expression while preserving the nonlinearity property. The both S-box transformations can be expressed in a matrix form.

$$S' = M \cdot S^{-1} + 1 \qquad (1)$$

Where the sign • is multiplication and the sign + is addition in the field $GF(2^8)$.The 8 × 1 vector S' denotes the bits of the output byte after the S-box transformations. The inverse S-box transformation can be get by multiplying both sides of equation (1) by M and it performs the inverse affine transformation followed by the multiplicative inverse in GF (2^8).

$$S^{-1} = M^{-1} \cdot S^{-1} + M^{-1} \cdot S^{-1} \qquad (2)$$

5   Linear and Differential Cryptanalysis

Linear and differential cryptanalysis uses the input-output correlation and the difference propagations of the cipher in order to extract partial or whole bits of the secret key. Linear cryptanalysis exploits a cipher's weakness expressed in terms of "linear expressions". In Matsui's terminology [11] a linear expression for one round is an equation for a certain modulo two sum of round input bits and round outputs bits as a sum of round key bits. The expression should be satisfied with probability much more than 0.5 to be useful.

In 1991 was introduced a crypto analytic technique known as differential cryptanalysis [14]. It was successfully applied to attack a variety of SPNs, including DES. Differential cryptanalysis requires knowledge of the XOR tables of S-boxes. For an $n \times n$ S-box, S, the XOR table has rows and columns indexed by $0, 1,...,2^n -1$, and the table entries are defined as follows: if $i, j \in \{0, 1,....,2^n- 1\}$, position (i, j) in the XOR table contains value $|\{X \in \{0, 1\}^n: S(X) \oplus S(X \oplus i)=j\}|$, s-block cipher is an S-box. To secure the cipher against these attacks, the nonlinearity of the S-box should satisfy: the maximum input-output correlation and the difference propagation probability should be minimum.

There are two ways to fight against linear and differential cryptanalysis. One is built S-boxes with low linear and differential probabilities. The other is to design the round transformation so that only trails with many active S-boxes occur. The round transformation must be designed in such a way that differential steps with few active S-boxes are followed by differential steps with many active S-boxes.

The object of this proposal is an AES cipher using key-dependent S-boxes. The fact that the S-boxes are unknown is one of the main strength of our cipher system, since both linear and differential cryptanalysis require known S-boxes. If the S-boxes are generated from the key in sufficiently random fashion, each S-box has a high probability of being complete, possessing fairly high nonlinearity. It is not apparent that the pseudorandom nature of the S-boxes introduces any weakness into the system. Ideal randomness of S-box cannot be achieved. Ideal randomness is not mathematically possible for the following reasons: the value of all elements in the S-box difference table should be even, since $a \oplus b = b \oplus a$. Since the S-box is bijective, the input difference of 0 will lead to an output difference of 0. So the element corresponding to row = 0 and column = 0 at the difference table will be 2^n and all other elements in row = 0 and column = 0 will be 0.

6   A Random Key Dependent S-box and Inverse S-box Generation algorithm

Input: key-dependent 176 bytes b from the output of the key expansion.
Output: integer numbers from the interval [0, 255] of the key-dependent S-box and the inverse S-box [12].

1: Initialization:

$i = 0$

$k = 1$

$l = 1$

2: Compute the first subtotal modulo 256:

$S(1) = (b(1) + b(2)) \bmod 256$

$Sbox(1) = S(1)$

3: while k<256

$i = i + 1$

$m = 1 + (k + i * l) \bmod 176$

$S(i + 1) = (S(i) + b(m)) \bmod 256$

$l = 0$

4: for $j = 1,\ldots,k$ do

Compare subtotal $S(i+1)$ with the elements $Sbox(j)$ and

count the number l of the S-box elements which are not equal to $S(i+1)$

end for

5: if $l = j$

$Sbox(k + 1) = S(i + 1)$

$k = k + 1$

end if

end while

6: for $k = 1,\ldots,256$ do

$invSbox(Sbox(k)+1) = k - 1$

end for

Here Randomness of the key-dependent S-box and inverse S-box is achieved by choosing the index m of the bytes b, which depends on the variables i, k, and l.

7   Conclusion

We presented a new approach to generate the AES random session keys and key-dependent S-boxes. The quality of this approach is tested by changing only one bit of the secret key to generate new S-boxes. The randomly key-dependent S-boxes make our approach resistant to linear and differential cryptanalysis. This approach will lead of the AES block cipher system. The main advantage of such approach is that an enormous number of S-boxes can be generated by changing secret key. It will generate more secure block ciphers, solve the problem of brute force attack and fixed structure S-boxes, and will increase security level.

References

1. Chen, T.-H., Horng, G., Yang, C.-S.: Public key Authentification schemes for local area networks (2008)
2. El-Ramly, S.H., El-Garf, T., Soliman, A.H.: Dynamic generation of S-boxes in block cipher systems. In: Eighteen National Radio Science Conference, pp. 389–397. Mansoura Univ., Egypt. (2001)
3. Masuda, N., Jakimovski, G., Aihara, K., Kocarev, L.: Chaotic block ciphers: from theory to practical algorithms. IEEE Trans. on Circuits and Systems – I: Regular Papers 53(6), 1341–1352 (2006)
4. Schneier, B.: Description of a new variable-length 64-bit block Cipher. Fast Software Encryption, 191–204 (1996)
5. Data Encryption Standard (DES), National Bureau of Standards. FIPS Publication 46 (1977)
6. Advanced Encryption Standard (AES). Federal Information Processing Standards. Publication 197, (November 26, 2001)
7. Menezes, A.J., van Oorschot, P.C., Vanstone, S.A.: Handbook of Applied Cryptography, Boca Raton (1997)
8. Keliher, L.: Linear Cryptanalysis of Substitution-Permutation Networks. PhD thesis, Queen's University, Kingston, Canada (2003)
9. Schneier, B.: Applied Cryptography: Protocols, Algorithms, and Source Code in C. Wiley, New York (1996)
10. Merkle, R.C.: Fast software encryption functions. In: Menezes, A., Vanstone, S.A. (eds.) CRYPTO 1990. LNCS, vol. 537, pp. 476–500. Springer, Heidelberg (1991)
11. Matsui, M.: Linear cryptanalysis method for DES cipher. In: Helleseth, T. (ed.) EUROCRYPT 1993. LNCS, vol. 765, pp. 386–397. Springer, Heidelberg (1994)
12. Kazlauskas, K., Kazlauskas, J.: Key-Dependent S-Box Generation in AES BlockCipher System. Informatica 20(1), 23–34 (2009)

Emulating a High Interaction Honeypot to Monitor Intrusion Activity

Anil Gopalakrishna and Alwyn Rosham Pais

Depatment of Computer Science and Engineering , NITK, Surathkal - 575025, India
{anilgopalakrishna1989,alwyn.pais}@gmail.com

Abstract. Intrusion activity monitoring is a complex task to achieve. An intruder should not be alerted about being monitored. A stealthy approach is needed, that does not alert the intruder about the presence of monitoring. Virtual Machine based High Interaction Honeypots help achieve stealthy monitoring. Most of the related research work use the concept of Virtual Machine Introspection that relies on System Call Interception. However most of these methods hook the sysenter instruction for interception of system calls. This can be defeated by an intruder since this is not the only way of making a system call. We have designed and implemented a High-Interaction Virtual Machine based honeypot using the open source tool Qebek. Qebek is more effective as it hooks the actual system call implementation itself. We have tested its capturability by running different types of malware. The Results obtained show that the system is able to capture information about processes running on the honeypot, console data and network activities, which reveal the maliciousness of the activities.

Keywords: Honeypot, Qebek, Intrusion Monitoring, Malware, System Call Interception.

1   Introduction

A honeypot is defined as 'a computational resource whose value lies in being attacked or compromised by intruders/invaders'. There are two important types of honeypots - Low Interaction, and High-Interaction. A low interaction honeypot hosts only the service/services that are required to be monitored. A High Interaction(HI) honeypot hosts a complete system with all the resources emulated. Using a high-interaction honeypot is more helpful in monitoring intrusions since it gives a wider perspective of the activities happening in the honeypot as compared to the low-interaction honeypot. There are many advantages of using honeypots for intrusion detection:

1. Any traffic flowing to the honeypot/honeynet is considered suspicious since the honeypot do not belong to the production network of an organization.
2. The risk of loss or damage to resources is minimal since honeypots are deployed to be attacked and have all the measures to revert quickly without loss of data.
3. Information about new/persistent attacks can be gained through a honeypot.
4. Post Intrusion activity monitoring using honeypots can be kept covert.

Sabu M. Thampi et al. (Eds.): SSCC 2013, CCIS 377, pp. 70–76, 2013.

1.1   Intrusion Activity Monitoring

The process of Intrusion Activity Monitoring begins post an intrusion. The main assumption in a honeypot is that every activity occurring in a honeypot is considered suspicious. Data collected from the honeypot is checked for malicious patterns. An intruder typically tries to download and run a malware in the honeypot. Information such as the host from which the malware was downloaded, the type of malware and what it is trying to do can be collected. The primary difference between Intrusion Detection and Intrusion Activity Monitoring is that, Intrusion Detection just gives out alerts on possible intrusions. Based on such alerts, certain users or applications are blocked. Intrusion Activity Monitoring continuously tracks and gives out alerts about malicious activities without blocking any user or application.

1.2   Motivation

Earlier work related to Intrusion Detection/ Intrusion Activity Monitoring using Virtualization High-Interaction Honeypots have used the approach of intercepting sysenter instruction to hook system calls made inside the Guest OS. However, this can be circumvented. If attackers/intruders gets control of OS kernel, they can

1.   Install a kernel rootkit that calls the syscall implementation.
2.   Register a new system call handler and make it a new syscall dispatcher.
3.   Register an interrupt handler to make syscall in user mode

The challenge here is to use an approach that leverages Virtual Machine Introspection based HI-Honeypots that has a system call hooking mechanism that cannot be circumvented or is highly difficult to do so.

This is where Qebek comes into the picture. Qebek is a Qemu based HI honeypot deployed on a virtual machine[1]. Qebek was developed to overcome the shortcomings of Sebek, an earlier version of Qebek that did not support virtualization. Sebek could be easily defeated since its presence could be detected by the intruder. However, Qebek monitoring happens in the Host machine and the honeypot is deployed as the guest machine. This is called `out-of-the-box' monitoring of a honeypot. To achieve out-of-the-box monitoring, two key concepts are required : System Call Interception and System View Reconstruction [5]. The hooking approach in Qebek is to hook the individual system call implementation directly, thereby making it impossible for an intruder to bypass the hooking mechanism. In this paper, we bring out an approach of Intrusion Activity Monitoring that uses Qebek to deploy a Virtualization based HI-Honeypot.

1.3   Outline of the Paper

The paper has been organized as follows. Section II throws light on the related work done in the field of Virtual machine based honeypot monitoring. Section III explains the design of the system. Section IV gives implementation details of the system including the deployment of honeypot, the database used to log data, and the application that gives a visualization of the captured data. Section V explains the results of testing the system with malware samples. Our paper concludes in Section VI.

2   Related Work

Honeypots have been widely used in the area of intrusion monitoring. They provide a stealthy mechanism to monitor intrusions without alerting the intruder. In [3], Martim d'Orey et. al, have developed a mechanism for automatic digital evidence collection using the open source tool sebek. However, Sebek can be defeated since it is an `in-house' monitoring tool which monitors intrusion activity within the honeypot. In [2], Nguyen Anh Quynh et. al, have designed a honeypot system, Xebek, using the XEN technology to overcome issues posed by Sebek, a honeypot tool. Xebek is stealthier than sebek and far more reliable. In [4], Xuxian Jiang et. al, have developed VMscope which is a virtualization based approach to view system internal events from outside the honeypot. Their prototype leverages and extends the concept of `Binary Translation'. Xuxian Jiang et. al, [5] have also developed VMwatcher, which is a stealthy malware detection using Virtual Machine based honeypot and semantic view reconstruction. Tal Garfinkel et. al, [6] have developed `livewire', a Virtual Machine Introspection based architecture for intrusion detection. The activity of the host is analyzed by directly observing hardware state and inferring software state based on a priori knowledge of its structure. Tamas K. Lengyel et. al,[7] have designed VMI-Honeymon, a High-Interaction Honeypot monitor based on VMI on XEN. They have shown that VMI-Honeymon is is effective in capturing both known and unclassified malware samples. Xiantao Zhang at. Al, [8] have implemented `vnida' which is a VMM based IDS. A separate intrusion detection domain (IDD) is added to provide intrusion detection services for all virtual machines.

3   System Design

The system is built on the architecture of Qebek so it extends the Qebek tool. Qebek logs mainly three types of data.

1. Process Information - Name of Process, Process ID and Parent Process ID.
2. Information Generated on the console by these processes.
3. Information about Network Activities - IP:Port Pair of Source and Destination.

The design is shown in Fig. 1. There are 5 modules of Qebek: Interception Module, Breakpoint System, SVR helper routines, Introspection Module and Output Module.

The interception module intercepts all instructions that cause a jump in the control flow, since invoking a system call also causes a jump. The breakpoint module consists of a hash table of all the breakpoints applied to the system calls. The SVR helper routines are invoked to reconstruct high OS-level information from low hardware-level information. The introspection module gathers required data for console activities, process creation and network activities. The output module outputs the information gathered by the introspection module onto the console. The Process monitor we have implemented using Qebek provides a real-time alert system. A Java application is built to extract data from the database and build a tree view of the processes, gather threat level information about each process and flag it as safe or unsafe and also gather domain information about the remote hosts being communicated by the honeypot. This system has been tested by running several samples of malware like backdoors, trojan, worms, rootkits etc.

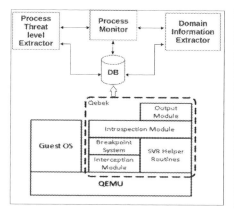

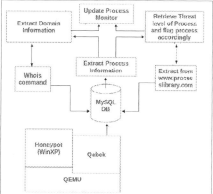

Fig. 1. Architecture of the System   **Fig. 2.** Flow of Events in the System

4   Implementation

Qebek(revision 66) is deployed on a system running Ubuntu 10.04. At the moment, Qebek has been successfully run only on Windows XP. Therefore, our honeypot is a Virtual Machine running Windows XP SP2. The database consists of three tables:

1.   EVENT : has information about each intercepted system call.
2.   IPINFO: Has domain information for each remote IP being communicated.
3.   PROCESS: Has information about the threat level of each process.

The flow of events in the system, depicted in Fig. 2, is explained as follows:

1. Raw data logged by Qebek is extracted and inserted into Database.
2. Each individual Event(System call intercept) is read from the database.
3. Based on the type of system call, only Domain information(for sys_socket) is extracted or domain information and threat level of process(for sys_read and sys_socket) is extracted.
4. To extract domain information, whois [13] command is used. Process threat level information is extracted from [12].
5. This information is inserted into the DB for further references.
6. Having all these information, process monitor is updated.

   Threat level of a process is decided as follows. For each entry in the process library website for a given process, marked as unsafe, we increment a threat value by one and flag it as unsafe and for each safe entry, we decrement it by 1. If there is no unsafe entry, it is flagged safe. Threat level ranges from a negative value(minimum of -2) to a positive value(maximum of 8). The values are dependent on the number of entries in process library. During experimental study, it was found that the values lie in the range -2 to 8. Threat values and their threat levels are as follows:

1.   Less than 0 and marked safe: No threat.
2.   Less than 0 and marked unsafe: Low threat.
3.   Zero and marked unknown: Uncertain Threat-level.
4.   Zero and marked unsafe: Low threat-level.
5.   Less than 2 but greater than 0: Medium Threat-level.

6. Less than or equal to 4 but greater than 2: High threat-level.
7. Greater than 4: Severe threat-level.

The process monitor is implemented as a GUI application. It has a tree view of all the processes running and is updated in real time. Each node of the tree is a process and the sub-nodes are child processes. Each process is marked safe or unsafe based on the threat value. Information about each process can be viewed in a separate window. For processes that invoked sys read system call, the console data collected is displayed. For processes that invoked sys socket call, domain information about the remote host being communicated is displayed. In both the cases, severity of threat of that process is also displayed.

5   Results

The system was tested by downloading and running malware from the malware repository offensive computing[11] on the honeypot. Table 1 shows the category of malware tested(includes split personality malware), the number of samples tested and the general observation about the captured activity. Split personality malware[9] [10]was developed to circumvent attempts of virtual machine based monitoring. Such a malware tries to detect the environment of the system that it is running on and tries to behave naive to avoid detection if it believes that it is running on a virtual machine, thereby being monitored.

Table 1. Category of malware tested, the number of samples tested & detected positively and the general observation about the captured activity

Category	No. of Samples Tested	No. of samples detected	General Observation
Constructors and Generators	5	3	Invokes the ntvdm.exe process which is the windows virtual dos machine. Presence of the ntvdm.exe could indicate the execution of a constructor or a generator.
Backdoors	8	4	Invokes the command prompt and other vital processes like net1.exe and sc.exe. Tries to delete itself by repeatedly executing the 'if exists, goto' command sequence.
Worms	5	5	Invokes one or more of the following processes: netsh.exe, net1.exe, cscript.exe, cacls.exe which are all vital windows processes used to monitor or modify ACLs, firewalls etc.
Trojans	8	4	Invokes the command prompt and executes the 'if exists, goto' command sequence to try and delete itself.
Spyware	9	6	Invokes a bunch of known malicious processes and some unknown processes

Table 1. (*Continued.*)

Category	No. of Samples Tested	No. of samples detected	General Observation
Exploits	2	2	Invokes ntvdm.exe and bunch of other unknown processes.
Email Worms	3	3	Tries to connect to some remote hosts.
Brontok Variants	10	8	Every variant of brontok invokes the at.exe which is a command that schedules other commands to run at certain points in time
Trojan.Proxy.Bypass.A	Creates a process csrse.exe which is registered on [12] as a backdoor.		
Heur.Trojan.Generic	Creates a process that invokes sys socket which tries to connect to a remote host in china. (Information based on 'whois' command)		
Net-worm.win32.kolab.ckp	Creates a process cPaner.com which invokes sys socket system call which tries to connect to a remote host in finland. (information from 'whois' command) . In addition it invokes the command prompt where it deletes many registry entries		
Trojan.spy.win32.Banker.pcu	Invokes the following processes: Schtasks.exe,sc.exe,reg.exe, netsh.exe, svchost.exe which are all known vital windows processes		
Trojan spy.win32.bancos.zm	Invokes the process Tasklist32.exe which is registered as an unsafe process		
Trojan.win32.killAV.or Backdoor.win32.Agobot.a ow Backdoor.win32.sdbot.fm e Trojandownloader.win32. agent.acrm, Worm.win32.autorun.pga	No information gathered		

Observation: It is quite clear that malware either tries to invoke a vital windows process like netsh.exe or cacls.exe which can alter the ACLs and firewalls, disguise itself into one such process, or invoke processes that is a known malicious process. In rare cases, it invokes processes about which there are not much information available. Out of 50 Samples of all categories of malware(excluding spit personality malware) that were tested, 35 showed positive detection. No information was collected in the case of 15 samples. Out of the 10 samples of Split personality malware that were tested, 5 showed clear signs of maliciousness in the information that has been gathered.

Inference: An accuracy of 70% has been achieved in detecting different categories of malware tested. Information about fifteen of the fifty malware samples were not gathered by the honeypot. This can be attributed to that fact that Qebek hooks only 8 Windows APIs at the moment.

6   Conclusion

This paper provides a solution for real-time monitoring of a High-Interaction Honeypot using the open source tool Qebek. We have demonstrated the effectiveness of this system in capturing malicious activity by testing with several categories of malware. Qebek is also a more secured solution as compared to other VMI - System call interception based monitoring approaches as it hooks individual system call implementations. Currently, Qebek hooks are available for only 8 windows APIs. Including more important APIs and extending the tool to Linux hosts will ensure completeness of monitoring. Our system can also be extended as a web application to be monitored from a remote host.

References

1. Song, C., Hay, B., Zhuge, J.: Know Your Tools: Qebek - Conceal the Monitoring, The honeynet project in Proceedings of 6th IEEE Information Assurance Workshop
2. Quynh, N.A., Takefuji, Y.: A Novel Stealthy Data Capture Tool for Honeynet System. In: Proceedings of the 4th WSEAS Int. Conf. on Information Security, Communications and Computers, Tenerife, Spain, December 16-18, pp. 207–212 (2005)
3. Andrade Carbone, M.P., de Geus, P.: A Mechanism for Automatic Digital Evidence Collection on High-Interaction Honeypots. In: Proceedings of the 2004 IEEE Workshop on Information Assurance and Security United States Military Academy, West Point, NY, June 10-11 (2004)
4. Jiang, X., Wang, X.: "Out-of-the-box" monitoring of VM-based high-interaction honeypots. In: Kruegel, C., Lippmann, R., Clark, A. (eds.) RAID 2007. LNCS, vol. 4637, pp. 198–218. Springer, Heidelberg (2007)
5. Jiang, X., Wang, X., Xu, D.: Stealthy Malware Detection and Monitoring Through VMM-Based "Out of the Box" Semantic View Reconstruction. ACM Transactions on Information and System Security V(N) (June 2008)
6. Garfinkel, T., Rosenblum, M.: A Virtual Machine Introspection Based Architecture for Intrusion Detection. In: Proc. Network and Distributed Systems Security Symposium
7. Lengyel, T.K., Neumann, J., Maresca, S.: Virtual machine introspection in a hybrid honeypot architecture. In: CSET 2012 - 5th Workshop on Cyber Security Experimentation and Test (2012)
8. Zhang, X., Li, Q., Qing, S., Zhang, H.: Vnida: Building an IDS Architecture Using VMM-based Non-intrusive Approach. In: Proceedings of SPIT-IEEE Colloquium and International Conference, Mumbai, India
9. Vishnani, K., Pais, A.R., Mohandas, R.: Detecting & Defeating Split Personality Malware. In: SECURWARE 2011: The Fifth International Conference on Emerging Security Information, Systems and Technologies (2011)
10. Balzarotti, D., Cova, M., Karlberger, C., Kruegel, C., Kirda, E., Vigna, G.: Efficient Detection of Split Personalities in Malware. In: NDSS 2010, 17th Annual Network and Distributed System Security Symposium, San Diego, USA, February 28-March 3 (2010)
11. Open Malware Repository, http://www.offensivecomputing.net
12. Process Library, http://www.processlibrary.com
13. Linux & Unix Whois command,
    http://www.computerhope.com/unix/uwhois.htm

On Pseudo-random Number Generation
Using Elliptic Curve Cryptography

Manali Dubal and Aaradhana Deshmukh

Department of Computer Engineering, SKNCOE, University of Pune, Pune, India
{manali.dubal,aadeshmukhskn}@gmail.com

Abstract. The recent branch of network security is Cryptography using Elliptic Curve Architectures which is based on the arithmetic of elliptic curves and discrete logarithmic problems. ECC schemes are public-key based mechanisms that provide encryption, digital signatures and key exchange algorithms. Elliptic curve algorithms are solely based on generation of random numbers which can be identified by pseudo-random number generator. This paper describes the mechanism of deriving random number and the possibilities of random number generator attack on ECC algorithms. The algorithm proposed here in can be used for generating random numbers in ECIES or any ECC based encryption decryption algorithm. Through the results obtained it is proved to be better in comparison to other algorithms.

Keywords: Elliptic curve cryptography, pseudo-random number generation algorithms (PRNG), related PRNG attacks, Elliptic curve Random Number Generator (ECRNG).

1 Introduction

PKC (Public Key Cryptography) depends on secret keys and if the adversary knew the secret key, it would know as much as the communicators know. It requires the generation of random numbers for formulating each of the private as well as public key. And the security of such systems depends on the generation of quantities that are of random size, large period and complexity.

Secrecy quantities - keys corresponds to the lack of information the adversary knows. It can be therefore assumed that keys must have certain amount of entropy that is to be kept secret. Entropy is the measurement of information which can be obtained from source node by observing mouse movements, computing resources the system have, disk access rate or even clock rate of system. These units are gathered, concatenated and stored in one pool known as entropy pool.

At the time of quantity generation, seed is extracted from the pool and given as input to the function that calculates the secret key through random number generation. Various methods of random number generation have been proposed and proven secure. ECRNG – Elliptic curve random number generator [1] uses ordinary elliptic curves to generate keys for one time usage. When the keys are required for further

Sabu M. Thampi et al. (Eds.): SSCC 2013, CCIS 377, pp. 77–89, 2013.

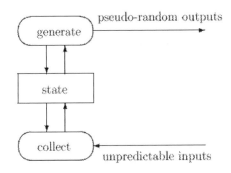

Fig. 1. Model of PRNG's

reuse, they must be stored 'on file' by administrator – concept of escrow keys, to which ECRNG does not provide solution to.

Several pseudorandom generators have been proposed which are using the form of elliptic curves such as [2]. Since [3] methods, different approaches for extracting pseudo randomness from elliptic curves have been proposed by [4] [5] [6].

This paper presents the scheme for sharing entropy by generating random numbers based on session using ECRNG and using same for Elliptic curve cryptosystems. This method reduces the actual cost of computation of random numbers and thereby decreases the time for key generation.

2   Related Work

2.1   Pseudo-number Generators

Many pseudo-number generators have been proposed and have proven to be insecure. Some of which are considered as follows

2.1.1   Netscape PRNG
Netscape used SSL to encrypt the messages. Three parameters were counted on to be the input for seed function: process id, parent process id and the system time. These factors were combined and given as input to hash function which is the seed for current random number generation. After each round of random number the seed is incremented by one. Hence if one seed is identified the rest of seeds used for generation can be determined. The process can be described as follows:

ALGORITHM 1. Seed Generation

Input: time $\rightarrow$ {sec, microsec}, ID$\rightarrow$\{process_id, parent_process_id\}
Output: Seed S

        Sys_a = lcpr(microsec)
        Sys_b = lcpr(process_id + sec + (parent_process_id <<12))
        S = MD5(Sys_a, Sys_b)
     return S
// where, lcpr(x) = return((0xDEECE66D*x + 0x2BBB62DC) >> 1)

ALGORITHM 2.   Pseudo-Random number generation

Input: Seed S
Output: Random number R
        R = MD5(S);
        S = S+1;
    return R

The secret key is the value R returned by the number generator algorithm. Several drawbacks have been encountered while implementing this algorithm. The browser's time is used as one of the factor for calculating seed, which can be known from the attacker's browser also. If the attacker uses UNIX system, the ps command can help in identifying the process_id as well as parent_process_id by listing all the respective processes. Again, every time the seed is incremented by 1, so if one of the seed is identified, then the sequence could be known easily.

2.1.2   ANSI X9.17 PRNG

The ANSI X9.17 PRNG generates secret key without changing the state of input to PRNG. For 64-bit block size, it is vulnerable to replay attacks.

ALGORITHM 3.   Seed generation (ANSI X9.17)

Input: Key k – generated by triple-DES
Output: Seed s
        $t_i \leftarrow E_k$ (system's current time)
        $output[i] \leftarrow E_k(t_i \oplus s[i])$
        $s[i+1] \leftarrow E_k (t_i \oplus output[i])$
    return s

The output s[i+1] depends on the previous output, so if the attacker knows the time factor and the key is compromised, the s[i+1] value is easy to recover. In other case, if the attacker has two outputs, and knows some of the bits of time factor, there is possibility of meet-in-the-middle attack because,

$$s[i+1] \leftarrow D_k (output[i+1]) \oplus t_{i+1}$$
$$s[i+1] \leftarrow E_k (output[i] \oplus t_i)$$

The only thing left is to make a list and check the value for correct seed. Of these two lists of seed, the common occurrences are the seeding values. Moreover, the protocol does not specify the entropy requirements of generation of seed.

2.1.3   NIST DSA PRNG

DSA PRNG was developed to generate pseudo-random numbers for digital signature algorithm (DSA).One way function is constructed using SHA-1 or DES. If DES is used the size of seed is 160 bits.

ALGORITHM 4. Seed generation – DSA PRNG

Input: changing state X_i, optional input I
Output: X_{i+1}, next state seed
        output[i] = hash(I+X_i mod 2^b)
        X_{i+1}=X_i+ output[i] + 1 (mod 2^b)
return X_{i+1}

If there is a method to control the inputs sent to I, the attacker can generate the same state again and again and the seed value would be repeated every time

3   Proposal

Elliptic curves are known for its best performance in fields of cryptography. The public key cryptography is based on elliptic curve architecture, where finite fields are used to generate base points and keys. ECC is used in this research to plot the EC points of curve to random bits and finally generate relation between private and public key, which could be used as escrow key for further communication.

3.1   Background on Elliptic Curve Cryptography

Elliptic curves have been used to solve a range of problems by mathematicians. The concept was first proposed by Neal Koblitz and Victor Miller to design public-key cryptographic systems.

Definition 3.1 An elliptic curve E over a field F is defined by an equation

$$E : y^2 +a_1 xy+a_3 y = x^3 +a_2 x^2 +a_4 x +a_6$$

where, $a_1,a_2,a_3,a_4,a_6 \in K$ and $\Delta \neq 0$, where Δ is the discriminant of E.

3.2   ECRNG – Elliptic Curve Random Number Generator

In ERNG, the algorithm generates the point P on field F_q of the elliptic curve obtained as per the parameters of tuple. It is assumed that,

1. the cofactor h = $E(F_q)$ / n ; normally has set of values {1,2,4}
2. n is the order of point P such that n*P equates to 0.
3. Another point Q is selected such that it is the additive multiple of point P.

As per [1], the current state of iteration is maintained in k_1, initially. The iteration index increments upon each output point of the ECRNG. The bit representation of the x-coordinate of point P(x,y) $\in$ E(F_q) is $\overline{x}$, which is converted into integer for further integral calculation purpose. The system generates R_i in $\frac{3}{2}$ log $_2$ s operations.

ALGORITHM 5.   ECRNG ALGORITHM

Input: Seed $k_1 \in [0,$ max $\{q\text{-}1$, n-1$\}]$, Q (initialization parameter), s_i (bit representation of x), point P(x,y)

Output: random number sequence

  $i \leftarrow 0;$
  $k_{i+1} \leftarrow x_i + i(\text{mod } p)$
  $R_i \leftarrow s_i * Q$
  $s_{i+1} \leftarrow x(s_i*P);$ x()–transforms x-coordinate to integer
  $r_i \leftarrow t(x(R_i))$; t() – truncation function
return r_i

Furthermore, there may be an integer f such that, Q = f *P and g * f = 1 mod n. Now, from algorithm, $s_{i+1} = s_i * P$ and $R_i = s_i * Q$. With integer g, it is easy to compute s_{i+1} from R_i, as $s_{i+1} = g * R_i$. The random number sequence $r_i = t(x(R_i))$ and R_i can be known from value of r_i. Once the $x(R_i)$ is obtained, the x-coordinate is known to adversary and this leads to the point decompression process and breakthrough of the y-coordinate which implies the value P(x,y).

3.3   Proposed ECRNG

The proposed scheme can be described by pictorials representation as below:

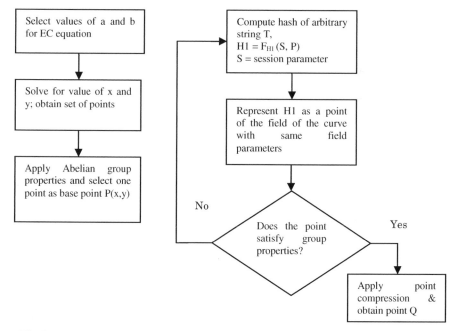

Fig. 2. Selecting point P(x,y)   **Fig. 3.** Generating point Q(x,y)

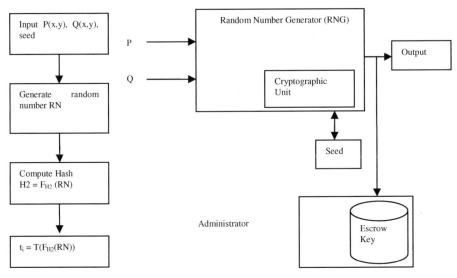

Fig. 4. Generation and truncation of RN　　　　**Fig. 5.** Storing keys (key escrow)

3.4　Mathematical Modeling of Proposed Scheme

The EC domain parameters remain same for random number generation. RNG is here a sub-function used in ECC algorithms. It can be defined mathematically as follows:

Input: EC Domain Parameters
Processing: $RN \rightarrow f(x)$;
where, $f(x)=T (F_{H2}(F_{H1} (S,P), Q))$, F_{H1} and F_{H2} are hash functions (F_{H1} being hash for arbitrary string, session parameter and point P, F_{H2} being hash for random number) and T being the truncation function of the final generated random number.
Output: Random number (RN)

4　Proof of Rightness

As the point P(x,y) is calculated before the generation of Q(x,y), it is clear that there is no dependency of point Q on point P. Thus if the public point P is known, there are no means to ensure determination of point Q. Though, for storing the keys for further use and to take advantage of unknown interdependency of P and Q, if there exists z ∈ Fq, such that P=z*Q, the relation z can be stored as derivative. In such case, z is known as escrow key and is handled and managed by administrator only.

5   Implementation Results

Testing is done for verification of the results obtained with the help of ECRNG and the proposed RNG. Test data include specific datasets for key size parameter having different characteristics. The field size is assumed to be {163,233,283,409,571}

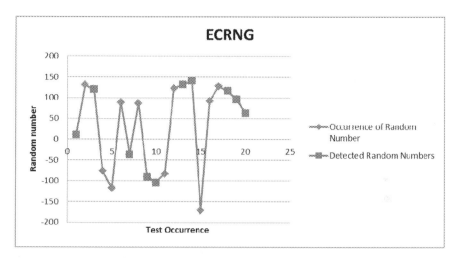

Fig. 6. Graph obtained for Dataset: 01 – ECRNG

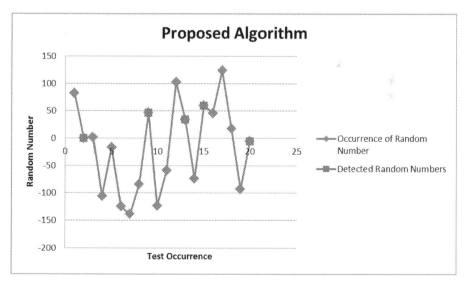

Fig. 7. Graph obtained for Dataset: 01 – Proposed algorithm

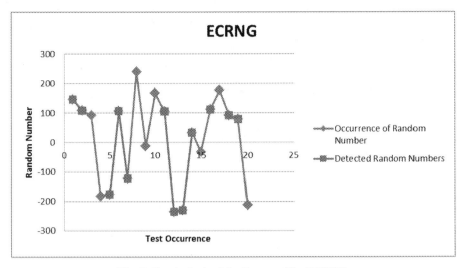

Fig. 8. Graph obtained for Dataset: 02 – ECRNG

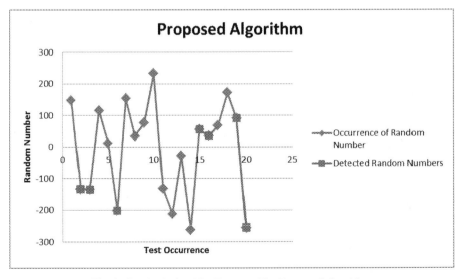

Fig. 9. Graph obtained for Dataset: 02 – Proposed algorithm

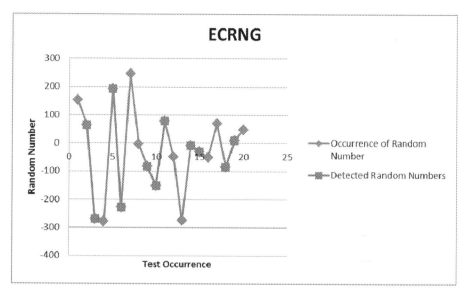

Fig. 10. Graph obtained for Dataset: 03 – ECRNG

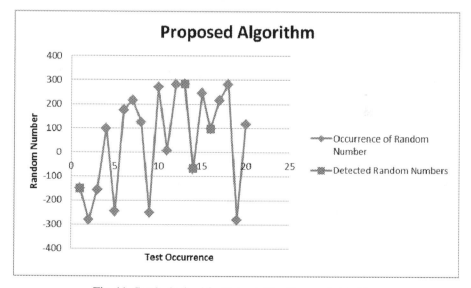

Fig. 11. Graph obtained for Dataset: 03 – Proposed algorithm

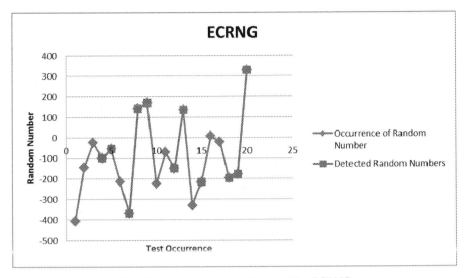

Fig. 12. Graph obtained for Dataset: 04 – ECRNG

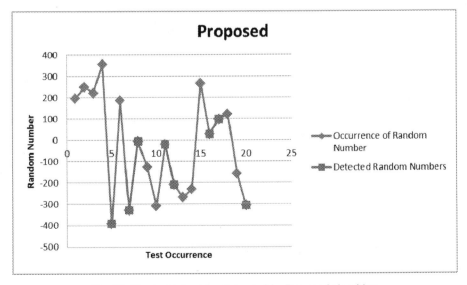

Fig. 13. Graph obtained for Dataset: 04 – Proposed algorithm

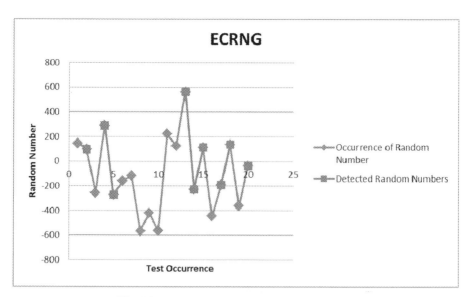

Fig. 14. Graph obtained for Dataset: 05 – ECRNG

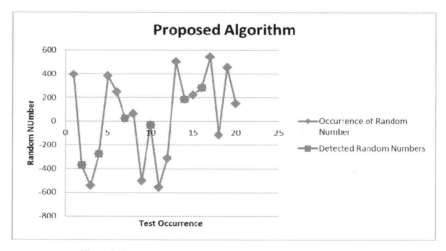

Fig. 15. Graph obtained for Dataset: 04 – Proposed algorithm

6   Analysis

The existing ECRNG algorithm and the proposed algorithm were applied to the datasets given in tables in appendix. The red marks show the detection of occurrence of random number in both the graphs. It can be observed that the detected random number are more in case of existing ECRNG as compared to proposed one. Thus it can be proved that the proposed algorithm will provide better security as compared to the existing one.

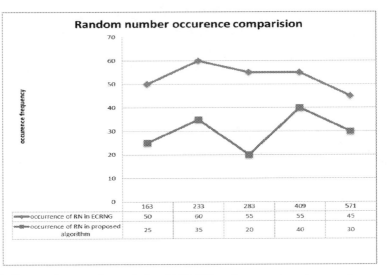

Fig. 16. Comparative security analysis of ECRNG and proposed random number generator algorithm for datasets 1 to 5

7   Conclusion

To summarize, the paper compares different RNG algorithms giving their advantages and limitations, presents new concept of deriving the private encryption point without relating to the public point. The derived relation between points (if exists), could be used as escrow key for future encryption purposes. Moreover, the random numbers are more securely generated using the proposed algorithm.

Acknowledgments. The first author expresses her sincere gratitude to second author for her constant support to make this research a fruitful venture.

References

1. Brown, D.R.L., Gjøsteen, K.: A Security Analysis of the NIST SP 800-90 Elliptic Curve Random Number Generator, IACR ePrint 2007/048 Crypto (2007)
2. Jao, D., Jetchev, D., Venkatesan, R.: On the bits of elliptic curve diffie-hellman keys. In: Srinathan, K., Rangan, C.P., Yung, M. (eds.) INDOCRYPT 2007. LNCS, vol. 4859, pp. 33–47. Springer, Heidelberg (2007)
3. Kaliski, B.S.: Journal of Cryptology 3, 187–199 (1991-1992)
4. Farashahi, R.R., Schoenmakers, B., Sidorenko, A.: Efficient pseudorandom generators based on the DDH assumption. In: Okamoto, T., Wang, X. (eds.) PKC 2007. LNCS, vol. 4450, pp. 426–441. Springer, Heidelberg (2007)
5. Caragiu, M., Johns, R.A., Gieseler, J.: Quasi-random structures from elliptic curves. J. Algebra, Number Theory Appl. 6, 561–571 (2006)

6. Chevassut, O., Fouque, P.-A., Gaudry, P., Pointcheval, D.: The twist-Augmented technique for key exchange. In: Yung, M., Dodis, Y., Kiayias, A., Malkin, T. (eds.) PKC 2006. LNCS, vol. 3958, pp. 410–426. Springer, Heidelberg (2006)
7. Longa, P.: High-Speed Elliptic Curve and Pairing-Based Cryptography. A thesis presented to the University of Waterloo (2011)
8. Batina, L., Mentens, N., Sakiyama, K., Preneel, B., Verbauwhede, I.: Low-Cost Elliptic Curve Cryptography for Wireless Sensor Networks. In: Buttyán, L., Gligor, V.D., Westhoff, D., et al. (eds.) ESAS 2006. LNCS, vol. 4357, pp. 6–17. Springer, Heidelberg (2006)
9. Gayoso Martinez, V., et al.: A Survey of the Elliptic Curve Integrated Encryption Scheme. Journal of Computer Science and Engg. (August 2010)
10. Kumar, A., et al.: Performance Analysis of MANET using Elliptic Curve Cryptosystem. In: IEEE – ICACT – 2012 (2012)
11. Fan, J., et al.: State – of –the art of Secure ECC implementations: a survey on known side-channel attacks and countermeasures. In: IEEE Symposium on Hardwar-Oriented Security and Trust (2010)

Appendix

Polynomial equation for datasets on which both the algorithms are applied to:

1.   163 bit field size: $p(t) = t^{163} + t^7 + t^6 + t^3 + 1$
2.   233 bit field size : $p(t) = t^{233} + t^{74} + 1$
3.   283 bit field size : $p(t) = t^{283} + t^{12} + t^7 + t^5 + 1$
4.   409 bit field size : $p(t) = t^{409} + t^{87} + 1$
5.   571 bit field size : $p(t) = t^{571} + t^{10} + t^5 + t^2 + 1$

Exploiting Functional Models to Assess the Security Aspect in Embedded System Design

Ingo Stierand[1] and Sunil Malipatlolla[2]

[1] Carl von Ossietzky Universität Oldenburg,
26111 Oldenburg, Germany
stierand@informatik.uni-oldenburg.de
[2] OFFIS - Institute for Information Technology,
26121 Oldenburg, Germany
sunil.malipatlolla@offis.de

Abstract. Conventionally, automotive embedded systems are assessed for evaluating various different aspects such as safety, functionality, and real-time. However, the inclusion of security aspect, which indeed is becoming increasingly important in modern day cars, has a significant impact on the above aspects, especially on functionality and real-time. This impact would be clearly visible in the functional model of the embedded system because including security features modifies the data flow in the system. Thus, the goal of this contribution is to assess and evaluate the security aspect in such systems by exploiting their functional models. Such an assessment further results in establishing a possible relation between real-time formal analysis and the existing security theory. For this, a formal approach well-known from real-time embedded domain is utilized in here.

Keywords: Real-Time, Embedded System, Formalization, Security Protocols, Validation.

1 Introduction

With an increased inclusion of electronics in automotive systems, they are becoming more and more vulnerable to attacks such as manipulation of data packets and malicious system updates. Thus, ensuring the security of such systems is a crucial task, particularly in safety relevant systems, where unintended modifications can lead to malfunctioning of a system. To achieve this, good methods are required to evaluate the security of a system. On the other hand, such an evaluation should not be isolated but must be done in an integrated manner. This means, though the system is initially modeled for functional and real-time aspect evaluation, a possible direction for evaluating the security aspect must further be given utilizing the same model.

In the above context, an automotive embedded sub-system, as depicted in Figure 1, is considered as the target system here. The system comprises of a sensor, an actuator, an Electronic Control Unit (ECU) with a processor and a

Sabu M. Thampi et al. (Eds.): SSCC 2013, CCIS 377, pp. 90–97, 2013.

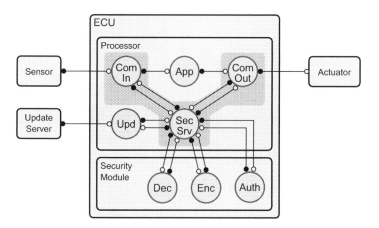

Fig. 1. An Example Embedded Sub-System with an ECU

security module, and an update server. It is a real-time system which has to satisfy its real-time properties, such as meeting deadlines, in addition to guaranteeing the functional correctness. The system realizes a simple real-time control application, where sensor data are processed by the control application in order to operate the plant due to an actuator. Though the concrete control application is not of interest in here, it might represent the engine control of a car or a driver assistant system such as an Automatic Breaking System (ABS).

In specific, Figure 1 depicts the functional model i.e., the control functionality performed by the App task and the update functionality executed by the Upd task. Encrypted data coming from the Sensor is decrypted through SecSrv utilizing the Dec function before feeding it to the task App. After performing the control operation, the output is again encrypted through SecSrv utilizing Enc block before forwarding it to the Actuator. Similarly, the update data from the Update Server is authenticated through SecSrv utilizing Auth block before loading into the system.

It can be seen that including the security module has a deep impact on the functional model of the system and thus the data flow in it. For example, due to the addition of authentication block for securing the system against malicious updates from the update server modifies the path of the data flow in the system. This is clearly visible in Figure 1, i.e., without an authentication block the data from the update server would have been directly loaded into the system by the Upd task instead of traversing through the tasks Upd, SecSrv, and the Auth block. Further, such a modification in the data flow due to the inclusion of security module has an impact on the real-time aspect of the system, as shown in our previous work [12].

On the other hand, such a functional model provides the capability for the system designer to model the possible attack points in its data flow path as detailed below. For example, an attacker may try to intercept the data from the

Sensor and clone it later if it is not encrypted or he may deceive the system for being the UpdateServer to load malicious update data into the system. Given this, the possible attack points are the communication channels between Sensor and ECU, and UpdateServer and ECU, respectively. Thus, the goal of this contribution is to assess the security aspect of such a system by exploiting its functional model and the corresponding data flow. For this, a formal approach, which is well-known for modeling the real-time systems, is utilized in here [3].

The rest of the paper is organized as follows. Section 2 gives a brief description of the existing work in the literature. Section 3 illustrates the proposed approach for assessing the security aspect utilizing the system functional model. We show that our functional models can be used as the input for security analysis, while ensuring that the semantics of both models are preserved. Section 4 sketches further steps towards integration by showing how the functional model can be exploited for confining the target security model. Section 5 concludes the paper and gives some hints on future work.

2   Related Work

Real-time task networks are well-established formalisms at the considered phase of system design, where the system functionality is mapped to a particular hardware architecture, including scheduling policies provided by the operating system(s). The relation between real-time systems and data flow models have been intensively studied over the last decade [2,10]. On the other hand, various security models are based on the data flow paradigm, such as the one from [13], which is mainly considered in this work. To the best of our knowledge, similar considerations for exploiting real-time formalisms in the security domain are yet to be made.

The authors Yip et al. in [15] proposed a new language run-time, referred to as *RESIN*, that helps to prevent security vulnerabilities, by allowing programmers to specify application-level data flow assertions. For this, it utilizes the mechanisms of policy objects associated with data, data tracking as data flows through an application, and filter objects that define data flow boundaries and control data movement. Though the goal of this work is to protect the software applications such as PHP and python against the existing vulnerabilities, our goal is to assess the security aspect based on data flow model in an embedded system.

The work in [6] proposes a generic framework for evaluating whether given information flows can cause security issues. The objective of the approach is to ensure that data objects do not leave the security class they are assigned to, or transitions into another class that is allowed by the information flow ($\rightarrow$) operator. The approach defines flows based on sequences of functions on the data objects. There also exist various well-established formalisms such as CSP [11] and Petri nets [5] that have been exploited for security analysis.

However, unlike the formalism utilized in here, none of the above approaches were originally developed for an architectural design.

3 Approach

3.1 Functional Real-Time Model

Real-time scheduling analysis [14] is an important building block in design processes for safety relevant systems. While early design phases consider the target hardware in a rather abstract way, if any, real-time scheduling analysis considers applications when they are deployed onto hardware with processors, buses and other components. Maybe the most popular formalisms to model real-time systems are so-called *task networks*, where tasks represent the individual software elements of the system. The tasks are connected in a graph structure, where the connections between tasks denote execution precedences. Typically, a real-time model also consists of a simple notion of hardware architectures, representing processing elements and buses in the case of distributed architectures. The tasks are allocated to the respective processing elements, representing their execution on the architecture elements.

In the following we introduce a particular class of task network models that allows to characterize individual data flows in the systems. The formalism actually is a simplified version of the one discussed in [3]. Each task is equipped with a set of input and output ports. The data flowing into and out of a task is modeled by a set of events that may occur at the respective ports. Tasks are connected by channels. A channel characterizes the flow of events between the individual tasks.

Definition 1. *A task network is a tuple* $N = (\Sigma, P, E, T, C)$ *where:*

- *Σ is a set of events,*
- *P is a set of ports,*
- *$E : \Sigma \to P$ induces for each port $p \in P$ a set $\Sigma(p) \subseteq \Sigma$ of events,*
- *T is a set of software tasks, where $t \in T$ is a tuple (P_i, ψ, P_o):*
  - *$P_i, P_o \subseteq P$ are the input and output ports of t,*
  - *$\psi : \bigcup_{p \in P_i} \Sigma(p) \to \Sigma$ is the execution function of the task. We require that $\psi(\sigma) \in \bigcup_{p \in P_o} \Sigma(p)$.*
- *$C \subseteq P \times P$ is a set of channels.* ◇

Note that the definition omits timing annotations, with which a task network can be checked whether it satisfies given timing requirements, as for example discussed in previous work [12].

The execution function ψ of a task defines the reaction of the task with respect to its activation by an incoming data object on its input port(s). Together with our notion of connectivity by channels, the formalism allows to model a wide range of (deterministic) data flows in a system. This is depicted for example in Figure 2, which illustrates the update service scenario of our initial system model (c.f. Figure 1) in more detail. It is assumed that the update service receives two different kinds of data packets, namely p and p'. A p packet denotes a packet with a valid authentication, while p' denotes a packet that has been modified by an attacker. The execution function ψ_{Upd} (depicted below task Upd) defines that

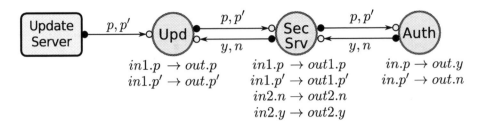

$$in1.p \to out.p \qquad in1.p \to out1.p \qquad in.p \to out.y$$
$$in1.p' \to out.p' \qquad in1.p' \to out1.p' \qquad in.p' \to out.n$$
$$in2.n \to out2.n$$
$$in2.y \to out2.y$$

Fig. 2. Task Network for Update Service

such packets are simply forwarded to the security service task SecSrv. The same forwarding takes place at task SecSrv. The authentication function, i.e., Auth, of the security module is assumed to return whether incoming packets are valid or not. This behavior is modeled by the execution function ψ_{Auth} that returns a y (yes) packet when the function has been called with a p packet, and n (no) otherwise. The answer is in advance relayed back to the update service function.

3.2 Towards Integration into Security Theory

Conventionally, a secure system is designed as follows: A set of security requirements is specified along with an attacker model with its capabilities before deploying the security protocols to achieve security. A rich set of theories exists for the verification of security protocols [4]. For example, based on a notion of protocols defining message transfers, term rewriting, and deduction rules; one can specify the abilities of an attacker and formally verify in advance whether the security protocol is vulnerable for the specified attacks [8,9].

Various well-established formalisms have been exploited for security analysis (such as CSP [11] and Petri nets [5]). As none of them was originally developed for architectural design, they have little relevance in actual system design for this design phase. Hence, our aim is to exploit real-time task networks, which is a well-established formalism that considers applications when they are deployed to a hardware architecture, for security analysis.

In order to model system functionality correctly, this clearly must involve the applied security protocols, as they might have a significant impact on the functionality and timing of the system. The proposed real-time model and its extensions [3] can be embedded in a natural way into security theories. This indeed could be done by relating our formalism to a respective CSP program [7] and then to apply security analysis as for example shown in [11]. For the present work however, we directly relate our formalism to the well-established Strand Space formalism developed in [13].

The Strand Space model exploits a basic notion of messages and message sequences:

Definition 2 ([13]). *A signed term is a pair $\langle d, a \rangle$ with $a \in \mathbf{A}$, and $d \in \{+, -\}$. We will write a signed term as $+a$ or $-a$. $(\pm \mathbf{A})^*$ is the set of*

finite sequences of signed terms. We will denote a typical element of $(\pm\mathbf{A})^*$
by $\langle\langle d_1, a_1\rangle, \ldots, \langle d_n, a_n\rangle\rangle$.

$\diamond$

Furthermore, the formalism defines a notion of protocols that are based on *strands*, which are essentially elements of $(\pm\mathbf{A})^*$:

Definition 3 ([13]). *A* Strand Space *is a set* S *with a trace mapping* $tr : S \to (\pm\mathbf{A})^*$.

$\diamond$

Given a task network N, it is easy to see how this relates to the above definitions. Considering the elements in the set Σ as messages that are transmitted between the protocol agents, provides us with the ground set of a Strand Space model: $\mathbf{A} = \Sigma$. Whether a message is received (denoted by $-$) or sent (denoted by $+$) can be obtained from the fact whether the message is observed at an input port or an output port respectively:

$$d(a) = \begin{cases} - & \text{if} \quad \exists t = (P_i, \psi, P_o) \in T : E(a) \in P_i \\ + & \text{if} \quad \exists t = (P_i, \psi, P_o) \in T : E(a) \in P_o \end{cases}$$

The translation gives rise to the integration of various important aspects of a system design. While the task network model is exploited for functional and real-time analysis, the translation allows the combination with security analysis. Based on the set $(\pm\mathbf{A})^*$ obtained by the translation, the security engineer is able to define the respective strands and bundles which form the basis (together with an understanding of the attacker capabilities) for the subsequent analysis. The main advantage of this integration is that all participants of the design have a common understanding of the design semantics.

The relation between the task network model and security formalisms as shown above is however, only a small part of what is needed in order to perform security analysis. In the following we concentrate on the notion of protocols, which is a crucial ingredient for security protocol analysis.

As said before, the Strand Space formalism defines the protocol sessions under consideration by finite sequences over messages, i.e., the elements of $tr(S)$. The causal and dependency relations, denoted by "$\to$" and "$\Rightarrow$" respectively, are essential for the formalism. They are also crucial for defining semantics of sending and receiving messages in a task network. Suppose a trace $\langle\langle d_1, m_1\rangle, \ldots, \langle d_n, m_n\rangle\rangle \in (\pm\mathbf{A})^*$. The reception of message m_i at the input port of a task, which corresponds to $\langle -, m_i\rangle$ in the trace, and the corresponding message sent by another task (which relates to $\langle +, m_i\rangle$) are causal related, i.e. we have the relation $\langle +, m_i\rangle \to \langle -, m_i\rangle$ in the corresponding Strand Space model. Additionally, the execution function of a task gives rise to the "$\Rightarrow$" relation of the corresponding Strand Space model. Given an actor (task) $t = (P_i, \psi, P_o)$, the dependency ($\Rightarrow$) relation of the strand is defined as:

$$\langle -, m_i\rangle \Rightarrow \langle +, m_{i+1}\rangle \quad \Longleftrightarrow \quad E(m_i) \in P_i \wedge E(m_{i+1}) \in P_o \wedge m_{i+1} = \psi(m_i)$$

4   Protocols and Verification

The relation proposed above is indeed only an initial step towards a more deeper integration of formal and security analyses. Nothing has been said for example about the capabilities of the intruder. More important, whether this would be possible without modifications of the underlying model in any case remains an open question. Explicit modeling of an intruder is not a well-established design step in current design processes for embedded systems.

It also remains open how the strand spaces for the security analysis of a given system are obtained. They essentially define the domain for the particular analysis. In the following we sketch the general approach for obtaining strand spaces from functional models.

Embedded systems are typically static systems. Dynamic behavior such as the addition of new functionality at run-time is rather uncommon. This is also reflected when using security protocols. We expect to see in a typical embedded system design only a fixed set of possibly available protocol behaviors. This fact can be exploited for deriving the parts of a security protocol actually used in a design in order to confine security analysis, and it should be possible to derive the relevant protocol behavior.

The security module in Figure 1, for example, provides a large set of possible protocol behaviors for authentication. In the depicted scenario however, only a single protocol instance is used, which is based on authenticating each incoming packet separately. This results in two possible protocol instances for the security protocol employed in the update service as shown in Figure 2, consisting of either the sequence SecSrv - p - Auth - y - SecSrv or SecSrv - p' - Auth - n - SecSrv between the SecSrv task (i.e., security service function) and the Auth block (i.e., authentication function).

The process of deriving the protocol behavior that is relevant for security analysis can also be done by exploiting formal analysis. For example, work in [3] proposes a translation scheme for our model into the formalism of timed automata [1]. Based on available model-checking tools this paves the way to obtain, for example, the relevant Strands for a given design model.

5   Conclusion

The goal of this contribution is to provide the basic notions for an integrated evaluation of the functional, real-time, and security aspect in the embedded system design utilizing formal mechanisms. For this, a functional model representing an example real-time system is considered as the target system and is modeled in the task network formalism. Then a possible relation is drawn between this formalism and the existing security theory, i.e., Strand Space formalism. However, drawing such a relation is only an initial step towards a more tighter integration between them. At the end, the presented formal approach is analyzed with an example to derive a protocol like behavior which is relevant for security analysis.

Acknowledgement. This work was supported by the Federal Ministry for Education and Research (BMBF) Germany, under grant code 01IS110355M, in project "Automotive, Railway and Avionic Multicore System (ARAMiS)" The responsibility for the content of this publication lies with the author.

References

1. Alur, R., Dill, D.L.: A Theory of Timed Automata. Theoretical Computer Science 126(2), 183–235 (1994)
2. Benveniste, A., Berry, G.: The Synchronous Approach to Reactive and Real-Time Systems. Proceedings of the IEEE 79, 1270–1282 (1991)
3. Büker, M., Metzner, A., Stierand, I.: Testing real-time task networks with functional extensions using model-checking. In: Proc. 14th IEEE International Conference on Emerging Technologies & Factory Automation, pp. 564–573. IEEE Press (2009)
4. Cortier, V., Kremer, S. (eds.): Formal Models and Techniques for Analyzing Security Protocols. IOS Press (2011)
5. Crazzolara, F., Winskel, G.: Petri nets in cryptographic protocols. In: Proceedings of the 15th International Parallel & Distributed Processing Symposium, IPDPS 2001, p. 149. IEEE Computer Society, Washington, DC (2001), http://dl.acm.org/citation.cfm?id=645609.662336
6. Denning, D.E.: A lattice model of secure information flow. Communications of the ACM 19(5), 236–243 (1976)
7. Faber, J., Stierand, I.: From high-level verification to real-time scheduling: A property-preserving integration. Reports of SFB/TR 14 AVACS 19, SFB/TR 14 AVACS (May 2007), iSSN: 1860-9821, http://www.avacs.org
8. Fröschle, S.: Adding branching to the strand space model. Electron. Notes Theor. Comput. Sci. 242(1), 139–159 (2009)
9. Fröschle, S., Sommer, N.: Reasoning with Past to Prove PKCS#11 Keys Secure. In: Degano, P., Etalle, S., Guttman, J. (eds.) FAST 2010. LNCS, vol. 6561, pp. 96–110. Springer, Heidelberg (2011)
10. Ghamarian, A.H., Geilen, M.C.W., Basten, T., Theelen, B.D., Mousavi, M.R., Stuijk, S.: Liveness and boundedness of synchronous data flow graphs. In: FMCAD 2006: Proceedings of the Formal Methods in Computer Aided Design, pp. 68–75. IEEE Computer Society, Washington, DC (2006)
11. Lowe, G.: Analysing Security Protocols Using CSP. In: Cortier, Kremer (eds.) [4] (2011)
12. Malipatlolla, S., Stierand, I.: Evaluating the Impact of Integrating a Security Module on the Real-Time Properties of a System. In: Schirner, G., Götz, M., Rettberg, A., Zanella, M.C., Rammig, F.J. (eds.) IESS 2013. IFIP AICT, vol. 403, pp. 343–352. Springer, Heidelberg (2013)
13. Fabrega, F.J.T., Herzog, J.C., Guttman, J.D.: Strand spaces: why is a security protocol correct? In: IEEE Symposium on Security and Privacy, pp. 160–171 (1998)
14. Tindell, K.W., Burns, A., Wellings, A.J.: Allocating hard real-time tasks: An NP-Hard problem made easy. Real-Time Systems 4, 145–165 (1992)
15. Yip, A., Wang, X., Zeldovich, N., Kaashoek, M.F.: Improving application security with data flow assertions. In: Proceedings of the ACM SIGOPS 22nd Symposium on Operating Systems Principles, pp. 291–304. ACM (2009)

Design of CAPTCHA Script for Indian Regional Websites

M. Tariq Banday[*] and Shafiya Afzal Sheikh

PG Department of Electronics and Instrumentation Technology,
University of Kashmir, Srinagar, 190 006,
Jammu and Kashmir, India
sgrmtb@yahoo.com

Abstract. To improve accessibility of Indian regional websites especially government websites content is offered in regional languages besides English language. However, these websites use CAPTCHA tests in English languages in regional language pages. This reduces usability and accessibility because non-native speakers of English language are required to pass CAPTCHA tests in English language. The accessibility of such websites can be improved substantially if secure CAPTCHA tests in regional languages are used. However, such an implementation is challenging as Indian regional languages are unique in many ways, are written differently and have different alphabets, glyphs, pronunciations, accents, etc. This paper reviews existing CAPTCHA scripts and Indian regional websites in terms of their usability, accessibility and multilingual support. It reports the design of CAPTCHA script in Hindi, Punjabi, Urdu and English languages which can be used to generate CAPTCHA tests in websites offering content in these languages. The designed CAPTCHA script offers features such as audio, localized onscreen keyboard, random patterns and fonts to improve usability and security.

Keywords: Web Accessibility, Multilingual Websites, CAPTCHA, Regional Languages, Human Interaction Proof, HIP.

1 Introduction

A website may be intended for international or regional audience and may offer its contents in only one language (monolingual) or in more than one language (multilingual). International and multilingual websites have specific requirements with respect to design, development, and deployment, and these requirements could call for different technical solutions. An international website is one that is intended for an international audience, and a multilingual website refers to a website that uses more than one language. An international website may or may not be multilingual, just as a multilingual website may or may not be international. Multilingual sites can exist in different forms. A site might offer language selection and then present the contents in only a single language at a time. A multilingual site might also mix

---

[*] Corresponding author.

Sabu M. Thampi et al. (Eds.): SSCC 2013, CCIS 377, pp. 98–109, 2013.

multiple languages within the same page, either because the audience is believed to be multilingual, or because there might be a need for embedded foreign text. An online foreign dictionary is a common example of such a site. A monolingual website presents its contents in only one language. Websites that present the same monolingual content to an international audience may be acceptable for a technical community with an agreed standard language. However it might still be useful to translate some types of information, such as tutorial and introductory text. A regional website might offer specific contents and features to its regional audience in a particular regional language or could simply offer translation of its offered contents and features in a particular regional language besides English or any other language considered as principal language.

Web accessibility is the ability of a person to understand and interact with the web contents using hardware and/or software that render the web contents. Given the multi-dimensional nature of the web which acts as source of information in the form of texts and multimedia, as an interacting technology and as a network interconnected with hyperlinks. W3C within the framework of Web Accessibility Initiative (WAI) (http://www.w3.org/WAI/) describes web accessibility to mean that people with a diverse range of hearing, movement, sight, and cognitive ability regardless of their hardware, software, language, culture, location, physical or mental ability can use it without any barriers. However, when websites, web technologies, or web tools are badly designed, they can create barriers that exclude people from using the web. W3C has published a set of twelve Web Content Accessibility Guidelines (WCAG 2.0) (http://www.w3.org/TR/WCAG20/) that are organized under four principles namely Perceivable, Operable, Understandable and Robust. Government of India (GOI) has also formulated 'Guidelines for Indian Government Websites' (http://web.guidelines.gov.in) to ensure that the websites belonging to any constituent of the Government of India at any level are user friendly, secure, accessible, easy to maintain and are in conformity to the world accepted standards. Realizing the fact that India is a country of diverse cultures with as many as 22 official languages, Government of India has issued several guidelines for inclusion of Hindi and other regional languages, in the websites of Government Departments.

A website or web portal may contain simple web pages, web forms, secure content, contact information, e-mail addresses and other similar information. Simple web pages are served to the clients on request without any type of security check. Some areas of a website may require users to login and others may not but at the same time to prevent misuse, they must not be accessible to bots such as web forms and web pages containing e-mail and other similar information. When the server receives a request for a web page which is not protected, access is granted directly. In case the content is protected, the website takes proper measure to allow access only to humans. CAPTCHA [1] challenges permit websites to determine whether the user of some resource is a human being or a web-bot. CAPTCHA challenges can protect web resources and services like online polls and surveys, e-mail services, chat systems, blogs, discussion boards, forums, downloadable documents, grievance redressal system, login & registration system, etc. Generally CAPTCHA challenges are in English language and therefore, can cause accessibility challenges to user of non-English or multilingual websites who are not well versed with English language.

A study [2] conducted to evaluate the usability of CAPTCHA challenges has found that CAPTCHA challenges are not only difficult for humans to solve but non-native speakers of English language are slower and less accurate on solving English language CAPTCHA tests. The study revealed that audio CAPTCHA takes 57% longer time to solve for non-native speakers of English language and highly educated people take less time in solving Image CAPTCHA tests. Similar results have been found through another study [3] conducted to evaluate the effect of script familiarization on CAPTCHA usability. It is therefore, desirable to have alternate CAPTCHA challenges for regional users which are secure and usable. A review of different types of CAPTCHA challenges, their working, limitations, effectiveness, usability and security issues have been discussed in the authors earlier studies [4], [5].

2   Analysis of Indian Regional Websites

To analyze and approximate the awareness, acceptance and compliance of W3C guidelines for websites and Indian government website guidelines, an analysis of as many as 150 Indian government websites and 120 non-government websites including corporate and society websites was carried. The result of this analysis are reported in table 1. The results are based on the analysis carried out on different browser types and versions running on different operating systems.

Table 1. Functionalities in Indian regional websites

Website Functionalities			Govt. Websites	Non-Govt. Websites
Multi-Lingual Functionalities		English	100%	95%
		Urdu	5%	10%
		Hindi	40%	5%
		Punjabi	2%	None
		Other Languages	2%	None
		Completeness	50%	70%
		Protected Feature(s)	70%	88%
		Uses CAPTCHA	47%	70%
		Localized CAPTCHA	None	None
CAPTCHA Functionalities	Type	Text Image	20%	30%
		Text Math	10%	20%
		Text Question	2%	7%
		Text Image Math	10%	10%
		Other	5%	3%
		Audio Alternative	20%	25%
		Reload Button	30%	35%
		Onscreen Keyboard	None	None
		Help	None	5%

The language distribution with respect to Indian regional languages indicates that a good number of analyzed websites especially government websites offer their content in Hindi language. Nearly half of the analyzed websites protect some features using various types of CAPTCHA challenges while as this goes up to 70% in case of non-government websites. Most of the websites that protect some resource through the use of CAPTCHA do not follow W3C guidelines pertaining to the use of CAPTCHA challenges. The completeness of multilingual features in case of government websites is only 50%. Localized CAPTCHA challenges have not been found in any analyzed website. Accessibility features like onscreen keyboard and help are not present in any government website. Audio alternative for CAPTCHA tests are present in 20% analyzed government and 25% non-government websites. The GOI Guidelines regarding multilingual versions are not being strictly adhered to as in some of the websites presentation of regional content is either very poor or cannot be properly displayed in current browsers.

3   CAPTCHA Scripts

Several open or closed source CAPTCHA scripts[1] that allow website developers to implement easy to use and accessible CAPTCHA challenges in web forms are available to prevent bots from filling up forms and causing security threats. CPATCHA scripts producing tests in languages other than English language may also offer several accessibility features to design CAPTCHA test that are easy for humans to solve but difficult for bots to simulate. Popular open source CAPTCHA scripts along with their multilingual and accessibility features are listed in table 2.

Column Legends: A-Multilingual Functionalities, B-Audio, C-Reload, D-Onscreen Keyboard, E-Help.

Almost all CAPTCHA scripts mentioned in table 2 are in English language except *BotDetech CAPTCHA*. This permits designing of CAPTCHA tests in major international languages including Hindi and Urdu. However, this script has not taken into consideration Glyph for languages like Urdu and also does not allow use of other Indian regional languages. Table 2 also compares CAPTCHA test functionalities in terms of audio alternative, image refresh, onscreen keyboard, help, and type. No CAPTCHA script listed in table 2 permits CAPTCHA tests to show onscreen keyboard. Help feature is present in only one CAPTCHA script. As many as 13 scripts do no use alternate CAPTCHA tests like audio for improving accessibility and 14 do not permit refreshing of CAPTCHA tests. Even the promising CAPTCHA script *BotDetech* CAPTCHA which allows various non-English languages does not permit help, refreshing of tests and onscreen keyboard. A major limitation with these services is that the users are unable to type the given characters using English keyboard causing challenges to users who do not possess enough computer skills to install keyboards. Further, the characters of a word are displayed separately instead of using glyphs and combining the characters wherever necessary for some languages. Furthermore, the tests lack dynamic CAPTCHA image generation algorithms and often use static images for tests. This results in reuse if these images causing severe security challenge.

---

[1] Script is a code fragment or some code in a web page which is written in some programming language and executed either on the server or on the client machine. CAPTCHA script is a server side script which is executed on server with responses delivered to the client.

Table 2. CAPTCHA scripts and accessibility features offered by each

S.	Script Name	A	B	C	D	E
1	Secure Image[2]	✗	✓	✓	✗	✗
2	Cool PHP CAPTCHA[3]	✗	✓	✓	✗	✗
3	Cryptographp[4]	✗	✗	✓	✗	✗
4	WP CAPTCHA-Free[5]	✗	✗	✓	✗	✗
5	Form-to-email script protected by CAPTCHA[6]	✗	✗	✗	✗	✗
6	freeCap[7]	✗	✗	✗	✗	✗
7	Ajax Fancy CAPTCHA[8]	✗	✗	✗	✗	✗
8	JCAPTCHA (Java)[9]	✗	✗	✗	✗	✗
9	TheCAPTCHA[10]	✗	✗	✗	✗	✗
10	Visual and Audio PHP CAPTCHA[11]	✗	✓	✗	✗	✗
11	Quick CAPTCHA 1.0 PHP[12]	✗	✗	✗	✗	✗
12	JCAP (JavaScript)[13]	✗	✗	✗	✗	✗
13	Hoomantest[14]	✗	✗	✗	✗	✗
14	Confident CAPTCHA[15]	✗	✓	✗	✗	✓
15	BotDetech CAPTCHA[16]	✓	✓	✗	✗	✗
16	CAPTCHATOR[17]	✗	✗	✗	✗	✗
17	adCAPTCHER[18]	✗	✗	✓	✗	✗
18	Simple JavaScript CAPTCHA[19]	✗	✗	✗	✗	✗
19	CAPTCHA 2.0[20]	✗	✗	✗	✗	✗

Besides the above mentioned scripts there are various other online CAPTCHA services that include *reCAPTCHA* (http://recaptcha.net) and *CAPTCHAS* (http://captchas.net/) which CAPTCHA tests to be designed in non-English languages.

---

[2] http://www. phpcaptcha.org
[3] https://code.google.com/p/cool-php-captcha/
[4] http://www.captcha.fr
[5] http://wordpress.org/extend/plugins/wp-captcha-free/
[6] http://www.snaphost.com/captcha/
[7] http://www.puremango.co.uk/2005/04/php_captcha_script_113/
[8] http://www.webdesignbeach.com/beachbar/
ajax-fancy-captcha-jquery-plugin
[9] http://jcaptcah.sourceforge.net/
[10] http://www.thecaptcha.com/
[11] http://www.ejeliot.com/pages/php-captcha
[12] http://www.web1marketing.com/resources/tools/quickcaptcha/
[13] http://www.archreality.com/jcap/
[14] http://fragged.org/dev/hOOmanTest_captcah_for_mootools.php
[15] http://www.confidenttechnologies.com/
[16] http://captcha.biz/
[17] http://captchator.com/
[18] http://www.adcaptcher.com
[19] http://sourcefirst.wordpress.com/category/javascript/
[20] http://milki.include-once.org/captcha/

However, these services and scripts are not available for designing CAPTCHA tests in Indian regional languages. Non-English language CAPTCHA challenges have been proposed in various studies e.g. Yalamanchili et al [6] proposed CAPTCHA for Indian regional language script Devanagari, Khan et al [7] proposed Arabic CAPTCHA for websites in Arabic language and Shirali-Shahreza et al in their studies [8], [9], [10], [11] proposed Persian, Arabic, Nastaliq CAPTCHA challenges for regional and illiterate users. In the current authors past study [12] an Urdu language CAPTCHA challenge was developed and its usability compared. The results suggested that accessibility of regional websites can be substantially improved by employing the use of secure and usable CAPTCHA challenges implemented in native language of the user.

4   Proposed CAPTCHA Script

This section describes a CAPTCHA script permitting generation of CAPTCHA tests in Hindi, Punjabi and Urdu languages besides English language. The script overcomes the challenges of existing multilingual scripts by permitting regional languages, improving presentation of CAPTCHA test (glyph), improving accessibility by providing onscreen keyboard in all permissible languages, audio alternative in all permissible languages, help and refreshing of CAPTCHA image. It does not use a static image set and instead generates images dynamically improving its security control. In the proposed script a CAPTCH image with a set of characters of the required language will be shown to the end user with a text box to fill in the given characters. A virtual keyboard is made available to the users by a click on the keyboard button which allows the user to enter the characters without requiring to install the regional language of CAPTCHA. To improve the accessibility, an alternate audio CAPTCHA test is also included. The user can also listen to the sounds of the characters present on the CAPTCHA image. The working of the script is detailed in figure 1.

When a client makes a request to the protected resource protected by the CAPTCHA test implemented through the proposed script, the script determines the language of the CAPTCHA test. The Unicode character set of the detected language is extracted from the underlying database to generate two words of 3 to 4 characters each. An image of 200X50 pixels is created in random background and noise in the form of lines, patterns, etc. applied to it. Two randomly generated words are rendered on the image in a random font with required glyph to produce the final CAPTCHA image. The CAPTCHA words along with other state information such as IP and GUID address of the client are stored in the database. Icons for displaying virtual keyboard, help, audio and refreshing are placed on the CAPTCHA frame. An input box for user entry is also generated in the CAPTCHA frame. The frame is returned to the client in response to its request which is then rendered in the webpage. The user response to the CAPTCHA test is submitted by the client to the script running on the web server. The script extracts words stored in its database corresponding to the requesting client using state information and compares it with the user response returning a success or failure notifications. In case user clicks on the keyboard icon a virtual keyboard of the CAPTCHA test language is programmatically created and displayed on the client. The user can enter response through this keyboard. A click on the help icon fetches a help file listing the help for user to solve the test. In case the

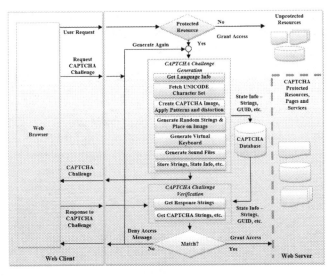

Fig. 1. Working of regional language CAPTCHA script

user clicks on the audio icon, a sound file is programmatically generated, downloaded and played on the browser reading the CAPTCHA characters. A click on the refresh icon regenerates the entire CAPTCHA challenge.

The algorithm used to generate CAPTCHA script in Hindi, Punjabi, Urdu and English languages is depicted in table 3.

Table 3. Algorithm for regional language CAPTCHA script

Step	Procedure
	A) Request CAPTCHA Challenge
1	Set CAPTCHA test language to detected/preferred language *LANG*. In absence of language information set *LANG* to English.
2	Create a blank image (*CAPIMG*) of 200x50 pixels with 96 DPI resolution.
3	Choose a random pattern from *X* predefined patterns and apply it to the CAPTCHA Image (*CAPIMG*) created in previous step.
4	Draw *N* random lines in random colors on the image.
5	Extract character set of the *LANG* from the database and store it into an array *CHARS*.
6	Randomly select *X* characters from array *CHARS* and form *WORD1*.
7	Randomly select *Y* characters from array *CHARS* and form *WORD2*.
8	Compare *WORD1* and *WORD2* with *M* recently used words stored in the underlying database tables in encrypted format, if match is found discard *WORD1* and *WORD2* and return to step 6, otherwise, continue to next step.
9	In case *LANG* is *URDU* then swap the words to display them in right to left order and replace the characters in *WORD1* and *WORD2* with proper glyphs to form properly connected *URDU* words.
10	Render *WORD1* and *WORD2* on the image in a random font and store in the database.
11	Store *WORD1* and *WORD2* along with *IP* address and GUID of the client and information in the underlying database table as a record in encrypted format.

Table 3. (*Continued.*)

Step	Procedure
12	Retrieve Primary Key (*ID*) of the record from the underlying database table and return to client i) Primary Key (*ID*), ii) path to image generation script for rendering the CAPTCHA image, icons and user response textbox along with necessary labels, iii) CAPTCHA image, and, iv) icons for displaying Virtual Keyboard (*ICO1*), generating Help (*ICO2*), playing Audio (*ICO3*) and Refreshing CAPTCHA Challenge (*ICO4*).

The client renders the CAPTCHA challenge in the webpage.

B) Response to CAPTCHA Challenge (User enters CAPTCHA response string in the text box)

1	Get the CAPTCHA response string (*RES*) from the client.
2	Get the *GUID* along with *IP* address of client and primary Key *ID*.
3	Verify *GUID*, if verified continue to next step otherwise quit with an error message.
4	Retrieve *WORD1* and *WORD2* from the underlying database table using primary key ID.
5	Compare response string (*RES*) with string formed from *WORD1* and *WORD2* for equality, if equal return test passed, otherwise, initiate steps for reloading CAPTCHA challenge.
6	Remove records of the of Mth CAPTCHA test.

The client permits access to protected area of the website or renders a new CAPTCHA challenge.

C) Response to CAPTCHA Challenge (User clicks on virtual keyboard icon)

1	Get the *GUID* along with *IP* address of client and primary Key *ID*.
2	Verify *GUID*, if verified continue to next step otherwise quit with an error message.
3	Return script for displaying Virtual Keyboard on the client in the language *LANG*. The language information is retrieved from the underlying database table.

The user response to virtual keyboard is entered in user response textbox.

D) Response to CAPTCHA Challenge (User clicks on help icon)

1	Get the *GUID* along with *IP* address of client and primary Key *ID*.
2	Verify *GUID*, if verified continue to next step otherwise quit with an error message.
3	Return script for rendering help text on the client.

The user reads the help message on the client.

E) Response to CAPTCHA Challenge (User clicks on audio icon)

1	Get the *GUID* along with *IP* address of client and primary Key *ID*.
2	Verify *GUID*, if verified continue to next step otherwise quit with an error message.
3	Retrieve *WORD1* and *WORD2* from the underlying database table using primary key ID.
4	Retrieve sound files for *WORD1* and *WORD2* from the underlying database table using primary key ID and create a temporary sound file (*AUDIO*) containing sounds of each character in order of their appearance in the CAPTCHA string.
5	Return the script for playing the sound file (*AUDIO*) which is send to the client along with the script.

The user listens to the sounds of characters contained in the CAPTCHA challenge.

F) Response to CAPTCHA Challenge (User clicks on Refresh icon)

1	Get the *GUID* along with *IP* address of client and primary Key *ID*.
2	Verify *GUID*, if verified continue to next step otherwise quit with an error message.
3	Generate CAPTCHA Challenge again.

The client renders a new CAPTCHA challenge in the webpage.

To strengthen the security of the proposed scheme randomization has been used in several steps of the algorithm. The random process of word generation is further strengthened by discarding use of recently generated M words. The characters, their number, font, font-size, and color used in each word of the CAPTCHA image is random thus making pattern learnability and their detection difficult by bots. A random wave effect has been added to the CAPTCHA image to increase the difficulty of finding cut points. It makes segmentation difficult. Thick lines at random locations in random colors and random background color make it difficult to segment and recognize the characters by programs. A shadow effect added to characters produces collapsing effect which acts as an anti-segmentation security measure. Further, the OCR technologies currently available are mostly based on Latin character set thus cannot be used to break the regional language CAPTCHA challenges easily. To further improve security several measures have been taken into considerations while designing CAPTCHA script. The script generates a low resolution image, random fonts are used for each language, and CAPTCHA strings generated in recent tests are not used for subsequent tests from a particular client. Further, background music and noise has been added to audio files that prevent extraction of characters by the automated systems. Further, with multiple invalid response, the script increases the complexity of the test by making the CAPTCHA string lengthy.

5   Implementation, Testing and User Study

The CAPTCHA script was developed using PHP 5.3.8 on Apache Server 1.7.7 with the underlying database stored in a MySql 3.4.5 database. The database was used to store UNICODE character set of Hindi, Urdu, Punjabi and English languages, audio files, help text, preferences, CAPTCHA strings and images, GUID and other state information. Background music and noise were added to sounds of each UNICODE character using Audacity (http://audacity.sourceforge.net/) which is a freely available open source cross-platform software for recording and editing, slicing and mixing sounds. Five API's namely *getCAPTCHA*, *getKeyboard*, *getHelp*, *getAudio*, *getResult*, and *capReload* were created to permit calls from varied programming environments. Calls from client to these API's return appropriate JavaScript in HTML code to the client. A call to *getCAPTCHA* API generates a new CAPTCHA challenge as discussed in the previous section. It generates CAPTCHA HTML code that can be embedded in the web page. It contains: i) an image tag with link to the image generation API on the server, ii) a refresh image tag with JavaScript which links to the reload API on the server, iii) a sound image tag with JavaScript which links to the sound generation API on the server. This also includes a sound player script, iv) a keyboard Image tag with JavaScript which calls the keyboard API and load the same from the server, v) a help image tag which links to the help page on the server, and, v) a textbox tag which will allow user to input the code as displayed on image or in sound. A call to *getKeyboard* API executes virtual keyboard and display a virtual keyboard on the client permitting the CAPTCHA respondent to respond without the use of multilingual keyboard or language support. A call to *getAudio* API generates a sound file in MP3 format on the server which is send to the client which then plays it using media player script supplied through *getCAPTCHA* API. Call to *getHelp* API loads a help page from the server. A call to *getResult* API returns a success signal or failure message with new CAPTCHA challenge. Clients can reload the CAPTCHA test with a call to *capReload* API.

To verify working and correctness of the CAPTCHA script, tests were carried out on local network. A network of five machines was set up. A machine was configured as a Webserver on which Apache version 1.7.7 and PHP version 5.3.8 were installed. Other machines were configured as clients on which various browsers were installed to allow users to access websites hosted on the Webserver. A sample website with pages in English, Hindi, Urdu and Punjabi languages was developed and installed on the Webserver. Each language page contained a web form that embedded a CAPTCHA challenge in respective languages using the developed CAPTCHA script. The website was successfully accessed through client machines using Internet Explorer, Google Chrome, Mozilla Firefox, and Opera browsers. A snapshot of the Hindi language CAPTCHA challenge embedded in a web form contained in a Hindi language page is shown in figure 2.

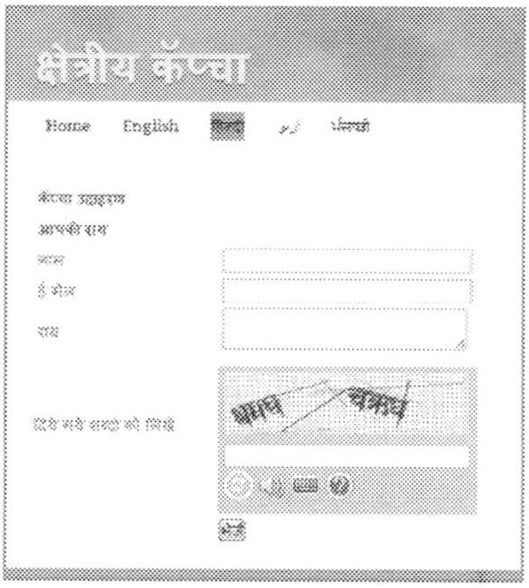

Fig. 2. Hindi language CAPTCHA challenge

Various functionalities of the CAPTCHA challenge were tested on all above mentioned browsers. A click on the reload button successfully reloaded the CAPTCHA challenge in the web form. A click on the audio icon successfully played the sounds in the respective language of characters in the CAPTCHA string. Virtual keyboard in respective language was successfully displayed and made correct entry in the user response text box. A sample virtual language keyboard for Hindi language CAPTCHA challenge as displayed by the script is shown in figure 3. A correct response was correctly recognized by the CAPTCHA script and the website permitted access to protected area of the website. An incorrect response was also correctly recognized by the CAPTCHA script. A message "Incorrect Security Code" was displayed and the CAPTCHA challenge was successfully reloaded in the web form.

Each language page containing CAPTCHA challenge embedded web form produced CAPTCHA challenge in respective language. The samples of the CAPTCHA images in English, Urdu and Punjabi language web forms are shown in figure 4. In each challenge virtual keyboards were successfully displayed and permitted user entry in respective languages and audio player successfully played audio files in respective languages. The help and reload functionalities in each implemented language also were successfully tested.

To access the usability of English language CAPTCHA in websites with content in regional languages and to identify the advantage of using regional language CAPTCHA in such websites, a user study with three groups of users was conducted. Each group comprised of ten regional language users who were having fluency in either Hindi, Punjabi or Urdu languages but little knowledge of English language. After coaching in browsing a website on a computer, they were asked to solve CAPTCHA challenge in English, Urdu, Hindi, and Punjab languages. The results were measured in terms of accuracy and time taken to solve CAPTCHA challenges. The results showed that the users were able to solve the CHAPTCHA in their regional languages more accurately and quickly. The users found it quite difficult to solve CAPTCHA challenges in English language.

Fig. 3. Virtual keyboard generated by the script for Hindi language CAPTCHA challenge

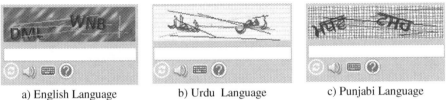

| a) English Language Challenge | b) Urdu Language Challenge | c) Punjabi Language Challenge |

Fig. 4. CAPTCHA Images in English, Urdu, and Punjabi languages challenges

The non-native, regional language CAPTCHA was the most difficult to solve for all groups of users. E.g. the users who whose native language was Urdu were able to solve Urdu CAPTCHA challenges with accuracy ranging from 90% to 98%. The same users solved English CAPTCHA with an accuracy of about 20% to 30%. However, CAPTCHA tests in other non-English and non-native languages were solved by about 5% to 7% users. Hindi language knowing user group solved Hindi CAPTCHA more accurately in comparison to solving English CAPTCHA. Similar results were obtained in the response time tests. The users were able to quickly solve the CAPTCHA challenges in their native languages. They took more time to respond to English CAPTCHA challenges. The response time was highest for attempting Non-native regional Language CAPTCHA challenges. The use of audio and virtual keyboard further improved the accuracy and response time.

6   Conclusion and Future Scope

Usability and accessibility of regional websites offering their content in regional languages is reduced by the use of English languages CAPTCHA challenges.

The accuracy and response time in solving such challenges for non-native speakers of English language is reduced. Some free and open source CAPTCHA scripts permit CAPTCHA tests to be responded in Indian regional languages, however, these lack the essential accessibility features and security mechanism. A secure and usable script for generating CAPTCHA challenges in Hindi, Punjabi, and Urdu languages besides English language has been realized in this study. The script produces CAPTCHA challenges with accessibility features such as localized onscreen keyboard, help, and audio make it usable. Random image patterns, use of multiple fonts and non-repetition of recent challenges make it secure against bots. The script can be further extended by permitting its implementation in all major languages of India. Its usability and security can be augmented by including more fonts and patterns and by improving its interface. Future work can also be undertaken to build an API accessible from all major programming environments offering CAPTCHA challenges in all major languages of India.

References

1. Ahn, L., Blum, M., Langford, J.: Telling Humans and Computers Apart Automatically. Communications of the ACM 47(2), 57–60 (2004)
2. Bursztein, E., Bethard, S., Fabry, C., Jurafsky, D., Mitchell, J.C.: How Good are Humans at Solving CAPTCHAs? A Large Scale Evaluation. Security and Privacy, 399–413 (2010)
3. Khalil, A., Abdallah, S., Soha, A., Hassan, H.: Script Familiarity and Its Effect on CAPTCHA Usability: An Experiment with Arab Participants. International Journal of Web Portals (IJWP) 4(2), 74–87 (2012)
4. Banday, M.T., Shah, N.A.: Image Flip CAPTCHA. ISeCure 1(2), 103–121 (2009)
5. Banday, M.T., Shah, N.A.: A Study of CAPTCHAs for Securing Web Services. IJSDIA 1(2), 66–74 (2009)
6. Yalamanchili, S., Kameswara Rao, M.: A Framework for Devanagari Script-based Captcha. arXiv preprint arXiv:1109.0132 (2011)
7. Khan, B., Alghathbar, K.S., Khan, M.K., AlKelabi, A.M., AlAjaji, A.: Using Arabic CAPTCHA for Cyber Security. In: Kim, T.-H., Fang, W.-C., Khan, M.K., Arnett, K.P., Kang, H.-j., Ślęzak, D. (eds.) SecTech/DRBC 2010. CCIS, vol. 122, pp. 8–17. Springer, Heidelberg (2010)
8. Shirali-Shahreza, M.H., Shirali-Shahreza, S.: Persian/Arabic Unicode Text Steganography. In: Fourth International Conference on Information Assurance and Security, ISIAS 2008, pp. 62–66. IEEE (2008)
9. Shirali-Shahreza, M.H., Shirali-Shahreza, M.: Advanced Nastaliq CAPTCHA. In: 7th IEEE International Conference on Cybernetic Intelligent Systems, CIS 2008, pp. 1–3. IEEE (2008)
10. Shirali-Shahreza, M.H., Shirali-Shahreza, M.: Localized CAPTCHA for illiterate people. In: International Conference on Intelligent and Advanced Systems, ICIAS 2007, pp. 675–679. IEEE (2007)
11. Shirali-Shahreza, M.H., Shirali-Shahreza, M.: Multilingual captcha. In: IEEE International Conference on Computational Cybernetics, ICCC 2007, pp. 135–139. IEEE (2007)
12. Banday, M.T., Shah, N.A.: Challenges of CAPTCHA in the accessibility of Indian regional websites. In: Proceedings of the Fourth Annual ACM Bangalore Conference, pp. 31–34. ACM (2011)

A Survey of Traditional and Cloud Specific Security Issues

Sumitra Binu[1,*] and Mohammed Misbahuddin[2]

[1] Christ University, Bangalore, India
sumitrabinu@gmail.com
[2] C-DAC, Electronic-City, Bangalore India
mdmisbahuddin@gmail.com

Abstract. The emerging technology popularly referred to as Cloud computing offers dynamically scalable computing resources on a pay per use basis over the Internet. Companies avail hardware and software resources as service from the cloud service provider as opposed to obtaining physical assets. Cloud computing has the potential for significant cost reduction and increased operating efficiency in computing. To achieve these benefits, however, there are still some challenges to be solved. Security is one of the prime concerns in adopting Cloud computing, since the user's data has to be released from the protection sphere of the data owner to the premises of cloud service provider. As more Cloud based applications keep evolving, the associated security threats are also growing. In this paper an attempt has been made to identify and categorize the security threats applicable to Cloud environment. Threats are classified into Cloud specific security issues and traditional security attacks on various service delivery models of Cloud. The work also briefly discusses the virtualization and authentication related issues in Cloud and tries to consolidate the various security threats in a classified manner.

Keywords: Cloud Computing, Security Issues, Service Delivery Models, Classification.

1 Introduction

Cloud Computing has brought about a change in the way in which computing services were traditionally being delivered. Essential resources consumed by households and businesses such as water, electricity and gas are delivered on a requirement basis through faucets and outlets. The sources and delivery mechanisms of these essentials are not of concern to the consumers. Cloud computing introduces the same concept to computing technology. This new computing model offers software, platforms and infrastructures as services over the Internet and the cloud service consumers are not aware of the physical location where these services are performed. From the plethora

---

* Corresponding author.

Sabu M. Thampi et al. (Eds.): SSCC 2013, CCIS 377, pp. 110–129, 2013.

of available definitions, we can interpret Cloud Computing as a new computing model that offers dynamically scalable resources such as Data, Software, and Storage as a service over the Internet. This computing model enables the Cloud users to increase their capacity and capability dynamically without investing in new infrastructure, training new personnel, licensing new software etc.

1.1   Cloud Computing Architecture

According to the National Institute of Standards and Technology (NIST), Cloud has four deployment models, three service delivery models and each model exhibits certain characteristic. Fig.1 illustrates the Cloud computing architecture. Similar to the classification of application software into multiple classes based on various parameters such as categories and intended user types, Cloud computing can also be divided into several service types and deployment models. Buyya et al.[1] in their work, divide Cloud computing services into three classes: Infrastructure-as-a-Service(IaaS), Platform-as-a-Service(PaaS) and Software-as-a-Service(SaaS). IaaS forms the bottom layer which offers the lowest level of separation between what consumers could expect and the resources that are readily available for them to utilize [2]. PaaS is the middle layer and is an environment where the Cloud provider offers as a service those applications which are ready to be developed or deployed. SaaS, the top most layer, provides application software as a service on demand. Each of the Cloud service delivery models are utilized within a particular deployment model. The different deployment models are Public, Private, Community and Hybrid Cloud. The four delivery models of the Cloud form the core of the Cloud and they exhibit certain characteristics like On-demand self service, Ubiquitous network access, Rapid elasticity, Measured service and Resource pooling [3][4].

1.2   Significance of Security in Cloud Computing

All the three layers of the Cloud promise a reduction in Capital expenditure by saving on hardware costs. The reductions in hardware, license and patch management costs contribute to lesser operational costs as well [5]. But along with these benefits, Cloud computing raises many security concerns, which makes potential customers think multiple times before they leap into the Cloud. Once the enterprise moves their data and execution tasks onto the Cloud which is managed by an external company, they lose control over their sensitive data. According to a recent survey by International Data Corporation (IDC), 87.5 % of the masses belonging to varied levels starting from IT executives to CEOs have said that security is the top most challenge to be dealt with in every cloud service [6]. Amongst the various threats faced by the different Cloud services, Security threat is considered to be of high risk [7] as demonstrated in the work of N.Kilari et al. [8]. These threats can be thwarted in an application by the introduction of some suitable elements.

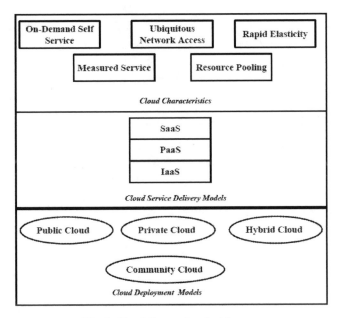

Fig. 1. Cloud Computing Architecture

Such an approach has been suggested by Ramgovind [9] and Nitin Singh Chauhan [10] in terms of six major principles of security which includes Confidentiality, Integrity, Authentication, Authorization, Non-Repudiation and Availability [11]. Out of these major principles in Cloud Security, availability which ensures continuous availability of resources to authorized users [12] seems to pose a major challenge in achieving the full benefits of Cloud. Cloud computing provides on-demand services to customers who expect minimum or no down time. Breaching such expectation would be detrimental to the future of Cloud [13].

1.3   Organization of the Paper

The rest of the paper is organized as follows: Section 2 discusses a few works done by researchers in the area of Cloud Security. Section 3 briefly examines the security challenges preventing the wide spread adoption of Cloud. There are a few threats that originated due to the inherent architecture of Cloud. These threats are not faced by traditional systems and hence require special mention. Section 4 elaborates the Cloud specific security issues. Section 5 is reserved for discussing the security issues faced by the SaaS, PaaS and IaaS service delivery models of Cloud and Section 6 concludes the work done.

2   Related Work

In recent years, many researchers have proposed, multifarious approaches to investigating security issues of Cloud computing. Meiko Jensen et al. [5] consider the technical security issues arising from the usage of Cloud services and the underlying technologies used to build these cross-domain inter-connected collaborations. But this work concentrates more on web services related security issues. Hassan Takabi et al. [3] have identified Cloud computing as an unstoppable force because of its potential benefits. The authors highlight the need to have appropriate mechanisms to handle the security and privacy risks in Cloud. The work discusses the security challenges including user authentication, access control, policy integration, trust management and service management and proposes a comprehensive security framework for Cloud computing . Hsin-Yi Tsai et al. [14] in their work explores the security issues in different service delivery models with respect to the security bench marks of Confidentiality, Integrity and Availability. These issues are discussed only from the perspective of Virtualization. S.Subashini and V.Kavitha [15] surveyed the security risks faced by the service delivery models, namely, IaaS, PaaS and SaaS. Authors suggest a security framework for Cloud that provides data security by storing and accessing data based on meta-data information. Rohit Bhadauria et al. [16] investigated the security threats related to Cloud computing in 2011. The authors surveyed different security risks such as SQL injection flaws, cross-site scripting, insecure storage etc. But the focus is on the various network layers such as Network level and Application level.

Although there is a considerable amount of ongoing research for identifying the security loop holes in Cloud, there is a need to consider the specific challenges faced by various architectural components of Cloud. Also the technologies used by Cloud for delivering its services raises various security issues, which needs to be identified and addressed. Providing a complete survey of Cloud security issues from the perspective of its architectural components, Virtualization technology, Technical issues and authentication becomes the motivation for this work.

3   Security Issues in Cloud

The acceptance of any new computing technology depends on the level of security it offers. The Cloud Service Provider's (CSP) claim that the customer's data is more secure within their data centers compared to the data residing in on-premise data center. These companies argue that their servers and data stored in them are sufficiently protected from any sort of invasion and theft [15]. But there have been many instances of Cloud Security breaches, bringing out the fundamental lapses in the security model of major CSP's. Though the CSP's claim that their down time is almost negligible, there have been instances where their security has been invaded and the whole system had been down for hours. Currently there are no standardized Cloud specific security metrics that Cloud customers can use to monitor the security status of their Cloud resources [5].

The security threats explored in the paper have been categorized into Cloud specific security threats and traditional security threats faced by the different service delivery models. Cloud specific security threats are applicable only to the Cloud environment. These security issues arise mainly due to the architectural features of Cloud. Again, Cloud has Internet as its backbone and web services act as an access mechanism for Cloud services. Hence the traditional security issues faced by the Internet and web services are also applicable to Cloud services. Traditional security issues are discussed in Sections 5 from the perspective of various service delivery models.

4   Cloud Specific Security Threats and Vulnerabilities

This section focuses on security threats and vulnerabilities that are specific to Cloud computing environment. These security concerns do not exist in the traditional application hosting and data delivery models, and requires a detailed understanding of how the threats are technically instigated in order to devise proper protection mechanisms. Fig. 2 traces out the Cloud specific security threats [2].

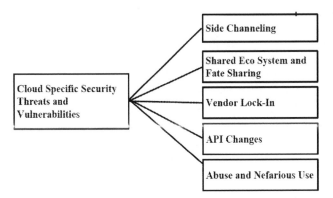

Fig. 2. Cloud Specific Security Threats

4.1   Side-Channeling

Multitenacy, which allows sharing of resources, facilitates selling of services at extremely low prices [17].Side-Channel attacks are launched by creating virtual machines on the same physical machine as that of the victim and then extracting sensitive information of the victim by exploiting shared CPU [18] or by examining traffic patterns [19]. For eg., a virtual machine-based root kit can instantiate a "rogue" hypervisor below the original one allowing malicious users to install unauthorized code into the system [20] .

4.2   Shared Ecosystem and Fate Sharing

A Cloud Service Provider (CSP) may provide security guidelines that come from his own knowledge base and best practices that are specific to the particular type of application the organization is deploying [21]. On the other hand, a third party's intervention affecting a shared ecosystem could bring a partial or total disruption of service to Cloud users. In April 2009, the FBI raided data centers in Texas, as part of an investigation targeting a set of companies with fraud allegations, resulting in loss of millions of dollars to the data center owners and customers and put some customers out of business or at risk of closure [22].

4.3   Vendor Lock-In

Vendor Lock-In or being tied with a vendor happens in two circumstances: (1) the cost of switching from one CSP to another surpasses the benefits of switching (2) In a SaaS deployment, the usage of proprietary APIs due to lack of common standards and protocols [23] makes it extremely difficult and complex to extract data from one Cloud provider and migrate to another. The worst outcome of Vendor Lock-In occurs when the Cloud service provider discontinues his services. When a Cloud online storage service, "The Link Up" shut down their services on 8th August, 2008, approximately 20,000 users were affected and about 45% of the customer data was lost [23].

4.4   API Changes

Cloud API's plays a very important role of functioning as an interface between Cloud infrastructure, services and applications allowing them to exchange data and carry out internal as well as external computations. Therefore , changes in the Cloud API's could result in lost connectivity, malfunctioning applications and new vulnerabilities exposed due to bugs introduced in the new APIs or change in Cloud configuration that do not provide the same level of protection as the previous version did. [24].

4.5   Abuse and Nefarious Use

This Cloud specific security threat is an attack launched by malicious users to gain control over computing, networking and storage resources. The attack is carried out by taking advantage of the loopholes in automated service registration process and anonymous resource usage models.

5   Security Issues as Applicable to Cloud Service Delivery Models

Cloud computing utilizes three delivery models viz., SaaS, PaaS and IaaS for offering software, application platform and Infrastructure services to the end users. The various models demand different level of security requirements in the cloud environment.

5.1   Security Issues in SaaS

In SaaS model the enterprise data is stored at the Cloud service provider's end, along with the data of other enterprises. Hence the confidentiality-of-data in rest is at risk and the SaaS vendor needs to ensure a proper boundary between the data of different users both at the application and physical level. Fig. 3 neatly lays down the security issues in SaaS model. The different security issues of SaaS [15] and a few strategies for securing SaaS applications are discussed in the following paragraphs.

5.1.1   Data Security

In SaaS model since the data is stored at the vendors end, it is the responsibility of the vendor to ensure that the stored data is not susceptible to security breaches due to application vulnerabilities or because of malicious employees. "A Better Practice Guide" by common wealth government recognizes Cloud security as a key risk factor, particularly when the data entrusted with the CSP is of sensitive nature and is to be held offshore [25]. Malicious users can launch attacks such as Cross-site scripting, SQL injection flaws, Cross-site request forgery by exploiting the weaknesses in the data security model and gain unauthorized access to data. Hence the SaaS providers should conduct assessment tests to validate the security of data against such attacks.

5.1.2   Network Security

The SaaS applications processes the sensitive data owned by enterprises, and store the result at SaaS vendor's end. Network traffic encryption techniques like Secure Socket layer (SSL) and the Transport Layer Security (TLS) can be used to secure the data flowing over the network. Tests for network penetration, packet analysis, identifying weaknesses in session management etc. need to be done by the CSP. Proper SSL configuration to protect user's credentials can be ensured by ascertaining the following security features [26]. i) Ensure that the certificate chain is valid ii) Use only secure protocols iii) Use only secure cipher suits iv) Control cipher suite selection v) Disable client initiated renegotiation vi) Mitigate Known Problems.

5.1.3   Data Locality

The SaaS model of Cloud provides applications which are used by the end users to process their data and the result is stored at the SaaS vendor's end. This means that many a times the customers are unaware of the location of their data, which can create security problems. Companies that operate in regulated industries need to consider the privacy laws before off-shoring their operations to Cloud. For eg, the Australian Banking and Insurance sectors need to abide by the terms and conditions dictated by the Australian Prudential Regulation Authority (APRA). The service contract in this case requires the service provider to comply with the Australian privacy laws, including the privacy act. Unfortunately, service providers based out of Australia may be reluctant to oblige to these rules. For a CSP, complying with privacy laws of home jurisdiction of each of their customers may be difficult and the laws in different jurisdictions may not be compatible or consistent [25].

5.1.4   Data Integrity

Ensuring Integrity requires the SaaS provider to implement mechanisms to protect data-in-transit, data-at-rest and network traffic from modification, execution etc. There are standards available for, managing data integrity such as WS-Transaction and WS-Reliability which are not mature enough. Architects and developers need to ensure that integrity of their database is ensured while moving to Cloud environment.

5.1.5   Data Access

Data of enterprises stored in the Cloud should be secured from unauthorized access. To restrict access to sensitive data, the different enterprises storing their data in the

Cloud, may have their own access control policies, and the SaaS model must be flexible enough to incorporate these policies.

5.1.6   Data Segregation

The SaaS model must ensure clear boundary, both at the application and physical level, between the data of different user's. In the case of Amazon Simple Storage Service (S3), the customer decides and maintains full control over access to their data and permission to modifying the bucket's Access Control List (ACL) is controlled by an ACL [27].

5.1.7   Authentication and Authorization

In a scenario where multiple users use the same computers but different accounts, there should be clear separation of user accounts to ensure the security of data, information and account [28]. Vast majority of SMB's have adopted SaaS and they use Active Directory (AD) tool and Light Weight Directory Access Protocol (LDAP) for managing users [29]. With SaaS, the software is at the vendor's end and hence to ensure the security of their data, the SaaS customers must remember to remove/disable accounts when an employee leaves the organization and create/enable accounts as they join.

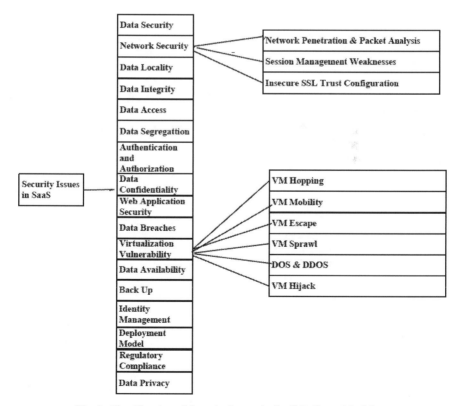

Fig. 3. Classification of Security Issues in SaaS Delivery Model

5.1.8   Data Confidentiality Issue

The fact that a business, a government agency or an individual is storing their data in Cloud and sharing the same with another person, leads to privacy and confidentiality related concerns such as the CSP being able to view the customer's data. SLA's must clearly mention the confidentiality requirements of the customer.

5.1.9   Web Application Security

In the Cloud environment, resources which are offered as a service, resides at a remote location and customer's access them via the web. One of the mandatory requirements of SaaS is that it has to be managed and accessed over the web [15]. Thus naturally, the security holes in web applications create a vulnerability to the SaaS applications. The SaaS vendor needs to periodically conduct assessment tests to evaluate the feasibility of attacks such as SQL, OS and LDAP injection flaws, Cross-site scripting etc., on his Cloud.

5.1.10   Data Breaches

The effect of data breach in a Cloud environment can be disastrous, since it has the potential to attack the data of multiple users and enterprises hosted in the cloud. SaaS service providers claim that they can provide better security to customers' data than by conventional means, but there are several instances of insider breaches.

5.1.11   Virtualization Vulnerabilities

Cloud computing uses the features of Virtualization technology to support resource pooling and multi-tenancy. Virtualization allows users to run multiple isolated machines known as Virtual Machines (VMs), on a single physical machine. Virtualization, one of the core components of Cloud, brings with it many security threats which in turn lead to virtualization vulnerabilities such as VM Hopping, VM mobility, VM Diversity and DOS attack [14].

a) VM Hopping: VM hopping attack enables an attacker on one VM to gain access to another victim VM residing on the same host machine to monitor the flow of traffic and the victim VM's resource usage. This attack belongs to the category of shared technology issues, which arise when the IaaS vendors deliver their services in shared infrastructure. [30].

b) VM Mobility: While moving around, the mobile VM's require security policies and baseline histories, without which they become vulnerable [31]. While VM portability facilitates quick deployment of VM's it could lead to security problems such as quick spread of vulnerable configurations designated by an attacker [14].

c) DOS and DDOS Attacks: One common method used to launch the DOS attack is to overload the target machine with bogus requests which prevents it from responding to legitimate requests in a timely manner [32]. On the other hand, a DDOS attack aims to make services or resources unavailable for indefinite amount of time by flooding the network with useless traffic [33] thus exhausting computer resources making it unavailable to legitimate users .DDOS attempts to imitate, pragmatic web service traffic, in order to create a large group of agents called Zombies, to launch an attack [34]. There are continued DDOS attacks on Amazon Web Services (AWS) making the services unavailable for hours at a time to AWS users [35].

d) VM Escape: Virtualization technology allows multiple guests VM's, operating systems and applications to run on a single physical server without the cost and complexity of running multiple machines [36]. VM's are vulnerable as they move [37] and in case of VM Escape, the attacker runs code on a VM that allows an Operating System running within it to break and interact directly with the hypervisor. In a Cloud, this would be disastrous as one tenant could affect the confidentiality and integrity of another tenant's virtual machine.

e) VM Hijack: To support the multi-tenancy characteristic of Cloud, a single server is made to host multiple VM's on it. Thus the host machine serves as the common storage system wherein the configuration files of all VM's are available and on accessing this information, an attacker can launch VM hijack attack on the VM's which are hosted on the same server [6].

f) VM Sprawl: Sharing both the application and physical hardware may result in information leakage and other exploitations. An inappropriate VM management policy will cause VM sprawling [38], a case where a number of VM's rapidly grow while most of them are idle or never be back from sleep causing resource of host machine being rapidly wasted . The right set of tools and expertise enables CSP's to control VM Sprawl effectively [39].

5.1.12   Data Availability

Availability of a SaaS offering is affected if the service/server is spoofed, penetrated or suspended. It is the responsibility of SaaS provider to ensure that his service offerings are available to the customers 24*7.

5.1.13   Back Up

Cloud hosts the data of multiple enterprises and the service provider needs to ensure that this data is available with minimum downtime in case of disasters. This is made possible by periodical backing up of the sensitive data.

5.1.14   Identity Management

Identity Management comprises of a series of activities that begins with assigning an ID to an individual or a process in a system , followed by checking the credentials to establish the identity, and controlling the access to resources in that system by enforcing restrictions on the established identities. S. Subashini and V. kavitha [15] in their work, discusses the three perspectives of Identity Management.

5.1.15   SaaS Deployment Model

SaaS deployment model also contributes to the security challenges faced by SaaS [40]. The SaaS vendors may choose to deploy their applications on a public Cloud or may decide to host it themselves. Public Cloud service providers such as Amazon AWS, IBM Smart Cloud etc. helps to secure SaaS solutions by offering infrastructure services that ensures perimeter and environment security. The service providers secure the SaaS applications using Intrusion Detection Systems (IDS), firewalls etc. These security services are to be built and assessed by the SaaS vendor in a self-hosted SaaS deployment [40].

5.1.16   SaaS Regulatory Compliance

The SaaS deployment must comply with certain regulatory and industry standards and the vendors must periodically assess their model to check the conformance [40]. The

SAS 70 standard governing the operating procedures for physical and perimeter security of data centers and service providers, Regulations such as ISO-27001, Sarbans-Oxley Act (SOX), Gramm-Leach-Bliley Act (GLBA), Health Insurance Portability and Accountability Act (HIPAA) and industry standards like Payment Card Industry Data Security Standard (PCI-DSS) should be followed to control and govern the access, storage and processing of sensitive data [27].

5.1.17   Data Privacy

Privacy has emerged as a major security challenge in the Cloud environment. The privacy regulations of different countries may not be compatible which makes it difficult for the CSP to comply with these rules. These might lead to conflicts when the sensitive data of one country is stored within a data centre located in another country. The Cloud service providers may be subject to the local laws of the countries in which their data centers are located. Laws of certain countries allow the respective government authorities to access and use the data residing in their country without considering the ownership of the data. Customers concerned about the privacy of their data may not agree to this level of government intervention and may be reluctant to move their data into Cloud. In such cases, the Service Level Agreement (SLA) should clearly specify, the customers' expectations on the privacy standards that should be maintained by the SaaS vendor.

5.2   Security Issues in PaaS

PaaS offers service that provides a complete software lifecycle management, from planning to design to building applications to deployment to maintenance. In PaaS, the provider might give some control to the people to build applications on top of the platform. But any security below the application level such as host and network intrusion will still be in the scope of the provider [15]. Fig. 4 gives an overview of the security issues faced by PaaS Clouds.

The PaaS model enables the users to submit their data for storage and applications for execution to the Cloud through the network .The user application or data are envisioned in a generic structure and this structure is called the user object [41]. The PaaS Cloud consists of several hosts which can store multiple user objects and the resources are shared efficiently and elastically by the assignment of objects to hosts and migration of objects among hosts. The security challenges of Cloud architecture are mainly due to the distribution of the user objects over the hosts of the Cloud. The distinct features of Cloud such as resource sharing, rapid elasticity, broad network access and measured service of Cloud can contribute to the security issues in PaaS, if not properly managed. The following sections are reserved for discussing the security issues due to the inherent features of Cloud.

5.2.1   Resource Pooling and Rapid Elasticity Concerns

In the Cloud environment, heterogeneous hardware and software resources are unified for efficient delivery of services. Heterogeneity may cause flaws because different resources may have incompatible security settings [42] and sharing of resources may lead to information leakage as each shared resource is a communication channel [43] [44]. Finally protection of distributed user objects stands as the most serious concern of PaaS Clouds.

Diversity may cause a set of resources to stop working due to interoperability issues which can be tackled by allowing the objects to access the resources through a common interface that supports all possible kinds of access scenarios. In their work [41] the authors propose the use of Trusted Computing Base (TCB) on every host to support interoperability. In a Cloud environment, protection of vulnerable hosts can be ensured by evaluating resource access request made by every object on the host which is done by implementation of TCB [41]. In a PaaS Cloud, there are three possible ways in which the security of a user object can be breached [41]. First, the service provider may access any of the objects residing on their host and SLA should clearly mention the extent to which the accessed objects can be used by the CSP. Second, co-resident users may attack each other's objects residing on the same host which can be eliminated by mechanisms that evaluate objects' resource access. Finally, a third party may directly attack a user object which should be defended by the object itself, by exhibiting the ability to reveal the sensitive information only to authorized users

5.2.2 Broad Network Access and Measured Service Issues

To secure a networked system, the SaaS vendor must ensure that the communications through the network are confidential and access to the resources by remote entities is controlled by proper authentication and authorization.

a) Communication Confidentiality: As in any other networked system, communication confidentiality is a key factor in PaaS Clouds. Communication channels which prevent eavesdropping can be established through TLS where a Public Key Infrastructure (PKI) exists.

b) Authentication: Even though many of the existing two-factor and multi-factor authentication mechanisms may be sufficient for Cloud, there needs to be a clear definition of standards to be followed by the authentication mechanisms. The requesting parties and objects must mutually authenticate each other to eliminate Man-in-the-Middle attacks.

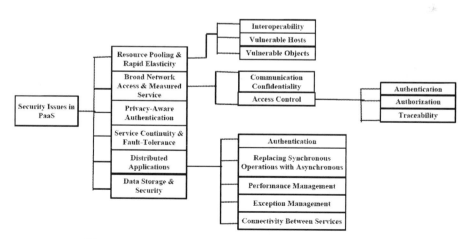

Fig. 4. Classification of Security Issues in PaaS Delivery Model

c) Authorization: Each host maintaining the access control policies of the objects residing within it and keeping them up-to-date during the reconfiguration periods may not be viable in a dynamic Cloud. A practical solution for these requirements is encapsulating and carrying the policies together with the objects.

d) Traceability: Traceability is achieved by logging the events occurring in a system. A PaaS Cloud must have an integrated undeniable logging mechanism and logging system must be protected against all kinds of users. M.T.Sandikkay and A.E Harmanci [41] discusses an undeniable logging protocol in their work on PaaS issues.

5.2.3   Privacy-Aware Authentication
Users should not leave more trace than necessary to protect their privacy in the Cloud where the resources are spread over several hosts [45]. Proxy certificates including only the required attributes of an authenticating entity and Zero Knowledge Proof (ZKP) mechanisms which enable an entity to prove its identity without revealing its Personally Identifiable Information (PII) are also proposed by researchers.

5.2.4   Service Continuity and Fault-Tolerance Issues
In a PaaS environment, a service may stop responding to user requests due to many reasons. In such a scenario, fault-tolerance and service-continuity can be achieved by adopting the Byzantine Quorum [46] approach.

5.2.5   Distributed Applications
Moving distributed applications to the Cloud environment can be a challenging task. In a scenario where we have an on-premise n-tier application , for security reasons we prefer to keep the data tier in a Private Cloud environment and migrate the business and presentation tier to the Public Cloud. Security challenges encountered during this type of migration includes authentication, replacing synchronous operations with asynchronous ones, performance management, exception management &error reporting, connectivity between services and applications.

5.2.6   Storage and Data Security
A public Cloud vendor stores the data in encrypted from, transports it to the customer systems in an encrypted form, processes it behind the firewall of the customer and stores the results on the public Cloud without encrypted data being exposed. However, applications work on unencrypted data, which means that the primary risks of data security come at the point of processing and not at the point of storage.

5.3   Security Issues in Iaas

In IaaS multiple users share the computing resources which may be residing on a single physical infrastructure and hence the service provider should ensure that one user cannot spy on the resource usage and memory status of another user. IaaS is susceptible to varying degrees of security threats based on the Cloud deployment model through which the service is being offered. The security issues applicable to IaaS Clouds are laid out in Fig. 5 and some of the attacks are discussed in the following paragraphs.

5.3.1   Network Security

While providing security at the Network level the various security parameters such as confidentiality, integrity, access control, privacy etc. should be considered. The problems associated with Network level security include DNS attacks, Sniffer attacks, Issues of Reused IP address, BGP Prefix Hijacking etc. few of which are discussed in the following paragraphs.

a) DNS Attacks: Grobauer et al. [47] in their work observes that the benefits of Cloud such as resource pooling and sharing of infrastructure component could contribute to cross-tenant attacks in IaaS. In the case of Domain Name Server (DNS) attacks, the attacker modifies the data on either the Authoritative Name Server (ANS) or the Cache Name Server (CNS).The user who calls a DNS server by name is routed to some other evil Cloud and accidentally reveals his credentials. A CSP that supports 20 organizations using its CNS will be providing forged DNS data to all these organizations in which they operate upon [48].

b) BGP Prefix Hijacking: BGP prefix hijacking attack on confidentiality, initiated by a faulty Autonomous System (AS) involves announcing an AS address space that belongs to someone else without her permission. Such wrong announcements often occur because of a configuration mistake which might result in the non-availability of Cloud based resources. In the news blog of CNET, Declan McCullagh discusses such a misconfiguration mistake which occurred in February 2008 when Pakistan Telecom made an error by announcing a dummy route for YouTube to its own telecommunications partner, PCCW, based in Hong Kong [2] rendering YouTube globally unavailable for two hours.

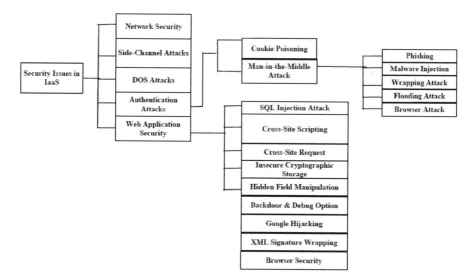

Fig. 5. Classification of Security Issues in IaaS Delivery Model

5.3.2   Side-Channel Attacks

An attacker could attempt to compromise the Cloud by placing a malicious virtual machine in close proximity to a target Cloud server and then launch side-channel attack. Multiple VM's sharing the same hardware resource provides malicious VM owners with the opportunity to extract sensitive information from other Co resident VM's. In their paper, Ristenpart et al., discusses information leakage in Amazon's EC2 [43].

5.3.3 DOS Attacks

Cloud system is more vulnerable to DOS attacks, since it supports resource pooling, so says security professionals. Twitter suffered a devastating DOS attack during 2009. The main objective of DOS attack is to overload the target machine with bogus service requests to prevent it from responding to legitimate requests. The server when it encounters the huge amount of requests will start to provide more resources such as virtual machine instances and service instances to handle the additional work load. The Cloud system, by allocating more and more resources to serve the bogus request is actually supporting the attacker rather than working against him.

5.3.4 Authentication Attacks

Authentication involves the process of ensuring that a person who presents a set of credentials is whom he or she claims to be and identity management aids in controlling access to the resources in a system by placing restrictions on the established identities. An authentication system should provide high security and more usability. Following paragraphs discuss a few attacks on authentication:

a) Cookie Poisoning: Cookie poisoning involves the modification of cookies of an authorized user to gain unauthorized access to resources. This masquerading attack on authenticity can be prevented to a certain extent by performing regular cookie clean up or by encrypting the cookie data.

b) Man-in-the-Middle Attack (MITM): MITM occurs when an attacker gains access to the communication channel established between two legitimate users. The attacker is then capable of performing unauthorized activities such as intercepting and modifying communications. The various types of Man-in-The Middle Attacks are as follows:

Wrapping Attack: A wrapping attack can be launched by, duplicating the user account and password during the login phase. This causes the SOAP messages exchanged between the browser and the server during the set up phase to be affected by the attackers [50].

Browser Attack: This attack is committed by sabotaging the signature and encryption during the translation of SOAP messages in between the web browser and web server, causing the browser to consider the adversary as a legitimate user and process all requests, communicating with web server [49].

Phishing: In phishing attack, the attacker masquerades as someone trustworthy and lure end users to select obscured links in emails by expressing some urgency, often ironically to protect the user's confidential data from malicious activities. In November 2007, an employee of SaaS vendor, SalesForce was victimized by a phishing attack that captured customer contact data and using the same to obtain SalesForce account information [50] of the customers.

5.3.5   Web Application Security

As the user community using Web 2.0 is increasing by leaps and bounds, security has become all the more an important issue to be immediately addressed. A few of the security risks faced by web applications are discussed in the following paragraphs:

a) SQL Injection Attacks: In the case of SQL injection attacks, an attacker inserts a malicious code into a standard SQL code which enables him to gain unauthorized access to the database and access sensitive data. On 1-Aug-2012, Cloud based storage provider Dropbox announced the details of a security breach that led to a spamming campaign. The company's investigation into the incident revealed that user names and passwords stolen from other web sites were used to sign into a number of Dropbox accounts, including one belonging to a Dropbox employee that contained a "Project Document" with user email addresses [51].

b) Insecure Cryptographic Storage: Insecure storage attack occurs due to the mistakes made by the developers while integrating the encryption techniques into a web application. The commonly made mistakes include insecure storage of keys, certificates and passwords, poor choice of algorithm, improper storage of secrets in memory etc. which can have a devastating effect on the security of the web site.

c) XML Signature wrapping [5]: XML signature and XML encryption are applied to SOAP messages used for secure communication in the web. XML Signature enables XML fragments to be digitally signed to ensure integrity or to authenticate the origin. XML Signature Element Wrapping is an attack on protocols using XML signature. Since web services are using the same and Cloud services are accessed through web services, the attack is applicable to Cloud also. In this attack, an attacker modifies the signed request sent by a legitimate client.

d) Browser Security [5]: In Cloud environment, computations are done on remote servers and the client system is used only for I/O. Modern web browsers with their AJAX techniques are capable of I/O but they raise many security issues. There are many security policies and mechanisms focusing on browser security, but still there are many issues requiring immediate attention.

6   Conclusion

The operational and economic benefits offered by Cloud have contributed to its adoption by many Small and Medium Business enterprises. The vast benefit of Cloud comes along with numerous security loop holes which questions the safety of the Cloud environment. Organizations before moving their data and applications into the Cloud environment should understand the security related intricacies behind this, much discussed technology. Cloud Computing is an emerging technology and any application relying on an emerging technology should carefully analyze the different threats in adopting the technology. A proper insight of security attacks on Cloud deployment models, service delivery models and the security issues due to the architectural features of Cloud is required for the development of a Security framework for Cloud services.   The classification of various selected threats and attacks on Cloud discussed in the paper exposes the limitations of Cloud from the security perspective. These limitations need to be immediately addressed to make Cloud a safer avenue for our data.

The work focuses on carrying out an in-depth examination of the security issues in various service delivery models of Cloud. We have attempted to identify the various Virtualization related vulnerabilities and attacks on authenticity in a dynamic Cloud environment and explain the same in the context of real life scenarios identified by researchers in the area of Cloud Security. Among all the security issues discussed in this paper, authentication related issues in the Cloud are the one that needs immediate attention because of the ever increasing rate in online frauds. Issues related to deployment models, virtualization related vulnerabilities etc. are discussed by many researchers and they have suggested many organizational means and defense mechanisms to address these issues. But authentication mechanisms in the Cloud have many security loop holes which are yet to be addressed. This paper elaborates the Cloud specific Security Threats and Traditional security threats faced by the cloud service providers and users. The work attempts to classify the threats on the basis of the different cloud service delivery models viz., Security-as-a-Service, Infrastructure-as-a-Service and Platform-as-a-Service.

References

[1] Buyya, R., Broberg, J., Goscinski, A.: Cloud Computing: Principles and Paradigms. Wiley, Hoboken (2011)

[2] Kahiyamo, T.: Cloud Computing Security: How Risks and Threats are Affecting Cloud Adopting Decisions. MBA Thesis (2012)

[3] Takabi, H., Joshi, J.B.D., Ahn, G.: SecureCloud: Towards a Comprehensive Security Framework for Cloud Computing Environments. In: Proc. IEEE 34th Annual Computer Software and Application Conference Workshops, July 19-23, pp. 393–398 (2010)

[4] http://csrc.nist.gov/groups/SNA/ Cloud-computing-cloud-def-v15.doc (accessed on: December 27, 2012)

[5] Jensen, M., Schwenk, J., Gruscka, N., Iacono, L.L.: On Technical Security Issues in Cloud Computing. In: Proc. IEEE International Conference on Cloud Computing, September 21-25, pp. 109–116 (2009)

[6] Lv, H., Hu, Y.: Analysis and Research About Cloud Computing Security Protect Policy. In: Proc. IEEE Int. Conference on Intelligence Science and Information Engineering, August 20-21, pp. 214–216 (2011)

[7] Bakshi, A., Yogesh, B.: Securing Cloud from DDOS Attacks Using Intrusion Detection System in VM. In: Proc. IEEE Second Int. Conference on Communication Software and Networks, February 26-28, pp. 260–264 (2010)

[8] Kilari, N., Sridaran, R.: A Survey on Security Threats for Cloud Computing. Int. Journal of Engineering Research and Technology 1(7) (September 2012)

[9] Ramgovind, S., Eloff, M.M., Smith, E.: The Management of Security in Cloud Computing. In: Proc. IEEE Conference Information Security for South Africa, August 2-4, pp. 1–7 (2010)

[10] Chauhan, N.S., Saxena, A.: Energy Analysis of Security for Cloud Application. In: Proc. Annual IEEE India Conference, pp. 1–6 (December 2011)

[11] Liu, W.: Research on Cloud Computing Security Problem and Strategy. In: Proc. IEEE 2nd Int. Conference on Consumer Electronics, Communications and Networks, April 21-23, pp. 1216–1219 (2012)

[12] Yu, X., Wen, Q.: A View About Cloud Data Security from Data Life Cycle. In: Proc. IEEE Intl. Conference on Computational Intelligence and Software Engineering, December 10-12, pp. 1–4 (2010)

[13] Kantarcioglu, M., Bensoussan, A., Ru, S.: Impact of Security Risks on Cloud Computing Adoption. In: Proc. IEEE 49th Annual Allerton Conference on Communication, Control and Computing, September 28-30, pp. 670–674 (2011)

[14] Hsin-Yi, T., Siebenhaar, M., Miede, A., Yulun, H., Steinmetz, R.: Threat as a Service? The Impact of Virtualization on Cloud Security. IT Professional 14(1), 32–37 (2011)

[15] Subashini, S., Kavitha, V.: A Survey on Security Issues in Service Delivery Models of Cloud Computing. Journal of Network and Computer Applications 34(1), 1–11 (2011)

[16] Bhadauria, R., Sanyal, S.: Survey on Security Issues in Cloud Computing and Associated Mitigation Techniques. International Journal of Computer Applications, 47–66 (June 2012)

[17] Halpert, B.: Auditing Cloud Computing: A Security and Privacy Guide. John Wiley & Sons, Inc., Hoboken (2011)

[18] Zhang, Y., Juels, A., Opera, A., Reiter, M.K.: HomeAlone: Co-Residency Detection in the Cloud Via side-Channel Analysis. In: Proc. IEEE Symposium on Security and Privacy, May 22-25, pp. 313–328 (2011)

[19] Carlson, C.: Side-Channel Attacks Threaten Data in the Cloud (May 30, 2012), http://www.fiercecio.com/storey/ side-channel-attacks-threaten-data-cloud/2012-05-30 (accessed on : January 25, 2013)

[20] Krutz, R.L., Vine, R.D.: Cloud Security: A Comprehensive Guide to Secure Cloud Computing. Wiley Publishing, Inc., Indianapolis (2010)

[21] Chen, Y., Pascon, V., Katz, R.H.: "What's New about Cloud Computing Security?" Technical Report (January 2010), http://www.eecs.berkeley.edu/pubs/Techrpts/2010/ EECS.2020-5.pdf (accessed on : January 25, 2013)

[22] Zetter, K.: FBI defends Disruptive Raid on Texas data Centers. (April 2009), http://www.wired.com/threatlevel/2009/04/data-centers-ra/ (accessed on: February 4, 2013)

[23] Armbrust, M., Fox, A., Griffith, R., Joseph, A.D., Katz, R., Konwinski, A., Lee, G., Patterson, D., Rabkin, A., Stoica, I., Zaharia, M.: Above the Clouds: A Berkeley View of Cloud Computing. Communications of ACM 53(4), 50–58 (2010)

[24] Carlin, S., Curran, K.: Cloud Computing security. International Journal of Ambient Computing and Intelligence 3, 14–19 (2011)

[25] Swinson, M.: Data Security and privacy Issues in Cloud Computing. (March 2012), http://WWW.mallesons.com/publications/marketAlerts/2012/ information-technologyupdate-march-2012/pages/ Data-Security-and-Privacy-Issues-in-Cloud-Computingaspx (accessed on: February 18, 2013)

[26] SSL/TLS deployment best practices. Version 1.0/; Ivan Ristic, Qualys SSL Labs (February 24, 2012), https://www.ssllabs.com/downloads/ SSL_TLS_Deployment_Best_Practices_1.0.pdf (accessed on : March 22, 2013)

[27] Rane, P.: Enterprise Applications in the Cloud: A SaaS Security Perspective (September 2010), http://esj.com/Articles/2010/02/09/ Cloud-saas-security.aspx?page=2&p=1 (accessed on : March 22, 2013)

[28] Kevin, G.: Software As A Service Security Facts You Should Consider (January 29, 2013), http://SaaSaddict.walkme.com/software-as-a-service-security-facts-you-should-consider/ (accessed on : March 22, 2013)

[29] Microsoft White Paper, MS Strategy for Lightweight Directory Access Protocol (2010) http://technet:microsoft.com/en-us/library/cc750824.aspx (accessed on: December 10, 2012)

[30] Jasti, A., Shah, P., Nagaraj, R., Pendse, R.: Security in Multitenancy. In: Proc. IEEE Int. Carnahan Conference on Security Technology, October 5-8, pp. 35–41 (2010)

[31] Owens, K.: Securing Virtual Compute Infrastructure in the Cloud. Hos-white-paper-securing virtual-computer-infrastructure in the cloud.pdf

[32] Sabahi, F.: Virtualization-level Security in Cloud computing. In: Proc. IEEE Third Int. Conference on Communication Software and Networks, May 27-29, pp. 250–254 (2011)

[33] Gul, I., Rehman, A., Islam, M.H.: Cloud Computing Security Auditing. In: Proc. IEEE the 2nd Int. Conference on Next Generation Information Technology, June 21-23, pp. 143–148 (2011)

[34] Joshi, B., Vijayan, A.S., Joshi, B.K.: Securing Cloud Computing Environment Against DDOS Attacks. In: IEEE Int. Conference on Computer Communication and Information, January 10-12, pp. 1–5 (2012)

[35] Rumor: Amazon Hit with Denial-of-Service-Attack, Again (June 6, 2008), http://www.appscout.com/2008/rumor-amazon-hit-with-denialof.php (accessed on: December 2, 2012)

[36] Tupakula, U., Varadarajan, V.: TVDSEC: Trusted Virtual Domain Security. In: Proc. IEEE 4th Intl. Conference on Utility and Cloud Computing, December 5-8, pp. 57–63 (2011)

[37] Trend Micro, "Making Virtual Machines Cloud-Ready," A Trend Micro White paper (2009), http://www.WhiteStratus.con/docs/making-vms-cloudready.pdf (accessed on: December 2, 2012)

[38] Lin, Z.: Virtualization Security for Cloud Computing Service. In: Proc. IEEE Intl. Conference on Cloud and Service Computing, December 12-14, pp. 174–178 (2011)

[39] Decarlo, A.L.: Myth Vs. Reality: Controlling VM Sprawl in the Cloud (January 2012), http://searchcloudprovider.techtarget.com/tip/Myth-vs-reality-Controlling-VM-sprawl-in-the-cloud (accessed on: March 22, 2013)

[40] Forrester Inc., Press Release "Top Corporate Software Priority is Modernizing Legacy Applications" (June 8, 2009), http://www.imakenews.com/avnet_bio/e_article001459482.cfm?x=bfQ4d5j,b817d1c4,w (accessed on: March 15, 2013)

[41] Sandikkaya, M.T., Harmanci, A.E.: Security Problems of Platform as a Service. In: 31st International Symposium on Reliable Distributed Systems (2012)

[42] Takabi, H., Joshi, J.B.D., Ahn, G.: Security and Privacy Challenges in Cloud Computing Environments. IEEE Security Privacy 8(6), 24–31 (2010)

[43] Ristenpart, T., Tromer, E., Shacham, H., Savage, S.: Hey, You Get Off My Cloud: Exploring Information Leakage in Third-Party Compute Clouds. In: Proc. of 16th ACM Conference on Computer and Communication Security, November 9-13, pp. 199–212 (2009)

[44] Saltzer, J.H., Schroeder, M.D.: The Protection of information in Computer Systems. Proceedings of the IEEE 63(9), 1278–1308 (1975)

[45] Rfc 3820: Internet X.509 Public Key Infrastructure,
http://ietf.org/html/rfc3820

[46] Lamport, L., Shostak, R., Pease, M.: The byzantine General Problem. ACM Trans. Program. Lang. Syst. 4(3), 382–401 (1982)

[47] Grobauer, B., Walloschk, T., Stocker, E.: Understanding Cloud Computing Vulnerabilities. IEEE Trans. Security & Privacy 9(2), 50–57 (2011)

[48] Sample, C.: Cloud Computing Security: Routing and DNS Security threats (June 2009), http://www.searchsecurity.techtarget.com/tip/DNS-attacks-compromising-DNS-in-the-cloud (accessed on: March 15, 2013)

[49] Meena, B., Challa, K.A.: Cloud Computing Security Issues with Possible Solutions. Int, Journal of Computer Science and Technology 2(1) (January-March 2012)

[50] Andree, Y.: Implications of SalesForce Phishing Incident (November 2007), http://www.ebizq.net/blogs/security_insider/2007/11/implications_of_salesforce_phi.php (accessed on: March 22, 2013)

[51] Prince, B.: Spam Campaign Caused by Stolen Drop box Employee Password (August 2010), http://www.eweek.com/c/a/Security/Spam-Campaign-Caused-by-Stolen-Dropbox-Employee-Password-344694/ (accessed on: March 15, 2013)

A Chaos Based Method for Efficient
Cryptographic S-box Design

Musheer Ahmad, Hitesh Chugh, Avish Goel, and Prateek Singla

Department of Computer Engineering, Faculty of Engineering and Technology,
Jamia Millia Islamia, New Delhi 110025, India

Abstract. Substitution boxes are integral parts of most of the conventional block ciphering techniques such as DES, AES, IDEA, etc. The strengths of these encryption techniques solely depend upon the quality of their nonlinear S-boxes. Therefore, the construction of cryptographically strong S-boxes is always a challenge to build secure cryptosystems. In this paper, an efficient method for designing chaos-based cryptographic S-box is presented. The chaotically-modulated system trajectory of chaotic map is sampled and pretreated to generate an initial 8×8 S-box. Elements shuffling through random circular-rotation and zig-zag scan pattern are carried out to improve its quality. The experimental results of analyses such as bijectivity, nonlinearity, strict avalanche criterion, equiprobable input/output XOR distribution, etc., demonstrate that the proposed S-box has better cryptographic properties as compared to the recently proposed chaos-based S-boxes, which justify its effectiveness for the design of strong block cryptosystem.

Keywords: S-box, chaotic map, block cipher, zig-zag scan, nonlinearity.

1 Introduction

Due to an ever increasing development and usage of digital techniques for transmitting, storing and editing the multimedia data, the primary concern of protecting the confidentiality, integrity and authenticity of sensitive data creates challenges for the professionals, researchers and academicians. One of the solutions to fulfill the need of data security is to design and deploy the effective encryption systems. In 1949, C. E. Shannon suggested two fundamental properties of confusion and diffusion for the design of cryptographically strong encryption systems [1]. The confusion is intended to obscure the relationship between the key and ciphertext data as complex as possible, which frustrates the adversary who utilizes the ciphertext statistics to recover the key or the plaintext. However, the diffusion is aimed to rearrange the bits in the plaintext so that any redundancy in plaintext is spread out over the whole ciphertext data. The conventional block cryptosystems achieve good confusion and diffusion by applying the rounds of substitution and permutation in their S-P networks [2]. The permutation-box (P-box) is linear; where as the substitution-box (S-box) is nonlinear in nature. S-boxes are the only portions which induce the nonlinearity to improve the statistical characteristics of the plaintext and

Sabu M. Thampi et al. (Eds.): SSCC 2013, CCIS 377, pp. 130–137, 2013.

provide the property of data confusion. As a result, they constitute the core component of most of the well-known block ciphers such as DES, AES, IDEA, BLOWFISH etc [2, 3]. The strengths of these ciphers primarily depend upon the quality of their S-boxes. Therefore, the design of cryptographic efficient S-boxes is a challenging task for designing strong block cryptosystem, as the weak S-boxes can lead to the weak cryptosystems. The challenges in the design of S-boxes are to achieve balancedness and avalanche effect, keep the maximum differential probabilities as low as possible to resist the differential cryptanalysis [4], and raise the nonlinearity scores as high as possible. But, the problem is that some of them contradict. For example, it is impossible to reach both the balancedness and the highest nonlinearity. The *bent*-Boolean functions, of size n-bit, can provide the highest possible nonlinearity score of $2^{n-1} - 2^{(n/2)-1}$, but they are not balanced [5]. Thus, some tradeoffs have to be made while designing efficient S-boxes.

Mathematically, an $m \times n$ S-box is a nonlinear mapping function S: $\{0, 1\}^m \rightarrow \{0, 1\}^n$, m and n need not be equal, which can be represented as $S(x) = [b_{n-1}(x)b_{n-2}(x) \ldots b_1(x)b_0(x)]$, where the b_i $(0 \leq i \leq n-1)$ is a Boolean function b_i: $\{0, 1\}^m \rightarrow \{0, 1\}$. An S-box can be keyed or keyless and static or dynamic. In the past decade, various methods have been proposed to design S-boxes; they are based on polymorphic-cipher [6], cellular automata [7, 8], *bent*-Boolean functions [9], evolutionary-computing [10, 11], power-mapping technique [12] and chaos [13-19] with acceptable cryptographic features. The features of chaotic systems such as ergodicity, high periodicity, mixing, random-behaviour and high sensitiveness to initial conditions make them promising candidates for the design of robust security systems to protect images, audios, videos etc. Nowadays, they are also explored to synthesize the nonlinear components of block ciphers i.e. the substitution boxes (S-box). The researchers are attempting to construct the strong chaos-based S-boxes having desirable properties in order to mitigate differential, linear and other cryptanalyses.

In this paper, chaotic systems are used to synthesize an S-box exhibiting better cryptographic properties than existing chaotic S-boxes. The system trajectory of the piece-wise linear chaotic map is chaotically modulated through chaotic logistic map and its modulated samples are recorded to generate an initial S-box. An efficient S-box is obtained after shifting the elements through zig-zag scan-pattern and random circular rotation. The rest of the paper is organized as follows: Section 2 gives the basic description of chaotic systems used and proposed method of designing S-box. The performance of the proposed S-box is analyzed in Section 3. Finally, the conclusions are drawn in Section 4.

2   Constructing Efficient Chaotic S-box

2.1   Chaotic Logistic and PWLCM Maps

The chaotic 1D Logistic map proposed by May [20] is one of the simplest nonlinear chaotic discrete systems that exhibits chaotic behavior, it is governed as:

$$x(n+1) = \lambda.x(n).(1 - x(n)) \tag{1}$$

Where $x(0)$ is initial condition, λ is the system parameter and n is the number of iterations. The research shows that the map is chaotic for $3.57 < \lambda < 4$ and $x(n) \in (0, 1)$ for all n.

The 1D piecewise linear chaotic map is composed of linear segments, in which limited numbers of breaking points are allowed. It is a dynamical system that exhibit chaotic behavior for all values of parameter $p \in (0, 1)$, the system is defined as [21]:

$$y(n+1) = \begin{cases} \dfrac{y(n)}{p} & 0 < y(n) \le p \\ \dfrac{1 - y(n)}{1 - p} & p < y(n) < 1 \end{cases} \qquad (2)$$

Where $y(0)$ is initial condition, $n \ge 0$ is the number of iterations and $y(n) \in (0,1)$ for all n. The research shows that the map has largest +ve lyapunov exponent at $p = 0.5$. Its bifurcation diagram shows that, for every value of control parameter p, the system trajectory of PWLCM map visits the entire interval $[0, 1]$.

2.2   Chaotic Modulation of PWLCM Map

In order to statistically improve the characteristics of the sequence generated by the piece-wise linear chaotic map (PWLCM), its normal system trajectory is modulated through chaotic logistic map. Firstly, the logistic map with appropriate initial conditions is iterated for t_o times to remove the transient effect. The current x-variable of logistic map is supplied to PWLCM map to generate its output y-variable, then a random number $n_i \in [1, 23]$ ($i = 1 \sim 256$) is extracted out of the current $y(i)$ variable. Now, the logistic map is iterated for n_i times to decide the next input of the PWLCM map which in turn produces next y-variable. The process is continued until 256 samples of y-values are obtained. The method of chaotic modulation of PWLCM map is depicted in Figure 1. The 256 samples of y-variable are recorded and shown in Figure 3. It is evident from the Figure 2 and 3 that latter shows regularities (marked by the circles) in the normal trajectory of PWLCM map, but such regularities are alleviated in the modulated trajectory of the map depicted in Figure 3. The averages of the two sequences shown in Figures are 0.5245 and 0.4955 (ideal value is 0.5). Hence, the modulated trajectory of PWLCM map has better randomness distribution.

2.3   Proposed Method

The steps of the proposed method are as follows:

S.1. Take proper initial conditions for $x(0)$, λ, p and t_o. Iterate chaotic Logistic map for t_o times and discard the values obtained.

S.2. Record 256 samples of chaotically modulated PWLCM map y-variables through the approach discussed in Section 2.2.

S.3. Preprocess the recorded samples as: $py(i) = y(i) * 10^6 - \text{floor}(y(i) * 10^6)$, $i = 1 \sim 256$.

S.4. Reshape the preprocessed 1D array $py(i)$ to a 2D matrix $P(j, k)$, $j, k = 1 \sim 16$.

S.5. Let $sy = sort(py)$ and reshape sorted array $sy(i)$ to a 2D matrix $S(j, k)$.

S.6. Find the (raster-scan) position of element $S(j, k)$ in matrix P and store it in new matrix $S_0(j, k)$, do it for all elements of S. This $S_0(j, k)$ is the initial 8×8 S-box.

S.7. Shift the elements of $S_0(j, k)$ through the zig-zag scan pattern (see Figure 3 of [22]) to produce $S_1(j, k)$. Now, let $mpos = 61$, $cnt = 1$.

S.8. Again, iterate the logistic map to generate a random number $rpos \in [1, mpos]$. Circularly shift (in *left* direction if cnt is odd, else in *right*) the cnt-th outer rows- &-columns of $S_1(j, k)$ by $rpos$ positions. $mpos = mpos - 8$, $cnt = cnt + 1$. Repeat this random circular shifting till $cnt \leq 8$. This step generates $S_2(j, k)$.

S.9. Again, shift the elements of $S_2(j, k)$ using zig-zag pattern to produce final S-box.

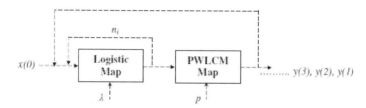

Fig. 1. Chaotic–modulation of piece-wise linear chaotic map

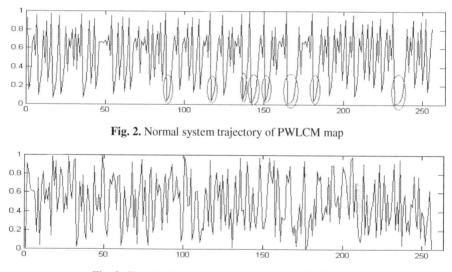

Fig. 2. Normal system trajectory of PWLCM map

Fig. 3. Chaotically-modulated trajectory of PWLCM map

3   S-box Performance Assessment

The initial values used for the simulation are: $x(0)=0.73$, $\lambda=3.997$, $p=0.491$ and $t_o=2500$. The S-box constructed using proposed method is depicted in Table 1. The performance of proposed S-box is tested under various statistical parameters to assess its suitableness for encryption. Performance tests such as *bijectivity*, *nonlinearity*, *strict avalanche criteria* and *equiprobable I/O XOR distributions* are applied to compare the features with few of the existing chaos-based S-boxes.

Bijectivity: A Boolean function f_i is bijective if it satisfies the condition [13]: $wt(\sum_{i=1}^{n} a_i f_i) = 2^{n-1}$, where $a_i \in \{0, 1\}$, $(a_1, a_2, \ldots, a_n) \neq (0, 0, \ldots, 0)$ and $wt(.)$ is hamming weight. It is required that every function f_i basically needs to be balanced. It is experimentally examined that the proposed S-box satisfies the bijective property.

Nonlinearity: A strong S-box should have high scores of nonlinearities. The nonlinearity N_f of Boolean function $f(x)$ can be evaluated as:

$$N_f = 2^{n-1}(1 - 2^{-n} \max |S_{\langle f \rangle}(w)|), \qquad \text{where} \quad S_{\langle f \rangle}(w) = \sum_{w \in GF(2^n)} (-1)^{f(x) \oplus x.w}$$

$S_{\langle f \rangle}(w)$ is the Walsh spectrum of $f(x)$ and $x.w$ denotes the dot-product of x and w. Nonlinearity scores for the eight Boolean functions of the proposed S-box are 108, 106, 104, 106, 108, 104, 106, 104 whose *mean* value is 105.75. These nonlinearity scores are compared with that of existing chaos-based S-boxes in Table 2. It is evident from the values that the proposed S-box offers higher *min*, *max* and *mean* value of nonlinearity scores. Hence, the proposed S-box outperforms on the basis of nonlinearity criteria.

Strict Avalanche Criteria: If a Boolean function satisfies the strict avalanche criteria, it means that each output bit should change with a probability of ½ whenever a single input bit is changed. An efficient procedure to check whether an S-box satisfies the SAC is suggested in [23]. Following the procedure, a dependency matrix, provided in Table 3, is calculated to test the SAC of the S-box. The SAC of the proposed S-box comes out as 0.5070 which is very close to the ideal value 0.5. Moreover, the comparisons drawn in Table 4 highlight that the proposed S-box provides comparable parameter values with respect to the strict avalanche criteria.

Table 1. Proposed chaotic substitution-box

161	41	0	247	163	32	150	214	169	122	189	248	61	102	104	75
70	203	197	124	142	132	221	53	243	225	98	121	233	36	234	46
95	116	54	71	107	55	143	49	45	65	192	141	182	79	64	183
56	184	119	186	92	73	217	117	110	129	140	139	162	137	198	72
115	90	108	20	29	13	42	33	219	205	187	22	216	245	12	235
84	101	120	28	138	69	224	109	202	204	9	10	144	218	196	244
114	77	210	232	30	165	222	123	128	176	135	172	91	130	37	246
31	231	148	94	180	178	154	88	87	38	160	6	131	14	118	81
179	100	103	60	157	226	19	89	158	105	74	251	208	26	173	134
125	126	164	149	43	223	52	27	39	51	153	133	85	238	8	127
240	63	207	47	156	239	193	48	3	209	253	50	175	5	62	168
97	201	67	215	16	25	146	167	35	68	57	111	242	185	220	96
229	15	188	106	155	76	145	230	136	250	199	59	66	249	228	78
191	181	40	255	206	213	113	152	80	190	58	171	212	17	18	112
147	227	241	21	174	200	1	44	195	93	82	151	170	194	11	252
166	211	23	7	159	177	237	86	34	254	4	83	99	2	24	236

Equiprobable I/O XOR Distribution: The differential cryptanalysis, introduced by Biham and Shamir to attack DES-like cryptosystems in [4], exploits the imbalance on the input/output distribution. In order to resist the differential cryptanalysis, the XOR value of each output should have equal probability with the XOR value of each input. If an S-box is closed in I/O probability distribution, then it is resistant against differential cryptanalysis. The differential probability for a function $f(x)$ is calculated as:

$$DP_f = \max_{\Delta x \neq 0, \Delta y} \left(\frac{\#\{x \in X \mid f(x) \oplus f(x \oplus \Delta x) = \Delta y\}}{2^n} \right)$$

Where X is the set of all possible input values and 2^n (here $n=8$) is the number of its elements. The differential probabilities (value/2^8) obtained for the proposed S-box are shown in Table 5. It is desired that the largest value of DP should be as low as possible. Now, it is evident that its largest element is 10 which is also the largest value in Tang's, Asim's, Wang's and Özkaynak's S-boxes. However, this value is better than the Jakimoski's and Chen's value of 12. This verifies that the proposed S-box is stronger than Jakimoski's and Chen's S-boxes and comparable to the others against differential cryptanalysis.

Table 2. Nonlinearity scores of S-boxes

S-box	Nonlinearities										
	1	2	3	4	5	6	7	8	Min	Max	Mean
Proposed	108	106	104	106	108	104	106	104	104	108	105.75
Jakimoski et al. [13]	98	100	100	104	104	106	106	108	98	108	103.25
Tang et al. [14]	100	103	104	104	105	105	106	109	100	109	104.50
Chen et al. [15]	100	102	103	104	106	106	106	108	100	108	104.37
Asim et al. [16]	107	103	100	102	96	108	104	108	96	108	103.50
Wang et al. [18]	104	106	106	102	102	104	104	102	102	106	103.75
Özkaynak et al. [19]	104	100	106	102	104	102	104	104	100	104	103.25

Table 3. Dependency matrix of proposed S-box

0.5468	0.5000	0.5000	0.4843	0.5312	0.5156	0.5000	0.5468
0.5468	0.5625	0.5000	0.5000	0.5156	0.4843	0.5312	0.5468
0.4843	0.4843	0.5156	0.5312	0.4531	0.5468	0.4375	0.4843
0.4843	0.5468	0.5312	0.5625	0.5156	0.4843	0.4843	0.4843
0.5000	0.5468	0.4218	0.5000	0.4218	0.5312	0.5468	0.5000
0.5312	0.5468	0.5312	0.5468	0.5468	0.4687	0.4843	0.5312
0.5000	0.5312	0.4843	0.4218	0.5468	0.4687	0.5156	0.5000
0.4531	0.5000	0.4843	0.5156	0.5000	0.5781	0.4843	0.4531

Table 4. Min-Max of dependency matrices and SAC of S-boxes

S-box	Min	Max	SAC
Proposed	0.4219	0.5781	0.5070
Jakimoski et al. [13]	0.3750	0.5938	0.4972
Tang et al. [14]	0.3984	0.5703	0.4993
Chen et al. [15]	0.4297	0.5703	0.4999
Asim et al. [16]	0.3906	0.5859	0.4938
Wang et al. [18]	0.4218	0.5681	0.4964
Özkaynak et al. [19]	0.4219	0.5938	0.5048

Table 5. Differential probabilities table in proposed S-box

8	8	8	6	6	6	8	6	8	10	6	10	6	6	4	6
8	6	6	6	6	6	8	6	6	8	6	6	6	6	8	6
8	8	6	6	6	6	6	6	6	6	8	6	6	6	8	8
6	6	6	6	6	6	6	6	6	6	8	6	6	6	8	8
6	6	6	6	6	10	8	8	4	6	10	6	6	6	8	8
8	6	6	6	4	6	10	6	6	8	6	8	6	6	8	8
6	6	6	6	8	6	6	6	6	6	6	6	10	6	8	8
6	6	6	6	6	6	6	8	6	6	8	6	6	6	6	6
6	6	6	6	6	6	6	6	6	6	6	6	6	8	8	6
6	6	6	6	6	6	8	8	6	8	6	6	8	6	6	8
8	6	6	6	6	8	6	6	10	8	8	10	6	8	8	8
6	6	8	6	6	6	6	6	6	8	10	6	8	8	6	6
6	8	6	8	6	8	6	6	6	6	6	8	6	8	6	8
6	8	8	8	8	10	8	6	6	8	6	6	8	10	8	6
6	6	6	8	6	6	6	6	8	6	6	8	6	8	8	6
6	6	8	8	6	6	8	8	6	6	6	6	6	8	8	-

4   Conclusion

In this paper, a cryptographic substitution-box is constructed by exploiting the random distribution characteristics of one-dimensional chaotic maps. For designing an efficient nonlinear S-box, the chaotically modulated trajectory of the PWLCM map is sampled and preprocessed to generate an initial S-box candidate. The shifting of whose elements through random circular rotation and zig-zag scan pattern results a cryptographically effective S-box. The experimental and comparative analyses show that the proposed S-box has better features than most of the existing chaos-based S-boxes, which verifies its high performance and suitableness for the design of strong block encryption systems.

References

1. Shannon, C.E.: Communication theory of secrecy systems. Bell Systems Technical Journal 28, 656–715 (1949)
2. Menezes, A.J., Oorschot, P.C.V., Vanstone, S.A.: Handbook of applied cryptography. CRC Press (1997)

3. Schneier, B.: Applied cryptography: protocols algorithms and source code in C. Wiley, New York (1996)
4. Biham, E., Shamir, A.: Differential cryptanalysis of DES-like cryptosystems. Journal of Cryptology 4(1), 3–72 (1991)
5. Dalai, D.K.: On some necessary conditions of boolean functions to resist algebraic attacks. PhD thesis, ISI Kolkata (2006)
6. Yin, Y., Li, X., Hu, Y.: Fast S-box security mechanism research based on the polymorphic cipher. Information Sciences 178(6), 1603–1610 (2008)
7. Bhattacharya, D., Bansal, N., Banerjee, A., Chowdhury, D.R.: A Near Optimal S-box Design. In: McDaniel, P., Gupta, S.K. (eds.) ICISS 2007. LNCS, vol. 4812, pp. 77–90. Springer, Heidelberg (2007)
8. Szaban, M., Seredynski, F.: Designing cryptographically strong S-boxes with the use of cellular automata. Annales UMCS Informatica Lublin-Polonia Sectio AI 8(2), 27–41 (2008)
9. Detombe, J., Tavares, S.: Constructing large cryptographically strong S-boxes. In: Zheng, Y., Seberry, J. (eds.) AUSCRYPT 1992. LNCS, vol. 718, pp. 165–181. Springer, Heidelberg (1993)
10. Chen, G.: A novel heuristic method for obtaining S-boxes. Chaos, Solitons & Fractals 36, 1028–1036 (2008)
11. Clark, J.A., Jacob, J.L., Stepney, S.: The Design of S-boxes by simulated annealing. New Generation Computing 23(3), 219–231 (2005)
12. Karaahmetoglu, O., Sakalli, M.T., Bulus, E., Tutanescu, I.: A new method to determine algebraic expression of power mapping based S-boxes. Information Processing Letters 113, 229–235 (2013)
13. Jakimoski, G., Kocarev, L.: Chaos and cryptography: Block encryption ciphers based on chaotic maps. IEEE Transaction on Circuits Systems 48(2), 163–169 (2001)
14. Tang, G., Liao, X., Chen, Y.: A novel method for designing S-boxes based on chaotic maps. Chaos, Solitons Fractals 23, 413–419 (2005)
15. Chen, G., Chen, Y., Liao, X.: An extended method for obtaining S-boxes based on three-dimensional chaotic Baker maps. Chaos Solitons Fractals 31, 571–577 (2007)
16. Asim, M., Jeoti, V.: Efficient and simple method for designing chaotic S-boxes. ETRI Journal 30(1), 170–172 (2008)
17. Yin, R., Yuan, J., Wang, J., Shan, X., Wang, X.: Designing key-dependent chaotic S-box with large key space. Chaos Solitons Fractals 42, 2582–2589 (2009)
18. Wang, Y., Wong, K.W., Liao, X., Xiang, T.: A block cipher with dynamic S-boxes based on tent map. Communications in Nonlinear Science and Numerical Simulations 14, 3089–3099 (2009)
19. Özkaynak, F., Özer, A.B.: A method for designing strong S-boxes based on chaotic Lorenz system. Physics Letters A 374, 3733–3738 (2010)
20. May, R.M.: Simple mathematical model with very complicated dynamics. Nature 261, 459–467 (1967)
21. Li, S., Chen, G., Mou, X.: On the dynamical degradation of digital piecewise linear chaotic maps. International Journal of Bifurcation and Chaos 15(10), 3119–3151 (2005)
22. Wallace, G.K.: The JPEG still picture compression standard. IEEE Transaction on Consumer Electronics 38, 18–34 (1992)
23. Webster, A.F., Tavares, S.: On the design of S-boxes. In: Williams, H.C. (ed.) CRYPTO 1985. LNCS, vol. 218, pp. 523–534. Springer, Heidelberg (1986)

A Multicast Authentication Protocol (MAP) for Dynamic Multicast Groups in Wireless Networks

Parag J. Jambhulkar, Soumyadev Maity, and Ramesh C. Hansdah

Dept. of Computer Science and Automation
Indian Institute of Science, Bangalore, India
{parag.cmps,soumya,hansdah}@csa.iisc.ernet.in

Abstract. In this paper, we have proposed a centralized multicast authentication protocol (MAP) for dynamic multicast groups in wireless networks. In our protocol, a multicast group is defined only at the time of the multicasting. The authentication server (AS) in the network generates a session key and authenticates it to each of the members of a multicast group using the computationally inexpensive least common multiple (LCM) method. In addition, a pseudo random function (PRF) is used to bind the secret keys of the network members with their identities. By doing this, the AS is relieved from storing per member secrets in its memory, making the scheme completely storage scalable. The protocol minimizes the load on the network members by shifting the computational tasks towards the AS node as far as possible. The protocol possesses a membership revocation mechanism and is protected against replay attack and brute force attack. Analytical and simulation results confirm the effectiveness of the proposed protocol.

Keywords: Multicast Communication, Dynamic Group, Wireless Networks, Least Common Multiple (LCM), Pseudo Random Function (PRF).

1 Introduction

The transmission of a message from one sender to multiple receivers is termed as a *multicast*. Multicast is preferable over multiple unicasts when the same message requires to be sent to different destinations. The popularity of multicast communication has grown considerably with the widespread use of the Internet. Typical applications over Internet which demand multicast communication includes software updates, live multiparty conferencing, on-line video game etc. Security issues like message authentication, secrecy, replay attack are more difficult to manage in multicast communication as compared to that in unicast or point-to-point communication. The task becomes more challenging in wireless networks due to constraints on the resources of nodes and their limited physical security.

Group key management is a fundamental service required to ensure the security of any multicast communication. As in case of a unicast, where the sender and receiver of the communication share a secret key, in a multicast communication also, the members of the multicast group require to share a common group

Sabu M. Thampi et al. (Eds.): SSCC 2013, CCIS 377, pp. 138–149, 2013.
© Springer-Verlag Berlin Heidelberg 2013

key among them. Generally, a group key is generated and distributed among the group members for each communication session. Group key management becomes more problematic when the group membership is *dynamic*. In a dynamic group, a new member can join the group or a member can leave the group at any time.

A lot of research has been carried out in the recent past to design efficient multicast authentication protocols in wireless networks. The existing protocols are basically of three types: (i)the centralized schemes, with one controller managing the entire network; (ii)the decentralized schemes, with subgroup controllers or cluster heads managing the clusters; and (iii)the distributed schemes, with no group controller and each group member contributing to the group key management. In the centralized schemes, group members need to bear less computation and storage burden, while in the distributed schemes, each group member needs to perform the necessary operations for group key management, imposing higher load on the group members. Performances of the decentralized schemes are in between the above mentioned two categories of protocols.

In this paper, we have proposed a novel centralized multicast authentication protocol (MAP) for wireless networks. The proposed protocol assumes a computationally enriched and physically secure trusted authentication server (AS) existing in the network. The protocol minimizes the load on the member nodes of the network by shifting the maximum computational tasks to the AS as far as possible. We use a pseudo random function (PRF) as a keyed one-way function to bind the secret keys of the network members with their identities. In this way, we achieve storage scalability on the AS node. In addition, we use the least common multiple (LCM) method to generate and distribute the group key for a multicast communication session. By doing this, we reduce both computational and control message overhead. There is no static multicast groups or clusters in the proposed MAP protocol. A multicast group $\mathcal{G}$ is specified only at the time of the multicast communication. The scheme is protected against replay attacks and brute force attacks. We have simulated the protocol using Castalia simulator. The analytical and the simulation results confirm the effectiveness of the proposed protocol.

The rest of the paper is organized as follows. In section 2, we give a brief overview of the related work. In Section 3, we describe the proposed MAP protocol in details. Section 4 analyzes the correctness and the security of the proposed scheme, whereas the efficiency of the MAP protocol is analyzed in section 5. Simulation results are given in section 6, and section 7 concludes the paper.

2   Related Work

The existing multicast group key management schemes in wireless networks are basically of three types, viz., a) Distributed Schemes b) Decentralized Schemes, and c) Centralized Schemes.

2.1   Distributed Schemes

In the distributed schemes, there is no group controller and each group member participates in the group key management process. Examples of such schemes can be found in [7], [4], [8].

2.2   Decentralized Schemes

Decentralized schemes have subgroup controllers or cluster heads to manage the multicast groups. Examples of such schemes include [9], [10], [3], [12], [13] .

2.3   Centralized Schemes

In the centralized schemes ([2], [1], [5], [11], [6]), there exists a single group controller which manages the multicast group key management for the entire network.

In the minimal key storage scheme given in [2], each member is allocated a unique Key. Both group controller and group member need to store two keys. Group member stores its individual secret key and the session group key. When any member leaves the group, Group Controller(GC) has to encrypt the new session key individually with the unique key of each of the group members. Hence, the communication overhead for updating the group of n members with the new key is O(n). To minimize the GC storage, a pseudo-random function is used with a random seed and index of group member to generate the individual node key. The GC has to store only two keys, the session key and the random seed. Hence, this scheme takes minimal memory storage for both group controller as well as group member.

Hierarchical Tree Approach, also called Logical Key Hierarchy Approach, is used in the scalable key management schemes given by Wallner et. al.[1] and Wong et. al.[5]. According to this scheme, each member is assigned to a unique leaf node of the tree. Hence, it fixes the number of leaves of a tree which is equal to the size of a group. Every node of the logical tree is assigned a Key Encryption Key(KEK). The set of keys assigned to the nodes along the path from a leaf node to the root are assigned to the member associated with that particular leaf node. These KEK's are used by a group controller(GC) to establish the Session Encryption Key(SEK) among the members. Member storage is equal to the depth d of a tree plus one, i.e.,d+1. As a member shares the root key and all the intermediate KEK's with other users, all the keys possessed by the member except the one at the leaf node have to be updated when the member is deleted. The number of key update messages is $kd - 1$ if one key is sent per message, where k is the degree of the tree and d is the depth of the tree. In the logical key hierarchy protocol, the group controller has to store all the keys corresponding to the nodes of the entire tree.

An improvement over Hierarchical Tree Approach scheme is Hybrid Tree Distribution given in [2]. Its main idea is to divide the group of size n into clusters of size m with every cluster assigned to a unique leaf node. Hence, there are n/m clusters as well as n/m leaves of a tree, and one will need to build a tree of depth $log(n/m)$. The hierarchical key tree is used as inter-cluster key management scheme to limit key update communication, and the minimal storage scheme is used as the intra-cluster scheme to reduce group controller storage requirement. In this scheme, the group member storage is of the order of O(log(n/m)). The key update overhead is of the order of O(m + log(n/m)). If m is not too large, the key update overhead is not severe.

Chinese Remainder Theorem based Group Key Management[11] uses Chinese remainder theorem to distribute the group session key among group members. A re-key message X is generated to distribute group session key by using the secrets of the group members and Chinese Remainder Theorem. The message X is transmitted along with each encrypted message. Only users in the secure group can find the group session key from X. Because X is common among all valid participants, the efficiency of the transmission of the re-key message, i.e., number of key update messages required is of the order of O(1). Each group member needs to store one group key and one private key.

Secure Group Key Management Scheme for Multicast Networks[6] has introduced a new entity, called the Sub-Group Controller(SGC). Similar to the hybrid tree scheme[2], a logical tree structure is constructed. All the users(N of them) are divided into clusters. Each cluster is related to the leaf of a tree. In this scheme, logical key tree is used for inter-cluster key management and chinese remainder theorem(CRT) scheme is used for intra-cluster key management. Each cluster is assigned an individual SGC which compute a common solution X based on the session encryption key and the public key of the users within that cluster. Each user after getting common solution X, applies CRT and decrypts it using its own private key in order to get the session encryption key. The complexity of this scheme for key update is O(N/M), where M is the cluster size. Each user has to store its own public key and private key. Each SGC stores public keys of users within its cluster.

3   The MAP Protocol

The proposed protocol assumes an authentication server (AS) existing in the network, which is responsible for providing the authentication services to all the network members. The AS is assumed to be completely secure against the perceived adversary of the network, and it is a computationally powerful device. The AS stores a secret value (α) using which the security credentials of the network members are calculated. Each network member x possesses a unique identity ID_x, and a secret key K_x. The protocol assumes loose time synchronization among the network nodes, and it also assumes an underlying routing protocol using which any node can communicate with any other node in the network.

3.1   Objectives

- Each multicast group $\mathcal{G}$ is dynamic in the sense that it is defined only when the corresponding multicast communication session begins.

- The protocol should be able to support two types of multicast communication scenarios, viz., a) from the AS to a multicast group and b) from any network member to a multicast group.
- The protocol should be completely storage scalable.
- The protocol should be protected against replay attacks and brute force attacks.
- Computational load should be shifted towards the AS node as far as possible.

3.2   Membership Issuance

Whenever a new user x wants to become a member of the network, it needs to come near the physical proximity of the authentication server (AS) and submit its request. The AS, after being satisfied about the genuineness of the user, generates a new unique identity (ID_x) for it. Next, it generates the secret key K_x for the user using its (AS) own secret key α as follows.

$$K_x = f_\alpha(ID_x)$$

The function 'f' is a pseudo random number generation function (PRF) which is used in this protocol as a keyed one-way function. α is given as the *seed*, and ID_x is given as the input to the PRF function. Finally, $\langle ID_x, K_x \rangle$ is transferred to the user x through a physically secure side channel. It is to be noted that, the AS and only the AS can always calculate the secret key of any network member.

3.3   Authentication Server to a Multicast Group Communication

Suppose that the AS wants to establish a communication session s with a multicast group $\mathcal{G}$ to securely send a number of messages to each member of the group. Let exp_time denote the desired expiration time(absolute) for the session s. The AS generates a session key K_s and a corresponding authenticator X_s by executing the steps as shown below.

1. $\forall i \in \mathcal{G}$, calculate the following values:
    (a) $K_i = f_\alpha(ID_i)$
    (b) $Info_i = ID_i \| exp\_time$
    (c) $C_i = MAC_{K_i}(Info_i)$
2. calculate l_s as the LCM of all C_is, i.e., $l_s = LCM(\{C_i | i \in \mathcal{G}\})$.
3. select a random number r_s for the session.
4. select a random session key K_s, such that, $\forall i \in \mathcal{G}(K_s < C_i)$.
5. calculate the authenticator X_s for the session key K_s as, $X_s = (l_s \times r_s + K_s)$.

Next, the AS multicasts the authenticator value X_s along with the expiration time exp_time to the members of the multicast group $\mathcal{G}$.

- $AS \rightarrow \mathcal{G} : X_s \| exp\_time$

Each member $i \in \mathcal{G}$, upon receiving the above information, calculates the session key K_s using its own secret key K_i as follows.

- $K_s = X_S \bmod (MAC_{K_i}(ID_i \| exp\_time))$

At this point, the session key K_s is established between the AS and the group members of the multicast group $\mathcal{G}$, using which the AS can send messages in a secure way as shown below.

- $AS \rightarrow \mathcal{G} : \ message \| MAC_{K_s}(message)$

It is to be noted that the group members would trust the session key as long as it has not expired.

3.4 A Member to a Multicast Group Communication

Now, suppose that a network member j wants to establish a session key with a multicast group $\mathcal{G}$. For this, member j has to send a request message to the AS. The request message contains the identity of the requester, the identities of each of the members in $\mathcal{G}$, and a time-stamp indicating the time of request. As a function of the time-stamp given in the message, a temporary key K_j^t is calculated by j using its secret key K_j as shown below.

- $Request = ID_j \| \{ID_i | i \in \mathcal{G}\} \| time\_stamp$
- $K_j^t = f_{K_j}(time\_stamp)$

To preserve the authenticity and the integrity of the request message, it is sent with its MAC value which is computed using the temporary key K_j^t, as shown below.

- $j \rightarrow AS : \ Request \| MAC_{K_j^t}(Request)$

The AS discards the request message if the time-stamp given on it is stale. Otherwise, the AS first calculates the secret key K_j of j using its own secret α as explained earlier. Using K_j, the AS calculates the temporary key K_j^t from the time-stamp given in the request message. With K_j^t, the AS can easily check the MAC value attached with the message.

If the server is satisfied, then it generates a session key K_s with expiration time exp_time along with its authenticator X_s, by executing exactly the same steps (step 1-5) as described in section 4.2, except that now $Info_i$, for each $i \in \mathcal{G}$, is calculated as $Info_i = ID_i \| ID_j \| exp\_time$. The AS sends the generated security credentials to the requester j encrypted by the temporary key K_j^t as shown below.

- $AS \rightarrow j : encrypt_{K_j^t}(X_s \| K_s \| exp\_time)$

The member j obtains K_s, X_s and exp_time by decrypting the message with K_j^t. It is to be noted that the encryption, in this case, not only ensures the confidentiality of key K_s, but also ensures the authenticity and the integrity of the message from AS to j.

Now, the member j multicasts the authenticator value X_s, the expiration time exp_time, and its own ID ID_j to the members of the multicast group $\mathcal{G}$.

- $j \rightarrow \mathcal{G} : \ ID_j \| X_s \| exp\_time$

Each member $i \in \mathcal{G}$ calculates the session key K_s using its secret key K_i as follows.

- $K_s = X_S \bmod (MAC_{K_i}(ID_i \| ID_j \| exp\_time))$

The established session key K_s can be used by j to send messages securely to the members of $\mathcal{G}$ until the session expires.

3.5   Membership Revocation

In the MAP protocol, each member node monitors the behaviors of its neighboring nodes. When a member x detects another member y as misbehaving, it confidentially sends a warning message to the authentication server, as shown below.

- $WarningMsg = ID_x \| ID_y \| time\_stamp$
- $K_x^t = f_{K_x}(time\_stamp)$
- $x \rightarrow AS: \ encrypt_{K_x^t}(WarningMsg)$

The AS keeps track of the count of warning messages against the member y, and as soon as the count exceeds a predetermined threshold value, the AS blacklists the member y. The AS neither sends an authenticated message nor gives any authentication services to a blacklisted member.

4   Correctness and Security Analysis

4.1   Correctness of the Session Key

From section 3.3 we see that, $\forall i (K_s < C_i)$. In addition, $l_s = LCM(\{C_i | i \in \mathcal{G}\})$. Hence, $\forall i (l_s \bmod C_i = 0)$. Now,

$$
\begin{aligned}
X_s \bmod C_i &= (l_s \times r_s + K_s) \bmod C_i \\
&= ((l_s \times r_s) \bmod C_i + K_s \bmod C_i) \bmod C_i \\
&= ((l_s \bmod C_i \times r_s \bmod C_i) \bmod C_i + K_s \bmod C_i) \bmod C_i \\
&= (K_s \bmod C_i) \bmod C_i \ [\because \ l_s \bmod C_i = 0] \\
&= K_s \ [\because \ K_s < C_i]
\end{aligned}
$$

Hence, each member $i \in \mathcal{G}$ calculates the correct session key K_s.

4.2   Security of the Session Key

In [4], the authors have analyzed the security of the LCM based key calculation mechanism and shown that the mechanism is provably secure against a possible brute-force attack. However, they also point out the LCM attack which says that in some cases, LCM of a set of numbers does not change even when new numbers are added to the set or some numbers are discarded. The proposed MAP protocol is free from such LCM attacks, as it incorporates into the authenticator value X_s, a random number r_s for each session s, which is not dependent on the LCM value l_s.

4.3   Security of the Secret Keys

From section 3.4 and 3.5, we can see that, a member x never uses its secret key K_x to send any message encrypted with it, rather, a confidential message is encrypted or attached with a MAC value which is computed with a temporary key K_x^t, generated using the secret key of the member. Hence, in the MAP protocol, the secret key of a member is neither sent unencrypted nor used to encrypt a message and send it over the insecure communication channel. Thus, an adversary is not able to obtain the secret key using brute-force attack. The only possibility to capture the secret key of a member is to capture the member itself. However, as explained in section 3.5, the membership revocation mechanism of the protocol is capable of eliminating a compromised member from the network.

4.4   Security against Replay Attack

In case of the multicast communications between the AS or a network member and a multicast group, the session keys are protected against replay attack as they are cryptographically attached with their expiration times. We assume that the size of the session keys and the complexity of the symmetric encryption algorithm that would be used in a possible implementation of the MAP protocol, are sufficiently strong enough to ensure that, the time required by the perceived adversary of the network to deduce a session key using brute force attack on the messages exchanged during the session is larger than the validity period of the session keys.

For the communications between a member and the AS, the possible replay attack is prevented by the use of time-stamps attached with the messages sent by the member. As the temporary keys used to authenticate the messages exchanged between the member and the server are one way functions of the corresponding time-stamp values, an old temporary key can never be used by an adversary.

5   Efficiency Analysis

In our protocol, each network member x, needs to store two pieces of information, viz., its identity (ID_x) and its secret key (K_x). Hence, the storage requirement to keep the security credentials of a member is not dependent on the total number of nodes in the network. On the other hand, the authentication server is able to calculate the secret keys of each of the members in the network with the help of a single key α. So, unlike the other centralized schemes, in the MAP protocol the server does not require to store per client secrets in its memory. In this way, the protocol achieves storage scalability for both network members and the server node.

The LCM based group key distribution mechanism used in the MAP protocol reduces the overall message overhead of the protocol. In many other existing schemes, each time a group key is updated, the group controller of a multicast group needs to send a separate message to each of its group members in order to distribute the session key. However, in our protocol, a single message (containing the authenticator X_s and the expiration time exp_time) is multicast to all of the group members from which each of the member can calculate the group session key.

Table 1 shows a comparison of the storage requirement and the key update overhead of the proposed MAP protocol with those of some of the other important existing multicast authentication protocols in wireless networks. Here, **GC** stands for group controller, which is the authentication server in our protocol, and **GM** stands for group member, which is any network member in our protocol. The network size is assumed to be n and the cluster size, for the static cluster based schemes, is assumed to be m.

Table 1. Storage Requirement and Key Update Overhead Comparisons

Protocol	Storage Requirement		Key Update Overhead
	GC	**GM**	
Minimal Key Storage Scheme [2]	$O(1)$	$O(1)$	$O(n)$
Hierarchical Tree Approach [1,5]	$O(n)$	$O(\log n)$	$O(\log n)$
Hybrid Tree Distribution [2]	$O(n)$	$O(\log(n/m))$	$O(m + \log(n/m))$
Chinese Remainder Method [11]	$O(n)$	2 keys	$O(1)$
Secure Group Key Management[6]	$O(n)$	2 keys	$O(1 + \log(n/m))$
The proposed MAP Protocol	$O(1)$	$O(1)$	$O(1)$

6   Simulation Results

We have further studied the performance of the proposed MAP protocol and compared it with some of the other existing schemes using the Castalia simulator [14]. Simulation parameters are given in table 2. We have used the TelosB mote hardware platform specifications. For multicasting of data packets from a node to a multicast group, we have used the multicast constant bit rate (MCBR) protocol in the application layer of the nodes. In the network layer of the nodes, we use the on-demand multicast routing protocol (ODMRP) to support multicast routing. In the simulations, we have varied the group size of a multicast group from 5 to 25.

Table 2. Simulation Configurations

Simulation Area	$50m \times 50m$
MAC Layer Protocol	IEEE 802.11 g/n
Transceiver data rate	$250\ Kbps$
Processor Clock rate	$8\ MHz$
RAM Size	$10\ Kb$
Flash Memory Size	$128\ Kb$
Battery Type	2 AA batteries
Mobility Model	Random Way-Point
Avg. node speed	$1 - 10\ m/s$

We have measured the average computational load imposed on the group controller (GC) node and on a group member (GM) node during the group key establishment process for one multicast session. For our protocol, the GC is the authentication server AS itself. We have compared the performances with the secure group key management (SGKM) protocol [6], which is a centralized scheme and uses a similar approach as in our protocol to distribute the group key. However, the SGKM protocol makes use of the Chinese remainder theorem (CRT) method in place of the LCM method to distribute the session key. Figure 1 shows the average computational loads on the GC nodes, and figure 2 shows the average computational load on the GM member nodes for both these protocols. From the figures, we can observe that, in our protocol, the load on the GC node is considerably lesser than that in the SGKM protocol. This is the advantage of using the computationally cheaper LCM method over the costly CRT method. We can also observe that the computational load on the group member nodes in the MAP protocol is comparable to that in the SGKM protocol. For both the protocols, the amount of load on the GM nodes is not affected when the group size increases.

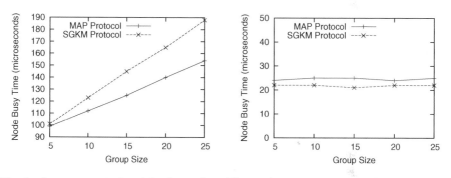

Fig. 1. Avg. computational load on the GC node

Fig. 2. Avg. computational load on a GM node

For the proposed MAP protocol, figure 3 shows the data packet delivery time required for a multicast from the authentication server to the group members of a multicast group. We have measured the maximum, average and minimum case delivery times for different values of the multicast group size. Figure 4 shows the average session key establishment delay suffered by a network member in our protocol. The session key establishment delay is measured as the duration of time from the instant when a member sends a multicast authentication request to the authentication server, to the instant when the member receives the required security credentials from the server. The results show that the proposed MAP protocol is computationally efficient and hence, perfectly suitable for resource constrained wireless networks.

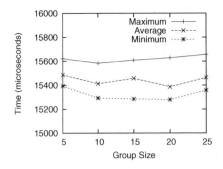
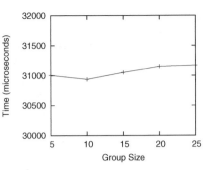

Fig. 3. Delivery time for the proposed MAP protocol

Fig. 4. Avg. session key establishment delay for the proposed MAP protocol

7 Conclusions

The protocol proposed in this paper provides an efficient mechanism for group key distribution among the members of a multicast group in wireless networks. A multicast group is defined only at the time of multicasting making the scheme completely dynamic. The scheme achieves storage scalability by using a pseudo random function, whereas it achieves computational and communication bandwidth consumption efficiency by using the least common multiple method. The protocol possesses an efficient membership revocation component, and it is protected against possible replay attacks and brute force attacks. The protocol is also secure against possible LCM attacks that can be launched on the other existing LCM based schemes.

References

1. Wallner, D.M., Harder, E.J., Agee, R.C.: Key management for multicast: Issues and architectures. RFC 2627 (June 1999)
2. Canetti, R., Malkin, T., Nissim, K.: Efficient communication-storage tradeoffs for multicast encryption. In: Stern, J. (ed.) EUROCRYPT 1999. LNCS, vol. 1592, pp. 459–474. Springer, Heidelberg (1999)
3. Abdel-Hafez, A., Miri, A., Orozco-Barbosa, L.: Authenticated Group Key Agreement Protocols for Ad hoc Wireless Networks. International Journal of Network Security 4(1), 90–98 (2007)
4. Balachandran, R.K., Ramamurthy, B., Zou, X., Vinodchandran, N.V.: CRTDH: an efficient key agreement scheme for secure group communications in wireless ad hoc networks. In: 2005 IEEE International Conference on Communications, ICC 2005, vol. 2, pp. 1123–1127. IEEE (May 2005)
5. Wong, C.K., Gouda, M., Lam, S.S.: Secure group communications using key graphs. IEEE/ACM Trans. Networking 8, 16–31 (2000)
6. Srinivasan, R., Vaidehi, V., Rajaraman, R., Kanagaraj, S., Chidambaram Kalimuthu, R., Dharmaraj, R.: Secure Group Key Management Scheme for Multicast Networks. International Journal of Network Security 11(1), 30–34 (2010)

7. Ingemarsson, I., Tang, D.T., Wong, C.K.: A conference key distribution system. IEEE Transactions on Information Theory 28(5), 714–720 (1982)
8. Zou, X., Thukral, A., Ramamurthy, B.: An Authenticated Key Agreement Protocol for Mobile Ad Hoc Networks. In: Cao, J., Stojmenovic, I., Jia, X., Das, S.K. (eds.) MSN 2006. LNCS, vol. 4325, pp. 509–520. Springer, Heidelberg (2006)
9. Dutta, R., Dowling, T.: Secure and Efficient Group Key Agreements for Cluster Based Networks. In: Gavrilova, M.L., Tan, C.J.K., Moreno, E.D. (eds.) Transactions on Computational Science IV. LNCS, vol. 5430, pp. 87–116. Springer, Heidelberg (2009)
10. Teo, J.C.M., Tanu, C.H.: Energy-Efficient and Scalable Group Key Agreement for Large Ad Hoc Networks. In: PE-WASUN 2005, Montreal, Quebec, Canada, October 10-13 (2005)
11. Zheng, X., Huang, C.-T., Matthews, M.: Chinese remainder theorem based group key management. In: Proceedings of the 45th Annual Southeast Regional Conference, March 23-24. ACM (2007)
12. Konstantinou, E.: Cluster-based Group Key Agreement for Wireless Ad Hoc Networks. In: Proc. of the Third International Conference on Availability, Reliability and Security - ARES 2008, pp. 550–557. IEEE Press (2008)
13. Drira, K., Seba, H., Kheddouci, H.: ECGK: An efficient clustering scheme for group key management in MANETs. Computer Communications 33, 1094–1107 (2010)
14. Castalia: A simulator for Wireless Sensor Networks and Body Area Networks, http://castalia.npc.nicta.com.au/pdfs/Castalia%20-%20User%20Manual.pdf

Clustering Based on Trust of a Node in Mobile Ad–Hoc NETworks

Pallavi Khatri[1,*], Shashikala Tapaswi[2], and Udai P. Verma[3]

[1] ITM University, Gwalior, India
[2] ABV – IIITM, Gwalior
[3] JU, Gwalior
pallavi.khatri.csit@itmuniverse.in

Abstract. The nodes in Mobile ad hoc networks join and leave the networks dynamically. At some point of time there is a possibility of enormous increase in the size of the network. Handling nodes in big network may put a burden on network management schemes and may introduce delays in the network. Dividing big networks in small groups called clusters may prove to be a good solution for handling them in a better and efficient manner. As MANET (Mobile Ad hoc networks) are self organized, the challenge of achieving security is critical. Evolving and managing trust relationships among the nodes in the network are important to carry efficient transmissions. This work proposes a trust based clustering algorithm which forms a cluster of trusted nodes only. Criteria used to select the nodes are the trust value of a node, weight of a node and its residual energy. A trusted cluster gives a better performance in terms of increase in throughput of the network which is well supported by the results produced by this approach.

Keywords: MANET, Security, Trust Value, Cluster.

1 Introduction

As the want for quicker communication with no geographical barriers is arising day by day, it's turning into tough job to deploy infrastructure network all over. All the devices of next generation demand a lot of mobility, less reliability on infrastructure and have reached the majority over the world. Best answer to those demands would be an infrastructure less ad hoc network where the nodes become a part of and leave the network dynamically. Nodes in ad hoc network are susceptible to attacks or could also be easily compromised. To achieve a definite level of security the necessity of recording information of nodes within the network is needed. Once the network is tiny, this task appears to be possible however just in case of huge networks this becomes tough. Increasing number of nodes within the network will be divided in smaller manageable groups referred to as clusters resulting in a hierarchical data structure of the network. Clusters are little groups consisting of a central watching

---

* Corresponding author.

Sabu M. Thampi et al. (Eds.): SSCC 2013, CCIS 377, pp. 150–161, 2013.

node referred to as a Cluster Head *(CH)* and its Cluster Members *(CM)* .The choice of clusters formation is usually arbitrary and does not take security in to account. A malicious node in the network may claim to become a cluster head and may attract the nodes to join its cluster. This will create a compromised cluster and will hamper the network efficiency with attacks and data loss. This work tries to bring in the concept of trust value of a node before choosing it either as a cluster head or a cluster member. This approach relies on trust value *(TVi)*, weight *(Wi)*, which is the number of neighboring nodes of the claiming node, and residual energy *(REi)* of a node *i* to elect it as Cluster Head *(CH)*. *CH* then selects the cluster members based on their trust value. Using trust value as a parameter for election of cluster head and clusters members gives better performance than many other approaches already proposed. It gives a new dimension to the formation of trusted clusters. Proposed scheme also uses a key management scheme for generation of a group key *(GK)* generated by a *CH* using its public key and its *ID* (Identity) and is distributed among the cluster members. This *GK* is used for encrypting and decrypting the data during transmission.

Rest of the paper is organized in following subsections. Section 2 discusses the various clustering schemes used in MANET and their limitations. In section 3 the details of the proposed protocol, approach, and notations are given. Simulation environment used for this study is detailed in section 4. The results obtained and discussions along with concluding remarks are done in section 5.

2   Related Work

In recent years lot of work has been done in the area clustered mobile ad hoc networks. Many clustering algorithms have been proposed in the past to efficiently divide the network in to small groups with aim of maintaining the efficiency of the network. In this section the works related to clustering the MANET have been discussed.

2.1   Clustering Schemes in MANET

Clustering using trust as a metric has been a very broad area of research in recent years. This section briefs about few strategies used for clustering in mobile ad hoc networks. Work in [1] proposes an on demand Weight Clustering Algorithm (WCA) which elects a cluster head based on the weight of a node. Security of the network is not taken care in this approach it simply concentrates on cluster formation. Leader election algorithm [2, 3] does not have any mechanism to detect the malicious nature of a node in the network. Scheme in [4] puts forth a Vice Cluster Head in Cluster Based Routing Protocol (VCH – CBRP) which is an extended version of CBRP (Cluster Based Routing Protocol). In this approach when a *CH* becomes idle, a vice node in the network declares itself as a *CH* provided it has a bidirectional link to one or more neighbors. This approach may fail when a node declared as vice moves out of the range of *CH*. Highest degree algorithm proposed in [5] is based on the number of its neighboring nodes which is defined as the degree of a node. A node having highest degree becomes a cluster head. Another *ID* (Identity) based algorithm [6] assigns a unique *ID* to each node and a node with lowest *ID* is chosen as cluster head. In [7] authors propose a clustering scheme based on the real distance between the nodes. This distance is measured on the basis of received signal strength of a message. This approach selects the most stable node but may not work efficiently because there is hardly any node in ad hoc network which is stable. Work in [8] proposed a cluster based trust aware routing protocol which protects the transmitted packets from the malicious node. This approach keeps a check on malicious node and if one is detected it is isolated from the network. Becheler et al. [9] uses a concept of threshold cryptography where a *CA* (Central Authority) is required to distribute the fragments of key to all the nodes in the cluster. This approach may be time consuming and will waste bandwidth of network and energy of a node when a new node tries to join the cluster. Approach in [10] proposes a clustering algorithm based on trust which overcomes the drawbacks of [9] but fails to detail the implementation of firewall in pure ad hoc networks. In [11] author proposed a self organized public key management system for fully self organized ad hoc networks. Each node here maintains a certificate repository before claiming to use the system but the drawback with this approach is that it assumes trust to be transitive which is not always true.

3   Proposed Protocol Details

Existing clustering algorithms discussed in section 2 concentrate on clustering the network by creating small groups but fail to take care of trust among the nodes while electing a *CH*. There are cases when a malicious node advertises itself to take care of it trust of node should be known. Many strategies check for the residual energy of all nodes while forming clusters but it will waste bandwidth of the network. Rather, checking residual energy for only those nodes which claim to be *CH* would be beneficial. Primary goal of this work is to propose and develop a trust based clustering algorithm which will help to enhance the performance of mobile ad hoc networks. Proposed work uses Trust Value, Residual Energy and weight of a node to elect it as a *CH*.

Trust Value of a node i can be calculated using equation (1):

$$TVi = f(Traffic\ statistics\ of\ a\ node) \tag{1}$$

Traffic statistics of a node used are number of packets dropped by a node, number of packets forwarded to wrong destination, number of false routing messages generated by a node and number of replay packets generated by a node.

Weight of a node which is the total number of 1 – hop neighbors it has can be evaluated using equation (2):

$$(Wi) = \Sigma\ all\ 1- hop\ neighbors\ of\ i \tag{2}$$

Each node in the network is equipped with an energy model. Every node consumes energy during every transmission and reception done through it (E_{loss}). Energy is also consumed in switching on the transmitter and receiver (E_{TR}) at a node and handling the overheads of the network (E_O). Every node a continuously monitor its energy and logs it every Δs seconds.

Assuming d as the distance between two nodes, the total energy (E_T) consumed in transmitting a packet of size m to a distance d is:

$$E_T(m,d)=E_{TR}*m+E_{loss}*m*d^2 \qquad (3)$$

Energy consumed in receiving a packet is:

$$E_R(m)=E_{TR}*m \qquad (4)$$

Combining equation (3) and (4) we get the total energy consumed in one transaction, this is given as:

$$E_{TOTAL}=E_T(m,d)+E_R(m)+E_O \qquad (5)$$

Residual energy of a node can be calculated using equation 5 as:

$$RE_{new} = RE_{old} - E_{TOTAL} \qquad (6)$$

RE_{old} is the Residual energy of a node till previous transaction. Using equation (1), (2) and (6) a cluster head which is eligible to send a claim() packet can be decided.

$$Eligible\,(CH) = max\,(TVi \cdot Wi \cdot REi) \qquad (7)$$

And operation is applied among these parameters to choose the CH.

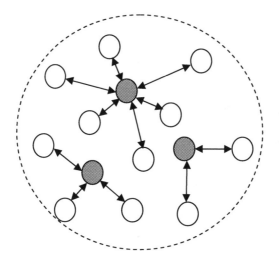

    Cluster Head

Cluster Member

Fig. 1. Clustering in network

Following assumptions are made before implementing the protocol:

1. All nodes in the network maintain the complete information of their 1 – hop neighbors. This is done by periodically broadcasting the hello packets.
2. A classical routing algorithm AODV [12] is running in the network.
3. Every node has a self generated key pair consisting of a secret key *(SK)* and a public key *(PK)*
4. Each cluster consists of a Cluster Head *(CH)* and its 1 – hop Cluster Members *(CM)*.
5. All the nodes in a cluster once it is formed are trusted.

Figure 1 shows the architecture of a clustered network which is obtained during this work. It consists of Cluster heads and Cluster members and bidirectional links joining them.

Proposed approach uses trust as a basic metric for making a cluster. Trust is the degree of belief that one node has on another. It is assumed that a TMS (Trust Management System) [13] is running at every node. Each node uses this TMS to evaluate its trust value and stores it in its routing table along with the trust values of all its 1 – hop neighbors. Nodes share this information in the network. Trust Management system allows forming three different trust relationships among the nodes in the network and categorizing the nodes on the basis of their trust values as given in Table 1:

Table 1. Trust Relationships

Nodes trust relationship	Trust Value
Fully Trusted (FT)	$TV_{max} = 1$
Partially Trusted (PT)	$TV_{avg} = 0.5$
Not Trusted (NT)	$TV_{min} = 0$

Trust of a node is evaluated based on the traffic statistics of a node. When a new node y enters the network, it sends a *join()* massage to its nearest Cluster Head. *CH* checks for its *TV* and if $TV_y >= TV_{threshold}$ it is allowed to be a member of the cluster. At this stage the trust value assigned to y is TV_{min} and eventually with every successful transaction done by y this value is incremented.

3.1   Cluster Head Election

Cluster control architecture used in this work is one hop clustering. For formation of a cluster the routing table of all the nodes which has recorded the details of its 1 – hop neighbors are read. Based on this weight of every node i, (Wi) is calculated which is the total number of 1 – hop neighbors of a node. A node having maximum weight claims to be a cluster head and broadcasts *claim()* to all its neighbors. Every neighbor receiving this claim() message will check the *TV* of the member who claims to be a cluster head in their surroundings and their respective routing tables and if *TV* >= $TV_{threshold}$, then the residual energy of the claiming node is evaluated. If this energy is found to be at some satisfactory level then the claiming node is declared as a cluster head.

Algorithm Cluster Head Election

```
N - Total number of nodes in the network
x, n - a node in the network
Wn - weight of a node n
TVn - Trust value of node n
CH - i^th cluster head
nnode - neighboring node
TVnnode - trust value of neighboring node
CM - cluster member
RT - Routing table
REx - Residual energy of x
```

1. For every node $n \in N$, Calculate W_n
2. For a node $x \in N$
   If $W_x = max (W_1, W_2, \ldots W_n)$
   Then node x broadcasts *claim()* message
3. For all 1 - hop neighbors receiving *claim()*
   Check TV_x in RT of *nnode* of x.
4. If $TV_x \geq$ $TV_{threshold}$ Then check RE_x
5. If RE_x is >> Min energy required for transmission
6. Then set a *FT* relationship between node x and evaluating *nnode*
7. Else if $TV_x = TV$ threshold and $RE_x = min(energy)$ set a *PT* relationship between node x and evaluating node.
8. Else set a *NT* relationship between x and evaluating node.
9. all nodes having *FT* or *PT* relation with claiming node x jointly declare x as a cluster head (*CH*)
10. This election is broadcasted in the network.

3.2   Cluster Member Selection

The 1 – hop nodes which receive *claim()* from elected *CH* send the *join()* message to the elected cluster head. The *CH* before allowing a node to be its cluster member checks for their *TV* and then allows it to be a *CM*.

Algorithm election Cluster member
NNODE: set of all 1 hop neighbors

```
1. For  every  node  having  a  FT  or  PT  relation  with
   elected CH
2. send join() message to respective CH
3. for every nnode ∈ NNODE sending join()
4. check TVnnode in RT(CH) and
        RT(NNODE - nnode)
5. if TVnnode >= TVthreshold then
      nnode = CM (CH).
```

3.3   Cluster Group Key Generation

All the Cluster Members of a cluster self generate their public keys and submit it to their respective Cluster Heads. Using these keys the *CH* computes a group key *(GK)* is distributed among all the cluster members of a specific cluster forming a key agreement zone between the Cluster head and its Cluster Members. All the cluster members contribute towards the computation of the *GK*. This *GK* is used for encryption / decryption of message exchanges within a group.

$$Group\ Key\ (GK) = f[PK(CMn)] \tag{8}$$

where n – all 1 hop neighbors of CH

Algorithm Cluster Group Key Generation.
```
1. For all CM ∈ CH
2. Generate a key pair (SK,PK)
3. Submit the public keys PK of all nnode to CH
4. CHi generates a group key (GKi) for ith cluster
5. Distribute GKi in all CM of ith cluster.
```

3.4   Recomputation of Group Key

A group key needs to be recomputed in the following cases.

1. Non Trusted *nnode* detected: Trust relationships among the *CH*s and *CM*s are periodically checked and till anode is having a *FT* or *PT* relationship with its *CH* it is allowed to be a part of this cluster. When a *CH* detects a non trusted neighbor it broadcasts this in the cluster and is excluded from the cluster. At this stage a new *GK* is computed and redistributed in the cluster.

2. Mobility / Death of a *nnode*: A node apart from being malicious can also move out of the RF (Radio Frequency) range of the cluster head due to mobility or may have died because of exhausted battery. A *CH* if not gets any hello packet from a specific *CM* after a specific interval tries to search for the *CM* through *nnode*. If *CM* is found it tries to establish a link with this node, else considering it as moved

to another cluster or dead its respective *RT* (Routing Table) entries are removed from *CHs* Routing table. At this stage a new *GK* is computed.

3. New *nnode* sends a *join()* : when a new *nnode* tries to join the cluster , sends its key to the *CH*. *CH* then computes a new *GK* and distributes it in the group.

3.5   Certificate Computation for *nnode*

Once all the cluster head have been elected they establish a session key among themselves using their key pair for inter cluster communication. Intra cluster communication takes place using Cluster Group key. *CHs* also generate a certificate for their respective *CMs* and broadcast it to all *CHs* or pass it them whenever required. The certificate *CERT* is computes as:

$$CERT^{CH}_{nnode} = SK_{CH}(PK_{CH}, PK_{nnode}, ID_{CH}, ID_{nnode}, validity)$$ (9)

$CERT^{CH}_{nnode}$ – certificate computed by *CH* for nnonde.

SK_{CH} – Secret Key of *CH*

PK_{CH} – Public Key of CH

PK_{nnode} –Public key of nnode

ID_{CH} – Identity of CH

ID_{nnode} – ID of nnode

validity – Validity period of Certificate

4   Simulation Environment

Simulation of the proposed protocol has been done on NS – 2.34 (Network Simulator) [14] and the results are produced and analyzed using tracegraph 2.02 [15] analyzer with the parameters given in Table 2.

Table 2. Simulation Parameters

Simulation Parameter	Value
Channel Type	Wireless Channel
MAC Type	802.11
Number of nodes	15
Routing Protocol	AODV
Dimension	500*500 m
Simulation Time	20s
Data Interval	0.5 s

Initial weight and initial energy of every node in the network is calculated. Using TMS in [13] the initial trust values of all the nods is evaluated and nodes are categorized as fully trusted (FT), partially trusted (PT) or non trusted (NT). Various initial node parameters are given in Table 3.

Table 3. Node Parameters

Node Number	Corresponding Weight	Initial Energy	Initial TV
0	5	64	0
1	4	192	1
2	5	110	0.5
3	2	127	0
4	1	154	1
5	3	131	0.5
6	4	56	0.5
7	3	90	0
8	4	31	0
9	5	168	1
10	1	82	0
11	2	87	0
12	3	166	0.5
13	1	150	1
14	1	127	1

Figure 2 shows the network scenario after all the clusters were formed.

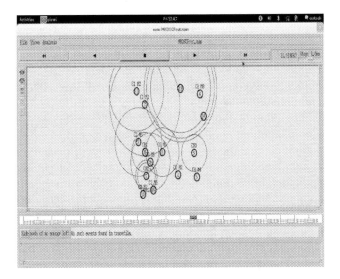

Fig. 2. Network Scenario

Applying algorithms for *CH* and *CM* four clusters were formed with *CH*s being node 1, 9, 6 and 12. The cluster members list is as given in Table 4.

Table 4. Cluster Details

Cluster Head	Cluster Members
Node 1	3,10,14
Node 6	7,11
Node 9	0,2,4,5,8
Node 12	13

5   Results and Conclusion

The proposed protocol is being compared with classical AODV protocol running for the same simulation environment and following results were obtained which prove the benefit of clustering in the network. At the same time the results also support the trust criteria used in forming the clusters by improving the network parameters.

Figure 3 gives the initial parameters of the nodes in the network which are used in deciding the first Cluster head of the network and gives node 1, 6, 9 and 12 as the initial *CH*s of the system.

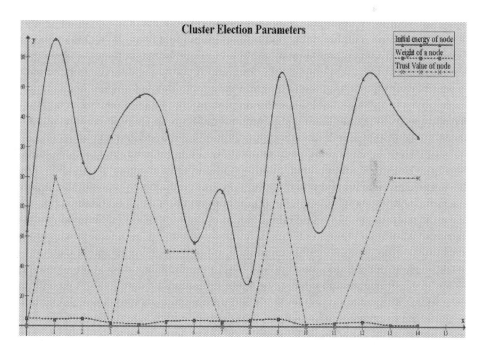

Fig. 3. Cluster Election Parameters

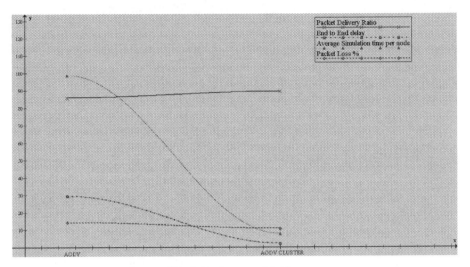

Fig. 4. Performance Metrics

Figure 4 show the improvement in the network parameters when trust based clustering is used. It clearly shows that average end to end delay of the network is decreased as the group to which a node transmits data is small. Average simulation time at every node also decreases. The trust incorporated in the network reduces the packet drop percentage in the network and as a result the packet delivery ratio of the network improves when trust based clustering scheme is used.

References

[1] Chatterjee, M., Das, S.K., Turgut, D.: An on-demand weighted clustering algorithm (WCA) for ad hoc networks. In: Proc. of IEEE GLOBECOM, San Francisco, pp. 1697–1701 (2000)

[2] Malpani, N., Welch, J., Vaidya, N.: Leader Election Algorithms for Mobile Ad Hoc Networks. In: Fourth International Workshop on Discrete Algorithms and Methods for Mobile Computing and Communications, Boston, MA (2000)

[3] Vasudevan, S., Decleene, B., Immerman, N., Kurose, J., Towsley, D.: Leader Election Algorithms for Wireless Ad Hoc Networks. In: Proc. of DARPA Information Survivability Conference and Exposition (2003)

[4] Yassein, M.B., Hijazi, N.: Improvement on Cluster Based Routing Protocol By Using Vice Cluster Head. In: Fourth International Conference on Next Generation Mobile Applications, Services and Technologies (2010)

[5] Gerla, M., Tsai, J.T.C.: Multicluster, mobile, multimedia radio network. Wireless Networks 1(3), 255–265 (1995)

[6] Baker, D.J., Ephremides, A.: The architectural organization of a mobile radio network via a distributed algorithm. IEEE Transactions on Communications, 1694–1701 (1981)

[7] Er, I.I., Seah, W.K.G.: Mobility-based D-hop Clustering Algorithm for Mobile Ad hoc Networks. In: IEEE WCNC, Atlanta, USA (2004)

[8] Safa, H., Artail, H., Tabet, D.: A cluster based trust-aware routing protocol for mobile ad hoc networks. Springer Science Business Media, LLC (2009)

[9]   Bechler, M., Hof, H.-J., Kraft, D., Pahlke, F., Wolf, L.: A Cluster-Based Security Architecture for Ad Hoc Networks. In: Proc. of IEEE INFOCOM (2004)

[10] Rachedi, et al.: Trust and mobility based clustering algorithm for secure ad hoc networks. In: Proc. of ICSNC 2006 (2006) ISBN: 0-7695-2699-3

[11] Hubaux, J.P., Buttyan, L., Capkun, S.: The Quest for Security in Mobile Ad Hoc Networks. In: Proc. of ACM Symposium on Mobile Ad Hoc Networking and Computing, pp. 146–155 (2001)

[12] Perkins, C.E., Royer, E.M.: Ad-hoc on-demand distance vector routing. In: Proc. of the Mobile Computing Systems and Applications, pp. 90–100

[13] Khatri, P., Tapaswi, S., Verma, U.P.: Trust evaluation in wireless ad hoc networks using fuzzy system. In: Potdar, V., Mukhopadhyay, D. (eds.) CUBE 2012, pp. 779–783 (2012)

[14] NS-2 simulation tool home page (2000), http://www.isi.edu/nsnam/ns/

[15] Malek, J.: Trace graph - Network Simulator NS-2 trace files analyser (2003), http://www.tracegraph.com/

A Novel Approach for Monitoring SQL Anti-Forensic Attacks Using Pattern Matching for Digital Forensic Investigation

Vaibhav T. Patil[1] and Amrita A. Manjrekar[2]

[1] Computer Science and Technology
patilvaibhav28@gmail.com
[2] Department of Technology, Shivaji University, Kolhapur
amrita5551@gmail.com

Abstract. Over the past few years the attacks on Software systems is increasing at an astonishing rate resulting in high revenue losses. Hence, Cyber/Digital forensics plays an important role by providing methods to acquire, asses, interpret, and use digital evidence to fetch conclusive details of cyber crime behavior. Recent trend in cyber crimes is the use of Anti-Forensic attacks to thwart the process of digital investigation by tampering the evidences.

The said system focuses on monitoring the Anti-Forensic attacks in the process of Digital Forensic Investigation. The system first identifies the different Anti-forensic attacks (Deletion /Modification /Hiding /Addition of evidences) by using a pattern matching algorithm, Finally the system effectively generates the reports and suggestions in accordance with the attacks. This system will prove helpful to the digital forensic investigators as well as other Government organizations in collecting post crime evidences and trace the identities of the attackers.

Keywords: Digital Forensics, Anti-Forensic attacks, Pattern Matching.

1 Introduction

Forensics, is the use of science to investigate and establish facts in a criminal or civil court. Physical evidence (e.g., bullets) and medical evidence (e.g., blood and DNA) are popular and well accepted in courts as well as the minds of the law enforcement community and the public. Less popular and much less well comprehended is the role of computer forensics and digital investigations.

Digital Forensics/Computer forensics is the acquirement, assessment, and reporting of information found on computers and networks that concern to a criminal or civil investigation. Almost every activity that someone does on a computer or a network leaves traces e.g. the deleted files, registry entries, Internet history cache and automatic Word backup files. E-mail headers and instant messaging logs give clues as to the intermediate servers through which information has traversed. Server logs provide information about every computer system accessing a Website [1].

Sabu M. Thampi et al. (Eds.): SSCC 2013, CCIS 377, pp. 162–167, 2013.

The term *anti-forensics* (AF) has recently been added into the language of digital investigators. While the digital forensic investigation aims at the analysis of digital evidence be accurate and provides an appropriate result, attackers try to defeat the process of investigation by making it difficult, challenging, or even impossible. A set of anti-forensic techniques and tools can be used to thwart the process of forensic investigation and also digital investigators [2].

Anti-Forensics Attacks refer to the use of tools and techniques that frustrate forensic tools, investigations and investigators [3].

Following are the primary goals of Anti-Forensic attacks [2]:

i. Evade detection by hiding, modifying, or wiping the traces generated by security solutions.

ii. Disconcert the collection of evidence from the compromised systems.

iii. Increase the effort required for the collection, analysis, and presentation of digital evidence.

2   Need of the System

Recently the attacks on IT systems are increasing at an alarming rate. The spectrum of these systems is very wide including servers to mobile devices and the losses caused as a consequence are in billions of dollars. Though, many criminals/offenders are successful to elude the responsibility due to the lack of supporting evidence to convict them [4]. So, under such circumstances, Cyber/Digital forensics plays a vital role by providing scientifically verified methods to acquire, assess, and report the cyber crime activities.

However the attackers are working on finding new ways of evading the investigation process. Recent trend in cyber crimes is the use of Anti-Forensic attacks to thwart the process of digital investigation by tampering the evidences. In spite of the fact that the incidents of cyber attacks on IT systems have increased tremendously and the losses are in millions of dollars there is not much research done in this area. Limited number of techniques are available to combat this problem.

So there is a need to devise a system that will facilitate the Digital Investigation Process by monitoring the Anti-Forensic Attacks. Hence an attempt is made to firstly identify the different Anti-forensic attacks (Deletion/Modification/Hiding/Addition of evidences). Finally the system effectively generates the reports and suggestions in accordance with the attacks.

This system will aid the digital forensic investigators as well as other government organizations in collecting post crime evidences and trace the identities of the attackers.

3   Related Work

As Digital Forensics has gained importance in recent years, Rekhis and Boudriga in [2] proposed an approach for digital investigation aware of anti-forensic attacks.

There are many techniques used for anti-forensic attacks which are highlighted in [3] by Garfinkel. It also mentions the novel detection techniques and countermeasures.

Arasteha *et al* describe a model checking approach to the formalization of the forensic analysis of logs in [4]. R.Harris in [5] made an attempt to arrive at a standardized method of addressing anti-forensics by defining the term, categorizing the anti-forensics techniques and outlining general guidelines to protect forensic integrity.

The anti forensics problem in various stages of computer forensic investigation from both a theoretical and practical point of view is explored in [6] by Pajek and Pimenidis. Different software tools and techniques that aid the Anti-Forensic attacks are also described.

Peron and Legary in [7] focused on what methods can be used to deceive someone who is in an investigative role into trusting an object which has been exploited.

Cesar Cerrudo in [8] describes the techniques security professionals can use to perform forensics analysis after a database attack. The author focuses specifically on Microsoft SQL Server 2005, however the information presented is also relevant to other database versions. The work gives the description of SQL Error Logs and Transaction logs in detail and also states the different queries to fetch these log records.

A new algorithm that searches multiple patterns simultaneously was proposed in [9] by Alqadi *et al*. The proposed algorithm is simple and can suit for multiple patterns matching in a file with unlimited size.

4   Overview of the System

With the rapid increase in the incidences of computer attacks, and the attackers getting smarter with the use of Anti-Forensic attacks it is necessary to design a system that will efficiently monitor the anti-forensic attacks and help keeping the system safe and secure.

The said system focuses on monitoring the Anti-Forensic attacks in the Digital Forensic Investigation. The input dataset for the system comprise of the log records obtained by firing queries in SQL Server 2005.

Outline of the proposed system is as follows:

i. The dataset is obtained by using different queries that generate log files in SQL Server 2005.

ii. The generated evidences are encrypted and securely preserved.

iii. Patterns are generated from these evidences for further investigation.

iv. The Anti-Forensic attack monitoring system takes the known patterns and the generated evidences under investigation as input. Pattern Matching algorithm like Multiple Skip Multiple pattern Matching Algorithm (MSMPMA) is applied to compare these inputs resulting in the detection and analysis of the Anti-Forensic attacks.

vi. The final step is the reporting and presentation of the investigation. Also some suggestions could be generated to help the administrator to keep the system safe and secure.

5   System Design

Fig. 1 illustrates the overall design of the said system. The system is divided into three principal modules viz. the Evidence generator module, the encryption decryption module and the anti-forensic attack monitoring module.

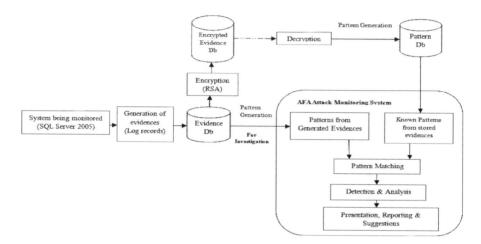

Fig. 1. System Design

6   System Description

6.1   Data Collection

The data set required as an input to the system is the log files referred to as evidences. The required log files are generated by firing different queries in SQL server 2005. The output of these queries will be the necessary log records.

6.2   Module Specification

Evidence Generation Module

Evidences in the form of log records are obtained by using different queries whose results are the required log records.

Encryption- Decryption Module

The evidences thus generated are encrypted using a standard encryption algorithm (e.g.RSA) and saved at a remote location to keep it safe and secure. Different patterns are generated from these evidences for further processing.

Anti-Forensic Attack Monitoring Module

Pattern Matching

The patterns of the generated evidences under investigation are compared with the known patterns using an effective pattern matching algorithm like Multiple Skip Multiple Pattern Matching Algorithm (MSMPMA) [9]. This will result in the detection of the Anti-Forensic attacks.

Detection and Analysis

The comparison between the generated and the stored evidences through the pattern matching algorithm results in the detection of the Anti-Forensic attacks. The detection requires analysis of the attacked system for further investigation.

Presentation and Reporting

The final step is to prepare the report of the attack, its consequences and probable solutions which will guide the administrator to combat such attacks in future.

7   Result Analysis

The implementation of the first two modules viz. the evidence generation module and the encryption-decryption module is successfully completed with desirable performance.

Fig. 2. Generated Log record

Fig.2. shows one of the six different log records generated by the first module.

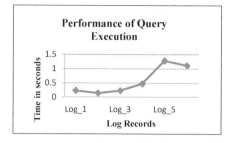

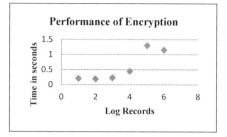

Fig. 3. Performance of Query Execution   **Fig. 4.** Performance of Encryption

Further Fig.3. shows the performance of the system in generating the required log records. In Fig.4. the performance of the encryption is illustrated. It compares the time taken for the encryption of the generated log records.

8   Conclusion

The first two modules of the system viz. the evidence generation module and the encryption decryption module are implemented with satisfactory performance. Further work is to complete the implementation of the anti-Forensic attack monitoring module and hence generate the reports and suggestions for the administrator. The system will definitely aid the entire process of digital forensic investigation and hence prove effective to the Cyber crime experts and other government organizations. The reports and suggestions generated by the system will assist the administrator in keeping the system safe and invulnerable.

References

1. Kessler, G.C.: The Role of Computer Forensics in Law Enforcement
2. Rekhis, S., Boudriga, N.: A System for Formal Digital Forensic Investigation Aware of Anti-Forensic Attack. IEEE Transaction on Information Forensics and Security 7(2) (April 2012)
3. Garfinkel, S.: Anti-forensics: Techniques, detection and countermeasures. In: Proc. 2nd Int. Conf. i-Warfare and Security (ICIW), Monterey, CA, March 8-9 (2007)
4. Arasteha, A.R., Debbabi, M., Sakhaa, A., Saleh, M.: Analyzing multiple logs for forensic evidence. Digital Investigation 4(1), 82–91 (2007)
5. Harris, R.: Arriving at an anti-forensics consensus: Examining how to define and control the anti-forensics problem. Digital Investigation 3(1), 44–49 (2006)
6. Pajek, P., Pimenidis, E.: Computer anti-forensics methods and their impact on computer forensic investigation. In: Jahankhani, H., Hessami, A.G., Hsu, F. (eds.) ICGS3 2009. CCIS, vol. 45, pp. 145–155. Springer, Heidelberg (2009)
7. Christian, S.J., Peron, M.: Legary.: Digital Anti-Forensics: merging trends in data transformation techniques. In: Seccuris Labs
8. Cerrudo, C.: SQL Server AntiForensics: Techniques and Countermeasures
9. Alqadi, Z.A.A., Aqel, M., El Emary, I.M.M.: Multiple Skip Multiple pattern Matching Algorithm(MSMPMA). IAENG International Journal of Computer Science 34(2) (2007)

Robust BPSO and Scene Change Based Digital Video Watermarking Algorithm in DWT-DFT-SVD Domain

Rahim Ansari[1], Mrutyunjayya Devanalamath[1], Maher Hussain[1], and V. Punya Prabha[2,*]

[1] Dept. of E and C, M. S. Ramaiah Institute of Technology, Bangalore
{rahimansari19,mrutyunjayamsrit,maherhussainmsrit}@gmail.com
[2] Dept. of E and C, M. S. Ramaiah Institute of Technology, Bangalore
punya.v@msrit.edu

Abstract. This paper proposes a Binary Particle Swarm Optimization (BPSO) and scene change based watermarking algorithm where BPSO is used to identify the robust pixels into which the watermark is to be inserted. Different watermarks are inserted into frames belonging to different scenes identified using a scene change detection algorithm. The watermarked video is obtained by inserting the singular values of Discrete Wavelet Transform (DWT) + Discrete Fourier Transform (DFT) sub-bands of the watermark into the singular values of Discrete Wavelet Transform + Discrete Fourier Transform sub-bands of video frames. Experimental results show the promising performance of the proposed algorithm for watermarking. Peak Signal to Noise Ratio (PSNR) values for the watermarked video in the range of 45 dB to 50 dB and maximum correlation of 0.9998 are achieved.

Keywords: Binary particle swarm optimization, Discrete wavelet transform, Discrete fourier transform, Singular value decomposition.

1 Introduction

In recent years there has been an explosion over the use and transfer of digital multimedia over the internet which has resulted in illegal access, use and modification of digital multimedia raising requirements of efficient techniques to be developed to protect digital content. Watermarking is a method of protecting digital multimedia (video, audio, text) from illegal access and tampering by embedding digital data known as watermark into it using a suitable algorithm.

Video watermarking poses greater challenges compared to image watermarking and is just not a mere extension of it since it involves lots of data and redundancy between frames. It can encounter inter-frame attacks such as frame averaging, frame dropping, statistical analysis and intra-frame attacks such as geometrical, noise and illumination attacks. Different watermarks can be inserted

---

* Corresponding author.

Sabu M. Thampi et al. (Eds.): SSCC 2013, CCIS 377, pp. 168–178, 2013.

into different scenes of the video as proposed by Ref. [1] to counter inter-frame attacks. Watermark can be embedded into the video in time domain (spatial domain watermarking) or frequency domain (frequency domain watermarking). Ref. [2] proposed watermarking in wavelet domain where video frames are transformed from RGB to YCbCr colorspace and watermark is inserted into the luminance component Y of frames. Watermarking in DWT+SVD domain was proposed by Refs. [3], [4], [5] where the watermark is embedded onto the singular matrices of the SVD decomposed wavelet coefficient of the luminance component Y of the video frames. H.264 compressed domain watermarking was proposed by Ref. [6], [7], [8] which exploits the specific characteristics of the compression standard and inserts the watermark in the I-frame. Refs. [9], [10], [11] proposed video watermarking scheme based on principal component analysis and wavelet transform where the watermark is inserted in the principal components obtained from LL and HH sub-bands of video frame.

The rest of the paper is organized as follows:- Section 2 reviews particle swarm optimization (PSO) and binary particle swarm optimization (BPSO), Section 3 describes the proposed watermarking algorithm including scene change detection, BPSO based robust video pixels identification algorithm, watermark embedding and watermark extraction. In Section 4 experimental results of the proposed algorithm are presented and Section 5 includes concluding remarks.

2   Particle Swarm Optimization (PSO)

Particle swarm optimization was proposed by Dr. Eberhart and Dr. Kennedy in 1995 Ref. [12]. It is a computational method based on the idea of collaborative behavior and swarming in biological populations inspired by the social behavior of bird flocking or fish schooling. Computation in PSO involves a collection of processing elements called particles which together are referred as a swarm. Each particle in the swarm is initialized with a random solution and the algorithm tries to find the optimum solution by updating it's generations and sharing of information between the particles.

Each particle in swarm is initialized with two variables position and velocity. The position and velocity of ith particle can be represented as $X = \{x_{i1}, x_{i2}, .., x_{iN}\}$ and $V = \{v_{i1}, v_{i2}, .., v_{iN}\}$ respectively where N in the number of dimensions in the search space.

PSO has two primary operations, velocity update and position update. During each iteration, fitness value of each particle is computed which is compared to it's previous best fitness value and the best fitness value of particle among the swarm. If the fitness value exceeds it's previous best fitness value, then it's personal best (pbest) is updated to particle's current position and if the fitness value exceeds best fitness value of particle among the swarm, then global best (gbest) is updated to particle's current position else both pbest and gbest are retained as before. Velocity and position of particle are updated using Eqs. [1,2] respectively.

$$V_i^{t+1} = w \times V_i^t + r_1 \times c_1 \times (pbest_i - X_i^t) + r_2 \times c_2 \times (gbest - X_i^t) \qquad (1)$$

$$X_i^{t+1} = X_i^t + V_i^{t+1} \tag{2}$$

Where w is a constant which determines the contribution of previous velocity on current velocity of a particle, r_1 and r_2 are random numbers, c_1 is a cognitive parameter and c_2 is a social parameter.

2.1   Binary Particle Swarm Optimization (BPSO)

In 1997 Dr. Eberhart and Dr. Kennedy released the binary version of PSO called as Binary Particle Swarm Optimization. In BPSO the position of the particle can take binary values i.e 0 or 1 in the N dimensional search space. Velocity of particle is updated using the same equation whereas position of particle is updated according to Eq. [3]

$$\text{If} \quad r < 1/(1 + \exp(-V_i^{t+1})) \quad \text{then} \quad X_i^{t+1} = 1 \quad \text{else} \quad X_i^{t+1} = 0 \tag{3}$$

3   Proposed Watermarking Algorithm

In the proposed algorithm, different scene's (collection of similar frames) in a video are identified by subjecting the video to scene change detection algorithm. For each scene identified, BPSO is applied to identify the robust pixels into which watermark has to be embedded. After identifying the robust pixels, frames are extracted from a video and one of the channels of frame is selected which is converted into a reduced robust channel by retaining only the identified robust pixels and removing other pixels from the channel. Four different frequency sub-bands are obtained by applying single level DWT to the reduced channel from which LH and HL sub-bands are chosen to which DFT is applied which are decomposed using Singular Value Decomposition (SVD) to obtain the singular matrices.

Similar procedure is applied to watermark i.e watermark is DWT+DFT+SVD transformed to obtain the singular matrices. Then the singular values of the watermark are inserted into the singular values of the reduced channel to obtain the watermarked reduced channel from which the watermarked channel is obtained by combining the watermarked pixels of the channel with unaltered pixels of original channel. Watermarked channel is combined with other channels to obtain watermarked frame which is combined with other watermarked frames to obtain the watermarked video.

3.1   Scene Change Detection

Scene change detection helps to identify different scene's in a video, hence different watermarks can be inserted into different scene's of a video which provides robustness against inter-frames attacks such as frame averaging, frame dropping and statistical analysis as mentioned in Ref. [1]. Scene change detection function provided by Matlab [13] has been used. In this method the edges in two consecutive video frames are computed which makes the algorithm less sensitive to small changes and then blocks of edges of the video frames are compared to one another. If the number of different blocks exceed a specified threshold, it is inferred that the scene has changed.

3.2 BPSO Based Robust Video Pixels Identification Algorithm

In order to identify the pixels which can be watermarked, initially a database is created from the frames belonging to the same scene. The first frame and few other frames belonging to a scene are extracted. Let the number of frames extracted be m. To each frame extracted different types of geometrical attacks such as rotation, filtering attacks such as gaussian filter, averaging filter and illumination attacks such as histogram equalization, gamma intensity correction are applied and difference image between the original frame and attacked frame is obtained. let the number of attacks applied to each frame be n. These attacks are applied to obtain modified frames which are used in determining the robust pixels through BPSO. In each iteration of BPSO, fitness value of each particle is computed which depends on particle's current position and created database. Base on fitness value obtained, gbest and pbest are updated. Let $R_1, R_2, R_3, \ldots, R_m$ represent the different classes each containing n number of difference frames represented as $S_1, S_2, S_3, \ldots, S_n$. Let $M_1, M_2, M_3, \ldots, M_m$ be the difference means of m classes and G represent the global difference mean of all the classes. The difference mean and global difference mean are calculated as in Eq. [4] respectively.

$$M_i = \frac{1}{n}\sum_{j=1}^{n}(X_i \times S_j) \qquad and \qquad G = \frac{1}{m}\sum_{i=1}^{m}M_i \tag{4}$$

where $i = 1, 2, 3, \ldots, m$ and X_i is the position of the particle. The fitness value F is calculated using Eq. [5]

$$F = \frac{1}{\sum_{i=1}^{m}\left((G - M_i)(G - M_i)^t\right)} \tag{5}$$

3.3 Watermark Embedding

The robustness of the algorithm is further increased by using a combination of DWT, DFT and SVD. By combining these transforms their individual properties of robustness to different types of attacks are exploited. The properties of DFT such as shift invariance, scaling are used and its less interpolation error compared to other transforms serves as an advantage to preserve the quality of the video. The Figs. [1,2] show the block diagram of Watermark Embedding and Watermark Extraction respectively. Watermark embedding is a process of inserting the watermark into host video to obtain the watermarked video. Steps:-

1. Scene change detection is performed on the video to identify different scenes.
2. BPSO is applied to each scene to obtain the pixels into which the watermark has to be embedded.
3. Video frames are extracted and one of the channels (R,G,B) is selected.
4. The selected channel is converted into a reduced robust channel by retaining only the identified robust pixels and removing the other pixels.
5. 2D-DWT (Haar) is applied to the reduced channel to obtain the four frequency sub-bands (LL,LH,HL,HH).
6. Apply 2D-DFT to LH and HL sub-bands and then SVD to the resulting 2D-DFT transformed sub-bands to decompose it into U, S and V matrices.
$$A_k = U_k S_k V_k^T \qquad \text{where} \quad k = 1, 2 \tag{6}$$

7. Apply 2D-DWT (Haar) to the watermark to obtain four sub-bands.
8. Apply 2D-DFT to LH and HL sub-bands and then SVD to obtain U, S and V matrices. $\qquad B_k = U_{1k} S_{1k} V_{1k}^T \qquad \text{where} \quad k = 1, 2 \tag{7}$

9. Insert the singular values of the watermark into the singular values of the host frame using the Eq. [8]
$$S_{2k} = S_k + \alpha S_{1k} \qquad \text{where} \quad k = 1, 2 \tag{8}$$

and α is the scale factor which controls the strength of the watermark to be inserted into the reduced channel.

10. Combine U_k, S_{2k} and V_k according to Eq. [9] to obtain C_k.
$$C_k = U_k S_{2k} V_k^T \qquad \text{where} \quad k = 1, 2 \tag{9}$$

11. Obtain watermarked LH and HL sub-bands by applying 2D-IDFT to C_1 and C_2.
12. Obtain the watermarked reduced channel by applying 2D-IDWT using the two non modified sub-bands and two watermarked sub-bands.
13. Obtain the watermarked channel by combining the watermarked pixels with the other unmodified pixels which is combined with the other two channels to obtain the watermarked frame.
14. Repeat steps 2 through 13 to obtain the watermarked frames for other scene of the video by embedding a different watermark.
15. Finally combine the watermarked frames to obtain the watermarked video.

3.4 Watermark Extraction

Watermark Extraction is a process of extracting the watermark from the watermarked video. Steps:-

1. Frames from the watermarked video are extracted and the scene to which the frame belongs is identified.
2. Channel into which the watermark was embedded is obtained and it is converted to reduced channel by retaining only the watermarked pixels.
3. Apply 2D-DWT (Haar) to the reduced watermarked channel which could be distorted due to the various attacks to obtain the four frequency sub-bands.

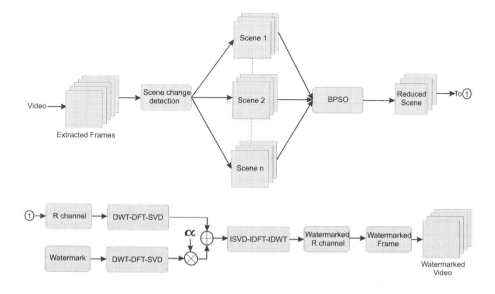

Fig. 1. Block diagram of Watermark Embedding

4. Apply 2D-DFT to LH and HL sub-bands in which the watermark was inserted during watermark embedding.
5. Apply SVD to the 2D-DFT transformed LH and HL sub-bands from step (4) to obtain U, S and V matrices.

$$A_k^* = U_k^* S_k^* V_k^{*T} \qquad \text{where} \qquad k = 1, 2 \qquad (10)$$

6. Obtain the singular matrix of LH and HL sub-bands of watermark using the Eq. [11].

$$S_{1k}^* = \frac{(S_k^* - S_k)}{\alpha} \qquad \text{where} \quad k = 1, 2 \qquad (11)$$

7. Combine S_{1k}^* with U_{1k} and V_{1k}^{T} according to the Eq. [12] to obtain B_k^*

$$B_k^* = U_{1k} S_{1k}^* V_{1k}^{T} \qquad \text{where} \quad k = 1, 2 \qquad (12)$$

8. Obtain the LH and HL sub-bands of the watermark by taking 2D-IDFT to B_1^* and B_2^*.
9. Obtain the watermark by applying 2D-IDWT to 2 sub-bands obtained above and other 2 sub-bands.

4   Analysis of Proposed Method and Experimental Results

In order to evaluate the algorithm MATLAB [13] is used as a platform and the proposed algorithm is applied to wildlife video. The size of the video considered is 512×512 (color video) and size of the watermark is 256×256. The Figs. [3a,3b]

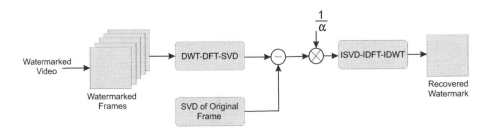

Fig. 2. Block diagram of Watermark Extraction

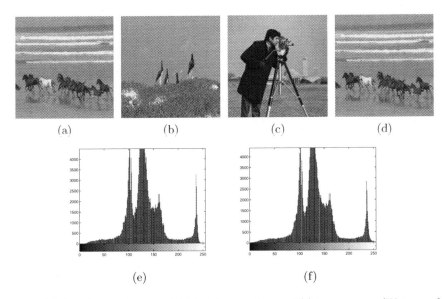

Fig. 3. (a) First frame of scene 1 (b) First frame of scene 2 (c) Cameraman (Watermark-256 × 256) (d) Watermarked frame of scene 1 (e) Histogram of Original Frame (f) Histogram of watermarked frame.

show the first frame of two different scenes extracted from the video and the Figs. [3c,3d] show Cameraman image as watermark and resulting watermarked frame of first frame of scene 1. The Figs. [4h,4i] show the R channel of video frame with robust pixels identified and reduced R channel containing only robust pixels with zeros padded at the end to accommodate the row with maximum pixels. The Figs. [3e,3f] show the histograms of host frame and watermarked frame which are similar which shows that by watermarking the host video's perceptual quality is slightly changed.

Two parameters correlation and PSNR are used to evaluate the proposed method. PSNR is calculated using Eq. [14] to evaluate the quality of the watermarked video and correlation between the original watermark and extracted watermark is calculated using Eq. [13] which shows the similarity between the original watermark and the extracted watermark and acts as a measure of the amount of information of the watermark which is unaltered.

$$corr(X,Y) = \frac{\sum\limits_{i=1}^{M}\sum\limits_{j=1}^{N}\left(X_{ij} - \overline{X}\right)\left(Y_{ij} - \overline{Y}\right)}{\sqrt{\left(\sum\limits_{i=1}^{M}\sum\limits_{j=1}^{N}\left(X_{ij} - \overline{X}\right)^2 \sum\limits_{i=1}^{M}\sum\limits_{j=1}^{N}\left(Y_{ij} - \overline{Y}\right)^2\right)}} \tag{13}$$

where X and $\overline{X}$ are the watermark and its mean respectively and Y and $\overline{Y}$ are the extracted watermark and its mean respectively.

$$PSNR = 10\log\left(\frac{255}{RMSE}\right) \tag{14}$$

$$RMSE = \sqrt{\frac{1}{MN}\left(\sum\limits_{i=1}^{M}\sum\limits_{j=1}^{N}\left(I\left(i,j\right) - \overline{I}\left(i,j\right)\right)^2\right)} \tag{15}$$

Where RMSE is root mean square error, $I\left(i,j\right)$ is the original host frame and $\overline{I}\left(i,j\right)$ is the watermarked frame.

In order to test the robustness of the proposed method, watermarked video is subjected to different types of intra-frame attacks such as geometrical, noise and illumination attacks. Geometrical attacks such as rotation (Rot), cropping (Crop) and compression (Comp), filter attacks such as gaussian filtering (Gaus), averaging (Avg), sharpening (Sharp), blurring (Blur) and motion blur (MB) and illumination attacks such as histogram equalization (Hist) and gamma intensity correction (GIC) are applied. The Figs. [4a,4b,4c,4d,4e,4f] show the frame of watermarked video subjected to motion blur, histogram equalization, rotation and extracted watermark from watermarked video frames respectively. To make the algorithm robust against inter-frame attacks such as frame averaging, frame dropping etc different watermarks are inserted into frames belonging to different scenes as proposed by [1].

In the proposed algorithm scale factor alpha was varied from 1 to 10 with increments of 1 and average values of PSNR between host frame and water-marked frame and correlation between watermark and extracted watermark are tabulated for watermark inserted in LH and HL sub-bands of host frame.

Table 1. PSNR values in dB of the watermarked frames

Scene	Frame	Pepper	Cameraman	Airplane	House	Boat
Scene 1	Frame 1	47.20	48.19	48.39	46.74	46.87
	Frame 10	47.13	48.08	48.30	46.67	46.76
	Frame 20	46.94	47.90	48.10	46.51	46.57
	Frame 30	46.93	47.90	48.13	46.48	46.57
	Frame 40	46.90	47.85	48.08	46.46	46.53
Scene 2	Frame 125	46.18	46.79	47.16	45.96	45.80
	Frame 135	46.16	46.78	47.16	45.94	45.79
	Frame 145	46.17	46.78	47.15	45.94	45.78

Table 2. Correlation coefficients of extracted watermark from R channel of watermarked video frames

Scene	Frame	Watermark	GIC	Hist	Rotation	Comp	Crop	Blur	Sharp	Avg	MB	Gaus
Scene 1	Frame 1	Pepper	0.9998	0.9419	0.9902	0.9831	0.9995	0.9417	0.9307	0.9860	0.9858	0.9865
	Frame 10		0.9997	0.9422	0.9907	0.9832	0.9995	0.9420	0.9311	0.9858	0.9853	0.9863
	Frame 20		0.9997	0.9426	0.9912	0.9837	0.9993	0.9424	0.9293	0.9852	0.9844	0.9857
	Frame 30		0.9997	0.9441	0.9910	0.9843	0.9993	0.9439	0.9292	0.9856	0.9851	0.9861
	Frame 40		0.9997	0.9457	0.9912	0.9854	0.9991	0.9455	0.9287	0.9856	0.9854	0.9861
Scene 2	Frame 125	Cameraman	0.9998	0.9464	0.9917	0.9826	0.9998	0.9462	0.8977	0.9785	0.9802	0.9789
	Frame 135		0.9993	0.9464	0.9917	0.9825	0.9998	0.9462	0.8987	0.9786	0.9803	0.9790
	Frame 145		0.9997	0.9467	0.9918	0.9826	0.9998	0.9465	0.8992	0.9788	0.9807	0.9792

Table 3. Correlation coefficients of extracted watermark from R channel of watermarked video frames

Scene	Frame	Watermark	GIC	Hist	Rotation	Comp	Crop	Blur	Sharp	Avg	MB	Gaus
Scene 1	Frame 1	Airplane	0.9986	0.9182	0.9873	0.968	0.9993	0.9178	0.9219	0.9854	0.9848	0.9860
	Frame 10		0.9986	0.9192	0.9884	0.9687	0.9992	0.9188	0.9227	0.9850	0.9842	0.9857
	Frame 20		0.9986	0.9201	0.9889	0.9696	0.9989	0.9197	0.9200	0.9843	0.9829	0.9850
	Frame 30		0.9986	0.9222	0.9889	0.9707	0.9989	0.9219	0.9201	0.9849	0.9839	0.9855
	Frame 40		0.9987	0.9248	0.9891	0.9726	0.9986	0.9244	0.9189	0.9850	0.9844	0.9856
Scene 2	Frame 125	House	0.9984	0.9185	0.9876	0.977	0.9998	0.9183	0.8441	0.9664	0.9691	0.9670
	Frame 135		0.9984	0.9186	0.9877	0.9769	0.9998	0.9184	0.8452	0.9665	0.9693	0.9672
	Frame 145		0.9984	0.9191	0.9879	0.9771	0.9998	0.9188	0.846	0.9668	0.9698	0.9675

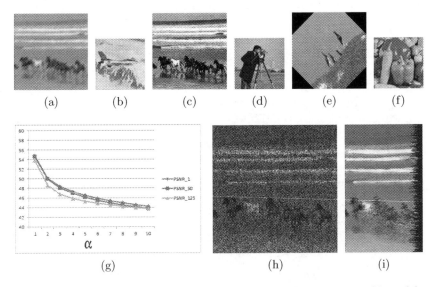

(a)   (b)   (c)   (d)   (e)   (f)

(g)   (h)   (i)

Fig. 4. (a) Motion blurred Frame (b) Extracted watermark from motion blurred frame (c) Hist-equalized Frame (d) Extracted watermark from Hist-equalized frame (e) Rotated frame $(45°)$ (f) Extracted watermark from rotated frame g) Comparison of PSNR of watermarked frames (h) R channel of first frame with robust pixels identified (i) Reduced R channel

Table 1 shows the average value of PSNR obtained for watermark inserted in R channel of frames of the video. In most of the watermarking schemes the value of α is restricted to 1, but in the proposed algorithm higher value of α (scale factor) is used since here the watermark is not directly embedded into the frames of video instead the singular values of two of the sub-bands are inserted into the frames due to which the video frames gets affected slightly. The Fig. [4g] shows the variation of PSNR for α varied from 1 to 10 for frame 1, 50 and 125 of the watermarked video which indicates that as the scale factor α increases PSNR decreases since with increase in α the weight of the watermark inserted also increases.

Tables 2 and 3 display the correlation coefficients obtained for watermark inserted in R channel of video frames. Sufficiently high correlation values are obtained as it can be observed from the table which indicates the robustness of the algorithm against different types of intra-frame attacks.

5 Conclusions

In this paper BPSO and scene change based video watermarking algorithm was proposed where BPSO is used to identify the robust pixels of video frames and scene change detection is used to insert different watermark in frames belonging to different scenes. The watermarked video is obtained by inserting the singular values of DWT+DFT transformed sub-bands into singular values of DWT+DFT transformed sub-bands of reduced video frames. The proposed method has been found to outperform both in terms of PSNR and correlation values compared to existing methods.

References

1. Chan, P.-W., Lyu, M.R.: A DWT-based Digital Video Watermarking Scheme with Error Correcting Code. In: Qing, S., Gollmann, D., Zhou, J. (eds.) ICICS 2003. LNCS, vol. 2836, pp. 202–213. Springer, Heidelberg (2003)
2. Preda, R.O., Vizireanu, D.N.: A Robust Digital Watermarking Scheme for Video Copyright Protection in the Wavelet Domain. Elsevier Journal, 1720–1726 (2010)
3. Faragallah, O.S.: Efficient Video Watermarking Based on Singular Value Decomposition in the Discrete Wavelet Transform Domain. Elsevier Journal (2012) (article in press)
4. Ansari, R., Devanalamath, M.M., Manikantan, K., Ramachandran, S.: Robust Digital Image Watermarking Algorithm in DWT-DFT-SVD Domain for Color Images. In: International Conference on Communication, Information and Computing Technology, ICCICT (2012)
5. Doerr, G., Dugelay, J.-L.: A Guide Tour of Video Watermarking. Signal Processing Image Communication Elsevier, 263–282 (2003)
6. Su, P.-C., Wu, C.-S., Chen, I.-F., Wu, C.-Y., Wu, Y.-C.: BA Practical Design of Digital Video Water- marking in H.264/AVC for Content Authentication. Elsevier Journal, 413–426 (2011)

7. Langelaar, G.C., Lagendijk, R.L.: Optimal Differential Energy Watermarking of DCT Encoded Images and Video. IEEE Transactions on Image Processing, 148–158 (2001)
8. Ghosh, P., Ghosh, R., Sinha, S., Mukhopadhyay, U., Kole, D.K., Chakroborty, A.: A Novel Digital Watermarking Technique for Video Copyright Protection. Computer Science and Information Technology, 601–609 (2012)
9. Mostafa, S.A.K., Tolba, A.S., Abdelkar, F.M., Elhindy, H.M.: Video Watermarking Scheme Based on Principal Component Analysis and Wavelet Transform. International Journal of Computer Science and Network Security (2009)
10. Boland, F.M., Kuannitlh, J.J.I., Uautzeiiberg, C.: Watermarking Digital Images for Copyright Protection. Proceedings of Image Processing and Its Applications (1995)
11. Junxiao, X., Qingbinc, L., Zhiyongc, L.: A Novel Digital Video Watermarking Algorithm. In: International Conference on Advances in Engineering, pp. 90–94. Published by Elsevier Ltd. (2011)
12. Kennedy, J., Eberhart, R.C.: A Disrete Binary Vertion of the Particle Swarm Algorithm. In: IEEE International Conference on Computational Cybernetics and Simulation, vol. 5, pp. 4104–4108 (1997)
13. http://www.mathworks.com

Slide Attacks against Iterated Hill Ciphers

Liam Keliher and Samuel Thibodeau

AceCrypt Research Group
Department of Mathematics and Computer Science
Mount Allison University
Sackville, New Brunswick, Canada
lkeliher@mta.ca

Abstract. In this paper we analyze two iterated Hill Cipher variants due to Sastry et al. The designers claim that their modifications to the classical Hill Cipher provide a high level of resistance to cryptanalysis. However, we describe how to break these iterated Hill Ciphers using a standard slide attack, and we present computational results from the implementation of our attack that confirm its effectiveness.

Keywords: cryptography, cryptanalysis, Hill Cipher, slide attack.

1 Introduction

This paper concerns the cryptanalysis of Hill Cipher variants. The Hill Cipher is a classical symmetric-key algorithm published by Lester Hill in 1929 [3]. In the Hill Cipher, each plaintext is a vector of integer values, and a plaintext is encrypted via a single multiplication with a square key matrix. This has the advantage of simplicity, but renders the cipher vulnerable to a straightforward known-plaintext attack based on linear algebra [15]. Despite this weakness (or perhaps because of it), the Hill Cipher is often described in cryptography textbooks, where it serves to introduce students to a number of important concepts, including simple block ciphers, modular arithmetic, linear algebra, and basic cryptanalysis.

A number of researchers have presented variants of the Hill Cipher that attempt to correct its security flaws [4, 11, 17, 18]. However, many of these ciphers have been subsequently attacked [5, 6, 8]. Modifications to the Hill Cipher are based on a variety of techniques, but one common approach is to add features borrowed from modern symmetric-key ciphers such as the Advanced Encryption Standard (AES) [2] — in particular, the iteration of a simpler encryption step called a *round*. Each round typically involves two or more internal *stages*, at least one of which is matrix multiplication (hence the connection to the original Hill Cipher).

This use of iterated rounds is the approach taken by Sastry et al. in a series of recent papers introducing several Hill Cipher variants [12–14]. Keliher noted that the cipher in [13] involves only simple *bitwise* operations in every stage, and can be trivially broken using a linear algebraic attack similar to the attack

Sabu M. Thampi et al. (Eds.): SSCC 2013, CCIS 377, pp. 179–190, 2013.

against the original Hill Cipher [7]. In contrast, the ciphers in [12, 14] contain rounds with stages that involve operations at both the bit level and the byte level, which appears to make them resistant to straightforward attacks such as the one in [7]. However, in the current paper we show that the modified Hill Ciphers in [12, 14] can be broken using a *slide attack*, a known/chosen-plaintext attack published by Biryukov and Wagner in 1999 [1].

For convenience we refer to the two Hill Cipher variants in [12, 14] as the Sastry et al. Hill Ciphers #1 and #2, shortened to SHC1 [12] and SHC2 [14]. Since these two ciphers are very similar, we focus primarily on SHC1. At the end of the paper we explain how our cryptanalysis of SHC1 also applies to SHC2 (and to a large family of related ciphers).

The remainder of this paper is organized as follows. In Section 2 we define some basic concepts from cryptanalysis. In Section 3 we present the Hill Cipher, and in Section 4 we give the structure of SHC1. In Section 5 we outline the slide attack. In Section 6 we describe how to use a slide attack against SHC1, and we summarize computational results from our implementation of the attack. In Section 7 we explain how our slide attack against SHC1 also works against SHC2 and closely related ciphers, and in Section 8 we conclude.

2   Basic Cryptanalysis Concepts

The primary goal of cryptanalysis applied to a symmetric-key cipher is to gain the ability to decrypt any ciphertext. Typically this involves learning the secret key, although sometimes an attacker can construct an algorithm that decrypts any ciphertext without determining the key (see [7], for example).

There are four standard general categories of attacks on symmetric-key ciphers, based on the type of data the attacker is able to obtain/capture:

1. **ciphertext-only:** attacker can obtain one or more ciphertexts
2. **known-plaintext:** attacker can obtain one or more plaintexts and the corresponding ciphertexts
3. **chosen-plaintext:** attacker can choose one or more plaintexts and obtain the corresponding ciphertexts
4. **chosen-ciphertext:** attacker can choose one or more ciphertexts and obtain the corresponding plaintexts

A well-designed cipher should be able to resist attacks in any of these categories (see [9] for additional categories). The *data complexity* of an attack is the number of plaintexts/ciphertexts that must be obtained in order for the attack to succeed, and the *time complexity* is the number of operations that must be performed. (There is no fixed definition of "operation," but often a natural unit of computational work, such as a single encryption, is used.)

The simplest attack is *exhaustive search of the key space* (also known as *brute force*). This is a known-plaintext attack in which the attacker first obtains a small number of plaintext-ciphertext pairs, $(\mathbf{P}_1, \mathbf{C}_1), (\mathbf{P}_2, \mathbf{C}_2), \ldots, (\mathbf{P}_N, \mathbf{C}_N)$, and then systematically tries all possible cipher keys until one is found that encrypts each $\mathbf{P}_i$ to the corresponding $\mathbf{C}_i$. With high probability, a candidate key that passes this test is the correct key. The data complexity of exhaustive search is small (often $N = 2$ or $N = 3$ is sufficient), but the time complexity is approximately equal to the size of the *keyspace* (the set of all keys), denoted $\#\mathcal{K}$, which is prohibitively large for most modern ciphers.

Exhaustive key search is viewed as a "baseline"—that is, an attack is considered to be significant if it has a lower time complexity than exhaustive search (but possibly a higher data complexity). This leads to another useful distinction:

- a **practical attack** is one that can be carried out in a reasonable amount of time using the computational resources available to the attacker
- an **academic attack** (or **theoretical attack**) has a data complexity or a time complexity that is too large to be practical, but still represents an improvement over exhaustive search

3   The Classical Hill Cipher

For the classical Hill Cipher, each plaintext is a vector $\mathbf{X} = (x_1, x_2, \ldots, x_n)^T$ (T denotes transposition) of length $n \geq 2$, where each x_i is an integer (mod m), with $m \geq 2$ (traditionally $m = 26$, since there are 26 letters in the English alphabet). A plaintext $\mathbf{P}$ is encrypted to the corresponding ciphertext $\mathbf{C}$ through multiplication with an $n \times n$ invertible key matrix $\mathbf{K}$, that is, $\mathbf{C} = \mathbf{KP}$ (mod m). The ciphertext is decrypted by computing $\mathbf{P} = \mathbf{K}^{-1}\mathbf{C}$ (mod m). In most situations, $\mathbf{K}$ is known only to the sender and the receiver.

The Hill Cipher is categorized as a *block cipher* because each plaintext consists of a fixed-size vector, or *block*, of values, and every block is encrypted in an identical fashion. In contrast, a *stream cipher* encrypts a continuous stream of smaller plaintext units such as bits or bytes, and the encryption operation can vary from unit to unit [9].

Here is the standard known-plaintext attack against the Hill Cipher: If an attacker can obtain n or more plaintext-ciphertext pairs such that n of the the plaintexts are linearly independent, the attacker places the linearly independent plaintexts in the columns of an $n \times n$ matrix $\mathbf{U}$, and places the corresponding ciphertexts in the columns of an $n \times n$ matrix $\mathbf{W}$. It follows that $\mathbf{KU} = \mathbf{W}$, and therefore $\mathbf{K} = \mathbf{WU}^{-1}$. Since the attacker knows $\mathbf{U}$ and $\mathbf{W}$, and can compute $\mathbf{U}^{-1}$ ($\mathbf{U}$ is guaranteed to be invertible because its columns are linearly independent), the attacker can determine the key $\mathbf{K}$, so the cipher is broken.

4   Sastry et al. Hill Cipher #1 (SHC1)

In SHC1, the key is also an invertible $n \times n$ matrix $\mathbf{K}$ with integer entries in the range $0 \ldots (m-1)$ (since all operations are performed (mod m)). A plaintext or ciphertext is an $n \times 2$ matrix (i.e., with two columns), also with entries in $0 \ldots (m-1)$. Sastry et al. use $m = 2^7 = 128$, which allows 7-bit values to be stored in each plaintext/ciphertext entry, but in general it is better to use

$m = 2^8 = 256$, since this allows any 8-bit value (byte) to be stored in each entry (this does not significantly alter the cipher). For $n = 8$ (an example value used in [12]), each plaintext/ciphertext contains 16 bytes = 128 bits, which is exactly the block size of standard symmetric-key ciphers such as the AES [2].

Let $\mathbf{P}$ denote a plaintext, and let $\mathbf{C}$ denote the corresponding ciphertext. SHC1 encrypts $\mathbf{P}$ through R rounds (the value $R = 16$ is used in [12]), each of which consists of two stages:

1. multiplication of the current block with the key matrix $\mathbf{K}$
2. permutation of the bits in the current block — Sastry et al. refer to this as *interlacing* (details below)

The last round is followed by a final multiplication with $\mathbf{K}$ to produce the ciphertext. Here is the pseudocode for encryption:

$$\mathbf{P}^0 = \mathbf{P}$$
for $r = 1$ to R
{
$$\mathbf{P}^r = \mathbf{K}\,\mathbf{P}^{r-1} \pmod{m}$$
$$Interlace\,(\mathbf{P}^r)$$
}
$$\mathbf{C} = \mathbf{K}\,\mathbf{P}^R \pmod{m}$$

And here is the pseudocode for decryption:

$$\mathbf{P}^R = \mathbf{K}^{-1}\,\mathbf{C} \pmod{m}$$
for $r = R$ down to 1
{
$$Un\text{-}Interlace\,(\mathbf{P}^r)$$
$$\mathbf{P}^{r-1} = \mathbf{K}^{-1}\,\mathbf{P}^r \pmod{m}$$
}
$$\mathbf{P} = \mathbf{P}^0$$

At any point in the encryption process, the current block $\mathbf{P}^r$ is an $n \times 2$ matrix. Since each entry consists of 8 bits, the left column of $\mathbf{P}^r$ can be represented as

$$\begin{pmatrix} a_{11}\ a_{12}\ a_{13}\ a_{14}\ a_{15}\ a_{16}\ a_{17}\ a_{18} \\ a_{21}\ a_{22}\ a_{23}\ a_{24}\ a_{25}\ a_{26}\ a_{27}\ a_{28} \\ \ldots \\ a_{n1}\ a_{n2}\ a_{n3}\ a_{n4}\ a_{n5}\ a_{n6}\ a_{n7}\ a_{n8} \end{pmatrix} \tag{1}$$

and the right column of $\mathbf{P}^r$ can be represented as

$$\begin{pmatrix} b_{11}\ b_{12}\ b_{13}\ b_{14}\ b_{15}\ b_{16}\ b_{17}\ b_{18} \\ b_{21}\ b_{22}\ b_{23}\ b_{24}\ b_{25}\ b_{26}\ b_{27}\ b_{28} \\ \ldots \\ b_{n1}\ b_{n2}\ b_{n3}\ b_{n4}\ b_{n5}\ b_{n6}\ b_{n7}\ b_{n8} \end{pmatrix} \tag{2}$$

where a_{ij} and b_{ij} are individual bits. The *Interlace*( ) operation permutes the bits of $\mathbf{P}^r$ by alternating bits from the left and right columns. For $n = 8$, the resulting left column of *Interlace* $(\mathbf{P}^r)$ is

$$\begin{pmatrix} a_{11}\ b_{11}\ a_{12}\ b_{12}\ a_{13}\ b_{13}\ a_{14}\ b_{14} \\ a_{15}\ b_{15}\ a_{16}\ b_{16}\ a_{17}\ b_{17}\ a_{18}\ b_{18} \\ a_{21}\ b_{21}\ a_{22}\ b_{22}\ a_{23}\ b_{23}\ a_{24}\ b_{24} \\ a_{25}\ b_{25}\ a_{26}\ b_{26}\ a_{27}\ b_{27}\ a_{28}\ b_{28} \\ a_{31}\ b_{31}\ a_{32}\ b_{32}\ a_{33}\ b_{33}\ a_{34}\ b_{34} \\ a_{35}\ b_{35}\ a_{36}\ b_{36}\ a_{37}\ b_{37}\ a_{38}\ b_{38} \\ a_{41}\ b_{41}\ a_{42}\ b_{42}\ a_{43}\ b_{43}\ a_{44}\ b_{44} \\ a_{45}\ b_{45}\ a_{46}\ b_{46}\ a_{47}\ b_{47}\ a_{48}\ b_{48} \end{pmatrix} \qquad (3)$$

and the resulting right column of *Interlace* $(\mathbf{P}^r)$ is

$$\begin{pmatrix} a_{51}\ b_{51}\ a_{52}\ b_{52}\ a_{53}\ b_{53}\ a_{54}\ b_{54} \\ a_{55}\ b_{55}\ a_{56}\ b_{56}\ a_{57}\ b_{57}\ a_{58}\ b_{58} \\ a_{61}\ b_{61}\ a_{62}\ b_{62}\ a_{63}\ b_{63}\ a_{64}\ b_{64} \\ a_{65}\ b_{65}\ a_{66}\ b_{66}\ a_{67}\ b_{67}\ a_{68}\ b_{68} \\ a_{71}\ b_{71}\ a_{72}\ b_{72}\ a_{73}\ b_{73}\ a_{74}\ b_{74} \\ a_{75}\ b_{75}\ a_{76}\ b_{76}\ a_{77}\ b_{77}\ a_{78}\ b_{78} \\ a_{81}\ b_{81}\ a_{82}\ b_{82}\ a_{83}\ b_{83}\ a_{84}\ b_{84} \\ a_{85}\ b_{85}\ a_{86}\ b_{86}\ a_{87}\ b_{87}\ a_{88}\ b_{88} \end{pmatrix} \qquad (4)$$

The *Un-Interlace*( ) operation is simply the inverse (reverse) of *Interlace*( ). For other values of n and m, *Interlace*( ) can be generalized in an obvious way.

5   The Slide Attack

It is easy to see that exhaustive key search is not effective against SHC1 when reasonable parameters are chosen. For example, when $n = 4$ and $m = 256$, it follows from [10] that the number of keys is

$$\#\mathcal{K} \ = \ 2^{7 \times 16} \prod_{t=0}^{3} (2^4 - 2^t) \ \approx \ 1.05 \times 10^{38} \qquad (5)$$

This is impractically large, so exhaustive search is impossible. Therefore, we look for other attacks that can break SHC1 with a much lower time complexity. One such attack is the slide attack.

Biryukov and Wagner introduced the slide attack in 1999 [1]. It is a known-plaintext or chosen-plaintext attack that targets iterated block ciphers in which *all rounds are identical, including the key values used inside each round.* Most iterated block published since 1999 have been designed to defend against slide attacks by ensuring that no two rounds are exactly the same, but this is not the case for SHC1/SHC2. One of the main observations of this paper is that *the use of identical rounds in SHC1/SHC2 is a significant design flaw.*

5.1   Attack Details

For a cipher with identical rounds, let **round**() denote a single round. The slide attack is based on the following assumptions:

- **Assumption 1:**   The attacker can capture a set of plaintext-ciphertext pairs $(\mathbf{P}_1, \mathbf{C}_1), \ldots, (\mathbf{P}_N, \mathbf{C}_N)$, where N may be large.
- **Assumption 2:**   There exist *pairs of pairs* $(\mathbf{P}_A, \mathbf{C}_A) / (\mathbf{P}_B, \mathbf{C}_B)$, with $1 \leq A, B \leq N$ and $A \neq B$, for which encrypting $\mathbf{P}_A$ through exactly one round produces $\mathbf{P}_B$, i.e., $\mathbf{P}_B = \textbf{round}(\mathbf{P}_A)$. Such a pair of pairs is called a *slid pair*.
- **Assumption 3:**   If the attacker can obtain an input $\mathbf{X}$ and the corresponding output $\mathbf{Y}$ *for a single round*, then this information can be exploited to find the key used inside that round (and hence inside every other round).

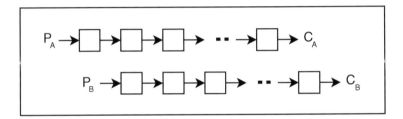

Fig. 1. Schematic of slide attack

From now on we refer to any pair of pairs (including a slid pair) as a *POP*. The idea behind the slide attack is illustrated in Figure 1. We make two observations:

1. If $(\mathbf{P}_A, \mathbf{C}_A) / (\mathbf{P}_B, \mathbf{C}_B)$ is a slid pair, then by definition $\mathbf{P}_B = \textbf{round}(\mathbf{P}_A)$, so $\mathbf{P}_A$ and $\mathbf{P}_B$ can be used to obtain the key used in a single round (based on *Assumption 3*).
2. If $(\mathbf{P}_A, \mathbf{C}_A) / (\mathbf{P}_B, \mathbf{C}_B)$ is a slid pair, then the encryption of $\mathbf{P}_B$ through R rounds is essentially the same as the encryption of $\mathbf{P}_A$ through R rounds, except that the encryption of $\mathbf{P}_B$ is shifted (slid) one round to the right. It follows that $\mathbf{C}_B = \textbf{round}(\mathbf{C}_A)$, and therefore $\mathbf{C}_A$ and $\mathbf{C}_B$ can also be used to obtain the key used in a single round.

In keeping with *Assumption 3*, given any two block-sized values $\mathbf{X}$ and $\mathbf{Y}$, define $\textbf{key}(\mathbf{X}, \mathbf{Y})$ to be the key that is needed to map $\mathbf{X}$ to $\mathbf{Y}$ through a single round. (*Note that such a key may not always exist.*) Clearly if $(\mathbf{P}_A, \mathbf{C}_A) / (\mathbf{P}_B, \mathbf{C}_B)$ *is* a slid pair, then $\textbf{key}(\mathbf{P}_A, \mathbf{P}_B) = \textbf{key}(\mathbf{C}_A, \mathbf{C}_B)$ is the correct key $\mathbf{K}$ used inside each round. On the other hand, given a random POP $(\mathbf{P}_i, \mathbf{C}_i) / (\mathbf{P}_j, \mathbf{C}_j)$, in general the attacker cannot know for certain that this POP is a slid pair since this would require being able to encrypt $\mathbf{P}_i$ through one round to see if the result is $\mathbf{P}_j$, which the attacker cannot do without knowing $\mathbf{K}$. However, the attacker can use the following test to determine whether or not $(\mathbf{P}_i, \mathbf{C}_i)$ / $(\mathbf{P}_j, \mathbf{C}_j)$ is *probably* a slid pair:

TEST: For any POP $(\mathbf{P}_i, \mathbf{C}_i)$ / $(\mathbf{P}_j, \mathbf{C}_j)$, if $\boldsymbol{key}(\mathbf{P}_i, \mathbf{P}_j)$ and $\boldsymbol{key}(\mathbf{C}_i, \mathbf{C}_j)$ both exist, and if $\boldsymbol{key}(\mathbf{P}_i, \mathbf{P}_j) = \boldsymbol{key}(\mathbf{C}_i, \mathbf{C}_j)$, then this POP is very likely a slid pair.

The reason this test works is that if $(\mathbf{P}_i, \mathbf{C}_i)$ / $(\mathbf{P}_j, \mathbf{C}_j)$ is a randomly chosen POP that is *not* a slid pair, then even if $\boldsymbol{key}(\mathbf{P}_i, \mathbf{P}_j)$ and $\boldsymbol{key}(\mathbf{C}_i, \mathbf{C}_j)$ both exist, they should be uncorrelated (for a reasonably strong cipher), and therefore the probability that they are equal is very small. If $\boldsymbol{key}(\mathbf{P}_i, \mathbf{P}_j)$ does equal $\boldsymbol{key}(\mathbf{C}_i, \mathbf{C}_j)$, then with high probability $(\mathbf{P}_i, \mathbf{C}_i)$ / $(\mathbf{P}_j, \mathbf{C}_j)$ is a slid pair and $\mathbf{k} = \boldsymbol{key}(\mathbf{P}_i, \mathbf{P}_j) = \boldsymbol{key}(\mathbf{C}_i, \mathbf{C}_j)$ is the correct key $\mathbf{K}$ used inside each round (we call $\mathbf{k}$ a *guess* for $\mathbf{K}$). The attacker can "double check" $\mathbf{k}$ by encrypting two or three plaintexts through the full cipher (R rounds) using $\mathbf{k}$ as the key. If these plaintexts encrypt to the corresponding ciphertexts, the attacker can be confident that $\mathbf{k} = \mathbf{K}$, and the cipher is broken.

Note that in describing the slide attack, we have not made use of the number of rounds, R, because *the slide attack is equally effective no matter how many rounds the cipher has.* This is interesting in light of a standard design assumption for symmetric-key ciphers, namely that the strength of a cipher increases as the number of rounds increases [9].

5.2 Attack Pseudocode

The above discussion leads to the following simple slide attack pseudocode:

> **Data Collection Phase:**
> capture N plaintext-ciphertext pairs $(\mathbf{P}_1, \mathbf{C}_1), \ldots, (\mathbf{P}_N, \mathbf{C}_N)$
>
> **Data Processing Phase:**
> for all i, j with $1 \le i, j \le N$ and $i \ne j$
> {
>   let $\mathbf{k} = \boldsymbol{key}(\mathbf{P}_i, \mathbf{P}_j)$
>   let $\mathbf{k}^* = \boldsymbol{key}(\mathbf{C}_i, \mathbf{C}_j)$
>   if $\mathbf{k}$ and $\mathbf{k}^*$ both exist, and if $\mathbf{k} = \mathbf{k}^*$
>   {
> $\mathbf{k}$ is a guess for $\mathbf{K}$, so double check $\mathbf{k}$
>   (if $\mathbf{k}$ passes the double check, terminate the
>   algorithm, since with high probability $\mathbf{k} = \mathbf{K}$)
>   }
> }

5.3   Data and Time Complexity

According to Biryukov and Wagner, the probability that the slide attack will succeed in finding the key increases as the number of plaintext-ciphertext pairs, N (the data complexity), increases. In particular, if $N = \sqrt{\#\mathcal{P}}$, where $\#\mathcal{P}$ is the total number of plaintexts, then the probability of success is approximately 50% [1]. Since the time complexity is proportional to the number of POPs, and since the number of POPs is approximately N^2, it follows that when $N = \sqrt{\#\mathcal{P}}$, the time complexity is in the order of $N^2 = \left(\sqrt{\#\mathcal{P}}\right)^2 = \#\mathcal{P}$. This will be better than exhaustive key search when $\#\mathcal{P}$ is less than $\#\mathcal{K}$.

It follows from the above that if *Assumptions 1, 2,* and *3* hold, and if the attacker is able to perform roughly $N^2 = \#\mathcal{P}$ operations, then the slide attack is a practical attack (with success rate approximately 50%). For many ciphers with identical rounds, $\#\mathcal{P}$ is prohibitively large, and therefore the slide attack is at best an academic attack, but for other ciphers it is practical. This is the case for SHC1/SHC2 with certain choices of parameters.

6   Applying the Slide Attack to SHC1

We now demonstrate how to use the slide attack as a known-plaintext attack against SHC1. One important problem is that *Assumption 3 does not hold for most values of $n \geq 2$*. In fact, *Assumption 3* only holds fully when $n = 2$ (in general, we ignore $n = 1$ for Hill Ciphers variants). This is because in order to find the value of an unknown $n \times n$ invertible matrix such as $\mathbf{K}$, we need n linearly independent input vectors and their corresponding output vectors [16]. When $n = 2$, if $\mathbf{X}$ is an input and $\mathbf{Y}$ is an output for one round of SHC1, and if $\mathbf{X}$ is invertible (note that $\mathbf{X}$ and $\mathbf{Y}$ are *square*), then the two columns of $\mathbf{X}$ are n linearly independent input vectors for $\mathbf{K}$, and the columns of *Un-Interlace*$(\mathbf{Y})$ are the matching output vectors.

On the other hand, when $n \geq 3$, the two columns of $\mathbf{X}$ do not give us the n input vectors we need. However, we can still adapt the basic slide attack to work against SHC1 when $n = 3, 4$, because for any slid pair $(\mathbf{P}_i, \mathbf{C}_i) \,/\, (\mathbf{P}_j, \mathbf{C}_j)$, the columns of $\mathbf{P}_i$ and the columns of $\mathbf{P}_j$ *together* give us four input vectors for $\mathbf{K}$ (we elaborate on this in Section 6.2). This approach fails for $n \geq 5$, though, since in this case a POP no longer contains enough information to determine $\mathbf{K}$.

On the basis of the above discussion, we present two versions of our attack.

6.1   Attack Version 1 $(n = 2)$

When $n = 2$ and $m = 2^B$, it follows that $\#\mathcal{P} = 2^{4B}$, so the slide attack has data complexity $\sqrt{2^{4B}} = 2^{2B}$ and time complexity 2^{4B} for a success rate of approximately 50%. Let $\mathbf{X}$ and $\mathbf{Y}$ be an input and an output, respectively, for one SHC1 round. We know that

$$\mathbf{Y} = Interlace\,(\mathbf{KX}) \tag{6}$$

so

$$Un\text{-}Interlace\,(\mathbf{Y}) = \mathbf{KX} \tag{7}$$

and therefore

$$Un\text{-}Interlace\,(\mathbf{Y})\,\mathbf{X}^{-1} = \mathbf{K} = \boldsymbol{key}\,(\mathbf{X}, \mathbf{Y}) \tag{8}$$

as long as $\mathbf{X}$ is invertible. It follows that any POP $(\mathbf{P}_i, \mathbf{C}_i)\,/\,(\mathbf{P}_j, \mathbf{C}_j)$ that passes the test in Section 5.1 satisfies

$$\mathbf{k} = Un\text{-}Interlace\,(\mathbf{P}_j)\,\mathbf{P}_i^{-1} = Un\text{-}Interlace\,(\mathbf{C}_j)\,\mathbf{C}_i^{-1} = \mathbf{k}^* \tag{9}$$

Here $\mathbf{P}_i$ and $\mathbf{C}_i$ are playing the role of $\mathbf{X}$, and $\mathbf{P}_j$ and $\mathbf{C}_j$ are playing the role of $\mathbf{Y}$. Clearly this requires that both $\mathbf{P}_i$ and $\mathbf{C}_i$ be invertible, which means that we will reject any POP for which this is not the case. However, we can loosen this restriction so that we reject fewer POPs by considering three cases:

- **Case 1:** If $\mathbf{P}_i$ and $\mathbf{C}_i$ are both invertible, compute $\mathbf{k}$ and $\mathbf{k}^*$ and test if $\mathbf{k} = \mathbf{k}^*$ as usual. If so, double check $\mathbf{k}$ (see Section 5.1).
- **Case 2:** If $\mathbf{P}_i$ is invertible but $\mathbf{C}_i$ is not, let $\mathbf{k} = Un\text{-}Interlace\,(\mathbf{P}_j)\,\mathbf{P}_i^{-1}$. Now test $\mathbf{k}$ by encrypting $\mathbf{C}_i$ through one round using $\mathbf{k}$ as the key. If the resulting output is $\mathbf{C}_j$, then $\mathbf{k}$ passes the test (this is the counterpart of testing if $\mathbf{k} = \mathbf{k}^*$ in **Case 1**). If so, double check $\mathbf{k}$.
- **Case 3:** This case is the mirror image of **Case 2**, with $\mathbf{P}_i$ and $\mathbf{C}_i$ interchanged, and with $\mathbf{P}_j$ and $\mathbf{C}_j$ interchanged.

As we will see in Section 6.3, Version 1 of our attack works as predicted. The main deficiency of Version 1 is that the time complexity (2^{4B}) is the same as the time complexity of exhaustive key search, since it is also the case that $\#\mathcal{K} = 2^{4B}$, which means that the attack is not significant. We rectify this by moving to $n = 3, 4$ in Version 2.

6.2   Attack Version 2 ($n = 3, 4$)

As noted earlier in Section 6, when $n = 3$ or $n = 4$, although we can no longer compute $\boldsymbol{key}\,(\mathbf{P}_i, \mathbf{P}_j)$ and $\boldsymbol{key}\,(\mathbf{C}_i, \mathbf{C}_j)$, a slid pair may still contain enough information to determine $\mathbf{K}$. For each POP $(\mathbf{P}_i, \mathbf{C}_i)\,/\,(\mathbf{P}_j, \mathbf{C}_j)$ in the data processing phase of the slide attack (Section 5.2), we carry out the steps below. For compactness, let $U(\mathbf{Z}) = Un\text{-}Interlace\,(\mathbf{Z})$ for any $n \times 2$ matrix $\mathbf{Z}$. As before, T denotes transposition.

1. Form the following $4 \times 2n$ matrix:

$$\mathbf{M} = \begin{pmatrix} \mathbf{P}_i^T & U(\mathbf{P}_j)^T \\ \mathbf{C}_i^T & U(\mathbf{C}_j)^T \end{pmatrix} \tag{10}$$

2. Using Gaussian elimination [16], attempt to transform the top n rows of the left half of $\mathbf{M}$ into the $n \times n$ identity matrix (with all operations performed (mod m)), and let $\mathbf{M}'$ be the resulting $4 \times 2n$ matrix. If this transformation is impossible, proceed to the next POP. If this transformation succeeds, there are three cases (these are the only possibilities):

- **Case 1:** If $n = 4$, let $\mathbf{k}$ be the transpose of the 4×4 matrix in the right half of $\mathbf{M}'$. Then $\mathbf{k}$ is a guess for $\mathbf{K}$, so double check $\mathbf{k}$.
- **Case 2:** If $n = 3$, and if the entire bottom (fourth) row of $\mathbf{M}'$ contains zeros, let $\mathbf{k}$ be the transpose of the 3×3 matrix in the top three rows of the right half of $\mathbf{M}'$. Then $\mathbf{k}$ is a guess for $\mathbf{K}$, so double check $\mathbf{k}$.
- **Case 3:** If $n = 3$, and if the left half of the bottom row of $\mathbf{M}'$ contains only zeros, but the right half of the bottom row contains at least one nonzero entry, proceed to the next POP.

Rationale: If the current POP is a slid pair, then the left half of $\mathbf{M}$ contains four input (row) vectors for $\mathbf{K}$, and the right half contains the corresponding output (row) vectors. In this case, Gaussian elimination will enable us to find $\mathbf{K}$ unless the four vectors in the left half of $\mathbf{M}$ are not sufficiently linearly independent, i.e., if the rank of the left half of $\mathbf{M}$ is *less than* n. We will detect this because it will be impossible to transform the top n rows of the left half of $\mathbf{M}$ into the $n \times n$ identity matrix. If the current POP is *not* a slid pair, then in general there is no simple correlation between the left and right halves of $\mathbf{M}$, so the probability is extremely low that the above process will produce a correct guess for $\mathbf{K}$. (Note that Case 3 represents a situation in which, first, the POP $(\mathbf{P}_i, \mathbf{C}_i)$ / $(\mathbf{P}_j, \mathbf{C}_j)$ is not a slid pair, and, second, some of the information placed in $\mathbf{M}$ corresponds to an *inconsistent* system of linear equations [16].)

Unlike Version 1, Version 2 of our attack has lower time complexity than exhaustive key search. For example, if $n = 3$ and $m = 256$, $\#\mathcal{P} = 2^{48}$ and $\#\mathcal{K} = 2^{72}$. In general, if $n = 3$ or $n = 4$, and $m = 2^B$,

$$\#\mathcal{P} = 2^{2nB} < \#\mathcal{K} = 2^{n^2 B} \tag{11}$$

6.3   Computational Results

We first implemented SHC1, and then implemented Version 1 and Version 2 of the slide attack as described above. All code was written in C++, compiled using GNU g++ with optimization switch -O3, and executed on a Dell Optiplex 790 with four 3.4 GHz cores running Ubuntu. Since the slide attack is computationally intensive, we used values of m less than $2^8 = 256$. Each time we carried out the attack for a particular choice of parameters, we ran multiple trials, and each trial used its own randomly generated key and plaintext-ciphertext pairs.

Version 1 Results. For $m = 2^5$ (so $\#\mathcal{P} = 2^{20}$), we ran 100 trials. The attack succeeded in finding the correct key in 46 of these 100 trials, which closely matches the predicted 50% success rate. Each trial took an average of 2.25 seconds. We then increased N from 2^{10} to 2^{11}, and ran another 100 trials. This time the attack was successful in 93 out of 100 trials, and each trial took an average of 9.27 seconds. This larger number of successful trials supports the theory of Biryukov and Wagner that the success rate of the slide attack increases as the data complexity increases [1].

Version 2 Results. For Version 2, we restricted our attention to $n = 3$, since $n = 4$ became too computationally demanding for short trials. For $m = 2^5$ (so $\#\mathcal{P} = 2^{30}$), we ran 20 trials. The attack was successful in 9 of these 20 trials, and each trial took an average of 2.7 hours. We then reduced m to 2^4 (so $\#\mathcal{P} = 2^{24}$) and ran 100 trials. The attack was successful in 51 of these 100 trials, and each trial took an average of 148 seconds.

Overall, our experimental results confirm that the slide attack works against SHC1 as predicted, despite the claims of Sastry et al. that SHC1 is able to resist existing cryptanalytic techniques [12].

7   SHC2 and Related Ciphers

SHC2 is identical in structure to SHC1, except that instead of the *Interlace( )* step in each round, SHC2 uses another bitwise permutation called *Interweave( )*. The *Interweave( )* operation involves placing the bits of the current block in a binary matrix, and then circularly shifting every second column upward (beginning with the first column) and circularly shifting every second row to the left (starting with the second row). Note that this has no effect on the resistance of SHC2 to the slide attack, since we can simply use *Un-Interweave( )* in place of *Un-Interlace( )* in our attack. In fact, replacing *Interlace( )* in SHC1 with *any* invertible bitwise permutation produces a cipher in the same "family" as SHC1 whose vulnerability to the slide attack is exactly the same as that of SHC1.

8   Conclusion

In this paper we have shown that two very similar iterated Hill Cipher variants due to Sastry et al. (SHC1 and SHC2) can be broken with slide attacks, despite the designers' claims that these ciphers are resistant to known cryptanalytic techniques. To support our claim, we implemented a slide attack against SHC1, and we presented the computational results of our work. We also explained why SHC2 (or any of a large number of related ciphers) has the same vulnerability to the slide attack as SHC1.

Acknowledgments. Funding for this research was provided by the Natural Sciences and Engineering Research Council of Canada (NSERC).

References

1. Biryukov, A., Wagner, D.: Slide Attacks. In: Knudsen, L.R. (ed.) FSE 1999. LNCS, vol. 1636, pp. 245–259. Springer, Heidelberg (1999)
2. Daemen, J., Rijmen, V.: The Design of Rijndael: AES - The Advanced Encryption Standard. Springer, Berlin (2002)

3. Hill, L.S.: Cryptography in an Algebraic Alphabet. Amer. Math. Monthly 36, 306–312 (1929)
4. Ismail, I.A., Amin, M., Diab, H.: How to Repair the Hill Cipher. J. Zhejiang Univ. Sci. A 7, 2022–2030 (2006)
5. Li, C., Zhang, D., Chen, G.: Cryptanalysis of an Image Encryption Scheme Based on the Hill Cipher. J. Zhejiang Univ. Sci. A 9, 1118–1123 (2008)
6. Lin, C.H., Lee, C.Y., Lee, C.Y.: Comments on Saeednia's Improved Scheme for the Hill Cipher. J. Chinese Inst. Engrs. 27, 743–746 (2004)
7. Keliher, L.: Cryptanalysis of a Modified Hill Cipher. Internat. J. Comp. Netw. Secur. 2, 122–126 (2010)
8. Keliher, L., Delaney, A.Z.: Cryptanalysis of the Toorani-Falahati Hill Ciphers. In: 22nd IEEE Symposium on Computers and Communications. IEEE Press, New York (to appear)
9. Menezes, A.J., van Oorschot, P.C., Vanstone, S.A.: Handbook of Applied Cryptography. CRC Press, Boca Raton (1997)
10. Overbey, J., Traves, W., Wojdylo, J.: On the Keyspace of the Hill Cipher. Cryptologia 29, 59–72 (2005)
11. Saeedinia, S.: How to Make the Hill Cipher Secure. Cryptologia 24, 353–360 (2000)
12. Sastry, V.U.K., Shankar, N.R.: Modified Hill Cipher with Interlacing and Iteration. J. Comp. Sci. 3, 854–859 (2007)
13. Sastry, V.U.K., Murthy, D.S.R., Bhavani, S.D.: A Block Cipher Involving a Key Applied on Both Sides of the Plain Text. Internat. J. Comp. Netw. Secur. 1, 27–30 (2009)
14. Sastry, V.U.K., Shankar, N.R., Bhavani, S.D.: A Modified Hill Cipher Involving Interweaving and Iteration. Internat. J. Netw. Secur. 11, 11–16 (2010)
15. Stallings, W.: Cryptography and Network Security: Principles and Practice, 5th edn. Prentice Hall, Boston (2011)
16. Strang, G.: Introduction to Linear Algebra, 4th edn. Wellesley-Cambridge Press, Wellesley (2009)
17. Toorani, M., Falahati, A.: A Secure Variant of the Hill Cipher. In: 18th IEEE Symposium on Computers and Communications, pp. 313–316. IEEE Press, New York (2009)
18. Toorani, M., Falahati, A.: A Secure Cryptosystem Based on Affine Transformation. J. Secur. Commun. Networks 4, 207–215 (2011)

Efficient Hierarchical Key Management Scheme Based on Polynomial Construction

B.R. Purushothama and B.B. Amberker

Department of Computer Science and Engineering
National Institute of Technology Warangal,
Warangal, Andhra Pradesh-506004, India
{puru,bba}@nitw.ac.in

Abstract. In this paper, we propose a hierarchical key management scheme based on polynomial interpolation technique. We review the existing hierarchical key management schemes based on polynomial interpolation technique for public space, private space, key derivation cost and forward/backward security requirements. The proposed scheme has several features. Only one key is stored by the user of any security class. The key derivation process requires only one polynomial evaluation and hash computations. We compare the proposed scheme with the schemes based on polynomial interpolation and show that our scheme is efficient. Our proposed scheme satisfies backward secrecy and forward secrecy requirements upon new class addition and existing class deletion respectively. Only one polynomial construction is required for rekeying during new class addition and existing class deletion. The proposed scheme is secure against common subordinate and collaborative attacks.

Keywords: Hierarchical, Key management, Polynomial Interpolation, Rekeying.

1 Introduction

Suppose $C = \{C_1, \ldots, C_n\}$ be the disjoint set of security classes. A security class can represent a person, a department or a user group in an organization. A partially ordered set (POSET) is a pair $(C, \leq)$. The relation "$\leq$" is reflexive, anti-symmetric and transitive defined on C. The relation $C_i \leq C_j$ between security classes C_i and C_j specifies that the users in security class C_i have higher clearance than the users in C_j. In other words, the users in C_i can access the data of users in C_j but the vice versa is not allowed. C_i is the predecessor of C_j and C_j is the successor of C_i. If $C_j \leq C_k \leq C_i$, then C_k is the immediate successor of C_i and C_j is the immediate successor of C_k. A hierarchy with the partially ordered relation can be represented by a directed graph G, where nodes corresponds to security classes and edges indicates the ordering. A user who is entitled to have access to certain class obtains access to that class and its descendants (successors) in the hierarchy. Figure 1 shows a hierarchy of 10 security classes. The following are the relations in the hierarchy; $SC_j \leq SC_1$ for $j = 2, \ldots, 10$, $SC_j \leq SC_2$ for $j = 5, 6, 8, 9$, $SC_j \leq$

Sabu M. Thampi et al. (Eds.): SSCC 2013, CCIS 377, pp. 191–202, 2013.

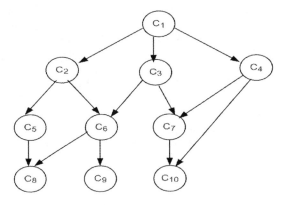

Fig. 1. A hiearchy with 10 security classes

SC_3 for $j = 6, 7, 8, 9, 10$, $SC_j \leq SC_4$ for $j = 7, 10$, $SC_8 \leq SC_5$, $SC_8 \leq SC_6$, $SC_9 \leq SC_6$, $SC_{10} \leq SC_7$, and for $i = 1, \ldots, 10$, $SC_i \leq SC_i$. For the relation $SC_8 \leq SC_1$, there is a path of length 3 in Figure 1. The users of the class SC_1 can access the data of the class C_8 but the users of class C_8 cannot access the data of C_1. Consider the relation $C_7 \leq C_3 \leq C_1$. Class C_7 is the successor and class C_3 is the immediate successor of class C_1.

A hierarchical key management scheme assigns keys to the security classes and distributes the subsets of the keys to a user, which permit the user to obtain access to the objects in his/her class and the all of the descendant classes. The hierarchical key management schemes are usually evaluated by the number of total keys the system must maintain, the number of keys each user receives, the size of the public information, the time required to derive keys of security classes, and the work needed when the hierarchy or the set of users change. Hierarchies of classes are used in many domains. Role Based Access Control (RBAC) models [14] are the traditional examples using the hierarchies. Hierarchies find useful in applications like content distribution wherein the users receive the content of different quality, cable TV, project development, defence in depth, military etc. Broadly, hierarchical access control is used in operating systems [7], databases [6] and in computer networking [12,13].

2   Security Requirements

In this section, we define the security requirements that a secure hierarchical key management scheme should satisfy upon new security class addition to the existing hierarchy and existing security class deletion from a hierarchy. Consider a POSET hierarchy with n security classes.

2.1   Backward Secrecy

Consider an event of adding a new security class to an existing hierarchy. Suppose $C_j \leq C_i, i, j \in [1, n], i \neq j$ be the existing relation. Let S_i and S_j be the set of successor classes of C_i and C_j respectively. Consider addition of new class $C_k, k \notin [1, n]$ such that $C_j \leq C_k \leq C_i$. Providing backward security means that, when a new class C_k is added, the users of C_k should not be able to access the past communications of C_j and classes in S_j.

2.2 Forward Secrecy

Consider an event of deleting an existing security class from a hierarchy. Suppose $C_j \leq C_k \leq C_i$ where, $i, j, k \in [1, n]$, $i \neq j \neq k$ be the existing relation. Let S_i and S_j be the set of successor classes of C_i and C_j respectively. Consider deleting class C_k such that the relation $C_j \leq C_k \leq C_i$ becomes $C_j \leq C_i$. Providing forward security means that, when a new class C_k is deleted, the users of C_k should not be able to access the future communications of classes in S_j.

3   Related Work

There are several hierarchical key management schemes based on the polynomial interpolation technique. Chang et al. [2] and Liew et al. [11] proposed schemes based on Newton's polynomial interpolation method and one-way functions. The key derivation process in [2] is inefficient as it requires a user of any class to carry out iterative (repeated) polynomial interpolations and one-way function evaluations. Suppose the length of the path from a class to a target successor class is l, then the scheme requires l polynomial interpolations followed by l one-way function evaluations to derive the key of the target successor class. The scheme in [11] follows the same approach of repeated polynomial interpolations and one-way function evaluations as in [2]. Therefore, the key derivation process is inefficient. Chang et al. [3] also uses the polynomial interpolation method for hierarchical key management; However, their scheme requires users of each class to store 2 keys and prior to construction of a polynomial of degree t for each class (assuming that each class has t successors) central authority (CA) should carry out $2t$ modular exponentiation operations. To derive the key of any successor class a user needs to carry out 3 modular exponentiations followed by a polynomial evaluation. Therefore, this key derivation process is also inefficient. Shen et al. [15] proposed a scheme based on polynomial interpolation and discrete logarithms. Hsu and Wu [10] pointed out a security weakness of Shen et al. scheme; where, the users in a class can have access to the data of classes which are not its successors. Precisely, if the two classes in the hierarchy have the same immediate successor, then the data owned by the successor is accessible to class which is not authorized to access it. Thus, the scheme is insecure. Also, the scheme suffers from large computational overhead. Das et al. [5] proposed a scheme based on polynomial interpolation. However, each user of a class has to store $n + 1$ secret keys, where n is the number of successors. Though, it is mentioned that there is no need of public information, the scheme inherently requires the public information proportional to the number of edges in the graph representing hierarchy. The scheme also uses encryption for assigning the keys to the classes. So, to assign the keys to the n security classes, it requires n encryption operations. Also, the scheme does not satisfy the forward secrecy and backward secrecy requirements upon new class addition and existing class deletion. In [16], each user of a class needs to store $O(n)$ secret keys (n is the number of nodes in the hierarchy). Giri et al. [8] have proposed a scheme based on Newton's polynomial interpolation technique where, the number of polynomial interpolations for a class is proportional to the number of successors of the class. Also, modular exponentiations are required for generating the keys and for computing the points for polynomial interpolations. The key derivation is inefficient as it requires 3 multiplications, 2 modular exponentiation, a hash computation, a decryption operation and a polynomial evaluation.

3.1   Our Contribution

We propose a hierarchical key management scheme based on the polynomial interpolation technique. In our proposed scheme, each user of a class stores only one key and one polynomial evaluation and only few hash function computations (bounded by the position of the target successor class in the level order traversal of the subtree rooted at a class to which user belongs in a hierarchy) are required to derive the key of any successor class. For each class, the public information is proportional to the number of it's successors. Our scheme is efficient compared to the other hierarchical key management schemes based on polynomial interpolation technique. Our scheme does not use any costly encryption, decryption or modular exponentiation during key computation and key derivation. Also, the scheme does not use any additional public information other than the public polynomials. We have compared our scheme with the other schemes existing in the literature and show that our scheme is efficient. Our proposed scheme handles the dynamic operations of new class addition to the hierarchy and existing class deletion from the hierarchy. We have commented on the security of the proposed scheme and show that indeed the proposed hierarchical key management scheme is secure.

We also provide a scheme that satisfies the forward and backward security requirements in hierarchical group communication. Only one polynomial construction is needed for rekeying upon new class addition and existing class deletion. We show that the proposed scheme is secure against collaborative and common subordinate attacks.

4   The Lagrange Form of the Interpolation Polynomial

Given a set of k points, $\{(x_1, y_1), \ldots, (x_j, y_j), \ldots, (x_k, y_k)\}$ where no two x_j are same, the *interpolation polynomial in the Lagrange form* is the linear combination,

$$P(x) = \sum_{j=1}^{k-1} y_j l_j(x) \tag{1}$$

of Lagrange's basis polynomials

$$l_j(x) = \prod_{1 \le i \le k, i \ne j} \frac{x - x_i}{x_j - x_i}$$

The degree of the polynomial $P(x)$ is less than or equal to $k - 1$.

Lagrange's form of polynomial interpolation and the complexity details are provided in [1,4,9].

5   Proposed Hierarchical Key Management Scheme

Our scheme uses a central authority (CA) who is responsible for managing the hierarchy of a set of disjoint classes $C_1, \ldots, C_n$. $GF(p)$ be the Galois Field, where p is a large prime, and h be the cryptographic hash function. We use the notation $h^i(x) = h^{i-1}(h(x)), i > 1$. For example, $h^3(x)$ is $h^2(h(x))$ which is $h(h(h(x)))$. All the polynomials are constructed using Lagrange's interpolation method given in section 4 using equation 1. The scheme consists of following phases.

1. **Key Generation and Key Assignment:** For each class C_i, CA chooses a distinct key K_i randomly from $GF(p)$ and securely distributes it to users of C_i.
2. **Public Information Generation:** For each class C_i, CA does the following. Let $S_i = \{C_j : C_j \le C_i\} - \{C_i\}$. Let $k = |S_i|$ be the size of S_i. Let $C_{j_1}, \ldots, C_{j_k}$ be the classes in S_i. Let $K_{j_1}, \ldots, K_{j_k}$ be the corresponding keys of classes in S_i. If $k > 1$, CA constructs a polynomial $P_i(x)$ with the points $\{(h(K_i), K_{j_1}), (h^2(K_i), K_{j_2}), \ldots, (h^k(K_i), K_{j_k})\}$ using Lagrange's polynomial interpolation equation 1. If $k = 1$, then CA randomly chooses a point (p_1, p_2) and constructs a polynomial $P_i(x)$ with the points $\{h(K_i), K_{j_1}), (p_1, p_2)\}$ (it should be noted that CA may pick more points randomly by fixing the degree of the polynomial). If $k = 0$, then C_i will have no outgoing edge and CA does not construct the polynomial $P_i(x)$. CA publishes the polynomial $P_i(x)$.
3. **Key Derivation:** Let $S_i = \{C_j : C_j \le C_i\} - \{C_i\}$. Let $C_{j_1}, \ldots, C_{j_k}$ be the classes in S_i. The user of class C_i can derive the key corresponding to class C_{j_l} for $1 \le l \le k$ by computing $P_i(h^l(K_i))$.

For instance, Figure 1 shows a hierarchy with 10 security classes. CA chooses $K_1, \ldots K_{10}$ randomly from $GF(p)$ and securely sends to users of $C_1, \ldots, C_{10}$ respectively. Here, $S_1 = \{C_2, \ldots, C_{10}\}$. CA constructs the polynomial $P_1(x)$ with the points $(h(K_1), K_2), (h^2(K_1), K_3), \ldots, (h^9(K_1), K_{10})$ using Lagrange's polynomial interpolation method and CA publishes $P_1(x)$. For C_2, $S_2 = \{C_5, C_6, C_8, C_9\}$. CA constructs the polynomial $P_2(x)$ with the points $(h(K_2), K_5), (h^2(K_2), K_6)$, $(h^3(K_2), K_8)$ and $(h^4(K_2), K_9)$ and publishes it. Likewise, CA constructs polynomials $P_3(x)$, $P_4(x)$ and $P_6(x)$. To construct $P_7(x)$, CA chooses randomly a point (p_1, p_2) and constructs $P_7(x)$ with points $(h(K_7), K_{10})$ and (p_1, p_2). CA publishes $P_7(x)$. Likewise, CA constructs $P_5(x)$.

To derive the key of the class C_2, the users of class C_1 compute $P_1(h(K_1))$. To derive the key of class C_8, users of C_2 compute $P_2(h^3(K_2))$. The level order

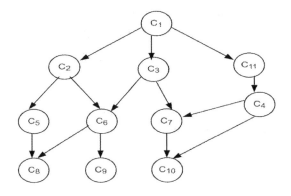

Fig. 2. Hierarchy after addition of security class

traversal of the subtree rooted at C_2 consists of the classes C_5, C_6, C_8, C_9 (excluding C_2). The position of the class C_8 is 3. So, three hash computations are required followed by a polynomial evaluation to get the key K_8.

5.1   Adding a New Class to an Existing Hierarchy

To add a new class C_t to the existing hierarchy, such that the relation $C_j \leq C_t \leq C_i$ holds, CA does the following.

1. CA chooses a distinct key K_t randomly from $GF(p)$ and securely gives it to users of C_t.
2. CA adds a node C_t between the classes C_i and C_j in the hierarchy.
3. For each predecessor C_i in $S = \{C_i : C_t \leq C_i\}$, CA does the following.
   (a) Let $C_{j_1}, \ldots, C_{j_k}$ be the classes in S_i where $S_i = \{C_j : C_j \leq C_i\}$. Let $K_{j_1}, \ldots, K_{j_k}$ be the corresponding keys of classes in S_i. CA computes the polynomial $P_i(x)$ using Lagrange's interpolation technique with the points $\{(h(K_i), K_{j_1}), (h^2(K_i), K_{j_2}), \ldots, (h^k(K_i), K_{j_k})\}$. CA publishes $P_i(x)$.
4. For the class C_t, CA does the following.
   (a) Let $C_{j_1}, \ldots, C_{j_k}$ be the classes in S_t where $S_t = \{C_j : C_j \leq C_t\}$. Let $K_{j_1}, \ldots, K_{j_k}$ be the corresponding keys of classes in S_t. CA computes the polynomial $P_t(x)$ using Lagrange's interpolation technique with the points $\{(h(K_t), K_{j_1}), (h^2(K_t), K_{j_2}), \ldots, (h^k(K_t), K_{j_k})\}$. CA publishes $P_t(x)$.

For example, consider and event of addition of a new class C_{11} to an existing hierarchy (refer Figure 1), such that the relation $C_4 \leq C_{11} \leq C_1$ holds. CA adds the class C_{11} to hierarchy as shown in Figure 2. CA chooses K_{11} randomly from $GF(p)$ and gives it securely to the users of C_{11}. The class C_1 is the predecessor of C_{11}. CA constructs the polynomial $P_1(x)$ with the points $(h(K_1), K_2), (h^2(K_1), K_3), (h^3(K_1), K_{11}), (h^4(K_1), K_5), (h^5(K_1), K_6), (h^6(K_1), K_7), (h^7(K_1), K_4), \quad (h^8(K_1), K_8), (h^9(K_1), K_9)$ and $(h^{10}(K_1), K_{10})$ using Lagrange's polynomial interpolation technique and publishes the new polynomial $P_1(x)$.

The successors of the newly added class C_{11} are classes C_4, C_7 and C_{10}. CA constructs the polynomial $P_{11}(x)$ with the points $(h(K_{11}), K_4), (h^2(K_{11}), K_7)$, and $(h^3(K_{11}), K_{10})$ using Lagrange's polynomial interpolation technique. As explained earlier the users of a class can derive the successor class keys using their own key.

5.2   Deleting a Class from the Existing Hierarchy

To delete a class C_t from the existing hierarchy where $C_j \leq C_t \leq C_i$, CA does the following.

1. For each predecessor C_i in $S = \{C_j : C_j \leq C_i\}$, CA does the following.
   (a) Let $C_{j_1}, \ldots, C_{j_k}$ be the classes in S_i where $S_i = \{C_j : C_j \leq C_i\} - \{C_t\}$. Let $K_{j_1}, \ldots, K_{j_k}$ be the corresponding keys of classes in S_i. CA computes the polynomial $P_i(x)$ using Lagrange's interpolation technique with the points $\{(h(K_i), K_{j_1}), (h^2(K_i), K_{j_2}), \ldots, (h^k(K_i), K_{j_k})\}$. CA publishes $P_i(x)$.
2. CA removes K_t.

6   Proposed Scheme with Forward and Backward Security

In this section, we modify the basic scheme described above such that the backward secrecy and forward secrecy of the classes is maintained when a new class is added to an existing hierarchy and an existing class is deleted from the hierarchy respectively. Our scheme employs a central authority (CA) who is responsible for managing the hierarchy of the set of disjoint classes $C_1, \ldots, C_n$. Let $S_i = \{C_j : C_j \leq C_i\} - \{C_i\}$. All the polynomials are constructed using the Lagrange's polynomial interpolation method. The scheme consists of following phases:

1. **Key Generation and Key Assignment:** For each class C_i, CA chooses a distinct keys K_i, R_i randomly from $GF(p)$ and securely distributes it to users of C_i. We call the key K_i as the *class key* and R_i as the *class rekeying key*. All the users in class C_i communicate securely using K_i.
2. **Public Information Generation:** For each class C_i, CA does the following. Let $S_i = \{C_j : C_j \leq C_i\}$. Let $k = |S_i|$ be the size of S_i. Let $C_{j_1}, \ldots, C_{j_k}$ be the classes in S_i. Let $K_{j_1}, \ldots, K_{j_k}$ be the corresponding keys of classes in S_i. If $k > 1$, CA constructs a polynomial $P_i(x)$ using Lagrange's interpolation technique with the points $\{(h(K_i), K_{j_1}), (h^2(K_i), K_{j_2}), \ldots, (h^k(K_i), K_{j_k})\}$. If $k = 1$, then CA randomly chooses a point (p_1, p_2) and constructs a polynomial $P_i(x)$ with the points $\{h(K_i), K_{j_1}), (p_1, p_2)\}$ (it should be noted that CA may pick more points randomly by fixing the degree of the polynomial). If $k = 0$, then C_i will have no outgoing edge and CA does not construct the polynomial $P_i(x)$. CA makes $P_i(x)$ public.
3. **Key Derivation:** Let $S_i = \{C_j : C_j \leq C_i\} - \{C_i\}$. Let $C_{j_1}, \ldots, C_{j_k}$ be the classes in S_i. The user of class C_i can derive the key corresponding to class C_{j_l} for $1 \leq l \leq k$ by computing $P_i(h^l(K_i))$.

It should be noted the given a relation $C_j \leq C_i$, the users of C_i can derive K_j. And, the users of class C_i do not have access to R_j. R_j is secret with only users of K_j and is not accessible to any other classes in the hierarchy.

6.1 Adding a New Class to an Existing Hierarchy

To add a new class C_t to the existing hierarchy such that the relation $C_j \leq C_t \leq C_i$ holds, CA does the following.

1. CA chooses distinct keys K_t, R_t randomly from $GF(p)$ and securely distributes it to users of C_t.
2. Let $S_t = \{C_j : C_j \leq C_t\} - \{C_t\}$ be the successors of C_t. Let K_{j_l} be the current key of class C_{j_l}, where $1 \leq l \leq |S_t|$. For each class C_{j_l} in S_t for $1 \leq l \leq |S_t|$, CA chooses a new key K'_{j_l} and constructs a public polynomial $P_s(x)$ with the points $(K_{j_1}, K'_{j_1}), \ldots, (K_{j_l}, K'_{j_l})$. CA does as above for providing backward secrecy to the classes in S_t.
3. The users of each class C_{j_l} in S_t evaluate $P_s(x)$ at K_{j_l} to get the new key K'_{j_l}. W l.o.g and for notational convenience we denote new key K'_{j_l} as K_{j_l}.
4. For each predecessor C_i in $S_i = \{C_i : C_t \leq C_i\}$, CA does the following.
   (a) Let $C_{j_1}, \ldots, C_{j_k}$ be the classes in S_i where $S_i = \{C_j : C_j \leq C_i\}$. Let $K_{j_1}, \ldots, K_{j_l}$ be the corresponding keys of classes in S_i. CA computes the polynomial $P_i(x)$ using Lagrange's interpolation technique with the points $\{(h(K_i), K_{j_1}), (h^2(K_i), K_{j_2}), \ldots, (h^l(K_i), K_{j_l})\}$. CA publishes $P_i(x)$.
5. For the class C_t, CA does the following.
   (a) Let $C_{j_1}, \ldots, C_{j_l}$ be the classes in S_t. Let $K_{j_1}, \ldots, K_{j_l}$ be the corresponding keys of classes in S_t. CA computes the polynomial $P_t(x)$ with the points $\{(h(K_t), K_{j_1}), (h^2(K_t), K_{j_2}), \ldots, (h^l(K_t), K_{j_l})\}$ using Lagrange's interpolation technique CA publishes $P_t(x)$.

6.2 Deleting a Class from the Existing Hierarchy

To delete a class C_t from the existing hierarchy where $C_j \leq C_t \leq C_i$, CA does the following.

1. Let $S_t = \{C_j : C_j \leq C_t\} - \{C_t\}$ be the successors of C_t. Let K_{j_l} be the current key of class C_{j_l}, for $1 \leq l \leq |S_t|$. Note that the users of C_t have access to the keys of the classes in S_t along with class key of C_t. For each class C_{j_l} in S_t for $1 \leq l \leq |S_t|$, CA chooses a new key K'_{j_l} and constructs a public polynomial $P_s(x)$ with the points $(R_{j_1}, K'_{j_1}), \ldots, (R_{j_l}, K'_{j_l})$. It should be noted that the key K_{j_l} cannot be used for constructing the polynomial as the users of class C_t have access to it. However, the users of C_t do not have access to R_{j_l}. This ensures the forward secrecy.
2. The users of each class C_{j_l} in S_t evaluate $P_s(x)$ at K_{j_l} to get the new key K'_{j_l}. W l.o.g and for notational convenience we denote new key K'_{j_l} as K_{j_l}.
3. For each predecessor C_i in $S = \{C_j : C_j \leq C_i\}$, CA does the following.

(a) Let $C_{j_1}, \ldots, C_{j_l}$ be the classes in S_i where $S_i = \{C_j : C_j \leq C_i\} - \{C_t\}$. Let $K_{j_1}, \ldots, K_{j_l}$ be the corresponding keys of classes in S_i. CA computes the polynomial $P_i(x)$ using Lagrange's interpolation technique with the points $\{(h(K_i), K_{j_1}), (h^2(K_i), K_{j_2}), \ldots, (h^l(K_i), K_{j_l})\}$. CA publishes $P_i(x)$.

4. CA removes K_t.

7   Analysis of the Proposed Scheme

Storage Cost. Consider a class with $t \leq n$ successors. Each user of class should store only one secret key. The public information of the class is the size of the constructed polynomial which is t. CA has to store the secret keys of n security classes of the hierarchy. Each user of a class in the second scheme should store two secret keys.

Computation Cost. CA should construct the polynomial for each class whose degree depends on the number of successors of the class. The cost of polynomial interpolation is $O(n \log^2 n)$ for degree n. The key derivation cost of user of a class requires hash computations equal to the position of the target successor class in the level order traversal of the subtree rooted at a class to which user belongs in a hierarchy and a polynomial evaluation (whose cost is $O(\sqrt{n})$).

8   Comparison

In this section, we compare our proposed scheme with the existing schemes by Chang et al. [3], Shen et al. [15], Das et al. [5] and Giri et al. [8] for public information storage, private information storage at user, private information storage at CA, Key generation and distribution cost per class, key derivation cost and for satisfying security requirements (forward and backward secrecy) upon new class addition and existing class deletion.

The comparison is given in Table 1. In Table 1, k is the security parameter (size of an element of $GF(p)$), E for exponentiation, c_H denotes computation cost of a hash function, c_D the cost of decryption, c_E the cost of encryption, c_M the cost of multiplication and n is the number of nodes in the hierarchy.

In Table 1, public space denotes the public information collectively for all the n nodes in the hierarchy. We have considered the case where a node can have n relations. The n^2 factor is a upper bound but given a partially ordered set, where relation is anti-symmetric, all the nodes will not have n relations, So, the public information in our proposed scheme is less than $O(n^2 k)$. The public information in our proposed scheme is exactly the number of relations present in the hierarchy. We have considered private space per class (at a user). In our proposed scheme a user of any class stores only one key. A user of any class in Chang et al. [3] scheme stores 2 keys. The schemes of Shen et al. [15] and Das et al. [5] the key of order $O(n)$ is stored at the user. Shen et al. scheme is shown to be insecure and the scheme of Das et al. does nt satisfy the forward and

Table 1. Comparison with the existing schemes

	Chang et al. [3]	Shen et al. [15]	Das et al. [5]	Giri et al. [8]	Ours
Public Space	$O((n^2+3)k)$	$O(nk)$	$O(nk)$	$O(n^2k)$	$O(n^2k)$
Private space at user	$2k$	$O(nk)$	$O((n+1)k)$	k	k
Private space at CA	$2nk$	$O(n^2k)$	$O(n^2k)$	$2nk$	nk
Key Distribution	$n^2E+O(n^2)$	$O(n^2)$	$n(c_E+c_H)+O(n^2)$	$2nE+nc_E+O(n^2)$	$nc_H+O(n\log^2 n)$
Key Derivation	$3E+O(n)$	$2E+O(n)$	$c_H+O(n)$	$3c_M+1E+c_H$ $+c_D+O(n)$	$c_Hl+O(\sqrt{n})$
Forward Secrecy	-	No	No	No	Yes
Backward Secrecy	-	No	No	No	Yes

backward secrecy requirements. The private storage at CA is nk in our scheme and is less compared to other schemes. So, our scheme requires the user and the CA to store only 1 and n keys respectively which can be the lower bound on key storage. We have considered the key generation and distribution cost per class with the assumption that the class has n successors. The key generation and distribution is costly in other schemes as they require modular exponentiation followed by polynomial interpolation. The scheme in [8] requires number of polynomial interpolations equal to the number of successors of a class. Also, it requires $O(n)$ number of exponentiations and encryptions for key generation. Our scheme requires only one polynomial interpolation per class. Using FFT polynomial interpolation requires $O(n\log^2 n)$ (where n is the degree) [9]. A user of a class requires hash computations and a polynomial evaluation to derive the key of any successor class. The number of hash computations varies depending on the number of successor classes of a class of which the user is part. In Table 1, l specifies position of the target successor class in the level order traversal of the subtree rooted at a class to which a user belongs. in a hierarchy. The other schemes use, costlier operations like modular exponentiations, encryption and decryption operations. As given in Table 1, key derivation cost is efficient in our proposed scheme.

9   Security Analysis

In this section, we provide insight into the security of the proposed scheme.

9.1   POSET Property

Consider any class C_i in the hierarchy with $S_i = \{C_j : C_j \le C_i\} - \{C_i\}$ and $k = |S_i|$ be the size of S_i. Let $C_{j_1}, \ldots, C_{j_k}$ be the classes in S_i. Let $K_{j_1}, \ldots, K_{j_k}$ be the corresponding keys of classes in S_i. Suppose $k > 1$. CA constructs a polynomial $P_i(x)$ using Lagrange's interpolation technique with the points $\{(h(K_i), K_{j_1}), (h^2(K_i), K_{j_2}), \ldots, (h^k(K_i), K_{j_k})\}$. CA publishes the polynomial $P_i(x)$. Consider the relation $C_{j_1} \le C_i$. The users of C_i have the secret key K_i. So, they can compute $h(K_i)$ and $P_i(h(K_i))$ to get K_{j_1}. However the users of C_{j_1} cannot get the key K_i. The probability that the users of C_{j_1} get K_i is $\frac{1}{p}$. So, the hierarchical key management maintains the POSET properties of the relations.

9.2   Collaborative Attack

In collaborative attack, two or more classes at lower level in the hierarchy cooperatively wish to derive the key of the superior class. Consider two classes C_i and C_j with the common parent class C_p. The keys are K_i, K_j and K_p respectively. Given $P_p(x)$, it is hard to derive K_p. The probability with which they can get K_p is $\frac{2}{p}$. For larger p, this is negligible.

9.3   Common Subordinate Attack

In common subordinate case, when the subordinate class C_j is accessible by two or more superior classes C_i and C_k, then the class C_i may gain access to the secret key of C_k through the common subordinate C_j. For the class C_j, the polynomials $P_i(x)$ and $P_k(x)$ are constructed at the points $(h(K_i), K_j)$ and $(h(K_k), K_j)$ respectively. Due to the one way property of hash function it is hard to get K_k.

9.4   Forward and Backward Secrecy

When a class is added, the class keys of all the successor classes are changed to prevent the new users from accessing the past communications of the successor classes. The same process is carried out when an existing class is deleted to prevent the deleted users from accessing the future communications.

10   Conclusion

We have proposed an efficient hierarchical key management scheme based on polynomial interpolation method. We have reviewed the existing polynomial based hierarchical key management schemes and highlighted the disadvantages of those schemes. In the proposed scheme, the key derivation process is efficient as any user of a class does only one polynomial evaluation and computes the number of hash operations bounded by the position of the target successor class in the level order traversal of the subtree rooted at a class to which user belongs in a hierarchy. The user of any class stores only one key in the basic scheme and two keys in the scheme providing forward and backward secrecy. The proposed scheme is secure against collaborative and common subordinate attacks. We have compared the proposed scheme with the existing schemes and shown that our scheme is efficient. As a future work, we try to reduce the key derivation cost by keeping the same amount of public information and storage at user and CA as that of the proposed scheme.

Acknowledgments. This work was supported by Information Security Education and Awareness - ISEA Fellowship, Department of Information Technology, Ministry of Communications and Information Technology and Ministry of Human Resource Development, Government of INDIA.

References

1. Aho, A.V., Hopcroft, J.E., Ullman, J.D.: The Design and Analysis of Computer Algorithms. Addison-Wesley (1974)
2. Chang, C.-C., Hwang, R.-J., Wu, T.-C.: Cryptographic key assignment scheme for access control in a hierarchy. Information Systems 17(3), 243–247 (1992)
3. Chang, C.-C., Lin, I.-C., Tsai, H.-M., Wang, H.-H.: A key assignment scheme for controlling access in partially ordered user hierarchies. In: International Conference on Advanced Information Networking and Applications (AINA), pp. 376–379 (2004)
4. Cormen, T.H., Leiserson, C.E., Rivest, R.L., Stein, C.: Introduction to Algorithms, 3 edn. MIT Press (2009)
5. Das, M.L., Saxena, A., Gulati, V.P., Phatak, D.B.: Hierarchical key management scheme using polynomial interpolation. SIGOPS Oper. Syst. Rev. 39(1), 40–47 (2005)
6. Denning, D., Akl, S., Heckman, M., Lunt, T., Morgenstern, M., Neumann, P., Schell, R.: Views for multilevel database security. IEEE Transactions on Software Engineering SE-13(2), 129–140 (1987)
7. Fraim, L.: Scomp: A solution to the multilevel security problem. Computer 16(7), 26–34 (1983)
8. Giri, D., Srivastava, P.D.: A cryptographic key assignment scheme for access control in poset ordered hierarchies with enhanced security. I. J. Network Security 7(2), 223–234 (2008)
9. Horowitz, E., Sahni, S.: Fundamentals of Computer Algorithms. Computer Science Press (1978)
10. Hsu, C.L., Wu, T.S.: Cryptanalyses and improvements of two cryptographic key assignment schemes for dynamic access control in a user hierarchy. Computers & Security 22(5), 453–456 (2003)
11. Liaw, H.T., Wang, S.J., Lei, C.L.: A dynamic cryptographic key assignment scheme is a tree structure. Computers and Mathematics with Applications 25(6), 109–114 (1993)
12. Lu, W.-P., Sundareshan, M.K.: A model for multilevel security in computer networks. IEEE Transaction on Software Engineering 16(6), 647–659 (1990)
13. McHugh, J., Moore, A.P.: A security policy and formal top level specification for a multi-level secure local area network. In: IEEE Symposium on Security and Privacy 1986, pp. 34–39 (1986)
14. Sandhu, R.S., Coyne, E.J., Feinstein, H.L., Youman, C.E.: Role-based access control models. Computer 29(2), 38–47 (1996)
15. Shen, V.R.L., Chen, T.S.: A novel key management scheme based on discrete logarithms and polynomial interpolations. Computers & Security 21(2), 164–171 (2002)
16. Tsai, H.M., Chang, C.C.: A cryptographic implementation for dynamic access control in a user hierarchy. Computers & Security 14(2), 159–166 (1995)

Hand Vein Authentication System Using Dynamic ROI

Munaga V.N.K. Prasad, Ilaiah Kavati, and Kanavu Ravindra

Institute for Development and Research in Banking Technology (IDRBT), Castle Hills,
Masab Tank, Hyderabad-57, India
mvnkprasad@idrbt.ac.in, {kavati089,ravindra270}@gmail.com

Abstract. This paper presents an efficient authentication system based on hand vein pattern. The stages involved in vein pattern authentication system are image acquisition, Region of Interest (ROI) Extraction, image enhancement, binarization, thinning, feature extraction and matching. We propose an algorithm for extraction of dynamic ROI from the hand vein image. The advantage of dynamic ROI extraction is that, ROI extracted for different hand images varies in size as the size of the hand varies and is possible to extract more features from a larger hand which otherwise is not possible with fixed ROI. A new thinning algorithm is used to extract one pixel thick medial axis vein network from the dynamic ROI and compared the results with matlab's thinning algorithm. The resulting thinned image may contain some artefacts, and we propose an algorithm to remove these artefacts. The minutiae features that represents the geometric information of the vein pattern is extracted which are bifurcation and ending points. Finally a matching algorithm is applied for authentication. The proposed system is efficient and got the lowest error rate.

Keywords: Hand vein, finger web, region of interest, thresholding, binarization, bifurcation, endpoint.

1 Introduction

A biometric system is basically an automated pattern recognition system that either makes identification or verifies an identity by establishing the probability that a specific physiological or behavioral characteristic is valid [1]. Biometrics plays a major role in today's security applications, including commercial (e.g. e-commerce, welfare-disbursement), various forms of access control (e.g. ATM's, boarder control, PC login), and so on. Various types of biometrics such as iris, face, fingerprints, hand geometry and vein patterns are being used for real-time identification and identity verification applications [14]. Among the various biometrics that can be used to identify a person, human hand veins exhibits some distinct advantages like ease of feature extraction, spoofing resistant, high accuracy, liveness detection and noncontact etc. Fig. 1 illustrates the generic vascular structure found on the back of the hand.

The human vascular structure is individually distinct and appears to be time invariant [12]. Human blood vessels are formed during the embryo stage with a variety of differentiating features, rendering each pattern unique, and their patterns

Sabu M. Thampi et al. (Eds.): SSCC 2013, CCIS 377, pp. 203–212, 2013.
© Springer-Verlag Berlin Heidelberg 2013

remain relatively constant over one's lifetime except in the case of injury or decease. An individual's identity can be authenticated using vein patterns in one's hands, and those patterns are located just under the surface of the skin and are invisible to the human eye, therefore vein patterns are much harder for intruders to copy [8].

The typical phases involved in the vein pattern authentication system are image acquisition, ROI extraction, binarization, thinning, feature extraction and matching. The acquisition of hand veins is generally done using infrared (IR) imaging. The IR imaging for veins is of two types namely near infrared (NIR) in the range of 0.75μm to 2μm and far infrared (FIR) in the range of 6μm to 14μm. After obtaining the images, the authentication system extracts the ROI from the hand to increase the accuracy and reliability of the system. The ROI is processed to increase the quality and then, the vein skeleton is extracted by a series of steps: normalizing, binarizing, filtering, smoothing, thinning, and pruning. Finally, the system extracts the features that represent the geometric information of the vein pattern, and matching is performed to authenticate the user.

Rest of the paper is organized as follows: section 2 describes the overview of the current development in hand vein pattern biometric. Section 3 presents the proposed dynamic Region of Interest (ROI) extraction. Noise removal, binarization of the ROI and the thinning is described in section 4. The feature extraction and matching of the key features are explained in section 5. The experiments and results from this work are presented in Section 6. Conclusions are described in section 7.

Fig. 1. An example vein patterns on the back of the hand

2   Related Work

In recent years, personal authentication using vein pattern has gained more and more research attention. It seems the first known work in the field of hand vein pattern was reported in 1990s [4], but it is not attracted much attention in that decade. Cross and Smith [9] have investigated the personal verification using hand vein patterns acquired using NIR camera. Authors used the medial axis representation as the feature of the vein pattern, and apply the constrained sequential correlation to match the vein signatures. Tanaka and Kubo [10] also employed the NIR images for personal verification and used phase only correlation technique to match the patterns. Lin et al [7] have detailed the usage of FIR imaging for the extraction of hand vein patterns and uses the combination of multi-resolution representations of the processed vein patterns for personal verification. Wang et al [8] present another approach for personal authentication using FIR hand vein images. Authors used the minutiae features of the vein pattern and employed the modified hausdorff distance to measure the similarity between the patterns.

Kumar et al [6] presents a new approach to authenticate individuals using NIR hand vein images that uses triangulation of minutiae features and knuckle shape information of the hand. The knuckle tips are used as key points for the image normalization and extraction of region of interest. The matching scores are generated in two parallel stages: hierarchical matching score from the four topologies of triangulation in the binarized vein structures, and from the geometrical features consisting of knuckle point perimeter distances in the acquired images. The weighted score from these two matching scores are used to authenticate the individuals. Yang et al [11] present a skeleton extracting algorithm for hand vein images. After a series of pre-processing: normalizing, filtering, segmenting, thresholding, smoothing, thinning, and pruning, the authors acquires clean and smooth vein pattern skeleton. Crisan et al [13] uses a new approach, where the vein detection process consists of an easy to implement device that takes a snapshot of the subject's veins under a source of near infrared radiation. Authors used the relative angles between vein segments, the number of end and bifurcation points, and the neighbors of each point for personal authentication.

3   Dynamic ROI Extraction

To increase the accuracy and reliability of the authentication system, the features of vein patterns extracted should be from the same region in different hands. The region to be extracted from the hand is known as ROI. ROI extraction can be either fixed [6, 7] or dynamic. The advantage of dynamic ROI is that ROI extracted for different hand images varies in size as the size of the hand varies and the extracted ROI's reference to the same region in the hand image irrespective of the size of the hands. So, it is possible to extract more features from the larger hand which otherwise is not possible with fixed region of interest extraction.

The process of dynamic ROI extraction is shown in Fig. 2. Firstly, the image I is binarized using a global thresholding method in order to extract the hand boundary. As shown in Fig. 2(b) global thresholding creates binary images from grey-level images by turning all pixels below some threshold to zero and all pixels above that threshold to one. Let I' is the binarized image of I, the global thresholding process is expressed using Eq. (1), where $I(x, y)$ denote the intensity value at position (x, y) in the image I and $I'(x, y)$ denote the value at position (x, y) in the image I'.

$$I'(x, y) = \left\} \begin{array}{ll} 1 & \text{if } I(x, y) \geq threshold \\ 0 & \text{otherwise} \end{array} \right. \qquad (1)$$

Then the boundary of the hand is extracted using morphological operators [2] on the binary image. An image A, and its boundary is denoted by β (A), can be obtained by first eroding A by B and then performing the set difference between A and its erosion. The boundary extraction process is defined using Eq. (2), where B is a suitable structuring element. A 3×3 matrix with element values 1 is used as the structuring element in the experiment.

$$\beta (A) = A - (A \ominus B) \tag{2}$$

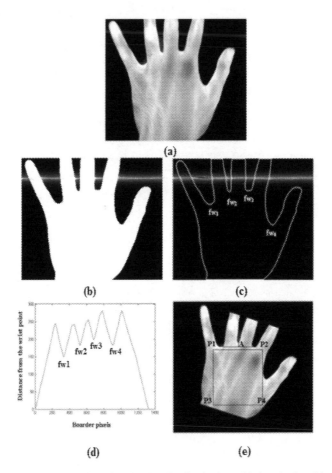

Fig. 2. Extraction of dynamic ROI: (a) hand vein image, (b) hand after binarization, (c) extracted hand boundary, (d) hand boundary distance profile, (e) locating the region of interest

The extracted boundary can be seen from the Fig. 2(c). Then for each boundary pixel, the Euclidean distance from the wrist middle point is calculated. Using these distances, a distance distribution diagram as shown in Fig. 2(d) is constructed whose pattern is similar to the geometric shape of the hand. In the diagram five local maxima (which resemble the five finger tips) and four local minima (which resemble the finger webs *i.e.* valley between fingers) can be seen. The line joining the finger webs fw_1 (the valley point between the small finger and ring finger) and fw_3 (the valley point between the middle finger and the index finger) is made parallel to the horizontal axis to make the images rotation invariant. The ROI is a rectangular region $R_{P1\ P2\ P3\ P4,}$ and defined using Eq. (3), where L represents the length, A is the distance between fw_2 and the line joining $fw_1\ fw_3$, c_1 and c_2 are two constants.

$$\left. \begin{array}{l} L_{P1\ P2} = L_{fw1\ fw3} + c_1 \times A \\[2mm] L_{P1\ P3} = L_{P1\ P2} + c_2 - A \end{array} \right\} \qquad (3)$$

The dynamic ROI located on the hand can be seen from the Fig. 2(e). It is observed that maximum possible region from the hand is extracted as ROI, which is not possible with fixed ROI. The main advantage to locate the ROI in this manner will increase the tolerance of the authentication system against hand rotation.

4   Binarization and Thinning

After obtaining the ROI, image enhancement techniques are applied in order to increase the quality of the ROI, as the images are low quality far infrared images. The first step in enhancement is applying histogram equalization technique [2] on the ROI to increase the contrast of the image and to reduce the possible imperfections in the image. The resultant ROI can be seen from the Fig. 3(b) and is subjected to binarization, to separate the vein structure from the image background. In order to binarize the image a locally adaptive threshold method has been applied. Due to small gray scale variations across the image, a global threshold method will not be a good choice to apply on the image. In contrast to the global threshold method which uses a single threshold, the adaptive threshold method [2] chooses different threshold value for every pixel in the image based on the mean value of all the pixels in the predefined neighborhood. The thresholding process is expressed using Eq. (4), where μ_{xy} is the mean value of the 31×31 neighborhood, for a pixel (x, y).

$$I'(x, y) = \left\{ \begin{array}{ll} 1 & \text{if } I\ (x,\ y) \geq \mu_{xy} \\[2mm] 0 & \text{otherwise} \end{array} \right. \qquad (4)$$

After thresholding process, connected noisy regions are identified in the binarized ROI and are eliminated which are below a predefined threshold value. There are some obvious protuberances and many spurs at the boundary (called boundary noise) of vein pattern, especially in horizontal. Median filter [2] of size 5×5 is used to reduce that noise. It preserves edges while removing noise. Then, a morphological opening operation is applied that smoothes the contour of object, breaks narrow isthmuses, and eliminates thin protrusions. The segmented ROI after noise reduction and smoothing is shown in Fig. 3(c).The resulting binary image is subjected to a thinning algorithm which generates the vein pattern structure of one pixel thick.

A thinning algorithm transforms a binary image into a skeleton and the skeleton is topologically equivalent to the image. Maintaining connectivity and ability to handle vein pattern boundary noise are the properties desired in thinning algorithms. Most of the thinning algorithms keep the connectivity of the region, but they cannot always get one-pixel thick skeleton and contains many spurs in the outline of the skeleton *i.e.* boundary noise. We use the thinning algorithm proposed by Ng et al [5] to handle these problems. It uses a flag map and smoothing templates for detecting thinned lines with multiple pixels thick and spurs with small connectivity.

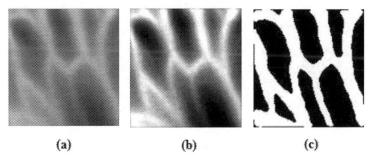

(a)   **(b)**   **(c)**

Fig. 3. Extraction of vein structure from the ROI: (a) extracted ROI, (b) after histogram equalization, (c) extracted vein patterns after noise removal and smoothing

However, the resulting image may also contain small unconnected and connected objects called thinning artefacts. A pruning technique is then applied to eliminate these false segments. Starting from every termination in the skeleton of the vein pattern, the technique tracks along the one pixel thick vein line until it reaches a crossing point or another termination. If the tracking length is less than a predefined threshold, the tracking line is marked as spur and deleted from the skeleton. The skeleton of the image is shown in Fig. 4(b).

5   Feature Extraction and Matching

After thinning the ROI, the key features which are relatively stable, unique and that represent the geometric information of the vein pattern are extracted. The minutiae features (vein ending and bifurcation) are considered as key features. A vein bifurcation is defined as vein point where vein forks or diverges into branch veins, and the vein ending is the point at which vein ends or disappears abruptly. This disappearance could be due to the abrupt ending of blood vessels or their poor visibility from the imaging system. In order to extract the minutiae points from the skeleton image, we examine the local neighborhood of every pixel P in a 3×3 window centered at P using cross number concept [3]. The cross number concept can be expressed using Eq. (5).

$$B = 0.5\sum_{i=1}^{8} | P_{i+1} - P_i |, \quad \text{Where } P_9 = P_1 \tag{5}$$

For a pixel P on the vein skeleton, its eight neighboring pixels are scanned as follows,

P_1	P_2	P_3
P_8	P	P_4
P_7	P_6	P_5

A pixel P is termed as bifurcation point if the value of B for the pixel is three or more. If the value of B is equal to one, the pixel P is an end point. A minutiae m_i can be represented by its position and type i.e., $m_i = (x_i, y_i, t_i)$ where (x_i, y_i) denotes the position and t_i is the type (vein bifurcation or ending) of the minutiae m_i. The extracted features are in Fig. 4(c).

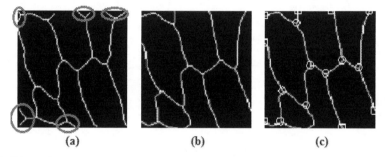

Fig. 4. Thinned images: (a) using MATLAB's 'skel' function (artefacts are highlightened), (b) using thinning algorithm [5], (c) extracted minutiae features (round symbol for bifurcation point and square symbol for end point)

Matching is the last phase in the vein pattern authentication system. Matching is used to authenticate the user i.e., to know whether the user is genuine (already registered) or imposter. Matching is done by comparing the minutiae features of a query template with the already stored templates. Let $M = \{m_1, m_2, ..., m_p\}$ and $N = \{n_1, n_2, ..., n_q\}$ are the two templates having p and q minutiae features respectively. We consider that a minutiae point $m_i = (x_i, y_i, t_i)$ of query template M is matched to a minutiae point $n_j = (a_j, b_j, t_j)$ of stored template N, if they satisfy the following set of conditions.

$$
\left. \begin{array}{l} t_i = t_j \\[2mm] \sqrt{(x_i - a_j)^2 + (y_i - b_j)^2} < Threshold \end{array} \right\} \tag{6}
$$

Match score of a query image against an enrolled image is defined using Eq. (7), where *count* is the number of query image minutiae features matched with the enrolled image, and p is the total number of query minutiae features. More the match score between two images, greater is the similarity between them.

$$\text{Match score} = \frac{count}{p} \times 100 \qquad (7)$$

6   Experiments and Results

The experiments are conducted on a far infrared hand vein pattern database of 178 images, approximately 3 prints each of 60 distinct hands and extracted the dynamic ROI's for these images. In the experiment, for extraction of dynamic ROI, the values of c_1 and c_2 in Eq. (3) are chosen empirically as 4 and 10 respectively. We got the smallest ROI size of 107×111 and largest ROI size of 137×141. We conducted an experiment using matlab's '*skel*' function for the extraction of the vein skeleton. The resulting image is shown in Fig. 4(a) and contains some artefacts which are highlightened. It can be observed from Fig. 4 that the thinning algorithm [5] used in this work performs well as it extracts the vein skeletons successfully and the shape of the vein pattern is well preserved.

The performance of the proposed authentication system is determined by False Acceptance Rate (FAR), False Rejection Rate (FRR) and Equal Error Rate (EER) [15]. FAR is the frequency that a non authorized person is accepted as authorized while FRR is the frequency that an authorized person is rejected access. The EER refers to a point where the FAR equals the FRR; a lower EER value indicates better performance. Fig. 5 shows the FAR and FRR at various thresholds and it can be seen that the Equal Error Rate (EER) is 0.05.

The genuine and imposter match scores distributions [15] are shown in the Fig. 6, it is observed that they are well separated, and maximum of the genuine scores are greater than threshold (T) and maximum of the imposter scores are less than T.

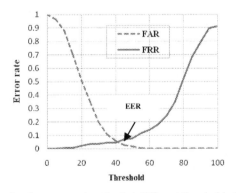

Fig. 5. Error rate curves for the proposed method at different thresholds (EER = 0.05 where the threshold is observed to be 42)

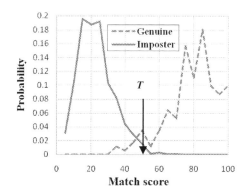

Fig. 6. The genuine and imposter match score distributions

7 Conclusion

This paper proposes a new dynamic ROI extraction method and implemented an efficient thinning algorithm [5] with artifact removal for vein pattern authentication. The dynamic ROI extraction made it possible to grab more features from the hand and made the system almost rotation invariant. The skeleton produced by the thinning algorithm is not only one-pixel thick, perfectly connected, but also has the desired property of handling boundary noise.

References

1. Wilson, C.: Vein Pattern Recognition: A Privacy-Enhancing Biometric. Taylor and Francis Group. CRC Press, Boca Raton (2010)
2. Gonzalez, R.C., Woods, R.E., Eddins, S.L.: Digital Image Processing using MATLAB, 2nd edn. Prentice Hall, Upper Saddle River (2010)
3. Maltoni, D., Maio, D., Jain, A.K., Prabhakar, S.: Handbook of Fingerprint Recognition. Springer, New York (2003)
4. MacGregor, R., Welford, R.: Veincheck: imaging for security and personal identification. Advanced Imaging 6, 52–56 (1991)
5. Ng, G.S., Zhou, R.W., Quek, C.: A Novel Single Pass Thinning Algorithm. IEEE Transactions on System Man and Cybernetics (1994)
6. Kumar, A., Prathyusha, K.V.: Personal authentication using hand vein triangulation and knuckle shape. IEEE Transactions on Image Processing 38, 2127–2136 (2009)
7. Lin, C.L., Fan, K.C.: Biometric verification using thermal images of palm-dorsa vein patterns. IEEE Trans. Circuits Syst. Video Technol. 14, 199–213 (2004)
8. Wang, L., Leedham, G., Cho, D.S.Y.: Minutiae feature analysis for infrared hand vein pattern biometrics. Pattern Recognition 41, 920–929 (2008)
9. Cross, J.M., Smith, C.L.: Thermographic imaging of the subcutaneous vascular network of the back of the hand for biometric identification. In: IEEE 29th Annu. Int. Carnahan Conf. Security Technology, Surrey, pp. 20–35 (1995)

10. Tanaka, T., Kubo, N.: Biometric authentication by hand vein patterns. In: Proceedings of SICE Annual Conference, Okayama, Japan, pp. 249–253 (2004)
11. Yang, L., Liu, X., Liu, Z.: A Skeleton Extracting Algorithm for Dorsal Hand Vein Pattern. In: International Conference on Computer Application and System Modeling, Taiyuan, pp. 92–95 (2010)
12. Jain, A.K., Bolle, R.M., Pankanti, S.: Biometrics: personal identification in networked society. Kluwer Academic Publishers, Dordrecht (1999)
13. Crisan, S., Tarnovan, I.G., Crisan, T.E.: Radiation optimization and image processing algorithms in the identification of hand vein patterns. Computer Standards and Interfaces 32, 130–140 (2010)
14. Jain, A.K., Flynn, P., Ross, A.: Handbook of Biometrics. Springer, New York (2007)
15. Jain, A.K., Ross, A., Nandakumar, K.: Introduction to Biometrics. Springer, New York (2011)

Vein Pattern Indexing Using Texture and Hierarchical Decomposition of Delaunay Triangulation

Ilaiah Kavati[1,2], Munaga V.N.K. Prasad[2], and Chakravarthy Bhagvati[1]

[1] University of Hyderabad, Hyderabad-46, India
[2] Institute for Development and Research in Banking Technology, Hyderabad-57, India
kavati089@gmail.com, mvnkprasad@idrbt.ac.in,
chakcs@uohyd.ernet.in

Abstract. In biometric identification systems, the identity corresponding to the query image is determined by comparing it against all images in the database. This exhaustive matching process increases the response time and the number of false positives of the system; therefore, an effective mechanism is essential to select a small collection of candidates to which the actual matching process is applied. This paper presents an efficient indexing algorithm for vein pattern databases to improve the search speed and accuracy of identification. In this work, we generate a binary code for each image using texture information. A hierarchical decomposition of Delaunay triangulation based approach for minutiae is proposed and used with binary code to narrow down the search space of the database. Experiments are conducted on two vein pattern databases, and the results show that, while maintaining 100% Hit Rate, the proposed method achieves lower penetration rate than what existing methods achieve.

Keywords: Hand vein, indexing, binary code, hierarchical decomposition, Delaunay triangulation, bifurcation, end point.

1 Introduction

A biometric system is essentially a pattern recognition system that recognizes a person based on physical and/or behavioral characteristics possessed by that person [10]. Authentication based on biometric technology has been an active area of research recently in security systems, because conventional means such as tokens, passwords have problems in terms of theft, loss, and reliance on the user's memory.

Biometric authentication can be achieved by either verification method or identification method. In verification mode, a quick response can be expected because the matching is executed only once, though the claimer has to enter his/her identity for every authentication session [14]. In identification mode, the user does not provide any identity claim, but recognition of a single query requires searching through the entire database containing a large collection of biometric images [15]. Since entire database is searched, the required processing will have longer response times and the identification performance is expected to suffer. Hence an effective and efficient

Sabu M. Thampi et al. (Eds.): SSCC 2013, CCIS 377, pp. 213–222, 2013.
© Springer-Verlag Berlin Heidelberg 2013

indexing mechanism is essential to select a small collection of candidates to which the actual matching process is applied. However, as the biometric data is unstructured, they cannot be indexed into alphabetical or numerical order [9]. The indexing method not only deals with unstructured data, but also has to deal with the challenges of intra-class natural variations and inter-class similarities.

The biometric indexing methods are generally based on either point [8,11] or triplets of points [1,2,12]. The authors in [11], extracted the minutiae points of the fingerprints and mapped them into a hash table using geometric hashing [7]. Similarly, Hunny et al. [8] extracted the key features of iris using Scale Invariant Feature Transform [6] and mapped them with the help of geometric hashing. However, the above methods require high computational and memory costs as each feature is inserted multiple times into the hash table to handle the intra class natural variations.

The triplets have been successfully used in biometric application to index biometric databases [1,2,12]. The triplets based techniques have proven more powerful than point based techniques, as the uncertainty of feature points and intra class natural variations do not affect the angles of a triangle [2]. In 1997, Germain et al. proposed an indexing scheme for fingerprint based on all possible triplets of minutiae that uses "Fast Look-up Algorithm for String Homology (FLASH)" [1] to generate the index and match. In this approach, length of each side of the triangle, local orientation and ridge count between vertices are used for flash index. Bhanu and Tan improved the work on minutiae triplets [2]. In their work, they used additional features such as triangle angles, handedness, type, and direction. However, the methods based on all possible triplets lead to high computational cost and possibility of mismatch as there are totally $O(n^3)$ triangles (where n is number of minutiae). Bebis et al. applied Delaunay triangulation instead of all triplets of the minutiae set [12] and experiments showed this approach had a better performance.

In this paper, we propose two invariant features to make the indexing algorithm more robust: texture binary code and hierarchical decomposition of Delaunay triangulation. Binary code is extracted for each image and is used to filter out the wrong correspondences during identification *i.e.* select genuine image from the database. The hierarchical decomposition of Delaunay triangulation classifies the triplets based on the combination of minutiae. The classified Delaunay triplets are used with the binary code that further reduces the search space of the database.

Rest of the paper is organized as follows. The proposed indexing scheme which is based on binary code and hierarchical decomposition of Delaunay triangulation has been described in section 2. Experimental results and analysis are presented in Section 3. Section 4 is the conclusion.

2   Proposed Indexing Approach

This section proposes an efficient indexing scheme for vein pattern images which is based on a binary code obtained from the texture and classified Delaunay triplets of the minutiae. The proposed approach follows these steps. 1) Computing binary code from the texture information, 2) Extraction of minutiae features, 3) Computing

Delaunay triplets from the extracted minutiae and hierarchical classification of triplets, 4) Index table generation, and 5) retrieval of candidate images which are similar to the query image.

2.1   Computing Binary Code from the Texture Information

The vein pattern image as shown in Fig.1 is segmented into n non overlapping sub images of size $x \times y$, and then the mean (μ_i) grayscale values of each sub image i ($1 \leq i \leq n$) is calculated. The method assigns a binary digit ($b_i = 1$ or 0) to each sub image i using Eq. (1), where T_1 is threshold.

$$b_i = \left.\begin{cases} 1 & \text{if } \mu_i > T_1 \\ 0 & \text{otherwise} \end{cases}\right. \tag{1}$$

Accumulate the bits of sub images in raster scan order to generate a binary code $B = \{b_1, b_2,.. b_n\}$ of the image. If two vein images belong to the same user their texture information is similar, and also the binary codes. During identification, the Hamming distance (the Hamming distance between two strings of *equal length* is the number of positions at which the corresponding symbols are different) between the binary codes is used to find out the potential list of candidate matches from the database and is described in Algorithm 1.

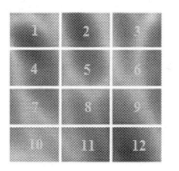

Fig. 1. Segmented Hand Vein image

Algorithm 1. Selection of potential candidates using binary code

---

Let Bq be the binary code of the query image q and B_x be the binary code of an image x from the database.

1.   Compute the Hamming distance $d = D_h (B_q, B_x)$.
2.   Select image x *as* potential candidate if $d \leq T_2$.
where T_2 is a predefined threshold.

2.2   Extraction of Minutiae Features

This section describes the extraction of minutiae features from the vein pattern images using image processing algorithms. The proposed algorithm extracts the minutiae of the vein pattern after a series of preprocessing steps such as image contrast enhancement, noise removal, binarization and thinning [13]. To enhance the contrast, the vein images are subjected to adaptive histogram equalization. The adaptive histogram equalization increases the contrast of the image and reduces the possible imperfections in the image. A vein image and its enhanced image are shown in Fig. 2(a) and Fig. 2(b). The enhanced images are further processed with median filter to suppress the noise content. The resulting image is binarized using locally adaptive threshold method [17] and finally thinning is performed to obtain the skeletons of the vein image. The binarized vein image is shown in Fig. 2(c). Then, the minutiae features are extracted using cross number concept [5]. The proposed system represents vein patterns in terms of their minutiae. The two most prominent minutiae used here are vein endings and vein bifurcations. Each minutiae is represented by its coordinates (x,y). The extracted minutiae of the thinned image are shown in Fig. 2(d).

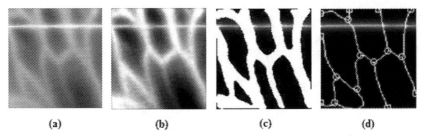

| (a) | (b) | (c) | (d) |

Fig. 2. Preprocessing of a vein image: (a) Cropped hand vein image from FIR database, (b) enhanced image, (c) binarized image, (d) minutiae of the thinned vein image (round symbol for bifurcation point and square symbol for end point)

2.3   Hierarchical Decomposition of Delaunay Triangulation

Once the minutiae have been extracted, their Delaunay triangulation is computed. Fig. 3 shows the Delaunay triangles of the minutiae for one of the vein pattern images in our database. The motivation of using Delaunay triangulation in this work is that the Delaunay triplets possess certain unique properties compared to other topological structures [12][16], including: (1) Delaunay triangulation partitions a whole region into many smaller pieces and exactly describes the closest neighbor structures of minutiae; (2) Insertion of a new point in a Delaunay triangulation affects only the triangles whose circum circles contain that point. As a result, noise affects the Delaunay triangulation only locally [12]; (3) The Delaunay triplets are not *skinny* which is desirable as the skinny triangles lead to instabilities and errors [3]; (4) The Delaunay triangulation creates only $O(n)$ triangles whereas, the approaches in [1, 2] uses all possible triangles of minutia set in an image and therefore, $O(n^3)$ triangles have to be compared during indexing. The computing cost greatly decreases using

Delaunay triangulation; (5) Compared to other topological structures, the Delaunay triangulation is less sensitive to distortion [4].

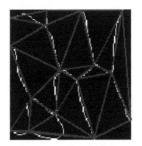

Fig. 3. Delaunay triangulation of set of minutiae

The triplets of the vein image are classified based on the combination of minutiae at the vertices of the triangle [18]. Fig. 4 shows an example of Delaunay triangle. Let Θ_{min}, Θ_{med} and Θ_{max} are the minimal, medial and maximal angles in the triangle respectively. The vertices of angle Θ_{max}, Θ_{med}, Θ_{min} are labeled as V_1, V_2, V_3 respectively. Then, based on the combination of types of minutiae at the vertices V_1, V_2, V_3 of the triangle, the Delaunay triplets are classified as eight types and is depicted in Table 1.

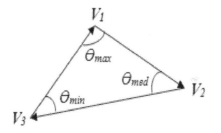

Fig. 4. Definition of minutiae triangle

2.4   Index Table Generation

This section explains the method of generating an index table for storing the classified minutiae triplets of the vein images. A 3D index $X = (t, \Theta_{med}, \Theta_{max})$ is formed for each triplet of the vein image, where t ($1 \leq t \leq 8$) is the triplet type. We use the (t, Θ_{med}, Θ_{max}) of the triplet as index into a 3D index table A of size 8×180×180. In the experiment, we use only two angles (Θ_{med}, Θ_{max}) of the triangle as index elements, because the third angle ($\Theta_{min} = 180 - (\Theta_{med} + \Theta_{max})$) can be easily determined if we know any two. Each triplet of the vein image is inserted into the index table as follows,

$$A (t, \Theta_{med}, \Theta_{max}) = (I, B_I) \tag{2}$$

where A $(t, \Theta_{med}, \Theta_{max})$ is the index table segment, I is the image identity to which the triplet belongs, and B_I is the binary code of the image. For each vein image in the database, same process is repeated and inserted into the index table. However, some segments of the index table may receive more than one entry. As a result, each bin may contain a list of entries of the form (I, B_I). The insertion of binary code along with image identity into the index table is used to filter out the wrong correspondences during identification. Algorithm 2 lists the process of indexing the vein images.

Table 1. Hierarchical Decomposition of Delaunay Triplets

Triplet Type	Vertex Minutiae Type*		
t	V_1	V_2	V_3
1	e	e	e
2	e	e	b
3	e	b	e
4	e	b	b
5	b	e	e
6	b	e	b
7	b	b	e
8	b	b	b

*e – end point, b – bifurcation point

Algorithm 2. Indexing

For each vein image I in the database,
    1.   Compute binary code B_I.
    2.   Extract the minutiae features after a series of preprocessing steps.
    3.   Apply Delaunay triangulation on the extracted minutiae set and classify the triplets according to Table 1
    4.   **For** each triplet in vein image I, do
          a. Compute 3D index $(t, \Theta_{med}, \Theta_{max})$ and access the Index table and put image identity I and binary code B_I into the indexed location.
    End For
End For

2.5   Retrieval of Candidate Images

Given a query and a large database, our objective in an indexing mechanism is to effectively retrieve a small set of candidates, which share topological similarity with the query. First, the query image binary code is computed as explained in section 2A. Then, its Delaunay triplets are generated and classified based on the minutiae that constitute the triplet.

For each triplet of the query image a 3D index $(t, \Theta_{med}, \Theta_{max})$ is computed and used to access the index table. Let $X = (t_i, \Theta_{med}, \Theta_{max})$, $X' = (t'_i, \Theta'_{med}, \Theta'_{max})$ be the indexes of the triplets for query and database image respectively, and let d be the hamming distance between their binary codes B and B'. The triplets X and X' are considered as matched, only if they satisfy the following set of conditions:

i. $\qquad t_i = t'_i$

ii. $\qquad |\Theta_{med} - \Theta'_{med}| < T_\Theta$

$\hfill (3)$

iii. $\qquad |\Theta_{max} - \Theta'_{max}| < T_\Theta$

iv. $\qquad d \leq T_2$

where T_Θ and T_2 are the thresholds. The triplets in the database that satisfy the conditions given in Eq. (3) are taken as successful correspondence for the query triplet and the corresponding image identity I is given a vote. This process is repeated for all the query triplets. Accumulate all the votes of the database images and declare the top N images as candidates whose vote scores are greater than a threshold T_3. The vote score of a database image against query image is given as,

$$\text{Vote score} = \frac{count}{p} \times 100 \qquad (4)$$

where *count* is the number of query triplets matched with the database image, and p is the total number of query triplets. Algorithm 3 lists the process of retrieving candidate images during identification.

3   Experiments and Results

Experiments have been carried out on NTU-NIR vein pattern database that consists of 738 images, 3 prints each of 246 distinct hands. In addition, we also conducted experiments on NTU-FIR vein pattern database consists of 194 images, approximately 3 prints each of 60 distinct hands. The first of these prints is used to construct the database, while the other two images are used to test the indexing performance. The images are cropped (NIR images: 320 × 248 pixels and FIR images: 120 × 120 pixels) to extract the features from the same region for different hands. In the experiments, binary code length and thresholds are selected empirically depending on the quality and size of the respective database images, and they are different for the two databases: for NIR database, binary code length = 16, $T_1 = 125$, $T_2 = 4$, $T_3 = 70\%$ and $T_\Theta = 8°$; for FIR database, binary code length = 12, $T_1 = 125$, $T_2 = 3$, $T_3 = 75\%$ and $T_\Theta = 6°$.

Algorithm 3. Retrieval

For Query image Q,
1. Compute binary code B_Q.
2. Extract the minutiae features after a series of preprocessing steps.
3. Apply Delaunay triangulation on the extracted minutiae set and classify the triplets according to Table 1.
4. **For** each triplet of query image Q, do
   a. Compute 3D index $(t, \Theta_{med}, \Theta_{max})$ and access the table.
   b. Take the triplets that satisfy the conditions given in Eq. (3) as successful correspondences and cast vote to respective image identities.
   End for
5. Accumulate the votes of all the database images and declare the top N images as best matches whose vote scores are greater than a threshold T_3.
End for.

The performance of the proposed algorithm is evaluated using two measures, namely Hit Rate (HR) and Penetration Rate (PR), where HR is defined as the percentage of test images for which the corresponding genuine match is present in the candidate list and PR is the average percentage of comparisons needed to identify a test image. Experiments have been carried out to evaluate the performances of the proposed algorithm, algorithm based on Delaunay triplets and algorithm based on all possible triplets. All the techniques have been implemented using MATLAB. The performance curves plotting the HR against PR at various thresholds are shown in Fig. 5, 6.

Fig. 5 shows the average percentage of database to be searched to identify a test image with the proposed method and the method using Delaunay triangulation for both the databases. It is observed that for FIR database, to achieve 100% hit rate, the search space of the proposed algorithm is 11.75%, which is around 7% less than the space of Delaunay triplet based algorithm whose search space is 18.22%. For NIR database, the search space of the proposed algorithm is 17.99%, which is around 15% less than the space of Delaunay triplet based algorithm whose search space is 32.99%. From the results it is evident that the performance of the proposed algorithm is better compared to Delaunay approach.

The performance of proposed algorithm against algorithm based on all possible triplets can be seen from the Fig. 6 for both FIR and NIR databases. The proposed method creates only $O(n)$ triplets which is very less in number compared to $O(n^3)$ triplets created by the all possible triangles algorithm. In all possible triangles approach, the presence of redundant triplets causes higher possibility of mismatch with wrong correspondences. This increases the size of the candidate set to which the actual matching has to be done and leads to more computing cost and search space compared to our method. It is seen from the Fig.6 that our algorithm performs better as it compare with less number of images to identify a test image.

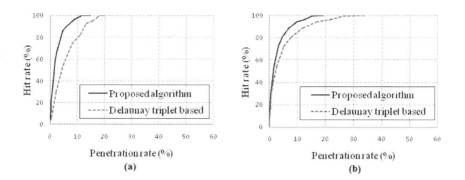

Fig. 5. Comparison of the proposed algorithm and the algorithm based on Delaunay triplets [16] on (a) FIR database, (b) NIR database

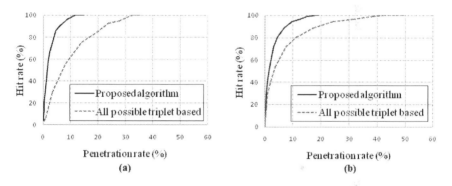

Fig. 6. Comparison of the proposed algorithm and the algorithm based on all possible triplets on (a) FIR database, (b) NIR database

4   Conclusion

In this paper, an efficient indexing algorithm using texture binary code and hierarchical decomposition of Delaunay triplets for minutiae of vein patterns are proposed. It has been shown that the proposed algorithm performs better for the vein pattern databases. The texture binary code proposed in the algorithm efficiently filter out the wrong correspondences i.e. inter-class similar images during identification, lead to significant decrease in the number of potential candidates to be matched. The decomposition of Delaunay triplets provides better classification in the database, and further reduces search space. The use of Delaunay triangulation reduces the computation cost, increase the response time as it produces only $O(n)$ triplets and is less sensitive to distortion compared to all possible triplets method.

References

1. Germain, R., Califano, A., Colville, S.: Fingerprint matching using transformation parameter clustering. IEEE Computational Science and Eng. 4, 42–49 (1997)
2. Bhanu, B., Tan, X.: Fingerprint indexing based on novel features of minutiae triplets. IEEE Transactions on Pattern Analysis and Machine Intelligence 25, 616–622 (2003)
3. Lamdan, Y., Schwartz, J., Wolfson, H.: Affine invariant model-based object recognition. IEEE Transactions On Robotics and Automation 6, 578–589 (1990)
4. Tuceryan, M., Chorzempa, T.: Relative Sensitivity of a Family of Closest-Point Graphs in Computer Vision Applications. Pattern Recognition 24, 361–373 (1991)
5. Maltoni, D., Maio, D., Jain, A.K., Prabhakar, S.: Handbook of fingerprint recognition. Springer, New York (2003)
6. Lowe, D.G.: Distinctive image features from scale-invariant keypoints. International Journal on Computer Vision 60, 91–110 (2004)
7. Lamdan, Y., Wolfson, H.J.: Geometric hashing: a general and efficient model-based recognition scheme. In: International Conference on Computer Vision, pp. 238–249 (1988)
8. Mehrotra, H., Majhi, B., Gupta, P.: Robust iris indexing scheme using geometric hashing of SIFT keypoints. Journal of Network and Computer Applications 33, 300–313 (2010)
9. Mhatre, A., Palla, S., Chikkerur, S., Govindaraju, V.: Efficient search and retrieval in biometric databases. Biometric Technology for Human Identification II 5779, 265–273 (2005)
10. Jain, A.K., Flynn, P., Ross, A.: Handbook of Biometrics. Springer, Heidelberg (2008)
11. Boro, R., Roy, S.D.: Fast and Robust Projective Matching for Finger prints using Geometric Hashing. In: Indian Conference on Computer Vision, Graphics and Image Processing, pp. 681–686 (2004)
12. Bebis, G., Deaconu, T., Georgiopoulos, M.: Fingerprint identification using Delaunay triangulation. In: Proceedings of International Conference on Information Intelligence and Systems, pp. 452–459 (1999)
13. Gonzalez, R.C., Woods, R.E., Eddins, S.L.: Digital Image Processing using MATLAB. Prentice Hall, Upper Saddle River (2010)
14. Jain, A.K., Hong, L., Bolle, R.: On-line fingerprint verification. IEEE Transactions on Pattern Analysis and Machine Intelligence 19, 302–313 (1997)
15. Jain, A.K., Pankanti, S.: Automated fingerprint identification and imaging systems. In: Advances in Fingerprint Technology, 2nd edn. Elsevier Science (2001)
16. Berg, M., Kreveld, M., Overmars, M., Schwarzkopf, O.: Computational Geometry: Algorithms and Application. Springer, Heidelbarg (1997)
17. Otsu, N.: A threshold selection method from gray-level histograms. IEEE Transactions on Systems, Man and Cybernetics 9, 62–66 (1979)
18. Kumar, A., Prathyusha, K.V.: Personal authentication using hand vein triangulation and knuckle shape. IEEE Transactions on Image Processing 38, 2127–2136 (2009)

Short Attribute-Based Group Signature without Random Oracles with Attribute Anonymity

Syed Taqi Ali and B.B. Amberker

National Institute of Technology Warangal,
Kazipet - 506004, AP, India
taqiali110@gmail.com, bba@nitw.ac.in

Abstract. Attribute Based Group Signature (ABGS) scheme is a kind of group signature scheme where the group members possessing certain privileges (attributes) only are eligible for signing the document. There are ABGS schemes secure under random oracle models, have signature length linear in terms of number of attributes and do not provide *attribute anonymity*. We have come up with an ABGS scheme which provides *attribute anonymity*, has short signature length independent of number of attributes and proven that it is secure under the standard model.

Keywords: Attribute based, group signature, attribute anonymity, standard model, short signature.

1 Introduction

Group signature (GS) allows a member of a group to sign a message anonymously so that outsiders and other group members cannot see which member has signed the message. The group is controlled by a group manager that handles enrollment of members and also has the ability to identify the signer of a message. Group signature schemes find several applications like company authenticating price list, press releases, digital contracts, anonymous credit cards, access control, e-cash, e-voting, e-auction.

Group signatures were first introduced by Chaum and van Heyst in [11], since then many other schemes were proposed secure in the random oracle model [7,12] and in the standard model [2,4,17,10,23]. In [2] Bellare et al. have given the formal definitions of the security properties of the group signature scheme, namely *Full-Anonymity* and *Full Traceablity*. Futhermore, in [4] Bellare et al. have strengthened the security model to include dynamic enrollment of members. Boyen et al. [10] and Liang et al. [23] given a group signature schemes that are secure in a restricted version of the BMW-model [2], where the *anonymity* of the members relies on the adversary can not make any query on the tracing of group signature.

Attribute Based Group Signature (ABGS) scheme is a group signature scheme where the group members satisfying the predicate with their assigned attributes are only eligible for signing the document [22]. In ABGS, each member is assigned a subset of attributes, verifier accepts the signed document only if the associated signature proves that it is signed by the member who possess sufficient

Sabu M. Thampi et al. (Eds.): SSCC 2013, CCIS 377, pp. 223–235, 2013.

attributes to satisfy the given predicate. The predicates in terms of attribute relationships (the access structures) are represented by an *access tree*. For example, consider the predicate Υ for the document M: (Institute = Univ. A) AND (TH2((Department = Biology), (Gender = Female), (Age = 50's)) OR (Position = Professor)), TH2 means the threshold gate with threshold value 2. Attribute $\mathcal{A}_1$ of Alice is ((Institute := Univ. A),(Department := Biology), (Position := Postdoc), (Age := 30), (Gender := Female)), and attribute $\mathcal{A}_2$ of Bob is ((Institute := Univ. A), (Department := Mathematics), (Position := Professor), (Age := 45), (Gender := Male)). Although their attributes, $\mathcal{A}_1$ and $\mathcal{A}_2$, are quite different, it is clear that $\Upsilon(\mathcal{A}_1)$ and $\Upsilon(\mathcal{A}_2)$ hold, and that there are many other attributes that satisfy Υ. Hence Alice and Bob can generate a signature on this predicate, and according to anonymity requirement of ABGS, a signature should not reveal any information except that the attribute of the signer satisfies the given predicate Υ.

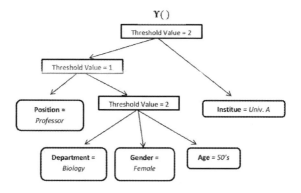

Fig. 1. Predicate example in Tree Structure

Thus the ABGS Scheme is a kind of group signature scheme where an user with a set of attributes can prove anonymously whether he possess these attributes or not [14]. The first ABGS was proposed by Dalia Khader [22] and listed *attribute anonymity* - the verifier should be able to verify whether the signer has required attributes without learning which set of attributes he used for signing, as a desirable feature to achieve. Later Dalia Khader proposed the ABGS scheme [21] with member revocation feature without achieving attribute anonymity. Emura et al. proposed the dynamic ABGS scheme [14], which is efficient when there is a frequent change in attribute's relationships but it does not provide attribute anonymity. Moreover the signature size in both the schemes depend on the number of attributes.

Attribute anonymity is as necessary as anonymity property and in certain cases it is mandatory. Consider the case where there is a unique attribute which belongs to only one group member along with other attributes and whenever the verifier finds that attribute in the signature then he can conclude that the signature is signed by that particular group member who alone owns that attribute;

thus anonymity itself is not preserved which is the basic security requirement in any group signature scheme. Many similar cases exist. Thus attribute anonymity is as important as anonymity property and we name *anonymity* property as a *user anonymity* property.

Maji et al. in [24] have introduced an Attribute-Based Signatures (ABS), where a signer can sign a message with any predicate that is satisfied by his attributes. Here, the signature reveals no information about the signer's identity or the attributes he holds but guarantees that the signer possesses the required attributes. Many ABS schemes in standard model have been proposed [24,20,15], among which the scheme presented by Herranz et al. [20] has constant length signature but for the threshold predicates and for general predicate (a monotone predicate), Escala et al. [15] have given the ABS scheme whose signature size is linear in terms of the size of the predicate. Notice that to build an ABGS scheme with attribute anonymity in standard model one can also combine an ABS scheme [20] with a group signature scheme [23], but it incurs additional cost of both the schemes.

Our Contribution. We propose a constant size ABGS scheme with attribute anonymity and proven that it is secure in the standard model. Our construction is based on the two-level signature scheme from [23] and the technique to build the access trees from [14]. We use non-interactive proof system technique [18] to hide the values in the group signature. We prove that our scheme preserves attribute anonymity unconditionally, user anonymity in CPA attacks under Subgroup Decision assumption, traceability under ℓ-MOMSDH and attribute unforgeability under DL and KEA1 assumptions, in the standard model. In contrast to other existing ABGS schemes [22,21,14] our scheme is built in standard model and achieves a constant size signature independent of number of attributes.

In Section 2, preliminaries are given and the formal definition and security model of ABGS scheme is described in Section 3. The proposed scheme is given in Section 4 followed by security analysis and comparison with previous schemes in Section 5. We conclude in Section 6.

2   Preliminaries

2.1   Bilinear Maps and Complexity Assumptions

Let $\mathbb{G}$ and $\mathbb{G}_T$ be cyclic groups of composite order n, where $n = pq, p, q$ are large primes of k bit length and $p \neq q$. Let g be a generator of $\mathbb{G}$. Let $\mathbb{G}_p$ and $\mathbb{G}_q$ be a subgroups of $\mathbb{G}$ of respective orders p and q.

Definition 1 (Bilinear Map). *The bilinear map e is an efficiently computable function, $e : \mathbb{G} \times \mathbb{G} \to \mathbb{G}_T$ with the following properties.*

- *Bilinearity : For any $h \in \mathbb{G}$, and $a, b \in \mathbb{Z}_n$, $e(g^a, h^b) = e(g, h)^{ab}$.*
- *Non-degeneracy: $e(g, h) \neq 1_{\mathbb{G}_T}$ whenever $g, h \neq 1_{\mathbb{G}}$.*

Definition 2 (Subgroup Decision Assumption [8]). *For all PPT algorithm*
$\mathcal{A}$, *the probability*

$$|Pr[w = g^r \wedge \mathcal{A}(n, \mathbb{G}, \mathbb{G}_T, e, g, w) = 1] - Pr[w = g^{pr} \wedge \mathcal{A}(n, \mathbb{G}, \mathbb{G}_T, e, g, w) = 1]|$$

is negligible function in k, *where* $r \in_R \mathbb{Z}_n^*$.

Definition 3 (ℓ-SDH Assumption [6]). *For all PPT algorithm* $\mathcal{A}$, *the probability*

$$Pr[\mathcal{A}(v, v^x, v^{(x^2)}, ..., v^{(x^\ell)}) = (v^{\frac{1}{x+c}}, c) \wedge c \in \mathbb{Z}_p]$$

is negligible function in k, *where* v *is the generator of* $\mathbb{G}_p$ *and* $x \in_R \mathbb{Z}_p^*$.

Definition 4 (ℓ'-Modified One More Strong Diffie-Hellman Assumption (ℓ'-MOMSDH) [23]). *For all PPT algorithm* $\mathcal{A}$, *the probability*

$$Pr[\mathcal{A}(v, v^x, u, c_1, v^{\frac{1}{x+c_1}}, c_2, v^{\frac{1}{x+c_2}}, ..., c_{\ell'}, v^{\frac{1}{x+c_{\ell'}}}) =$$
$$(v^c, v^{\frac{1}{x+c}}, u^{\frac{1}{c+m}}, m) \wedge c \neq c_i, \text{ for } i = 1, ..., \ell']$$

is negligible function in k, *where* u, v *are the generators of* $\mathbb{G}_p$, $x \in \mathbb{Z}_p^*, c_i \in \mathbb{Z}_n$ *and* $m \in \mathbb{Z}_n$.

Definition 5 (DL Assumption). *For all PPT algorithm* $\mathcal{A}$, *the probability*

$$Pr[\mathcal{A}(v, v' = v^\xi) = \xi]$$

is negligible function in k, *where* $v \in_R \mathbb{G}_p$ *and* $\xi \in_R \mathbb{Z}_p^*$.

Definition 6 (Knowledge of Exponent Assumption 1 (KEA1) [19,3]).
For any adversary $\mathcal{A}$ *that takes input* q, v, v^a, *where* v *is a generator of a cyclic group* $\mathbb{G}_q$ *of order* q *and returns a pair of elements* v', v'^a *from* $\mathbb{G}_q$, *there exists an extractor* $\bar{\mathcal{A}}$, *which given the same inputs as* $\mathcal{A}$ *returns* ξ *such that* $v^\xi = v'$.

KEA1 has been shown to hold in generic groups (i.e., it is secure in the generic group model) by A. Dent [13] and independently by Abe et al. [1].

Definition 7 (Access Structure [21]). *Let* $Att = \{att_1, att_2, ..., att_m\}$ *be a set of attributes. For* $\Gamma \subseteq 2^{Att} \backslash \{\emptyset\}$, Γ *satisfies the* monotone *property if* $\forall B, C \subseteq Att, B \in \Gamma$ *and* $B \subseteq C$, *then* $C \in \Gamma$ *holds. An* access structure *(respectively, monotone access structure) is a collection (respectively, monotone collection)* Γ *of non-empty subsets of* Att, *i.e.,* $\Gamma \subseteq 2^{Att} \backslash \{\emptyset\}$.

2.2   Access Tree

An access tree T is used for expressing an access structure (predicate Υ) by using a tree structure. An access tree T consists of threshold gates as non-leaf nodes and attributes as leaves. Let l_x be the number of children of node x, and k_x $(0 < k_x \leq l_x)$ be the threshold value on the threshold gate of node x. A threshold gate represents the number k_x of l_x children branching from the current node x need to be satisfied in order to imply that the parent node is satisfied. Note that if number of children is equal to threshold value it indicates an AND gate and if the threshold value is one then it indicates an OR gate. Satisfaction of a leaf is achieved by owning an attribute.

3   Attribute-Based Group Signatures: Definitions and Security

In this section, we give some basic models and security definitions which are similar to the one given in papers [22,14,23,9] with added attribute anonymity. **Notations:** Let k be the security parameter, Att be the universal set of attributes, Υ used to denote the predicate, T_Υ be an access tree representing the predicate Υ, $\mathcal{T}_\Upsilon$ the public values associated with T_Υ, gpk the group public key used to verify the validity of the group signature, ik the issuing key used for issuing private keys to users, ok the opening key used for opening the signer's identity from the given group signature, id $\in \{0,1\}^k$ represents the user identity, k_{id} be the user's private key, $\mathcal{A}_{\mathrm{id}} \subseteq Att$ the attributes of the user with identity id. $\Upsilon(\zeta) = 1$ denotes that the attribute set ζ satisfies the predicate Υ.

Definition 8 (ABGS). *An ABGS scheme consists of the following six algorithms. Unless specified all the algorithms are probabilistic.*

- *params* ← Setup(1^k): *It takes the security parameter k as an input and generates system parameters params.*
- (gpk, ik, ok) ← KeyGen(*params*): *It takes the system parameters params as an input and outputs group public key gpk, an issuing key ik for enrolling group members and an opening key ok for identifying the signers.*
- k_{id} ← Join($gpk, ik, \mathrm{id}, \mathcal{A}_{\mathrm{id}}$): *This algorithm generates the private key for the user with identity id. It takes ik, user identity id and subset of attributes $\mathcal{A}_{\mathrm{id}} \subseteq Att$, and outputs a user private key k_{id} which is to be given to the user.*
- σ ← Sign($gpk, k_{\mathrm{id}}, \zeta, M, \Upsilon$): *It takes gpk, k_{id}, an attribute set $\zeta \subseteq \mathcal{A}_{\mathrm{id}}$, a message M and a predicate Υ, and outputs a group signature σ.*
- $0/1$ ← Verify(gpk, M, Υ, σ): *This is a deterministic algorithm which outputs a boolean value. If it is 1 it claims that σ is a valid group signature on M with respect to Υ, otherwise invalid.*
- $\mathrm{id}/\perp$ ← Open(gpk, ok, σ) : *This is a deterministic algorithm which takes an opening key ok and a group signature σ, and outputs either id or $\perp$. If id then the algorithm claims that the group member with an identity id has produced σ, and if $\perp$, it claims that no group member produced σ.*

There are three types of entities in ABGS scheme:

- The group manager GM, who sets up the group by running the Setup and KeyGen algorithms. GM keeps issuing key ik and opening key ok secret. Using issuing key GM enrolls an user into the group by allotting some privilege (in terms of attributes) say $\mathcal{A}_{\mathrm{id}} \subseteq Att$ and issuing a user's private key k_{id}, by running the Join algorithm. GM runs Open algorithm to reveal the signer's identity from the group signature.

– Group members, or signers, who are having their private keys k_{id}'s. They run Sign algorithm to produce a group signature on a document M with predicate Υ; if they possess valid attribute set which satisfies the predicate.
– Outsider, or verifier, who can only verify the group signature using the group public key, gpk.

Definition 9 (Correctness). *We call an ABGS scheme is correct if for all honestly generated* $(gpk, ik, ok) \leftarrow$ KeyGen$(params)$, *for all* $k_{\text{id}} \leftarrow$ Join$(gpk, ik, \text{id}, \mathcal{A}_{\text{id}})$ *the following equations hold.*

$$1 \leftarrow \text{Verify}(gpk, M, \Upsilon, \text{Sign}(gpk, k_{\text{id}}, \zeta, M, \Upsilon))$$

$$: \zeta \subseteq \mathcal{A}_{\text{id}} \text{ and } \Upsilon(\zeta) = 1$$

$$\text{id} \leftarrow \text{Open}(gpk, ok, \text{Sign}(gpk, k_{\text{id}}, \zeta, M, \Upsilon))$$

We write Sign$(gpk, ik, \text{id}, \zeta, M, \Upsilon)$ (i.e., in place of user private key k_{id}, we use issuing key ik and user identity id) to denote the following task: pick the corresponding k_{id} from the list (we assume that a list $\{(\text{id}, k_{\text{id}})\}$ is maintained) and returns the group signature $\sigma \leftarrow$ Sign$(gpk, k_{\text{id}}, \zeta, M, \Upsilon)$, and if the related k_{id} is not present in the list (i.e., k_{id} is not generated yet) then choose $\mathcal{A}_{\text{id}} \subseteq Att$ randomly such that $\exists \zeta \subset \mathcal{A}_{\text{id}}, \Upsilon(\zeta) = 1$ and gets $k_{\text{id}} \leftarrow$ Join$(gpk, ik, \text{id}, \mathcal{A}_{\text{id}})$, stores it in a list and finally returns the intended group signature $\sigma \leftarrow$ Sign$(gpk, k_{\text{id}}, \zeta, M, \Upsilon)$.

For convenience, in the definitions below we denote sign oracle as Sign$(gpk, ik, ., ., ., .)$ to generate the group signature requested by an adversary with the query that includes user identity id, a message M and a predicate Υ. And we denote join oracle as Join$(gpk, ik, ., .)$ to generate a user private key $k_{\text{id}} \leftarrow$ Join$(gpk, ik, \text{id}, \mathcal{A}_{\text{id}})$ upon input id and an attribute set $\mathcal{A}_{\text{id}} \subseteq Att$ queried by the adversary.

Definition 10 (User Anonymity (CPA[1])). *We say that the ABGS scheme preserves* User Anonymity *if for all PPT* $\mathcal{A}$, *the probability that* $\mathcal{A}$ *wins the following game is negligible.*

– **Setup** : *The simulator* $\mathcal{B}$ *generates* $(gpk, ik, ok) \leftarrow$
KeyGen$(params)$. $\mathcal{B}$ *gives gpk to* $\mathcal{A}$.
– **Phase1** : $\mathcal{A}$ *is given access to the oracles* Join$(gpk, ik, ., .)$ *and* Sign$(gpk, ik, ., ., .)$.
– **Challenge** : $\mathcal{A}$ *outputs* M^*, Υ^* *and two identities* ID_1, ID_2 : $\exists \zeta_1 \subseteq \mathcal{A}_{ID_1}, \zeta_2[2] \subseteq \mathcal{A}_{ID_2}$ *and* $\Upsilon^*(\zeta_1) = \Upsilon^*(\zeta_2) = 1$ *to be challenged. The simulator* $\mathcal{B}$ *randomly selects* $x \in_R \{1, 2\}$ *and responds with a group signature* $\sigma^* \leftarrow$ Sign$(gpk, k_{ID_x}, \zeta_x, M^*, \Upsilon^*)$. *The constraints are the private keys of* ID_1 *and* ID_2 *to the join oracle, and group signatures on* (M^*, Υ^*, ID_1) *and* (M^*, Υ^*, ID_2) *to the sign oracle should not be queried before.*

---

[1] Note: If we provide Open oracle to the adversary then the *User Anonymity* will be enhanced to CCA-security notion.
[2] ζ_2 can be equal to ζ_1. Since we are concerned only about the user anonymity the attribute anonymity is separately considered in *Attribute Anonymity* definition.

- Phase2 : $\mathcal{A}$ can make all queries similar to Phase1 under the constraints mentioned above.
- Output : $\mathcal{A}$ outputs a bit x', and wins if $x = x'$.

The advantage of $\mathcal{A}$ is defined as $Adv_{\mathcal{A}} = |Pr(x = x') - \frac{1}{2}|$.

Thus there should not exists any PPT adversary to distinguish the two group signatures with non negligible probability.

Definition 11 (Attribute Anonymity). We say that the ABGS scheme preserve Attribute Anonymity if, for all honestly generated $(gpk, ik, ok) \leftarrow$ KeyGen$(params)$, for all predicates Υ, for all attribute sets $\mathcal{A}_{id} \subseteq Att$ such that there exist $\zeta_1, \zeta_2 \subseteq \mathcal{A}_{id}$ and $\Upsilon(\zeta_1) = \Upsilon(\zeta_2) = 1$, for all $k_{id} \leftarrow$ Join$(gpk, ik, id, \mathcal{A}_{id})$ and all messages M, the distributions Sign$(gpk, k_{id}, \zeta_1, M, \Upsilon)$ and Sign$(gpk, k_{id}, \zeta_2, M, \Upsilon)$ are identical.

In other words, even the computationally unbounded adversary cannot link a signature to a set of attributes used to generate it.

The *Traceability* definition is same as given in [2].

Definition 12 (Attribute Unforgeability). We say that the ABGS scheme preserves Attribute Unforgeability if for all PPT $\mathcal{A}$, the probability that $\mathcal{A}$ wins the following game is negligible.

- Setup : The simulator $\mathcal{B}$ generates $(gpk, ik, ok) \leftarrow$ KeyGen$(params)$. $\mathcal{B}$ gives gpk to $\mathcal{A}$.
- Queries : $\mathcal{A}$ is given access to the oracles Join$(gpk, ik, ., .)$ and Sign$(gpk, ik, ., ., .)$.
- Output : $\mathcal{A}$ outputs a message M^*, a predicate Υ^* and a group signature σ^*.

$\mathcal{A}$ wins if (1) Verify$(gpk, M^*, \Upsilon^*, \sigma^*) = 1$,
(2) Open$(gpk, ok, \sigma^*) = id$ and
(3) $\nexists \zeta \in \mathcal{A}_{id} : \Upsilon(\zeta) = 1$.

Thus it should be impossible for any PPT adversary to satisfy the predicate with invalid set of attributes.

Definition 13 (Collusion resistance of Attributes). We say that the ABGS scheme preserves Collusion resistance of Attributes if for all PPT $\mathcal{A}$, the probability that $\mathcal{A}$ wins the following game is negligible.

- Setup : The simulator $\mathcal{B}$ generates $(gpk, ik, ok) \leftarrow$ KeyGen$(params)$. $\mathcal{B}$ gives gpk to $\mathcal{A}$.
- Queries : $\mathcal{A}$ is given access to the oracles Join$(gpk, ik, ., .)$ and Sign$(gpk, ik, ., ., .)$.
- Output : $\mathcal{A}$ outputs a message M^*, a predicate Υ^* and a group signature σ^*.

$\mathcal{A}$ wins if (1) Verify$(gpk, M^*, \Upsilon^*, \sigma^*) = 1$, and (2) $\mathcal{A}$ has obtained $k_{id_1}, ..., k_{id_k}$: $\Upsilon^*(\cup_{j=1}^{k} \mathcal{A}_{id_j}) = 1$ and $\Upsilon^*(\mathcal{A}_{id_j}) \neq 1$ for $j = 1, ..., k$.

Thus the users with invalid set of attributes each, cannot collude with each other to pool a valid attribute set for producing a valid group signature.

4   Short Attribute Based Group Signature Scheme with Attribute Anonymity

In this section, we propose our short attribute based group signature scheme with attribute anonymity. First we present the Two-level signature scheme [23] and Assignment of Secret Values to Access Trees [14] which are used in our proposed scheme.

4.1   Two-Level Signature Scheme

We use the two level signature scheme proposed by Liang et al. in [23] which is existential unforgeable against chosen message attacks under ℓ-SDH and ℓ'-MOMSDH assumption. In the first level, the certificate is signed by the group manager and in the second level a short signature on message M is produced. This signature scheme is based on the short signature proposed by Boneh et al. in [5].

4.2   Assignment of Secret Values to Access Trees

We use the *Bottom-up Approach* for the construction of access tree of the predicate given by Emura et al. in [14]. This includes the following three functions:

1. `AddDummyNode`(T): This algorithm takes as input an access tree T, adds dummy nodes to it and returns the *extended access tree* T^{ext}.
   Let D_T be a set of dummy nodes added. Let $s_j \in \mathbb{Z}_q^*$ be a secret value for an attribute $\text{att}_j \in Att$. Let $S = \{s_j\}_{\text{att}_j \in Att}$.
2. `AssignedValue`(S, T^{ext}): This algorithm takes as input S and T^{ext} and returns a secret value for each dummy node $\{s_{d_j}\}_{d_j \in D_T} \in \mathbb{Z}_q^*$ and a root secret $s_T \in \mathbb{Z}_q^*$.
3. `MakeSimplifiedTree`($Leaves, T^{ext}$): This algorithm takes as input the attributes set $Leaves \subseteq Att$ satisfying the tree T, and returns the product of Lagranges coefficients $\Delta_{leaf}(\forall leaf \in Leaves \cup D_T^{Leaves})$, Such that

$$\sum_{\text{att}_j \in Leaves} \Delta_{\text{att}_j} s_j + \sum_{d_j \in D_T^{Leaves}} \Delta_{d_j} s_{d_j} = s_T \qquad (1)$$

holds, where $D_T^{Leaves} \subseteq D_T$ is the set of dummy nodes related to *Leaves*.

For details of these algorithms we refer readers to [14].

4.3   Proposed ABGS Scheme

- `Setup`(1^k): It takes the security parameter k as an input and output the system parameters.
  1. Select the primes p and q of size k. Let the groups $\mathbb{G}$ and $\mathbb{G}_T$ be of order $n = pq$ for which there exists a bilinear map e from $\mathbb{G} \times \mathbb{G}$ to $\mathbb{G}_T$. Let $\mathbb{G}_p$ and $\mathbb{G}_q$ be the subgroups of $\mathbb{G}$ of order p and q, respectively.

2. Define the universal set of attributes, $Att = \{att_1, ..., att_m\}$, $m = O(k)$.
3. Define Collision resistant hash function, $\mathcal{H} : \{0,1\}^{m'} \rightarrow \mathcal{Z}_n$, $m' = O(k)$.
4. Output the system parameters,

$$params = (n, p, q, \mathbb{G}, \mathbb{G}_T, e, \mathbb{G}_p, \mathbb{G}_q, Att, \mathcal{H})$$

- KeyGen($params$): It takes the system parameter $params$ as an input and output the group public key gpk, issuing key ik and the opening key ok.
  1. Select the generators $g, u \in \mathbb{G}$ and $h \in \mathbb{G}_q$.
  2. For each attribute att_i select the attribute secret $s_i \in \mathbb{Z}_q^*$. Let $S = \{s_i\}_{att_i \in Att}$.
  3. Compute the public values of the attributes $\{h_{att_i} = h^{s_i}\}_{att_i \in Att}$.
  4. Select the secret $z \in_R \mathbb{Z}_n^*$ and compute $Z = g^z$.
  5. Output the group public key,

$$gpk = (g, u, h, Z, \{h_{att_i}\}_{att_i \in Att})$$

  The issuing key $ik = (z, S)$ and the opening key $ok = q$.
  The gpk also include the description of $(n, \mathbb{G}, \mathbb{G}_T, e)$, $Att, \mathcal{H}$.
- Join($gpk, ik, \mathrm{id}, A_{\mathrm{id}}$): It takes group public key, issuing key, user identity id and subset of attributes $A_{\mathrm{id}} \subseteq Att$, and outputs user private key k_{id}.
  1. Select the unique identifier $s_{\mathrm{id}} \in \mathbb{Z}_n^*$.
  2. Compute $g_{\mathrm{id}} = g^{\frac{1}{s_{\mathrm{id}}+z}}$.
  3. Compute the attribute certificates $\{g_{\mathrm{id},i} = g_{\mathrm{id}}^{s_i}\}_{att_i \in A_{\mathrm{id}}}$.
  4. Output the user private key,

$$k_{\mathrm{id}} = (k_{\mathrm{id}}^{(1)}, k_{\mathrm{id}}^{(2)}, k_{\mathrm{id}}^{(3)}) = (s_{\mathrm{id}}, g_{\mathrm{id}}, \{g_{\mathrm{id},i}\}_{att_i \in A_{\mathrm{id}}})$$

- BuildTree(gpk, ik, Υ): It generates a public values for the predicate Υ.
  1. Let T_Υ be the tree that represents the predicate Υ.
  2. Get extension tree $T^{\mathrm{ext}} \leftarrow$ AddDummyNode(T_Υ).
  3. Get secret values for each dummy node and the secret value of root of T^{ext} using $(\{s_{d_j}\}_{d_j \in D_T}, s_T) \leftarrow$ AssignedVaule(S, T^{ext}).
  4. Output the public values of tree T_Υ.

$$\mathcal{T}_\Upsilon = (\{s_{d_j}\}_{d_j \in D_T}, h_T = h^{s_T}, g_T = g^{s_T}, T^{\mathrm{ext}})$$

- Sign($gpk, k_{\mathrm{id}}, \zeta, M, \Upsilon$): It generates a group signature σ on message $M \in \{0,1\}^{m'}$ with user private key k_{id} who satisfy the predicate Υ with his subset of attributes $\zeta \subseteq A_{\mathrm{id}} : \Upsilon(\zeta) = 1$.
  1. Get the public values of Υ from the public repository[3].
  2. Compute $\rho = (\rho_1, \rho_2, \rho_3) = (g^{s_{\mathrm{id}}}, g_{\mathrm{id}}^{s_T}, u^{\frac{1}{s_{\mathrm{id}}+\mathcal{H}(M)}})$
     where $\rho_2 = g_{\mathrm{id}}^{s_T}$ is computed as follows,
     - Select $\zeta \subseteq A_{\mathrm{id}} : \Upsilon(\zeta) = 1$.

---

[3] GM runs BuildTree algorithm to generate the public values of the predicate Υ and stores it in a public repository. Note that if the public values of the required predicate is present in the public repository then the user will not approach GM.

- Get $\qquad$ $(\{\Delta_{\text{att}_j}\}_{(\forall \text{att}_j \in \zeta)}, \{\Delta_{d_j}\}_{(\forall d_j \in D_T^\zeta)})$ $\qquad$ ←
  MakeSimplifiedTree(ζ, T^{ext}).

- Compute $\qquad \rho_2 \qquad = \qquad \Pi_{\text{att}_i \in \zeta} g_{\text{id},i}^{\Delta_{\text{att}_i}} g_{\text{id}}^{(\Sigma_{d_j \in D_T^\zeta} \Delta_{d_j} s_{d_j})} \qquad =$

  $g_{\text{id}}^{\Sigma_{\text{att}_i \in \zeta} \Delta_{\text{att}_i} s_i} g_{\text{id}}^{\Sigma_{d_j \in D_T^\zeta} \Delta_{d_j} s_{d_j}} = g_{\text{id}}^{s_T}$.

  Hiding the ρ values.

3. Choose $t_1, t_2, t_3 \in_R \mathbb{Z}_n$, and compute $\sigma_1 = \rho_1 h^{t_1}$,
   $\sigma_2 = \rho_2 h^{t_2}$ and $\sigma_3 = \rho_3 h^{t_3}$.
4. Compute $\pi_1 = \rho_2^{t_1}(Z\rho_1)^{t_2} h^{t_1 t_2}$,
   $\pi_2 = \rho_3^{t_1}(g^{\mathcal{H}(M)}\rho_1)^{t_3} h^{t_1 t_3}$.
5. Output a group signature: $\sigma = (\{\sigma_i\}_{i=1}^3, \pi_1, \pi_2) \in \mathbb{G}^5$

Notice that the attribute certificates are only used in computing ρ_2. Also notice that the signature size is independent of number of attributes $|\zeta|$.

- Verify$(gpk, M, \Upsilon, \sigma)$:
  1. Compute $T_1 = e(\sigma_1 Z, \sigma_2)e(g, g_T)^{-1}$ and $T_2 = e(\sigma_1 g^{\mathcal{H}(M)}, \sigma_3)e(g, u)^{-1}$
  2. Verify the following equations:

$$T_1 \overset{?}{=} e(\pi_1, h) \tag{2}$$

$$T_2 \overset{?}{=} e(\pi_2, h) \tag{3}$$

Returns 1 if the above equations holds, else return 0.

Equation (2) establishes that the signer is a valid member holding required attributes that satisfies the predicate Υ and equation (3) establishes that the group signature is on message M.

- Open(gpk, ok, σ): Parse the signature and get σ_1. Calculate $(\sigma_1)^q$ and test:

$$(\sigma_1)^q = (g^{s_{\text{id}}} h^{t_1})^q \overset{?}{=} (g^{s_{\text{id}}})^q$$

All the $(g^{s_{\text{id}}})^q$ can be pre-computed and stored as a list by the opener. It returns the corresponding id if it matches any such value from the list, else returns 0. Time to find the identity id is linearly dependent on the number of initial users.

5 Security Analysis

Theorem 1. *The proposed ABGS scheme is correct, preserves attribute anonymity, preserves user anonymity under subgroup decision assumption, is traceable under the chosen message existential unforgeability of the two-level signature scheme, preserves attribute unforgeability under DL and KEA assumptions, and preserves collusion resistance of attributes.*

Proof. The proofs will appear in full version of this paper. $\qquad\qquad \square$

5.1   Comparison

In the proposed scheme, the group signature contains 5 elements from $\mathbb{G}_n$. In Table 1 we compare our proposed scheme with the existing ABGS schemes. Let $\phi = |\zeta|$, where ζ be the set of attributes associated with a signature and $m = |Att|$. Let $m' \le m$ be the number of attributes assigned to any user and r be the number of revoked members. Let RO denotes the Random oracle model, SGD denotes the Subgroup Decision assumption, (ℓ, m, t)-aMSE-CDH denotes the (ℓ, m, t)- augmented multi-sequence of exponents computational Diffie-Hellman and let e represents the bilinear operation. In Table 1, we compare our scheme with the other schemes proposed in [21], [14] and [20,23]. Also note that the verification cost of the proposed scheme is constant, where as other schemes verification cost is linear in terms of attributes.

Table 1. Comparison with other schemes

	Dalia Khader [21]	Emura et al. [14]	Herranz et al. [20] +Liang et al. [23]	Our Scheme
User Anonymity	CPA	CCA	CPA	CPA
Attribute Anonymity	no	no	yes	yes
Signature Length	$O(\phi)$	$O(\phi)$	$15|\mathbb{G}_p| + 5|\mathbb{G}_n| = O(1)$	$5|\mathbb{G}_n| = O(1)$
User's Signing Key Length	$(m'+1)|\mathbb{G}_p| + |\mathbb{Z}_p^*|$	$(m'+1)|\mathbb{G}_p| + 2|\mathbb{Z}_p^*|$	$(m+m')|\mathbb{G}_p| + |\mathbb{G}_n| + |\mathbb{Z}_p|$	$(m'+1)|\mathbb{G}_n| + |\mathbb{Z}_n^*|$
Assumptions	DLDH, ℓ-SDH	DDH, ℓ-SDH, DL	DLin ,(ℓ,m,t)-aMSE-CDH SGD, ℓ'-MOMSDH	SGD, ℓ-SDH, ℓ'-MOMSDH, DL, KEA
Model	RO	RO	Standard	Standard
Signing	$(7+2\phi)\mathbb{G}_p + (5+\phi)\mathbb{G}_T + (\phi+1)e$	$(9+3\phi)\mathbb{G}_p + (1+\phi)\mathbb{G}_p + 8\mathbb{G}_T + 3e$	$(6m+6m'+\phi(\phi-1)+14)\mathbb{G}_p + (m'+22)\mathbb{G}_n$	$(22+2\phi)\mathbb{G}_n$
Verification	$(6+2\phi)\mathbb{G}_p + (8+2\phi)\mathbb{G}_T + (\phi+2r+1)e$	$(11+2\phi)\mathbb{G}_p + (\phi+1)\mathbb{G}_2 + 14\mathbb{G}_3 + 6e$	$((4m+6m')\mathbb{G}_p + 33e + 21\mathbb{G}_T) + ((3)\mathbb{G}_n + 6e + 2\mathbb{G}_T)$	$3\mathbb{G} + 2\mathbb{G}_T + 6e$

6   Conclusion

We have proposed an ABGS scheme having the attribute anonymity with the constant size signature, and proven that it is secure under standard model. Also the scheme reduces the computational cost on both signer and verifier side. Further, to make our scheme more practical, a user as well as attribute revocation feature need to be added and need to enhance the security of user anonymity to CCA security notion. Our scheme is better than the existing ABGS schemes in terms of efficiency along with additional features viz. attribute anonymity and constant size signature, in the standard model.

Acknowledgments. This work was supported by Ministry of Human Resource Development (MHRD), Government of INDIA.

References

1. Abe, M., Fehr, S.: Perfect nizk with adaptive soundness. In: Vadhan, S.P. (ed.) TCC 2007. LNCS, vol. 4392, pp. 118–136. Springer, Heidelberg (2007)
2. Bellare, M., Micciancio, D., Warinschi, B.: Foundations of group signatures: Formal definitions, simplified requirements, and a construction based on general assumptions. In: Biham, E. (ed.) EUROCRYPT 2003. LNCS, vol. 2656, pp. 614–629. Springer, Heidelberg (2003)

3. Bellare, M., Palacio, A.: The knowledge-of-exponent assumptions and 3-round zero-knowledge protocols. In: Franklin [16], pp. 273–289
4. Bellare, M., Shi, H., Zhang, C.: Foundations of group signatures: The case of dynamic groups. In: Menezes, A. (ed.) CT-RSA 2005. LNCS, vol. 3376, pp. 136–153. Springer, Heidelberg (2005)
5. Boneh, D., Boyen, X.: Short signatures without random oracles. In: Cachin, C., Camenisch, J.L. (eds.) EUROCRYPT 2004. LNCS, vol. 3027, pp. 56–73. Springer, Heidelberg (2004)
6. Boneh, D., Boyen, X.: Short signatures without random oracles and the sdh assumption in bilinear groups. J. Cryptology 21(2), 149–177 (2008)
7. Boneh, D., Boyen, X., Shacham, H.: Short group signatures. In: Franklin [16], pp. 41–55
8. Boneh, D., Goh, E.-J., Nissim, K.: Evaluating 2-DNF formulas on ciphertexts. In: Kilian, J. (ed.) TCC 2005. LNCS, vol. 3378, pp. 325–341. Springer, Heidelberg (2005)
9. Boyen, X., Waters, B.: Compact group signatures without random oracles. In: Vaudenay, S. (ed.) EUROCRYPT 2006. LNCS, vol. 4004, pp. 427–444. Springer, Heidelberg (2006)
10. Boyen, X., Waters, B.: Full-domain subgroup hiding and constant-size group signatures. In: Okamoto, T., Wang, X. (eds.) PKC 2007. LNCS, vol. 4450, pp. 1–15. Springer, Heidelberg (2007)
11. Chaum, D., van Heyst, E.: Group signatures. In: Davies, D.W. (ed.) EUROCRYPT 1991. LNCS, vol. 547, pp. 257–265. Springer, Heidelberg (1991)
12. Delerablée, C., Pointcheval, D.: Dynamic fully anonymous short group signatures. In: Nguyên, P.Q. (ed.) VIETCRYPT 2006. LNCS, vol. 4341, pp. 193–210. Springer, Heidelberg (2006)
13. Dent, A.W.: The hardness of the dhk problem in the generic group model. IACR Cryptology ePrint Archive 2006, 156 (2006)
14. Emura, K., Miyaji, A., Omote, K.: A dynamic attribute-based group signature scheme and its application in an anonymous survey for the collection of attribute statistics. JIP 17(1), 216–231 (2009)
15. Escala, A., Herranz, J., Morillo, P.: Revocable attribute-based signatures with adaptive security in the standard model. In: Nitaj, A., Pointcheval, D. (eds.) AFRICACRYPT 2011. LNCS, vol. 6737, pp. 224–241. Springer, Heidelberg (2011)
16. Franklin, M. (ed.): CRYPTO 2004. LNCS, vol. 3152. Springer, Heidelberg (2004)
17. Groth, J.: Fully anonymous group signatures without random oracles. In: Kurosawa, K. (ed.) ASIACRYPT 2007. LNCS, vol. 4833, pp. 164–180. Springer, Heidelberg (2007)
18. Groth, J., Sahai, A.: Efficient non-interactive proof systems for bilinear groups. In: Smart, N.P. (ed.) EUROCRYPT 2008. LNCS, vol. 4965, pp. 415–432. Springer, Heidelberg (2008)
19. Hada, S., Tanaka, T.: On the existence of 3-round zero-knowledge protocols. In: Krawczyk, H. (ed.) CRYPTO 1998. LNCS, vol. 1462, pp. 408–423. Springer, Heidelberg (1998)
20. Herranz, J., Laguillaumie, F., Libert, B., Ràfols, C.: Short attribute-based signatures for threshold predicates. In: Dunkelman, O. (ed.) CT-RSA 2012. LNCS, vol. 7178, pp. 51–67. Springer, Heidelberg (2012)

21. Khader, D.: Attribute based group signature with revocation. IACR Cryptology ePrint Archive 2007, 241 (2007)
22. Khader, D.: Attribute based group signatures. IACR Cryptology ePrint Archive 2007, 159 (2007)
23. Liang, X.-H., Cao, Z.-F., Shao, J., Lin, H.: Short group signature without random oracles. In: Qing, S., Imai, H., Wang, G. (eds.) ICICS 2007. LNCS, vol. 4861, pp. 69–82. Springer, Heidelberg (2007)
24. Maji, H.K., Prabhakaran, M., Rosulek, M.: Attribute-based signatures. In: Kiayias, A. (ed.) CT-RSA 2011. LNCS, vol. 6558, pp. 376–392. Springer, Heidelberg (2011)

Security Analysis of an Efficient Smart Card-Based Remote User Authentication Scheme Using Hash Function

Ashok Kumar Das[1], Vanga Odelu[2], and Adrijit Goswami[3]

[1] Center for Security, Theory and Algorithmic Research
International Institute of Information Technology, Hyderabad 500 032, India
iitkgp.akdas@gmail.com, ashok.das@iiit.ac.in
[2] Department of Mathematics
Rajiv Gandhi University of Knowledge Technologies, Hyderabad 500 032, India
odelu.vanga@gmail.com
[3] Department of Mathematics
Indian Institute of Technology, Kharagpur 721 302, India
goswami@maths.iitkgp.ernet.in

Abstract. In a remote user authentication scheme, a remote server verifies whether a login user is genuine and trustworthy. Several remote user authentication schemes using the password, the biometrics and the smart card have been proposed in the literature. In 2012, Sonwanshi et al. proposed a password-based remote user authentication scheme using smart card, which uses the hash function and bitwise XOR operation. Their scheme is very efficient because of the usage of efficient one-way hash function and bitwise XOR operations. They claimed that their scheme is secure against several known attacks. Unfortunately, in this paper we find that their scheme has several vulnerabilities including the offline password guessing attack and stolen smart card attack. In addition, we show that their scheme fails to protect strong replay attack.

Keywords: Cryptanalysis, Password, Remote user authentication, Smart card, Security, Hash function.

1 Introduction

Remote user authentication plays an important role in order to identify whether communicating parties are genuine and trustworthy where the users are authenticated by a remote server before allowing access to services. Several password-based schemes (for example [4], [7], [9]) or biometric-based schemes (for example [2], [3], [6]) have been proposed for remote user authentication. As pointed out in [7], an idle password-based remote user authentication scheme using smart cards needs to satisfy the following requirements: (1) without maintaining verification tables; (2) a user can freely choose and update password; (3) resistance to password disclosure to the server; (4) prevention of masquerade attacks; (5) resistance to replay, modification, parallel session and stolen-verifier attacks;

Sabu M. Thampi et al. (Eds.): SSCC 2013, CCIS 377, pp. 236–242, 2013.
© Springer-Verlag Berlin Heidelberg 2013

(6) a easy-to-remember password; (7) low communication cost and computation complexity; (8) achieve mutual authentication between login users and remote servers; (9) resistance to guessing attacks even if the smart card is lost or stolen by attackers; (10) session key agreement; (11) resistance to insider attacks; and (12) prevention of smart card security breach attacks.

In 2012, Sonwanshi et al. proposed a remote user authentication scheme based on passwords using the smart card [9]. Their scheme is based on the one-way hash function and bitwise XOR operation. Due to efficiency of the hash function as well as bitwise XOR operation, their scheme is very efficient in computation. They claimed that their scheme is secure against various known attacks such as (i) resilient to Denial-of-Service (DoS) attack; (ii) resilient to offline password guessing attack; (iii) resilient to impersonation attack; (iv) resilient to parallel session attack; and (v) resilient to stolen smart card attack. However, in this paper we show that their scheme is insecure. We show that their scheme is vulnerable to the offline password guessing attack and stolen smart card attack. In addition, we show that their scheme fails to protect strong replay attack.

The rest of this paper is organized as follows. In Section 2, we review Sonwanshi et al.'s remote user authentication scheme using smart card. In Section 3, we show that Sonwanshi et al.'s scheme is vulnerable to offline password guessing attack and stolen smart card attack. In this section, we also show that their scheme fails to protect strong replay attack. Finally, we conclude the paper in Section 4.

2   Review of Sonwanshi et al.'s Smart Card Based Remote User Authentication Scheme

In this section, we briefly review the recently proposed Sonwanshi et al.'s scheme [9]. Their scheme consists of four phases: registration phase, login phase, authentication phase and password change phase. For describing this scheme, we use the notations given in Table 1.

Table 1. Notations used in this paper

Symbol	Description
U_i	User
S_j	Remote server
ID_i	Identity of user U_i
PW_i	Password of user U_i
X	Permanent secret key only known to the remote server S_j
$h(\cdot)$	Secure one-way hash function (e.g., SHA-1 [1])
$A\|\|B$	Data A concatenates with data B
$A \oplus B$	XOR operation of A and B

The different phases of Sonwanshi et al.'s scheme are described in the following subsections.

2.1   Registration Phase

In this phase, the user U_i needs to register with the remote server S_j providing his/her own identity ID_i and hashed password $h(PW_i)$ via a secure channel. This phase has the following steps:

Step R1. U_i first selects ID_i and PW_i. U_i then sends the registration request message $\langle ID_i, h(PW_i) \rangle$ to S_j via a secure channel.

Step R2. After receiving the message in Step R1, S_j computes $A_i = h(X||ID_i)$ and $B_i = A_i \oplus h(ID_i||h(PW_i))$, and issues a smart card containing the information $(A_i, B_i, h(\cdot))$ and sends the smart card to U_i via a secure channel.

2.2   Login Phase

If the user U_i wants to access services from the remote server S_j, U_i needs to perform the following steps:

Step L1. U_i inserts his/her smart card into a card reader of the specific terminal and inputs his/her identity ID_i^* and password PW_i^*.

Step L2. The smart card then computes $B_i^* = A_i \oplus h(ID_i^*||h(PW_i^*))$ using the stored value of A_i in its memory, and then verifies the condition $B_i^* = B_i$. If they do not match, it means that U_i enters his/her ID_i and PW_i incorrectly and this phase terminates immediately. Otherwise, the smart card executes Step L3.

Step L3. The smart card uses the current system timestamp T_u to compute $CID = h(PW_i^*) \oplus h(A_i||T_u)$ and $E_i = h(B_i||CID||T_u)$, and sends the login request message $\langle ID_i, CID, E_i, T_u \rangle$ to S_j via a public channel.

2.3   Authentication Phase

In this phase, S_j authenticates U_i. For this purpose, after receiving the login request message $\langle ID_i, CID, E_i, T_u \rangle$ from U_i, S_j executes the following steps:

Step A1. S_j verifies the format of the message and ID_i. S_j then checks the validity of the timestamp by $|T_u - T_u'| < \triangle T$, where T_u' is the current system timestamp of S_j and $\triangle T$ is the expected transmission delay. If these conditions are valid, S_j computes $A_i^* = h(X||ID_i)$ using its secret key X, $h(PW_i^*) = CID \oplus h(A_i^*||T_u)$, and $B_i^* = A_i^* \oplus h(ID_i||h(PW_i^*))$. S_j then computes $E_i^* = h(B_i^*||CID||T_u)$ and checks whether $E_i^* = E_i$. If it does not hold, S_j rejects the user U_i as an illegal user and the phase terminates immediately. Otherwise, S_j goes to execute Step A2.

Step A2. S_j computes $F_i = h(A_i^*||B_i^*||T_s)$, where T_s is the current system timestamp of the remote server S_j. S_j sends the acknowledgment message $\langle F_i, T_s \rangle$ to the user U_i via a public channel.

Step A3. After receiving the acknowledgment message in Step A2, U_i checks the validity of the timestamp by $|T_s - T'_s| < \triangle T$, where T'_s is the current system timestamp of U_i and $\triangle T$ is the expected transmission delay. If this is valid, U_i further computes $F_i^* = h(A_i||B_i||T_s)$ and checks whether $F_i^* = F_i$. If it holds, U_i computes a secret session key shared with S_j as $SK_{U_i,S_j} = h(A_i||T_u||T_s||B_i)$. Similarly, S_j also computes the same secret session key shared with U_i as $SK_{U_i,S_j} = h(A_i^*||T_u||T_s||B_i^*)$ for their future secure communications.

The registration, login and authentication phases of Sonwanshi et al.'s scheme are summarized in Table 2.

Table 2. Summary of message exchanges during the registration phase, the login phase and the authentication phase of Sonwanshi et al.'s scheme [9]

User (U_i)	Remote server (S_j)
Registration phase	
$\langle ID_i, h(PW_i) \rangle$	
	$\langle Smart\,Card(A_i, B_i, h(\cdot)) \rangle$
Login phase	
$\langle ID_i, CID, E_i, T_u \rangle$	
Authentication phase	
	$\langle F_i, T_s \rangle$

2.4   Password Change Phase

For security reasons, it is expected that the user U_i needs to change his/her password at any time locally without contacting the remote server S_j. This phase consists of the following steps:

Step P1. U_i inserts his/her smart card into a card reader of the specific terminal and inputs identity ID_i and old password PW_i^{old}. The smart card then computes $B_i^* = A_i \oplus h(ID_i||h(PW_i^{old}))$, and verifies the condition $B_i^* = B_i$. If the condition does not hold, this phase terminates immediately.

Step P2. The user U_i is asked to input his/her chosen new changed password PW_i^{new}. The smart card then computes $B_i^{**} = A_i \oplus h(ID_i||h(PW_i^{new}))$. Finally, the smart card updates B_i with B_i^{**} in its memory.

3   Cryptanalysis on Sonwanshi et al.'s Scheme

In this section, we show that Sonwanshi et al.'s scheme is insecure against different attacks, which are given in the following subsections.

3.1   Offline Password Guessing Attack

As in [9], we also assume that if an adversary (attacker) gets the user U_i's smart card, the attacker can retrieve all sensitive information stored in the smart card's memory by monitoring the power consumption of the smart card [5], [8]. Thus, the attacker knows the values A_i and B_i. By eavesdropping the login request message $\langle ID_i, CID, E_i, T_u \rangle$ during the login phase, the attacker also knows ID_i containing in the message, since the message is sent via a public channel.

Note that $A_i = h(X||ID_i)$ and $B_i = A_i \oplus h(ID_i||h(PW_i))$. X is a secret number kept to the server S_j only and it is usually a 1024-bit number. So, deriving X from A_i is a computationally infeasible problem for the attacker due to the one-way collision resistant property of the hash function $h(\cdot)$. However, knowing A_i, B_i, and ID_i, the adversary executes an offline password guessing attack and then derives the user U_i's password PW_i iterating on all possible choices of PW_i. Our attack has the following steps:

Step 1. The adversary computes $h(ID_i||h(PW_i)) = A_i \oplus B_i$.
Step 2. The adversary selects a guessed password PW_i'.
Step 3. Knowing ID_i from the login request message $\langle ID_i, CID, E_i, T_u \rangle$, the adversary computes the hash value $h(ID_i||h(PW_i'))$.
Step 4. The adversary compares the computed hash value $h(ID_i||h(PW_i'))$ with the derived hash value $h(ID_i||h(PW_i)) = A_i \oplus B_i$.
Step 5. If there is a match in Step 4, it indicates that the correct guess of the user U_i's password PW_i. Otherwise, the adversary repeats from Step 2.

As a result, the adversary can succeed to guess the low-entropy password PW_i of the user U_i. The detailed steps of the offline password guessing attack of Sonwanshi et al.'s scheme are illustrated in Table 3.

3.2   Stolen Smart Card Attack

Suppose the user U_i's smart card is lost/stolen by an attacker. The attacker can then extract the information $(A_i, B_i, h(\cdot))$ from the memory of the smart card using the power analysis attacks [5], [8], where $A_i = h(X||ID_i)$ and $B_i = A_i \oplus h(ID_i||h(PW_i))$. Again the attacker knows the identity ID_i of the user U_i from the login request message eavesdropped by that attacker. The attacker can derive the hash value $h(ID_i||h(PW_i)) = A_i \oplus B_i$ using the extracted A_i and B_i. Using the offline password guessing attack as stated in Section 3.1, the attacker can retrieve the password PW_i of the user U_i. As a result, once the attacker knows ID_i and PW_i of the user U_i, the attacker can use this smart card in order to successfully login to the remote server S_j. Hence, Sonwanshi et al.'s scheme fails to protect stolen smart card attack.

3.3   Fails to Protect Strong Replay Attack

Suppose an adversary intercepts the login request message $\langle ID_i, CID, E_i, T_u \rangle$ during the login phase, and replays the same message to the remote server S_j

Table 3. Summary of offline password guessing attack on Sonwanshi et al.'s scheme [9]

User (U_i)	Attacker	Remote server (S_j)
	1. Obtain U_i's smart card and gets the information (A_i, B_i).	
2. $\langle ID_i, CID, E_i, T_u \rangle$ $\xrightarrow{\hspace{2cm}}$		
	3. Eavesdrops the login request message in Step 2 and stores ID_i of U_i.	
	4. Knowing A_i and B_i, computes $h(ID_i \| h(PW_i)) = A_i \oplus B_i$.	
	5. Guesses a password PW_i'.	
	6. Computes $h(ID_i \| h(PW_i'))$ using ID_i from Step 3.	
	7. Compares $h(ID_i \| h(PW_i'))$ with $h(ID_i \| h(PW_i))$. If there is a match, PW_i is derived. Otherwise, the attacker executes from Step 5 to guess another password.	

within a valid time interval. Then S_j treats this message as a valid message, because the condition $|T_u - T_u'| < \triangle T$ will be satisfied, where T_u' is the current system timestamp of S_j and $\triangle T$ is the expected transmission delay.

Similarly, the attacker can intercept the message $\langle F_i, T_s \rangle$ during the authentication phase and replay the same message within a valid time interval. In this case, S_j also treats this message as valid as the condition $|T_s - T_s'| < \triangle T$ will be satisfied, where T_s' is the current system timestamp of U_i and $\triangle T$ is the expected transmission delay. Of course, this attack depends on the expected time interval $\triangle T$. If this interval is very short, then the attacker could not succeed. Thus, this attack is weak.

To overcome such weakness, one can adopt the similar strategy as suggested in [2], where instead of using timestamp one can use random nonce for this purpose.

4   Conclusion and Future Works

Recently Sonwanshi et al. proposed an efficient smart card based remote user authentication using the one-way hash function and bitwise XOR operation. Though their scheme is efficient in computation, in this paper we have shown that their scheme is still vulnerable to offline password guessing attack and stolen smart card attack. Further, their scheme fails to protect strong replay attack. In future work, we aim to propose an improved scheme which needs to be secure and efficient. We also encourage the readers to come up with their proposed improvements in order to remedy these weaknesses found in Sonwanshi et al.'s scheme.

Acknowledgements. The authors would like to acknowledge the anonymous reviewers for their helpful comments and suggestions.

References

1. Secure Hash Standard, FIPS PUB 180-1, National Institute of Standards and Technology (NIST), U.S. Department of Commerce (April 1995)
2. Das, A.K.: Analysis and improvement on an efficient biometric-based remote user authentication scheme using smart cards. IET Information Security 5(3), 145–151 (2011)
3. Das, A.K.: Cryptanalysis and further improvement of a biometric-based remote user authentication scheme using smart cards. International Journal of Network Security & Its Applications 3(2), 13–28 (2011)
4. Hwang, M.S., Li, L.H.: A new remote user authentication scheme using smart cards. IEEE Transactions on Consumer Electronics 46(1), 28–30 (2000)
5. Kocher, P.C., Jaffe, J., Jun, B.: Differential power analysis. In: Wiener, M. (ed.) CRYPTO 1999. LNCS, vol. 1666, pp. 388–397. Springer, Heidelberg (1999)
6. Li, C.T., Hwang, M.S.: An efficient biometric-based remote authentication scheme using smart cards. Journal of Network and Computer Applications 33, 1–5 (2010)
7. Li, C.-T., Lee, C.-C., Liu, C.-J., Lee, C.-W.: A Robust Remote User Authentication Scheme against Smart Card Security Breach. In: Li, Y. (ed.) DBSec. LNCS, vol. 6818, pp. 231–238. Springer, Heidelberg (2011)
8. Messerges, T.S., Dabbish, E.A., Sloan, R.H.: Examining smart-card security under the threat of power analysis attacks. IEEE Transactions on Computers 51(5), 541–552 (2002)
9. Sonwanshi, S.S., Ahirwal, R.R., Jain, Y.K.: An Efficient Smart Card based Remote User Authentication Scheme using hash function. In: Proceedings of IEEE SCEECS 2012, pp. 1–4 (March 2012)

Formal Security Verification of a Dynamic Password-Based User Authentication Scheme for Hierarchical Wireless Sensor Networks

Ashok Kumar Das[1], Santanu Chatterjee[2], and Jamuna Kanta Sing[3]

[1] Center for Security, Theory and Algorithmic Research
International Institute of Information Technology, Hyderabad 500 032, India
iitkgp.akdas@gmail.com, ashok.das@iiit.ac.in
[2] Research Center Imarat
Defence Research and Development Organization, Hyderabad 500 069, India
santanu.chatterjee@rcilab.in
[3] Department of Computer Science and Engineering
Jadavpur University, Kolkata 700 032, India
jksing@ieee.org

Abstract. In 2012, Das et al. proposed a new password-based user authentication scheme in hierarchical wireless sensor networks [Journal of Network and Computer Applications 35(5) (2012) 1646-1656]. The proposed scheme achieves better security and efficiency as compared to those for other existing password-based user authentication schemes proposed in the literature. This scheme supports to change dynamically the user's password locally at any time without contacting the base station or gateway node. This scheme also supports dynamic node addition after the initial deployment of nodes in the existing sensor network. In this paper, we simulate this proposed scheme for formal security verification using the widely-accepted Automated Validation of Internet Security Protocols and Applications (AVISPA) tool. AVISPA tool ensures that whether a protocol is insecure against possible passive and active attacks, including the replay and man-in-the-middle attacks. Using the AVISPA model checkers, we show that Das et al.'s scheme is secure against possible passive and active attacks.

1   Introduction

A wireless sensor network (WSN) consists of a large number of tiny computing nodes, called sensor nodes or motes. These sensor nodes are small in size and they have very limited resources such as small memory storage, low computing processor, short communication range, and also they run in battery power. After deployment of sensor nodes in a target field (deployment field), they form an adhoc infrastructure-less wireless network, where nodes communicate with each other within their communication ranges and data are finally routed back to the nearby base station(s) via multi-hop communication path. In recent years, WSNs have drawn attention in several applications including military (for example,

Sabu M. Thampi et al. (Eds.): SSCC 2013, CCIS 377, pp. 243–254, 2013.
© Springer-Verlag Berlin Heidelberg 2013

battlefield surveillance), healthcare applications and other real-time applications. A large number of nodes could be dropped on a particular area from truck/plane and there after each node coordinates with their neighboring nodes and together they form a network which is finally linked to the nearby base station (BS). Information gathered from the area of deployment are then passed on to the base station, where the base station performs costly operations on behalf of sensor nodes. A survey on WSNs can be found in [6].

User authentication is one of the primary services required to provide security in WSN applications. Consider the scenario where the information from nodes are gathered periodically in the BS. The gathered information may not be always real-time data. Thus, if we allow the base station to wait for next read cycle, the information gathered from the nodes may not be real-time and as a result, appropriate decisions could not make quickly for critical real-time applications. To access the real-time data from nodes inside WSN, the users (called the external parties) should be allowed so that they can access directly the real-time data from nodes and not from the BS as and when they demand. In order to get the real-time information from the nodes, the user needs to be first authorized to the nodes as well as the BS so that illegal access to nodes do not happen. In 2012, Das et al. proposed a new password-based user authentication scheme in hierarchical wireless sensor networks [15]. The proposed scheme achieves better security and efficiency as compared to those for other existing password-based user authentication schemes proposed in the literature. This scheme supports to change dynamically the user's password locally at any time without contacting the base station or gateway node. This scheme also supports dynamic node addition after the initial deployment of nodes in the existing sensor network. In this paper, we validate the formal security of Das et al.'s scheme using the widely-accepted AVISPA tool. Using the AVISPA model checkers, we show that Das et al.'s scheme is secure against possible passive and active attacks, including the replay and man-in-the-middle attacks.

The rest of this paper is organized as follows. In Section 2, we review Das et al.'s novel dynamic password-based user authentication scheme in HWSNs. In Section 3, we simulate Das et al.'s scheme for the formal security verification using AVISPA tool. In this section, we first give an overview of AVISPA tool and then give details of implementation aspects and analyze the simulation results. Finally, we conclude the paper in Section 4.

2   Review of Das et al.'s Scheme

In this section, we briefly review the recently proposed Das et al.'s scheme [15]. We describe the different phases related to this scheme. For describing this scheme, we use the notations given in Table 1.

In this scheme, a hierarchical wireless sensor network [10], [14] is considered, which consists of two types of sensors: a small number of powerful High-end sensors (called the H-sensors) and a large number of resource-constrained Low-end sensors (called the L-sensors). The H-sensors have much larger radio transmission range and also larger storage space than the L-sensor nodes, whereas the

Table 1. Notations used in this paper

Symbol	Description
U_i	User
BS	Base station
S_j	Sensor Node
CH_j	Cluster head in the j-th cluster
PW_i	Password of user U_i
ID_i	Identity of user U_i
ID_{CH_j}	Identifier of cluster head CH_j
$h(\cdot)$	A secure one-way hash function (e.g., SHA-1 [4])
E	Symmetric key encryption algorithm (e.g., AES [1])
D	Symmetric key decryption algorithm (e.g., AES [1])
X_s	A secret information maintained by the base station
X_A	A secret information shared between user and base station
y	A secret random number known to user
T	Timestamp
$A\|B$	Data A concatenates with data B
$A \oplus B$	XOR operation of A and B

L-sensors are extremely resource-constrained. For example, the H-sensors can be PDAs and the L-sensors are MICAz/IRIS sensor devices [5]. The target field is considered as two dimensional and is partitioned into a number m of equal-sized disjoint clusters so that each cluster consists of a cluster head CH_j (here it is an H-sensor node) and a number n_i of L-sensor nodes. An L-sensor node is called a regular sensor node and an H-sensor node as a cluster head (CH). The number n_i of regular sensor nodes is taken in each deployment cluster in such a way that the network connectivity in each cluster is high so that every sensor node can communicate securely among each other and finally with their neighbor cluster head in that cluster. The sensors are deployed randomly in each cluster and each cluster head is deployed in that cluster around the center of that cluster. Finally, the base station (BS) can be located either in the center or at a corner of the network depending on the situation and application.

Das et al.'s scheme consists of the following phases: pre-deployment phase, post-deployment phase, registration phase, login phase, authentication phase, password change phase and dynamic node addition phase. For the purpose of formal security verification using AVISPA tool, first five phases are described briefly in the following subsections.

2.1   Pre-deployment Phase

The (key) setup server (the base station) performs the following in offline before deployment of the sensor nodes and cluster heads in a target field (deployment field). The setup server assigns a unique identifier, say ID_{CH_j} and selects randomly a unique master key, say MK_{CH_j} to each cluster head CH_j. Similarly, for each deployed regular sensor node S_i, the setup server also assigns a unique identifier, say ID_{S_i} and a unique randomly generated master key, say MK_{S_i}. Once all the cluster heads and sensors are assigned to their corresponding identifiers and master keys, the setup server loads the following information into the memory of each cluster head CH_j ($j = 1, 2, \ldots, m$): (i) its own identifier, ID_{CH_j} and (ii) its own master key MK_{CH_j}. The setup server also loads the following information into the memory of each deployed regular sensor node S_i in the cluster C_j: (i) its own identifier, ID_{S_i} and (ii) its own master key MK_{S_i}.

2.2 Post-deployment Phase

In this phase, after deployment of regular sensor nodes in their respective clusters and the cluster heads in their respective clusters, they locate their physical neighbors within their communication ranges. For secure communication between regular sensor nodes, and between regular sensor nodes and cluster head in a cluster, nodes require to establish pairwise secret keys between them. The unconditionally secure key establishment scheme [14] for pairwise key establishment between nodes in each cluster and between cluster heads is used in this scheme for establishing the secret keys between neighbors in the network.

2.3 Registration Phase

In this phase, the user U_i needs to register with the base station (BS). For this purpose, the user U_i and the base station (BS) need to perform the following steps:

Step R1: U_i first selects a random number y, its identifier ID_i and password PW_i. U_i then computes the masked password $RPW_i = h(y\|PW_i)$. After that U_i provides the computed masked password RPW_i and ID_i to the base station via a secure channel.

Step R2: After receiving the information from U_i, BS computes $f_i = h(ID_i\|X_s)$, $x = h(RPW_i\|X_A)$, $r_i = h(y\|x)$, and $e_i = f_i \oplus x = h(ID_i\|X_s) \oplus h(RPW_i\|X_A)$. The secret information X_s is only known to the BS, whereas the secret information X_A is shared between U_i and BS.

Step R3: BS selects all m deployed cluster heads, CH_1, CH_2, ..., CH_m, which will be deployed during the initial deployment phase in the network, and computes the m key-plus-id combinations $\{(K_j, ID_{CH_j}) \mid 1 \leq j \leq m\}$, where $K_j = E_{MK_{CH_j}}(ID_i\|ID_{CH_j}\|X_s)$ is computed using the master key MK_{CH_j} of CH_j.

Step R4: For dynamic cluster head addition phase, assume that another m' cluster heads, CH_{m+1}, CH_{m+2}, ..., $CH_{m+m'}$ will be deployed later after the initial deployment in the network in order to deploy some nodes due to some compromised cluster heads, if any, and add some fresh cluster heads along with sensor nodes.

For this purpose, the BS computes another m' key-plus-id combinations $\{(K_{m+j}, ID_{CH_{m+j}}) \mid 1 \leq j \leq m'\}$, where $K_{m+j} =$

$E_{MK_{CH_{m+j}}}(ID_i||ID_{CH_{m+j}}||X_s)$. Note that $ID_{CH_{m+j}}$ is the unique identifier generated by the BS for the cluster head CH_{m+j} to be deployed during the dynamic node addition phase and $MK_{CH_{m+j}}$ the unique master key randomly generated by the BS for CH_{m+j}, which is shared between it and the BS.

Step R5: Finally, the BS generates a tamper-proof smart card with the following parameters: (i) ID_i, (ii) y, (iii) X_A, (iv) r_i, (v) e_i, (vi) $h(\cdot)$, and (vi) $m+m'$ key-plus-id combinations $\{(K_j, ID_{CH_j}) \mid 1 \le j \le m+m'\}$, and sends the smart card with these information to the user U_i via a secure channel.

Note that $m+m'$ encrypted keys are stored into the memory of the smart card of a user U_i, which are different from those for another user U_j, because these keys are encrypted using the master keys of cluster heads along with the different identifiers of users, the identifiers of cluster heads and the secret information X_s.

2.4   Login Phase

In order to access the real-time data from nodes inside WSN, the user U_i needs to perform the following steps:

Step L1: U_i first inserts his/her smart card into the card reader of a specific terminal and provides his/her password PW_i'.

Step L2: The smart card then computes the masked password of the user U_i as $RPW_i' = h(y||PW_i')$ using the stored secret number y. Using the computed masked password, the smart card further computes $x' = h(RPW_i'||X_A)$ and $r_i' = h(y||x')$, and then verifies whether the condition $r_i' = r_i$ holds. If this condition does not hold, this means that the user U_i has entered his/her password incorrectly and the phase terminates immediately. Otherwise, the following steps are executed.

Step L3: Using the system's current timestamp T_1, the smart card computes the hash value $N_i = h(x'||T_1)$.

Step L4: The user U_i then selects the cluster head, say CH_j from which the real-time data can be accessed inside WSN. Corresponding to CH_j, the smart card selects the encrypted master key of CH_j, K_j from its memory and computes the ciphertext message $E_{K_j}(ID_i||ID_{CH_j}||N_i||e_i||T_1)$. Finally, the user U_i sends the login request message $\langle ID_i||ID_{CH_j}|| E_{K_j}(ID_i||ID_{CH_j}||N_i||e_i||T_1)\rangle$ to the BS, via a public channel.

2.5   Authentication Phase

After receiving the login request message $\langle ID_i||ID_{CH_j}||E_{K_j}(ID_i||ID_{CH_j}||N_i||e_i||T_1)\rangle$ from the user U_i, the BS needs to perform the following steps in order to authenticate the user U_i by the BS and the cluster head CH_j:

Step A1: The BS computes the key K using the stored master key MK_{CH_j} of the cluster head CH_j as $K = E_{MK_{CH_j}}(ID_i||ID_{CH_j}||X_s)$. Using this computed key K, the BS decrypts $E_{K_j}(ID_i||ID_{CH_j}||N_i||e_i||T_1)$ in order to retrieve the information $ID_i, ID_{CH_j}, N_i, e_i$, and T_1.

Step A2: The BS checks if retrieved ID_i is equal to received ID_i and also if retrieved ID_{CH_j} is equal to received ID_{CH_j}. If these hold, the BS further checks if $\mid T_1 - T_1^* \mid < \triangle T_1$, where T_1^* is the current system timestamp of the BS and $\triangle T_1$ is the expected time interval for the transmission delay. Now, if it holds, the BS further computes $X = h(ID_i \| X_s)$, $Y = e_i \oplus X$, and $Z = h(Y \| T_1)$. If $Z = N_i$, then the BS accepts U_i's login request and U_i is considered as a valid user by the BS. Otherwise, the scheme terminates.

Step A3: Using the current system timestamp T_2, the BS computes $u = h(Y \| T_2)$ and produces a ciphertext message encrypted using the master key MK_{CH_j} of the cluster head CH_j as $E_{MK_{CH_j}}(ID_i \| ID_{CH_j} \| u \| T_1 \| T_2 \| X \| e_i)$. The BS sends the message $\langle ID_i \| ID_{CH_j} \| E_{MK_{CH_j}}(ID_i \| ID_{CH_j} \| u \| T_1 \| T_2 \| X \| e_i) \rangle$ to the corresponding cluster head CH_j.

Step A4: After receiving the message in Step 3 from the BS, the cluster head CH_j decrypts $E_{MK_{CH_j}}(ID_i \| ID_{CH_j} \| u \| T_1 \| T_2 \| X \| e_i)$ using its own master key MK_{CH_j} to retrieve ID_i, ID_{CH_j}, u, T_1, T_2, X, and e_i. CH_j then checks if retrieved ID_i is equal to received ID_i and also if retrieved ID_{CH_j} is equal to received ID_{CH_j}. If these hold, CH_j further checks if $\mid T_2 - T_2^* \mid < \triangle T_2$, where T_2^* is the current system timestamp of the CH_j and $\triangle T_2$ is the expected time interval for the transmission delay.

If this verification holds, CH_j computes $v = e_i \oplus X = h(RPW_i \| X_A)$, $w = h(v \| T_2) = h(h(RPW_i \| X_A) \| T_2)$. CH_j further checks if $w = u$. If it does not hold, this phase terminates immediately. Otherwise, if it holds, the user U_i is considered as a valid user and authenticated by CH_j.

CH_j also computes the secret session key SK_{U_i,CH_j} shared with the user U_i as $SK_{U_i,CH_j} = h(ID_i \| ID_{CH_j} \| e_i \| T_1)$. Finally, CH_j sends an acknowledgment to the user U_i via other cluster heads and the BS and responds to the query of the user U_i.

Step A5: After receiving the acknowledgment from CH_j, the user U_i computes the same secret session key shared with CH_j using its previous system timestamp T_1, ID_i, ID_{CH_j} and e_i as $SK_{U_i,CH_j} = h(ID_i \| ID_{CH_j} \| e_i \| T_1)$. Note that both user U_i and cluster head CH_j can communicate securely in future using the derived secret session key SK_{U_i,CH_j}.

The summary of message exchanges during the registration phase, the login phase and the authentication phase of Das et al.'s scheme [15] is provided in Table 2.

3 Formal Security Verification of Das et al.'s Scheme Using AVISPA Tool

In this section, we first describe in brief the overview of AVISPA tool along with the high-level protocol specification language (HLPSL). We then give the implementation details of Das et al.'s scheme in HLPSL. Finally, we discuss the analysis of the simulation results using AVISPA back-end.

Table 2. Summary of message exchanges during the registration phase, the login phase and the authentication phase of Das et al.'s scheme [15]

Entity	Entity
Registration phase	
U_i	BS
$\langle ID_i, RPW_i \rangle$ $\longrightarrow$	
	$\langle Smart\,Card(ID_i, y, X_A, r_i, e_i, h(\cdot),$ $\{(K_j, ID_{CH_j}) \mid 1 \leq j \leq m + m'\}) \rangle$ $\longleftarrow$
Login phase	
U_i	BS
$\langle ID_i \| ID_{CH_j} \| E_{K_j}(ID_i \| ID_{CH_j} \| N_i \| e_i \| T_1) \rangle$ $\longrightarrow$	
Authentication phase	
BS	CH_j
$\langle ID_i \| ID_{CH_j} \| E_{MK_{CH_j}}(ID_i$ $\| ID_{CH_j} \| u \| T_1 \| T_2 \| X \| e_i) \rangle$ $\longrightarrow$	
	$\langle$ acknowledgment to BS $\rangle$ $\longleftarrow$
	$\langle$ query response/data to user $U_i \rangle$ $\longleftarrow$

3.1   Overview of AVISPA

AVISPA (Automated Validation of Internet Security Protocols and Applications) is a push-button tool for the automated validation of Internet security-sensitive protocols and applications, which provides a modular and expressive formal language for specifying protocols and their security properties, and integrates different back-ends that implement a variety of state-of-the-art automatic analysis techniques [2], [7]. We have used the widely-accepted AVISPA back-ends for our formal security verification [9], [11], [12], [13]. AVISPA implements four back-ends and abstraction-based methods which are integrated through the high level protocol specific language, known as HLPSL [17]. A static analysis is performed to check the executability of the protocol, and then the protocol and the intruder actions are compiled into an intermediate format (IF). The intermediate format is the start point for the four automated protocol analysis techniques. IF is a lower-level language than HLPSL and is read directly by the back-ends to the AVISPA tool. The first back-end, the On-the-fly Model-Checker (OFMC), does several symbolic techniques to explore the state space in a demand-driven way [8]. The second back-end, the CL-AtSe (Constraint-Logic-based Attack Searcher), provides a translation from any security protocol specification written as transition relation in intermediate format into a set of constraints which are effectively used to find whether there are attacks on protocols. The third back-end, the SAT-based Model-Checker (SATMC), builds a propositional formula which is then fed to a state-of-the-art SAT solver and any model found is translated back into an attack. Finally, the fourth back-end, TA4SP (Tree Automata based on Automatic Approximations for the Analysis of

Security Protocols), approximates the intruder knowledge by using regular tree languages.

Protocols to be implemented by the AVISPA tool have to be specified in HLPSL (High Level Protocols Specification Language) [17], and written in a file with extension hlpsl. This language is based on roles: basic roles for representing each participant role, and composition roles for representing scenarios of basic roles. Each role is independent from the others, getting some initial information by parameters, communicating with the other roles by channels. The intruder is modeled using the Dolev-Yao model [16] (as in the threat model used in Das et al.'s scheme) with the possibility for the intruder to assume a legitimate role in a protocol run. The role system also defines the number of sessions, the number of principals and the roles.

The output format (OF) of AVISPA is generated by using one of the four back-ends explained above. When the analysis of a protocol has been successful (by finding an attack or not), the output describes precisely what is the result, and under what conditions it has been obtained. In OF, the first printed section SUMMARY indicates that whether the tested protocol is safe, unsafe, or whether the analysis is inconclusive. The second section, called DETAILS either explains under what condition the tested protocol is declared safe, or what conditions have been used for finding an attack, or finally why the analysis was inconclusive. Other sections such as PROTOCOL, GOAL and BACKEND are the name of the protocol, the goal of the analysis and the name of the back-end used, respectively. Finally, after some comments and statistics, the trace of an attack (if any) is also printed in the standard Alice-Bob format.

3.2   Specifying the Protocol

We have implemented Das et al.'s scheme [15] in HLPSL language. In our implementation, we have three basic roles: alice, bs and bob, which represent the participants: the user U_i, the base station (BS) and the cluster head CH_j, respectively. We have further specified the session and environment in our implementation.

In Figure 1, we have implemented the role for U_i in HLPSL. During the registration phase, the user U_i sends the registration request message $\langle ID_i, RPW_i \rangle$ securely to the BS with the help of the $Snd()$ operation. Here the type declaration $channel\,(dy)$ indicates that the channel is for the Dolev-Yao threat model. U_i waits for the smart card containing the information in the message $\langle ID_i, y, X_A, r_i, e_i, h(\cdot), \{(K_j, ID_{CH_j}) \mid 1 \leq j \leq m + m'\} \rangle$ securely from the BS from the $Rcv()$ operation. The intruder has the ability to intercept, analyze, and/or modify messages transmitted over the insecure channel. In the login phase, the user U_i sends the login request message $\langle ID_i || ID_{CH_j} || E_{K_j}(ID_i || ID_{CH_j} || N_i || e_i || T_1) \rangle$ to the BS. The user then waits for an acknowledgment regarding successful authentication from the cluster head CH_j via the BS.

Figure 2 shows the implementation for the role of the BS in HLPSL. During the registration phase, after receiving the message $\langle ID_i, RPW_i \rangle$ securely from

```
role alice (Ui, CHj, BS  : agent,
        MKchj : symmetric_key,
        SKubs : symmetric_key,
        H : hash_func,
        Snd, Rcv: channel(dy))

played_by Ui
def=
  local State : nat,
        RPWi, PWi, Xs, Xa, Yy, ACK,
        T1, T2, IDi, IDchj: text

  const alice_server, server_bob, subs1,
        subs2, subs3, subs4, subs5 : protocol_id

  init State := 0

  transition
   1. State = 0 ∧ Rcv(start) =|>
      State' := 1 ∧ RPWi' := H(Yy.PWi)
  ∧ Snd(Ui.BS.{IDi.RPWi'}_SKubs)
  ∧ secret({Xs}, subs1, BS)
      ∧ secret({PWi}, subs2, Ui)
      ∧ secret({MKchj}, subs3, {BS,CHj})
      ∧ secret({SKubs}, subs4, {Ui,BS})
      ∧ secret({Xa,Yy}, subs5, {Ui,BS})
   2. State = 1 ∧ Rcv(BS.Ui.{IDi.Yy.Xa.H(Yy.H(H(Yy.PWi).Xa)).H.
      xor(H(IDi.Xs),H(H(Yy.PWi).Xa)).H.
      {IDi.IDchj.Xs}_MKchj.IDchj}_SKubs) =|>
      State' := 2 ∧ T1' := new()
      ∧ Snd(Ui.BS.IDi.IDchj.
          {IDi.IDchj.H(H(H(Yy.PWi).Xa).T1')
          .xor(H(IDi.Xs),H(H(Yy.PWi).Xa)).
          T1'}_({IDi.IDchj.Xs}_MKchj))
      ∧ witness(Ui, BS, alice_server, T1')
   3. State = 2 ∧ Rcv(BS.Ui.ACK) =|>
      State' := 3
end role
```

Fig. 1. Role specification in HLPSL for the user U_i

```
role bs (Ui, CHj, BS  : agent,
        MKchj : symmetric_key,
        SKubs : symmetric_key,
        H : hash_func,
        Snd, Rcv: channel(dy))
played_by BS
def=
  local State : nat,
        PWi, Xs, Xa, Yy, ACK,
        T1, T2, IDi, IDchj: text

  const alice_server, server_bob, subs1,
        subs2, subs3, subs4, subs5 : protocol_id

  init State := 0

  transition
   1. State = 0 ∧ Rcv(Ui.BS.{IDi.H(Yy.PWi)}_SKubs) =|>
      State':=1  ∧ secret({Xs}, subs1, BS)
                 ∧ secret({PWi}, subs2, Ui)
                 ∧ secret({MKchj}, subs3, {BS,CHj})
                 ∧ secret({SKubs}, subs4, {Ui,BS})
                 ∧ secret({Xa,Yy}, subs5, {Ui,BS})
                 ∧ Snd(BS.Ui.{IDi.Yy.Xa.H(Yy.H(Yy.PWi).Xa)).
                   xor(H(IDi.Xs),H(H(Yy.PWi),Xa)).H.
                   {IDi.IDchj.Xs}_MKchj.IDchj}_SKubs)
   2. State = 1  ∧ Rcv(Ui.BS.IDi.IDchj.
                   {IDi.IDchj.H(H(H(Yy.PWi).Xa).T1')
                   .xor(H(IDi.Xs),H(H(Yy.PWi).Xa)).
                   T1'}_({IDi.IDchj.Xs}_MKchj)) =|>
      State' := 2 ∧ T2' := new()
                 ∧ Snd(BS.CHj.IDi.IDchj.{IDi.IDchj.
                   H(xor(xor(H(IDi.Xs), H(H(Yy.PWi).Xa)),
                   H(IDi.Xs)).T2').T1.T2'.H(IDi.Xs).
                   xor(H(IDi.Xs), H(H(Yy.PWi).Xa))}_MKchj)
                 ∧ witness(BS, CHj, server_bob, T2')
   3. State = 2 ∧ Rcv(CHj.BS.ACK) =|>
      State' := 3 ∧ Snd(BS.Ui.ACK)
                 ∧ request(Ui, BS, alice_server, T1)
end role
```

Fig. 2. Role specification in HLPSL for the base station, BS

the user U_i from the $Rcv()$ operation, the BS sends a smart card containing the information in the message $\langle ID_i, y, X_A, r_i, e_i, h(\cdot), \{(K_j, ID_{CH_j}) \mid 1 \le j \le m + m'\}\rangle$ securely to the user U_i. In the login phase, the BS receives the login request message $\langle ID_i||ID_{CH_j}||E_{K_j}(ID_i||ID_{CH_j}||N_i||e_i||T_1)\rangle$ from the user U_i. During the authentication phase, the BS sends the authentication request message $\langle ID_i||ID_{CH_j}|| E_{MK_{CH_j}}(ID_i||ID_{CH_j}||u||T_1||T_2||X||e_i)\rangle$ to the cluster head CH_j. BS then waits for an acknowledgment regarding successful authentication from the cluster head CH_j.

In Figure 3, we have implemented the the role of the cluster head CH_j in HLPSL. During the authentication phase, after receiving the authentication request message $\langle ID_i||ID_{CH_j}|| E_{MK_{CH_j}}(ID_i||ID_{CH_j}||u||T_1||T_2||X||e_i)\rangle$ from the BS, the cluster head CH_j sends an acknowledgment regarding successful authentication to the BS. In HLPSL specification, witness(A,B,id,E) declares for a (weak) authentication property of A by B on E, declares that agent A is witness for the information E; this goal will be identified by the constant id in the goal section. request(B,A,id,E) means for a strong authentication property of A by B on E, declares that agent B requests a check of the value E; this goal will be

```
role bob (Ui, CHj, BS  : agent,
        MKchj   : symmetric_key,
        SKubs : symmetric_key,

        H : hash_func,
        Snd, Rcv: channel(dy))
played_by CHj
def=
 local State : nat,
        PWi, Xs, Xa, Yy, ACK,
        T1, T2, IDi, IDchj: text
 const alice_server, server_bob, subs1,
        subs2, subs3, subs4, subs5 : protocol_id

 init State := 0
 transition

  1. State   = 0 ∧ Rcv(BS.CHj.IDi.IDchj.{IDi.IDchj.
               H(xor(xor(H(IDi.Xs), H(H(Yy.PWi).Xa)),
               H(IDi.Xs)).T2').T1'.T2'.H(IDi.Xs).
               xor(H(IDi.Xs), H(H(Yy.PWi).Xa))}_MKchj)  =|>
            State' := 1 ∧ secret({Xs}, subs1, BS)
                        ∧ secret({PWi}, subs2, Ui)
                        ∧ secret({MKchj}, subs3, {BS,CHj})
                        ∧ secret({SKubs}, subs4, {Ui,BS})
                        ∧ secret({Xa,Yy}, subs5, {Ui,BS})
                        ∧ Snd(CHj.BS.ACK)
                        ∧ request(BS, CHj, server_bob, T2')
 end role
```

```
role environment()
def=
 const ui, chj, bs: agent,
       mkchj: symmetric_key,
       skubs : symmetric_key,
       h  : hash_func,
       ack, pwi, xs, xa, yy, t1, t2,
       idi, idchj: text
       alice_server, server_bob,
       subs1, subs2, subs3, subs4, subs5 : protocol_id

 intruder_knowledge = {ui, chj, bs, idi, idchj, h}

 composition
  session(ui, chj, bs, mkchj, skubs, h)
  ∧ session(ui, chj, bs, mkchj, skubs, h)
  ∧ session(ui, chj, bs, mkchj, skubs, h)
 end role

 goal
   secrecy_of subs1
   secrecy_of subs2
   secrecy_of subs3
   secrecy_of subs4
   secrecy_of subs5
   authentication_on alice_server
   authentication_on server_bob
 end goal
 environment()
```

Fig. 3. Role specification in HLPSL for the cluster head CH_j

Fig. 4. Role specification in HLPSL for the environment and goal

identified by the constant id in the goal section. The intruder is always denoted by i.

We have given the specifications in HLPSL for the role of session, goal and environment in Figures 4 and 5. In the session segment, all the basic roles: alice, bs and bob are instanced with concrete arguments. The top-level role (environment) defines in the specification of HLPSL, which contains the global constants and a composition of one or more sessions, where the intruder may play some roles as legitimate users. The intruder also participates in the execution of protocol as a concrete session. The current version of HLPSL supports the standard authentication and secrecy goals. In our implementation, the following five secrecy goals and two authentications are verified:

- secrecy_of subs1: It represents that X_s is kept secret to the BS.
- secrecy_of subs2: It represents that PW_i is kept secret to the user U_i.
- secrecy_of subs3: It represents that MK_{CH_j} is secret to BS and the cluster head CH_j.
- secrecy_of subs4: It represents that $SKubs$ is secret to U_i and BS.
- secrecy_of subs5: It represents that X_a and y are secret to U_i and BS.
- authentication_on alice_server: U_i generates a random timestamp T_1, where T_1 is only known to U_i. If the BS gets T_1 from the message from U_i, the BS authenticates U_i on T_1.
- authentication_on server_bob: BS generates a random timestamp T_1, where T_2 is only known to BS. If the cluster head CH_j receives T_2 from the message from the BS, CH_j authenticates BS on T_2.

3.3   Analysis of Results

We have chosen the back-end OFMC for an execution test and a bounded number of sessions model checking [8]. For the replay attack checking, the back-end checks whether the legitimate agents can execute the specified protocol by performing a search of a passive intruder. After that the back-end gives the intruder the knowledge of some normal sessions between the legitimate agents. For the Dolev-Yao model check, the back-end checks whether there is any man-in-the-middle attack possible by the intruder.

We have simulated Das et al.'s scheme under the back-end OFMC using the AVISPA web tool [3]. The simulation results are shown in Figure 6. The formal security verification analysis of Das et al.'s scheme clearly shows that this scheme is secure against active attacks including replay and man-in-the-middle attacks.

```
role session(Ui, CHj, BS: agent,
    MKchj : symmetric_key,
        SKubs : symmetric_key,
        H : hash_func  )

def=

    local  SI, SJ, RI, RJ, BI, BJ: channel (dy)

    composition
        alice(Ui, CHj, BS, MKchj, SKubs, H, SI, RI)
        ∧ bs(Ui, CHj, BS, MKchj, SKubs, H, BI, BJ)
        ∧ bob(Ui, CHj, BS, MKchj, SKubs, H, SJ, RJ)
end role
```

```
% OFMC
% Version of 2006/02/13
SUMMARY
 SAFE
DETAILS
 BOUNDED_NUMBER_OF_SESSIONS
PROTOCOL
 /home/avispa/web-interface-computation/
 ./tempdir/workfileOORcJO.if
GOAL
 as_specified
BACKEND
 OFMC
COMMENTS
STATISTICS
 parseTime: 0.00s
 searchTime: 0.58s
 visitedNodes: 55 nodes
 depth: 6 plies
```

Fig. 5. Role specification in HLPSL for the session

Fig. 6. The result of the analysis using OFMC back-end

4   Conclusion

We have reviewed the recently proposed Das et al.'s password-based user authentication scheme for large-scale hierarchical wireless sensor networks. We have then simulated Das et al.'s scheme for the formal security verification using the widely-accepted AVISPA tool. We have implemented the roles for the user, the sensor and the base station (gateway node) using the HLPSL language, which is a role-oriented language. We have also implemented the roles for the session, goal and environment using the HLPSL language. We have finally executed this protocol under the OFMC back-end. The results of the analysis using the OFMC back-end clearly shows that Das et al.'s scheme is secure against passive and active attacks.

References

1. Advanced Encryption Standard (AES), FIPS PUB 197, National Institute of Standards and Technology (NIST), U.S. Department of Commerce (November 2001), http://csrc.nist.gov/publications/fips/fips197/fips-197.pdf
2. Automated Validation of Internet Security Protocols and Applications, Avispa Tool Documentation, http://www.avispa-project.org/package/user-manual.pdf (accessed on March 2013)
3. Automated validation of internet security protocols and applications, AVISPA Web Tool, http://www.avispa-project.org/web-interface/expert.php/ (accessed on January 2013)
4. Secure Hash Standard, FIPS PUB 180-1, National Institute of Standards and Technology (NIST), U.S. Department of Commerce (April 1995)
5. Wireless Sensor Networks, Crossbow Technology Inc., http://www.xbow.com (accessed on September 2011)
6. Akyildiz, I.F., Su, W., Sankarasubramaniam, Y., Cayirci, E.: Wireless sensor networks: A Survey. Computer Networks 38(4), 393–422 (2002)
7. Armando, A., et al.: The AVISPA Tool for the Automated Validation of Internet Security Protocols and Applications. In: Etessami, K., Rajamani, S.K. (eds.) CAV 2005. LNCS, vol. 3576, pp. 281–285. Springer, Heidelberg (2005)
8. Basin, D., Modersheim, S., Vigano, L.: OFMC: A symbolic model checker for security protocols. International Journal of Information Security 4(3), 181–208 (2005)
9. Chatterjee, S., Das, A.K., Sing, J.K.: An Enhanced Access Control Scheme in Wireless Sensor Networks. Ad Hoc & Sensor Wireless Networks (in presss, 2013)
10. Das, A.K.: An unconditionally secure key management scheme for large-scale heterogeneous wireless sensor networks. In: First IEEE International Conference on Communication Systems and Networks (COMSNETS 2009), pp. 1–10 (2009)
11. Das, A.K.: A secure and effective user authentication and privacy preserving protocol with smart cards for wireless communications. Networking Science 2(1-2), 12–27 (2013)
12. Das, A.K., Chatterjee, S., Sing, J.K.: A novel efficient access control scheme for large-scale distributed wireless sensor networks. International Journal of Foundations of Computer Science (in press, 2013)
13. Das, A.K., Massand, A., Patil, S.: A novel proxy signature scheme based on user hierarchical access control policy. Journal of King Saud University - Computer and Information Sciences (2013), http://dx.doi.org/10.1016/j.jksuci.2012.12.001
14. Das, A.K., Sengupta, I.: An effective group-based key establishment scheme for large-scale wireless sensor networks using bivariate polynomials. In: 3rd IEEE International Conference on Communication Systems Software and Middleware (COMSWARE 2008), pp. 9–16 (2008)
15. Das, A.K., Sharma, P., Chatterjee, S., Sing, J.K.: A dynamic password-based user authentication scheme for hierarchical wireless sensor networks. Journal of Network and Computer Applications 35(5), 1646–1656 (2012)
16. Dolev, D., Yao, A.: On the security of public key protocols. IEEE Transactions on Information Theory 29(2), 198–208 (1983)
17. von Oheimb, D.: The high-level protocol specification language hlpsl developed in the eu project avispa. In: Proceedings of APPSEM Workshop (2005)

VM Profile Based Optimized Network Attack Pattern Detection Scheme for DDOS Attacks in Cloud

Sanchika Gupta and Padam Kumar

Department of Electronics and Computer Enginnering
Indian Institute of Technology Roorkee, Roorkee, Uttarakhand, India-247667
dr.sanchikagupta@gmail.com, padamfec@iitr.ernet.in

Abstract. Cloud computing is a well-known internet platform based technology that provides access to rented, remotely located and distributed IT resources such as computing infrastructure, storage, online web and utility application on a pay per usage model. As it is a widely used service by individual users to corporate organizations and contains valuable data and applications, it is known to be vulnerable to risks and threats such as network level threats, host level threats and virtualization layer vulnerabilities etc. However for counterattacking these vulnerabilities traditional defense measures exists but are not efficient, scalable and optimized to be used in cloud. The paper identifies the drawbacks in the current schemes used for handling network attacks (primarily DDOS) and provides a new direction in which the same level of security capabilities for network can be obtained with minimal expense of resources which is the prime requirement for any scheme for being applicable in cloud environment. The paper describes a prototype implementation of the concept with details of experimental setup and initial results.

Keywords: Cloud, DDoS, VM, Profile, IDS, Detection, Network, Attacks, Vulnerability, defense, security, threats.

1 Introduction

Cloud computing is a current buzz word in the area of computing and data storage. It provides network based access to a shared pool of resources on a pay per usage model [1]. The resource's includes utility applications, word processing software's, remote code execution platforms (backend supports for user's own created applications), remote data storage facilities, computing infrastructure etc [2]. The important point that makes everything easy in cloud is that virtual replicas of physical resources can be dynamically created according to cloud user needs and can be allocated, managed and released with minimal managerial efforts from cloud service providers [3]. Cloud provides services at three layers of computing which includes SaaS (Software as a Service), PaaS (Platform as a Service) and IaaS (Infrastructure as a Service) [4]. As user's secret data is stored on cloud, which provide shared resource usage between several cloud users (that can include internal adversaries and external attackers) Information security and trust establishment is an immediate need in cloud

Sabu M. Thampi et al. (Eds.): SSCC 2013, CCIS 377, pp. 255–261, 2013.

[5]. Some of the security concerns need stronger access control and logging requirements in cloud, network security establishments for thwarting well known cloud network attacks including DDOS [6], stronger host based security measures for detection of malicious programs and security from virtualization layer based attacks including VM hoping, VM Escape etc. [7]. This paper focuses on security of cloud from network layer DDOS attacks with proposal and experimental results of an efficient technique to thwart such attacks and which is based on network profile information of virtual machines. The motivation of the research lies in the fact that there is an alarming rate of network layer attacks [8] [9] on cloud since past and there is an immediate need of optimized defense measures for thwarting them in Cloud environment. The proposed solution provides new lightweight and VM profile based approach for network attack pattern detection in cloud. The prototype implementation has been tested with a set of attack patterns and initial results show it to be efficient and optimized.

2 Related Work

Because of the potential threats to cloud infrastructure from network based attacks, such as DDOS, researchers have started looking into prevention and defense measures to thwart them. However the analysis for a perfect Network IDS that will work specifically for cloud in terms of efficiency and completeness is still under discussion. Traditional methods for network intrusion detection that are used in certain specific environments as well are proved computationally complex to be used in cloud. Hai Jin et al. [10] Proposed VMFence which is used to monitor network flow and file integrity in real time. But this architecture is computationally complex as it checks for attack patterns from data coming from all VM's connected to the central domain. Daniel Smallwood et al. [11] described the effectiveness of a utility that was developed to improve retrospective packet analysis and which was tested with data Centre traffic from a ISP providing cloud services. There results indicate that they outperformed existing techniques in terms of query function performance. However the concept of deep packet inspection for network intrusion detection works efficiently for small and simpler enterprise networks, but in the case of distributed and complex network topologies like cloud, deep packet inspection schemes will demand noticeable amount of resources. Chi-Chun Lo et al. proposed an idea of cooperative IDS [12] on cloud computing region. These IDSs cooperate with each other with exchange of alerts to reduce the impact of a DoS attack. But this architecture demands extra communication cost in cooperation and delays. S. Roschke et al. proposed extensible intrusion detection system management architecture in the cloud [13]. This architecture consists of several sensors which report back alerts to a central management unit. As the sensors are distributed and resides over VM's a higher level of trust cannot be expected from the data coming from them. C. Mazzariello [14], et al. proposed a network based IDS for cloud computing environment in which the issue of detecting DoS attacks on services hosted in a cloud is addressed. The system is able to detect the flooding attack but in this architecture the overloaded cluster controller comes as a bottleneck. S.N. Dhage, et al. [15] proposed intrusion detection system in cloud computing environment in which each instance of the IDS has to monitor a single user. But here host can subvert the individual IDS deployed at a VM and hence after then the system will not be able to detect network intrusions correctly. From the knowledge gained from above related work done in the area of IDS in Cloud, we identified that the schemes proposed are good but they lacks two important thing which are trust and efficiency. The schemes do not perform optimized detection which is an immediate need for their applicability in cloud i.e. they search the patterns in network traffic even after knowing that some systems are not a severe victim of it in the past and will have a negligible probability in near future. The techniques also decrease the trust of detection when they run in a distributed way on VM's instead on a centralized domain. Also cooperation based techniques are good but increase communication cost and delays in detection. Our proposed scheme runs on a privileged central domain and performs optimized rule matching with the use of VM profile's that describe a VM network characteristic information and is described in section 3.

3   Proposed Work

The proposed scheme has specific characteristics such as: It classifies the network traffic coming from various VM's in cloud computing environment. Hence network traffic of cloud is viewed as traffic coming from individual physical network interfaces. The approach creates individual profiles for each VM for all possible attacks patterns. The profile of a VM contains the attack pattern (the rule) and the threshold that needs to be tested. (We have currently focused on detection of TCP SYN flooding attacks). The technique decreases the computational resources needed for attack patterns detection exponentially based on VM network behavior which provides a lightweight but complete method for packet inspection based network intrusion detection in cloud. The scheme description is as follows: While initializing a VM to a cloud user, the process of initial rule creation, establishes the set of rules and their thresholds. In this step we run the rule pattern detection over a period of N packets and the same process is repeated M times. N is defined as the number of packets (basically a period) over which we are looking for rule matching packets (which are TCP SYN packets in our prototype implementation). M is the repetition value of the rule that determines how many times the same process over N packets is followed to gain the correct network behavior of a rule (TCP SYN flooding detection rule). Our rule based detection follows the steps for detection which are as follows:

1. It extracts the threshold for the rule pattern from initial rule establishment phase. It runs the rule matching operation over N packets i.e. accumulate number of rule matched patterns per N packets and match it with the threshold P to determine whether there is an ongoing DDOS attack or not. This is as per traditional schemes for detecting TCP SYN DDOS attacks based on threshold.
2. If during the first run of the rule over the network, the traffic reveals that there is no ongoing attack (i.e. threshold is not crossed) the detection frequency is decreased by a power of 2. This means now the attack pattern is searched (rule matching) once after every second packet. If the same happens for the second time the detection is again decreased with the same ratio. Now the pattern is

matched once after the 4th packet. Similarly in the first case when the threshold is not exceeded by the network traffic, the period of threshold detection, which is N packets is moved to a period of 2N packets while in the next case it is moved to 4N packets.

3. This exponential decrease of attack pattern detection is performed till a limit which depends upon the limit up to which the decreased speed of detection is accepted. But the decrease in speed of detection is acceptable because of these reasons: In case of DDOS attacks such as TCP SYN floods the rate in which packets are sent is too high and hence if a correct value of N is chosen it will not create noticeable delay in detection even if the attack matching is decreased S times. Also the detection rate vibrates between the specified limit. The detection is exponentially decreased until a limit which is S after which it again starts with normal detection strategy and again detection schemes decrease its matching for attack pattern exponentially. This is followed until the attack is detected. Hence the speed of detection doesn't get decreased for always. But it moves to its normal speed 1/S times.

4. However if the rule matching packets crosses the attack detection threshold in any of the detection stage the detection is moved to the traditional detection strategy that is rule detection per packet with threshold detection every N packets and will remain in the stage till a period of Y*N times before exponentially decreasing the attack pattern detection. This is to ensure that the attack which is detected has been properly tackled and verified for its non-existence. When TCP SYN flood is detected then after moving to the base speedy detection strategy, it collects IP addresses from where the SYN packets are coming. Then the communication with the IP addresses is stopped for a period of t seconds. The rule for which is as follows: Let's suppose there are Z Source IP addresses from which TCP SYN flooding packets are received during attack. We sort IP address based on the number of TCP SYN packets obtained in N packets. So we stop communication with the IP address if: #TCP SYN packets = P/Z +- d, where d is the variation parameter defined as Max (#TCP SYN from an IP)/Z.

The communication is stopped by rule creation in IP tables for the attacking IP addresses. The scheme not only identifies TCP SYN flooding from external IP addresses, but it also identifies VM that are launching TCP SYN flooding attacks to the external world. For example if a VM user is trying to launch TCP SYN flooding attack to other VM or to other external system the event is logged and the communication of the System is disconnected from the external world for a period of t seconds. During Network behavior based rule updation the VM after a predefined period of time or packets (dependent upon dynamicity of network behavioral conditions it can be small or large and is a customizable parameter) is again put to initial rule establishment step in background with rule based detection. But now the rule is updated with the network conditions and VM behavior. VM network behavior for the rule is updated from the values obtained by again applying the initial rule creation. After M times, the values obtained are looked for the most frequent highest value (for say h). The threshold is updated only if the value is higher than present threshold and which is as follows: Threshold = Threshold + f * (Threshold-h). Where f is a small value, generally 0.125, which steadily changes the threshold according to current network conditions but also does not disturb it in case of short dynamic busty traffic. The implementation of the scheme is done as a prototype for TCP SYN flooding attack detection technique.

4   Implementation Details, Results and Discussions

Network traffic is sniffed from the Ethernet interface of the central privileged domain by setting it to promiscuous mode. After sniffing the packets the traffic is classified based on the VM's from which it is obtained. Each of the VM has a separate database that stores behavior of TCP SYN packet per N number of packets. We identified that each VM has different Network usage scenarios. On the initial run and looking for TCP SYN packets per 50 TCP Packets we identified that each individual VM has a different behavior and is dependent upon VM usage scenario. The value of N = 50 is chosen taking into account The TCP backlog value that is 128 for slow connections and 1024 normally. We want that the TCP SYN flooding should be detected timely even if we exponentially decrease the detection of rule to an extent. By setting value to 50 we can move towards decreasing the detection speed to a value of period 4N. Even then we are sure that if TCP SYN flood happens in this case it will not fill the TCP queue fully as the value of 4N will be 200 less than 1024 which is normal case of TCP backlog value. And when the Flood is detected it can be handled gracefully with an acceptable detection speed. For each VM the threshold for TCP SYN flooding attack detection is identified by storing the #TCP SYN packets per N (50) packets 1000 times and then identifying the maximum value from the 1000 runs. The maximum value is set as the attack detection threshold for TCP SYN flooding attack detection. During initial rule creation stage of a particular VM we found this value of threshold as 20, hence we set threshold P=20. During rule based detection we identified the optimization in rule pattern matching operation. We have taken the value of S=4 hence the pattern will be matched once every 4th packet and with effective N = 4N =200. The optimization in terms of rule matching operations is shown below. The total number of TCP packets over which the rule is fired is 20 million. In case of our scheme in which the detection is optimized by varying the detection strategy the amount of rule pattern searches in N+2N+4N+2N+N packets (which are 500 packets) will be 5N(200 packets). While in case of traditional method of attack detection through rule pattern searching in a continuous way for detecting SYN flooding attack will be 10N (500 packets). Hence the amount of pattern matches will be decreased and will be equal to: (10N – 5N)/10N * 100 = 50%. According to the proposed dynamicity of the attack pattern searching strategy the probability of detection of attack at the same time as with traditional measures on N packets will be: Probability of timely detection = (2/5)*100 = 40%.This is because of the fact that the detection comes to normal detection strategy two times every cycle, when it moves from N to 4N period and back to N. The tradeoff of speed of detection with the proposed technique is also defended by the fact that denial of service attacks such as TCP SYN flood has aim of overloading the system with enormous number of attack packets so as to fill the TCP connection queue making it unable to handle any incoming valid TCP connection packet. Hence in such cases even with big period of

detection (up to a limit) the attacks can easily get detected because of the huge
frequency in which they are fired. And it is a fact that a system remains more time in
its normal mode of operation compared to the time it is in attack hence decreasing the
detection speed in this manner will eventually save computation resources needed for
rule matching operations. A snapshot of working is shown in figure1.

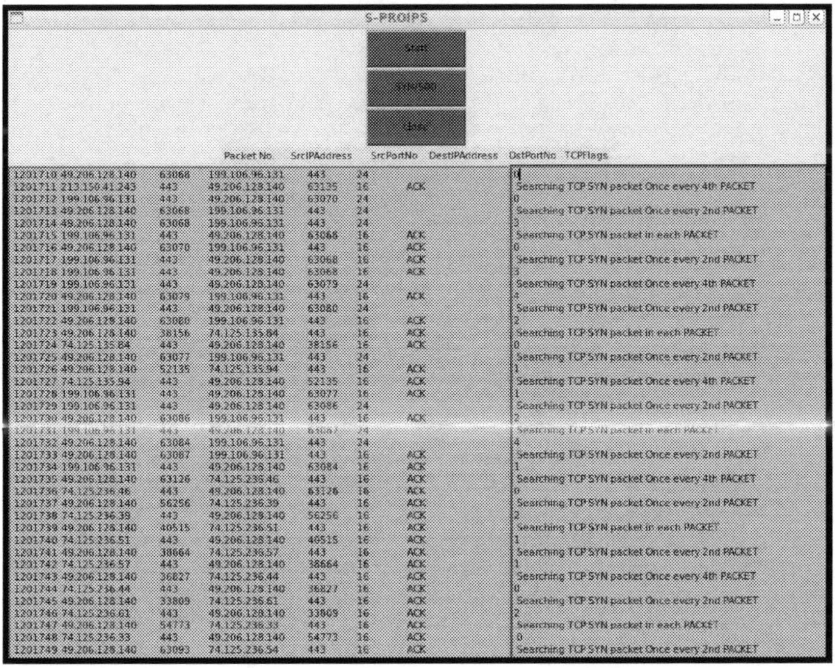

Fig. 1. The Intrusion Detection Scheme GUI in its Normal Run

5   Conclusions

Paper describes a very lightweight and complete approach for rule based DDOS
network intrusion detection in Cloud. The scheme is centralized and hence does not
suffers from overloading as it keeps minimal information about communicating
entities and do minimal analysis for the detection. It saves huge amount of resources
that are wasted for continuous rule based pattern matching for network intrusion
detection. As the scheme does not have any dependency on VM's and runs on
centralized domain it has higher trust compared to other distributed schemes and also
it does not incurs delay in detection. With proper parameters used for detection in a
specific cloud environment a higher value of optimization can be achieved with what
is reported in our analysis and results. The scheme not only stops DDOS attacks from
external VM;s but also stops malicious entities that uses cloud resources for such
attacks to the outside world. A complete implementation with other rule for detection
of various other DDOS attacks in cloud is under progress.

References

1. Grance, P.M.A.T.: Effectively and Securely Using the Cloud Computing Paradigm, v0.25 (2009), http://csrc.nist.gov/organizations/fissea/2009-conference/presentations/fissea09-pmell-day3_cloud-computing.pdf
2. Brown, E.: NIST Issues Cloud Computing Guidelines for Managing Security and Privacy. National Institute of Standards and Technology Special Publication 800-144 (2012)
3. Susmita, H., et al.: Implementing private cloud at IIT Roorkee: an initial experience. Book Implementing private cloud at IIT Roorkee: an initial experience, Series Implementing private cloud at IIT Roorkee: an initial experience, pp. 453–458. ACM (2012)
4. Nist, S.P.: 800-53 Rev. 2. Recommended Security Controls for Federal Information Systems (2007)
5. Gupta, S., et al.: A secure and lightweight approach for critical data security in cloud. In: 2012 Fourth International Conference on Proc. Computational Aspects of Social Networks (CASoN), pp. 315–320. IEEE (2012)
6. Gupta, S., Horrow, S., Sardana, A.: A Hybrid Intrusion Detection Architecture for Defense against DDoS Attacks in Cloud Environment Contemporary Computing. In: Parashar, M., Kaushik, D., Rana, O.F., Samtaney, R., Yang, Y., Zomaya, A., et al. (eds.) IC3 2012. CCIS, vol. 306, pp. 498–499. Springer, Heidelberg (2012)
7. Gupta, S., et al.: A light Weight Centralized File Monitoring Approach for Securing Files in Cloud Environment. In: Proc. of the 7th International Conference for Internet Technology and Secured Transactions (ICITST 2012), pp. 382–387. IEEE (2012)
8. Bloomerg, Attack on Sony Play station Network exploiting Amazon Cloud Services (2011), http://www.bloomberg.com/news/2011-05-15/sony-attack-shows-amazon-s-cloud-service-lureshackers-at-pennies-an-hour.html/
9. Top Threats to Cloud Computing (2012), https://cloudsecurityalliance.org/research/top-threats/
10. Jin, H., et al.: A VMM-based intrusion prevention system in cloud computing environment. The Journal of Supercomputing, 1–19 (2011)
11. Smallwood, D., Vance, A.: Intrusion analysis with deep packet inspection: Increasing efficiency of packet based investigations. In: 2011 International Conference on Proc. Cloud and Service Computing (CSC), pp. 342–347. IEEE (2011)
12. Chi-Chun, L., et al.: A Cooperative Intrusion Detection System Framework for Cloud Computing Networks. In: 2010 39th International Conference on Proc. Parallel Processing Workshops (ICPPW), pp. 280–284 (2010)
13. Roschke, S., et al.: Intrusion Detection in the Cloud. In: Eighth IEEE International Conference on Proc. Dependable, Autonomic and Secure Computing, DASC 2009, pp. 729–734 (2009)
14. Mazzariello, C., et al.: Integrating a network IDS into an open source Cloud Computing environment. In: 2010 Sixth International Conference on Proc. Information Assurance and Security (IAS), pp. 265–270 (2010)
15. Dhage, S.N., et al.: Intrusion detection system in cloud computing environment. International Journal of Cloud Computing 1(2), 261–282 (2012)

Implementation and Embellishment
of Prevention of Keylogger Spyware Attacks

Mohammad Wazid[1], Robin Sharma[2], Avita Katal[3], R.H. Goudar[4],
Priyanka Bhakuni[5], and Asit Tyagi[6]

[1,3,4,6] Department of CSE, Graphic Era University, Dehradun, India
[2,5] Department of IT, Graphic Era University, Dehradun, India
{wazidkec2005,sharmaisrobin,avita207,rhgoudar,
priyankabisht99,asittyagi30}@gmail.com

Abstract. Internet has become the essential requirement of modern society. People using Internet frequently for their day to day work includes online banking transaction, email and online chat with friends etc. Malwares are very light programs, they are designed to cause harm to your system. Hackers can steal the credentials of your online banking account by the help of spyware (a kind of malware). Malware attacks are very often in Cyber World such kinds of attacks are very difficult to detect and defend. Keylogger spyware is a combined script attack. A keylogger spyware contains both scripts keylogger and spyware in a single program. A hacker can steal the credentials and confidential information from the infected user's system by performing this attack. In this paper we have implemented a prevention mechanism for keylogger spyware attacks. It contains three phases keylogger spyware attack, honeypot based detection and prevention of keylogger spyware. The detection of keylogger spyware is performed by the help of honeypot. There is a honeypot agent program deployed in client's system monitors malicious activities and reports them to the honeypot. All keylogger spyware attack related information sent by honeypot agent program is stored in the database maintained at honeypot. If a keylogger spyware program is detected in a system then it will be permanently removed by the help of prevention server. The implemented mechanism is capable to prevent such kind of attacks using a combination of malwares.

Keywords: Keylogger, Spyware, Keylogger Spyware Algorithm, Honeypot Agent Algorithm, Honeypot Algorithm, Keylogger Spyware Inspection Algorithm, Prevention Algorithm at Client Side, Prevention Algorithm at Prevention Server.

1   Introduction

Malwares are designed to cause harm to a system, to steal confidential information from a system, they can also be used to earn revenue. Type includes keylogger, spyware, adware, rootkit etc. They are very light in nature. A system user can not feel their presence. In short we can say that they are programs that are intentionally developed to cause harm to a system. It has become essential to provide efficient security solution to

Sabu M. Thampi et al. (Eds.): SSCC 2013, CCIS 377, pp. 262–271, 2013.
© Springer-Verlag Berlin Heidelberg 2013

those systems which are used in day to day online banking transaction. A keylogger spyware is a different kind of malware attack which uses two malware programs in a combined script. A keylogger which captures all the key strokes in a log file and other is spyware which emails this to hacker's specified address. So all the credentials can be easily stolen using keylogger spyware. In this paper we have implemented a prevention mechanism for keylogger spyware attacks. The detection is performed by honeypot, there is a honeypot agent program deployed in client's system detects the presence of keylogger spyware and reports anomaly data to the honeypot. All keylogger spyware attack related information sent by honeypot agent program is stored in the database maintained at honeypot. It will be inspected by the administrator to check presence of keylogger spyware program in a client's system. If a keylogger spyware program is detected in a system then it will be permanently removed by the help of prevention server. The overall paper is organized as: in Section 2 we have discussed related work. Section 3 defines problem definition followed by the methodology of work in Section 4 contains the methodology of this work. Section 5 contains various proposed algorithms for keylogger spyware detection and prevention. The work done is concluded in section 6 along with the discussion of future work.

2   Literature Survey

In paper [1] authors have proposed a framework for detection and prevention of keylogger spyware attack. It is capable of defending against such kind of attacks using a combination of malwares. The paper [2] focuses on the honeynet technology used for network security. It provides new powerful means, the optimization of system to improve the honeypot for target, integrity from system detection rate and safety. Experiments show that the improved honeypot system achieves higher detection rates and higher safety. In paper [3] an intrusion detection module based on honeypot technology is presented. This detection technique makes use of IP Trace back technique. The use of mobile agents provides it with the capability of distributed detection and response. This module by making the use of honeypot technology traces the intrusion source farthest. In paper [4] both honeypot client and server technologies are used in combined way of malware collection and analysis. The main objective of this paper was the analysis of collected malwares from honeypots. Classification of honeypots is done as server honeypots and client honeypots. In paper [5] authors presented the four main methodologies that are used in intrusion detection and prevention systems (IDPS/IPS). The discussed methodologies are: anomaly based, signature based, stateful protocol analysis and hybrid based. In paper [6] a distributed intrusion detection system based on honeypot is proposed. It can detect intruders not only outside but also inside the system. The system provides a complete, controllable, reliable proactive protection for computers and network. For the shortcoming of traditional intrusion detection system (IDS) in complex and unknown attack detection. In paper [7] authors explain a new generation of malware attack for VoIP infrastructures and services. If strong security measures are not deployed then these malwares produces a real threat to the deployed VoIP architectures. The proposed bot architecture stack of different protocols provides the bot with an application interface to use these protocols. The introduced "VoIP bots" support a wide set of attacks ranging from Spam Over Internet Telephony (SPIT) to distributed denial of service attack (DDoS). They are tested against several VoIP platforms. In paper [8] authors discuss some problems (i.e. Gap between spamtraps and phoneytokens, online verification of phoneytokens etc) of existing anti phishing solutions based on honeypots. A framework is proposed which can transform the real e-banking system into a honeypot having honeytokens to deal with the above mentioned problems. In paper [9] authors proposed a worm detection and defense system named bot-honeynet which combines the best features of honeynet, anomaly detection and botnet. Bot-honeynet is designed to not only detect worm attacks but also defend against malicious worms. In paper [10] authors propose a hybrid and adaptable honeypot-based approach that improves the currently deployed IDSs for protecting networks from intruders. The main idea of this paper is to deploy low-interaction honeypots that act as emulators of services and operating systems and have them direct malicious traffic to high-interaction honeypots, where hackers engage with real services.

People have discussed about malware attacks, some of them provide the intrusion detection and prevention systems for these kind of attack. But nobody has provided an effective solution for joint script malware attacks.

3   Problem Definition

Malware can be of many types i.e. keylogger, spyware, rootkit etc. We can use them in a combination i.e. keylogger spyware as a common program. In this paper we have implemented a prevention mechanism for keylogger spyware attacks. It is based upon honeypot, there is a honeypot agent program deployed in client' system reports anomaly data to the honeypot. The reported information will be stored in the maintained database at honeypot contains all the entries of the malicious activities taking place in client's system. It contains Timestamp, IP address of the client and the process ID of the email sending process. The presence of keylogger spyware program is detected during an inspection process. If keylogger spyware program is detected in a client's system then that can be removed by the help of prevention server. The implemented prevention mechanism is capable to detect and defend such kind of attacks using a combination of malwares.

4   Methodology

The malware attack becomes very deadly if they are used in a combination. In this work we have designed an attacking scenario for keylogger spyware, a combination of keylogger and spyware program. The keylogger script stores every keystroke into a file and generates a log file then the spy script email this log file to the designer's specified address.

The implemented prevention mechanism is divided into three phases keylogger spyware attack, honeypot based detection and prevention of keylogger spyware program.

4.1   Keylogger Spyware Attack

We have designed an attacking scenario for keylogger spyware attack on user's system as shown in figure 1. There are 2 users, accessing various services via Internet i.e. online banking, email etc. A malicious server hosting keylogger spyware enters into the system in the form of application software as it appears useful software to a user which he is in need of leading him to download it. Once the downloaded program is installed, it starts capturing every keystroke. A log file is generated corresponding to each keystroke (i.e. asd file) included spy script within the installed malicious software email this log file to the specified address of the hacker.

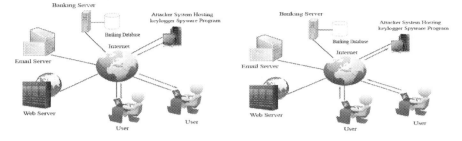

Fig. 1. Keylogger Spyware Attack   Fig. 2. Email Process: Transfer of confidential information from user's system

The red colored arrows in figure 1 show the entry of keylogger spyware program into user's system. Figure 2 shows automatic email process performed by the spyware script periodically i.e. after every 1 minute. It is shown by blue colored arrows in figure 2.

Fig. 3. Email sent by Mohammad Wazid   Fig. 4. Snapshot of spylog file received at robhack7@gmail.com

Mohammad Wazid a system user sends an email to rsachan28@gmail.com at 7:54 pm on 28th March, 2013, as shown in figure 3.The keylogger spyware generated a log file (asd) as shown in figure 4 corresponding to each keystroke. The information contains in generated log file has the important credentials of the user i.e. for Mohammad Wazid the username is wazidkec2005 and password is jp@050124. Thus the credentials and entire message both are leaked.

Figure 5 shows the snapshot of email received at hackers specified address i.e. robhack7@gmail.com. The log file (asd) shown in figure 4 are received at this email id at 7.54 PM on 28th March, 2013.

Fig. 5. Spyware log file received at hacker's email account

4.2   Honeypot Based Detection

It has become essential to detect the existence of keylogger spyware program in a user's system. For detection purpose we have used honeypot agent program deployed in client's system and a honeypot, both are communicating to each other. Honeypot agent program deployed in client's system detects the malicious activity being performed by the keylogger spyware if present. This information is reported to the honeypot appliance having honeypot program and a database. The maintained database has having all the entries of the malicious activities taking place in client's system. The database contains three fields i.e. Timestamp, IP address of the client system and the Process ID of the email sending process.

Figure 6 shows keylogger spyware monitoring process performed by deployed honeypot agent. The red arrows show the entry of keylogger spyware into the user's system having honeypot agent program. Figure 7 shows the communication between honeypot agent program and honeypot appliance. The information sent by the honeypot agent program is entered in the database maintained at honeypot appliance. The maintained database is further used in the inspection process of malicious programs.

Figure 8 shows the snapshot of database containing information sent by the honeypot agent program to the honeypot appliance. This database is having three columns Timestamp, IP address and Process ID of the email sending process. The PID 2856 of an email sending process is detected again and again in a system having IP address 121.245.65.202.

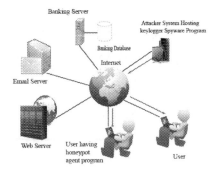

Fig. 6. Deployment of Honeypot Agent

Fig. 7. Communication between Honeypot agent and Honeypot

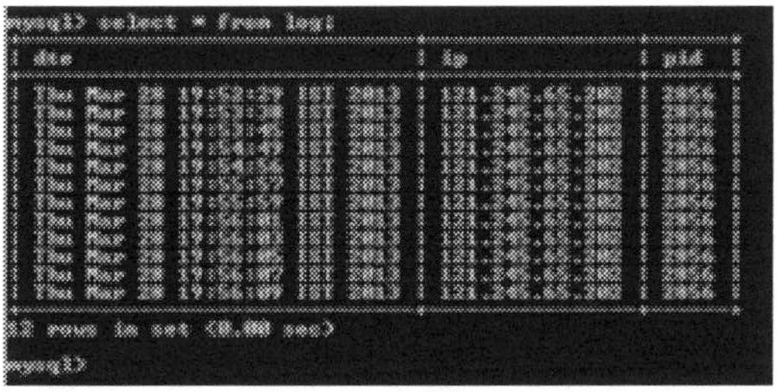

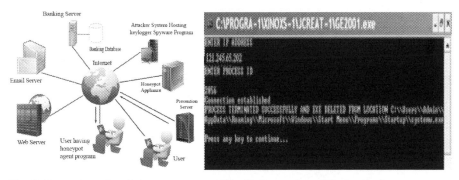

Fig. 8. Entries in the maintained database at Honeypot

4.3   Prevention of Keylogger Spyware

The prevention of keylogger spyware is performed by the help of deployed prevention server.

Fig. 9. Prevention of malicious program   **Fig. 10.** Prevention of Keylogger Spyware
performed by Prevention Server

If the existence of keylogger spyware is detected in a system, it can be resolved by the help of deployed prevention server. The performed prevention process of keylogger spyware is shown in figure 9. Figure 10 shows, how a keylogger spyware program is removed from the infected system. We have used wmic command to get the information of running executable programs in a system with their PIDs and their location on hard disk drive. We run a prevention program at prevention server in which we enter the IP address (i.e. 121.245.65.202) of infected system and the PID (i.e. 2856) of keylogger spyware program. When prevention program successfully executed it will completely remove that keylogger spyware from the infected system and a message will be shown on the screen of prevention server "PROCESS TERMINATED SUCCESSFULLY AND EXE DELETED FROM THE LOCATION C:\\Users\\Admin\\AppData\\Running\\Microsoft\\Windows\\Start Menu\\Programs\\Startup\\system.exe" as shown in figure 10.

5   Proposed Algorithms

For the proposed mechanism following algorithms are designed:

5.1   Keylogger Spyware Algorithm [1]

```
Keylogger_Algorithm ( )
{
//Algorithm for keystroke capturing
   While (true)
      {
```

- *Open* the log file in write mode.
- *Get* the system time using *time.h* API in C and enter that time in log file.
- *Append* the time in the log file.
- *Get* the activity by tapping the keystrokes and mouse clicks. It can be done in using *windows.h* and *Winuser.h* API available in C compilers.
- Enter the activity into log file as soon as the valid status of particular key is pressed or mouse click is observed.
- *Close* the file and terminate all the file pointers.
- *Open* the file in append mode to avoid the overwriting and synchronization problem.

```
      }
}
Spyware_Algorithm ( )
{
//Algorithm for sending periodic emails
   While (true)
      {
      Keylogger_Algorithm ( )
```

- Make the program to sleep for sometime so that keylogger can tap sufficient data and log into log file. The time period can be 1 minute or 5 minute or anything as per requirement.
- *Get* the system name.
- *Select* that log file.
- Perform the attachment and send the email to specified email address with system name written in subject or body of email.
- *Terminate* keylogger process.

```
      Keylogger_Algorithm ( )
      }
}
```

5.2   Honeypot Agent Algorithm

Honeypot_Agent_ Algorithm ( )

// TCP processes are those processes that are using the TCP protocol at transport layer in the layered architecture of the network
// APPL_SMTP processes are those processes that are using SMTP protocol at //Application Layer
// BUFFER is a Buffer having PIDs that can be implemented by using BufferedReader Class of JAVA at Client side
// sleep (2): go into sleep mode for 2 seconds

1. Get the PID's of all the TCP processes by using the *COMMAND* netstat –o –p.
2. Store the PID's of the APPL_SMTP processes in a BUFFER.
3. if the result of Step-2 is NULL then
     Sleep (2)
     GOTO step-1
otherwise
     GOTO step-4
4. Using TCP Socket establish the connection with honeypot.
5. Send the BUFFER content with the time stamp and client's IP address to honeypot.
6. Close the connection with honeypot and GOTO step-1.

This program runs in client's system.

5.3   Honeypot Algorithm

Honeypot_Algorithm ( )

// BUFFER is a Buffer having PIDs that can be implemented by using BufferedReader Class of JAVA at Client side

1. Open TCP connection with honeypot agent.
2. Get the BUFFER content with time stamp and IP address.
3. Maintain the log information at honeypot and insert BUFFER|| time stamp || IP address in this log.
4. Close the connection with honeypot agent.
5. Goto step-1.

This program runs at honeypot appliance and communicates with honeypot agent program.

5.4   Keylogger Spyware Inspection Algorithm

Keylogger_ Spyware_ Inspection_ Algorithm ( )

// detected_IP_address is IP address of client's system stored in database maintained at honeypot

// detected_PID is the process ID of email sending process stored in database maintained at honeypot

// time_stamp is a time when email was sent from user's system

if *detected_IP_address* & *detected_PID* is same after every nT *time_stamp* value then

keylogger spyware is present in the user's system
otherwise

System is safe

This program runs at honeypot appliance to check the existence of a keylogger spyware program in a client's system.

5.5 Prevention Algorithm at Client Side

Client_ Prevention_Algorithm ( )
{
// Client side prevention algorithm
//PID: Process ID of processes running on a machine
//HDD: Hard Disk Drive

- *Open* the *TCP Socket* and *bind* with any port number available.
- *Wait* for Server side program to respond.
- After getting the Server response with a *PID* of malicious program, save that *PID* into a variable.
- *Run* the *wmic* command to get the list of all the processes with their executable location on HDD and their *PID*.
- Filter the above output and get the location of the executable of the malicious program with the help of its *PID* send by Server side program.
- After getting the location, *delete* the file from the location.
- *Send* message to Prevention Server that program has been deleted.
- *Close* the *TCP connection* with Prevention Server.

}
This program runs in client's system.

5.6 Prevention Algorithm at Server Side

Server_Prevention_Algorithm ( )
{
//Server side prevention algorithm
//PID: Process ID of processes running on a machine

- *Connect* to Client side program running in Client system.
- *Send* the *PID* of malicious process to Client side program.
- *Wait* for termination message coming from Client side program.
- As soon as message is received, *close* the *TCP Connection* with Client.

}

This program runs at prevention server and communicates with the prevention program running in client's system.

6   Conclusion

We have implemented a prevention mechanism for keylogger spyware attack. If a keylogger spyware is detected in a client's system then the work of prevention is started. The keylogger spyware can be completely removed by the help of prevention server. During the experimentation it has observed that proposed prevention mechanism is capable to prevent the keylogger spyware attacks.

In future we can design some other kind of cyber attacks by using different malwares (i.e. hijacker with rootkit) and we can provide the solution to those attacks.

References

1. Mohammad, W., Robin, S., Avita, K. Goudar, R.H., Singh, D.P., Bhakuni, P., Tyagi, A.: A Framework for Detection and Prevention of Novel Keylogger Spyware Attacks. In: Proceedings of 7th International Conference on Intelligent Systems and Control (2013)
2. Zhen, J., Liu, Z.: New honeypot system and its application in security of employment network. In: IEEE Symposium on Robotics and Applications (2012)
3. Liu, D., Zhang, Y.: An Intrusion Detection System Based on Honeypot Technology. In: ACM International Conference on Computer Science and Electronics Engineering (2012)
4. Sanjeev, K., Rakesh, S.: Bhatia J. S.: Hybrid Honeypot Framework for Malware Collection and analysis. In: 7th IEEE International Conference on Industrial and Information Systems (2012)
5. David, M., Rajeev, A.: A study of Methodologies used in Intrusion Detection and Prevention Systems (IDPS). In: Proceedings of IEEE Southeastcon (2012)
6. Yun, Y., Jia, M.: Design and implementation of distributed intrusion detection system based on honeypot. In: 2nd IEEE International Conference on Computer Engineering and Technology (2010)
7. Mohamed, N., Radu, S., Olivier, F.: VoIP Malware: Attack Tool & Attack Scenarios. In: IEEE International Conference on Communications (2009)
8. Li, S., Roland, S.: A Novel Anti-Phishing Framework Based on Honeypots. IEEE eCrime Researchers Summit (2009)
9. Yao, Y., Lv, J.-W., Gao, F.-X., Yu, G., Deng, Q.-X.: Detecting and Defending against Worm Attacks Using Bot-honeynet. In: 2nd IEEE International Symposium on Electronic Commerce and Security (2009)
10. Hassan, A., Haider, S., Malek, S., Iyad, K., Zaid, A.M.: A hybrid honeypot framework for improving intrusion detection systems in protecting organizational networks. Elsevier Journal of Computers & Security 25(4), 274–288 (2006)

Data Anonymization According to the Combination of Attributes on Social Network Sites

Sanaz Kavianpour, Bharanidharan Shanmugam, and Zuraini Ismail

Advanced Informatics School, Universiti Teknologi Malaysia,
Kuala Lumpur, Malaysia
ksanaz3@live.utm.my, {bharani,zurainisma}@ic.utm.my

Abstract. The popularity of social network sites has increased extremely during the previous years. Social network sites provide an intimacy interactive platform on the Internet for exchanging information among users. Users may disclose their ideas, comments, pictures or videos, secrets about their business or other private information that may be used by inappropriate user to threaten users' future decisions or positions. Thus, the goal of this paper is to explain how users' data can be anonymized to mitigate privacy concerns through information dissemination. The results depicts that although anonymization of data cannot protect the privacy of data completely, it can reduce the possibility of re-identification.

Keywords: Social network sites, privacy, anonymity.

1 Introduction

Social Network Sites (SNSs) are web-based services that allow users to make profiles, make relationships, share information such as photos, interests and activities or go through other users' information and activities [1].There are four subjects that define the structural differences among SNSs [2]. First, profile visibility that includes the amount of information which users can make public or private on the site. Second, self-presentation that contains styles of using profiles such as professional or social by users to present themselves on the site. Third, the profile customization that differentiates users based on their likes, dislikes and so on. Forth, privacy policies that forms social settings which can be specified by the site or users.

Social network sites (SNSs) databases store huge quantity of personal data either sensitive or non-sensitive. In compare with other websites, SNSs seems to be of interest to attackers due to the large number of users and the abundance availability of personal information that whereby mutual trust is common among users. SNSs do not have enough privacy protection tools [3] plus with majority of users lack the awareness in handling privacy issues [4] for the information protection. Most of privacy settings need to be configured manually and most of users do not mind to configure them.

SNSs release users' data to the public for various reasons such as research objectives or advertisements purposes. Google, Microsoft, Yahoo and American

Sabu M. Thampi et al. (Eds.): SSCC 2013, CCIS 377, pp. 272–280, 2013.

Online (AOL), the biggest players on the Internet expend billions of dollars in new advertising technologies [5] by mining the data from social networks. SNSs facilitate information sharing across infinite distances and provide easy access to the shared information for users [6]. Thus, as a result of that privacy becomes a prominent issue among SNSs users.

Private information can be access by unauthorized people when large amount of data is published through data mining techniques such as web crawlers. Data gathering through SNSs can be destructive for users' privacy. Users may lose control over their personal information, despite observing privacy setting options set by the specific SNS. Hence, such unawareness may result to unwanted information dissemination, and also improper use of information by unauthorized users. This provides the necessity to do further work in investigating how information disclosure by users can be anonymized to mitigate privacy concerns of users.

Thus, the rest of the paper is organized as follows. Conceptualizations of privacy are defined in section 2. Privacy on social network sites is described in section 3. The role of data anonymization is explained in section 4. Then, the proposed anonymization algorithm is presented in section 5 and the results of the evaluation are discussed respectively. In section 6, we summarize and in section 7 we conclude the comprehensive concept of the paper.

2   Conceptualizations of Privacy

Privacy has been studied in relationship development [7] and in interpersonal relations, trust and identity in mediated environments [8]; and in a digital realm [9]. Privacy is a dominant topic in psychology, sociology and communication [10]. Although privacy has deep historical roots and worldwide concept, it has fuzzy definitions.

The ability of an individual or group to isolate themselves or their information in order to reveal them selectively is privacy in general [11]. The right of not being attacked by the government, corporations or individuals is part of many countries privacy laws such as the Data Protection Directive in Europe which control processing of personal data within the European Union [12]. Privacy laws include the basic concepts of consent, control and disclosure.

Privacy view has changed by the technologies which have designed to enable the collection and manipulation of personal data of the Internet [13]. The designs are based on the accepted definition of privacy which sheds light on the value of privacy in the context of digital technologies and the Internet.

3   Privacy on Social Network Sites

Social networking sites accumulate hundreds of millions users personal data under a single administrative domain and they are under the control of their host servers regulatory and policy domains [14]. This provides a significant target for attackers to analyze privacy vulnerabilities with the intention to compromise privacy. In general, privacy is the ability of an individual or group to isolate themselves or their information to reveal them selectively. Users' privacy will be vulnerable to privacy violations via security attacks and unintentional disclosures. SNSs give the provider rights to reuse users' data such as sharing data with third-party advertisers and websites [15]. This may results in identity fraud by use of users' profiles data and unlimited default access that is provided by SNSs [16]. Users may lose control of data once their profiles are downloaded and stored by site operators to create a digital dossier of personal information. Thus, Users' privacy may be violated by users' improper behaviors such as teenagers' sexting.

According to the Altman, people are eager to have private spaces [17] and SNSs connect users in networked spaces. Not all users have enthusiasm to share any information with everyone at all the time [18]. Structure of SNSs is comparable with structure of physical spaces [2] as they also have equivalent spaces that shape users environment for online transactional behaviors [19].

Information dissemination on SNSs should be controlled to preserve privacy [20]. Preserve users' privacy and control users personal information is complicated once they disperse information on public domains. Privacy settings which are provided by social networking sites are not adequate to protect users as most of users place private and sensitive personal information without any concerns on their profiles. Therefore there is an urgent need which should consider by owners and administrators of social networking sites to diminish the occurrence of pornographers, identity theft and other privacy concerns.

4   Data Anonymization

Data publishing to the public is required for various types of analysis such as public health [21]. Although many benefits can be gained from dissemination of collected data, many privacy concerns can be created for users. The privacy concerns are as significant especially for micro-data as they encompass detailed personal data in its original form such as social security number or name.

User or enterprise micro- data need to be protected when it released or shared to the public. Many privacy protection techniques have been done on certain datasets [22]. Among these privacy protection techniques, anonymity is popular because of two main reasons as follows. First, contrarily to any privacy protection such as secure multi-party computation, implementation of anonymization is easier and less expensive. Second, anonymized data disclosure of sensitive data is acceptable by privacy laws that should be considered while data publishing [23].

There are various ways for anonymizing users by hiding the attributes. Conventionally, some of these methods have been used in order to anonymize customers' information that should be stored on micro data strips. However, since the advent of online social networks in recent years, these methods have got the attention of researchers more than any other times.

Anonymization is to publish publicly user personal and private information unknown and with some information masked [24]. By applying anonymization, people can study and use real data with less concerns of users' privacy. It will also persuade third-parties to use new mining techniques to gain access to real data. The utility of data is the main point that should be considered during anonymizing. Thus, to protect privacy of data, information loss should be measure to reduce distortion of data. Although anonymization adds uncertainty to data, it is one of the best techniques to preserve partially users' privacy especially on social network sites.

5   The Proposed Anonymization Algorithm

Social network can be considered as a graph G (N, E, A). N is the number of nodes that indicates a user and E is the number of edges which indicates the relation between nodes. Each node has some attributes that are represented by A. The attributes in graph G are identifiers (ID), quasi-identifiers (QS) and sensitive (S) (A= {ID, QS, S}). Identifiers are those attributes that can be used uniquely to identify a user such as name or social security number (SSN). Quasi-identifiers are those attributes which their combination can be used to identify a user such as age or zip code. Sensitive attributes are very private and personal such as disease or hobby.

The most popular concepts for providing anonymity are namely k-anonymity [25], ℓ-diversity [26] and t-closeness [27]. Despite their popularity, these three concepts have some weaknesses. In k-anonymity, although released data cannot be re-identified from at least k-1 other released data, there are vulnerable to two types of attacks background knowledge and homogeneity of data. To cover k-anonymity limitations, ℓ-diversity was proposed and it provided sufficient diversity among sensitive attributes. Due to ℓ-diversity, semantic relationships among the attribute values and different levels of privacy because of the same level of diversity were occurred. Another algorithm that is called t-closeness insures ℓ-diversity shortcomings. According to t-closeness, the distribution of sensitive attributes in same class cannot be match with the distribution of sensitive attributes in the whole data set, but it provides lack of definite measure to estimate the distance between multiple sensitive attributes that makes the relationship between t and the level of privacy more difficult. Hence, this paper will explore these three basic concepts in capitalizing their strengths and proposing the new algorithm to cover their weaknesses.

Results from previous researches have shown that just removing identifiers from the disseminated data is inadequate to preserve privacy as quasi-identifiers attributes can be used to re-identify the users in the disseminated data by linking to the outsources information such as public voting or registration data. Thus, anonymization technique is required to preserve privacy of users wherever data is diffused such as social network sites.

The proposed anonymization algorithm performs anonymization according to the following technique. Three different levels should be considered for the set of attributes as follows.

Table 1. Attributes level

Level	Attributes
$L_1=\{ I_1,I_2 , ..., I_n, Q_1,Q_2, ...,Q_n, S_1,S_2,...,S_n \}$	$ID = \{I_1,I_2 , ..., I_n\}$ $QS = \{Q_1,Q_2, ...,Q_n\}$ $S = \{S_1,S_2,...,S_n\}$
$L_2=\{ Q_1,Q_2, ...,Q_n,S_1,S_2,...,S_n \}$	$QS = \{Q_1,Q_2, ...,Q_n\}$ $S = \{S_1,S_2,...,S_n\}$
$L_3=\{ Q_1,Q_2, ...,Q_n \}$	$QS = \{Q_1,Q_2, ...,Q_n\}$

Level (1) contains all three sets of attributes. In this level, identifiers will not be removed. This level is considered for requests from those Third-parties who have high authorization for full access to the data such as government. These third-parties can send request for different combinations of attributes. In this set, the attributes selection can be categorized as two types: the one in which sequence of selection is important and another one in which sequence of selection is not important. Sequence of selection is important as it varies the level of anonymization. The total number of attributes combination from set L_1, important sequence of attributes selection and Unimportant sequence of attributes selection can be calculated according to the formulas that are shown in Table 2.

In order to calculate the level of anonymization, it is required to measure the amount of information sharing (IS) and the likelihood of information sharing ($P_{(IS)}$). These two metrics can be calculated based on the following formula (1) and (2).

$$IS_{(Amount\ of\ information\ sharing)} = \frac{N(L_1|m)}{N(L_1)} *m \qquad (1)$$

$$P_{(IS)} = \frac{N(L_1|m)}{N(L_1)} \qquad (2)$$

m indicates the number of selected attributes from the attributes set L_1. The amount of information sharing and its likelihood provide the required level of anonymization according to the requested attributes. If the amount and likelihood be high, it requires more anonymization. Otherwise less anonymization is required to protect data.

Table 2. Required Formula

Level	Total number of attributes combination	Important sequence of attributes selection	Unimportant sequence of attributes selection
Level (1)	$T_{(L_1)} = \dfrac{n!}{I_n!\, Q_n!\, S_n!}$	$L_{1(m)} = \dfrac{n!}{(n-m)!}$	$L_{1(m)} = \dfrac{n!}{(n-m)!m!}$
Level (2)	$T_{(L_2)} = \dfrac{n!}{Q_n!\, S_n!}$	$L_{2(m)} = \dfrac{n!}{(n-m)!}$	$L_{2(m)} = \dfrac{n!}{(n-m)!m!}$
Level (3)	$T_{(L_3)} = 2^n - 1$	————	$L_{3(m)} = \dfrac{n!}{(n-m)!\, m!}$

Level (2) contains quasi-identifiers and sensitive attributes. In this level, identifiers will be removed. This level is considered for requests from those Third-parties who have medium authorization for medium access to the data such as analyst. These third-parties can send request for different combinations of attributes. Similar to the level (1), the attributes selection has two types: the one in which sequence of selection is important and another one in which sequence of selection is not important. The total number of attributes combination from set L_2, important sequence of attributes selection and Unimportant sequence of attributes selection can be calculated according to the formulas that are shown in Table 2. It is required to measure amount of information sharing and the likelihood of information sharing to calculate the level of anonymization. These two metrics can be calculated based on the following formula (3) and (4).

$$IS_{(Amount\ of\ information\ sharing)} = \frac{N(L_2|m)}{N(L_2)} * m \tag{3}$$

$$P_{(IS)} = \frac{N(L_2|m)}{N(L_2)} \tag{4}$$

m indicates the number of selected attributes from the attributes set L_2. Similar to level (1), the amount of information sharing and its likelihood provide the required level of anonymization according to the requested attributes. If the amount and likelihood be high, it requires more anonymization. Otherwise less anonymization is required in order to protect data.

Level (3) contains quasi-identifiers. In this level identifiers and sensitive attributes will be removed. This level is considered for requests from those Third-parties who have low authorization for low access to the data such as advertisement. These third-parties can send request just for quasi-identifiers. The total number of attributes selection from set L_3 and the value for selecting m attributes from L_3 can be calculated based on the formulas that are shown in Table 2.

Similar to the level (1) and level (2), the amount of information sharing and the likelihood of information sharing should be measured to calculate the level of anonymization. These two metrics can be calculated based on the following formula (5) and (6). If the amount and likelihood be high, it requires more anonymization. Otherwise less anonymization is required in order to protect data.

$$IS_{(Amount\ of\ information\ sharing)} = \frac{N(L_3|m)}{N(L_3)}*m \qquad (5)$$

$$P_{(IS)} = \frac{N(L_3|m)}{N(L_3)} \qquad (6)$$

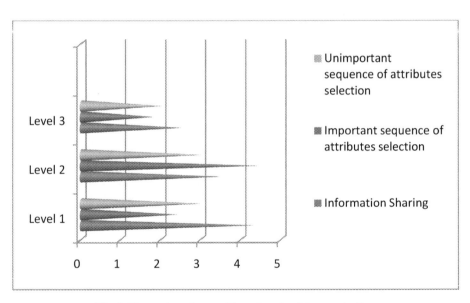

Fig. 1. Comparison Among Three Levels of Anonymization

The results depict that in the two sets of attributes L_1 and L_2, the possibility of information sharing is more than L_3, as these two sets contain identifier and sensitive attributes. And also the sequence of attributes selection has an important role in the amount of information sharing. The amount of information sharing defines the required level of anonymization. The proposed anonymization algorithm performs less anonymization by minimizing the data perturbation according to the third-parties requests. This type of anonymization protects data privacy while reducing information loss.

6   Summary

The paper presents an approach in providing anonymity for users' data on social network sites. The anonymization of attributes can be according to three different levels. The main objective of the data anonymization is to provide anonymity for social network users to preserve privacy and anonymity of users through social interactions; and protect users from being re-identified. Therefore, once users' data is used by the government, advertisers and the third parties, the user identity cannot be revealed from it.

7   Conclusions

In this paper, we describe that social network sites release users' data to the public for various reasons as the nature of activities on social network sites are sharing information and traversing through other users' information. Distinguishing the final audience of social data is difficult, as well as controlling the social contexts which transfers among individuals are not completely possible. Whether it is enterprise data or personal data, the need to be protected is of utmost important. Private realm of users should be keep away from public knowledge in order to prevent information leakage. However, these privacy concerns are not completely covered by SNSs, thus effects the preservation of users' privacy and anonymity. To achieve this, we propose an anonymization algorithm which provides anonymity for users' data in order to mitigate privacy concerns through data publishing. This study can be useful for designing secure social networks for future usage. It is expected the provided level of anonymity could mitigate the possibility of information leakage and re-identification in order to preserve users' identity.

Acknowledgements. The authors would like to thank Research Management Centre, Universiti Teknologi Malaysia for supporting this research work through Foreign Academic Visitor Fund via grant number R.K130000.7738.4D066.

References

1. Ellison, N.B.: Social network sites: Definition, history, and scholarship. Journal of Computer Mediated Communication 13, 210–230 (2007)
2. Papacharissi, Z.: The virtual geographies of social networks: A comparative analysis of Facebook, LinkedIn and A Small World. New Media and Society 11(1-2), 199–220 (2009)
3. Schlenkrich, L., Sewry, D.A.: Factors for Successful Use of Social Networking Sites in Higher Education. Research Article, SACJ (49) (2012)
4. Paula, S.: Ethical Issues in Social Networking Research, http://www.deakin.edu.au (accessed January 1, 2013)
5. Hansell, S.: AOL removes search data on vast group of web users. New York Times (2006)
6. Katona, Z., Zubcsek, P., Sarvary, M.: Network Effects and Personal Influences: The Diffusion of an Online Social Network. Journal of Marketing Research XLVIII, 425–443 (2010)
7. Young-ok, Y., Kazuya, H.: Computer-Mediated Relationship Development: A Cross-Cultural Comparison. Journal of Computer-Mediated Communication 11(1), 133–152 (2005)
8. Metzger, M.J.: Privacy, trust, and disclosure: Exploring barriers to electronic commerce. Journal of Computer-Mediated Communication (2004)

9. Gavison, R.: privacy: Legal aspects. Available at SSRN 1885008 (2011)

10. Margulis, S.T.: On the status and contribution of Westin's and Altmans'theories of privacy. Journal of Social Issues 59, 411–429 (2003)

11. Eloff, J.: Information Security Innovation. SAP Research (2012)

12. Sandra, C., Henderson, C., Snyder, A.: Personal information privacy: implications for MIS managers. Department of Management, College of Business, Auburn University, 415 W, Magnolia (March 1999)

13. Starke-Meyerring, D.: The Implications of Blogs for Professional Writing: Speed, Reach, Engagement and the Art of the Self in the Participatory Web. Studies in Writing 21, 125 (2007)

14. Pallis, G., Zeinalipour-yazti, D., Dikaiakos, M.: Online social networks: status and trends. New Directions in Web Data Management 1, 213–234 (2011)

15. Zhang, C., Sun, J., Zhu, X., Fang, Y.: Privacy and security for online social networks: challenges and opportunities. IEEE Network 24, 13–18 (2010)

16. Gross, R., Acquisiti, A.: Information revelation and privacy in online social networks. In: Proceedings of the 2005 ACM Workshop on Privacy in the Electronic Society, pp. 71–80. ACM (2005)

17. Solove, D.: A taxonomy of privacy. University of Pennsylvania Law Review 154, 477 (2006)

18. Altman, I.: Privacy regulation: Culturally universal or culturally specific? Journal of Social Issues 33(3), 66–84 (1977)

19. Boyd, D.M.: Social network sites as networked publics: Affordances, dynamics, and implications. In: Papacharissi, Z. (ed.) Networked Self: Identity, Community, and Culture on Social Network Sites, pp. 39–58 (2010), http://www.danah.org/papers/2010/SNSasNetworkedPublics.pdf (retrieved)

20. Marisela Gutierrez, L.: Unfriend, Unfollow, Unsubscribe: Unsociability on social network sites (May 2012)

21. Hui, W., Ruilin, L.: Privacy-preserving publishing microdata with full functional dependencies. Published by Elsevier: Data & Knowledge Engineering 70, 249–268 (2011)

22. Willenborg, L., De Waal, T.: Statistical Disclosure Control in Practice. Springer (1996)

23. Yongcheng, L., Jiajin, L., Jian, W.: Survey of Anonymity Techniques for Privacy Preserving. In: International Symposium on Computing, Communication, and Control (ISCCC), Singapore, vol. 1 (2009)

24. Hay, M., Miklau, G., Jensen, D., Weis, P., Srivastava, S.: Anonymizing Social Networks, University of Massachusetts Amherst Computer Science Department, Technical Report No. 07-19 (2007)

25. Ninghui, L., Wahbeh, Q., Dong, S.: Provably Private Data Anonymization: Or, k-Anonymity Meets Differential Privacy. CERIAS Tech Report. Center for Education and Research Information Assurance and Security Purdue University, West Lafayette, IN 47907- 2086 (2010)

26. Mayil Vel Kumar, P., Karthikeyan, M.: L diversity on k-anonymity with external database for improving privacy preserving data publishing. International Journal of Computer Applications (0975 – 8887) 54(14) (2012)

27. Mvr, N., Js, V., Rnv, V., Ch, R.: Closeness: privacy measure for data publishing using multiple sensitive attributes. International Journal of Engineering Science & Advanced Technology 2(2), 278–284 (2012)

Secure Multimedia Transmission in P2P Using Recurence Relation and Evolutionary Algorithm

Ramesh Shahabadkar and Ramchandra V.Pujeri

Anna University, Chennai, India
ramesh.shahabadkar@gmail.com
KGiSL Institute of Technology Coimbatore, India

Abstract. Distribution and sharing of multimedia contents is extensively higher in number as compared to other applications in Peer-to-Peer network. The prior work in the same issues is conducted to explore that there are comparatively few work done when it comes to ensuring security over transmitting multimedia contents over highly vulnerable P2P network. Therefore, this paper introduces a cost-effective and trivial model using recurrence relation of degree 2 and evolutionary algorithm for performing multimedia content encryption. A novel technique of performing encryption using a simple partitioning technique is used to ensure the security of the transmitted frames over any types of network. The novelty of the proposed system is that evolutionary algorithm is used for strengthening the encryption process further and final results were evaluated with respect to maximized entropy of frames, minimized Pearson Product Moment Correlation Coefficient (PPMCC) among the adjacent pixels and key analysis.

Keywords: P2P Network, Multimedia Security, Evolutionary Algorithm, Recurrence Relation.

1 Introduction

The area of modern communication system using Peer-to-Peer (P2P) network is currently adopted by many user for the multimedia sharing purpose [1]. The evolution to streaming and multicast (e.g., TV) was just a consequence. The P2P (Peer-to-Peer) technology is now well-known by the public, mainly because of the great success of some applications, such as file sharing applications (Kazaa, eDonkey, BitTorrent, etc.) but also more recently such as video streaming applications (PPLive, PPStream, UUSee, SopCast, etc. [2][3]). However, the P2P networks still suffer from bad reputation because of the large number of illegal contents that are distributed by those applications. The usage of the social networking applications [4] e.g. (Facebook and MySpace) are also on rise as the user find broader set of tools to perform highly customized communication as well as it also enable the user to share their personal data over the internet. Such application has also higher versions of accessibility from various computing devices. Usually social networking applications are client (browser) specific application that permits the user to share their multimedia (image and video) data as well as it also allows the other end of recipient to perform downloading too.

Sabu M. Thampi et al. (Eds.): SSCC 2013, CCIS 377, pp. 281–292, 2013.

Usage of such application also involves cost of maintenance from server viewpoint. Therefore, a peer-to-peer based techniques is the best alternative solution to overcome such load of networking and thereby minimizes cost of maintenance too. But, as peer-to-peer architecture is basically an overlay architecture on top of internet protocols, thereby the communication usually takes place directly from one peer to another peer in absence of any intermediate server. Due to this design of peer-to-peer system, it poses potential threats from security viewpoint in terms of secure communication and accessing confidential data [5]. Such types of application using peer-to-peer networking system are usually shared on public network where the vulnerability of transmitted data (especially over wireless network) poses a potential threat to confidentiality, privacy, as well as integrity as shown in Fig.1. Excavating the history will highlight multiple formats of attacks in the work of Information Technology [6] introduced by P2P network. The popular product of P2P i.e. Napster has already witnessed such intrusions. Hence, there is a critical need of more investigation towards research domain in order to furnish a better security protocols for preventing unauthorized intrusions or attacks in such P2P networks.

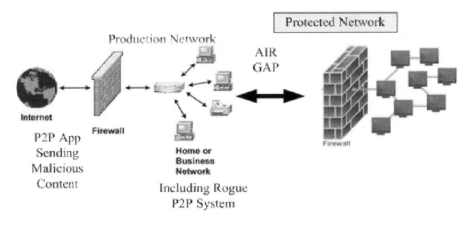

Fig. 1. Vulnerabilities of P2P network

Due to absence of web or application server to monitor the communication systems in P2P, it basically allows the intruders to formulate various versions of attacks e.g. break-in attack, malicious mischief, espionage etc to name a few. Usage of P2P network allows the user to download various application that may be pirated or malicious in nature completely harming the entire traffic system routing towards the user and its connected network peripherals too. Hence, security policies are highly vulnerable and susceptible for network breach in P2P applications [7]. Not only security aspect, consistent usage of P2P networks like BitTorrent, Kazaa, etc renders the network completely slow due to high bandwidth consumption. Such issues also give rise to Quality of Service (QoS) problems over internet usage. Unfortunately, the existing P2P networking system resists the corporate network security by furnishing decentralized security administration, decentralized shared data storage system, and a method to prevent critical perimeter defences e.g. Firewalls, AntiRootKits etc.

In the proposed method, the recurrence relation of degree 2 and a key extracted from the multimedia contents are used to encrypt the image. The technique discussed is used to generate a number of encrypted digital contents that are almost near to impossible to decrypt by intruder. These encrypted multimedia contents are considered as the initial population for the evolutionary algorithm which is considered for deployment in the study for the purpose of optimizing the encryption to higher degree. In the end, the best cipher-frame is chosen as the final encryption frame. Section 2 discusses about the prior research work. Section 3 highlights about the proposed system followed by research methodology in Section 4. Section 5 discusses about the performance analysis followed by conclusion in Section 6.

2   Related Work

Muller et al. [7] have presented experiments with efficient Content Based Image Retrieval in a P2P environment, thus a P2P-CBIR system. Although according to the work, peer data summaries can be used within the retrieval process for increasing efficiency, but security aspects are ignored. Jung and Cho [8] have proposed a watermarking platform for protecting unauthorized content distribution in P2P networks. The proposed platform dynamically generates 2D barcode watermark according to consumer's data and inserts the watermark into downloaded audio source in wavelet domain. However, the proposed watermarking platform is not able to prohibit illegal usage of digital audio content.

Chu et al. [9] have investigated the requirements for multimedia content sharing among Peer-to-Peer (P2P) networks and proposed a novel business models along with Digital Rights Management (DRM) solutions. The aim of this DRM research is to set new business models for content owners to benefit from the massive power of content distribution of P2P networks with least intrusion and interference to end consumer's privacy and anonymity.

Kumar and Sivaprakasam [10] have proposed a new encryption mechanism is included in which a message is transformed into a binary image which cannot be identified as a cipher text or stegno object. The approach is very much better for transmitting a confidential data from client to server. However, P2P network reliability is not ensured as the experiments were performed on adhoc network.

Mathieu et al. [11] have proposed a P2P system that ensures the security of contents, by controlling that only authorized contents are exchanged between peers and by being able to identify the people that redistribute illegal contents if it happens. This is mostly addressed by the use of watermarking functions in the video contents processing and by the deployment of specific peers that can monitor and detect misbehavior of the peers.

Meddour et al. [12] have performed a study where the authors have investigated various available techniques that use the potential features of P2P techniques for enhancing the existing multimedia streaming protocols. The author specified that current open issues in multimedia P2P streaming are a) appropriate video coding scheme, b) managing peer dynamicity, c) peer heterogeneity, d) efficient overlay network construction, e) selection of the best peers, f) monitoring of network conditions, and g) incentives for participating peers.

Berson [13] has discussed the security aspects of Skype. Tang et al. [14] have proposed their work on real-time P2P application for live multimedia streaming termed as GridMedia that was used for broadcasting real-time events over the internet. Hughes and Walkerdine [15] have discussed their work on distributed multimedia encoding techniques as a tool to exploit the extra-computational resources of standing computing devices using P2P network.

Reforgiato et al. [16] have presented their work that uses multiple point for broadcasting their multimedia contents over heterogeneous content distribution P2P networking system. The authors have used MPEG-4 encoder without any losses at the base layer stream.

Hagemeister [17] has described the framework for a distributed censorship-resistant policy drafting system. By relying on a DTN as well as a P2P network, the system can work even without internet access.

We have attempted to explore some prior work done towards securing image or video contents over P2P network and examined some attacks and issues with P2P networks. In the multimedia content distribution scenario, this server is usually hosted and maintained by the content providers. This results in peer user's anonymity interference and content provider's efforts in server maintenance. It was found that majority of the work done past is either on cryptography or using DRM or watermarking, where the prime concern is the privacy and anonymity issues of content consumers. Since DRM systems track user transactions, purchases, and access history, end consumers' detail activities are recorded at content retailer's database and thus raise divergences regarding multimedia content protection versus privacy protection. Due to the inherent charecteristics of decentralization, P2P network suffers from security loopholes as there is no central monitoring or control system to mitigate the online threats or attacks. No much work towards securing image or video content while transmission is explored very recently or even in past.

3   Proposed System

The proposed system introduces a novel framework of secure multimedia transmission in P2P network. The system uses the potentials of recurrence relation of degree 2. Recurrence relation [18] were applied in various fields in past as it basically defines recursively a sequence once one or more initial terms are given where each further term of the sequence is defined as a function of the preceding terms. The recurrence relation is represented as:

$$X_{n+1} = rx_n(1-x_n) \tag{1}$$

Where, x_n is a number with a range of 0-1 and it signifies the ratio of current population to the highest potential population at year n, r is a positive number that represents a combined rate for reproduction and starvation. Equation (1) shows a nonlinear difference equation that is intended to encapsulate two impacts e.g. a) reproduction where the population will increase at a rate proportional to the current population when the population size is small and b) starvation (density-dependent mortality) where the growth rate will decrease at a rate proportional to the value obtained by taking the theoretical "carrying capacity" of the environment less the current population.

Recurrence relation is applied over the encryption process to generate certain initial values that will be used further for optimization of encryption processes. As the optimization technique will require a population (scores of best encryption), hence, recurrence relation formulation assists in generation those initial values that will be a part of computation for best population selection (strongest encryption over the multimedia contents) using a fitness function.

The proposed system uses recurrence relation of degree 2 and a key extracted from the extracted multimedia contents are used to encrypt the file. The proposed technique using recurrence relation is used to generate quantity of the population (encrypted digital of multimedia files to be transmitted). These encrypted digital contents are considered as the initial population for the evolutionary algorithm. Then, the evolutionary algorithm is used to optimize the encryption process as much as possible. At the end, the optimal ciphered multimedia content is selected as the final encryption content. The paper also discusses the techniques deployed in use of recurrence relation and evolutionary algorithms and consecutively, the accomplished results were analyzed with concluding remarks. Therefore, the prime aim of the proposed study is to formulate a secure, efficient, and computationally less expensive process that ensures safer protection of multimedia contents. In order to accomplish the proposed aim, following objectives needs to be considered:

- To design 2 modules to implement the proposed system e.g. Peer-1 for performing encryption and peer 2for performing decryption module.
- To design a framework for accepting the input frames and perform portioning to 4 equal parts based on the specified dimension of the frames
- To implement recurrence relation of degree 2 by selecting specific pixels as encryption key for forming the initial value and for performing encryption towards the input frames.
- To estimate the initial value of the recurrence relation.
- To strengthen the encryption technique using secret key.
- To optimize the encryption method using Evolutionary algorithm.
- To restore and access the encrypted frames for performing decryption operation by peer-2 client.
- To perform the entire operation considering image entropy, correlation coefficient, and key analysis.

4   Research Methodology

The proposed system assumes a highly vulnerable P2P connectivity on either wired network or in wireless network. However, the current work only emphasizes on the security aspect of the multimedia contents to be transmitted by Peer-1 to Peer-N. The current work considers a frame as an input towards the framework which it partitions in 4 equal quadrants based on the cumulative dimension of input frame. To make the computation easier, the colored frames are converted to grayscale that is subjected to the actual algorithm. The proposed system considers using recurrence relation for performing encryption on all the pixels presents in each of the 4 partitioned image blocks. The proposed system considers the input of video file of MP4 format of size 268 KB as shown below in Figure 2, which is finally converted to grayscale for ease in computation.

Fig. 2. Extracted frames for the input to the model

Step-1: The system considers 5 pixel selections from each parts of image as the encryption key for designing the initial value of recurrence relation of degree 2 and for performing encryption on that partitioned part. The selections of such pixels are based on the quantity of the population being formed.

Step-2: The preliminary value of the recurrence relation of degree 2 is evaluated from the following equation by using the values of the gray scales of the five pixels in step-1.

$$P_x = \{P \times 1, P \times 2, P \times 3, P \times 4, P \times 5\}(in\,decimal) \,. \tag{2}$$

Where Pi represents an 8-bit block. Then the following equation is used to convert Px into ASCII number.

$$B = \{P1,1, P1,2, P1,3....P2,1, P2,2...P5,7, P5,8\}(inASCII) \,.$$

Here, Pi,j represents jth bit of the ith block. After Px is converted into an ASCII number, the string B with length of 40 bits is generated. Therefore, by using the following equation, the preliminary values for starting the execution of the recurrence relation of degree 2 is extracted,

$$U_{o,k} = \frac{P_{1,1}x2^{39} + P_{1,2}x2^{38} + ... + P_{2,1}x2^{31} + ... + P_{5,7}x2^1 + P_{5,8}x2^0}{2^{40}} \,. \tag{3}$$

Where, k is set of integers for the purpose of indexing each multimedia packets to be used in encryption process. By deploying this relation, the preliminary value of the recurrence function (Uo,k), which lies in the interval 0 to 1 is obtained.

Step-3: The previous step is iterated for each part of the plain frames. Hence, at the end, there will be 4 distinct preliminary values for each portioned portion of the frames.

Step-4: For encryption the pixels in each part of the image, the preliminary value of that part and following equation is deployed,

$$CurrentValue = round(U_{i,k}x255) \otimes OldValue. \tag{4}$$

In the above equation, XOR operation is performed, and OldValue represents the existing value of the pixel and CurrentValue represents the new value of the pixel after it is encrypted. The value of Ui,k refers to the ith value of the recurrence relation in the kth part of the original frame that is determined for each step by using equation (1).

All the pixels in each part, except the 5 pixels used as the key, are sequentially (row by row) encrypted in this way. Finally, the first member of the population is built. These steps are repeated for the entire partitioned image to get the rest of the population.

5   Performance Analysis

With the application of a multimedia encryption algorithm to any multimedia contents, its pixels values change when compared with the original frames. The proposed framework was design to make such alterations in pixel values in extremely irregular and sophisticated fashion for maximizing the higher degree of pixel differences between the original and encrypted multimedia contents. The core of the technique considers the higher flexibility in encryption by creating maximum random patterns that have no chance of disclosing any private characteristics of the original multimedia contents. However, it should be noted that there should not be any sorts of dependent between the encrypted and original multimedia contents. The encoded multimedia content should have very low value of correlation compared to original multimedia content. Another critical factor in evaluating an encrypted multimedia content is the visual inspection process.

The proposed study has also considered diffusion as one of the significant factor for measuring the randomization of the encryption process. It is strongly believed that if the proposed algorithm has better diffusion features than the correlation between the original and encrypted multimedia contents will be very much complex and thereby highly unpredictable. In order to scale up the diffusion charecteristics of the proposed study, a bit of pixel is changed in source content and the error estimation between the encrypted multimedia contents accomplished from original source content were evaluated. The parameters for evaluation of the proposed security process are discussed below:

Estimating Entropy for Frames:-Entropy is one of the prominent features in randomization and is basically a mathematical modelling for data communication and storage systems. Equation 1 is introduced for obtaining entropy.

$$H(S) = \sum_{i=0}^{2^N-1} P(s_i)\log(\frac{1}{P(s_i)}) \tag{5}$$

In which, N is the number of gray levels used in the multimedia contents, and $P(s_i)$ illustrates the probability of having a ith gray level in the multimedia contents. In multimedia contents that are generated in a completely random way, the proposed formulation considers N as 8 to be an ideal value.

Pearson Product-Moment Correlation Coefficient:-A good encryption algorithm is one in which the correlation coefficient between pairs of encrypted adjacent pixels in the horizontal, vertical, and diagonal positions are at the least possible level. The correlation coefficient is calculated by using equation 5

$$r_{xy} = \frac{|\text{cov}(x, y)|}{\sqrt{D(x)} x \sqrt{D(y)}}$$

(6)

In the above relation, x and y are the gray levels in two adjacent pixels of the frames. In calculating the correlation coefficients, the following equations are employed:

$$\text{cov}(x, y) = \frac{1}{N} \sum_{i=1}^{N} (x_i - E(x))(y_i - E(y))$$

(7)

$$E(x) = \frac{1}{N} \sum_{i=1}^{N} x_i$$

$$D(x) = \frac{1}{N} \sum_{i=1}^{N} (x_i - E(x))^2$$

To test the correlation coefficient between two adjacent vertical pixels, two adjacent horizontal pixels, and two adjacent diagonal pixels in a cipher-frame, the following procedure is used: first, 2500 pairs of pixels are randomly selected, and then the correlation coefficient is obtained by using equation5 (the results of which are shown in Table 1).

Table 1. PPMCC of two adjacent pixels in two images

	Plain-Frame	Cipher-Frame
Vertical	0.9711	0.0093
Horizontal	0.9445	-0.0054
Diagonal	0.9217	-0.0009

C. Key analysis: - A suitable encryption algorithm must be sensitive to small changes in keys. Moreover, the key must be long enough to resist against brute-force attacks. In this work, a 40-bit long key is suggested which produces a key space equivalent to 240 (and hence this key seems to be long enough).To test the sensitivity of the key in the proposed method, first the frame is encrypted using the proposed method. Then, this same frame is encrypted once again using the proposed method, with the difference that this time, in the stage of producing the initial population (when each member of the population is being produced), one bit of the key of the member is changed; and the population is formed in this way. After this new population is formed, the rest of the proposed method is executed, and in the end final frame is obtained. The experiment also shows the similarity of the two encrypted images (the white points are the common points of the two encrypted frames). The two encrypted frames are about 99.76% different.

A. Results Obtained: After forming the initial population, the evolutionary algorithm is used to optimize the encrypted images. The evolutionary algorithm introduced in this study uses the crossover operation. The proposed system is experimented on 32 bit Windows OS with 2.84 GHz Intel core i3 processor considering Matlab as the programming tool. The proposed system considers frames (still image) and converts it in grayscale in case the origin image is colored as shown in Figure 3(a). The input frame is then partitioned into 4 equal quadrants (portions) as seen in Figure 3(b). The preliminary values are estimated exactly after that along with implementation of recurrent relation and secret key which is user defined.

Fig. 3(a). Input   **Fig. 3(b).** Partitioning into 4 equal quadrants

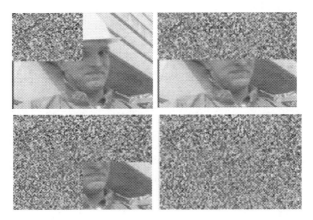

Fig. 4. Process of performing encryption in each partitioned frames portion

Finally a decryption mechanism is performed considering the encrypted image as input image along with previously used secret key. Following are the results accomplished.

Fig. 5. Input Image (previously encrypted)

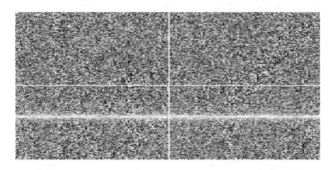

Fig. 6. Partitioning into 4 equal quadrants

Fig. 7. Process of performing decryption in each partitioned (encrypted frames)

The proposed study considers correlation coefficient between the pairs of adjacent pixel value of each frames extracted from video as the fitness function. At each stage, the new generations produced and the previous ones are evaluated using the fitness function and 50% of the population with the minimum PPM-correlation coefficient and 10% of the remaining population is selected for the next generations. In every generation, the initial values and correlation values that are considered as encryption parameters are checked during optimization internally by the evolutionary algorithm. This is an iterative process until it finds the best correlation coefficient as the best generation when it doesn't show much significant change in dual successive stages of iterations. Followed by the previous step, the generation with minimum correlation value is finally considered for encryption.

6 Conclusion

The proposed system highlights a new method for performing encryption over the multimedia contents by using recurrence relation of degree 2 and evolutionary algorithm. The system uses recurrence relation for the preliminary encryption and the evolutionary algorithm is deployed to strength then encryption process in P2P network further more secure. The accomplished results from correlation coefficients and the entropies of the images also prove the high efficiency of this method.

References

1. Do, T., Hua, K.A., Tantaoui, M.: P2VoD: Providing Fault Tolerant Video-on-Demand Streaming in Peer-to-Peer Environment. Proceedings of the IEEE, 20–24
2. Ciullo, D., Garcia, M.A., Horvath, A., Leonardi, E., Mellia, M., Rossi, D., Telek, M., Veglia, P.: Dissecting PPLive, SopCast, TVAnts. ACM (2008)
3. http://zeenews.india.com/news/net-news/cyber-criminals-targeting-social-networking-sites-to-steal-money_827996.html
4. Graffi, K., Mukherjee, P., Menges, B., Hartung, D., Kovacevic, A., Steinmetz, R.: Practical Security in P2P-based Social Networks. IEEE (2009)
5. Saroliya, A., Mishra, U., Rana, A.: A pragmatic analysis of peer to peer networks and protocols for security and confidentiality. International Journal of Computing and Corporate Research 2(6) (2012)
6. http://ntrg.cs.tcd.ie/undergrad/4ba2.02-03/p10.html
7. Muller, W., Eisenhardt, M., Henrich, A.: Efficient content-based P2P image retrieval using peer content descriptions. SPIE Electronic Imaging (2004)
8. Jung, E.H., Cho, S.Y.: A Robust Digital Watermarking System Adopting 2D Barcode against Digital Piracy on P2P network. International Journal of Computer Science and Network Security 6(10) (2006)
9. Chu, C.C., Su, X., Prabhu, B.S., Gadh, R., Kurup, S., Sridhar, G., Sridhar, V.: Mobile DRM for Multimedia Content Commerce in P2P Networks. IEEE (2006)
10. Kumar, S., Sivaprakasam, P.: A New Approach for Encrypting and Decrypting Data in Images among users in Ad hoc Network. European Journal of Scientific Research 92(3), 425–430 (2012)
11. Mathieu, B., Guelvouit, G.L., Desoubeaux, M.: Mitigating illegal contents via watermarking in video streaming P2P network. In: Proceedings of IEEE Advanced Networks and Telecommunication Systems (2010)
12. Meddour, D.E., Mushtaq, M., Ahmed, T.: Open Issues in P2P Multimedia Streaming. MULTICOMM (2006)

13. Berson, T.: Skype security evaluation. Anagram Laboratories (2005)
14. Tang, Y., Luo, J.G., Zhang, Q., Zhang, M., Yang, S.-H.: Deploying P2P Networks for Large-Scale Live Video-Streaming Service. IEEE Communications Magazine (2007)
15. Hughes, D., Walkerdine, J.: Distributed video encoding over a peer-to-peer network. PREP (2005)
16. Reforgiato, D., Lombardo, A., Schembra, G.: A P2P Platform based on Rate-Controlled FGS encoding for Broadcast Video Transmission to Heterogeneous Terminals with Heterogeneous Network Access. GTTI (2009)
17. Hagemeister, P.: Censorship-resistant Collaboration with a Hybrid DTN/P2P Network. Masters Thesis (2012)
18. http://en.wikipedia.org/wiki/Recurrence_relation

Hybrid Approach for Improvising
Credit Card Fraud Detection Based on Collective Animal
Behaviour and SVM

V. Dheepa[1] and R. Dhanapal[2]

[1] Research and Development Centre
Bharathiar University, Coimbatore-641 046, TamilNadu, India
dsvdeepasaro@gmail.com
[2] Research Department of Computer Applications
Easwari Engineering College, Chennai-600 089, TamilNadu, India
drdhanapal@gmail.com

Abstract. The explosive growth of Information Technology in the last few decades has resulted in automation in every possible field. This has also led to electronic fund transfers and increased usage of credit cards and debit cards. Credit card fraud costs consumers and the financial industry billions of dollars annually. In this paper we propose a hybrid approach to credit card fraud detection, where a combination of supervised and unsupervised approaches was used to detect fraudulent transactions. This includes a behaviour based clustering approach where we use patterns from collective animal behaviours to detect the changes in the behaviour of credit card users to minimize the false positives. This approach also opens the avenue to predict the collective behaviours of highly organized crime groups involved in credit card fraud activities which as an option is not explored so far.

Keywords: Credit card fraud detection, SVM, Collective animal behavior.

1   Introduction

1.1   Need for Credit Card Fraud Detection Systems

The necessity for a credit card system could be avoided if the user reports missing cards or anomalies in the transaction. But according to information from credit card incidents and control measures [1] [2] it is given clearly with proof that it is not possible for users to detect all types of credit card frauds. Though physical card theft could be reported, it is just very meagre and the actual loss is because of highly organized theft of card credentials and its use for funding illegal activities. The control system currently in place requires a lot of human work involving the analyst. This approach may not be welcome by the customers of the banking system as they may have to undergo several verifications even if it a genuine transaction. A hybrid approach [3] could enhance the predicting ability of the system thereby minimizing the analysis and the time required for processing the fraudulent transactions.

Sabu M. Thampi et al. (Eds.): SSCC 2013, CCIS 377, pp. 293–302, 2013.
© Springer-Verlag Berlin Heidelberg 2013

1.2   The Need for a Hybrid Approach

Hybrid approach [3] [4] is the process of combining multiple approaches into a single problem for improving the accuracy of the system. In general, machine learning techniques are classified into two broad categories, and each has their own positives and negatives. The proposed data-customised approach combines elements of supervised and unsupervised methodologies aiming to compensate for the individual deficiencies of the methods.

A supervised learning algorithm analyzes the training data and produces a function, which has the maximum probability of predicting the output. The problems encountered by the supervised learning techniques are bias and variance provided by the function and data complexity, dimensionality of the input space, noise in the output values, etc. Unsupervised learning refers to the problem of trying to find hidden structure in unlabeled data [7]. Since the examples given to the learner are unlabeled, there is no error or reward signal to evaluate a potential solution. Synergistic Hybrid option of using supervised followed by unsupervised or vice versa can be used for achieving better accuracy.

Here we use a unsupervised approach at the beginning followed by a supervised approach and then another stage of analysis for predicting. The hybrid approach though effective must be used properly as each method will have its own advantages and disadvantages. In this approach the usage of behaviour based systems in the first level for predicting the fraudulent transactions based on the past data using a clustering approach that involves multilevel clustering, which is a kind of unsupervised approach. [10] [11] Then we apply the SVM based classification approach which is basically a supervised learning approach which is best suited for the binary classification. Then we go for the cluster analysis based on collective animal behaviour where we try and find out patterns in the natural behaviour of various animals and create a model that is analogous to that in predicting the change in the behaviour of each of the user's behaviour [12]. This method helps us to eliminate the false positives[9]. Pre-processed must be performed without affecting the quality of the data, to make it suitable for the second level processing. [5] Especially the requirements of the SVM [13] approach for data input format is different from that of others.

Collective animal behaviour [14] describes the coordinated behaviour of large groups of similar animals and the emergent properties of these groups. Determining the rules by which an individual animal navigates relative to its neighbours in a group can lead to advances in the deployment and control of groups of swimming or flying micro-robots such as UAVs. [15] In our process we can use this collective animal behaviour to determine if an outlier is actually a fraudulent transaction or a legitimate transaction occurring during certain predefined occasions.

Multi-clustering is the process of performing clustering on a single data from different points. Multiple views are considered and clustering is performed on the basis of each of these views. The views are determined by the user and Clustering is performed on the basis of all the available views.

Support vector machine is a method used in pattern recognition and classification. It predicts or classifies patterns into two categories; fraudulent or non fraudulent. It is well suited for binary classifications. As any artificial intelligence tool, it has to be trained to obtain a learned model. SVM is correlated to and having the basics of non-parametric applied statistics, neural networks and machine learning. [20][21][22][23].

2   Fraud Detection Process

2.1   Pre-processing the Dataset

The available data might not be in the format that can be directly used by the system, hence pre-processing becomes a basic necessity for the process. The highly imbalanced state of data might result in a biased result. Preventing the fraud data that is very minimal from being eliminated as noise during the data cleaning approach is also an important use of pre-processing. [26] Derived attributes and their usage should be initially determined and their state should be properly maintained. The data transformation techniques are used for achieving precise results.

```
1 22.08 11.46 2 4 4 1.585 0 0 0 1 2 100 1213 0
0 22.67 7 2 8 4 0.165 0 0 0 2 160 1 0
0 29.58 1.75 1 4 4 1.25 0 0 0 1 2 280 1 0
0 21.67 11.5 1 5 3 0 1 1 11 1 2 0 1 1
1 20.17 8.17 2 6 4 1.96 1 1 14 0 2 60 159 1
0 15.83 0.585 2 8 8 1.5 1 1 2 0 2 100 1 1
1 17.42 6.5 2 3 4 0.125 0 0 0 2 60 101 0
```

Fig. 1. A Sample Preprocessed Data

The actual data collected from the data set is in the format represented in Figure 1. We analyze the available attributes and prepare a dataset that could be made usable. The SVM requires a special format for reading the data. The expected format of input for an SVM is

[label] [index1]:[value1] [index2]:[value2] ...

Where label represents the final classified label, index values range from 1,2...n and value1, value2.... represents the corresponding column values.

Hence the data provided in the Figure1 is further processed and is converted into the form usable by the SVM.

```
-1 1:-1 2:-0.731729 3:-0.5 5:0.0769231 6:-0.25 7:-0.988421 8:-1 9:-1 10:-1 11:-1 13:-0.84 14:-1
-1 1:-1 2:-0.52391 3:-0.875 4:-1 5:-0.538462 6:-0.25 7:-0.912281 8:-1 9:-1 10:-1 11:1 13:-0.72 14:-1
+1 1:-1 2:-0.761805 3:-0.178571 4:-1 5:-0.384615 6:-0.5 7:-1 8:1 9:1 10:-0.671642 11:-1 13:-1 14:-1
+1 1:1 2:-0.806917 3:-0.416429 5:-0.230769 6:-0.25 7:-0.862456 8:1 9:1 10:-0.58209 11:-1 13:-0.94
14:-0.99684
+1 1:-1 2:-0.937444 3:-0.958214 5:0.0769231 6:0.75 7:-0.894737 8:1 9:1 10:-0.940299 11:-1 13:-0.9
14:-1
-1 1:1 2:-0.889624 3:-0.535714 5:-0.692308 6:-0.25 7:-0.991228 8:-1 9:-1 10:-1 11:-1 13:-0.94 14:-
0.998
```

Fig. 2. Input Data for SVM

2.2   Multi-clustering

The user provides properties that have a high probability of affecting the buying behaviour. The processed data is then clustered from the point of view of each of these probabilities. Hence every single data is added to multiple clusters. This helps is a behaviour based organization of data. [19]

The data sample depicted in Figure 1 is provided as the input for multi-clustering. The attributes that are to be used for clustering is selected by the user. We use the, K-mean Clustering algorithm [17 multi clustering], which is a simple and fast clustering method, which has been popularly used. So we apply it to group the items. Firstly, items are grouped into a given number of clusters. After completion of grouping, the probability of one object j to be assigned to a certain cluster is calculated as follows

$$P(j,k) = 1 - \frac{Ec(j,k)}{MaxEc(k)}$$

where $P(j,k)$ means the probability of object j to be assigned to cluster k; the $Ec(j,k)$ means the function to calculate Euclidean distance between an object j and cluster k; $MaxEc(k)$ means the maximum Euclidean distance from centered point of cluster k. Mean Absolute Error (MAE) [19] is a measure of deviation of predicted ratings from their actual ratings.

The MAE is represented as follows

$$MAE = \frac{\sum_{i=1}^{n} | p_i - r_i |}{n}$$

where pi is a predicted rating, ri is the actual ratings and n is the number of actual ratings in the test set.

The lower the MAE, the more accurate the predictions are permitting to provide better recommendations.

2.3   SVM Based Approach

SVM is a supervised approach that is best suited for binary classification.

The problem taken in hand is a binary classification problem and it can be defined as

Given l samples: (x1 , **y1**), (**x2** , **y2**),… (**xl** , **yl**)

Where $xi \in R^d$, for $i = 1,2,...l$ is a feature vector of length d and $yi = \{+1,-1\}$ is the class label for data point xi,

We find a classifier with the decision function f(x) such that $y = f(x)$, where y is the class label for **x.** These l samples are called "training data". The performance of the classifier is measured in terms of classification error on unseen "testing data" which is defined in the equation below

$$E(y, f(x)) = \begin{cases} 0 & if\ y=f(x), \\ 1 & otherwise \end{cases}$$

The SVM is provided the appropriate training data and the classifier function is determined. Data is passed from the pre-processing phase to the SVM. The classifier function is applied on this data and the result is obtained. If this result is found to be positive, i.e. if the record is classified as a legitimate record, the analysis ends. If the record is classified as a fraudulent record, then it is passed on to the next phase for verification. Since an SVM can be applied to only two-class tasks, uncertainty is classifications exist and the parameters of the solved model are difficult to implement. [25] [27]

2.4   Collective Animal Behaviour Approach

The collective animal behaviour approach is the process of finding the co-ordinated behaviour of a group of a similar species. Hence, in our approach we can say that users under the same category demonstrate a similar behaviour. All clusters that contain the currently analyzed user are considered for evaluation. All users under the each cluster are analyzed for a similar behaviour. [16]

If the users behaviour in any one of the clusters matches and exceeds the provided threshold, then the transaction is labelled as legitimate. This helps providing a higher level of accuracy in labelling a fraudulent transaction. In the problem at hand, false positives pose a great threat in degrading the goodwill of an organization; hence accuracy in predicting a fraudulent transaction should be maintained very high. [17] [18]

3   Analysis of the Results

The current process is evaluated with various sets of data containing different number of data items and the obtained values are recorded in a confusion matrix.

Table 1. Confusion Matrix

		Predicted	
		Positive	**Negative**
Actual	Positive	TP	FP
	Negative	TN	FN

Where,

TP - True positive, FP- False positive, TN – True Negative and FN – False Negative.

The two performance measures, sensitivity and specificity are used for evaluating the results.

Sensitivity is the accuracy on the positive instances.

$$Sensitivity = TP/TP + FN$$

where TP is True Positive Rate and FN is False Negative Rate.
Specificity is the accuracy of the negative instances

$$Specificity = TN/TN + FP$$

where TN is True Negative Rate and FP is False Positive Rate.

tp	fp	tn	fn	fpr	tpr
0	0	1	0	0	0
3	0	3	0	0	1
5	0	6	0	0	1
7	1	7	1	0.125	0.875
10	1	9	1	0.1	0.909091
11	1	13	1	0.071429	0.916667
15	1	14	1	0.066667	0.9375
16	1	18	1	0.052632	0.941176
20	2	18	1	0.1	0.952381
22	2	20	2	0.090909	0.916667
23	3	23	2	0.115385	0.92
24	3	27	2	0.1	0.923077
26	4	29	2	0.121212	0.928571
29	4	31	2	0.114286	0.935484
30	4	35	2	0.102564	0.9375
32	4	38	2	0.095238	0.941176
34	4	41	2	0.088889	0.944444

Fig. 3. A sample confusion matrix set with TPR and FPR

The simulation is conducted with a dataset containing a total of 690 records. The Australian credit approval dataset was used for the processing. The process was broken at regular intervals to find the values of TP, FP, TN and FN. These function as the basis for calculating the TPR and FPR. These readings are tabulated and the ROC is plotted.

From the figure, we can see that during the initial stages, when the number of entries are minimal, the plots point to 0,0 and 0,1 points. As the number of entries keep increasing, we can see that the plotted points are clustered towards the northwest corner and are above the diagonal. This proves that our process provides a high level of accuracy, almost meeting the perfect standard of 0,1.

Precision is the fraction of retrieved instances that are relevant, while recall is the fraction of relevant instances that are retrieved. Both precision and recall are therefore based on an understanding and measure of relevance. Hence we can use this measure to find the relevance of the readings.

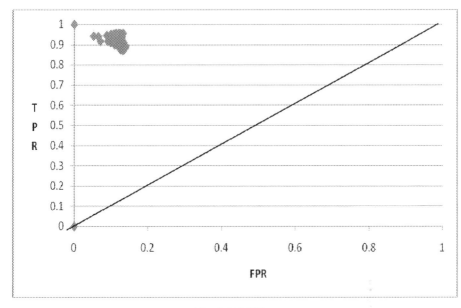

Fig. 4. ROC Plot

Accuracy is determined by the location of the points in the PR space. As the points move towards the top right, we can guarantee better accuracy. In Figure 5, a dense concentration of points is observed, which implies that our process provides better accuracy.

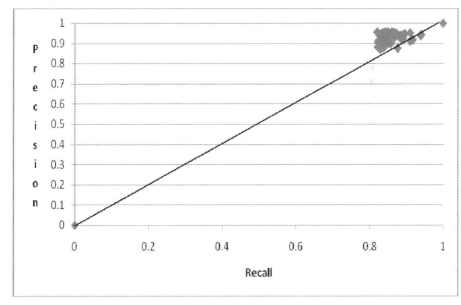

Fig. 5. PR Curve

Usually, precision and recall scores are not discussed in isolation. Instead, either values for one measure are compared for a fixed level at the other measure or both are combined into a single measure, such as their harmonic mean the F-measure, which is the weighted harmonic mean of precision and recall.

$$F = 2 \cdot \frac{precision \cdot recall}{precision + recall}$$

This is also known as the F_1 measure, because recall and precision are evenly weighted

precision	recall	F measure
0	0	0
1	1	1
1	1	1
0.875	0.875	0.875
0.909091	0.909091	0.909091
0.916667	0.916667	0.916667
0.9375	0.9375	0.9375
0.941176	0.941176	0.941176
0.909091	0.952381	0.930233
0.916667	0.916667	0.916667
0.884615	0.92	0.901961
0.888889	0.923077	0.90566
0.866667	0.928571	0.896552
0.878788	0.935484	0.90625
0.882353	0.9375	0.909091
0.888889	0.941176	0.914286
0.894737	0.944444	0.918919
0.871795	0.944444	0.906667
0.853659	0.945946	0.897436

Fig. 6. Precision, Recall and F-Measure – Sample values

Here, the F-Measure of our values shows a rate of 0.869341 and we obtain an average accuracy rate of 0.892489. The MAE is calculated to be 0.3334, hence the performance during multi-clustering is also found to be efficient. Hence we can prove that our process shows a higher accuracy rate and better performance.

4   Conclusion and Future Enhancements

The process described [28] is mostly supervised and hence need to be fine-tuned according to the application data that is being considered for analysis, while [29] uses only SVM, which is a binary classifier. The false positive rates in SVM are found to be higher, which is not acceptable in real time-scenarios. The current process is found to improve the accuracy rate of prediction, especially in the areas of false positives, further the generalized structure helps in faster incorporation towards any dataset. The process could be made better if the output is in a human readable form because the actual output from a SVM based output is not human interpretable in nature. Since this particular application requires that the fraud data be considered for further analysis by the analysts it is better if we can use some fuzzy based approach where we can use natural languages for labelling the data. Further, this process can also be used for finding the patterns in organized crime and hence help in predicting the behaviour of malicious users.

References

1. Pavia, J.M., Veres-Ferrer, E.J., Escura, G.F.: Credit Card Incidents and Control Systems. International Journal of Information Management, 501–503 (2012)
2. Bhattacharyya, S., Jha, S., Tharakunnel, K., Christopher Westland, J.: Data Mining For Credit Card Fraud: A Comparative Study. Decision Support Systems 50, 602–613 (2011)
3. Krivko, M.: A Hybrid Model for Plastic Card Fraud Detection Systems. Expert Systems with Applications 37, 6070–6076 (2010)
4. Duman, E., Hamdi Ozcelik, M.: Detecting Credit Card Fraud by Genetic Algorithm and Scatter Search. Expert Systems with Applications 38, 13057–13063 (2011)
5. Panigrahi, S., Kundu, A., Sural, S., Majumdar, A.K.: Credit Card Fraud Detection: A Fusion Approach Using Dempster–Shafer Theory And Bayesian Learning. Information Fusion 10, 354–363 (2009)
6. Vatsa, V., Sural, S., Majumdar, A.K.: A Game-Theoretic Approach to Credit Card Fraud Detection. Springer, Heidelberg (2005)
7. Elías, A., Ochoa-Zezzatti, A., Padilla, A., Ponce, J.: Outlier Analysis for Plastic Card Fraud Detection a Hybridized and Multi-Objective Approach. Springer, Heidelberg (2011)
8. Sańchez, D., Vila, M.A., Cerda, L., Serrano, J.M.: Association Rules Applied To Credit Card Fraud Detection. Expert Systems with Applications 36, 3630–3640 (2009)
9. Ngai, E.W.T., Hu, Y., Wong, Y.H., Chen, Y., Sun, X.: The Application of Data Mining Techniques in Financial Fraud Detection: A Classification Framework and an Academic Review of Literature. Decision Support Systems 50, 559–569 (2011)
10. Gadi, M.F.A., Wang, X., do Lago, A.P.: Credit Card Fraud Detection with Artificial Immune System. Springer, Heidelberg (2008)
11. Jha, S., Guillen, M., Christopher Westland, J.: Employing Transaction Aggregation Strategy to Detect Credit Card Fraud. Expert Systems with Applications 39, 12650–12657 (2012)
12. Quah, J.T.S., Sriganesh, M.: Real-Time Credit Card Fraud Detection Using Computational Intelligence. Expert Systems with Applications 35, 1721–1732 (2008)
13. Sun, A., Lim, E.-P., Liu, Y.: On Strategies For Imbalanced Text Classification Using SVM: A Comparative Study. Decision Support Systems 48, 191–201 (2009)

14. Zhang, H.-T., Chen, M.Z., Stan, G.-B., Zhou, T., Jan, M.: Maciejowski, Collective Behavior Coordination with Predictive Mechanisms. IEEE Circuits and Systems Magazine (2008)
15. Sumpter, D.J.T.: Phil. Trans. R. Soc. B. The Principles of Collective Animal Behaviour 361, 5–22 (2006)
16. Cuevas, E., Gonzalez, M., Zaldivar, D., Perez-Cisneros, M., Garcia, G.: An Algorithm for Global Optimization Inspired by Collective Animal Behaviour, vol. 2012, Article ID 638275, 24 pages. Hindawi Publishing Corporation Discrete Dynamics in Nature and Society (2012)
17. He, S., Wu, Q.H., Saunders, J.R.: Group Search Optimizer: An Optimization Algorithm Inspired by Animal Searching Behavior. IEEE Transactions on Evolutionary Computation 13(5) (October 2009)
18. Lu, J., Liu, J., Couzin, I.D., Levin, S.A.: Emerging Collective Behaviors of Animal Groups. In: Proceedings of the 7th World Congress on Intelligent Control and Automation, Chongqing, China, June 25-27 (2008)
19. Puntheeranurak, S., Tsuji, H.: A Multi-Clustering Hybrid Recommender System. In: Seventh International Conference on Computer and Information Technology. IEEE (2007)
20. Phoungphol, P., Zhang, Y., Zha, Y., Srichandan, B.: Multiclass SVM with Ramp Loss for Imbalanced Data Classification. In: IEEE International Conference on Granular Computing (2012)
21. Tang, Y., Jin, B., Sun, Y., Zhang, Y.-Q.: Granular Support Vector Machines for Medical Binary Classification Problems. IEEE (2004)
22. Tang, Y., Zhang, Y.-Q., Chawla, N.V., Krasser, S.: SVMs Modeling for Highly Imbalanced Classification. IEEE (2009)
23. Hsu, C.-W., Chang, C.-C., Lin, C.-J.: A Practical Guide to Support Vector Classification (2010)
24. Dheepa, V., Dhanapal, R.: Behavior Based Credit Card Fraud Detection Using Support Vector Machines (2012)
25. Dheepa, V., Dhanapal, R., Manjunath, G.: Fraud Detection in Imbalanced Datasets using Cost Based Learning (2012)
26. Yan-li, Z., Jia, Z.: Research on Data Preprocessing In Credit Card Consuming Behavior Mining. Energy Procedia 17, 638–643 (2012)
27. Lemnaru, C., Cuibus, M., Bona, A., Alic, A., Potolea, R.: A Distributed Methodology for Imbalanced Classification Problems. In: 11th International Symposium on Parallel and Distributed Computing (2012)
28. Chen, R.-C., Luo, S.-T., Liang, X., Lee, V.C.S.: Personalized Approach Based on SVM and ANN for Detecting Credit Card Fraud. 0-7803-9422-4/05/$20.00 C2005. IEEE
29. Wei, X., Yuan, L.: An Optimized SVM Model for Detection of Fraudulent Online Credit Card Transactions. In: International Conference on Management of e-Commerce and e-Government (2012)

Recent Trends in Collection of Software Forensics Artifacts: Issues and Challenges

Deepak Gupta and Babu M. Mehtre

Institute for Development and Research in Banking Technology
Established by Reserve Bank of India
Masab Tank. Castle Hills Road No 1, Hyderabad-500057, India
{GDeepak,BMMehtre}@idrbt.ac.in

Abstract. Digital forensics helps an investigator to find traces of any malicious activity of user, done by using a particular piece of software. In recent years, analysis of computer software products has been done for collection of forensics artifacts, using traditional digital forensic approach. But as the traditional forensics has now been established as a standard, more people are familiar with the forensic processes. They know where traces can be left behind and how to get rid of them so as to eliminate possible evidence. Thus anti forensic techniques are imposing as disruptive challenge for investigators. In this paper we discuss recent trends in the field of artifacts collection and highlight some challenges that have made finding and collecting forensics artifacts a very hard job. We examine whether it is possible for a forensics investigator to rely on old traditional approach or not. Furthermore in conclusion we suggest possible solutions and new areas where we can find evidences.

Keywords: Cyber Forensics, Digital Evidence, Information Security, Software artifact Forensics, Recent Trends.

1 Introduction

Nowadays various software products (both free and priced) are available out of which some of them are being used either to carry out malicious activity or assisting in doing it. For example downloading pornographic content using any download assisting software, bullying or harassing someone over internet using Skype or other chatting software is direct use of software in cyber crime. While opening any pirated archive files using *WinRAR* or *WinZip* is considered as assisting in carrying malicious activity. Software artifacts are kind of by-products produced during installation and/or use of software products. Forensics of Software Artifacts is collection of these byproducts during cyber investigation to relate with crime.

But unfortunately in today's changing scenarios, there are various ways available by which these artifacts can be modified, tempered or erased. That makes collection of evidences very hard or futile exercise. Automatic, Selective and Secure Deletion of digital evidence [1] explains mechanism to delete data or evidences in such a manner

Sabu M. Thampi et al. (Eds.): SSCC 2013, CCIS 377, pp. 303–312, 2013.

that no forensic investigation can detect or retrieve it. It makes our job futile exercise. This paper explores some areas where investigators search for evidences and then discuss challenges in collection of these evidences.

The rest of the paper is organized as follows. In Section 2, we discuss recent trends in artifacts collection and give overview of some very frequently examined areas by forensics investigators to extract artifacts from a computer. In Section 3, we discuss various challenges that make collection of these artifacts a hard job. Then in Section 4, we will demonstrate some experimental results and show how these issues are affecting investigation process. Finally the conclusion of this work is given in Section 5.

2   Recent Trends in Software Artifact Collection

In the last two decades many techniques as well as tools are being presented for collection of digital forensics artifacts. Apart from simply stored data, investigators search some specific areas that users generally are unaware of, and provide some very crucial information during digital crime investigation process. In recent years various papers have been published which discuss about finding digital forensics artifacts of different software products. Usually these software products are widely used and can assist someone in carrying out malicious activity. For example Paper [2] and [3] talks about various artifacts left by tools *Download accelerator* and *Internet Download manager* which are widely used to manage download from internet. Paper [4] talks about Windows 7 registry forensic evidences created by 3 popular BitTorrent clients. [5] Talks about forensic artifacts created by opening of ".zip" archive files opened using *WinRAR*. While another paper [6] analyze artifacts left by *Window Live Messenger*, also known as *MSN messenger* that is an instant messaging client.

Similarity among all these recently published papers is that they all use similar traditional forensics approach in which all investigate same areas like windows registry, log files, temporary files and *AppData* folder to identify and collect various artifacts. Here we are giving overview of some of these fields which are being investigated very often by forensic investigators for artifacts.

2.1   Windows Registry

Windows registry stores configuration database of Microsoft Windows operating system. This storage includes settings and options. Registry contains lots of crucial information that is very much valuable to a forensic investigator [7]. Registry can be used to fetch information like personal settings, programs executed, passwords, preferences, most recently used files. This editor is divided into 2 panels where left panel displays entire registry tree and right panel shows individual values. In windows 7, this left panel will show 5 hives that are

- HKEY_CLASSES_ROOT contains file name extensions associations and COM class registration information such as programmatic identifier, class identifier and interface identifier

- HKEY_CURRENT_USER contains the user profile for the user who is currently logged on to the computer. that includes various information like program installed, desktop settings, network connections, printers, and application preferences
- HKEY_LOCAL_MACHINE contains all information about the hardware and software settings being used for all users of the same machine
- HKEY_USERS contains user-specific configuration information for all currently active users on the computer
- HKEY_CURRENT_CONFIG contains all information about the current hardware configuration

During collection of software forensic artifacts we can fetch information like which software was recently executed, list of uninstalled software, files recently saved/downloaded, location of software and many more.

2.2   AppData Folder Analysis

The AppData folder in new version of windows is more equal to the Documents and Settings folder in Windows XP. This AppData folder is a hidden folder in windows that contains user data and settings and protects them from unwanted changes. It contains many valuable artifacts such as program settings, IE cookies, toolbar settings, browsing history, temporary files created by applications, libraries; send to items, templates and many more. This folder contains 3 sub folders inside it, namely Local, LocalLow and Roaming. Each folder has its own significant.

- **Local** Folder mainly contains folders related to installed programs. Also there is a folder of Microsoft where history of Windows activities can be found. There is a temp folder which stores all the temporary files.
- **LocalLow** is mainly for IE, Java and Adobe protected mode data.
- **Roaming** folder contains machine independent application specific data. The data stored in this folder, roam around with the user profile.

2.3   System Event Logs

Event logs are special files that record significant events on computer [8], such as when a user logs on to the computer or when a program encounters an error. This event log service stores event related to application security and system event. These logs can be used to trace any user activity on particular system components. Windows typically stores these logs in a machine.

- **Application** event log contains the data generated from any installed application
- **System** event log stores messages generated from windows services. They are divided as error, warning and information
- **Security** log contains security related events that are generated from auditing policy
- **Setup** logs are additional logs in Computers that are configured as domain controllers.
- **Forwarded Events** log contains log forwarded by other computes

2.4   Temporary Files

Mostly temporary files [9] are created by computer programs. There could be various reasons behind creation of these files. For example when a program need to store data temporarily it creates a temporary file or when an executable cannot allocate enough memory to its task it stores the data in temporary files. Many times even after the completion of their task many applications leave these files undeleted. Now these files can come in handy for an investigator during investigation as these files hold so much information without user's knowledge of their existence.

2.5   Web Browsing Activity

Most of us use web browsers like internet explorer, Mozilla Firefox, Apple safari to access internet in daily life. We access various important websites such as online banking, emails, social networking, keyword search and many more. The information related to these sites along with our personal information like passwords, cart information is being stored as internet history and cookies by these web browsers. This information can be accessed by any investigator [10]. Even after you delete the history, temporary files and cookies, these can be recovered and evidences can be found. So investigation can fetch information like list of files downloaded, websites visited and passwords using web browser forensics.

2.6   Deleted Data

After simply deleting the data by using delete button doesn't actually mean that the data is forever gone and nobody can get their hands on that information. What actually happens is that when we delete a file, you are removing it from the directory and flagging this part of drive as available for new data. So by using any data recovery tool investigator can recover your deleted data [11]. And by this investigator can retrieve lots of crucial artifacts.

3   Challenges in Artifacts Collection

So far we have discussed about various areas from where investigators search for artifacts. Now we'll talk about some challenges that are making our job of retrieving these artifacts really tough.

3.1   Encryption

The very simple way to irritate a forensic investigator is by hiding your files, partitions or complete hard disk using encryption. Encryption is the process of encoding message in such a way that no authorize person can read it [12]. It is in fashion for a very long time and with time it is continuously evolving. Nowadays instead of just encrypting single files, some new trends like complete hard disk or specific partition encryption is being faced by investigator very often. Various powerful encryption tools are freely available over internet like *crypt4free, TrueCrypt*, which are being used in hiding data.

Nowadays software like *SafeHouse* creates hidden storage area (also called as virtual drive that is more like an encrypted volume within a volume) that allows storing all private files and folders. Volume size can also be adjusted according to user's requirement. That makes our job more challenging. Although it is possible to break the encryption but still it takes great load of time and processing power to break this encryption and time is luxury in investigation process that we can't afford to lose.

3.2 Artifacts Contraception

Trail contraception methods prevent artifacts generation by interfering with the normal process of windows of storing data. There are different kinds of artifact contraception method that works differently and prevent traces to be created. Some of them are discussed here:

3.2.1 Use of Portable Software
Portable software is an executable program that runs independently without any need of installation. These kinds of applications can be stored on removable storage media such as USB flash drive or portable hard disks. So once after storing a portable application in portable device it can be used in any number of compatible machines. These applications don't leave program files or data on host system. Generally they also don't write to windows registry or configuration files on user's profile in system. There are lots of portable tools available on internet for various functionalities. For example *Firefox portable* and *chrome portable* are for web browsing, *µTorrent portable* version for P2P sharing is available and distributed freely.

So by using portable application one can get rid of various artifacts like registry data, temporary files configuration files, etc.

3.2.2 Sandbox Environment
Sandbox is an isolated environment initially used by software developers to text new programming code. But nowadays various software products like *Sandboxie* create isolated environment to general users. So what it does is to run various computer programs in an isolated environment and prevent them from making any permanent change to other programs and data in computer. Once we sandbox is closed along with the program running, it'll automatically dump all the changes made by that program in such manner that it is not reflected anywhere in computer.

So by using sandbox environment one can avoid various traces like browsing history, cookies, cache temporary files and many more

3.2.3 Virtual Machines
The very basic meaning of virtual machine is simulation of a computer within a physical computer. A virtual machine also referred as "VM" is kind of a computer application that creates a virtual environment, also referred as "virtualization". This

allows a user to run any number of operating systems on a single computer at the same time. As a VM is a file or say set of files, it can be carried on a removable media and can be accessed on nearly any computer. These VMs can be encrypted and disposing them is really very easy task.

When a person wants to carry any malicious intent, it simply setup a VM and performs all activities using this VM only. Once he is done, he can dispose it using any secure deletion software. Or if VM resides in any portable device, then his only task is to hide this device from investigator.

Forensic analysis of VM is still a challenging job for an investigator [13] as first it has to find the traces of VM's existence. And even after finding the traces of existence, he can't tell what activities were being done using this VM until unless he gets his hands on that VM.

So by using virtual machines and disposing it successfully one can skip mostly all the artifacts that leads him to crime.

3.2.4   Use of Live OS

A live OS also referred as a live CD, live DVD, live USB or live disc is a bootable computer operating system that runs in the computer's memory, Rather than loading from the hard disk drive. So without even installing an OS, live disc allow users to work on an operating system. It runs without making any changes to the existing operating system on the computer.

The key trick is that the live environment runs completely in RAM so artifacts like cookies, registry, and temporary files don't get saved in secondary storage. So creation of various artifacts can be avoided using live OS.

3.2.5   Private Browsing

Private Browsing allows user to browse Internet without saving any personal information like which sites and pages visited, cookies, passwords, Search bar entries, download list entries, and cache web content.

So if a user used private browsing to surf internet, then it's really challenging task for an investigator to track and find artifacts related to his web activity.

3.3   Artifacts Deletion

The next challenge for an investigator is artifacts deletion, in which various artifacts that we have discussed in section 2 are being deleted either manually or using some tools. Here we are discussing some common artifacts deletion.

3.3.1   Deleting Event Logs

Event logs deletion is really very easy task. It can be done manually as well as by using some freely distributed tools. There are several ways to do it manually, for example one is to simply clear all logs from Event viewer that resides in "Administrative tools" in control panel.

In the same way there is large number of freely distributed software products are available over internet to perform this task very easily and user friendly. For example *CCleaner* is very useful and widely used tool that delete all the logs with one click of mouse.

3.3.2   Cleaning Windows Registry

Windows registry is another artifact that can be tempered, modified and cleaned. As it stores so many crucial information like list of all installed and uninstalled software product, recently save files, it impose as a real challenge is somebody modified the registry keys. This registry Cleaning can be done by both manually as well as using some tools. Although manually tempering with registry is very risky as any mistake can cause whole windows to crash down but still it is being done widely. It can be done manually by opening the registry editor and modifying or deleting the specific registry key value.

To automatically clean registry we have large number of software available like *CCleaner, AML registry cleaner*.

3.3.3   Cleaning Internet History and Temporary Program Files

As we discussed in section II, internet history, and cookies can reveal a great load of private information of user's web activity. Cleaning internet history is relatively very easy task. All you have to do is open your web browser find the location of history and cookies and delete it. It also can be done with the help of various tools like *CCleaner*.

There are many manual ways to deleted temporary files. For example one is to search temporary files by typing "%temp%" in run dialogue box and then delete them permanently. Many tools can also perform this task just by one click.

3.4   Secure Data Deletion Techniques

As we previously discussed in section 2 that simply deleting data doesn't mean that it is gone forever. There are many tools to recover deleted data. To get rid of this many cyber criminals are using various tools and techniques that provide automatic, selective and secure deletion of data [1]. For secure deletion basic approach generally includes following given steps

1) Delete the data/file
2) Delete the metadata (path name and other details) related to that data/file
3) Rewriting the physical location where the previous data was stored

It's not like that all tools follow these same steps but mostly idea is same. In recent years some techniques for this secure deletion are being proposed like The Gutmann method [14].

Nowadays there are several tools available in market which provide functionality of secure data deletion like *Heidi Eraser, Secure Erase*. These tools are imposing as real challenge for retrieving artifacts by recovering deleted data.

3.5   Creation of Fake Trails

So far we have talked about hiding from investigator by removing trails. But a criminal can also create some fake trails that will leave investigator confused and diverted. To confuse an investigator all they have to do is to modify or create some new fake logs, edit the registry.

There are some tools available over internet that can provide you the functionality of altering the windows event log/server logs, creation of fake registry, faking MAC (medium access control) address, and many more.

4   Experimental Results

We performed forensic analysis on some frequently used software products and tried to examine the difference made by these challenges we talked in section 3. For all the experiments, we used hardware platform with CPU Intel Core I5-2430M, RAM 4 GB DDR3, hard disk SATA 500GB, running Microsoft Windows 7 Professional and NTFS file system.

We examined artifacts left behind by following software products: *Mozilla Firefox, Google Chrome, µTorrent, Internet Download Manager (IDM)* and *WinRar*. Initially we did all the investigation in normal environment. We installed each software and collected forensic artifacts related to them. The results are shown in Table 1. *"Yes"* in table means that we were able to retrieve artifacts from a specific location while *"No"* means that no artifacts related to that activity was found. If particular activity is not related to tool then we placed "--" in the table. It is evident that we were able to retrieve almost all the forensics artifacts in normal situation. Then in a separate machine we used portable versions of these software products, hosted in a USB disk and this time we were not able to find any single evidences. Results are shown in Table 2. Finally we installed and used same tools in sandbox environment and again we were not able to find any artifacts, left behind by these software products. The comparative results are given in Table 1, 2 and 3 which demonstrate the impact of these issues.

Table 1. Different Artifacts Left Behind By Use of Various Software Products

Software Products	Artifacts			
	Windows Registry	*AppData Folder*	*Temporary Files*	*History*
Firefox	*Yes*	*Yes*	*Yes*	*Yes*
Chrome	*Yes*	*Yes*	*Yes*	*Yes*
µTorrent	*Yes*	*Yes*	*Yes*	--
IDM	*Yes*	*Yes*	*Yes*	*Yes*
WinRar	*Yes*	*Yes*	*Yes*	--

Table 2. No Artifact Found While Using Portable Version

Software Products (portable Version)	Artifacts			
	Windows Registry	*AppData Folder*	*Temporary Files*	*History*
Firefox	*No*	*No*	*No*	*No*
Chrome	*No*	*No*	*No*	*No*
µTorrent	*No*	*No*	*No*	--
IDM	*No*	*No*	*No*	*No*
WinRar	*No*	*No*	*No*	--

Table 3. No Artifact Found While Using Sandbox Environment

Software Products	Artifacts			
	Windows Registry	*AppData Folder*	*Temporary Files*	*History*
Firefox	*No*	*No*	*No*	*No*
Chrome	*No*	*No*	*No*	*No*
µTorrent	*No*	*No*	*No*	--
IDM	*No*	*No*	*No*	*No*
WinRar	*No*	*No*	*No*	--

As you can see in Table 2 and 3, no artifacts were found while using the techniques, mentioned in section 3. In the same way when we used virtual machine and live disks and again no artifacts were found.

5   Conclusion

So in these changing times when a criminals having so many tools and techniques available to dodge a forensic investigation as we have seen in this paper, we can easily assess that traditional forensic approach is no longer feasible. We must have to stop relying on this approach to collect the forensic artifacts and have to look beyond the disk forensic and some other areas too for artifacts collection.

Some new areas that we need to explore more for forensic analysis are physical memory, hibernation files, page files and configuration files, system restore files and backup files. These all areas contain very crucial artifacts and if utilized properly by an investigator, can help in many complex cases.   Data Carving is also new trend in forensic investigator that can assist an investigator to find some crucial artifacts.

References

1. Castiglione, A., Cattaneo, G.: Automatic, Selective and Secure Deletion of Digital Evidence. In: International Conference on Broadband and Wireless Computing, pp. 392–398 (2011)
2. Yasin, M., Wahla, M.A., Kausar, F.: Analysis of Download Accelerator Plus (DAP) for Forensic Artefacts. In: Fifth International Conference on IT Security Incident Management and IT Forensics, pp. 142–152 (2009)
3. Yasin, M., Cheema, A.R., Kausar, F.: Analysis of Internet Download Manager for collection of digital forensic artefacts. Digital Investigation 7(1-2), 90–94 (2010)
4. Lallie, H.S., Briggs, P.J.: Windows 7 registry forensic evidence created by three popular bittorrent clients. Digital Investigation 7(3-4), 127–134 (2011)
5. Fellows, G.: WinRAR temporary folder artefacts. Digital Investigation 7(1-2), 9–13 (2010)
6. Van Dongen, W.S.: Forensic artefacts left by Windows Live Messenger 8.0. Digital Investigation 4(2), 73–87 (2007)
7. Carvey, H.: The Windows Registry as a forensic resource. Digital Investigation 2(3), 201–205 (2005)
8. Event Log, http://windows.microsoft.com/en-IN/windows7/ What-information-appears-in-event-logs-Event-Viewer
9. Windows Temporary files, http://support.microsoft.com/kb/92635
10. Oha, J., Leeb, S., Leea, S.: Advanced evidence collection and analysis of web browser activity. Digital Investigation 8(suppl.), S62–S70 (2011)
11. Shinder, L., Cross, M.: Chapter 7 – Acquiring Data, Duplicating Data, and Recovering Deleted Files. Scene of the Cybercrime, 2nd edn., pp. 305–346. Syngress Publication (2008)
12. Smid, M.E., Branstad, D.K.: Data Encryption Standard: past and future. Proceedings of the IEEE 76(5), 550–559 (2002)
13. Bares, R.A.: Hiding in a Virtual World: Using unconventionally installed operating system. In: International Conference on Intelligence and Security Informatics, pp. 276–284 (2009)
14. Gutmann, P.: Secure Deletion of Data from Magnetic and Solid-State Memory. In: Proceedings of the 6th conference on USENIX Security Symposium, Focusing on Applications of Cryptography, vol. 6, pp. 77–89. USENIX Association, Berkeley (1996)

Service Dependencies-Aware Policy Enforcement Framework Based on Hierarchical Colored Petri Net

Yosra Ben Mustapha and Hervé Debar

Telecom Sudparis, SAMOVAR UMR 5157
9 rue Charles Fourier, 91011 EVRY, France
{yosra.ben_mustapha,herve.debar}@telecom-sudparis.eu

Abstract. As computer and network security threats become more sophisticated and the number of service dependencies is increasing, optimal response decision is becoming a challenging task for security administrators. They should deploy and implement proper network security policy enforcement mechanisms in order to apply the appropriate countermeasures and defense strategy.

In this paper, we propose a novel modeling framework which considers the service dependencies while identifying and selecting the appropriate Policy Enforcement Points during an intrusion response process. First, we present the security implications of the service dependencies that have been developed in the literature. Second, we give an overview of Colored Petri Nets (CPN) and Hierarchical CPN (HCPN) and its application on network security. Third, we specify our Service Dependencies-aware Policy Enforcement Framework which is based on the application of HCPN. Finally and to illustrate the advantage of our approach, we present a webmail application use case with the integration of different Policy Enforcement Points.

1 Introduction

As computer and network security threats are becoming more sophisticated as described in [1] and the number of service dependencies is increasing, optimal response decision is becoming a challenging task for security administrators. Applying appropriate countermeasures and defense strategy implies the deployment of proper network security policy enforcement while taking into account service dependencies and their different interactions. Most of the current automated Intrusion Response Systems (IRS)s are based on the risk assessment and the cost-sensitive analysis as detailed in [2–4]. They are still suffering from several drawbacks as described in [5]. Usually, they provide isolated response applied in a single Policy Enforcement Point (PEP) of the Information System.

The lack of formal representation of the interaction between service dependencies and policy enforcement mechanisms is a motivation for our proposed approach. Moreover, there is still a gap between service dependencies, attack graphs and policy enforcement reaction decisions. Thus, our main objective is

Sabu M. Thampi et al. (Eds.): SSCC 2013, CCIS 377, pp. 313–321, 2013.

to design and develop new strategies to optimize policy enforcement response decision against single alert first, then, multiple alerts.

We propose to extend the existing service dependency model by including a clear and explicit representation of policy enforcement mechanisms (Firewalls, User Directories, . . .). We consider the service architecture and its dependencies in order to explore several enforcement possibilities in a response decision. Contrary to the majority of research which consider the security as a service, we distinguish between a service component and a security component. By doing so, we aim at giving a clear representation of PEPs in the service dependencies model. In fact, in the existing Service Dependency Models, as described in [6,7], the interaction between two dependent services is only constrained by the presence of required privileges. This hides the concrete and explicit presence of PEPs in the dependencies model.

Therefore, we propose to deploy Hierarchical Colored Petri Nets (HCPN) by introducing the notion of substitution transitions to represent PEPs. Each PEP is characterized by its enforcement capabilities. We model these capabilities by specifying the substitution transition functions. In this paper, we propose a novel modelling framework which considers service dependencies while selecting appropriate PEPs in an intrusion response process. First, we present the security implications of the service dependencies that have been developed in the literature. We also detail the definition of Policy Enforcement and Access Control. Second, we give an overview of deploying Colored Petri Nets (CPN) as well as Hierarchical CPN (HCPN) and motivations to apply this latter in network security issues. Third, we specify our Service Dependencies-aware Policy Enforcement Framework which is based on the application of the HCPN. Last but not least in order to illustrate the advantage of our approach, we present a webmail application use case with the integration of different Policy Enforcement Points.

2   Policy Enforcement Point Definition

According to [8], *the Policy Decision Points (PDPs) process Access Control policies, along with other data such as network state information, and take policy decisions regarding what policies should be enforced and how this will happen. These policies are sent as configuration data to the appropriate Policy Enforcement Points (PEPs), which reside on the managed devices and are responsible for installing and enforcing them.*

The concept of PEP was also introduced in [9] as an entity that performs access control by making decisions requests and *enforcing* authorization decisions by the PDP. Referring to the latest version of [9], the PEP comes in many forms. It can be part of a remote-access gateway, part of a web server or email user-agent, etc. In [10], the PEP is defined as the most security critical component, which protects the resources and enforces the PDP's decision. Generally, the PDP and the PEP are combined to control access and enforce the security policy.

In [11], authors specifies that the logical level integration allows the enforcement of policies through a PEP. Usually, in applications where multiple architecture is layered, the PEP is located between the presentation layer and the logical layer, intercepting the calls, using the controls, and in case the invocation is authorized, it can be executed.

3   Service Dependencies Model and Security Implications

Recently, the application of service dependencies in the response decision process is gaining an expanding interest, [6, 7, 12, 13]. As mentioned in [6], the high number of service dependencies increases the challenge of response decision and policy enforcement. Therefore, authors propose to use service dependencies as frames for attack impact and response costs evaluation.

In [12], authors present in depth explanation about the use of service dependency to enforce policy-based response. They propose to find the best suitable set of PEPs capable of applying a response that has been already selected. Authors define the PEP capability as the ability of the PEP to apply a security rule on a specific set of subjects, actions and objects.

In [7], authors demonstrate how service dependencies have security implications and extend the work presented in [12]. First, they consider that a service is a set of components C_i. A simple service model is composed of connected components. The basic model M_S of the service S is defined by $M_S = \{(C_i, PC_i, SC_i)\}, i \in \{1 \ldots n\}\}$. PC_i and SC_i are respectively the providers of resources to C_i and the subscribers of resources provided by C_i. This model is extended by adding (1) the privileges granted to the service Pr_C, (2) the credentials accredited to this service Cr_C and (3) the trust it has regarding other privileges and/or credentials Tr_C. This modelling approach links dependent services by defining these sets: providers and subscribers and required privileges of each service.

The proposed model has been used in order to assist the administrators in selecting the appropriate Policy Enforcement Point (PEP). Authors does not formally define this latter -PEP- and consider each service as a PEP having limited access control capabilities. But, this approach does not allow us to dynamically and automatically identify PEPs capable to implement a proper response decision.

In [13], authors combines service dependency graphs with attack graphs in order to enable security analysts to make more informed decisions. According to them, there is a gap between system components and service dependencies graphs and attack graphs. Therefore, they propose to combine attack and dependency graphs to provide security analysts with a better picture of the cyber situation.

4   Colored Petri Nets: Definitions and Related Works

4.1   Brief Definition of Petri Nets

Petri Nets formalism was introduced by C. A. Petri in 1962, [14] for the mathematical representation of discrete distributed systems. Known also place/transition nets, it graphically depicts the structure of systems as a direct bipartite graph with annotations. Places and transitions are respectively denoted by circles and rectangles. Directed edges (arcs) connect places to transitions and vice versa. A transition can be fired only if the input place(s) have the required number of tokens.

4.2 Colored Petri Nets: CPNs and Hierarchical CPNs

Colored Petri Nets (CPNs) are an extension of original Petri Nets. Contrary to ordinary Petri Net which do not define types for tokens and modules, using CPNs, we are able to assign tokens with different data value called token colors. Moreover, connections between places and transitions are labeled by a color function. These CPN additional features allows us to model more complex and large systems. However, both Petri Nets and CPNs do not ensure modularity modelling of such systems with multi level and heterogeneous activities. Hierarchical CPNs have been proposed to answer to such modelling requirements. HCPNs make the modelling of distributed systems and different level of abstraction feasible. Similar to modular programming, HCPNs is composed of smaller CPNs (called subpage) that are represented in the upper net (called superpage) by *substitution transitions*. Due to space limitation, we invite the reader to refer to reference [15] and [16] to get more details about the CPNs and HCPNs formalism.

CPNs and HCPNs are used in a wide variety of application domains [17], for instance distributed systems [18], information systems, communication protocols, security protocols [19–21], data networks, security policy enforcement mechanisms [22], attack modeling [23], etc.

In [24], HCPNs verify and analyze Web Service Composition. CPNs have been also applied to model service dependencies as described in [25]. Authors model service privileges by CPN tokens. A dependency between two services will be

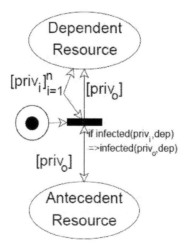

Fig. 1. CPN dependency [25]

then satisfied if and only if all the required privileges exist in the input places (the dependant service), see figure 1.

The resulting model represents both services and PEP without distinction; since authors confound service and PEP. This modeling approach has some drawbacks regarding the representation of the service and the policy enforcement capabilities of the monitored systems.

5 Service Dependency-Aware Policy Enforcement Framework

In this section, we first define the concepts that are deployed in the proposed framework. Then, we describe the main components of our proposed framework.

5.1 Definitions

Service. A service is an implementation of an interface which provides resources to its users. We define a service as a tuple composed of the following attributes:

- Name: the name identifying the service
- Service-ID: service identifier.
- Description: brief functional description of the service
- A-SD (Service Dependency) List: a list of the antecedent service(s) on which the service depends
- D-SD List: a list of the dependent service(s) which depend on the service

Attack and Threat Context. An attack is a potential malicious event detected by an IDS. Usually attacks are only discernible in terms of IDS alerts. In addition, this definition of attack makes it interchangeable with the IDS alert. Thus, we will not always explicitly state that an attack is represented by the alerts. We also assume that Intrusion Detection Systems and Alert Correlation techniques provide us with clear identification of the attack.

Each attack is characterized by the following attributes respecting the Intrusion Detection Message Exchange Format IDMEF [26]:

- CreateTime: The time when the attack is detected.
- Source: The source attribute includes information about the attacker. It can be a tuple of { IP address, Port, protocol }
- Target: The target includes information about the exploited entity. It can be a tuple of { IP address, Port, protocol, service, User }
- Classification: The attack type. Usually, it refers to the exploited vulnerability.
- Assessment: impact assessment, action, confidence.

Threat context are used referring to these alert attributes and respecting the Or-BAC formalism as described in [26]. For each detected attack, a new threat context is activated. Our proposed framework performs while considering this context.

Policy Enforcement Point. We define each PEP by the following attributes:

- Role Set (RS): The set of subjects that can be controlled and protected by the PEP. Referring to this set, we are able to identify if the PEP is capable to counter a detected threat with a specific enforcement action or not.
- Activity Set (AS): The set of activities that the PEP can analyze and mitigate in case of attack.
- View Set (VS): The set of objects that can be protected by the PEP.

We identify these sets referring to the configuration of the PEP. This latter is represented by the set of configured rules which are usually represented as follows:

$$rule : Conditions \rightarrow Decision(s) \qquad (1)$$

Decision(s) is an instance from the set of elementary decisions $\{d_1, d_2, d_3, \ldots, d_p\}$ when *Conditions* on Subject, Objects and Actions are satisfied.

5.2   Proposed Framework

Our proposed approach supports reasoning about the global optimality of a chosen set of responses and their application points (PEPs). Global optimality means that a response decision must take into account the fact that there exist dependencies between different services and different PEPs capable of enforcing the same mitigation decision.

In a first stage, we propose to extend the existing service dependency CPN model as described in [7, 12] by including a clear representation of policy enforcement mechanisms. In fact, we should be aware of the service architecture and its dependencies in order to explore possibilities to enforce the response decision at different points. Contrary to the approach proposed in [6, 7, 12, 25], we distinguish service components and a PEPs. By doing so, we give an explicit representation of PEPs in the service dependencies model as described in figure 2. In fact, in the existing Service Dependency model, the activation of a transition between two services is constrained by the existence of specific tokens as explained earlier. This hides the concrete and explicit presence of PEP in the service dependencies model. Thus, analyzing potential *attack paths* to a particular service while including the PEPs becomes challenging using such service dependencies framework. Therefore, we propose to deploy HCPNs by introducing the notion of substitution transitions to represent the PEPs. Figure 2 presents an overview of the proposed approach. Each substitution transition is mapped to a PEP capability as defined earlier by defining the ML functions using CPN tool.

6   Illustrative Example: Enforced E-Mail Application

To demonstrate the usability of our proposed framework, we consider the case of a simple network offering three main services: Webmail application, Internet Message Access Protocol (IMAP) and Post Office Protocol (POP). In order

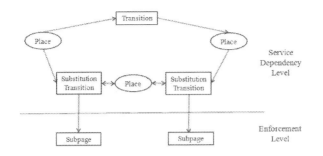

Fig. 2. Overview of the proposed Framework

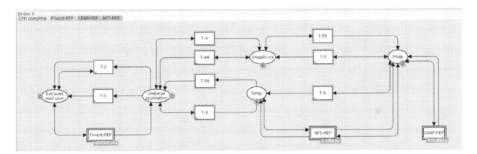

Fig. 3. Use Case: webmail application

to offer the e-mail service to the client, dependencies between webmail application, IMAP and POP services have to be satisfied. This is enforced by the
deployment of proper PEPs that are in our case: the LDAP (Lightweight Directory Access Protocol) server, the NFS (Network File System) and the Network
Firewall. The firewall monitors the access to the webmail server at the network
level. The LDAP controls access to user accounts and the NFS is capable to
control the access to the requested files. Each described PEP has its proper
access control capabilities that are mapped to appropriate functions in the substitution transitions (labelled boxes). We implement our framework using the
CPN Tools simulator, [27]. The use case is illustrated in Figure 3. Each PEP has
its corresponding subpage (referenced by labelled boxes: FW-PEP, LDAP-PEP
and NFS-PEP) which implement the capability functions. These functions support the security administrator in selecting the appropriate PEP by identifying
whether the PEP is capable to mitigate the detected attack.

7   Conclusions and Future Works

In this paper, we propose to integrate Policy Enforcement Point in the service dependencies model in a well presented framework. A significant benefit of

deploying HCPN in our proposed framework is to provide the security administrator with a clear representation of service dependencies and their interactions with Policy Enforcement Points. This support the administrator in detecting which security constraints are violated to access a set of dependent services. The proposed framework is capable to dynamically assist the response process in selecting the Policy Enforcement Points capable of applying dynamic response rules. At present, we are focusing on formally modeling and developing PEP capability functions in order to detect the most appropriate PEPs that are capable to mitigate a detected attacks.

Acknowledgement. The research leading to these results has received funding from the European Commission's Seventh Framework Programme (FP7/2007-2013) under grant agreement no. 257495, "Visual Analytic Representation of Large Datasets for Enhancing Network Security (VIS-SENSE)".

References

1. Hachem, N., Mustapha, Y.B., Granadillo, G.G., Debar, H.: Botnets: Lifecycle and Taxonomy. SAR-SSI (2011)
2. Gonzalez Granadillo, G., Débar, H., Jacob, G., Gaber, C., Achemlal, M.: Individual countermeasure selection based on the return on response investment index. In: Kotenko, I., Skormin, V. (eds.) MMM-ACNS 2012. LNCS, vol. 7531, pp. 156–170. Springer, Heidelberg (2012)
3. Stakhanova, N., Basu, S., Wong, J.: A Taxonomy of Intrusion Response Systems. Int. J. Inf. Comput. Secur. (2007)
4. Strasburg, C., Stakhanova, N., Basu, S., Wong, J.S.: Intrusion Response Cost Assessment Methodology. In: Proceedings of the 4th International Symposium on Information, Computer, and Communications Security. ACM (2009)
5. Hachem, N., Debar, H., Garcia-Alfaro, J.: HADEGA: A novel MPLS-based mitigation solution to handle network attacks. In: 2012 IEEE 31st International on Performance Computing and Communications Conference, IPCCC (2012)
6. Kheir, N., Debar, H., Cuppens-Boulahia, N., Cuppens, F., Viinikka, J.: Cost evaluation for intrusion response using dependency graphs. In: International Conference on Network and Service Security, N2S 2009 (2009)
7. Debar, H., Kheir, N., Cuppens-Boulahia, N., Cuppens, F.: Service Dependencies in Information Systems Security. In: International Conference on Mathematical Methods, Models, and Architectures for Computer Network Security (2010)
8. Boutaba, R., Polyrakis, A.: Towards Extensible Policy Enforcement Points. In: Sloman, M., Lobo, J., Lupu, E.C. (eds.) POLICY 2001. LNCS, vol. 1995, pp. 247–261. Springer, Heidelberg (2001)
9. eXtensible Access Control Markup Language (XACML) (2003), https://www.oasis-open.org/committees/download.php/2406/oasis-xacml-1.0.pdf
10. Zaborovsky, V., Mulukha, V., Silinenko, E.: Access Control Model and Algebra of Firewall Rules (2011)
11. Betarte, G., Gatto, A., Martinez, R., Zipitria, F.: ACTkit: A Framework for the Definition and Enforcement of Role, Content and Context-based Access Control Policies. IEEE Latin America Transactions (2012)

12. Kheir, N., Debar, H., Cuppens, F., Cuppens-Boulahia, N., Viinikka, J.: A Service Dependency Modelling Framework for Policy-based Response Enforcement. In: Flegel, U., Bruschi, D. (eds.) DIMVA 2009. LNCS, vol. 5587, pp. 176–195. Springer, Heidelberg (2009)
13. Albanese, M., Jajodia, S., Pugliese, A., Subrahmanian, V.S.: Scalable Analysis of Attack Scenarios. In: Atluri, V., Diaz, C. (eds.) ESORICS 2011. LNCS, vol. 6879, pp. 416–433. Springer, Heidelberg (2011)
14. Petri, C.A.: Communication with automata. Ph.D. dissertation, Darmstadt University of Technology (1962)
15. Jensen, K., Kristensen, L.M., Wells, L.: Coloured Petri Nets and CPN Tools for modelling and validation of concurrent systems. Int. J. Softw. Tools Technol. Transfer, 213–254 (2007)
16. Lakos, C.: From coloured petri nets to object petri nets (1995)
17. Gehlot, V., Nigro, C.: An Introduction to Systems Modeling and Simulation with Colored Petri Nets. In: Proceedings of the, Winter Simulation Conference (2010)
18. Lv, Y.Q., Lee, C.K.M.: Application of Hierarchical Colored Petri Net in Distributed Manufacturing Network. In: Proceedings of the 2010 IEEE IEEM (2010)
19. Long, S.: Analysis of Concurrent Security Protocols Using Colored Petri Nets. In: International Conference on Networking and Digital Society (2009)
20. Chen, Z., Chen, X.-W., Zhang, Z.-W.: IPSec Modeling Based Color Petri Nets. In: International Conference on Communications, Circuits and Systems Proceedings, vol. 3, pp. 1655–1659 (2009)
21. Xu, Y., Xie, X.: Modeling and analysis of security protocols using colored petri nets. Journal of Computers 3 (2011)
22. Ayachit, M.M., Xu, H.: A Petri Net Based XML Firewall Security Model for Web Services Invocation. In: Proceedings of the Iasted International Conference Communication, Network, and Information Security (October 2006)
23. Wu, R., Li, W., Huang, H.: An Attack Modeling Based on Hierarchical Colored Petri Nets. In: International Conference on Computer and Electrical Engineering (2008)
24. Yang, Y., Tan, Q., Xiao, Y.: Verifying Web Services Composition based on Hierarchical Colored Petri Nets. In: Proceedings of the first International Workshop on Interoperability of Heterogeneous Information Systems. ACM (2005)
25. Kheir, N., Cuppens-Boulahia, N., Cuppens, F., Debar, H.: A Service Dependency Model for Cost-Sensitive Intrusion Response. In: Gritzalis, D., Preneel, B., Theoharidou, M. (eds.) ESORICS 2010. LNCS, vol. 6345, pp. 626–642. Springer, Heidelberg (2010)
26. Debar, H., Curry, D., Feinstein, B.: The Intrusion Detection Message Exchange Format (IDMEF). RFC 4765, Internet Engineering Task Force (March 2007), http://www.ietf.org/rfc/rfc4765.txt
27. Vinter Ratzer, A., Wells, L., Lassen, H.M., Laursen, M., Qvortrup, J.F., Stissing, M.S., Westergaard, M., Christensen, S., Jensen, K.: CPN tools for editing, simulating, and analysing coloured petri nets. In: van der Aalst, W.M.P., Best, E. (eds.) ICATPN 2003. LNCS, vol. 2679, pp. 450–462. Springer, Heidelberg (2003)

Monitoring Information Leakage in a Web Browser

Nemisha Sharma[1], Swati Kare[1], Sanket Chichani[1], Vidhi Naredi[1],
Jyoti Nandimath[1], Arun Mishra[2], and Arati Dixit[2]

[1] Department of Computer Engineering, Shrimati Kashibai Navale College of Engineering,
Pune, India
[2] Department of Computer Engineering, Defence Institute of Advanced Technology,
Pune, India
{nemisha1991,kareswati,sanket.chichani08,vidhinaredi26,
jyoti.nandimath,adixit98}@gmail.com, arundoes@yahoo.co.in

Abstract. This paper outlines the potential problem of information leakage
between programs running inside a web browser. A program to which user's
information is voluntarily provided can leak it to other malicious programs;
likewise, a program may steal information from another program. A number of
ways through which such leakage may take place using the operating system's
inter process communication mechanism is listed. The proposed solution
includes a 'controller' that monitors all processes running in a browser for their
access to the kernel's services through system calls, intercepts and thwarts an
attempt at communication with another process.

Keywords: Web browser, confinement, inter process communication, system
call, leakage of data, security.

1   Introduction

Today, as the utilities of the web are growing, so are the attacks a user is prone to. A
person using the internet through a program called a '*web browser*' can be a subjected
to phishing attacks, malware, spoofing sites, password theft, SQL injection attacks
and so on. These attacks can be detected sooner or later, however, if a seemingly
harmless process covertly reads information meant for another process on the net, or
the target process itself is secretly communicating confidential information to
someone else, there will generally be no indication that the security of the data has
been compromised. To achieve such an unauthorized access to information, a cleverly
written program can be downloaded and run by a pop-up or some such miscellaneous
element in a browser, which will covertly read passwords, online banking information
etc. entered in a page form. In another case, a process having access to user's data
may leak it to any third party process which may request for it.

The problem of creating a controlled environment, in which a possibly
untrustworthy program may run safely, and may even be trapped as a result of trying
to leak information, has been termed as 'the confinement problem' in 'A Note on the
Confinement Problem' [1] by Lampson. A variety of work has been done in the field

Sabu M. Thampi et al. (Eds.): SSCC 2013, CCIS 377, pp. 322–329, 2013.

of confining applications, mainly consisting of identifying various covert and side channels, and creating secure environments within which untrusted programs are given restricted access to the system's resources, mainly the operating system and the file system. The key idea behind the latter is the Principle of Least Privilege, which ensures that the damage caused by a compromised application is limited by the restricted environment in which it executes. [2]

In this paper, however, we focus on the security of user's information supplied to a process running inside a web browser, and propose a system which will thwart attempts of passing such information on to unauthorized processes. In particular, we deal with the inter process communication facility provided by the operating system to enable communication between two processes on the same host. We observe that such a communication may take place between a process in the user's machine and a process residing on a different machine through a communication network, but an untrustworthy third party process may not necessarily be unwanted; we may want to navigate to some ads, play flash games or download some content featured in them, making it undesirable to restrict all traffic to and from unknown locations. This paper, therefore, deals with prohibiting communication using IPC between processes running on the same host.

2   Implementation

2.1   Overview

As a solution to the above discussed problem, we propose a 'controller' application which will execute in the background along with the web browser. The controller is responsible for monitoring all processes that execute within the browser for possible attempts at information leakage through IPC. In our implementation of the controller, we have intercepted the starting of the execution of every new process and forked a child that will be assigned the task of monitoring that process. Thus, the main body (the parent process) of the controller is devoted to listening for new processes, while the children are made to monitor every discovered process. Thus, multiple processes can execute, being simultaneously monitored. We have chosen the Linux operating system and Mozilla's Firefox web browser in our implementation.

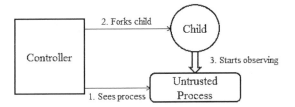

Fig. 1. Handling a new process

Assumptions. We List out the Underlying Assumptions for Our Solution:

- A process to which we voluntarily provide our confidential information, in this context, can be assumed to perform its task as advertised. For example, if one provides one's email address and password to a social networking site, hoping to find friends through mail contacts, it is assumed that one will succeed. In this sense, this authorized process can be called 'trusted'. However, there is no guarantee that this process may not leak, i.e. transmit to someone else the input data it received from the user. [1] We therefore assume that the so-called 'trusted' process, to which we provide our information, can itself be a partner in crime to unauthorized processes, which do not have explicit access to user's data. We must assume this because we cannot assume otherwise- as there will be generally be no indication if an authorized process leaks.
- Every process running within the browser is entirely self-sufficient, meaning it doesn't depend on any other process to do the task it advertises to do. This applies to both the main service processes of the website, and the miscellaneous processes that come attached with advertisements, pop-ups, etc. This assumption leads us to define the security policy for our confinement application- no two processes are allowed to communicate with each other using IPC.
- Processes with malicious intent may well be expected to keep trying the same system calls that will get them the information they desire. Keeping this in mind, we kill erring processes rather than letting them run.

Inter Process Communication. [3] IPC is the Transfer of Data among Processes Using Certain System Calls. We Have Studied Four Types of Inter Process Communication:

- Shared memory allows one block of memory to be shared by several processes such that when one process changes it, all other processes can see that modification, making it the fastest form of IPC. The system call shmget is used to allocate a shared memory segment. Its first argument is an integer key value that specifies which segment to create. If two or more processes agree upon a key value beforehand, they can use that pre-decided value to obtain access to the same memory segment, thus making it easy to exchange information amongst them. Also, knowing the segment identifier SHMID returned by shmget, a process may attach the segment for its own access using shmat. This information is readily available through the ipcs command.
- Mapped memory is similar to the above described shared memory, except that the block of memory is associated with a file in the file system. Once again, if an intruder knows the name of the file beforehand (provided the access permissions have been favorably set), confidential information can be read from it.
- Pipes allow sequential communication between related processes.
- A first-in, first-out file (FIFO) is a named pipe which allows communication between any two processes, i.e. the processes need not be related to each other. A FIFO is a pipe which is also associated with a file in the file system. For communicating, one process opens the FIFO file for writing, while the other opens it for reading.

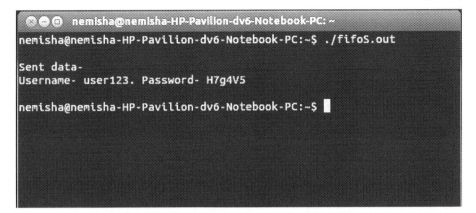

Fig. 2. A FIFO writer program sends out confidential information

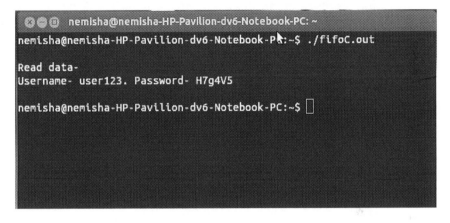

Fig. 3. A FIFO reader obtains the confidential information

2.2 Interception Mechanism

The core of our system is the interception of system calls and allowing or disallowing them based on whether they seek to facilitate communication between processes. We can intercept system calls before they are executed by doing static library interposing [4], binary editing [4], `ptrace` or the `/proc` virtual file system [2] [4]. The disadvantages of static library imposition are that applications cannot always be relinked to the interposed library, and applications can always bypass the interposed library by using the same `syscall` interface used by the library. [4] Binary editing is rejected because we cannot have a dynamically loaded library at runtime. [4] The confinement systems Janus [2] and Mapbox [4] use the `/proc` virtual file system which provides access running states and addresses spaces of each process running in the system.

Given our assumption that all processes are self-sufficient and do not need to communicate at all for their working, we keep our implementation basic, by disallowing all IPC calls. This can be well achieved by both `ptrace` and `/proc`.

However, due to our assumption we do not require the system call arguments, return values, information like signals and stack size etc. available with /proc. Plus, our plan of action for each IPC call is the same, and we do not require different call handlers to be registered for each call. Due to these reasons, we use the ptrace system call in our implementation. In the future, for more fine-grained control of processes, involving examining the arguments and return values of system calls, the /proc virtual file system would be a more efficient choice.

2.3   Flow of Control

The flow of control for one system call is shown below.

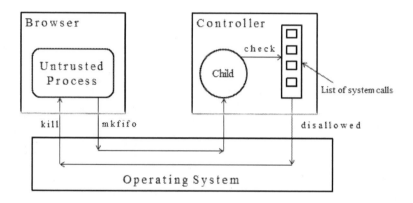

Fig. 4. Flow of control

We have shown that the controller runs along with the browser. For every process forked within the browser, the controller forks a child and supplies him with the process id of that process. The child lays in rest for the next system call to be made by the process. Suppose a process running within the browser makes an attempt to create a FIFO file. Once the mknod system call (used for FIFO) has been issued, the operating system alerts the responsible child and the child awakens to execution. The child identifies the system call identifier (SYS_mknod) from the contents of the EAX register of the process at the current time. It checks this identifier against a list of denied system calls. Upon finding it, it sends a kill signal to the process, and the process gets killed.

Using the ptrace system call, the child attaches itself to the running process. In effect, the observer actually becomes the traced process's parent and the result is as if the process has issued a ptrace call with PTRACE_ME to the OS. This allows the child to trace the process even though it is not really the parent of the process.

The ptrace system call intercepts the process both while its entry into and its exit from the kernel. To reduce the amount of overhead introduced while monitoring system calls, we ignore the intercepted exit of the process from the kernel and let it continue its working. Thus, the checking of the system call is only done during entry into the system call.

2.4   Usage

The necessary condition in the success of the controller is that it should start up along with the browser, so that it starts listening for system calls before any process gets a chance to execute them. To achieve this, we could create a bash wrapper script or an alias that starts the browser and the controller together. Both of these solutions require each user to individually perform the required steps, which is not desirable.

A more suitable solution incorporates using Firefox's *extension*, which is a type of browser 'add-on' that adds new features to Firefox or modifies existing functionality. Our implementation of the controller, which is a C program, can be wrapped inside an XPCOM Component, which is a cross-platform component object model, and deployed as an extension.

3   Results

To evaluate the success of our implementation, we wrote some 'intruder' programs which aim to communicate information to each other. For each form of IPC, we listed out some of the possible ways in which information can be leaked. Our list, though not exhaustive, shows that methods to leak information require the help of the same system calls for each form of IPC, and so the exact illegal method adopted to gain access to information is irrelevant.

Our implementation is capable of thwarting several leakage attacks at once. For each process, an observer child remains in memory only as long as the process exists. The interception of all system calls made by a process adds a non-trivial overhead to its working. By replacing the `ptrace` interception mechanism with the `/proc` virtual file system, callbacks can be registered on a per-syscall basis, [2] allowing the harmless calls to be executed without any overhead. Some processes that were waiting for information but did not attempt any forbidden system call (e.g. the FIFO reader) were left in an indefinite wait-state, as a result of which their observers were left waiting too. This needs to be prevented by implementing some sort of a timeout mechanism. The following figures show the execution of the FIFO writer process while the controller runs in the background:

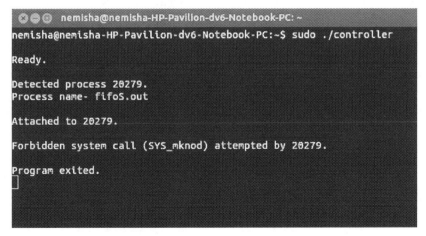

Fig. 5. The controller intercepts an attempt to create a FIFO file

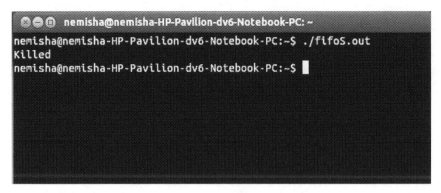

Fig. 6. The FIFO writer is killed for making the mknod system call

4   Related Work

The confinement problem was first defined and explored by Lampson in 'A Note on the Confinement Problem' [1]. He formulated the problem of protecting the confidentiality of information and identified a number of ways in which information can be leaked. Since then, quite a lot of work has been done in identifying and preventing covert and side channels. Wang and Lee identified covert and side channels due to processor architecture [5] and gave hardware solutions for them. Demme, et al. [6] devised a metric for measuring information leakage. Much of the research done in this field focused on confining programs that performed encryption.

The modern versions of the confinement problem include the protection of the system from attacks. Janus [1] was developed at Berkeley to provide a confined environment to untrusted helper applications spawned by browsers like Netscape. Janus uses its own language to write user-configurable policy modules. Mapbox [4] divides several applications into classes based on their behavior and provides a confined environment customized for each class. Deeds [7] develops a history-based access-control mechanism for mediating accesses from mobile code and uses it for Java. It maintains a selective history of accesses for an application and uses this information to grant or deny further access. These applications, though quite successful, say nothing about the confidentiality of user's information. In another approach called 'Proof Carrying Code' [8], Necula and Lee suggest a technique in which the producer of an untrusted code provides a proof that the code adheres to a predefined set of safety rules as chosen by the user. The user who runs the code can verify the proof at loadtime. However, this method is more suited in environments where these constraints on the code can be easily enforced. In a web application environment, such constraints are not feasible as they demand the entirety of web programs to be rewritten.

5 Conclusion

We conclude that seemingly harmless processes, which may escape firewalls and network security, can be used to steal confidential information being entered in the browser with little or no indication. We also show how the operating system's IPC mechanism can be used for this purpose. We list certain assumptions about processes running within a browser, using which we devise and implement a controller for preventing information leakage from the browser. Our implementation is capable of providing some assurance to the user that the data being given to a desired process will not be compromised.

References

1. Lampson, B.W.: A Note on the Confinement Problem. Communications of the ACM 16(10) (October 1973)
2. Wagner, D.A.: Janus: an approach for confinement of untrusted applications. University of California, Berkeley
3. Advanced Linux Programming, http://www.advancedlinuxprogramming.com/
4. Raje, M.: Behavior-based Confinement of Untrusted Applications. University of California, Santa Barbara
5. Wang, Z., Lee, R.B.: Covert and Side Channels due to Processor Architecture. In: 22nd Annual Computer Security Applications Conference, ACSAC (2006)
6. Demme, J., Martin, R., Waksman, A., Sethumadhavan, S.: Side Channel Vulnerability Factor. In: 39th Annual International Symposium on Computer Architecture, ISCA (2012)
7. Acharya, A., Edjlali, G., Choudary, V.: History Based Access Control for Mobile Code. In: Proceedings of the 5th ACM Conference on Computer and Communications Security (1998)
8. Necula, G., Lee, P.: Proof Carrying Code. IEEE Symposium on Security and Privacy (1997)

Securing Biometric Data with Visual Cryptography and Steganography

Deepak Aeloor and Amrita A. Manjrekar

Department of Technology, Shivaji University Kolhapur
deepakaeloor@gmail.com
aam_tech@unishivaji.ac.in

Abstract. Visual cryptography is the technique used to encrypt the data which is in the form of visual information such as images. Since the biometric templates stored in the database is usually in the form of images, the visual cryptography can be efficiently employed to encrypt the templates from attacks. The technique of steganography is used in combination to the visual cryptography for imparting additional security to biometric data. The biometric information such as the private face image is decomposed into two shares and stored in separate database tables such that the private image can be revealed only when both shares are simultaneously available. Each individual share is covered with a different image which is selected from a public host image database. The LSB steganography is applied to keep the user name and password hidden inside the final shares of visual cryptographic phase there by provides a mutually interconnected security mechanism.

Keywords: Visual Cryptography, Shares, Biometrics, face authentication, Steganography.

1   Introduction

The word biometrics is originated from two individual words such as 'bio' and metrics. 'Bio' means something that is related to life or living being and 'metric' refers to measurement. Thus biometrics can be defined as any type of calculation or measurement of living being based on their biological traits which can be either physical or behavioural characteristics. The application which most people associate with biometrics is security as a form of identification and access control. The biometric traits such as face, fingerprints, iris, gait and voice are most commonly used for verification of the identity of a person. The biometric form of human identification has several advantages over the password and PIN based methods. The person to be identified is required to be physically present at the time-of-identification. Identification based on biometric techniques obviates the need to remember a password or carry a token. The biometric system uses the concept of pattern recognition in which the physical appearance and behavioural characteristics pertaining to a human being is measured and computed for determining the authenticity. It is also used to identify individuals in groups that are under surveillance.

Sabu M. Thampi et al. (Eds.): SSCC 2013, CCIS 377, pp. 330–340, 2013.

A biometric system can be broadly classified into two categories based on the function. The first type is known as identification system which only performs the identification of a human being. The second type is the verification (authentication) system which identifies a user and matches the user with the previously stored data. Identification is a one to many relationships that can be used to determine a person's identity even without his knowledge or consent. On the other hand Verification is a One to One relationship that can be used to verify a person's identity.

Biometric authentication system consists of three main stages of operation. The first stage is the capture process which consists of acquiring raw biometric data from a subject (e.g., face image, finger print) by a sensing device such as a fingerprint scanner or video camera. The second phase of processing is to extract the features that are unique to the particular user from the biometric information gathered from the user. Next phase does the process of enrolment. During the enrolment phase a processed form of user details are stored. This processed information does not resemble the actual biometric data and are usually in the form of mathematical values or relations. These mathematical data are stored in a storage medium for future comparison during an authentication [1].

Biometric identifiers are the distinctive, measurable characteristics used to label and describe individuals. Biometric identifiers are often categorized as physiological versus behavioral characteristics. A physiological biometric considers the physical features of a human being such as one's voice, DNA, hand print or behavior. Behavioral biometrics is related to the behavior of a person, which consist of features such as typing rhythm, gait, gesture, facial expression and voice. Some researchers have coined the term behavior metrics to describe the latter class of biometrics.

A biometric authentication system can use several different features of a person which includes his physiology, chemistry or way of behaving. Out of all the available features pertaining to a person, the selection of any one of the trait or feature for the biometric computation is based on some basic properties that are required for that particular biometric trait. Some of the required properties are: **1) Universality:** refers that the biometric feature under consideration should be present in all the person who are using the system. **2) Uniqueness**: means the trait should be only one of its kind and should not be similar to others. **3) Permanence:** specifies that the biometric feature under consideration should remain permanent for that particular user and it should not be something that varies over time. That means a trait with 'good' permanence will be remains unchanged time. **4) Measurability (collectability):** relates to the easiness for acquiring a data and to undergo computation on the acquired data. The acquired data should also permit the extraction of the relevant feature sets. **5) Performance:** refers to the accuracy, speed, and robustness of the system when using a particular biometric trait. **6) Acceptability:** refers to how comfortable the users of a population are towards the use of a technology and the willingness to get their biometric trait captured and assessed. **7) Circumvention:** this property considers whether the trait can be imitated by un authorized user by using an artifact or substitute.

The main aim is to develop a biometric authentication system which uses the face image that helps to restrict the access to confidential data by unauthorized users along with giving security to the biometric templates by a combination of Visual cryptography and Steganography. While considering independently face recognition, visual cryptography and steganography are all known concepts. The combination of all the three types of security enhancing mechanisms are never tried before. This unique combination also results in synergic effect. With the availability of modern high performance hardware and latest software technologies, the security of any system can be easily breached and compromised. In such a situation the one and only one option which provides a higher degree of security is biometric authentication methods. Even if biometric authentication is capable to prevent the unauthorized access to the system, it does not guarantee that the authentic person can always access a system with ease even if an intruder modified or altered the secret database of the authentication system. The motivation behind this system is to avoid the problem of access denial to a genuine user by external attacks. To attain this goal the most common method of image encryption technique that is visual cryptography is employed together with the biometrics. This system results in adding security to the conventional face authentication systems.

In this paper, the concept of visual cryptography is explored for securing the privacy of biometric information such as face image by the creation of shares or transparencies out of the original image by performing decomposition of the image. The decomposed image or shares do not reveal any information about the original image. The information of the underlying image can be revealed only when both images are simultaneously available. During the enrolment process, the private biometric data is sent to a trusted third-party entity. Once the trusted entity receives it, the biometric data is decomposed into two images and the original data is discarded. The decomposed components are then transmitted and stored in two different database servers such that the identity of the private data is not revealed to either server. During the authentication process, the trusted entity sends a request to each server and the corresponding sheets are transmitted to it. Sheets are overlaid (i.e., superimposed) in order to reconstruct the private image thereby avoiding any complicated decryption and decoding computations that are used in watermarking steganography, or cryptosystem approaches. Once the matching score is computed, the reconstructed image is discarded. Further, cooperation between the two servers is essential in order to reconstruct the original biometric image.

2   Related Works

The security of a biometric system solely lies in the ability of the system to protect the biometric data and templates from external attacks and modifications. One technique that is used to avoid this unauthorized modification of biometric data is to use the concept of biometric watermarking [5]. The concept of watermarking is to introduces some extra information into the biometric feature templates which results in certain distortion to the images.. Two application scenarios in the context of iris recognition were introduced, for investigating the performance of the biometric recognition systems when the watermarking technique is introduced. They are namely, protection of iris images by watermarking them and protection of iris templates by hiding them in cover images as watermarks. The observation to this investigation was that the watermarking iris image does not introduce detectable decreases on iris recognition performance whereas in the case of severe attacks to the iris watermark, the recognition performance drops significantly.

The iris recognition is performed based on a mathematical and computational method called discrete cosine transform (DCT). It consists of calculating the differences of discrete cosine transform (DCT) coefficients of overlapped angular patches from the normalized iris image for the purpose of feature extraction [4].

Ratha *et al.*[6] explains several problems that are unique to biometric authentication systems and propose solutions to many of those problems. This paper mainly focuses on finger print recognition as a model but the concepts and solutions can be extended for the analysis of other biometric authentication methods. Methods are proposed for preserving the privacy of the individuals enrolled in the biometric database. Instead of the original biometric template, a transformed biometric template is stored in the database in this technique. This transformed biometric templates are known as a private template or a cancellable biometric. The transformation made by adding a series of noise pixels into the biometric template.

Davida *et al.*[7] introduced an idea for user identification schemes with the help of a secure offline authentication process, based on a biometric system that can measure a user's biometric accurately. This scheme wraps a biometric template with authorization information and thereby enhances the identification and authorization in secure applications. The compromising of private biometrics data of a user that is enclosed in the authorization information are minimized with the help of specially developed schemes without the use of secure hardware tokens. The scope and feasibility of using the biometrics for the development of high level applications are also studied.

A fast, accurate and robust algorithm is developed by using Active Appearance Model (AAM) concept which exhibits a efficient direct optimization technique that helps to match both shape and size simultaneously [8]. This method does not attempt to solve a general optimization problem each time to fit the model to a new image. Instead, it exploits the fact that the optimization problem is similar each time so that it can learn these similarities offline. Irrespective of the high dimensionality of the search spaces, this technique allows the rapid convergences to be found out. It also described a method of matching statistical models of appearance to images. The training set acts as a base for learning and understanding the set of model parameters, grey-level variations and control modes of shapes.

The Extended Visual Cryptography [9] is an enhanced version of traditional visual cryptographic technique developed by Moni Noar and Adi Shamir. This type of cryptography encodes a number of images resulting in shares and when the shares are stacked together, the hidden message or hidden image will appears without a trace of original images. As in normal visual cryptography, the extended visual cryptography does not require any type of complex computation for the decryption process. It can be done in ease with human visual system. This system takes three pictures as input and generates two shares which are in the form of clear images which correspond to two of the three input pictures. The third picture which is the secret image that has to be kept protected is reconstructed by overlapping the transparencies generated by printing the two output images. Basic visual cryptographic methods are capable of dealing only with grayscale or binary images where are the extended visual cryptography scheme is suitable for colored images. Extended visual cryptography improves the quality of the output images.

3   Proposed Work

With the availability of modern high performance hardware and latest software technologies, the security of any system can be easily breached and compromised. In such a situation the one and only one option which provides a higher degree of security is biometric authentication methods. Even if biometric authentication is capable to prevent the unauthorized access to the system, it does not guarantee that the authentic person can always access a system with ease even if an intruder modified or altered the secret database of the authentication system. To avoid this problem the most common method of image encryption technique that is visual cryptography is employed together with the biometrics.

3.1   Components of System

In this system, the biometric information of a user (i.e. face image) is decomposed into shares that do not reveal any information about the actual image. The actual image can be reconstructed only if the two shares are available at the same time and by performing overlapping of those shares. The project has three significant components.

Public Host Image Database: The public host image database is a collection of images that can be used to encrypt the shares generated out of the user's private face image. Instead of using a random set of images, the public host image database is usually populated with face images. Using of face images has several benefits as compared to random images [2]. The attributes such as age, gender, ethnicity, etc. of the private face images can be maintained in the host images and it results in keeping the clarity and visibility of the image generated after encryption process. When a host image is selected which does not matches with the features of the private face image, then it results in distortion of the generated image. The face images used in the host image database is usually of celebrities to host the private face database. Another benefit of the using face image in host image database is that with the help of a minimum number of face images, several private face images can be encrypted accurately. Using random images other than the face images as hosts may result in revealing the presence of a secret face. While decomposing the face image into random noise structures may be preferable, it can pique the interest of an eavesdropper by suggesting the existence of secret data.

Trusted Third Party Entity*:* The trusted third party is a component which is capable of performing both storing and decomposing of the image that has to be stored in the biometric database. The role of trusted third party is to simplify the role of encryption and decryption process. The trusted third party only processes the information and act as a medium between the external user and the database. The trusted third party does not act as a substitute to the encryption and decryption process. The encryption and decryption process are one the functions provided be trusted third party. The image which has to be stored in the database is taken either with a camera present along with the system or it is manually stored by capturing the image by an external digital camera at the time of enrollment phase. The enrollment phase also takes a user identification number, username and password from the user as present in conventional authentication systems. The image input in the previous step is temporarily stored in a database table until it gets encrypted in the next step. The image is decomposed into two different images or shares by visual cryptography and the initial image is discarded. Two face images stored in the host database are selected. The face image decomposed in the previous stage is encrypted pixel by pixel using the two host images selected from host database. The two shares are moved to two different database tables. During authentication phase the real time image of the person who claims authenticity is captured with the help of a camera (webcam). Other user specific details such as username, password and primary key are also gathered from the user in this phase. Base on the user identification number, the encrypted shares the trusted entity sends a request to each database tables. The corresponding sheets are transmitted to the third party entity. Sheets are overlaid (i.e., superimposed) to reconstruct the private image. At the same stage the actual hidden username password is also decrypted and cross matched with the new entry. Only if the three fields, User identification number, password and username is properly cross matching, then only the facial feature of new image is calculated and compared with the decrypted user image. Once the matching score is computed, the reconstructed image is discarded. If the image reconstructed is matching with the newly taken image, then authentication is provided to that particular user.

Steganographic Component: The system provides an added security by employing steganographic techniques. The commonly used Username and password system of authentication is modified in this method. Normally the username and password are stored as such in the database, here in this system the user name and password are kept hidden in the transparencies of face image generated in the previous stage. The reason for using steganography instead of other text encryption cryptographic methods is that to reduce the overall computational complexity. In this system an attacker will not be even able to recognize the correct transparencies that correspond to a particular user. In such a case the chance for an attacker to correctly get the two shares from different database and also able to properly retrieve the textual data kept in random pixels of the image is comparatively very less. This is done using LSB steganography technique.

3.2   Host Image Selection

In [2] the selection of compatible hosts is a tedious process which requires the calculation of transformation cost (T_c). The cost of aligning each image in the public dataset with the private image is computed as transformation cost (T_c). The smallest registration cost is computed after the costs are sorted in order to locate two host images, H_{s1} and H_{s2}. However, this method is a complex process and requires very high computational time. To avoid such unwanted complexity in the system the host images are selected randomly from the database and used for the encryption of the face images. The random selection of the face images from the host image database is such a way that there is a maximum similarity between the faces by computing the facial features of the user image and the host image. The system doesn't compare a single user image with all the images in the host database, but the randomly selected image is compared and can be changed by the trusted third party at the time of encryption. GEVCS is used to hide the secret image O in the two host images H_{s1} and H_{s2} resulting in two sheets denoted as, S_1 and S_2 respectively. The secret private image can be reconstructed by superimposing of S_1 and S_2. The reverses process of the pixel expansion is performed for retrieving the final target image that retains the original image size.

3.3   Working Algorithms for Facial Image Encryption

The sequence of steps followed for the encryption of a face image is summarized here. At first the private face image which has to be encrypted is entered into the system with the help of a camera attached to the system or by loading a digital image which is already stored in the system. Next select two face images from the public host image database. Selection of host image is done randomly or as desired by the trusted third party. After selecting two host images (H_{s1} H_{s2}) they are aligned with the face image O. In the next step the aligned host and private images are cropped to capture only the facial features. Then encrypt the facial image in host images H_{s1} and H_{s2}, using Grey-level extended visual cryptography scheme resulting in shares S_1 and S_2. The Grey level extended visual cryptography has different stages within it. Initially consider three pixels at a time, such that one pixel is from the secret image ant the remaining two pixels are from the host images. Divide the pixels into sub pixels using pixel expansion method. Determine the triplet t_1, t_2, and t_T, where t_1 and t_2 are the pixels in the share and t_T is the target pixel. t_T is the target pixel constructed by the combination of pixels t_1, and t_2, Construct the collection matrix C. C is a set of xm Boolean matrices where m is the pixel expansion. Select matrix B from C for encoding each pixel. Superimpose the shares S_1 and S2 to retrieve the actual secret face image.

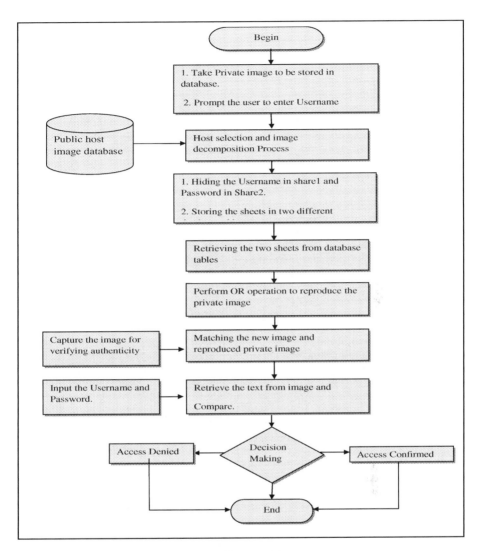

Fig. 1. Block diagram of the system

3.4   Working Algorithms for LSB Steganography

The principle of steganography is to hide one message within the other without modifying the actual message. Usually an image is used as the cover image and a text is used as the information to be hidden. The LSB [12] based steganography have five different steps. Firstly the cover image is read from the user and the text message which has to be hidden in the cover image. Secondly convert the text message into binary format. In the third step calculate the least significant bits of each pixels of the cover image. In the next step replace the least significant bits of the cover image with the each bit of secret message one by one. And finally write the steganographic image.

4   Results and Specifications

4.1   Face Detection

The system possesses two significant features during face detection. Efficient and robust frontal facial detection is the first one. That is whenever the facial features are not clearly focused by the camera then the face detection seems to be difficult. The second notable feature is the multiple face detection in an image. The system also supports head rotation, i.e. -30 to +30 degree in- plane rotation and -30 to +30 out of plane rotation. Some of the technical features of Face detection are specified in following table. Table.1. In facial feature detection, an array of 66 (x,y) co-ordinate of facial feature point is stored.

Table 1. Technical Specification of Face Detection

No	Feature	Measurement
1.	Detection Speed	241 Frames/ Sec (Depends on Resolution
2.	Real-Time Detection	0.0041 Secs (241 Frames /Sec with webcam resolution)
3.	Reliable Detection	0.267 Sec with Digicam resolution
4	No. of facial features	66 Facial features
5.	Facial features Time Detection	0.104 Sec (Not including face detection phase)
6.	Eye centre point detection	0.0064 Secs (Not including face detection stage)

4.2   Face Matching

Face matching compares two images with their facial features and the similarity level between the two images are returned. Some of the technical features of Face matching are specified in Table 2.

Table 2. Technical Specification of Face Matching

Sr. No.	Features	Measurement
1.	Enrolment Time	0.02 Sec (50 FPS with webcam resolution)
2.	Template Size	16 Kb
3.	Matching Speed	49700 faces/Sec

A set of images that are taken out of the IMM database are used for the computation of the performance of the system. The two reasons for selecting the IMM database is that the facial landmarks of individual images were annotated and available free of cost in internet. For the efficient working of AAM scheme these annotations were necessary. The IMM Face Database is an annotated database containing 6 face images each of 40 different people which includes both male and female. Out of the 6 images, randomly selected 3 frontal face images per subject were used in the experiments. In the following experiments, the match scores were generated using the Face.SDK. Table 3 shows the various False Acceptance Rate (FAR) and False Rejection Rate for some of Threshold (Similarity level) on a set of 6 facial images of 10 different individuals taken from IMM database.

Table 3. FAR and FRR for Common Similarity Levels

Threshold/ Similarity level	FAR	FRR
100	0 %	100 %
90	0 %	100 %
80	10%	90%
70	20%	80%

5   Conclusion

This paper explored the possibility of improving the security of the biometric systems by the encryption of the stored biometric templates. A similar set of procedures that includes cryptographic computations can be applied for other biometric traits also. In the case of fingerprints and iris templates, the decomposition of the templates using (2, 2) VCS results in two noise-like images, and the spatial arrangement of the pixels in these images varies from block to block. So it is difficult to recover the original template without accessing both the shares. The XOR operator is used to superimpose the two noisy images and fully recover the original template. In addition, the contribution of this paper includes a methodology to protect the privacy of a face database by decomposing an input private face image into two independent sheet images such that the private face image can be reconstructed only when both sheets are simultaneously available. The system follows a random mode selection of the host images that are likely to be compatible with the secret image based on geometry and appearance. GEVCS is then used to encrypt the private image in the selected host images. It is observed that the reconstructed images are similar to the original private image.

References

[1] Jain, A., Flynn, P., Ross, A.: Handbook of Biometrics. Springer, New York (2007)
[2] Ross, A., Otheman, A.: Visual cryptography for biometric privacy. IEEE Trans. Information forensic and Security 6(1) (March 2011)

[3] Naor, M., Shamir, A.: Visual cryptography. In: De Santis, A. (ed.) EUROCRYPT 1994. LNCS, vol. 950, pp. 1–12. Springer, Heidelberg (1995)

[4] Mulla, R., Amrita, M.: Iris Recognition Using DCT. In: Computational Intelligence and Information Technology, pp. 258–263. Springer

[5] Dong, J., Tan, T.: Effects of watermarking on iris recognition performance. In: Proc. 10th Int. Conf. Control, Automation, Robotics and Vision, pp. 1156–1161 (2008)

[6] Ratha, N., Connell, J., Bolle, R.: Enhancing security and privacy in biometrics -based authentication systems. IBM Syst. J. 40(3), 614–634 (2001)

[7] Davida, G.I., Frankel, Y., Matt, B.J.: On enabling secure applications through off-line biometric identification. In: Proc. IEEE Symp. Security and Privacy, pp. 148–157 (1998)

[8] Cootes, T., et al.: Active appearance models. IEEE Trans. Pattern Anal. Mach. Intell. 23(6), 681–685 (2001)

[9] Nakajima, M., Yamaguchi, Y.: Extended Visual Cryptography for Natural Images

[10] Jena, D., Jena, S.K.: A Novel Visual Cryptography Scheme. IEEE (2008)

[11] Incze, A.: Pixel Sieve Method of Visual Cryptography. In: Proc. IEEE Symp. Security and Privacy (March 2009)

[12] Marvel, L.M., Boncelet, C.G., Retter, C.T.: Spread Spectrum Image Steganography. IEEE Transaction on Image Processing 8(8) (August 1999)

Forensics Analysis of Sandboxie Artifacts

Deepak Gupta and B.M. Mehte

Institute of Development and Research in Banking Technology
Established by Reserve Bank of India
India
{GDeepak,BMMehtre}@idrbt.ac.in

Abstract. SandBox is an isolated environment nowadays being used as an anti-forensics tool by many (criminals) to perform malicious activity. The paper investigates the effectiveness of sandbox environment in widely used tool named as Sandboxie, and outline how to perform investigation when this tool is used to perform a criminal or illegal act. For the purpose of experimental investigation we have considered two test cases and several scenarios. In the first case we assumed that user simply used sandboxie and terminated it, while in second case we assumed the user also deleted the sandboxie contents after using it. In this investigation process, first common places where evidences are usually found in general scenarios are examined, and then other locations in local machine are examined using special forensics tools. Also the main/physical memory (RAM) is captured and examined for traces. Through these experiments we showed that no trails could be found in common places for any activity if a user deletes his sandboxie content. However, the complete isolation does not occur and some traces can be found into the main memory (RAM) as well as in unallocated clusters on the disks. This is a valuable evidence for digital investigator.

Keywords: Digital Forensics, Information Security, Digital Evidences, Anti-forensics.

1   Introduction

Nowadays people perform lots of activity on their windows machine like Files downloading, internet browsing, or creating/deleting file or executing some tools. The Windows is designed in such a fashion that it records and retains lots of information related to user activities. This includes Windows registry, Event logs, Deleted data, cache files and many more. These files are stored on local computer and it is an easy job for a (digital) forensics investigator to easily access and retrieve information during his investigation of suspect's activity.

In recent years however many anti-forensics tools and techniques are available to users to get rid of these traces and to dodge any digital investigation. Many free tools are available over internet, which provide a trace free environment to a criminal to carry out his malicious intent without leaving any data trails on his computer and *Sandboxie* is one such a tool that provides an isolate environment.

Sabu M. Thampi et al. (Eds.): SSCC 2013, CCIS 377, pp. 341–352, 2013.
© Springer-Verlag Berlin Heidelberg 2013

This paper aims to investigate the artifacts created/left by the activities done in Sandboxie environment and also outlines how to investigate when these activities have been used to perform criminal or illegal act. For investigation purpose, we considered different user activity scenarios and perform analysis on these scenarios. The paper assumes that the reader is known to the basic steps in forensics examination of a computer hard disk and will not cover in this process.

The rest of the paper is organized as follows. In section 2, we discuss literature review about sandbox environment and Sandboxie. In section 3 we discuss Methodology in which we discuss about the different scenarios included in experiment. Section 4 will discuss the analysis process and results. Then finally in section 5 analysis of results as well as conclusion is given.

2   Literature Review

Sandbox is an isolated environment initially used by software developers to test new programming code. But nowadays various software products like Sandboxie [1] create isolated environment to general users. So these tools allow various computer programs to run in an isolated environment and prevent them from making any permanent change to other programs and data in computer. Once sandbox is closed along with the program running within it, it'll automatically dump all the changes made by that program in such a manner that it is not reflected anywhere else in the computer. So by using sandbox environment one can avoid various traces like browsing history, cookies, cache, temporary files and many more.

Sandboxie is a sandbox-based isolation program developed by Ronen Tzur, for 32- and 64-bit Windows NT-based operating systems. It creates a sandbox-like isolated operating environment in which applications can run or installed without permanently modifying the local or mapped drive. The latest version by the time paper was written was 3.76 which were released on 16 December 2012. So if this program is really doing what it claims to be then users will have a great privacy while working on their computers. On the other hand cyber criminal can take advantage of this tool and use it to eliminate the traces of their illegal activities. This makes collection of artifacts very hard and futile exercise for a forensics investigator. Therefore we decided to conduct some tests that would provide a better understanding of this feature, the artifacts left by the use of it and how it could affect investigations in the digital forensics field.

In past couple of years, some paper have been published which used advance forensics analysis to discover evidences left by some anti-forensic techniques. Forensic analysis of private browsing artifacts [2] uses the RAM forensics to find traces of activities done in private browsing mode while [3] use the advance forensics to find out password of an encrypted volume by analyzing hibernation file. To the best of our knowledge nobody has addressed sandboxie issue so far. This is the first attempt to address such kind of anti-forensic tool by investigating the artifacts left by using sandboxie.

3   Methodology

This section describes test and analysis we conducted on Sandboxie including various scenarios. In order to perform the test, several hardware and software tools have been used. We used 2 windows machines with the same configuration for the experimental purpose. The following is the system configuration (list of all the hardware and software that are used).

- Hardware platform with CPU Intel Core i5-2430M, RAM 4 GB DDR3, hard disk SATA 500GB, running Microsoft Windows 7 Professional and NTFS file system.
- Sandboxie version 3.76
- Mozilla Firefox version 20.0
- FTK Imager Lite 3.1.1.8 for capturing physical memory, RAM.
- Hex Workshop 6.7 for analyzing RAM.
- Recuva version 1.45.858 for retrieving deleted files..
- Cache and History Viewers

First we installed Sandboxie and all other software mentioned above in both workstations and then started our tests considering following scenarios. In PC-1 we conducted the analysis just after the experiments while in PC-2 first we deleted the sandboxie content and then conducted the analysis. All the experiments were conducted in the sandboxie default box. Fig. 1 displays deletion of user content in sandboxie environment.

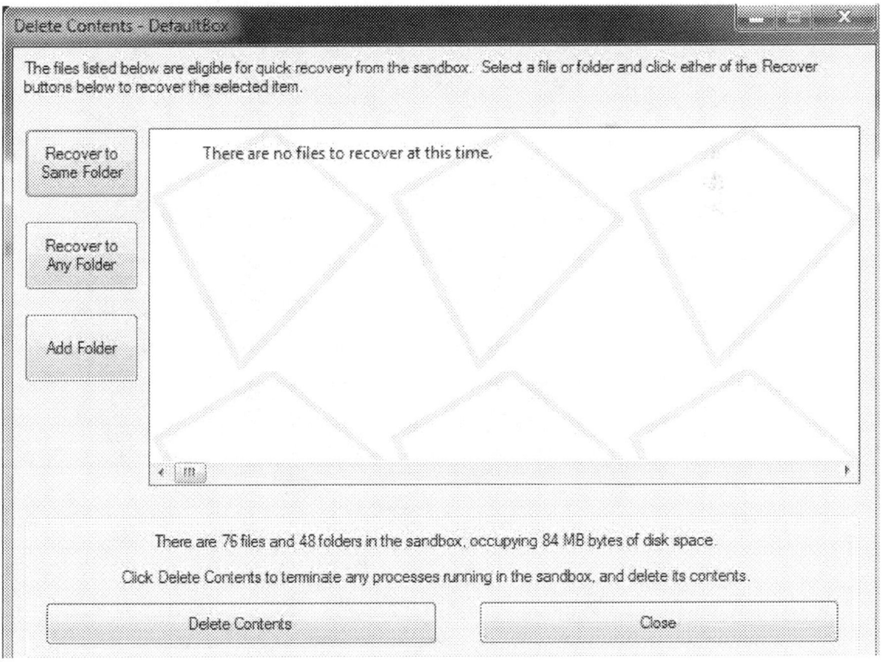

Fig. 1. Deleting contents of SandBoxie

3.1   Internet Browsing

First we made a small list of URLs and keywords to be entered in the web browser to replicate a user's browsing activity. These URLs and keywords were unique to ensure the accuracy of the test. Table 1 contains the list of the URLs and keywords we made to conduct this test.

Table 1. Unique URL, Keywords, Used in the Test

URLs	Keywords
astalavista.com	baadal – google.com
hackersonlineclub.com	urgrove – ask.com

Then the test was carried out by first opening Mozilla Firefox in sandbox environment and entering all these URLs in address bar and different keywords searched using different search engines. This was to emulate the behaviors of users in real life. Finally the browser was turned off along with the Sandboxie. Figs. 2, 3 illustrate some of the test performed.

Fig. 2. URLs entered in Firefox running in Sandboxie environment

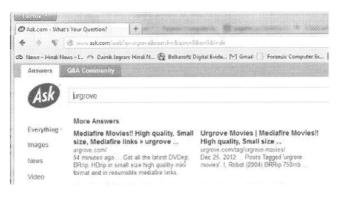

Fig. 3. Keywords in Firefox running in Sandboxie

3.2   File Creation

For this next scenario we started sandbox environment again and this time we created several files of different type in different drive. Table 2 contains the list of all files we created to conduct this experiment. Figs. 4 and 5 shows files created.

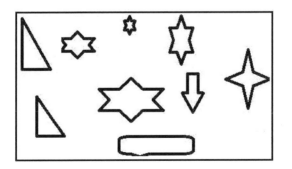

Fig. 4. Secret.txt

Fig. 5. Arc.bmp

Table 2. List of the files created

File Name	Type
Secret.txt	Notepad File
Arc.bmp	MS Paint File

After we created the files, we opened and modified them and closed with termination of Sandboxie. One we terminated the Sandboxie the files were automatically gone. After ending this session analysis was conducted again by capturing physical memory and analyzing it.

3.3   File Downloads

For this scenario we again open web browser in Sandboxie mode and downloaded some files from internet. The lists of files/tools downloaded along with their location are given in the Table 3.

Table 3. List of Files Downloaded

File Name	Location
Network_Security_assessment.pdf	Gmail attachment
sky_sunrays-wide.jpg	http://www.hdwallpapers.in

Once we download these files we opened them for once and then closed them along with terminating the sandboxie which causes us these downloaded files to be dumped. After this, we ended test by capturing physical memory and deleting content of sandboxie in PC2.

3.4   Software Installed/ Executed

Next thing we did was to intimate installing and execution of software in the sandboxie environment. For this we used BitTorrent in sandboxie and executed it for once. Finally we terminated the sandboxie and captured physical memory for analysis purpose. Fig. 6 shows the execution of BitTorrent in sandboxie environment.

Fig. 6. BitTorrent installed and executed in Sandboxie

4   Analysis and Results

This Section describes our findings from the tests and analysis we conducted on 2 different machines considering same scenarios. After conducting each test, and before conducting any analysis, we captured an image of physical memory using FTK Imager and set it aside. On PC-1 we examined common areas [2] [3] like registry analysis, AppData folder, and windows logs in computer to find out whether any traces of the test could be found. Then we found some pretty decent traces which are good digital evidences. While in PC-2, as we deleted sandboxie default box contents, so this basic analysis could not provide good results. So we moved to advance forensics analysis. For that we used Hex workshop to analyze captured physical memory and finally we used *Recuva* to retrieve the deleted data from unallocated clusters.

4.1   Analysis on PC-1

Through our analysis we came to know that sandboxie creates a folder named as "sandboxie" in primary disk drive and store all its configuration settings, files and related information in this folder. By investigation this folder we found that it creates different folders for each drive where it stores all files created in the sandboxie environment. All files we created in different disk drives during our experiment were found here. It also creates folder named as "AppData" in "user" folder, just like windows and stores user's data and settings. From this folder we were able to retrieve installation file of BitTorrent and browsing history of Firefox. Sandboxie also creates traces inside the windows registry under "HKEY_USER\Sandbox_Username_DefaultBox" where we found the traces of BitTorrent. So, in short, if a user doesn't have knowledge about working of sandboxie and he doesn't delete his content after using this tool, one can easily find traces of his activities.

But on the other hand if user deleted the content of his sandboxie using simple option provided within tool itself, none of the above discussed evidence will be found. Then we have to rely on advance forensics. Figs. 7, 8 show some of the results of our findings.

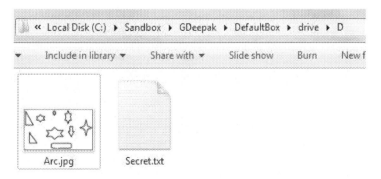

Fig. 7. Files found in "Sandbox" folder

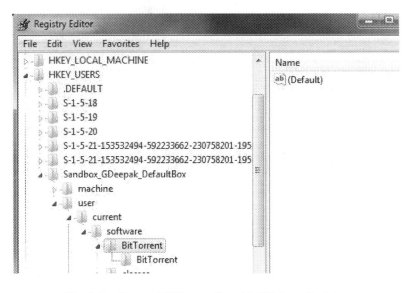

Fig. 8. Sandbox and BitTorrent Found in Windows Registry

4.2   Analysis on PC-2

Now in PC-2 as we deleted the sandbox content, still to be sure we started our analysis by examining common places for windows common artifacts, but no trace was found so we moved to advance forensics analysis.

4.2.1   Internet Browsing

During common area analysis, there were no traces of web browsing activity performed during sandboxie mode. We didn't find any URL or keywords we used during our test. Also no trace in "sandbox" folder was found. We moved to second step and started analyzing captured image of physical memory. We did a string search on all URLs and keywords used during our test. For example, there were 247 entries for the visited URL "**astalavist.com**", 131 entries for the queried keyword "**baadal**", we were also able to find blocks of HTML code that constructs web site we visited. Fig. 9 shows our findings in Physical memory and Table 4 displays summary of results.

0	1	2	3	4	5	6	7	8	9	A	0123456789A
25	32	46	77	77	77	2E	61	73	74	61	%2Fwww.asta
6C	61	76	69	73	74	61	2E	63	6F	6D	lavista.com
25	32	46	62	6F	75	6E	63	65	2E	70	%2Fbounce.p
68	70	25	33	46	73	69	74	65	25	33	hp%3Fsite%3
44	61	48	52	30	63	43	55	7A	51	53	DaHR0cCUzQS
55	79	52	69	55	79	52	6E	64	33	64	UyRiUyRnd3d
79	35	30	62	33	42	70	65	43	35	6A	y50b3BpeC5j

Fig. 9. "Astalavista.com" found in physiscal memory

Table 4. Summary of Internet Browsing Results

Analysis of Cache and Web history	Analysis of Physical Memory	Advance Analysis Results
No Trace of URLs & Keywords were found in the web browsing history	■ Many Traces were found ■ 247 entries for "astalavista.com" ■ 131 entries for "hackersonlineclub.com" ■ 32 entries for "baadal" ■ 12 entries for "urgrove"	■Some Mozilla Firefox ".squlite" file were retrieved from unallocated clusters that shows search history result for "Baadal"

4.2.2 File Creation

For this we started our analysis by examining common places like Windows registry, recent items, and Index.dat files, and as expected, no trace was found. Next we analyzed the Physical memory where we were able to find traces of the created files. Finally using *Recuva* we were able to retrieve these files from unallocated clusters. Figs 10, 11 display our findings of evidence and Table 5 displays summary of results.

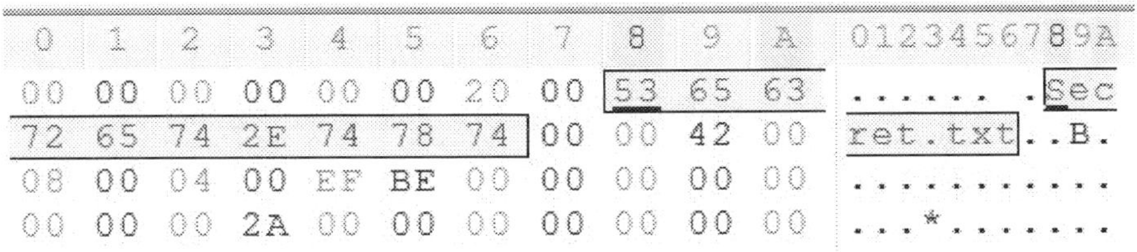

Fig. 10. "Secret.txt" Found in Physical Memory

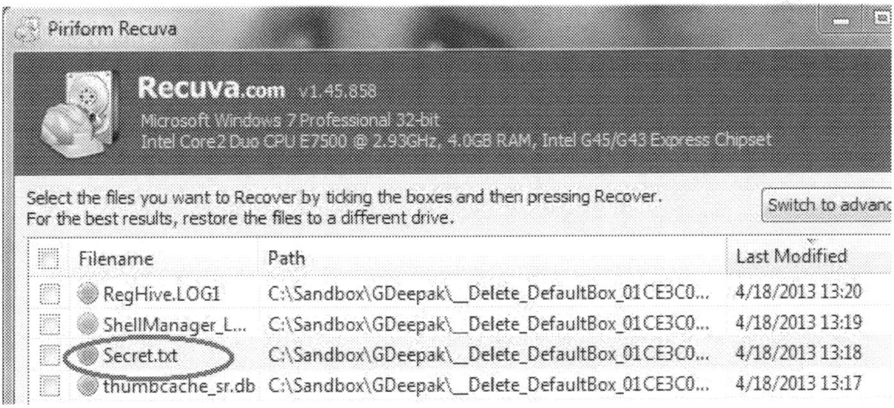

Fig. 11. "Secret.txt" recovered using Recuva

Table 5. Summary of File Creation Results

Analysis of Registry and other areas	Analysis of Physical Memory	Advance Analysis
- No Trace was found in common areas like Open- SaveMRU, LastVisitedMRU, Recent Files, Index.dat)	▪ 1 instance of "Secret.txt" was found ▪ 1 trace of "arc.bmp" was found	▪Both files were recovered from unallocated clusters using Recuva

4.2.3   File Download

To analyze traces of file download we followed the same approach. We started with examining common places like Windows registry, recent items files etc. As expected, no trace was found again. Next, we analyzed the Physical memory and this time unfortunately no traces were found in RAM that can relate us to downloaded files. Finally using advance forensics we were able to recover those files completely from deleted data with the help of *Recuva*. Fig. 12 shows our findings of evidence and table 6 displays summary of results.

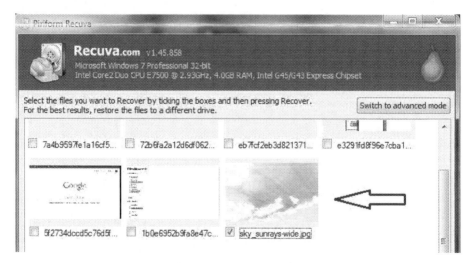

Fig. 12. "sky_sunrays-wide.jpg" recovered from deleted data

Table 6. Summary of File Download Trails

Analysis of Registry and other areas	Analysis of Physical Memory	Advance Analysis
▪ No Trace was found in common areas like OpenSaveMRU, LastVisitedMRU, Recent Files, Index.dat)	▪ No traces were found in physical memory	▪ Recovered both files from unallocated cluster

4.2.4   Software Installed/Executed

To find the traces of installed/executed software, the same approach as mentioned above was followed and as expected, common places didn't provide any significant results. While analyzing the RAM, unfortunately this time we got no traces. Finally performing advance forensics we were able to retrieve some "reghive.log" files from sandboxie folder that were related to registry entries created by Sandboxie, still we were not able to make quite significance out of them. Table 7 displays the summary of our analysis.

Table 7. Summary of Results

Analysis of Registry and other areas	Analysis of Physical Memory	Advance Analysis
▪ No traces were found to in common areas	▪ No traces were found in RAM	▪ We were able to retrieve "reghive.log" file but didn't make quite significance

5   Conclusion

Most of the activities performed using computer always leaves some Traces behind which can be a source of potential digital evidence in any investigation. However sandboxie isolated environment can prevent forensics investigators from finding these information when examining subject computers. This paper examined the artifacts that are left by performing various activities in sandboxie mode. Further experiments in this area should also include other tools which provide same features. Some other areas like super cookies, prefetch list, jump list, hibernation files can also be explored during the analysis. These all areas contain crucial artifact in normal scenarios and if looked examined deeply, can provide better insight.

The results mentioned in the previous sections suggest the level of isolation, privacy provided by sandboxie is sufficient for an average user. No trails could be found in common places for any activity if a user deletes his sandboxie content after use. So until and unless the user doesn't have advance knowledge in computer technology, he'll be not able to find any trace of activities performed in sandboxie isolated environment. However the complete isolation does not occur and sandboxie dumps significant amount of data into the main memory (RAM) as well as in unallocated clusters on the disks. So if sandboxie was used and computer is still running, there is high probability that data related to activities in sandboxie can be retrieved from RAM. And even if computer was turned off after sandboxie session, there are still chances that data could be retrieved from unallocated clusters. This could help forensic examiner while investigating a case where suspected activities were being performed using sandboxie.

References

1. Sandboxie, http://www.sandboxie.com
2. Said, H., Al Mutawa, N., Al Awadhi, I.: Forensic analysis of private browsing artifacts. In: International Conference on Innovations in Information Technology (IIT), pp. 197–202 (2011)
3. Mrdovic, S., Huseinovic, A.: Forensic analysis of encrypted volumes using hibernation file. In: 19th Telecommunications Forum (TELFOR), pp. 1277–1280 (2011)
4. Junghoon Oha, J., Leeb, S., Leea, S.: Advanced evidence collection and analysis of web browser activity. Digital Investigation 8(suppl.), 62–70 (2011)
5. Carvey, H.: The Windows Registry as a forensic resource. Digital Investigations 2(3), 201–205 (2005)

An Improved Secure Communication Scheme Using Adaptive Parameter Synchronization

Arti Dwivedi[1,2,*], Ashok K. Mittal[1], and Suneet Dwivedi[2]

[1] Physics Department, University of Allahabad, Allahabad, UP 211002, India
[2] K Banerjee Centre of Atmospheric and Ocean Studies, University of Allahabad,
Allahabad, UP 211002, India
arti2dwivedi@gmail.com

Abstract. An improved secure communication scheme based on adaptive parameter synchronization of the Rossler systems is proposed. Some additive parameters are introduced, which are used for chaos shift keying. It is shown that the synchronization time scale can be made much smaller than the chaotic oscillation time scale of the transmitting oscillator. The advantages of a communication scheme based on this rapid synchronization are analytic simplicity, rapid parameter convergence leading to greater speed of communication, avoidance of chaotic fluctuations in the parameters before convergence, and enhanced security. These advantages are demonstrated by comparison with a similar communication scheme having synchronization time greater than the chaotic oscillation time scale.

Keywords: Chaotic systems, Adaptive synchronization, Parameter estimation, Secure communication, Return map.

1 Introduction

The idea of synchronizing two identical chaotic systems and its use for secure communication was introduced by Pecora and Carroll [1-2]. Chaotic variables can be used as carriers of secure messages because they are noise-like. They can easily hide the messages they carry. A b*ona-fide* recipient, who knows the details of the transmitting chaotic system, but not the initial values used, can use synchronization to recover the message. Several approaches for encoding and decoding messages using chaos synchronization have been suggested [3-10]. The early approaches required the recipient to have a precise knowledge of the transmitting parameters [3-4]. Later, parameter adaptation schemes were introduced, in which the receiving system incorporated suitably chosen parameter adaptation laws, so that the receiver parameters also converged to the transmitter parameters along with synchronization of the chaotic variables [5-6]. This allowed coding a message by chaos shift keying, in which a transmitter parameter is switched between two different parameter values to code a binary message [7-9].

There are three time-scales involved in digital communication which is based chaos shift keying and chaotic synchronization: (i) T_c, the average oscillation time of

---

* Corresponding author.

Sabu M. Thampi et al. (Eds.): SSCC 2013, CCIS 377, pp. 353–365, 2013.
© Springer-Verlag Berlin Heidelberg 2013

the chaotic master system, (ii) T_s the time in which the transmitter and receiver systems synchronize and (iii) T_d, the bit duration time, for which a parameter value is held constant at a value representing a specific symbol in the message. If synchronization has to be used for decoding of digital messages, clearly T_d cannot be less than T_s. A perusal of the literature shows that typically $T_s > T_c$ This obviously limits the speed of information transmission. Moreover, as the system parameters are held constant for a long time, an intruder can identify the distinct attractors corresponding to the different parameter values, for example, by using return maps [10]. This weakness can be removed if the bit duration time, T_d, is made much less than the typical chaotic time scale, T_c. In this case, any portion, of the intercepted signal, that corresponds to a bit i.e., the time for which the parameters of the transmitting system are held constant, would be too small to reveal any property of the corresponding attractor or any pattern that can help an intruder decode a message. In Section 2, we show how T_d can be made much less than T_c using synchronization based on adaptation of receiver parameters to additive coding parameters of the transmitter. In Section 3, we describe in detail the encoding-decoding scheme that uses multi-parameter adaptation for transmitting several messages in parallel. In Section 4, we discuss the advantages of our approach, comparing it with a recently published [6] communication scheme. Conclusions are summarized in Section 5.

2   Rapid Synchronization Based on Parameter Adaptation

The Rossler system was designed so that its attractor was chaotic, like the Lorenz attractor, but was easier to analyze. The variables in this system are dimensionless and do not have any physical definition. However, electronic systems can be designed to provide physical realizations of this system.   Several studies [11-15] have used Rossler systems for synchronization and secure communication.

A parameter adaptation scheme for synchronization of two Rossler systems was discussed in [6]. The drive system was governed by the Equations

$$\dot{x}_1 = -x_2 - x_3$$
$$\dot{x}_2 = x_1 + p_1 x_2 + p_2 \tag{1}$$
$$\dot{x}_3 = 0.2 + x_3(x_1 - 7)$$

with $p_1 = 0.2$ and $p_2 = 0$. The slave system was a similar Rossler system, with a coupling term and with parameter adaptation rules governed by:

$$\dot{y}_1 = -y_2 - y_3$$
$$\dot{y}_2 = y_1 + q_1 y_2 + q_2 + \varepsilon_2(y_2 - x_2)$$
$$\dot{y}_3 = 0.2 + y_3(y_1 - 7)$$
$$\dot{\varepsilon}_2 = -\gamma_2(y_2 - x_2)^2 \tag{2}$$
$$\dot{q}_1 = -\delta_1 y_2(y_2 - x_2)$$
$$\dot{q}_2 = -\delta_2(y_2 - x_2)$$

where $\gamma_2 = 20$, $\delta_1 = \delta_2 = 2$. It was assumed that the receiver has no knowledge of the parameters p_i, so they were replaced by unknown parameters q_i, which were governed by suitably chosen adaptation laws in the receiver system, so that the receiver parameters q_i converged to the transmitter parameters p_i.

In the above reference, two binary messages were coded at the transmitting end by switching the parameter p_1 between the values 0.2 and 0.3 and the parameter p_2 between values 0 and 0.2 depending on the bit value of the messages. At the receiving end, parameter convergence was used to simultaneously recover the two messages. As in other prevailing chaos based communication schemes, the bit duration time, T_d, was much larger than the chaotic oscillation time T_c.

It will be advantageous to make T_d less than T_c, for two reasons: (i) the transmission speed will increase and (ii) the transmitted chaotic variables will correspond to a symbol of the message for a very short time and therefore different instances of the same symbol will give rise to different portions of the attractor, making it very difficult for an intruder to decode the different symbols.

In order to make T_d less than T_c, it is necessary to make the synchronization time T_s less than T_c. Synchronization takes place only if the solutions of the synchronization error Equations converge to the null solution. The synchronization error Equations are obtained by subtracting the transmitter Equations from the receiver Equations. These Equations, in general, have coefficients which depend on the chaotic variables. Therefore the instantaneous error growth rate depends on the chaotic variables. As the chaotic variables fluctuate wildly, the instantaneous error growth rate will also fluctuate wildly. Over time scales greater than the chaotic oscillation time, T_c, the chaotic variables traverse a substantial portion of the chaotic attractor. So the average growth rate over such time scales becomes independent of the instantaneous values of the chaotic variables. When, on an average, the growth rate is negative, synchronization takes place.

However, over time scales much smaller than the chaotic oscillation time T_c, the average error growth rate depends on the values that the chaotic variables take over this time scale. Therefore, when the error equations have coefficients which depend on the chaotic variables, it is difficult, if not impossible, to ensure synchronization in this small time interval, independent of the values of the chaotic variables during this interval. There will be short intervals of time during which the errors will increase, even as the errors vanish over a long period of time. It follows that if the coefficients of the synchronization error Equations depends on chaotic variables, the synchronization time, Ts has to be larger than the chaotic oscillation time, T_c.

On the other hand, if the error equations do not have coefficients which depend on the chaotic variables, the error growth rate will also not depend on the chaotic variables. In this case, it is easy to make the errors vanishingly small in short time intervals. Thus synchronization can be achieved in time much less than the chaotic oscillation time, T_c.

In view of the above arguments, we make modifications in the transmitting and receiving systems discussed in [6] so that the resulting synchronization error equations are linear with constant coefficients. Instead of (1), we consider the transmitter system governed by the Equations

$$\dot{x}_1 = -x_2 - x_3 + R_1$$
$$\dot{x}_2 = x_1 + 0.2x_2 + R_2 \tag{3}$$
$$\dot{x}_3 = 0.2 + x_3(x_1 - 7) + R_3$$

Here all the variables are dimensionless and have no units. The additive parameters R_i can be varied to code the secret message that needs to be conveyed. The receiver system is governed by a similar system, with unknown parameters denoted by R_1 ', R_2 ', R_3 ' modified by an appropriately chosen control system and laws for parameter adaptation. These parameters are assigned arbitrary initial values. Although the receiver system has no knowledge of the transmitter system parameters, it synchronizes with the transmitter, and the receiver parameter values rapidly converge to the corresponding values of the transmitter parameters.

To design the control system, the receiver system

$$\dot{y}_1 = -y_2 - y_3 + R_1 ' + u_1$$
$$\dot{y}_2 = y_1 + 0.2y_2 + R_2 ' + u_2 \tag{4}$$
$$\dot{y}_3 = 0.2 + y_3(y_1 - 7) + R_3 ' + u_3$$

is considered, where the controllers u_1, u_2, u_3 are allowed to be functions of the transmitter and receiver variables and of the receiver parameters , but not of the transmitter coding parameters. Then the synchronization errors are governed by the Equations

$$\dot{e}_1 = -e_2 - e_3 + e_{R_1} + u_1$$
$$\dot{e}_2 = e_1 + 0.2e_2 + e_{R_2} + u_2 \tag{5}$$
$$\dot{e}_3 = y_3 y_1 - x_3 x_1 - 7e_3 + e_{R_3} + u_3$$

where $e_i = y_i - x_i, e_{R_i} = R_i ' - R_i, i = 1, 2, 3$

One way of doing this is to find a Lyapunov function V, which is a positive definite function of the errors, whose time derivative is negative definite. We consider a test Lyapunov function $V = \dfrac{1}{2}\displaystyle\sum_{i=1}^{3}(e_i^2 + e_{R_i}^2)$ such that $\dot{V} = \displaystyle\sum_{i=1}^{3}(e_i\dot{e}_i + e_{R_i}\dot{e}_{R_i})$ is negative definite. A possible choice that gives rise to convergence is

$$u_1 = -pe_1$$
$$u_2 = -(0.2 + p)e_2$$
$$u_3 = e_1 + (7 - p)e_3 - y_1 y_3 + x_1 x_3$$
$$\dot{R}_1 ' = -e_1 \tag{6}$$
$$\dot{R}_2 ' = -e_2$$
$$\dot{R}_3 ' = -e_3$$

where $p > 0$. With this choice we get

$$\dot{e}_1 = -pe_1 - e_2 - e_3 + e_{R_1}$$
$$\dot{e}_2 = e_1 - pe_2 + e_{R_2}$$
$$\dot{e}_3 = e_1 - pe_3 + e_{R_3}$$
$$\dot{R}_1' = \dot{e}_{R_1} = -se_1 \tag{7}$$
$$\dot{R}_2' = \dot{e}_{R_2} = -se_2$$
$$\dot{R}_3' = \dot{e}_{R_3} = -se_3$$

Therefore, $\dot{V} = -p(e_1^2 + e_2^2 + e_3^2)$. The controllers and the parameter evolution laws were chosen, so as to make the error equations linear with constant coefficients. The system of Equations (7) can be expressed as a matrix Equation $\dot{e} = Le$. We have introduced here (a large positive) scale factor s in the parameter convergence law to increase the rate of synchronization. We choose the values $p = 80$, $s = 1600$ and find that the eigenvalues of the matrix L are: -45.3 ± 6.05i, -34.7 ± 4.63i, -40, -40. The system (7) has a globally stable equilibrium solution $e_1 = e_2 = e_3 = e_{R1} = e_{R2} = e_{R3} = 0$ because the real part of every eigenvalue of L is negative. Thus the controlled receiver governed by Equations (4) and (6) synchronizes with the transmitter system (3) and the additive parameters R_1', R_2', R_3' converge to the parameters R_1, R_2, R_3 respectively. Because of the rapid and smooth parameter convergence, it is possible to choose a large number of closely spaced values of the parameters R_i, for coding the messages. Thus the message may be coded using a larger number of symbols thereby decreasing the time required for transmitting the same information. As the separation, between successive values in the parameter set R_1, R_2, R_3 used for coding, can be chosen to be relatively small, the attractors for different parameter values are not visibly different, making it even more difficult for an intruder to infer the message.

3   Encoding-Decoding Messages by Multiparameter Adaptation

For communication of three digital messages $\{C_i(n)\}$, $i = 1, 2, 3$ where $C_i(n)$ denotes the nth symbol of the ith message and belongs to the set of p integers $\{0, 1, 2 \ldots\ldots\ldots,(p-1)\}$, the additive parameters R_i encode the digital messages according to the rule $R_i(t) = R_{i0} + 2C_i(n)\Delta R_i$ for $nT_d < t < (n+1)T_d$ where we have chosen $R_{10} = 0.5$, $R_{20} = 1.5$, $R_{30} = 1$, $\Delta R = 0.025$ and $p = 10$. The coding parameter values are held constant for time T_d before changing their values according to the next symbols of the messages. Before transmitting the actual message, pre-agreed header symbols are transmitted for the time $0 < t < T_d$. Receiver parameter values are maintained identical to the transmitter parameter values and the parameter evolution laws are suspended during this period. If this is not done, large initial synchronization errors would cause the receiver parameters to assume unacceptably large negative values before synchronization and the synchronization time would also be relatively large.

To recover the message at the receiving end, the recipient defines $\tilde{C}_i'(t) = \{R_i'(t) - R_{i0}\} / (2\Delta R)$ and decodes the nth symbol of the ith message as the integral value nearest to $\tilde{C}_i'((n+1)T_d)$. A small value of T_d can be chosen as one does not need to wait for nearly complete synchronization for decoding a transmitted symbol. Using this approach an error free message can be communicated with switching time T_d as small as 0.15 (Fig 1). The pre-agreed header bit '0' is transmitted by holding the parameters R_i constant at the values R_{i0} during the time $0 < t < T_d$. During this time the receiver parameters are also held constant at the values R_{i0}, while the parameter evolution laws remain suspended.

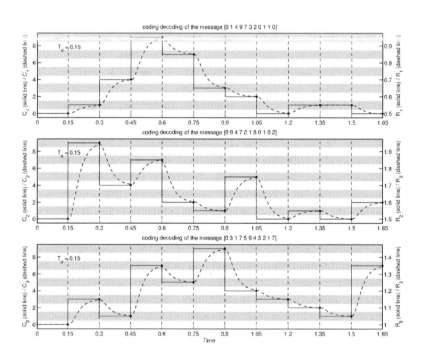

Fig. 1. Plot showing simultaneous decoding of three decimal messages with bit duration time 0.15. The solid lines represent the digital messages transmitted and also show the value of the coding parameters R_i at time t. The dashed curves show the values of the corresponding receiver parameters R'_i at time t. The message is decoded by observing R_i' only at integer multiples of bit duration time T_d and approximating the corresponding C_i' by the nearest integer.

In Fig 1, the solid lines represent the transmitted message. The left vertical axis reads the message symbols C_i and the corresponding coding parameters R_i at time t. The curved dashed lines represent the corresponding receiver parameters R_i' at time t. The message is decoded by observing these parameters at integral multiples of bit duration time T_d (as indicated by dashed vertical lines), reading the corresponding C_i' values on the left vertical axis and taking the nearest integer approximation as the decoded value. The shaded bands provide a simple representation of this process.

It is not possible for an intruder to obtain the master Equations, or infer any characteristic of different attractors, from the transmitted variables, because the parameters change values in a time, $T_d = 0.15$, which is much smaller than the average oscillation time period $(T_c = 6.15 \pm 0.11)$ of the transmitter system. Smooth convergence allows a very large number of closely spaced parameters to be used for coding a large set of symbols, further enhancing the security and simultaneously increasing the information transmission rate. The number of parameter values that are used for coding a message is very large and decoding is done by choosing the nearest allowed parameter at specific times. The intruder does not have the information about the number of parameters used in coding and the switching time. All these features combine to make it very difficult for an intruder to decode the message.

4 Advantages of Small Synchronization Time

Rapid synchronization allows small switching time and therefore high communication speed. Smooth synchronization allows the possibility of using closer parameter values for switching. This increases the rate at which information can be communicated. When the switching time is small compared to the chaotic oscillation time scale, parameter values change very rapidly and only a very small portion of the attractor is traversed during the time a parameter is held constant. This makes it very difficult for an intruder to identify the different attractors corresponding to the different parameter values used. Moreover, an intruder does not have the information about the number of parameters used in coding and about the switching time, making unauthorized decoding even more difficult.

We discuss these advantages by comparing the proposed scheme with that of [6]. Both schemes apply parameter adaptation to synchronize Rossler systems. However, for the decoding scheme in [6], the bit duration time was 100, which is much larger than the average oscillation time of the master system. For a given decoding scheme, the decoding accuracy will improve if the bit duration time is increased and if the separation between parameter values used for coding is increased. The transmission speed increases if the bit duration time is decreased. Also more symbols can be used for coding if the parameter separation is reduced. Therefore, one has to seek the smallest bit duration time and the smallest parameter separation that permit correct decoding. Fig 2 shows that for the decoding scheme of [6], even for a value of T_d as large as 15 and level separation of 0.2 in p_1 and 0.5 in p_2, the messages are not correctly decoded. It is necessary to increase these values to get error-free decoding.

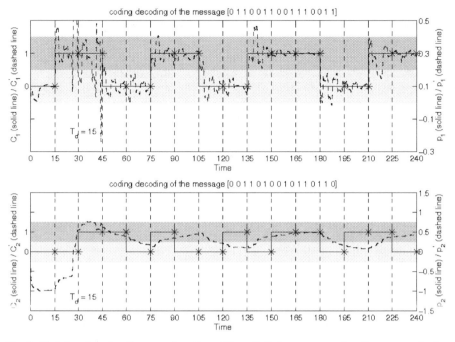

Fig. 2. Plot showing simultaneous decoding of two digital messages using the communication scheme of [6] with bit duration time 15. The piece-wise constant functions represent the digital messages transmitted and also show the value of the coding parameters p_i at time t. The dashed curves show the values of the corresponding receiver parameters p'_i at time t.

Further, because of the fluctuations, it is not possible to decode messages by observing the parameter values at fixed time intervals. It will be necessary to use filtering before decoding. Even then the decoding will have errors as is evident form the figure.

In comparison, for our scheme, $T_d = 0.15$, so that the symbol transmission rate is at least 100 times greater than that possible by the encoding-decoding scheme of [6]. Moreover the level separation between parameters used for coding is 0.05. So it is possible to use many more symbols for coding messages further increasing the information transmission rate several folds. Further, because the parameter variation is smooth, only observation of the parameter values at fixed time intervals suffices to decode the message; no elaborate filtering is necessary,

Fig 2 shows wild fluctuations on time scales smaller than T_c, Thus T_d has to be larger than T_{c}. This is typically the case, if the coefficients of the error Equations in [6] contain chaotic variables. For different short time durations, the Error equations would vary greatly, depending on the values that the chaotic coefficients may take during these time durations, causing different error growth rates for different durations. In other words, for rapid synchronization, it is not sufficient to make the maximum global Lyapunov exponent have a large negative value, it is also necessary that all local Lyapunov exponents have large negative values. It is difficult, if not impossible, to ensure this. In [6] it is stated that by increasing the value of γ_2 in their paper, the synchronization time can be decreased. However, we have found that it is not possible to significantly reduce the synchronization time by this technique. Thus the bit duration time, T_d, is necessarily much larger than the chaotic oscillation time T_c, of the transmitter.

In our scheme, the synchronization error Equations are linear with constant coefficients. The instantaneous error decay rate is constant independent of the instantaneous values of the chaotic variables. It can be made as large as desired by changing the parameters in the adaptive and control terms of the receiver equations. In this way, the synchronization time, T_s, can be made much smaller than the chaotic oscillation time, T_c. Convergence of the variable parameters in the receiving system can be made rapid and smooth. This allows the use of closer and more numerous parameter values for coding compared to the scheme in [6]. Moreover, it greatly enhances the security of the transmission, because the chaotic system switches from one attractor to another much before it traverses a significant part of any attractor. This precludes the possibility of an intruder identifying the message by applying the return map technique [10] or any other technique based on distinguishing between the attractors corresponding to different parameters.

Perez and Cerdiera [10] demonstrated how a return map technique can be used by an intruder to decipher a message. In this technique, a return map is constructed from the intercepted signal. The n'^{th} local maxima and minima, of the intercepted signal are denoted by X_n and Y_n. A graph is plotted between $A_n = (X_n + Y_n)/2$ and $B_n = (X_n - Y_n)$. In the absence of parameter switching, this map consists of a few branches, each branch appears to be a quasi-curve. When a parameter value is switched, each branch shifts laterally by a small amount. When the bit duration time, T_d, is large compared to the chaotic oscillation time scale, T_c, several succeeding local maxima and minima are found during one bit duration time. The corresponding points on the return map fall on only one of the two slightly separated quasi-curves. This allows identification of each quasi-curve with one of the bits. As several successive maxima and minima correspond to the same bit, it is possible for an intruder to decipher the message. This technique fails if the bit duration time is small compared to the chaotic oscillation time. We demonstrate this by comparing the return maps for the scheme of [6] with the scheme proposed in this paper. The two cases are the same in all respects, except the bit duration time, T_d..

In Fig 3 we plot the return map as described in [10] for the system governed by eqn (1) with parameter $p_1 = 0.2$ while the parameter p_2 is switched between the values 0 and 0.2, according to the bit value of the message to be communicated, with a bit duration time of 100. In Fig 4, the return map is plotted for the system described by eqn (3) with parameters R_1 and R_3 equal to zero, whereas the parameter R_2 is switched between the values 0 and 0.2, with bit duration time 0.15. The signals intercepted (x variable) by an intruder in the two cases differ only in regard to the bit duration time, everything else is identical. It is seen that the return map of figure 3 consists of two distinct quasi-curves, corresponding to the two different parameter values used in chaos shift keying. This map can be used by the intruder to decipher the message as described in [10].

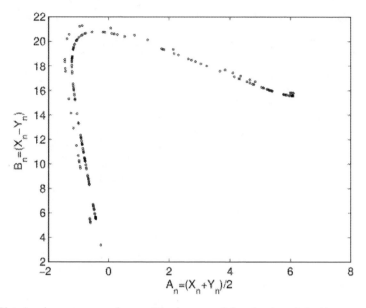

Fig. 3. Plot showing return map for eqn (1) where $p_1 = 0.2$ and p_2 is switched between 0 and 0.2 with bit duration time, $T_d = 100$. X_n and Y_n denote the n'th maxima and minima of the intercepted signal.

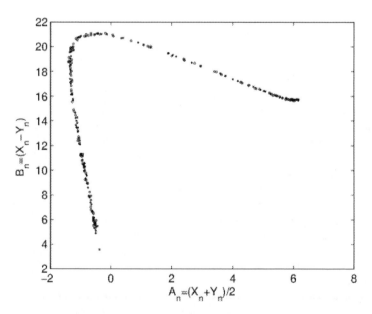

Fig. 4. Plot showing return map for Eqn. (3) with parameters R_1 and R_3 equal to zero, and R_2 is switched between 0 and 0.2 with bit duration time, $T_d = 0.15$. X_n and Y_n denote the n'th maxima and minima of the intercepted signal.

In contrast, the return map of figure 4 fails to reveal any property that can be used to decipher the message. Because of rapid switching between parameters, most of the points on this map are obtained from values of maxima and minima which correspond to different parameter values. Hence they do not reflect any property pertaining to either of the parameter values. The security is further enhanced when the parameters R_1 and R_3 are also used for coding and each parameter is switched among several values, instead of just two.

5   Conclusion

A scheme of additive parameter adaptive control is proposed to synchronize two Rossler systems. The main contribution of our paper is to demonstrate the advantages of modifying the receiver system by controllers and parameter adaptation laws in such a way that the synchronization error Equations becomes linear with constant coefficients, whose eigenvalues have large negative real parts. This simple modification allows synchronization to be achieved in a time, T_s, less than the average chaotic oscillation time, T_c, leading to rapid and smooth convergence of the receiver parameters to the transmitter parameters. This allows transmission of digital messages with small bit duration time, leading to increased transmission speed and enhanced security.

In particular, we demonstrated the advantages of our scheme by comparing it with the scheme discussed in [6]. It is shown that our scheme has several advantages like analytic simplicity of the system, rapid convergence leading to greater speed of communication, avoidance of chaotic fluctuations in the parameters R_1 ', R_2 ', R_3 ' before convergence, and enhanced security due to inapplicability of the technique of return maps for message identification by an intruder.

The ideas given in this paper can be combined with ideas from some other papers. For example, in [16, 17] an attempt was made to code the secret message using a nonlinear function of a chaotic variable and a time-dependent parameter of the transmitter, the latter serving as a secret key. However, the parameter is held constant for a time much longer than the chaotic oscillation time. So even though the parameter is changing, it is not changing fast enough to preclude the possibility of parameter identification by an intruder. So the security is essentially reduced to the secrecy of the non-linear function and not to the secret key according to which the parameter values change. It would be worth trying to modify the approach of [11, 12] so that the parameter is changed in a time shorter than the chaotic oscillation time.

In this paper, we have not considered real world effects like uncertainty and variability of parameters and noise. In [18-20] adaptive controller techniques were developed for synchronization of such uncertain systems. However, this synchronization was not used for secure communication. The possibility of applying such synchronization techniques along with our approach for obtaining faster and more secure communication in the presence of real world uncertainties will be explored in future research.

In [21] a secure communication scheme based on synchronization of fractional chaotic systems was proposed. In [22] neural controllers were used for obtaining synchronization of chaotic systems and for communication of secure messages. In both these schemes messages were communicated by chaotic masking and not by switching of parameters. It would be worth trying to improve upon these techniques, using the approach of our paper, so that chaotic communication based on parameter switching with switching time less than chaotic oscillation time can be achieved.

References

[1] Pecora, L.M., Carroll, T.L.: Synchronization in chaotic systems. Phys. Rev. Lett. 64, 821–825 (1990)
[2] Pecora, L.M., Carroll, T.L.: Driving systems with chaotic signals. Phys. Rev. A 44, 2374–2384 (1991)
[3] Zhou, C.-S., Chen, T.-L.: Communication via Chaotic Synchronization Based on Contraction Maps. Chinese. Phys. Lett. 13, 572–575 (1996)
[4] Cuomo, K.M., Oppenheim, A.V.: Circuit Implementation of Synchronized Chaos with Applications to Communications. Phys. Rev. Lett. 71, 65–68 (1993)
[5] Zhou, C.-S., Lai, C.-H.: Decoding information by following parameter modulation with parameter adaptive control. Phys. Rev. E. 59, 6629–6636 (1999)
[6] Xing, G.J., Huang, D.B.: Encoding-decoding message for secure communication based on adaptive chaos synchronization. J. Shanghai Univ. 12, 400–404 (2008)
[7] Feki, M.: An adaptive chaos synchronization scheme applied to secure communication. Chaos, Solitons and Fractals 18, 141–148 (2003)
[8] Palaniyandi, P., Lakshmanan, M.: Controlled Parameter Modulations in Secure Digital Signal Transmissions. International Journal of Bifurcation and Chaos in Applied Sciences and Engineering 17, 4187–4193 (2007)
[9] Yang, T., Chua, L.O.: Secure communication via chaotic parameter modulation. IEE Transactions on Circuits and Systems I: Fundamental Theory and Applications 43, 817–819 (1996)
[10] Perez, G., Cerdeira, H.A.: Extracting Messages Masked by Chaos. Phy. Rev. Lett. 74, 1970–1973 (1995)
[11] Chen, S., Hu, J., Wang, C., Lu, J.: Adaptive synchronization of uncertain Rossler hyperchaotic system based on parameter identification. Phys. Lett. A 321, 50–55 (2004)
[12] Arefi, M.M., Jahed-Motlagh, M.R.: Robust synchronization of Rossler systems with mismatched time varying parameters. Nonlinear Dyn. 67, 1233–1245 (2012)
[13] Garcia, J.H., Jaimes-Reategui, R., Pisarchik, A.N., Murguia- Hernandez, A., Medina-Gutierrez, C., Valdivia-Hernadez, R., Villafana-Rauda, E.: Novel communication scheme based on chaotic Rossler circuits. IOP Journal of Physics: Conference Series 23, 276–284 (2005)
[14] Sambas, A., Sanjaya, M., Mustafa Mamat, W.S., Diyah, H.: Design and analysis bidirectional chaotic synchronization of Rossler circuit and its application for secure communication. Applied Mathematical Sciences 7, 1–21 (2013)
[15] Garcia-Lopez, J.H., Jaimes-Reategui, R., Chiu-Zarate, R., Lopez-Mancilla, D., Ramirez-Jimenez, R., Pisarchik, A.N.: Secure computer communication based on chaotic Rossler oscillators. The Open Electrical and Electronic Engineering Journal 2, 41–44 (2008)

[16] Zaher, A.A.: An improved chaos-based secure communication technique using a novel encryption function with an embedded cipher key. Chaos, Solitons and Fractals 42, 2804–2814 (2009)

[17] Zaher, A.A., Abu-Rezq, A.: On the design of chaos-based secure communication systems. Commun. Nonlin. Sci. Numer. Simulat. 16, 3721–3737 (2011)

[18] Li, W., Liu, Z., Miao, J.: Adaptive synchronization for a unified chaotic system with uncertainty. Commun. Nonlin. Sci. Numer. Simulat. 15, 3015–3021 (2010)

[19] Salarieh, H., Alasty, A.: Adaptive synchronization of two chaotic systems with stochastic unknown parameters. Commun. Nonlin. Sci. Numer. Simulat. 14, 508–519 (2009)

[20] Pourmahmood, M., Khanmohammadi, S., Alizadeh, G.: Synchronization of two different uncertain chaotic systems with unknown parameters using a robust adaptive sliding mode controller. Commun. Nonlin. Sci. Numer. Simulat. 16, 2853–2868 (2011)

[21] Kiani-B, A., Fallahi, K., Pariz, N., Leung, H.: A chaotic secure communication scheme using fractionalchaotic systems based on an extended fractional Kalman filter. Commun. Nonlin. Sci. Numer. Simulat. 14, 863–879 (2009)

[22] Sheikhan, M., Shahnazi, R., Garousi, S.: Synchronization of general chaotic systems using neural controllers with application to secure communication. Neural Comput. & Applic. 22, 361–373 (2013)

A Side View Based Video in Video Watermarking Using DWT and Hilbert Transform

Loganathan Agilandeeswari[1], K. Ganesan[1], and K. Muralibabu[2]

[1] School of Information Technology and Engineering, VIT University, Vellore
[2] Global Institute of Engineering and Technology, Vellore
agila.l@vit.ac.in

Abstract. In this paper, an efficient side view based video in video watermarking technique using DWT and Hilbert transform has been proposed. First, convert the cover video to side-view video using pre-processing steps. This pre-processing helps to switch the frames video references with dimensions equivalent to the number of frames like width and the same height than the original video. The proposed algorithm is a non-blind watermarking algorithm, means that the receiver needs the original host data in order to extract the watermark from the received watermarked video. The experimental result shows that, the algorithm runs with good imperceptibility levels, with an average PSNR value 42. It also robust against most of the attacks such as image processing, geometrical and video processing attacks when compared to the existing video watermarking techniques.

Keywords: DWT, Hilbert Transform, Pre-processing, PSNR, blind watermarking.

1 Introduction

The development of high-speed Internet, multimedia processing, and compression technology allows the widespread use of multimedia applications. This leads to the strong need to protect such multimedia information, especially its authentication and copyright. Consequently, digital watermarking emerges as one possible and popular solution [1-5].

This paper focusses on the authentication of video content by embedding watermark video into the cover video, which makes our approach robust against all possible attacks. There are several ways to insert watermark data into the video. The simple way involves considering the video as a sequence of still images or frames, and then embeds each watermark frame into each cover frame independently[6]. Here, we proposed a robust and imperceptible video watermarking algorithm which combines two powerful mathematical transforms: Discrete Wavelet Transform [7], and the Hilbert Transform [8]. DWT is more computationally efficient than other transform methods like DCT and DFT. It is very suitable to identify the areas in the host video frame where the watermark can be embedded. The Hilbert transform has been widely used in image processing and phase observation on account of its edge

Sabu M. Thampi et al. (Eds.): SSCC 2013, CCIS 377, pp. 366–377, 2013.

enhancing properties. The classic Hilbert filter enhances the image along one dimension. It is possible to create two-dimensional masks by performing the product of two Hilbert masks. The representation of Hilbert transform of an image matrix Z of size n×m with elements Z_{ij},

$$Z_{ij} = a_{ij} \cos\Theta_{ij}, \text{ where, } i = 1,2,3, \ldots n, j = 1,2,3, \ldots m. \qquad (1)$$

In this, a_{ij} are the amplitudes and Θ_{ij} are the phases obtained from vector-wise Hilbert transform applied on Z. Principle Component Analysis(PCA) is used to hybridize the algorithm as it has the inherent property of removing the correlation among the data. In addition to this, to increase the level of authentication, we pre-processed the video before embedding and extracting the watermark.

The rest of the paper is organized as follows: In Section 2 brief review of the existing watermarking system is given.Section 3 describes the proposed watermarking scheme. Section 4 shows experimental results. Conclusions and Future Work are given in the Section 5.

2   Related Works

This section discusses some of the famous existing watermarking techniques. Novel adaptive approaches to video watermarking have been proposed by Ge etal [9]. In order to guarantee the robustness and perceptual invisibility of the watermark, he uses both intra-frame and inter-frame information of video content. The MPEG-based technique for digital video watermarking has been proposed by Hsu & Wu [10].They embedded watermarks in both intraframe and non-intraframe with different residual masks. The embedding process involves, first the degradation of the original watermark using pixel based permutation and block-based permutation, followed by this, embedding can be done in the middle frequency coefficients in DCT domain, which is collected in zig-zag order.

The DWT based algorithm proposed by Hong et al [11] where the middle frequencies are modified and a flag is generated for the extraction process. During the extraction process another flag is generated from the watermarked image in order to compare with the original flag. Here, authors used the generated flag as watermark instead of original watermark image. Doerr & Dugelay [12] have proposed video watermarking based on spread spectrum techniques in order to improve robustness. Here each watermark bit is spread over a large number of chip rate (CR) and then modulated by a pseudo-random sequence of binary. This algorithm's robustness increases with the increase of the variance of the pseudo-noise sequence.The wavelet transform based video watermarking scheme was proposed by Liu et al [13] which dealt with embedding multiple information bits into the uncompressed video sequences. The embedding in LL sub-band used for reducing error probabilities of detection of BHC code.

A new type of watermarking scheme proposed by Niu et al [14] using two-dimensional and three – dimensional multi resolution signal decomposing. The watermark image which is decomposed with different resolution is embedded in the corresponding resolution of the decomposed video. The robustness of watermarking is enhanced by coding the watermark information using the Hamming error correction code.A novel blind watermark algorithm based on SVD and DCT by Fen Lie et al [15] describes that this algorithm satisfies the transparence and robustness of the watermarking system as well. The experimental results show that this approach is robust against common signal processing attacks.Haneih [16] have proposed a multiplicative video watermarking scheme with Semi-Blind maximum likelihood decoding for copyright protection. They first divide the video signal into non-overlapping pixel cubes. Then, the 2D Wavelet transform is applied on each plane of the selected cubes. For extraction, a semi-blind likelihood decoder is employed.The digital video watermarking algorithm using Principal Component Analysis by Sanjana et al [17] proposed the imperceptible high bit rate watermark. It was robust against various attacks such as filtering, contrast adjustment, noise addition and geometric attacks.Nisreen et al [18] proposed a comprehensive approach for digital video watermarking is introduced, where a binary watermark image is embedded into the video frames. Each video frame is decomposed into sub-images using 2 level discrete wavelet transform then the Principle Component Analysis (PCA) transformation is applied for each block in the two bands LL and HH. The watermark is embedded into the maximum coefficient of the PCA block of the two bands. Agilandeeswari et al [19] have proposed a novel method for embedding video in video using Discrete wavelet transform and Singular value decomposition. This approach was robust against all types of image processing attacks.

3   Proposed Algorithm

The detailed steps required for proposed watermarking algorithm is discussed in this section. First, convert the cover video to side-view video using pre-processing steps. After pre-processing the side-view of the video becomes the front face. Now, perform embedding operation on this front face using DWT and Hilbert Transform, by selecting a suitable block using PCA score. The embedded video is again rotated to get the normal view. Finaly, video watermark is extracted using extraction process. The detailed explanation of the each steps is decribed as follows:

A. Side View Video Pre-processing

The pre-processing of video before embedding and extracting the watermark is shown in fig.1. The video is essentially the collection of frames that can be considered as a 3D matrix. During the pre-processing, this 3D matrix format is rotated to one side, and the side-view of the matrix becomes the front face. Thus the embedding takes place on this front face. After the embedding process is completed, the watermarked matrix is again rotated in the direction opposite to that done earlier. The actual front view of the video is obtained, with the watermark video embedded criss-cross onto the host video.

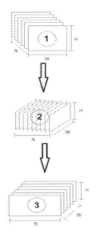

Fig. 1. Side view video pre-processing

B. Embedding Algorithm

This subsection discusses the proposed embedding algorithm. The following fig.2 shows its flowchart representation.

Step 1: Conisder the gray scale cover video C and   watermark video W.

Step 2: Pre-process the cover video to get the side view video in order to embed   the watermark frames.

Step 3: Convert Input Cover Video and Watermark video into frames.

Step 4: Perform 2-level DWT on each gray scale Cover video frame C as,

$$DWT\{C\} = \{LL1, HL1, LH1, HH1\} \tag{2}$$
$$DWT\{LL1\} = \{LL2, HL2, LH2, HH2\}$$

The above equation results in four muli-resolution subbands as LL1, HL1, LH1 and HH1 for the first level and eight multi-resolution subbands for the second level as LL2, HL2, LH2 and HH2.

Step 5: Let's represent the DWT frame D with elements D_{ij} and the watermark frame W with elements W_{ij}.

Step 6: Apply PCA based subband selection algorithm on D as,

   (i)   Find zero mean A_i for each block B_i, $A_i = E(B_i - m_i)$ (3)

  (ii)   Calculate covariance matrix $Cm_i = A_i \times Ai^T$ (4)

 (iii) Transform each block into PCA components by calculating the eigenvectors corresponding to eigenvalues of the covariance matrix as,

$$Cm_i \, \varphi = \gamma_i \, \varphi, \tag{5}$$

     where φ is the eigen vectors matrix and γ is the eigenvalues matrix.

 (iv) Calculate PCA transformation of each block to get a block of uncorrelated coefficients using,

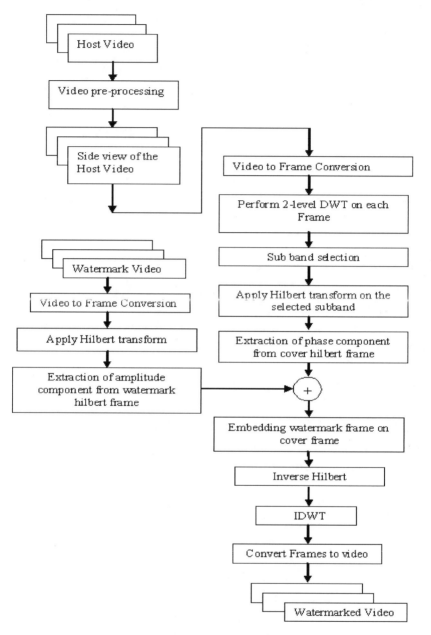

Fig. 2. Embedding Algorithm

$$Pc_i = \varphi^T A_i \qquad (6)$$

where, Pc_i is the principle component of the ith block.

Step 7: Choose the subband with highest PCA score and named it as subband S_1.

Step 8: Perform Hilbert transform on S_1 of image D and W as,

$$D_{ij} = p_{ij} \cos\theta_{ij} \tag{7}$$

$$W_{ij} = q_{ij} \cos\Phi_{ij} \tag{8}$$

where, p_{ij} and q_{ij} are amplitude components of D and W repectively

$\qquad \theta_{ij}$ and Φ_{ij} are phase components of D and W respectively.

Step 9: Embedding the Watermark frame in the subband which has highest score as,

- (i) Divide the selected subbands into non-overlapping blocks of size equal to the size of the watermark frame.
- (ii) Compute the score for each block using Step 6.
- (iii) Extract the phase component and the amplitude component of the hilbert cover frame and watermark frame respectively.
- (iv) Modify the coefficients of the selected hilbert block of the subbands with watermark frame as follows,

$$\psi_{ij} = \theta_{ij} + \alpha\, q_{ij} \tag{9}$$

where, α represents robustness factor

$\qquad q_{ij}$ represents amplitude component of the Watermark frame

$\qquad \theta_{ij}$ represents phase component of the original frame.

Step 10: Reconstrution of modified subband DWT Coefficient using inverse hilbert.

Step 11: Obtain the watermarked frame D^w using Inverse DWT as,

$$D^w = p_{ij} \cos \psi_{ij} \tag{10}$$

Step 12: Repeat Step 4 to 11 for all the frames of a video

Step 13: Reconstruct the frames back to original view mode.

Step 14: Combine the resultant embedded frames to get watermarked video.

C. Extraction Algorithm

The detailed explanation of extraction algorithm is given in this subsection and its flowchart representation is shown in fig.3.

Step 1: Convert watermarked video into frames

Step 2: From the input watermarked image D^w, we can extract watermark W, if we know, p_{ij}, θ_{ij}, Φ_{ij} for all the values of i and j and the robustness factor α.

Step 3: Perform 2-level DWT on D^w

Step 4: Apply PCA based subband selection procedure.

Step 5: Perform Hilbert tranform on D^w and extract its phase component ψ_{ij} from equ. (10) as,

$$D^w = p_{ij} \cos \psi_{ij}$$

Now, divide both sides of equ. (10) by p_{ij} and also replace it by equation (8), we get,

$$D^w / p_{ij} = \cos \psi_{ij}$$
$$\psi_{ij} = \cos^{-1} (D^w / p_{ij})$$
$$\theta_{ij} + \alpha\, q_{ij} = \cos^{-1} (D^w / p_{ij})$$
$$q_{ij}{}' = [\cos^{-1} (D^w / p_{ij}) - \theta_{ij}] / \alpha \tag{11}$$

Step 6: Thus the extracted watermark can be created using the equation below,

$$W_{ij}{}' = q_{ij}{}' \cos\Phi_{ij} \tag{12}$$

Step 7: Combine all the extracted watermark frames to get watermark video.

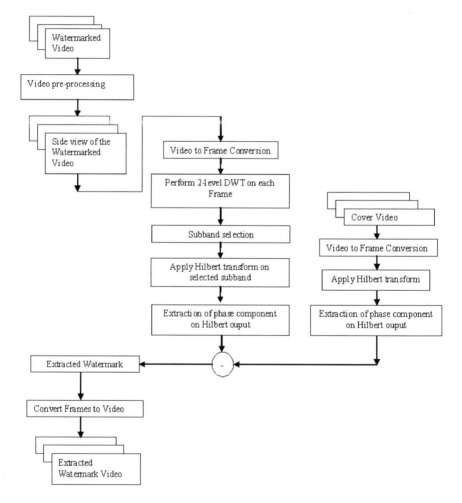

Fig. 3. Extraction Algorithm

4   Experimental Results

The performance of the proposed watermarking technique has been measured in terms of its imperceptibility and robustness against all possible attacks like image processing attacks, geometric attacks and video processing attacks. We used the following sample video sequences 'grayrhino.avi' of length 114 frames with the frame size of 320 X 240 as a cover video and 'traffic.avi' as the watermark video with a framesize of 160 X 120. Fig. 4(a) and 4(b) shows the original and the watermarked video frames respectively. Fig. 4(c) is the original watermark video and Fig. 4(d) is the extracted watermark video. For the frame decomposition, two level DWT with Haar wavelet   has been used for better reconstruction.

The PSNR (Peak Signal-to-Noise ratio) and the correlation coefficient are the two measures used to imperceptibility levels and the robustness of the proposed algorithm. It is given as,

$$PSNR = 10 \log_{10} \left(\frac{255^{\wedge}2}{MSE} \right) \tag{13}$$

Fig. 4.a Original Video Frame   **Fig. 4.b** Watermarked Video Frame   **Fig.4.c** Original Watermark video   **Fig.4.d** Extracted Watermark

$$MSE = \frac{1}{T} \left(\sum_{t=1}^{T} (O(t) - A(t))^2 \right) \tag{14}$$

$$Correlation\ Co-Efficient = \frac{\sum ((X_i - X_m)(Y_i - Y_m))}{\sqrt{\sum (X_i - X_m)^2} \sqrt{\sum (Y_i - Y_m)^2}} \tag{15}$$

The PSNR values, Correlation coefficient values along with sample watermarked frame and extracted watermark are given in table 1.

Frame Dropping: The process of dropping one or more frames randomly in the watermarked video sequence is known as frame dropping. If the dropping rate is too high, the quality of the watermarked video will decrease rapidly, so in our experiment we drop one frame randomly. The chance of missing the corresponding watermark frame is also less, since the size of cover video is double the size of watermark video. We drop maximum (n / 2, where n- total number of frames). But the quality of the watermarked video degrades severely.

Table 1. Extracted watermark Frame, Pre-processed video And watermarked frame after the Attacks with its PSNR And Correlation Coefficient Value

Attack Type	PSNR	Correlation Coefficient	Pre-processed video	Watermarked Frame	Extracted Watermark Frame
Gaussian Noise	33.1654	0.7677			
Poisson Noise	28.5402	0.5125			
Salt and Pepper Noise	29.2658	0.8050			
Median Filtering	33.4165	0.8198			
Contrast Adjustment	42.6543	0.5117			
Rotation	33.3374	0.6610			
Cropping	33.8165	0.6710			
Frame Dropping	32.4353	0.7852			

Table 1. (*Continued.*)

| Frame Swapping | 33.4212 | 0.8431 | | | |
| Frame Averaging | 31.6781 | 0.8540 | | | |

Frame Swapping: The process of switching the order of frames randomly within a watermarked video sequence is known as frame swapping. The quality of the video will degrade, when we swap too many frames. Since we have embedded same watermark in each frame of the cover video, frame swapping will not affect the extraction of all the watermarks.

Frame Averaging: Like frame dropping and frame swapping watermark extraction will not be affected by frame averaging, this is true due to the same information is embedded twice in the cover video.

The results obtained indicate that the usage of the side-view has better robustness and imperceptibility as compared to the existing front-view watermarking [17][19]. These finding is summarized in table 2.

Table 2. Comparison Of Existing Watermarking Algorithm with our Proposed Approach

Type of Attacks	Existing Watermarking Algorithm[17]		Existing Watermarking Algorithm[19]		Proposed Watermarking Algorithm	
	Avg.PSNR in 'db'	Correlation Coefficient	Avg.PSNR in 'db'	Correlation Coefficient	Avg.PSNR in 'db'	Correlation Coefficient
Gaussian	27.0321	0.7134	29.1654	0.7677	33.1654	0.7943
Poisson	24.1342	0.6241	24.5402	0.5125	28.5402	0.6150
Salt & Pepper	24.2685	0.7905	25.2658	0.8050	29.2658	0.8343
Contrast adjustment	29.0145	0.5017	29.4165	0.8198	33.4165	0.8412
Median filtering	35.6041	0.8011	38.6543	0.5117	42.6543	0.5430
Cropping	28.3454	0.6506	29.3374	0.6610	33.3374	0.6780
Rotation	28.0145	0.6490	28.8165	0.6710	33.8165	0.6712
Frame Dropping	25.4353	0.7564	28.4353	0.7852	32.4353	0.8012
Frame Swapping	28.3141	0.8392	29.4212	0.8431	33.4212	0.8634
Frame Averaging	26.4582	0.7530	27.6781	0.8540	31.6781	0.8840

From the PSNR values in the table 2, we conclude that the proposed video watermarking algorithm produces better quality video after embedding the watermark video.

5   Conclusions and Future Work

In this paper, we have presented a robust video in video watermarking algorithm for content authentication based on DWT and Hilbert Transform. Also a new idea of performing embedding steps over pre-processed video to increase the level of authentication security has been introduced.The experimental analysis shows that our approach is robust against various attacks such as, Gaussian attack, Poisson Attack, Salt and Pepper attack, Median filtering, Contrast Adjustment, Rotation and Cropping and various video related attacks such as Frame dropping, Frame averaging and Frame swapping. Here, we concentrated on embedding a video i.e., different watermark frames in all the frames of the cover video. The comparison table.2 shows that our approach is good when compared to the existing watermarks. As a future work, we can go for embedding the watermarks on the frame which doesn't have any motion by applying the motion estimation algorithms on the cover video, which may helps us in finding the location of embedding.

References

[1] Lu, C.S., Liao, H.Y.M., Sze, C.J.: Structural digital signature for image authentication: an incidental distortion resistant scheme. In: Proceedings of the Multimedia Security Workshop 8th ACM International Conference on Multimedia, pp. 115–118 (2000)
[2] Lin, C.Y., Chang, S.F.: A robust image authentication method surviving JPEG lossy compression. In: Proceedings of SPIE International Conference on Storage and Retrieval of Image/Video Database, vol. 3312, pp. 296–307 (1998)
[3] Lin, E.T., Podilchuk, C.I., Delp, E.: Detection of image alterations using semi-fragile watermarks. In: Proceedings of SPIE Conference on Security and Watermarking of Multimedia Contents, pp. 152–163 (2000)
[4] Lee, C.-H., Lee, Y.-K.: An Adaptive Digital Watermarking Technique for Copyright Protection. IEEE Trans. Consumer Electronics 45, 1005–1015 (1999)
[5] Cox, I.J., Miller, M., Bloom, J.A.: Digital Watermarking. Morgan Kaufmann (2002)
[6] Hsu, C.T., Wu, J.L.: DCT-based watermarking for video. IEEE Trans. Consumer Electronics 44, 206–216 (1998)
[7] Mallat, S.: A theory for multi-resolution signal decomposition: The wavelet representation. IEEE Trans. Pattern Anal. and Machine Intel. 11(7), 674–693 (1989)
[8] Agarwal, R., Krishnan, R., Santhanam, M.S., Srinivas, K., Venugopalan, K.: Digital Watermarking: An approach based in Hilbert Transform. arXiv:1012.2965 (2010)
[9] Ge, Q., Lu, Z., Niu, X.: Oblivious video watermarking scheme with adaptive embedding mechanism. In: Proc. Int. Conf. Machine Learning and Cybernetics, Xian, China, vol. 5, pp. 2876–2881 (2003)
[10] Hsu, C.T., Wu, J.L.: A DCT-based watermarking for videos. IEEE Transactions on Consumer Electronics 44(1), 206–216 (1998)

[11] Hong, I., Kim, I., Han, S.S.: A blind watermarking technique using wavelet transform. In: Proc. IEEE Int. Sym. Industrial Electronics, Pusan, Korea, vol. 3, pp. 1946–1950 (2001)

[12] Doerr, G., Dugelay, J.L.: A guide tour of video watermarking. Signal Processing: Image Communication 18(4), 263–282 (2003)

[13] Liu, H., Chen, N., Huang, J., Huang, X., Shi, Y.Q.: A robust DWT-based video watermarking algorithm. In: Proc. IEEE Int. Sym. Circuits and Systems, Scottsdale, Arizona, vol. 3, pp. 631–634 (2002)

[14] Niu, X., Sun, S., Xiang, W.: Multiresolution watermarking for video based on gray-level digital watermark. IEEE Transactions on Consumer Electronics 46(2), 375–384 (2000)

[15] Liu, F., Han, K., Wang, C.Z.: A Novel Blind Watermark Algorithm based on SVD and DCT. In: IEEE Conference, pp. 283–286 (2009)

[16] Khalilian, H., Bajic, I.V.: Multiplicative Video watermarking with Semi-Blind Maximum Likelihood Decoding for Copyright Protection. In: IEEE Conference, pp. 125–130 (2011)

[17] Sinha, S., Bardhan, P., Pramanick, S., Jagatramka, A., Kole, D.K., Chakraborty, A.: Digital Video Watermarking using Discrete Wavelet Transform and Principal Component Analysis. International Journal of Wisdom Based Compuitng 1(2), 7–12 (2011)

[18] Yassin, N.I., Salem, N.M., El Adawy, M.I.: Block Based Video Watermarking Scheme Using Wavelet Transform and Principle Component Analysis. IJCSI International Journal of Computer Science Issues 9(1)(3) (January 2012) ISSN (Online): 1694-0814

[19] Agilandeeswari, L., Muralibabu, K.: A Novel block based Video in Video Wateramrking Algorithm using Discrete Wavelet Transform and Singular Value Decomposition. In: International Journal of Advanced Research in Computer Science and Software Engineering (IJARCSSE), pp. 878–886 (2013)

Malware Detection Using API Function Frequency with Ensemble Based Classifier

Pratiksha Natani and Deepti Vidyarthi

Defence Institute of Advance Technology (DIAT) DU, Pune
pratiksha.natani@gmail.com, deepti@diat.ac.in

Abstract. Malicious code, known as malware, when executed can steal information, damage the system or may cause unavailability of system resources. In order to safeguard information systems from malware, effective detection of malware is a top priority task. Malware exhibits malicious behaviors like connecting to a remote host, downloading file from remote host, creating file in system directory etc. These behaviors can be mapped to functions used by malicious files which are imported from system's dynamic link libraries i.e. Application programming interface (API) functions. Hence, we propose a technique to detect malware using API function frequency as feature vector for classifying malicious file. We use Ensemble based classifier for classification, as it is proven to be stable and robust classification technique. Experiments are conducted over 200 files and the technique classified malicious files effectively. Bagging used in ensemble classifier provides better results as compared to ensemble boosting. Comparison with other known techniques is also listed.

Keywords: Ensemble based Classifier, Boosting, Bagging, Cuckoo Sandbox.

1   Introduction

Malware is a malicious code which can harm computer to get sensitive information from system. Malware can be classified as Trojans, backdoor, rootkits, viruses, worms, adware & spyware. To detect malware, antivirus companies use signature based or heuristic based detection. Signature based detection is fast and effective if signature of malware is known. But malware writer uses techniques like polymorphism (Encrypting malware with unique key during regeneration of malware) and metamorphism (obfuscating code during regeneration of malware) to evade signature detection. Heuristic techniques are useful but they are expensive and complex. Apart from these there are many behavior detectors which use behaviors of malware as signature. These detectors can detect polymorphic or metamorphic malware because they focuses on semantic interpretation rather than syntactic. But main disadvantage of behavior detectors is that they generate false positives. In our proposed technique behavior of malware is used as basis for detection of malicious files.

Sabu M. Thampi et al. (Eds.): SSCC 2013, CCIS 377, pp. 378–388, 2013.
© Springer-Verlag Berlin Heidelberg 2013

Windows Portable Executable (PE) format is used for executable, object code, Dynamic Link Library (DLLs) and others. The PE format is a data structure that captures the information necessary for the Windows OS loader to manage the wrapped executable code. It includes dll references for linking, Import Address Table (IAT) and Export Address Table (EAT), resource management data and thread-local storage (TLS) data. Import Address Table (IAT) contains information about API functions imported from various system dll (kernel32.dll, user32.dll, gdi32.dll, advapi32.dll etc.) or other dll files which is used by executable, DLLs, object code and others. These API functions can be mapped to behavior of any particular file.

Proposed technique uses behavior as basis for detection of malicious files and mapped those behaviors to API functions which are frequently used by malicious files.

In section 2 of this paper, available techniques are explored. In section 3, machine learning for malware detection is explained. Sections 4 and 5 define basics of ensemble based classifier. In section 6 and section 7, proposed technique and experimental result and performance is explained respectively. Finally, section 8 and section 9, compare with other available techniques and conclude the proposed approach and describes future work.

2 Related Work

Basis for malware detection can be found in [1] which provides information about worm detection using signature based and anomaly based detection. Comparison of both the techniques is also elaborated and hybrid detection technique is proposed. Different behavioral detection techniques are explained in [2]. It provides basis for behavioral detection techniques and define model for detection. Information is also provided related to different behavior detection techniques used by anti-viruses. Extensive survey is provided on automated dynamic analysis tools and techniques in [3]. It defines many approaches of dynamic analysis for malware. It also provides information about available sandboxes and their effectiveness. A method for classifying malicious files using a fuzzy clustering method with the Native API call is explained in [4]. Proposed method in [4] is compared with classifying methods for evaluation. In [5], frequency of instructions is used to distinguished malicious files from normal files. Experimental results show that there is a clear distinction in frequency distribution of malicious and normal files.

3 Machine Learning for Malware Detection

The real world applications deal with classifying data and recognizing patterns from the data. There exist numerous supervised, semi supervised and unsupervised data classification algorithms such as Artificial Neural Networks (ANN), decision trees, Support Vector Machine (SVM), Ensemble based classifiers etc. In [6] & [7], different techniques of data mining are explained and experiment is conducted on different sets of data to define best data mining algorithm for malware detection.

4   Ensemble Based Classifier

In machine learning, ensembles [8], [9], & [10] are used as they produce better results in terms of accuracy and stability. The idea of ensemble based classifiers is to combine a set of classifiers instead of a single classifier. Weak learners will produce varying results making the classifier unstable and less accurate. The use of multiple classifiers, instead of a single classifier will reduce bias, because multiple classifiers will learn better. Hence, ensembling is used to improve the performance of these unstable learners.

5   Ensemble Methods

Various learning algorithms are employed by ensembles to improve the classifiers performance. Boosting & bagging are popular ensemble methods.

5.1   Boosting

Boosting [8], [9] is a technique to improve the performance of any learning algorithm. AdaBoost (Adaptive Boosting) [8], [9] is boosting algorithm formulated by Yoav Freund and Robert Schapire. It is an adaptive algorithm, as it tweaks the classifiers for data misclassified by previous classifiers. Even though the classifiers used may be weak, the algorithm will finally improve the model. The weak classifiers are considered, because they will have negative values in the final aggregation of the classifiers and will work as their inverses. The technique repeatedly runs a weak learner on various distributed training data. These classifiers can be merged to form a strong classifier, hence reducing the error rate to increase the accuracy. Boosting algorithms have certain limitations. The algorithm fails to perform if the data is noisy.

5.2   Bagging

Bagging [8], [9] ensemble is a technique where each classifier is trained on a set of training data that are drawn randomly. The training is again carried out by replacing the training data with a dataset from the original training set. This training set is called a bootstrap replicate of the original training dataset. In bootstrapping, the replicate consists of average, 63.2% of the original training set, with multiple problems being trained many times. The predictions are made by considering the majority of votes in the ensemble. The aim of bagging is to reduce the error due to variance of the classifier.

6   Proposed Approach

In our approach behaviors of malicious files are used as basis for detection of malware. To collect information about malicious behaviors malware analysis is conducted over 100 malicious files, downloaded from [12], in virtual environment.

These behaviors are used to identify 24 API functions which are frequently used by malicious files and are defined in Table 1.

To collect information about API functions, file is run in Cuckoo automatic malware analyzer [13]. Cuckoo is a sandbox which runs a file in virtualized environment and extracts information about activities of a file. Cuckoo generates a report which gives information about how many API functions are called and how many times each API function is being called.

After getting this information, frequency of each function is calculated. Suppose a file named as A has used N number of API functions represented as $X_1, X_2, X_3 \ldots \ldots X_N$ then frequency of each function is calculated by using following formula (1):

$$\frac{\text{Number of times Xi function called in file}}{\text{Total number of distinct function called by file (N)}} \tag{1}$$

Frequency of API functions is extracted from different files (normal and malicious files). File A can be represented as feature of $\{Y_1, Y_2, Y_3 \ldots \ldots Y_M\}$ where Y_i is frequency of identified API function. These frequencies of 24 API functions are used as input for ensemble based classifier. Two methods of ensemble based classifier are used i.e. AdaBoost and Bagging.

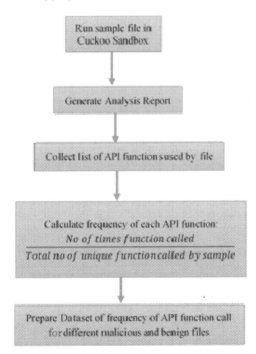

Fig. 1. Flowchart of Feature Extraction from files

7   Implementation and Experimental Setup

Virtual environment is setup to conduct malware analysis. Setup for malware analysis consists of Windows 7 and Windows XP virtual machine on Windows 7 host machine. For malware analysis, several tools are installed on virtual machine:

1. ProcessExplorer
2. ProcessMonitor
3. RegShot
4. Wireshark
5. ApateDNS
6. GMER
7. VB32 AntiRootkit
8. ImportREconstructor
9. Ollydbg
10. WinDbg
11. ProcDump
12. AutoRun

Total 100 malware samples consisting of Trojans, backdoor, rootkits, worms are analyzed using these tools. Malicious behaviors identified by the analysis are as follows:

1. Communication with Remote Host
2. Create Executable files
3. Modify registry for startup
4. Obtain system information
5. Inject into other processes
6. Create or modify windows services
7. Log keystrokes
8. Install or modify drivers
9. Make system/hidden directories
10. Create processes
11. Load Suspicious Executable

Table 1. Identified 24 API functions

Function Name	
ControlService	NtAllocateVirtualMemory
CreateProcessInternal	NtClose
CreateRemoteThread	NtCreateSection
DeviceIOControl	NtDelayExecution
FindFirstFile	NtDeviceIOControlFile
HttpSendRequest	NtFreeVirtualMemory
InternetReadFile	OpenSCManager
IsDebuggerPresent	OpenService
LdrGetProcedureAddress	ReadProcessMemory
LdrLoadDll	RegEnumKey
RegEnumValue	WriteProcessMemory
VirtualProtect	WSAStartUp

API functions identified according to the identified malicious behaviors are as listed in Table-1.

7.1   Experimental Setup for API Collection

For collecting information about API functions used by different files, virtual setup is established. It consists of an Ubuntu 12.04 VM in which cuckoo sandbox is installed. For analysis of files, Windows XP virtual machine is configured which is managed by cuckoo. Block diagram of cuckoo setup is shown in Fig. 2. Cuckoo submits files for analysis to Windows XP virtual machine and collects activity traces of file and generates different reports. Reports consist of html report, dump of network traffic and csv report which includes API functions used by file.

Information about API functions is collected from csv report. Frequency of each API function used by file is calculated using formula (1).

7.2   Feature Extraction

Frequency of malicious functions, which is feature vector for ensemble based classifier, is extracted for different files (malicious and normal). Different experiments are conducted over different set of files.

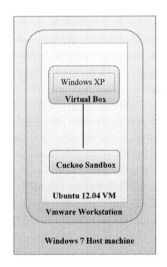

Fig. 2. Block Diagram of Cuckoo Sandbox Setup

Table 2. Experimental Result for AdaBoostM1 and Bagging

Ensemble Classifier	No of Iterations	TPR and FPR
EnsembleAdaBoostM1	AdaBoostM1 (100)	TPR = 88.46%
		FPR = 22.73 %
	AdaBoostM1 (1000)	TPR = 92.31%
		FPR = 22.73 %
	AdaBoostM1 (5000)	TPR = 88.46%
		FPR = 13.64 %
EnsembleBag	Bag (100)	TPR = 88.46 %
		FPR = 18.18%
	Bag (1000)	TPR = 88.46%
		FPR = 13.64 %
	Bag (5000)	TPR = 88.46%
		FPR = 13.64 %

Table 3. Experimental Result for AdaBoostM1 and Bagging

Ensemble Classifier	Training Time (seconds)	Testing Time (seconds)
EnsembleAdaBoost(100)	6.25	1.46
EnsembleAdaBoost(1000)	37.42	14.57
EnsembleAdaBoost(5000)	187.83	62.21
EnsembleBag(100)	4.90	1.52
EnsembleBag(1000)	28.06	11.67
EnsembleBag(5000)	132.88	63.12

7.3   Experimental Result

Experiment is conducted over 200 files in which 50 files are normal system utilities files and 150 are malicious files. To train ensemble based classifier, training set consists of 76 files in which 25 files are normal and 51 are malicious files. Test set consists of 124 files in which 25 files are normal and 99 files are malicious.

Two types of Ensemble based classifier are used:

AdaBoost

AdaBoostM1 is used for binary classification. Experiment is conducted for 100 and 1000 round of iterations. Performance of AdaBoostM1 (1000) is better than AdaBoostM1 (100). But for AdaBoostM1 (5000), false positive rate is very less as compared to AdaBoostM1 (1000).

Bagging

Bagging is used for binary classification. Experiment is carried out over 100 and 1000 iterations. Here too, Bag (1000) gives better performance than Bag (100). Bag (5000) gives same result as Bag (1000).

7.4   Performance Evaluation and Time Consumption

To evaluate performance of classifier following metrics are used:

True Positive Rate

TPR is ratio of number of malicious files correctly detected by total number of malicious files tested.

$$\text{True Positive Rate (TPR)} = \frac{TP}{TP + FN}$$

False Positive Rate

FPR is ratio of false positive by total number of normal files tested.

$$\text{False Positive Rate (FPR)} = \frac{FP}{FP + TN}$$

Accuracy Rate

Accuracy rate is defined as ratio of total number of correct classification by total number of files tested.

$$\text{Accuracy Rate} = \frac{TP + TN}{TP + TN + FP + FN}$$

Where,

TP is True Positive i.e. a malicious file classified as malicious.

TN is True Negative i.e. normal file classified as normal.

FP is False Positive i.e. normal file classified as malicious.

FN is False Negative i.e. malicious file classified as normal.

Table 2 shows TPR and FPR for experiments conducted using ensemble based classifier.

Receiver Operating Characteristics (ROC) curve is used for evaluating performance of classifier graphically. ROC curve is 2D plot in which X-axis represent false positive rate and Y-axis represent true positive rate. ROC curve is plotted for conducted experiments as shown in Fig.3, 4, 5, & 6. As we can see from Table-2 and Fig. 3 and 4 for AdaBoostM1, performance of AdaBoostM1 (1000) is better than AdaboostM1 (100) but false positives in both cases are 22.73%. Performance of each of Bag (1000) and Bag (5000) is better than Bag (100) because false positive rate is less. As we can see from Fig. 7, EnsembleAdaBoost at 5000 iterations gives same result as Bag (1000) and it is better than AdaBoostM1 (1000).

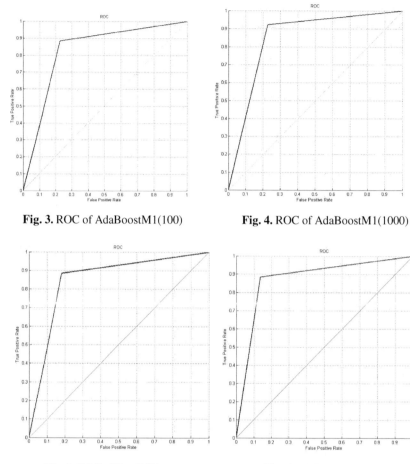

Fig. 3. ROC of AdaBoostM1(100)   **Fig. 4.** ROC of AdaBoostM1(1000)

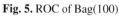

Fig. 5. ROC of Bag(100)   **Fig. 6.** ROC of Bag(1000)

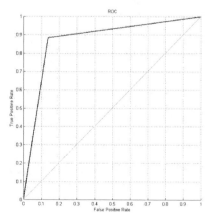

Fig. 7. ROC of AdaBoostM1(5000)

Table 3 represents time consumption of proposed approach for both AdaBoost and Bag classifiers. Training time and testing time for both classifiers for different iterations is shown. As represented in Table 4 time consumption for 5000 iterations for both classifiers is high and may increase with size of data.

8   Comparison with Other Methods

In Table 4, proposed approach is compared with other known techniques.

Table 4. Comparison with other techniques

Detection Technique	True Positive Rate	False Positive Rate
Signature Method [6]		
-Bytes	33.75%	0%
RIPPER [6]		
-DLLs used	57.89%	9.22%
-DLL function calls	71.05%	7.77%
-DLLs with counted function calls	52.63%	5.34%
Naïve Bayes [6]		
-Strings	97.43%	3.80%
Ensemble Based Classification (AdaBoost)		
-Frequency of API function calls	88.46%	13.64%
Ensemble Based Classification (Bag)		
-Frequency of API function calls	88.46%	13.64%

True positive rate (TPR) of proposed approach is better than Signature method and RIPPER as shown in Table 4. False positive rate (FPR) of this approach is high as compared to other approaches. So this work can be extended to reduce false positive rate and also improve true positive rate.

9   Conclusion and Future Work

In this paper we describe a methodology to detect malicious files by using malicious behaviors. API function calls are mapped to these behaviors and frequency of these functions is used to classify file as malicious or normal. Main disadvantage of behavior detector is false positives. As we can see from above experimental results, EnsembleAdaBoost at 1000 iterations results in TPR 92.31% but FPR is very high as compared to EnsembleBag. But AdaBoostM1 at 5000 iterarions gives same result as EnsembleBag. So we can conclude that performance of EnsembleBag at 1000 iterations and EnsembleAdaBoost at 5000 iterations give better result than EnsembleAdaBoost at 1000 iteration. This work can be extended by considering API functions used for rootkits. Rootkits use Native API functions i.e. functions imported from ntoskrnl.exe. These functions can be included with these API functions for rootkit detections. False positive rate of proposed approach can be improved as we can see from Table 4 it is very high as compared to other techniques.

References

1. Li, P., Salour, M., Su, X.: A Survey of Internet worm Detection and Containment. IEEE Communications Survey 10, 20–35 (2008)
2. Jacob, G., Debar, H., Filliol, E.: Behavioral Detection of Malware: From a Survey Towards an Established Taxonomy. Journal Computer Virology 4, 251–266 (2008)
3. Egele, M., Scholte, T., Kirda, E., Kruegel, C.: A Survey on Automated Dynamic Malware-Analysis Techniques and Tools. ACM Computing Survey 44(2) (Feburary 2012)
4. Kwon, O., Bae, S., Cho, J., Moon, J.: Study of Fuzzy Clustering Methods for Malicious Code using Native API Call Frequency. In: IEEE Symposium on Computational Intelligence in Cyber Security, pp. 24–29 (2009)
5. Han, K.S., Kang, B., GyuIm, E.: Malware Classification using Instruction Frequencies. In: Proceedings of RACS 2011 ACM Symposium on Research in Applied Computation, pp. 298–300 (2011)
6. Mathew, G., Schultz, E., Eskin, E., Stolfo, S.J.: Data Mining Methods for Detection of New Malicious Executables. In: Proceedings in IEEE Conference, pp. 38–49 (2001)
7. Zico Kolter, J., Maloof, M.A.: Learning to Detect and Classify Malicious Executables in the Wild. Journal of Machine Learning Research 7, 2721–2744 (2006)
8. Zenobi, G., Cunningham, P.: Using Diversity in Preparing Ensembles of Classifiers Based on Different Feature Subsets to Minimize Generalization Error. Department of Computer Science. Trinity College Dublin, pp. 1–15
9. Rokach, L.: Ensemble Methods for Classifiers, ch. 45, Department of Industrial Engineering, pp. 957–962. Tel-Aviv University
10. Menahem, E., Shabtai, A., Rokach, L., Elovici, Y.: Improving Malware Detection by Applying Multiinducer Ensemble. Elsevier Computational Statistics and Data Analysis 53, 1483–1494 (2009)
11. VmWare Workstation, https://my.vmware.com (dated August 01, 2012)
12. Malware.lu, http://malware.lu/ (dated February 10, 2013)
13. Cuckoo Sandbox, http://www.cuckoosandbox.org/ (dated February 10, 2013)

Privacy Issues in Single and Multi–hop Wireless Mesh Network

Sagar Kakade, Ravi Sawant, and Deepak C. Karia

Department of Electronics and Telecommunication
Sardar Patel Institute of Technology
University of Mumbai,
Mumbai 400058, India
{sagarkakade7799,rvsawant3,deepakckaria}@gmail.com

Abstract. Wireless mesh networks (WMN) provide fine solutions for commercial, personal and corporate purposes since it has the features of self-configuration, instantly deployable, low-cost. Mesh network utilizes the open medium property of Wireless channel, has a fixed topology, the limited network size and thus it is prone to attacks. Wireless network security protocols are easily prone to attacks such as brute-force attacks in case of wired equivalent privacy (WEP) and to some extent Wi-Fi Protected Access (WPA) as well. we are designing a layered encryption technique referred to as Onion that will make it more secure against global adversary attacks.

General Terms: Security, Design.

Keywords: Mesh Networks, Privacy, Onion routing.

1   Introduction

Wireless mesh networks are being widely preferred over other networks due to the advantages of being simple to implement, low cost, and providing a reliable service over wide area networks. And this also improves the working efficiency of multi-hop WMNs with additional advantage of having high throughput and enhanced user capacity over long distance communications.

A multi-hop WMN has several nodes with each node acting as a router which can be a personal computer or laptop. All this interconnected nodes are usually stationary. These types of wireless networks have a decentralized infrastructure and are relatively inexpensive. The nodes function as repeaters with each node re-transmitting data to its adjacent or distant nodes like from user A to an end user B. This results in a wireless network which is span over a long distance having covered a wide area coverage which can be extended as per requirement in case of both, coverage and capacity. This additional requirement can be fulfilled by just adding more nodes. But this mesh networks are vulnerable to attacks.

To solve the above problem, we have designed a communication protocol, called Onion Ring, to defend against a global attacker and to protect node privacy by using both cryptography and redundancy. In onion routing , instead

Sabu M. Thampi et al. (Eds.): SSCC 2013, CCIS 377, pp. 389–396, 2013.

of establishing a direct connection between the two hosts that want to communicate, the connection is routed through a set of routers called onion routers and there by allow the communication to be anonymous [1]. Every node only has information about its previous hop and the next hop i.e., the person who he is communicating with and the person with whom he is supposed to communicate. The information passed on between the users is encrypted. Thus any router does not have any idea of who is the initiator of the connection neither does he have the information on the destination. Only the last node on the route which establishes a connection with the destination finally has information on the destination. Data appearing at each onion router is different and padded at different levels to keep the length of the data constant.

The paper is organized as follows. In Section 2 we list existing system, security assumptions. In Section 3 we review traditional ways of Onion Routing,implementation of onion routing and onion layer. In Section 4 we present our proposed plan of Onion Ring Routing in the Mesh network, we present Onion ring that can defend against a global adversary. In Section 5 we present its implementation in NS2. In Section 6 we address the four different cases involved in Onion Ring Routing. In Section 8 we conclude and discuss future research directions.

2   Existing System

To hide an active node that connects the gateway router among a group of mesh nodes and thus making an active node untraceable by Creating dummy nodes for protection against global adversaries from tracing the main active node,also exploring routing redundancy for node anonymity, by having decoy itself as the Gateway router. Onion routing does not hide a communication end. It achieves anonymity by making communication ends unlink-able. In the Mesh network, one of the communication ends is the Gateway router. If the other end that is the Mesh node, is known, the communication privacy is cracked. Therefore to achieve privacy in the Mesh network, the active Mesh nodes have to be hidden. The privacy achieved by Onion routing is not exact what is needed in the Mesh network

A. Assumptions

It is assumed that the wireless channels are symmetric.. We assume that the gateway router knows the network topology. Thus routing information can be obtained when any new mesh node joins the network,as routing update is required. We assume that error control is used at the link layer in the network topology , therefore an erroneous packet is not caused by wireless transmission. It discovers its neighbours first,then it uses RIP [2] or OPSF [3] to find a route to the Gateway router and update the network topology. Thus it is vulnerable to outside attacks. We also assume that a Mesh node establishes a symmetric key with any of its one-hop neighbouring Mesh node.

3   Proposed System: Onion Ring Routing

Traditional Onion routing may not be efficient to preserve privacy for a Mesh node because

1) it reveals the communication ends;
2) it cannot defend against global attacker. In this paper, we design a protocol called ring routing that jointly uses Onion routing and communication redundancy, and therefore hides communication ends.

The following description assumes that the onion routing network runs on top of TCP, however it can be implemented on top of other protocols. We have implemented this protocol in NS2.The protocol is named as OR protocol. Fig 3. shows our proposed plan of onion ring routing.

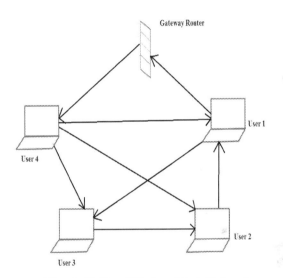

Fig. 1. Exiting Wireless Mesh Network

A. Onion Routing

Onion routing is a set of proxies which help in encrypted communication [4]. The initiator first establishes an initiating connection with Application Proxy on his machine through which the communications are routed to the Onion Proxy which defined the route to the destination and constructs the onion,so called the onion layer routing. Onion Proxy establishes the connectionof the first node in the route and passes on the onion to it. The flow-graph for onion routing is shown above in Fig.1. The First node on receiving the onion sends it to its own router, which basically strips of a layer of onion to get details about the next node on the route and accordingly modifies the onion and sends it to the next router. This way the onion moves in between the routers defined in the route and finally reaches the last node in the route. Each layer contains information about the next hop and also a key for encryption of data to be transmitted.

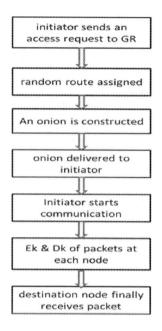

Fig. 2. Block Diagram

Once the communication is established between initiator and destination, data can be exchanged between the two. The data is transmitted by repeatedly encrypting it with the keys derived from the key seed material. The encryption is done with the key of the last route first and so on and finally with the key of the first router. The encrypted message moves through the nodes removing a layer of encryption at each node and finally the data reaches the destination in plain text. As the data moves through the network, it appears different at different stages and thus prevents snooping by comparing the packets. Every onion layer is also associated with an expiration time. Thus every router stores a copy of onion till the time expires and hence if a duplicate onion appears within this period, it is ignored and also the onion is ignored if it appears after the expiration time. Thus replay attack is controlled. The advantages of onion routing is that it is not necessary to trust each cooperating router; if one or more routers are compromised, anonymous communication can still be achieved. This is because each router in an Onion Router network accepts messages, re-encrypts them, and transmits to another onion router. An attacker with the ability to monitor every onion router in a network might be able to trace the path of a message through the network, but an attacker with more limited capabilities will have difficulty even if he controls one or more onion routers on the messages path.

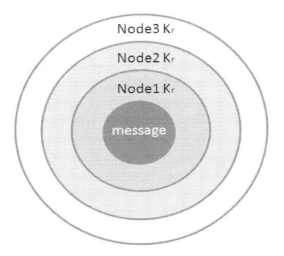

Fig. 3. Onion layered encryption

B. Implementation of Onion Routing

Implementation of Onion Routing [5] in communication of a client which wants to communicate certain messages with a host server and the client has the information about the server but the server does not know anything about client. The following steps are involved in our implementation

1. Network Set-up: starts the Onion Router servers and establishes the long standing connections between Onion Routers.
2. Starting Services: Starting the Onion Proxy, Application Proxy, host server.
3. Connection Set-up : Client establishes anonymous connection with host server.
4. Data transfer: Transfer of messages from client to serve.

Table 1. Onion Layer specifications

1 Byte	version number of current system
1 Byte	encr.mech. for forword and backword hash currently 0 for both
2 Byte	port of next node in route - 0 if final node
4 Byte	IP Address of next node in route - null if final node
4 Byte	Expiration time of onion
16 Byte	Key Seed Material
28 Byte	Total

C. Onion Ring Implementation in NS2 : RingOr.tcl

This file is the actual file which ns2 executes. It is written in a scripting language called tcl (tool command language). This file initializes ns2, sets the nodes and their positions, connects nodes and also establishes connection between them. The nodes are nothing but objects of OrClass. OrClass is implements in C++ which has functions to send, received, encrypt and decrypt data in Onion Routing format. This file also schedules various events and executes the 4 cases described below. After the simulation is done, it opens the Network Animator to view the animation of the simulation.

D. Onion Header Implementation in NS2: Or.cc/Or.h

These are the C++ files which have the actual functions of packet sending and receiving. These files define a custom OR packet header called hdr-or. This header encapsulates the normal IP header and adds some extra information to it. The extra information contains the next hop in the OR network, sending time, receiving time, and data.

The header format is used by a custom OR agent called Or-Agent. This Agent class has the actual methods to send and receive OR packets and interpret them. The send function is called from the tcl file whenever a node wants to send some data. When a node received the data, recv function is called. The encryption/decryption algorithm implemented currently is a simple ex-OR based symmetric encryption. However, in further implementations, this can be extended to include sophisticated asymmetric encryption algorithms.

4   Result Analysis

In this case, the Gateway Router (GR) is shown to send request carrier. Encryption and Decryption of message takes place between the source and the destination. Decryption of message in Onion Ring Routing is shown below in Fig.4. If any of the nodes has some data to send, they modulate the request

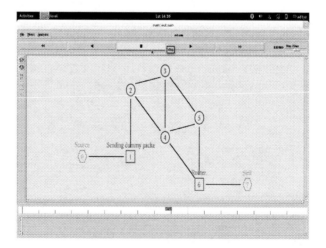

Fig. 4. Wireless Mesh Simulation using Random Routing

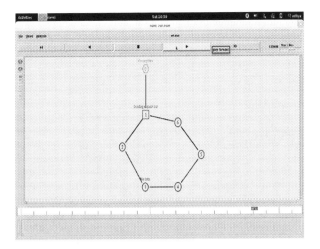

Fig. 5. Case Simulation in Onion Rring Routing

carrier and send the data on it. A node never initiates a session on its own as this would mean disclosing the source of packet to an external observer. In this case, the GR sends a carrier which is encrypted. None of the nodes have any data to send. Hence the GR receives the same carrier which it has got.

Now node 4 has some data to send. However as it can not initiate a session on its own, it waits for the request carrier. When the next request carrier is sent by the GR, Node 4 receives it and modulates it with its own data (which is encrypted). This is then forwarded to the next node. When this carrier reaches back to the GR, it knows that the carrier has data from node 4 as it has the public key of all the nodes in ring. It decrypts the data and sends it to external network with source ID of its own. Internally, it stores and entry that Node 4 has send a request out so when it receives a reply, it can route it back properly .

The external network sends a response to the request by node 4. However, for the external network the source address of the request was sent as the GR. Hence the GR receives the response. It then lookups the actual Node for which the response is meant, in this case it was Node 4. It encrypts the response and sends as a response carrier. All the nodes receive the response and forward it with their own encryption. When Node 4 receives the response, it detects that it is meant for it. It decrypts the data and takes the response.

However, it cannot stop here else an external observer can easily deduce that the source and destination node for this transaction and from that get the session keys. Hence Node 4 again encrypts a dummy packet and forwards it as a response carrier. This is then received by the GR which indicates a successful transaction.

This is an edge case scenario where two Nodes have data to be sent in the same request carrier cycle. In this case, Node 4 and 5 both have data to be sent. Node 4 modulated the request carrier with its own data and forwards it. However, Node 5 cannot detect that Node 4 has already modulated the data as both Node's session keys are different. Node 5 assumes that the carrier is unmodulated and modulates it with own data. This overwrites Node 4 data and hence the GR receives this packet as if data from Node5.

Now node 4 should have a time out period within which it should receive a response. If it does not receive a response within that period, it should resend the data. This is a known shortcoming of the Ring OR network which cannot be easily addressed.

5   Conclusion and Future Scope

Here we presented a protocol called Onion Ring Routing. The purpose of Onion Ring Routing is to protect the anonymity of a user who wants to communicate over a network. In particular, it will hide the destinations of all communications initiated by the user. Any outside observers will not be able to tell whom the user is communicating over the network. We have implemented the onion ring protocol over TCP-IP protocol. To achieve this goal, the encryption/decryption algorithm implemented currently is a simple ex-OR based symmetric encryption. However, in further implementations, this can be extended to include sophisticated asymmetric encryption algorithms.

The future work will be simulation study on the routing performance of the Onion ring .Also we are focusing on to increase the throughput in Onion Ring.The future work will also include intelligent generation of the rings, i.e., generating rings according to the profiles of the Mesh nodes.

Acknowledgement. We thank our guide Dr. Deepak Karia for his guidance and assistance in our project and for being a constant source of inspiration to us. Also, we are thankful to our institute, Sardar Patel Institute of Technology, Mumbai, India for providing the facilities to carry out our project work.

References

1. Reed, M.G., Syverson, P.F., Goldschlag, D.M.: Anonymous Communication and Onion Routing. IEEE Journal on Selected Areas in Communication Special Issue on Copyright and Privacy Protection (1998)
2. Routing Information Protocol, RFC, http://www.faqs.org/rfcs/rfc1058.html
3. OPSF Version 2, RFC, http://www.faqs.org/rfcs/rfc2328.html
4. Tor: "An anonymous Internet communication system" =http://tor.eff.org
5. Dingledine, R., Mathewson, N., Syverson, P.: Tor: The Second- Generation Onion Router. In: 13th USENIX Security Symposium (2004)
6. http://www.isi.edu/nsnam/ns

Scalable Key Transport Protocol Using Chinese Remainder Theorem

Manisha Y. Joshi[1] and R.S. Bichkar[2]

[1] M.G.M.'s College of Engineering, Nanded
[2] G.H. Raisoni College of Engineering, Wagholi, Pune

Abstract. In any conditional access system, the broadcast content is encrypted with the secret key to protect it from unauthorized users. The secret key is shared by server and a authorized user and a key transport protocol is used to transfer the secret key securely to these users. In this paper we introduce a scalable key transport protocol based on Chinese remainder theorem for single as well as multiple access control. In this protocol, user or user device has to carry only two keys. To decode the broadcast message, only one modular division and one decryption is sufficient. The main advantage of our scheme is that, a server can update the scrambling key or group key in one message, without changing user's key. The proposed protocol is scalable and it can be used for multiple access control, which is useful in Pay TV, without increasing communication and computation overhead on user as well as the server.

Keywords: key transport protocol, Chinese remainder theorem, pay-TV, conditional access system.

1 Introduction

In the era of pay per view and conditional access systems, efficiency of access control system is a very important issue. Access control systems are responsible for scrambling of the video signal broadcasted by server. A video stream is scrambled with secret key and broadcasted. Only the authorized user or subscriber receives the video signal broadcasted by the server. This process is also called as broadcast encryption [1]. To maintain the confidentiality and access control, a receiver has to preserve the secret key, generally called as user's long time secret key which has been shared by the server and a receiver. As the number of users is dynamic, server has to change the scrambling key from time to time. Thus, there is a need of scalable key transport protocol for single and multiple access control.

Key transport protocols are used to send the session key or private key to the intended receivers. In these protocols, the sender (generally key server) is responsible to generate the key and transfer it to receiver securely. Hence the receiver or its device has less responsibility and less resource requirement compared to the sender. Because of this feature these are preferred in the client server environment. Rest of the paper is organized as follows; section 2 gives a brief review of the related work.

Sabu M. Thampi et al. (Eds.): SSCC 2013, CCIS 377, pp. 397–402, 2013.

This includes   Chiou and Chen's secure lock scheme [2] and key transport protocol based on secret sharing scheme by Eskicioglu and Delp [4]. Section 3 explains our proposed scheme for single access control. Section 4 presents an extension of scheme for multiple access control application. Section 5 presents analysis of the proposed scheme and its comparison with other scheme. Finally, section 6 concludes the paper.

2   Related Work

There are several solutions for key distribution based on logical hierarchical key tree [5, 6]. In these solutions n users have to keep $\Theta(\log_2 n)$ keys and carry out the same number of encryptions as well as decryptions [7]. Hence it is not efficient when receiver's devices are less powerful. Use of Chinese remainder theorem for broadcast encryption was first proposed by Chiou and Chen [2]. They have used this theorem to construct a secure lock and have suggested both public key and symmetric key based solution. While using symmetric key based solution, each of n users has to maintain n moduli   or integer m_1, m_2, ... m_n, relatively prime with each other and n secret keys k_1, k_2, ... k_n and secure lock is a function of n moduli. The main disadvantage of this scheme is that if group size changes server has to redistribute new updated number of moduli n' to all user. Hence this scheme is not scalable for dynamic group. Our proposed scheme is derived from this scheme but in our scheme each user u_i has to keep only two keys $(m_i \ k_i)$ instead of n key pairs. If new user joins or existing user leaves, server has to update the scrambling key as well as key database and communicate to existing users. The existing users need not to change their keys. This makes our scheme more scalable.

The key transport protocol presented by Eskicioglu et al. uses secret sharing scheme [3]. In this scheme, one share of secret i.e. one point (x_i, y_i) of polynomial passing through origin, is with i^{th} user device and another secret i.e. another point (x_0, y_0) is with key the server. Server sends its share and scrambled video signal. Receiver computes scrambling key, which is intercept of polynomial using its own share and received share. As scrambling key is a function of server and user share, if any new user joins or existing user leaves, server has to regenerate the shares and redistribute among the users. Thus although this scheme reduces computation at receiver's side, it is not scalable for a set of dynamic users.

3   Scalable Key Transport Protocol Using CRT (SKTPCRT) for Single Access Control

As our scheme is based on Chinese remainder theorem, the statement of the Chinese remainder theorem (CRT) is discussed prior to the proposed protocol.

3.1   Chinese Remainder Theorem

Let there be n integers $m_1, m_2, \ldots m_n$, such that, $gcd\,(m_i, m_{i+1}) = 1$ i.e m_i and m_{i+1} are co prime and n residue $a_1, a_2, \ldots a_n$, There is an integer $x \equiv x(mod\ M)$ such that,

$$x \equiv a_1 (mod\ m_1)$$

$$x \equiv a_2 (mod\ m_2)$$

$$x \equiv a_3 (mod\ m_3)$$

$$x \equiv a_n (mod\ m_n)$$

$$M = \prod_{i=1}^{n} m_i$$

$$x \equiv x(mod\ M)$$

$$x = \left(\sum_{i=1}^{n} a_i\, c_i\, y_i\right) mod\ M$$

Where, $y_i = M/m_i$, $c_i = y_i^{-1}\ mod\ m_i$

3.2   Registration and Pre Distribution of Keys

Server generates, $n + 1$ pair of integers, each called as a key pair (m_i, k_i), where, $0 \le i \le n$. There are $m_0, m_2, \ldots, m_n$ such that $gcd\,(m_i, m_{i+1}) = 1$. There are $\{k_0, k_2, \ldots, k_n\}$ keys for n users and one for server. Key pair (m_0, k_0) is not allotted to any user. All the key pairs are securely communicated to n users by either smart cards or using any secure authenticated protocol like SSL [8]. Let vs be the video signal which server want communicate securely. Server generates secret key S which is used to scramble the video signal for a group G.

3.3   Scalable Key Transport Protocol Using CRT (SKTPCRT)

i.   Server encrypts key S using each users key k_i and generates sub key S_i for each user i.e. $S_i = E_{k_i}\{S\}$, where $0 \le i \le n$

ii.   Server computes a lock X using Chinese remainder theorem as follows
$$X = \left(\sum_{i=0}^{n} S_i\, C_i Y_i\right) mod\ M,\ \text{where,}$$
$$M = \prod_{i=0}^{n} m_i\,, S_i = E_{k_i}\{S\},\ Y_i = M/m_i\,,\ C_i = Y_i^{-1}\ mod\ m_i,$$

iii.   Server broadcast or multicast the message $\{X\}\ \|\ E_S\{vs\}$

iv.   Each user computes $S_i = X\ mod\ m_i$ and decrypts S_i using its key k_i i.e. $S = D_{k_i}\{S_i\}$. Here the encryption/decryption can be performed by any standard symmetric cipher such as DES, AES [9, 10].

v.   User or user's device will decrypt the video signal $vs = D_S\{E_S\{vs\}\}$

There is need to change the scrambling key S if any new member subscribes to the CAS, called as **Join** and if any member's subscription ends and he doesn't want to continue, called as **leave.**

3.4   Join

New member registration is similar to that mentioned in the registration phase. New pair of keys (m_{new}, k_{new}) is generated for new user and new scrambling key S' is generated by server. Where m_{new} is relatively prime with M calculated in step 2 in the previous section and k_{new} is fresh.

Lock X is recomputed as follows

    i. $M = M \times m_{new}$

    ii. $S_i = E_{k_i}\{S'\}$, $Y_i = {}^{M}/m_i$ $C_i = Y_i^{-1} \bmod m_i$ where $,0 \le i \le n+1$

    iii. $X = \left(\sum_{i=0}^{n+1} S_i\, C_i Y_i\right) \bmod M$

    iv. Server broadcast or multicast the message $\{X\} \parallel E_S\{vs\}$

    v.   Each user computes $S_i = X \bmod m_i$ and $S' = D_{k_i}\{S_i\}$.

    vi. User or user's device will decrypt the video signal $vs = D_{S'}\{E_{S'}\{vs\}\}$

3.5   Leave

When a user u_l leaves the group, its key pair (m_l, k_l) is deleted from key database and new scrambling key S' is generated by server. Secure lock X is recomputed using following steps

    i. $M = {}^{M}/m_l$

    ii. $S_i = E_{k_i}\{S'\}$, $Y_i = {}^{M}/m_i$ $C_i = Y_i^{-1} \bmod m_i$ where $,0 \le i \le n-1$

    iii. $X = \left(\sum_{i=0}^{n-1} S_i\, C_i Y_i\right) \bmod M$

    iv. Server broadcast or multicast the message $\{X\} \parallel E_{S'}\{vs\}$

    v.   Each user computes $S_i = X \bmod m_i$ and $S = D_{k_i}\{S_i\}$ User or user's device will decrypt the video signal $vs = D_{S'}\{E_{S'}\{vs\}\}$

4   Scalable Key Transport Protocol (SKTPCRT) for Multiple Access Control

In the multiple access control we have assumed that, there are l channels called as main set of channels $A = \{C_1, C_2, C_3, .. C_l\}$ and there are j subsets which are called as groups G_1, $G2$,......,Gj for example $G_1 = \{C_1, C_l\}, G_2 = \{C_1, C_4, ..., C_l\}$. Each user subscribes for one group at a time. User has facility to change the group. After changing a group user will not able to access previous group.

i. Server generates secret key $S_1, S_2, S_3 \ldots .. S_j$ which is used to scramble the video signal for a group G_j and sub key S_{ij} for each ith user of jth group i.e. $S_{ij} = E_{k_i}\{S_j\}$, where $0 \leq i \leq n_j$

ii. Server computes various locks $X_1, X_2, \ldots \ldots X_j$ using Chinese remainder theorem as follows, $Xj = \left(\sum_{i=1}^{n_j} S_i C_i Y_i\right) mod\ M, \quad M_j = \prod_{i=1}^{n} m_{ij}, \quad S_{ij} = E_{k_i}\{S_j\}, \quad Y_i = {Mj}/{m_i} \quad C_i = Y_i^{-1}\ mod\ m_i$

iii. Server broadcast or multicast the message $\{X_1, X_2, \ldots, X_j\}$ for j groups

iv. Each user of respective group computes $S_{ij} = X_j\ mod\ m_i$ and decrypts the scrambling key using its own key k_i i.e. $S_j = D_{k_i}\{S_{ij}\}$.

When any user u_{ij} want to change group from G_1 to G_2, group keys of group G_1 and G_2 are changed. Scrambling key for group G_2 is constructed and distributed using our join algorithm discussed in previous section, except that there is no need to generate new key pair, as user still has a registered member. Scrambling key for group G_1 is constructed and distributed using our leave algorithm in previous section except that the user's key pair is not deleted from key database. It is retained as user is still authorized user and only changing the group.

5   Analysis of SKTPCRT

In our scheme key pair (m_l, k_l) is kept secret by user hence only authorized user will be able to reveal encrypted scrambling key and that is decrypted by user itself. As encryption/decryption is performed by standard symmetric block cipher, the proposed protocol is secure from known plaintext attack as well as brute force attack.

Table 1. Comparison of SKTPCRT with other schemes

Parameters for comparison → Schemes ↓	Number of keys stored by user	Number of messages needed to transfer the key	Computation by users	Scalable to dynamic group	Can be used for multiple group access
Chiou and Chen's	n-1	1	$E+S+ M_D$	No	No
Key transport protocol by Eskicioglu et.al	1	1	$E+\theta(t^2)$	No	No
Proposed protocol (SKTPCRT)	2	1	$E+M_D$	Yes	Yes

n-number of users ,S-search, t-degree of polynomial , E-Encryption/decryption, M_D- modular division,

Secure lock X is function of key pair (m_0 , k_0) which is with server, thus if any key like m_i is compromised, no one can forge the lock X. Hence our protocol is secure against impersonate attack and man in middle attack.

To compute the secure lock heavy computations are required but that will be computed by server. Server can use computationally efficient processor as well use divide and conquer algorithm [2] to implement the Chinese remainder theorem. Table 1 shows the comparison of our protocol with other schemes.

6   Conclusions

In this paper we have presented scalable key transport protocol (SKTPCRT) which is useful for single and multiple access control. As user has to store only two secret keys it is storage efficient. User has to perform only one modular division and one decryption to get access to the signal, it has advantage where receivers are having less resources. SKTPCRT is more applicable in conditional access system than group key management.

Protocol is efficient as only one message is sufficient to get access. An authorized user is not affected with new member joining or leaving.

References

1. Fiat, A., Naor, M.: Broadcast encryption. In: Stinson, D.R. (ed.) CRYPTO 1993. LNCS, vol. 773, pp. 480–491. Springer, Heidelberg (1994)
2. Chiou, G.H., Chen, W.T.: Secure broadcast using secure lock. IEEE Trans. Software Engineering 15(8), 929–934 (1989)
3. Shamir: How to share a secret. Communications of the ACM 22(11), 612–613 (1979)
4. Eskicioglu, A.M., Delp, E.J.: A Key Transport Protocol based on secret sharing, Application to information security. IEEE Transactions on Consumer Electronics 48(4), 816–824 (2002)
5. Wang, S.-Y., Laih, C.-S.: Efficient Key Distribution for Access Control in Pay-TV Systems. IEEE Transactions on Multimedia 10(3), 480–491 (2008)
6. Liu, B., Zhang, W., Jiang, T.: A scalable key distribution scheme for conditional access system in digital pay-TV system. IEEE Trans. Consumer Electron. 50(2), 632–637 (2004)
7. Wallner, D., Harder, E., Agee, R.: Key management for multicast: issues and architecture. National Security Agency, RFC 2627 (June 1999)
8. Rescorla, E.: SSL and TLS: Designing and Building Secure Systems. Addison-Wesley, Reading (2001)
9. Schneier, B.: Applied Cryptography. Wiley, New York (1996)
10. Daemen, J., Rijmen, V.: Rijndael: The Advanced Encryption Standard. Dr. Dobb's Journal (March 2001)

Author Index